D1190323

CHAUCER: THE CRITICAL HERITAGE

VOLUME 2 1837–1933

THE CRITICAL HERITAGE SERIES

GENERAL EDITOR: B. C. SOUTHAM, M.A., B. LITT. (OXON.)
Formerly Department of English, Westfield College, University of London

For a list of books in the series see the back end paper

CHAUCER.

THE CRITICAL HERITAGE

VOLUME 2 1837-1933

Edited by
DEREK BREWER
Emmanuel College, Cambridge

ROUTLEDGE & KEGAN PAUL
LONDON, HENLEY AND BOSTON

First published in 1978
by Routledge & Kegan Paul Ltd
39 Store Street,
London WC1E 7DD,
Broadway House,
Newtown Road,
Henley-on-Thames,
Oxon RG9 1EN and
9 Park Street,
Boston, Mass..02108, USA
Printed in Great Britain by
Redwood Burn Ltd
Trowbridge & Esher
© Derek Brewer 1978
No part of this book may be reproduced in
any form without permission from the
publisher, except for the quotation of brief
passages in criticism

British Library Cataloguing in Publication Data

Chaucer, the critical heritage. —(The Critical
heritage series).
1. Chaucer, Geoffrey—Criticism and
interpretation—Addresses, essays, lectures
I. Brewer, Derek Stanley II. Series
821'.1   PR1924   78-40016

ISBN 0 7100 8497 8

General Editor's Preface

The reception given to a writer by his contemporaries and near-contemporaries is evidence of considerable value to the student of literature. On one side we learn a great deal about the state of criticism at large and in particular about the development of critical attitudes towards a single writer; at the same time, through private comments in letters, journals or marginalia, we gain an insight upon the tastes and literary thought of individual readers of the period. Evidence of this kind helps us to understand the writer's historical situation, the nature of his immediate reading-public, and his response to these pressures.

The separate volumes in the *Critical Heritage Series* present a record of this early criticism. Clearly, for many of the highly productive and lengthily reviewed nineteenth- and twentieth-century writers, there exists an enormous body of material; and in these cases the volume editors have made a selection of the most important views, significant for their intrinsic critical worth or for their representative quality—perhaps even registering incomprehension!

For earlier writers, notably pre-eighteenth century, the materials are much scarcer and the historical period has been extended, sometimes far beyond the writer's lifetime, in order to show the inception and growth of critical views which were initially slow to appear.

In each volume the documents are headed by an Introduction, discussing the material assembled and relating the early stages of the author's reception to what we have come to identify as the critical tradition. The volumes will make available much material which would otherwise be difficult of access and it is hoped that the modern reader will be thereby helped towards an informed understanding of the ways in which literature has been read and judged.

B.C.S.

For Helena

Contents

Introduction

I

The present volume takes up the criticism of Chaucer at
the moment when a new accent cf ultimately great importance begins to be heard: that of American, more strictly,
US, criticism. The first comment is that of Emerson, who
immediately strikes a fresh and characteristic note,
though there is no sharp break with the preceding tradition. The last comment in this second volume is also by a
scholar from the USA. It is taken from the first work of
the learned and sympathetic Rosemond Tuve, heralding a new
age of professionalism, a new recognition of the intellectual, artistic and social range of Chaucer's poetry. Her
contribution is notably more powerful, and more specialised, than that of her distinguished older contemporaries
of that same year, though it maintains something of their
gracefulness. The year 1933 was chosen as the *terminus ad
quem* for critical comment because that year seemed to mark
the decisive point of change in the balance between the
amateur and professional criticism of Chaucer. It marks
the point of overlap between the long tradition of the
amateur critic - amateur both as lover and as unprofessio-
nal - and the beginning of the professional, even scientific criticism in which the concept of the love of an
author would too often appear ludicrous. About the early
1930s, too, and doubtless not accidentally, becomes more
visible the beginning of the break-up of the long and honourable traditions of Neoclassical and Romantic criticism
which were so closely connected with the critic's status
of gentleman-amateur. From the middle 1930s onwards, the
professional criticism of Chaucer by salaried academics,
not gentlemen (which had of course begun in a small way in
the nineteenth century), now dominates. This is not to
deny a professional competence, where it is needed, to the

1

great figures in Chaucer criticism whose work fills the
latter pages of this volume: but their work retains an air
of almost innocent pleasure in and zest for literature, a
certain elegance of style, an appeal to the educated
'common reader', which, though not entirely lost in more
recent years, are hardly marked characteristics of the
modern 'Chaucer industry'. The overlapping of the amateur
and the professional in the work that appears in the
latter pages of the present volume produced the best criticism we have, which can and should be read not only in
historical perspective but for its direct illumination of
Chaucer's quality and its own learning and humanity.

It may be remarked, however, that the twentieth-century
comments collected here do not often derive from the general periodicals, written for non-specialist readers,
which provide the main source of comment in the nineteenth
century. The contributions of Huxley, Virginia Woolf, and
Praz were indeed published in general literary periodicals,
but they are in a minority, and most of the extracts are
drawn from specialist journals or similar sources, though
they are far less technical in tone, and of much broader
appeal, than such writings would normally be today.

In the development from amateur to professional we see
some of the paradoxes of twentieth-century culture. The
more professional criticism at its best may be, because
more specialised, more learned and penetrating, less
simply a reflection of current predispositions. Furthermore, the great increase of education and the now fully
accepted study of vernacular literature as a university
discipline and a desirable educational tool in schools,
have ensured that a higher proportion of the population
of Great Britain has at least had a brush with Chaucer at
school, and have made professional criticism possible by
providing jobs. On the other hand, the prestige and quality of general literary culture have declined in society
as a whole relative to other interests, notably science
and sport, while modern literary culture itself appears to
be going through a phase of hostility to traditional virtues and to intellect.

Strangely enough, a recognition of the specialised and
thus fragmented culture of the latter part of the twentieth century may bring us a clearer understanding of some
characteristics of Chaucer's literary culture, fragmented
in a different way, than could the heroic attempt of Neoclassicism and Romanticism to establish at least a secondary, unified, Nature of sweetness and light; but that is a
story beyond the scope of this volume. Its complex development is only just beginning to show in the work of
Empson, Lewis and others in the early 1930s. In general,

the comments collected together in the present volume,
from 1837 to 1933, are essentially those of the nineteenth
century. They deploy the legacy of Neoclassical criticism
with its Romantic extensions, qualifications and compensations, not fundamentally changing that inheritance, but,
so to say, spending it. It seems now finished, and has
given excellent value. The volume of criticism in that
hundred years is roughly equal to that of the preceding
nearly five hundred, though of course each volume is the
product of selection. A similarly proportional selection
from the last fifty years would no doubt equal or exceed
the quantity of all the previous centuries' criticism put
together.

The nineteenth-century criticism of Chaucer offers a
varied field of pleasant reading. One is continually impressed by its warmth, copiousness, energy, and intelligence, if sometimes wearied by its longwindedness. It
still deserves the term amateur even in the case of such
a prolific and attractive journalist as Leigh Hunt (No. 6),
who wrote for a living. While at its weakest such criticism may be merely 'genteel' and vapid, it draws virtue
from being the product of love, or at least of liking.
Nineteenth-century critics also have a quality attributed
by Wordsworth to poetry itself: the directness and full-
ness of 'a man speaking to men'. They continued the earlier tradition of men writing from choice and interest
for assumed equals, with unaffected enjoyment of their
author or equally unaffected blame. They wrote out of
experience of life about 'life' (or history) in literature. For them literature was a part of life, and 'life'
almost the whole of literature. It is true that they may
be plainly wrong, frequently prolix, sometimes sentimental, occasionally inconsistent, now and again uncomprehen-
ding, and too often careless of evidence; they neglect
Chaucer's Gothic earthiness; but they have a directness
and a warmth which is refreshing. Nothing is forced,
over-ingenious, ill-tempered or perverse. And one may
say, in the most general terms, that something like this
largeness and sincerity of mind is the main impression
they appear to have of Chaucer - surely a true impression.
Even when such an impression attributes to Chaucer, and
indeed expresses in itself, a certain naivety, it records
an ability to take much of Chaucer's work at its face-
value, an ability which some late twentieth-century over-
interpretation would do well to recover.

II

The continuity of the impression made by Chaucer's works
on nineteenth-century critics as compared with eighteenth-
century critics is at once apparent, and of course witnes-
ses to the simple truth of the quality of the poetry, and
of the response of criticism, which no study of critical
discovery and change, and no relativism of outlook can
destroy.   Chaucer's work is indeed, as critics in all centuries constantly remark, very varied; often humorous;
often tender and with pathos; full of vivid description
and characterisation; even, in parts, 'dramatic'.   Such,
in general, has been perceived from Chaucer's own lifetime.   Even the emphasis on 'The Canterbury Tales' to the
almost total exclusion of other works has its early antecedents.   Comments on such matters deserve to be frequently reiterated in each generation.   They are fully illustrated in the extracts in the present volume, but they
need no further discussion here in their general form.
More specifically, Chaucer's 'realism' begins to be
more strongly emphasised, as we would expect in a century
which sees the triumph of the realistic novel, the practical successes of British society as a whole, and the
strong development of the scientific materialism always
implicit in Neoclassical literary theory.   Chaucer's realism is frequently mentioned, for example by 'Christopher
North' (No. 4), Ruskin (No. 9), and Mackail (No. 34).   It
probably emerges in Bagehot's sense of Chaucer's 'practical' nature (No. 10) and in Ker's interesting perception,
in his magisterial article (No. 29), of Chaucer's writing
as 'the commonplace transformed'.   The same general
notion probably underlies Aldous Huxley's statement of
Chaucer's utter materialism (No. 40); Manly's view of
Chaucer's meritorious progress in rejecting rhetoric and
moving from 'art' to 'nature' (No. 43); Praz's conception
of Chaucer's prosaic English shopkeeping character (No.
44); and Housman's commendation of Chaucer's 'sensitive
fidelity to nature' (No. 51).
This is to make the highest concept of art an identification of art with 'nature' (even with a concealed premise
of idealism and social control that certain aspects of
'nature' should not appear in 'art').   In such a situation
'nature' may triumph over 'art' in the critic's estima-
tion, 'art' itself may seem like falseness, and Chaucer's
successful artistry may then be interpreted, as it was,
for example, by Landor (No. 13), as non-art; writing that
is childlike, realistic, and therefore by implication
'true'.   Chaucer's naivety was noticed, or invented, in
the Romantic period, the first person to use the term

being apparently John Galt in 1812 (Vol. 1, No. 93), and
it is referred to a number of times in the present volume,
American critics being attracted to the notion (e.g.,
Thoreau, No. 3, Lowell, No. 17). Naivety in turn rein-
forces the concept of Chaucer's childlikeness, or, a very
different matter, his childishness, as in Landor (No. 13),
or Mackail (No. 34).

Chaucer's 'realism' could also lead in other directions
in the nineteenth and twentieth centuries, e.g., to 'rationalism', already suggested above in Huxley's view of his
materialism, but that would prolong the line of development too far from the texture of his poetry. The constant
emphasis on Chaucer's realism, a basically Neoclassical
quality derived from the demand upon literature to 'imitate' 'life', and already strongly emphasised by Dryden
(Vol. 1, No. 66), obviously responds to an extremely important, prominent and (for Chaucer's own time) novel quality in his writing. The problem for critics has always
been, how to relate his realism to other aspects of his
work which are certainly non-realistic, unless the critic,
like Aldous Huxley, totally disregards these other
elements.

III

To return to the texture of the poetry indicated by the
word 'realism', the diction of Chaucer, in association
with his 'realism', began to be discovered by Romantic
critics to be 'plain', as noted, for example, by Southey
(Vol. 1, No. 101), in total opposition to the response
of Chaucer's fifteenth-century readers. Emerson is
strong on Chaucer's plainness (No. 1) and the point is
repeated, e.g., by the anonymous reviewer of 1859 (No.
11) who maintains that there is only one possible style:
'natural, straightforward, workman-like, and simple'. The
denial of alternative possibilities in the choice of style,
very characteristic of some modern thought about literature, is almost to deny the possibility of art. It is
suggested again by the emphasis on Chaucer's 'naturalness'
by the admirable scholar Lounsbury (No. 28), and by the
less scholarly Raleigh (No. 31). A true sense of the
nature of the possible richness of Chaucer's style only
develops right at the end of our period with Professor
Empson's brilliant comments on allusion and ambiguity (No.
46), C.S. Lewis's equally valuable perception of Chaucer's
'sententiousness', and Mario Praz's rather more patronising exposition of his relation to Dante.

IV

The fruitful sense of Chaucer's relation to the culture of
his time, a Romantic product for once really different
from Neoclassical concepts, and which in Chaucer criticism
dates from Thomas Warton (Vol. 1, No. 83) and particularly
Godwin (Vol. 1, No. 87), is to be detected variously in
many essays and comments. It hardly allows itself to be
summarised briefly. In the nineteenth century, as still
in the late twentieth, we are far from a satisfactorily
systematic account either of literary culture itself or of
its relation to society as a whole. Works of literary
genius are perhaps by definition anomalous. But in the
nineteenth century many perceptions of the relationships
of Chaucer's work to his general social culture and the
condition of England help to paint a fuller picture of the
work and culture of Chaucer's own time. They are valuable
even when later scholarship has used them in order to
change them.

The relationship of Chaucer to his whole culture is
very generally expressed by Emerson (No. 1), who is particularly sensitive to the way the poet acts as a spokesman
for his culture. Here Emerson's total lack of a sense of
differences and of history - surely no writer was ever so
naturally a 'Platonist', finding one thing like another,
as he - is a strength in responding to Chaucer's Gothic
representativeness. Emerson's chronological confusion,
or, to be plain, downright ignorance of the simplest historical fact, as that Caxton lived a century after Chaucer, reveals his corresponding weakness, the absence of
any ability to perceive difference and development.

Chaucer's multiplicity of interest is also recognised
by the very interesting comparison, made by James Lorimer,
of Chaucer with Goethe (No. 7). (In the nineteenth century the comparison of Chaucer with classical precedents,
Homer, Ennius, Virgil, so common in earlier centuries, is
rarely if ever made. Chaucer is regarded as too clearly
different.)

The national mind is also found expressed in Chaucer by
Ruskin (No. 9). For him Chaucer is 'the most perfect type
of a true English mind in its best possible temper', and
'quite the greatest, wisest and most moral of English
writers', though this is not unequivocal praise since it
includes that jesting and coarseness ('fimesis') which
Ruskin regards as so deplorable yet so integral a part of
English strength.

F.D. Maurice feels that Chaucer 'entered into fellowship with common citizens' (No. 15) and is the best type
of English poet. Both Mackail in 1909 (No. 34) and

W.W. Lawrence in 1911 (No. 35) respond in a somewhat similar and refreshing way to Chaucer's representative multiplicity (which is also frequently at least implied in the
many references to his dramatic power). But F.J. Snell
(No. 30) a few years earlier, in 1901, with modest and
perhaps in consequence disregarded originality, takes it
further and accepts calmly what Ruskin deplores, that
Chaucer's variety shows that he is not, in all his writings, a 'responsible' poet, thus reversing the Neoclassical and Romantic requirement that a great poet, or at
least, great poetry, should be a great moral teacher.
Finally, Chaucer's representative quality is flatly denied
in a brief, journalistic, but penetrating sketch in 1933
by Chesterton, who asserts that there never was a less
representative poet than Chaucer (No. 49).

Minto (No. 21) makes a valuable attempt to relate Chaucer to the chivalric system, though in intellectual rather
than social terms.   There are various views about Chaucer's
own status in his society, and of his consequent attitudes.
Morris maintains the older view and contrasts Chaucer the
gentleman with 'the people' (No. 27), while Smith sees him
as a Conservative (No. 14).   James Lorimer (No. 7), however, in 1849, finds Chaucer to be 'of the progressive
party'.   Chaucer the bourgeois, so frequently met with in
Chaucer criticism of the latter part of the twentieth century, makes his first appearance in a penetrating comment
by that strange bourgeois, Swinburne (No. 26), and is developed in 1927 in Praz's Italianate view of the staid,
mercantile, bourgeois poet (No. 44); though Tout, with the
authority of a great historian of the period, describes
him as a prudent courtier.

Another aspect of Chaucer's representative genius and
relation to his culture is the nineteenth century emphasis
on his 'Englishness'.   Once again Emerson (No. 1) is early,
if not first, with this note, expressed as a compliment
but obviously not with the patriotic self-confidence that
the English nineteenth century felt to be as appropriate
as the late twentieth century feels it inappropriate.   The
Scottish writer of passage No. 7 expresses Victorian patriotism in 1849; it appears again in Ruskin (No. 9), again
in No. 22 (by W. Cyples) in 1877, and in touches elsewhere.

Another aspect of Chaucer's relationship to the culture
of his own time, which links up with a perception of his
rationalism noted above, is discussion of his religious
position, which again is related to a view of his personal
temperament.   For the sixteenth century, and even for
Wordsworth (Vol. 1, No. 88), partly on the basis of texts
wrongly attributed to him, Chaucer was something of a
rationalist, and consequently, a religious reformer, but

the general opinion in the nineteenth century tends to see
him as something of a rationalist and therefore somewhat
lukewarm in religion and not a reformer. For Alexander
Smith (No. 14) and 'Matthew Browne' (No. 16) he is a Conservative and a Laodicean, not the stuff martyrs are made
of. This topic was picked up by Tatlock in a massively
learned article (No. 39) which does not fundamentally
change this opinion, though it has not gone unchallenged
by more recent Chaucer criticism. Chaucer's temperament
is seen as easy-going, kindly, in accordance with his absence of ecclesiastical rigour, for example by the advanced and kindly theologian F.D. Maurice (No. 15), as by
other kindly men like Thoreau (No. 3) and Lowell (No. 17),
and through this tolerant geniality we are led back again
to Chaucer's dramatic capacity to represent many different
kinds of men, and his consequent representative quality.

The culmination of this study of Chaucer's relationship
to his own society and culture is to be found in the works
by Tatlock and Tout already mentioned, and in the equally
learned and readable study by Lowes (No. 47) which felici-
tously touches on, and may be said to summarise, so many
of the learned topics started in the nineteenth century,
while raising others, such as the importance of the oral
element in Chaucer's poetry, which are still being worked
out. Tatlock, Tout and Lowes are all represented here by
substantial and central contributions, which however are
only a small proportion, in terms of bulk, of their extensive, usually more technical, work, on Chaucer, fourteenth
century life, and the relationship between them.

V

These very varied studies on Chaucer's relationship to his
own culture exemplify a well-known and profound development in the nineteenth century by no means limited to
Chaucer studies: namely, the new sense of historical
change, of the past being validly different from the present. This change is often associated with Romanticism,
and in so far as any large-scale cultural change can be
associated with individual men it is associated with the
work and influence of Sir Walter Scott. Signs of it are
to be noticed in the period before that covered by this
volume as early as Gray and Hurd (Vol. 1, Nos 81 and 82)
and elsewhere, including the historical survey of criticism
by Hippisley that concludes Vol. 1, but it is in the latter
part of the nineteenth century and first third of the
twentieth that it flourishes. Many of the examples already
referred to directly illustrate the sense of history, but

it is revealed perhaps even more vividly in the new sense
of relativity of judgment, adumbrated by Hippisley, continued by Horne (No. 2), but most fully expressed, as one
might expect, by Miss Spurgeon herself in her introduction
to her collection of criticism of and allusions to Chaucer,
which does not prevent her own view of Chaucer himself
being very characteristically late Romantic (No. 41). But
if, as she says, critics describe and judge themselves,
she comes out very well with her large, humane, learned
and cheerful view of Chaucer. In a more critical way,
though with equal magnanimity, C.S. Lewis shows a sense of
historical depth and change by his comparison of Chaucer's
'Troilus' with Boccaccio's 'Il Filostrato' (No. 48), and
begins to retrieve, for the first time since the seventeenth century, a sympathetic feeling for Chaucer's traditionally 'sententious' style. Lewis argues that Chaucer
'medievalises' Boccaccio, and perhaps thus unconsciously
reveals his own roots in the Romantic medievalisation that
accompanies the sense of historical change, though Lewis
safeguards his Romantic medievalism by powerful learning
and literary insight. Neither Spurgeon nor Lewis slips
into a purely relativistic view of literary value.

VI

The description of Nature (conceived of mainly as natural
scenery) is a marked characteristic of nineteenth-century
poetry which finds a slight but interesting echo in Chaucer criticism. Ruskin (No. 9) asks some very interesting
questions, and Brooke (No. 18) makes a relatively full
survey which demonstrates many nineteenth-century characteristics. He finds Chaucer's landscape limited, but
'exquisitely fresh, natural and true in spite of its being
conventional'. This admirable essay on Chaucer's landscape becomes in part a study of Chaucer's visual imagination, and makes some effective comparisons with the paintings of the early Italian Renaissance painters. It is a
pioneering work whose lead was not followed till the
middle of the twentieth century. The very last extract in
this volume, by Rosemond Tuve (No. 52), from her first
book, is as learned, subtle and penetrating as one would
expect on Chaucer's relationship to the poetic tradition
of describing the seasons. She shows there is no simple
and direct response to unmediated experience.

VII

On the whole, nineteenth-century critics have little feeling for the relation of poetry to earlier poetry: they tend to judge poetry as a direct response to experience, in accordance with Neoclassical anti-rhetorical principles taken over, even emphasised, by Romanticism. Critics find it easy enough, therefore, to note Chaucer's humour as frequently as did eighteenth-century critics. Chaucer's humour, and the necessarily autonomous, fantasising, self-sufficient, and therefore non-imitative quality that inheres in all humour even when 'realistic', are partly at the root of Arnold's famous complaint that Chaucer lacks 'high seriousness' (No. 24), just as they are also no doubt partly at the root of Arnold's corresponding sense of Chaucer's genial worldliness and humanity. Perhaps Swinburne's similar comment on Chaucer's lack of sublimity has a similar source (No. 26).

In the nineteenth century there is also a question of the decency of Chaucer's humour, though no one gets very excited about it. Sometimes his humour is partially excused as 'broad' (No. 18) or it may be partially condemned, as by Ruskin (No. 9), who coins the useful word 'fimetic', but it is normally felt to be 'healthy' (as surely it is), and usually kindly, as by Lowell (No. 17). It thereby contributes to, or is a product of, the view of Chaucer's poetic, or indeed actual, personality, as genial and tolerant. An approach to a more analytical discussion is made by Leigh Hunt (No. 6), but apart from him Chaucer's humour is barely analysed until the very beginning of the twentieth century, when Hart in 1908 analyses 'The Reeve's Tale' in terms of comic 'poetic justice' derived, no doubt unconsciously, as already noted (Vol. 1, introduction), from the premises of eighteenth-century Neoclassicism. In the same year (No. 33) Saintsbury makes a less systematic but useful attempt to argue that it is humour which unifies Chaucer's apparent miscellaneity. He also makes one of the rare attempts to deny, at least by implication, the almost universally accepted concept of the fully dramatic nature of the separate 'Tales', when he observes that the specific tellers may be forgotten. But the old dramatic principle, and Chaucer's sense of humour, were then winningly reunited in Kittredge's most influential essay on 'The Canterbury Tales' as a 'connected human comedy', which also effectively denied the miscellaneity of the 'Tales' (No. 36). But human comedy is mainly a term to signify drama, and even with Hart there is no thoroughgoing analysis of Chaucer's humour in the period covered by these volumes, frequent as are the references to it.

VIII

In discussing humour one would have thought that Chaucer's irony could hardly be overlooked, but the distrust of Neo-classical writers for ambiguity of any kind presumably inhibited eighteenth-century critics, and Chaucer's irony only slowly achieved recognition in the nineteenth century. There is a reference by John Payne Collier in 1820 to Chaucer's ambiguities; Isaac D'Israeli in 1841 remarked that 'Chaucer's fine irony may have sometimes left his commendations, or even the objects of his admiration, in a very ambiguous condition'; but these are brief passing references which may be found in Spurgeon (see Bibliographical Note) and have not been reprinted here. The first substantial reference is by Leigh Hunt (No. 6), one of the most attractive of Chaucer's critics, who begins something of a technical analysis of Chaucer's work in several directions, including his humour, as noted above. After Hunt in 1846, an interesting contribution on Chaucer's irony is made by Lloyd in 1856 (No. 8). Hales picks up the topic in 1873 (No. 20), and Raleigh in 1905 (No. 31), but it is not much emphasised in the period covered by this book, in contrast to its perhaps excessive dominance in the understanding of Chaucer in the second half of the twentieth century, which no doubt follows the emphasis by the American New Critics of the mid-twentieth century on the centrality of irony to poetry. Within this present volume the more recent view is foreshadowed by Professor Empson's remarkable work, of great originality, on ambiguity in general, with its interesting examination of Chaucer.

IX

The predominance of the realistic and humorous Chaucer did not completely exclude other responses. The beauty of his work, or Chaucer's own sense of beauty, are often mentioned in passing and occasionally emphasised, as for example by the anonymous author of No. 11, or by Stopford Brooke (No. 18) (and merely to note this prompts the reader to wonder how many professional students of literature in the late twentieth century would consider 'beauty' a subject worth mentioning or discussing, and how much we have in consequence narrowed in sensibility).

On the whole, nineteenth-century critics seem to mention Chaucer's sensibility and tenderness more frequently than those of the eighteenth (or of the late twentieth), and they also sometimes associate with his tenderness something of love and romance. Yet love is not mentioned as

often as might be expected, considering that it is Chaucer's main topic, and the principal thread on which so much
nineteenth-century literature was strung. No doubt romantic love in Chaucer was felt to be more 'ideal' and less
'real' than domestic comedy or natural scenery, and there
was also perhaps felt to be some complication in the relation of love to sexuality. Nevertheless, love was not neglected. 'Christopher North' (John Wilson) in 1845 (No. 4)
notes that a new love-poetry arises in early medieval
Europe, and remarks on the 'predominancy of the same star'
in many poets of different vernaculars who make 'one might
almost say, man's worship of women the great religion of
the universe'. This is perhaps the earliest example of the
recognition of 'the allegory of love' and of the religion
of love, which was not fully developed until C.S. Lewis's
famous and influential book 'The Allegory of Love' (1936).
Wilson sees this exaggeration of love as a curious 'amiable
madness' that long dominated 'the poetical mind of the reasonable Chaucer'; for him it evokes tedium and the image of
childishness. Wilson prefers poems that tread 'the plain
ground'. His typical nineteenth-century preference stul-
tified his own insight and it is not surprising that love
in Chaucer's poetry then remained practically unremarked
for thirty years, and then became the subject of an essay
which astonishingly considers that the general interest
in sex is waning. The author also makes the much more
likely observation that Chaucer is little read (No. 22).
The author, William Cyples, does not value highly that
nine-tenths of Chaucer's work which he considers to be
melancholy, outlandish, immoral 'erotics'; but, granted
his premises, it is a sensible and perceptive piece of
criticism, and at least the writer responds, though nega-
tively, to something that is really there. Arnold, too,
is rather dismissive (No. 24), while Sir Adolphus Ward,
(No. 23) rather than recognise an interest in love is more
inclined to emphasise Chaucer's satire of women. The topic
was re-opened by W.G. Dodd in 'Courtly Love in Chaucer and
Gower' (Harvard Studies in English, Volume I, 1913, reprinted Peter Smith, Gloucester, Mass., 1959). Dodd introduces into English Chaucer criticism 'the system of courtly
love' from slightly earlier French and American scholars
of French literature, and he summarises 'the code of
courtly love' from the 'De Arte Honeste Amandi' by Andreas
Capellanus. Dodd then proceeds to demonstrate the presence of 'the code' in Gower and Chaucer, largely by a
summary of the relevant poems. Though most of Dodd's particular premises and conclusions have been subsequently
attacked and in some cases refuted, such is the fate of
scholarship; Dodd's is in its own terms an admirable piece

of work. It has so little literary criticism, however,
that nothing has been selected from it for the present
volume. It was not till some years after C.S. Lewis himself followed Dodd's trail in 1936 with wit, wisdom, eloquence and literary passion, that the subject caught fire.
Even then Lewis, for all his genius, was no doubt helped
by the much greater post-war literary (and perhaps non-
literary) taste for sex and adultery. Lewis's recognition
of love is represented in the present collection by his
brilliant essay on 'Troilus' (No. 48), which touches in
brief so many different points of Chaucer's genius.

The nineteenth century had little more taste for romance in Chaucer than for love. W.P. Ker's remark about
'The Knight's Tale' that it is 'romance and nothing more'
(No. 29), though followed by praise, nevertheless reflects his own preference for the dourness and tragic
muddle of life found in Norse saga. The remark also sums
up a general (though not total) nineteenth-century dislike
for, or failure to understand, fantasy-structures, and
preference for naturalistic presentation, which even the
self-conscious fantasies of William Morris continually
demonstrate, thus carrying on the Neoclassical tradition
in its alliance with an empirical scientific materialism.
Now and again a note of approval of romance is found, as
in the appreciation by J.W. Mackail (No. 34), though he
also repeats some commonplaces, and has a certain patronising attitude towards romance too frequently met even
in the late twentieth century.

With love and romance are often associated pathos, and
pity, which had long been intermittently recognised in
Chaucer's work, and which are well brought out by Hales
(No. 20), though astonishingly denied by the usually
sensible Lawrence (No. 35), who is more orthodox when he
also denies Chaucer the Neoclassical virtue of sublimity.
Lewis's essay (No. 48), though not directly on Chaucer's
pity and pathos, again contributes to a proper understanding of it, as of romance, by his salutory insistence on
taking many parts of Chaucer's work at their face value,
with their 'historial', sententious, unironic seriousness.

X

Chaucer's works are rarely considered as allegory in the
nineteenth century. The earliest conscious recognition
of a strong allegorical element seems to be in the piece
by 'Christopher North' already referred to, where he
treats Chaucer as a 'love allegorist', though dismissively
(No. 4). Naturally the obviously allegorical translation

of 'Le Roman de la Rose' is normally accepted as such, with a few other pieces, though not with pleasure, but allegory is not a topic of general interest. (Even C.S. Lewis's 'Allegory of Love' (1936), which falls outside the scope of the present selection, treats - surely rightly - Chaucer's principal work as literal, not allegorical.)

XI

Throughout the nineteenth century there was a growing, though somewhat wavering and unsteady, appreciation of Chaucer's artistry. This naturally comprises many detailed and various observations that do not lend themselves to brief generalisation. Moreover, it was in conflict with other preconceptions, such as the strong Romantic vein emphasising 'sincerity' and 'nature'; the older but persistent Neoclassical concern with the imitation of the materially 'there'; and the specifically nineteenth-century emphasis on childishness and naivety. This cluster of concepts combined to depreciate the artificiality and conventionality that are inherent in art or in any purposive human activity. In some ways the anti-art concepts of the nineteenth century came to a climax in Manly's famous lecture on Chaucer and the Rhetoricians (No. 43), in which he represents Chaucer as emancipating himself from the constrictions of rhetorical art and as turning at last to 'nature'.

But Manly's lecture is more subtle than that, and is part of the growth of a recognition of Chaucer's artistry. The lecture itself was ultimately, because of the information and scholarship it contained, greatly to promote our sense of the basically rhetorical nature of Chaucer's art, as well as our sense of how Chaucer bettered instruction. Manly's discussion of rhetoric was prompted directly by the publication of E. Faral's 'Les Arts Poétiques du XIIe et du XIIIe Siècle' (Paris, 1924), which is a good example of how scholarship can open new vistas for criticism.

An early indirect recognition of Chaucer's artistry is provided by Horne's careful analysis of the translations of Chaucer (No. 2), which has many sharp observations; while 'Christopher North's' comments on allegory (No. 4 (already several times referred to) also imply recognition of art. The best early analyses seem to be those excellent pieces by Leigh Hunt (No. 6), where the experience of a fellow-practitioner, however minor, a clear mind and a generous temperament, combine to produce interesting and instructive reading. From Hunt onwards Chaucer continues

to be referred to as a great narrative poet. Narrative
poetry as such was not regarded in the nineteenth century
as the highest kind of poetry, but something of its special quality was coming to be recognised. The unknown
writer of No. 11 carried the discussion further with his
valuable notion of 'the poetry of situation' in narrative,
which he then goes on to connect with the more usual concept of Chaucer's dramatic power. The notion that the
larger patterns which are conveyed by extended narrative
may themselves have a meaning beyond the narrated sequence
of events is one that may lie behind the discussions of
narrative, but it never becomes quite explicit. Both
Lounsbury (No. 28) and Ker (No. 29), admirable scholars
and sound critics, convey a strong sense of Chaucer's artistry, even while (especially in Lounsbury's case) balan-
cing it with a sense of Chaucer's 'naturalness'. The balance may be summed up, perhaps, in the notion they share
(which perhaps Ker derived from Lounsbury), of how Chaucer
could transform the 'commonplace'. Virginia Woolf in a
beautifully sensitive and percipient piece, which notices
many aspects of Chaucer's work, responds to Chaucer's narrative skill with the appreciation of a practising novelist, though without noticing much detail. Like others she
sees Chaucer as particularly conveying a kind of 'ordinariness', and calls this quality, with Neoclassical appropriateness, 'the morality of the novel'.

Lowes and Lewis are the critics who really bring the
informed learning of the literary historian to a consideration of Chaucer's art in general, though they also consider many other matters. In the twentieth century, for
the first time, we begin to get a full sense of Chaucer's
place within the great process of European literary culture, though it is worth recalling that this had been
adumbrated earlier, especially by Coleridge (Vol. 1, No.
96).

The most specific key to Chaucer's artistry has only
been somewhat uncertainly used even towards the end of the
period covered by these volumes, and that has already been
referred to: the key of rhetoric. Manly was the great
discoverer, though Manly did not quite know how to use it.
Lewis is the first critic really to understand Chaucer's
poetic rhetoric, though with characteristic modesty he assumes that every one else knows it too (No. 48).

One other aspect of Chaucer's artistry attracts a certain amount of discussion: his metre. This is connected
with an historical understanding of his language, which
had developed sufficiently by the eighteenth century for
Gray (Vol. 1, No. 81) for example, to have a clear idea of
his regularities and of the need to sound final - *e* in

some words where it represents an earlier full inflection.
By the early nineteenth century most critics were not inclined to make a difficulty of Chaucer's scansion, though
Nott (Vol. 1, No. 94) had confused the issue. In the present volume a brief but highly judicious contribution from
1863 on the subject of final -e represents the work of a
great and generous American scholar, F.J. Child (No. 12),
and remains excellent guidance. Gerard Manley Hopkins (No.
24) refers to Chaucer's scansion in a way that is perhaps
more interesting from the point of view of Hopkins's own
well-known interest in scansion than from the point of
view of understanding Chaucer's. The extracts are from
letters and it would not be right to take them as formal
public comment; but it is remarkable that as late as 1880,
in his thirty-sixth year, the great exponent of sprung-
rhythm had not read 'Piers Plowman'. It seems probable
that Hopkins had been misled about metre by Nott's remarks on Wyatt and Surrey. A year later he is claiming
that Chaucer is much more smooth and regular than is
thought by Mr Skeat (Hopkins even wrote to Skeat, and
received a polite, though baffled, reply from that scholar harassed by too much work). Skeat himself is not represented in this collection because he restrained himself from criticism and his scholarly work is easily
available in his great six-volume edition of Chaucer's
'Works' (see Bibliographical Note).

XII

Discussion of metre has obviously verged on the discussion of scholarship, which it is not the primary aim of
these volumes to record. Yet scholarship and criticism
cannot be clearly separated, any more than they can be
identified. Knowledge, if it does not always precede
perception, is most certainly a part of it, and the quality of a mind's knowledge inevitably affects the quality
of its insight. Many a critical folly would be avoided by
the possession of even elementary information. At the
same time, knowledge is not merely inert information, and
critical insight in some ways leads to knowledge. The
dominance of certain critical ways of thought has been
constantly seen, in the course of surveying six centuries
of commentary on Chaucer, to determine what kind of knowledge of Chaucer's work can be acquired at any given
period.
    Knowledge and criticism of Chaucer, in so far as they
can be differentiated, belong also to other systems of
thought as well as to the tradition of literary study.

Knowledge of Chaucer the man belongs also to the system
of historical thought and investigation which developed
in the nineteenth century so much more rapidly than that
strange hybrid, literary history. In the late eighteenth
century Tyrwhitt had exercised as scholarly a scepticism
about the evidences for Chaucer's life, as for the canon
of his work (Vol. 1, No. 84). Tyrwhitt's scepticism was
somewhat offset by the extremely unscholarly Godwin's enthusiasm for what may be called 'cultural' history, which
was itself based on the uncritical accumulations of biographical nonsense that went back to Speght (Vol. 1, No.
53) and Leland (Vol. 1, No. 24), not to speak of
Shirley's unreliable gossip (Vol. 1, No. 9). Now for the
first time, apart from Tyrwhitt, and much more thoroughly
than he, historical scholarship was brought to bear in
1845 by Sir Harris Nicolas on a scientific search for and
examination of documents that would establish a reliable
basis for knowledge of Chaucer's life (No. 5). In relation to what had previously been thought, most of Sir
Harris Nicolas's conclusions were negative. Chaucer, far
from attending both Oxford and Cambridge Universities, as
was natural for Humanist scholars to assume, attended
neither, if positive evidence is to be required. And so
with much else. Sir Harris Nicolas's work is the foundation stone on which rests the now very considerable
modern knowledge of Chaucer's career. The work continued,
especially under the aegis of the Chaucer Society, which
published the valuable documentary collection of Life-
Records in 1900. This work remained the standard source
of knowledge of Chaucer's life until 1966, but it does not
call to be illustrated here.

The general growth of historical scholarship of all
kinds in the nineteenth century, and its relation to Chaucer studies, has already been touched on above. The great
achievements of historical Chaucer scholarship itself,
however, are those of the twentieth century: Kittredge
(No. 36): Tatlock (No. 39); Manly (though in work other
than that represented here, notably 'New Light on Chaucer', 1926); Tout (No. 45); Lowes (No. 47); Tuve (No. 52).
The work of all these scholars remains not only humane and
readable but valuable as knowledge, even though we no
longer quite share their premises.

The more specific scholarship of Chaucer studies increased in the nineteenth century. The man who complained
most about its deficiencies and did most to remedy them in
the field of historical English literary studies, was the
remarkable F.J. Furnivall. He founded the Chaucer Society
(now long since defunct) in 1868, and his titanic and
multifarious labours are represented here by his vigorous

report, on the borders of criticism, 'Work at Chaucer' (No.
19), written for 'Macmillan's Magazine' in 1873. (It is
hard to imagine a general periodical which would carry
such an account today.) Furnivall provides a very useful
summary, which therefore need not be repeated here, of the
progress of the various branches of scholarship up to his
time: study of the language, Chaucer's canon and text, his
life, study of rhymes, chronology of composition, manuscripts. All these provide problems which, unlike many
critical questions, admit of right (or wrong) answers, at
least in principle, and which are a main, though not the
only, foundation-stone of a true understanding of Chaucer.
It is perhaps particularly worth emphasising how important
is the establishment of an internal chronology of the
order of composition of the various works, which in Chaucer studies followed the creation of such a chronology in
the case of Shakespeare. This is specifically a nineteenth-century achievement. When one reads a great critic,
such as Samuel Johnson, who wrote before the development
of the historical sense and its accompanying techniques,
without any sense of the relative immaturity of one work
compared with the maturity of another, one cannot but be
astonished by the way that, for example, 'Titus Androni-
cus' and 'King Lear' are taken at the same level and assumed to provide the same sort of evidence for Shakespeare's characteristic genius. In the case of Chaucer,
what we now know to be his earlier works were previously
taken as evidence of his incapacity, without any sense of
their historical and personal place. The result was the
dominance of certain of 'The Canterbury Tales' and the
absence of relative judgments based on a detailed understanding of the development of Chaucer's genius, and of
the true balance in his work between innovation, convention and tradition. The establishment of some degree of
historical perspective in the nineteenth century, chiefly
by ten Brink, began to enable scholars and critics of
Chaucer to consider his earlier works, and perhaps particularly 'Troilus', with deeper understanding and consequently greater enjoyment.
     Another scholarly question with important implications
for criticism which was settled in the nineteenth century
was the question of the canon of Chaucer's works. The rejection of spurious works had been begun by Tyrwhitt, and
was continued more scientifically by Bradshaw and ten
Brink. The list of authentic works was definitively
summed up, apart from a very few minor problems, by W.W.
Skeat, 'The Chaucer Canon' (1900), following on his edition of works falsely attributed to Chaucer in 'Chaucerian
and Other Pieces' (1897), a supplementary volume to his

'Complete Works of Geoffrey Chaucer'. Tests of authenticity are of different kinds, but are mainly linguistic, or
if stylistic, below that usual level of conscious choice
which constitutes the more literary element of style.   In
other words, tests of authenticity are objective, though
intrinsically of little general interest.   It is paradoxical that criticism, which is usually rated nowadays, not
altogether wrongly, as a 'higher' activity than scholarship, is nevertheless incapable of establishing with certainty either the exact canon of the admired author, or
whether various works were written early, midway or late
in his life.   Criticism is also fickle.   'The Flower and
the Leaf' was admired as one of Chaucer's best poems by
the great poets Dryden and Wordsworth, not to speak of
other writers, yet since it was expelled from the canon it
has been largely neglected.   The truth is that a writer's
authentic works themselves constitute a system with their
own inter-relationships.   A given poem or prose work draws
part of its significance from its relation to other works
by the same author.   When that relation is apparently destroyed the now 'spurious' work loses significance in itself.   Nothing, or at least no work of art, exists in
total isolation.
   From another point of view, the final rejection from
the canon of Thomas Usk's 'Testament of Love' (see Vol.
1, No. 2), for whose presence there was never any excuse,
had earlier readers actually read it, affected the view
taken of Chaucer's life and personality, since Usk's
self-accusation of betrayal of friends had been attributed to Chaucer.   'The Plowman's Tale' and 'Jack Upland'
(both now clearly shown to be spurious), when attributed
to the canon, had also affected men's judgment of the
system of Chaucer's work thus constituted, which then
incorporated works of a reforming religious spirit, and
influenced readers' notions of what sort of man he must
have been.   A poet's life is itself a system, related to
the system constituted by his work, and this relationship
naturally affects the systems themselves.
   One final point may be made about the canon of Chaucer's writings.   Throughout the eighteenth and nineteenth
centuries 'The Canterbury Tales' dominated readers' interests (as one may suspect the work always has done for
ordinary readers), but the number of references to 'Troilus and Criseyde' increases in the twentieth century, not
to the exclusion of 'The Canterbury Tales', but to reach
something like parity of esteem by scholars.   The increasing sense of chronological development also begins to
allow the shorter poems, and especially 'The Parliament of
Fowls', a warmer appreciation.   W.P. Ker (No. 29) gives

perhaps the crucial example of this development of the
appreciation of Chaucer's hitherto lesser-known works.

XIII

In the century covered by the present volume, from 1837
to 1933, we move without a break but with a real transformation away from the quaintness of 'old Chaucer', the
simple-minded fellow, a great poet almost by accident, to
a much stronger sense of the great artist. In the twentieth century there also enters yet another note, very different from the patronising familiarity that is most noticeable in the eighteenth century but is still occasionally heard even today. A note of bafflement now arises in
reading Chaucer, which does not apparently derive only
from his historical remoteness. Chaucer is now found to
have a peculiar elusiveness, perhaps reflected in some of
his ironies, in the ambiguities that Professor Empson
began to trace, or in the 'ordinariness' that is not at
all ordinary. Virginia Woolf records this elusiveness
most sensitively, and we may think that it accords with
something that was genuinely in Chaucer himself, that
perhaps he himself recognised, which he conveyed when he
represented the Host in 'The Canterbury Tales' as commen-
ting on him as 'elvyssh by his contenaunce' (VII, 703).
This brief episode between the Host and the poet records,
from the very beginning, that curious mixture of sensa-
tions of familiarity and strangeness that Chaucer and his
works evoke in the more fully instructed modern reader.
An aspect, or a source, of the mixture of familiarity
and elusiveness, is the curious combination of ease, with
which most of Chaucer's poetry can be understood and
enjoyed by anyone who will take a little trouble with the
language, together with the difficulty of finding suitable
critical concepts to grasp the whole of his work. The
concepts derived from Neoclassical sources (and there were
no others till a period after this selection closes) are
only partly applicable to Chaucer, as to Shakespeare (and,
one might add, to many later writers as well). As the
Neoclassical concepts weaken or change in the earlier part
of the twentieth century, so criticism becomes more ten-
tative, less self-confident, more probing. Critics become
more conscious of the multiplicity of Chaucer's work; of
his unfamiliar rather than merely faulty modes of perspective; of a status for a poet different from what has been
conventionally expected; of a verbal art more casual yet
more elaborate than has been conceived since the sixteenth
century.

XIV

It is notable that in the nineteenth century (as in other
centuries) Chaucer and his work were rarely assimilated
to the Romantic 'medieval' *frisson* shared by so many different persons, and an important element in nineteenth-
century general culture. The outstanding example of Romantic 'medievalism' associated with Chaucer is remarkable
as much for its isolation as its beauty: Morris's great
Kelmscott Chaucer with the Burne-Jones illustrations. In
general Chaucer's work does not seem to lend itself to the
dark mystery of a Christabel, the swashbuckling adventure
of an Ivanhoe, the adolescent fantasy of love and adventure of St Agnes' Eve. Chaucer's realistic 'ordinariness'
seems usually to have broken through the coloured mists of
Romantic medievalising.

More surprisingly, because realism is historically
often associated with satire, relatively rare mention is
made of Chaucer's satirical edge in the nineteenth and
early twentieth centuries, though Sir Adolphus Ward's reference to Chaucer's satire (No. 23) has already been
noted. Other critics remark on Chaucer's satire, but the
emphasis is far more on his genial toleration.

XV

The richness and humanity of nineteenth- and early twentieth-century criticism of Chaucer needs no defence, and
much of it deserves to be read in its own right. It will
benefit from its own bequest to modern readers; an historical perspective, a sympathy for the differences of
the past.

Literary criticism is a multifarious and hybrid phenomenon, where genius is not always accurate, and accuracy
not always helpful. It has few essential premises and
relies on many variables and imponderables. It reflects
more than many intellectual activities the colours of individual circumstances, feeling, knowledge and imagination. Poetry lives in the minds of its readers, and the
same poetry takes on many differing configurations and
creates a sequence of many differing images of itself when
viewed in a uniquely long critical tradition such as has
been displayed in the two present volumes.

Granted all this, it is also true, and it has been one
of the main purposes of the present essay to point out,
that the tradition of criticism itself constitutes a factor in what critics think, feel and say. An individual
piece of criticism is to a larger extent than is often

realised part of a tradition, that is, of a partly self-
enclosed, systematic, historically developing, and therefore to some extent historically conditioned structure,
with its own conventions and characteristics, just like
poetry, or language. Or rather, an historical body of
criticism is a number of various systems (again like the
poetry or language to which it corresponds), complex in
themselves, each enclosed by larger systems, and often en-
folding smaller systems. Naturally, criticism is no more
completely self-enclosed than language and poetry. Like
language and poetry it is genuinely also 'about' something
other than itself. Though some intellectual fashions in
the early 1970s urge us to believe that works of art, or
even language-systems, are essentially autonomous and
self-enclosed, empirical common sense resists such an extreme view, while welcoming the valuable part-truth.

The partially systematic self-enclosed nature of criticism can be seen easily enough in the way fifteenth-
and sixteenth-century critics repeat the judgments of Lydgate, or eighteenth- and nineteenth-century critics repeat
Dryden's judgments about the characters of the 'General
Prologue'. Blake's pronouncements have the force of
genius, but they are as judgments relatively hackneyed.
It would have been easy in putting this collection together to have provided evidence of this kind of repetitive
system in the criticism so extensive and convincing as to
have created a monstrous book, crushing in interest and
impractical to publish. Therefore I have excluded, where
I could, criticism that merely repeated what had already
been said. Even so, the reader will find plenty of repetition, given partly as evidence of continuity of witness,
occasionally because of interest in the man who expressed
it, but also included because the new is inextricably
intertwined with the old, and both need to be given in
order that the statement should be properly understood.
There are also many inter-relationships, many lesser
structures or systems, set up between different pieces of
criticism, which the reader will perceive, though they are
not always editorially commented on. They are 'systematic' in the sense that they can be largely explained in
terms of the critical tradition, its premises and requirements at any given time. That they can be so explained
does not necessarily mean, even when they seem wrong to
us, that the critics have not read the poems, or have been
obtuse, or insincere, or even that the qualities they see
because they have learnt to look for them, or have learnt
to want them, are not in the poems. Chaucer's poetry is
itself part of the larger cultural tradition, of which the
criticism is another part, and there are often real

correspondences between the criticism and the poetry, though they may receive different emphases in different periods. This does not imply that a piece of criticism, or even a tradition of critical statements, may not be just wrong. Men are fallible, of which the present collection gives plenty of evidence. Criticism is at least partly an intellectual activity, and if it could not occasionally be wrong it could never be significantly right, and would thus forfeit any claim to intellectual value. But the present collection also illustrates the extreme complexity of the critical processes even in the relatively unselfconscious, or differently conscious, periods before our own.

Bibliographical note

The general aim of the two volumes is to present a copious selection of the criticism of Chaucer in English from his own day until 1933. Though necessarily selective, I believe nothing of significance has been omitted. The two volumes divide conveniently almost in mid-nineteenth century.

Speght was the first editor to include 'the judgments and reports of some learned men, of this worthy and famous Poet' 'Workes', 1598, c.i a). Urry collected more such 'Testimonies'. Hippisley, with an extract from whose work our first volume concludes, appears to be the first to attempt an articulated account of the course of such comments. The process culminates in the great collection made by Miss C.F.E. Spurgeon, 'Five Hundred Years of Chaucer Criticism and Allusion', 3 vols, Cambridge, 1925 (reprinted 1961), whose entries reprint in full or in selected extracts the comments she lists. Further references to other criticisms and allusions have been made in the bibliographies by D.D. Griffith, 'Bibliography of Chaucer 1908-1953', Seattle, 1955; and W.R. Crawford, 'Bibliography of Chaucer, 1954-63', Seattle, 1967. The present work has added a few more comments not previously noted elsewhere, but this has not been a principal object. W.L. Alderson and A.C. Henderson, 'Chaucer and Augustan Scholarship', Berkeley, 1970, is a detailed study of one aspect of the reception of Chaucer with new bibliographical information. The work by A. Miskimin, 'The Renaissance Chaucer', Yale University Press, 1975, appeared too late to be used.

The present work has an orientation different from that of Miss Spurgeon. Her intention was, especially in the earlier period, to collect as far as possible every reference, however repetitious, and whether literary or not, although for the nineteenth century she was forced to be very

selective. The present collection has a more specifically
critical orientation. There could be no question of re-
printing the great number of adaptations or textual reminiscences, for their bulk is great and their critical interest minimal. Nor have simple allusions, references, nor
quotations, been recorded, except in rare instances where
they have further, representative, interest. The number
of references to Chaucer listed in the fifteenth and sixteenth centuries has consequently been much reduced,
though some new ones have been added. The actual number
of references, allusions, etc. from subsequent centuries
is also somewhat reduced: for example, Scott's numerous
allusions to Chaucer find no place in this collection because they are of little critical interest, and such as
they have, arising out of their mere number, is adequately
represented by Miss Spurgeon. Keats read, enjoyed and
imitated Chaucer; he exulted in the possession of a copy
of Speght's edition of 1598 (wrongly dated 1596; letter of
31 July 1819 to Dilke), but once again, his brief comments
are of no special Chaucerian interest as criticism and
have not been included. In contrast, many of the passages
reprinted in the present volumes are in themselves more
extensive than the extracts printed by Miss Spurgeon, in
order to help the passages to be seen as autonomous critical units, and at least to suggest their own premises.
The nineteenth-century passages in particular are more extensive than those reprinted by Miss Spurgeon, and differ
considerably in material and emphasis. Nevertheless Miss
Spurgeon's work has naturally offered a most valuable
guideline even when I have departed from it, and it cannot
be replaced.

In many cases, especially before the nineteenth century,
I have perforce reprinted mostly the same text as that of
Miss Spurgeon, but I have in almost every case gone back
to the originals and have often reprinted a more extensive
passage. In only a very few cases over the whole work has
a first edition or a manuscript not been used as a base.
I only hope I have been as accurate as Miss Spurgeon, but
even her texts have a few minor errors which I have corrected, and in some cases, most notably that of Gray, I
have been able to give a text more accurate than any at
present current.

The texts have been presented with the minimum of edi-
torial interference. The original spelling and punctua-
tion have been retained but marginal comments and footnotes, except where necessary for understanding, have been
removed. In some modern scholarly essays in Volume 2 a
large selection of footnotes has necessarily been retained. I have not attempted to alter the mode of

reference to Chaucer's text in any period, variable as it
is.   The source of each comment has been given as briefly
as possible in the headnote to the comment, except where
it is more conveniently noted with the extracts themselves.   All the comments by one single writer are grouped
together even when separated in time.   The headnotes aim
to give such information about the writer, where it is
available, as may enable him to be 'placed', for his comment to be better understood.   Some main aspect of the
comment is also usually touched on, partly, but not always,
with reference to the principal points of the Introduction;
without, of course, any pretence to completeness.   The
main sources of biographical details are those monuments
of self-effacing scholarship, 'The Dictionary of National
Biography'; A.B. Emden, 'A Biographical Register of the
University of Cambridge to 1500', and his equivalent three
volumes for Oxford; J. Foster, 'Alumni Oxonienses'; J. and
J.A. Venn, 'Alumni Cantabrigienses'; 'Who was Who 1871-
1916';'Who's Who' for subsequent years; 'The Dictionary of
American Biography'; 'Who Was Who in America'.

The principal editions of Chaucer's 'Works' up to 1933

A. MANUSCRIPTS

Chaucer died in 1400. Manuscripts of his works, or at
least of his later works, circulated for reading during
his lifetime, as we may deduce from his little poem to
Adam, his scribe, from 'Lenvoy de Chaucer a Bukton', and
from Deschamps' poem (Vol. 1, No. 1); but all the manuscripts we now have were written in the fifteenth century.
In number they vary from the eighty-odd complete or fragmentary copies of 'The Canterbury Tales' through the
twenty-odd complete or fragmentary copies of 'Troilus and
Criseyde' to the unique copy of 'Adam Scriveyn'. Some are
splendid compilations fit for a king, others are solid
bookshop products, some others (of short poems) are copies
by interested amateurs. The shorter poems are sometimes
placed in small groups, but no manuscript aims to put together the complete Works - the very concept did not
exist.

B. EARLY PRINTS

Caxton first printed 'The Canterbury Tales' about 1478,
and reprinted it about 1484. Wynkyn de Worde and Pynson,
his successors, reprinted it again. Similarly Caxton and
his successors reprinted separately a number of other
works by Chaucer. Copies of these editions are now exceedingly rare.

C. FURTHER EDITIONS

(1) 1532, 'The Workes of Geoffrey Chaucer', etc., folio
blackletter, edited by W. Thynne, printed by T. Godfray.

This contains most of Chaucer's genuine works, together
with the non-Chaucerian verse 'Testament of Cressida', the
prose 'Testament of Love', and other spurious poems. It
is in effect a collection of Chaucer and Chaucerian works,
and resembles in appearance one of the great fifteenth-
century manuscript volumes. It contains the Preface by
Sir Brian Tuke (see Vol. 1, No. 22) and other prefatory
matter, all of which was continued in the later booksellers' reprints.

Thynne (d. 1546), educated at Oxford, became an official in the king's household, and in 1526 chief clerk of
the kitchen. He sought assiduously for texts of Chaucer,
and the 1532 edition is the first edition with claims to
completeness. He presumably recognised that several items
were not by Chaucer, though many careless readers attributed them to him. For a list, see Leland, c. 1540 (Vol. 1,
No. 24). The dedication of his edition was written by Sir
Brian Tuke (cf. Vol. 1, No. 22). Thynne wrote nothing on
Chaucer that has survived but is noted here for the sake
of his edition, the foundation of all subsequent editions
until that begun by Urry, published 1721 (cf. Vol. 1, No.
71 and below, item 8). 'A Short Title Catalogue of Books
Printed 1475-1640', The Bibliographical Society, 5068.
(2) 1542, 'The workes of Geoffrey Chaucer', etc., folio,
blackletter. Two issues, imprints by W. Bonham and John
Reynes. Contents are as in Thynne, save that 'The Plowman's Tale' is added after 'The Canterbury Tales'.
'Short Title Catalogue', 5069, 5070.
(3) c. 1550, 'The workes of Geoffrey Chaucer', etc., folio,
blackletter; published by W. Bonham, R. Kele, T. Petit,
R. Toye. Except for the differing printer's name there
is no difference between these issues. Contents are as
in Thynne, save that 'The Plowman's Tale' is now incorporated within 'The Canterbury Tales', immediately preceding 'The Parson's Tale'. 'Short Title Catalogue', 5071-
4.
(4) 1561, folio, blackletter. Edited by John Stowe, printed by Ihon Kyngston for Ihon Wight. There are two
issues: (a) 'The workes of Geoffrey Chaucer', etc., which
has a series of woodcuts illustrating 'The General Prologue' and is much the rarer of the two, only six copies
being known to me; (b) 'The woorkes', etc., which has no
woodcuts in 'The General Prologue'. John Stowe (c. 1525-
1605), whose education is unknown, was son of a tallow
chandler and citizen of London. Stowe himself was a tai-
lor but also a most diligent antiquary, now famous for his
'Survey of London', 1598; his first production, however,
was this edition of Chaucer. He was a collector of manuscripts, some of which are now the treasured possessions

of great libraries, though Stowe himself was very poor in
later life. One, presumably, of his manuscripts was the
large collection of verse which is now R.3.19 of Trinity
College, Cambridge, and from which, it is thought, came
the many mediocre pieces of fifteenth-century verse, 'a
heap of rubbish' in Tyrwhitt's words, which were added to
Chaucer's verse in this edition. But a number of the
additions were authentic poems by Chaucer, and others,
such as Lydgate's 'Story of Thebes', intend no deception.
The volume maintains its character as 'Chaucer and Chaucerian'. 'Short Title Catalogue', (a) 5075, (b) 5076.
(5) 1598, 'The Workes of our Antient and Learned English
Poet Geffrey Chaucer', folio, blackletter, edited by T.
Speght, imprints by G. Bishop, A. Islip for B. Norton, and
A. Islip for T. Wight. (See Vol. 1, Nos 51, 53.) Hetherington points out that Speght disclaims responsibility for
the edition, already nearly complete before he learnt of
it. It is essentially a bookseller's reprint of the 1561
edition, having been entered at Stationers' Hall in 1592
and 1594, to which Speght contributed the Life and Notes.
Stowe made some hitherto unprinted material available to
him. In this edition were first printed the spurious
'Chaucer's Dream', now known as 'Isle of Ladies', and
'The Flower and the Leaf'.
   Although Speght's editing was slight in that he paid
no attention to the text, apart from 'The General Prologue' to 'The Canterbury Tales', the prefatory and ex-
planatory matter make the volume different in kind from
the straightforward unadorned reprints made earlier in
the century in which Chaucer is presented as a 'contemporary'. Chaucer has here become 'ancient and learned'!
Among other additions Speght initiates the process, of
which the present book is the latest example, of printing
a selection of comments on Chaucer's poems, briefly quoting Thynne, Ascham, Spenser, Camden and Sidney's commendations. Chaucer has become a classic - an idea which, with
its veneration for literary achievement, is itself Neoclassical, not Gothic. 'Short Title Catalogue', 5077-9.
(6) 1602, 'The Workes of . . . Geffrey Chaucer', folio,
blackletter, edited by T. Speght, imprints by Adam Islip
and G. Bishop. This edition is re-set, more fully punctu-
ated, and with frequent marginal fists inserted to mark
'sentences and proverbs'. Chaucer's 'A.B.C.' is here
printed for the first time, and 'Iacke Upland' added.
Speght benefited from the 'Animadversions' of William
Thynne, who is thanked. See Vol. 1, Nos 51, 53. 'Short
Title Catalogue', 5080-1.
(7) 1687, 'The Works of . . . Jeffrey Chaucer', folio.
Reset in handsome, rather mannered blackletter. Not all

the errata of the 1602 edition are corrected. The period
between this and the preceding edition is the longest between any editions. This edition is essentially a reprint
of the 1602 edition, with spurious brief conclusions to
the 'Cook's' and 'Squire's Tales' added. The spelling
Jeffrey is distinctive, and used for the first time. The
blackletter style was antiquated and this must have been
one of the last large books printed in such type.
J. Harefinch was responsible. See the valuable study by
W.L. Alderson and A.C. Henderson, *Chaucer and Augustan
Scholarship,* University of California Publications: English Studies 35: 1970.
(8) 1721, 'The Works of Geoffrey Chaucer', edited by John
Urry and others, folio. (Cf. Vol. 1, No. 71). This large
handsome volume continues the process of presenting Chaucer as an 'ancient'. As in editions of the Latin Classics,
pride of place is given to a large engraving of the editor,
Urry (who died before completing his work), and an engraving of Chaucer follows on the next leaf. The prefatory
matter is rewritten and increased. The Glossary is much
improved. Chaucer's 'Retracciouns' to 'The Canterbury
Tales' are printed for the first time.
   John Urry (1666-1715), born in Dublin of Scottish parents, graduated B.A. from Christ Church, Oxford, and was
also elected Student (i.e. fellow) in 1686. He was per-
suaded by Bishop Atterbury to publish an edition of Chaucer largely because his Scotch-Irish accent was considered an advantage. Notwithstanding the claims on the
title-page to have consulted manuscripts, his edition
mended Chaucer's metre (sadly mangled in the earlier
printed editions) quite arbitrarily without due regard to
the manuscripts, and has been universally condemned since
Tyrwhitt's scathing remarks in his edition of 'The Canterbury Tales, (Vol. 1, No. 84). But his principles were not
so foolish. The British Library copy of the edition contains the agreement to publish by Bernard Lintot of 26
August 1715, which provides for 1000 copies to be sold at
£1 10s. 0d. and 250 more on large paper at £2 10s. 0d.
But Urry died very soon after this agreement was made, and
ultimately the edition was completed by Timothy Thomas,
helped by W. Thomas, presumably his brother, who contributed together a sensible Preface and useful Glossary
(mainly William's). The Life was written mainly by John
Dart (Vol. 1, No. 71). The spurious tales of 'Gamelyn'
and 'Beryn', not before printed, were added. The copy in
the British Library is annotated in manuscript by Timothy
Thomas (1694-1751), a Welsh clergyman, who graduated B.A.
from Christ Church in 1716. Of William little is known.
See Alderson and Henderson, above, item 7.

(9) 1737, 'The Canterbury Tales of Chaucer', edited by the Reverend Thomas Morell. This comprises only 'The General Prologue', and 'The Knight's Tale', but prints them in a Middle English text, with variant readings, notes and references, together with modernised versions by Dryden and others. Morell used some thirteen manuscripts and his edition is the first to do what Urry's claimed to do, namely attempt a scientifically constructed text. See Alderson and Henderson, above, item 7; and Vol. 1, Nos 73, 74.

(10) 1775, 'The Canterbury Tales of Chaucer', edited by T. Tyrwhitt, 5 vols, 1775-8. The fifth volume, containing the Glossary, appeared in 1778. See Vol. 1, No. 84. Tyrwhitt's textual method was still unsystematic, but nevertheless an advance on all previous editors. He was also the first editor not merely to refrain from adding further works to Chaucer's credit or discredit, but to make an attempt, largely successful, to sort the genuine works from the spurious, which he did by the criterion of style.

(11) 'The Works of Chaucer' in John Bell's 'The Poets of Great Britain Complete from Chaucer to Churchill', Vols 24mo, 1782-3. Chaucer's works appear in Vols 1-14, with text from Tyrwhitt supplemented by Urry, like numerous other booksellers' reprints of the next few decades.

(12) 1845, 'The Works of Chaucer' in Pickering's Aldine Poets, 6 vols, 1845. This edition has the memoir by Sir Harris Nicolas. For the first time the life is scientifically examined, but the text is not greatly improved.

(13) 1894, 'The Complete Works of Geoffrey Chaucer', edited by W.W. Skeat, The Clarendon Press, Oxford, 6 vols. A supplementary Vol. VII, 'Chaucerian and Other Pieces', containing most of pieces formerly attributed in error to Chaucer, appeared in 1897. The second edition, 1899, is that current. Skeat's text is eclectic, but his command of Middle English and his textual intuition were outstanding. The edition as a whole is out of date, but the Glossary in especial is still valuable, and the whole is a fine work of humane scholarship.

(14) [1933], 'The Complete Works of Chaucer', edited by F.N. Robinson, Oxford University Press, 1 vol. A new text, and in the Notes a remarkably full reference to current scholarship; weak Glossary.

These brief comments on some editions have been compiled from E.P. Hammond, 'Chaucer: A Bibliographical Manual', 1908; J.R. Hetherington, 'Chaucer 1532-1602; Notes and Facsimile Texts', published by the author, Vernon House, 26 Vernon Road, Birmingham 16; W.L. Alderson and A.C. Henderson, 'Chaucer and Augustan Scholarship',

University of California Publications: English Studies,
35, University of California Press, 1970; and from personal observation. A facsimile of the 1532 edition, based
on the British Library copy, was edited by W.W. Skeat,
1912. Another facsimile (based on the copy in Clare College Library, Cambridge, formerly owned by Sir Brian Tuke
himself), and supplemented with facsimiles of the material
added in the editions of 1542, 1561, 1598, and 1602 was
published by The Scolar Press, Menston, Yorkshire, 1969,
edited by Derek Brewer.

Comments

1. RALPH WALDO EMERSON, THE IDENTITY OF ALL MINDS

1837, 1845 (1850), 1856

The great contribution to Chaucer studies from the USA
begins with Emerson (1803-82), man of letters and trans-
cendentalist, who refers to Chaucer several times. He
associates Chaucer with other great writers in a timeless
unity of world literature, as in extract (a) from the
lecture on The American Scholar, delivered in 1837 (Cen-
tenary Edition, I, pp. 91-2). In extract (b), from the
lecture on Shakespeare in the series 'Representative Men'
given in 1845 (first published 1850), he perceives how a
writer such as Chaucer, not seeking an idiosyncratic originality, is as it were a spokesman of, not a legislator
for, a whole tradition of culture, though here timeless-
ness becomes so independent of chronology and historical
process as to make Chaucer the borrower from Caxton (Cen-
tenary Edition, IV, pp. 196-8, 215-17). But Emerson recognised some difference in extract (c) from 'English Traits'
(1856), where he praises Chaucer's plainness of speech as
emphatically as Lydgate has praised his ornateness (Cen-
tenary Edition, V, pp. 233-4). Emerson groups Chaucer
with other major poets who create a general significance
of meaning in human life extending beyond utilitarian
practicality, though in English, as he seems to claim,
based on a feeling for material reality.

(a)

It is remarkable, the character of the pleasure we derive
from the best books. They impress us with the conviction,
that one nature wrote and the same reads. We read the
verses of one of the great English poets, of Chaucer, of
Marvell, of Dryden, with the most modern joy, - with a
pleasure, I mean, which is in great part caused by the abstraction of all *time* from their verses. There is some
awe mixed with the joy of our surprise, when this poet,
who lived in some past world, two or three hundred years
ago, says that which lies close to my own soul, that which
I also had well-nigh thought and said. But for the evidence thence afforded to the philosophical doctrine of the
identity of all minds, we should suppose some pre-estab-
lished harmony, some foresight of souls that were to be,
and some preparation of stores for their future wants,
like the fact observed in insects, who lay up food before
death for the young grub they shall never see.

(b)

Shakespeare knew that tradition supplies a better fable
than any invention can. If he lost any credit of design,
he augmented his resources; and, at that day, our petulant
demand for originality was not so much pressed. There was
no literature for the million. The universal reading, the
cheap press, were unknown. A great poet, who appears in
illiterate times, absorbs into his sphere all the light
which is anywhere radiating. Every intellectual jewel,
every flower of sentiment, it is his fine office to bring
to his people; and he comes to value his memory equally
with his invention. He is therefore little solicitous
whence his thoughts have been derived; whether through
translation, whether through tradition , whether by travel
in distant countries, whether by inspiration; from whatever source, they are equally welcome to his uncritical
audience. Nay, he borrows very near home. Other men say
wise things as well as he; only they say a good many
foolish things, and do not know when they have spoken
wisely. He knows the sparkle of the true stone, and puts
it in high place, wherever he finds it. Such is the
happy position of Homer, perhaps; of Chaucer, of Saadi.
They felt that all wit was their wit. And they are librarians and historiographers, as well as poets. Each
romancer was heir and dispenser of all the hundred tales
of the world, -

Presenting Thebes' and Pelops' line
And the tale of Troy divine.

The influence of Chaucer is conspicuous in all our early
literature; and, more recently, not only Pope and Dryden
have been beholden to him, but, in the whole society of
English writers, a large unacknowledged debt is easily
traced. One is charmed with the opulence which feeds so
many pensioners. But Chaucer is a huge borrower. Chau-
cer, it seems, drew continually, through Lydgate and
Caxton, from Guido di Colonna, whose Latin romance of the
Trojan war was in turn a compilation from Dares Phrygius,
Ovid, and Statius. Then Petrarch, Boccaccio, and the
Provençal poets, are his benefactors: the Romaunt of the
Rose is only judicious translation from William of Lorris
and John of Meun: Troilus and Creseide, from Lollius of
Urbino: The Cock and the Fox, from the 'Lais' of Marie:
The House of Fame, from the French or Italian: and poor
Gower he uses as if he were only a brick-kiln or stone-
quarry, out of which to build his house. He steals by
this apology, - that what he takes has no worth where he
finds it, and the greatest where he leaves it. It has
come to be practically a sort of rule in literature, that
a man, having once shown himself capable of original writing, is entitled thenceforth to steal from the writings
of others at discretion. Thought is the property of him
who can entertain it; and of him who can adequately place
it. A certain awkwardness marks the use of borrowed
thoughts; but, as soon as we have learned what to do with
them, they become our own.
     Thus, all originality is relative. Every thinker is
retrospective....
     One more royal trait properly belongs to the poet. I
mean his cheerfulness, without which no man can be a
poet, - for beauty is his aim. He loves virtue, not for
its obligation, but for its grace: he delights in the
world, in man, in woman, for the lovely light that sparkles from them. Beauty, the spirit of joy and hilarity,
he sheds over the universe. Epicurus relates that poetry
hath such charms that a lover might forsake his mistress
to partake of them. And the true bards have been noted
for their firm and cheerful temper. Homer lies in sunshine; Chaucer is glad and erect; and Saadi says, 'It
was rumoured abroad that I was penitent; but what had I
to do with repentance?' Not less sovereign and cheerful,
- much more sovereign and cheerful, is the tone of Shakspeare....
     Shakspeare, Homer, Dante, Chaucer, saw the splendour
of meaning that plays over the visible world; knew that a

tree had another use than for apples, and corn another
than for meal, and the ball of the earth, than for tillage
and roads: that these things bore a second and finer harvest to the mind, being emblems of its thoughts, and conveying in all their natural history a certain mute commentary on human life.

(c)

A taste for plain strong speech, what is called a biblical
style, marks the English.... It is not less seen in
poetry. Chaucer's hard painting of his Canterbury pilgrims satisfies the senses.... This mental materialism
makes the value of English transcendental genius.

The marriage of the two qualities (materialism and
intellectuality) is in their speech.

2. RICHARD HENGIST HORNE, TRANSLATIONS

1841

Hengist Horne (1803-84), a man of many talents and much
energy, was educated at the Military School at Sandhurst,
and led an intermittently adventurous life, which did not
check a voluminous output of epic poems, drama, novels,
stories, translations, a report on working children, etc.,
among which is included the Introduction and three translations of 'The Poems of Geoffrey Chaucer Modernized',
1841. These extracts from the Introduction give an intelligent survey of some translations and modernisations of
Chaucer from Dryden onwards with a fresh and more historical critical view of Dryden's achievement. Horne concludes by quoting the most Tennysonian line Chaucer ever
wrote.

(p.v) The present publication does not result from an
antiquarian feeling about Chaucer, as the Father of English Poetry, highly interesting as he must always be in
that character alone; but from the extraordinary fact, to
which there is no parallel in the history of the literature

of nations, - that although he is one of the great poets
for all time, his works are comparatively unknown to the
world.   Even in his own country, only a very small class of
his countrymen ever read his poems.   Had Chaucer's poems
been written in Greek or Hebrew, they would have been a
thousand times better known.   They would have been translated.   Hitherto they have had almost everything done for
them that a nation could desire, in so far as the most
careful collation of texts, the most elaborate essays, the
most ample and erudite notes and glossaries, the most elaborate and classical (as well as the most trite and vulgar)
paraphrases, the most eloquent and sincere admiration and
comments of genuine poets, fine prose writers, and scholars - everything, in short, has been done, except to make
them intelligible to the general reader.

Except in the adoption of a modern typography, Chaucer's
poems have always appeared hitherto, under no better aus-
pices for modern appreciation than on their first day of
publication, some three centuries and a half ago.   Concerning the various attempts to render several of his poems
available to the public, which have been made at intervals
by poets and lovers of Chaucer, a few remarks will shortly
be submitted.   With whatever reverence or admiration these
latter may have been received by the readers of those poets
who introduced such specimens among their own works, it is
certain that they produced no perceptible effect in the
popularity of the original author.

Whether there has been a feeling in the public about
Chaucer, amounting to a sort of unconscious resentment at
the total inability to read his poems without first best-
owing the same pains upon his glossary, which has been more
willingly accorded to poetry and prose in the Scottish dialect; or whether on account of certain passages which in
the present stage of refinement appear offensive to a
degree that the good folks of Chaucer's time, as well as
the poet himself, could never have contemplated, it is not
necessary to determine.   Such an antipathy to the study of
his language does exist....

(p. xii) With every respect, then, for the genius, and
for everything that belongs to the memory of Dryden, the
grand charge to which his translations from Chaucer are
amenable is that he has acted upon an erroneous principle.
While it is manifest that much of Chaucer needs but little
more than modern orthography and an occasional transposi-
tion of words, in order to retain such portions as entire
and as intelligible as the productions of the most lucid
writer of the present time, - Dryden considered that nothing whatever of the original substance should be retained.
He translates Chaucer, without any exceptions, as he would

Ovid, Virgil, or Homer, and there seem no characteristic differences. Some idea may be formed of the manner in which Chaucer's foundation is built over, by the fact that the character of the poor Parson in the Prologue to the Canterbury Tales contains only fifty-two lines, - while Dryden's version of it occupies one hundred and forty lines. However the execution may be admired, it is quite clear that the grand and sonorous pomp of the style is directly opposite to the extreme simplicity of the original. Chaucer says of his poor Parson, that, -

> To drawen folk to heaven with faireness,
> By good ensample, was his business.

Dryden says of his, -

> For, letting down the golden chain from high,
> He drew his audience upward to the sky!

The lofty idea here suggested of a figure standing in the clouds, and letting down 'the golden chain' for his audience, can surely never be received as the companion or representative of the meek and unostentatious man of God who went in all weathers to visit his sick parishioners, -

> Upon his feet, and in his hand a staff.

In Dryden's version of the 'Knight's Tale' these lines occur:-

> Next stood Hypocrisy, with holy fear;
> Soft smiling and demurely looking down,
> But hid the dagger underneath the gown:
> The assassinating wife, the holy fiend;
> And far the blackest there, the traitor-friend.

The original of all this is one line, -

> The. smiler with the knife under the cloak.

It is hard to lose such a line for the sake of a trifling matter of spelling. The 'obsolete' outcast is merely this, -

> The smiler with the knif under the cloke.

There is in Chaucer the strength of a giant combined with the simplicity of a child. The latter is quite metamorphosed in Dryden's swelling verse. Whenever he

attempts simplicity, which is very rarely, he fails. Let
the reader compare his account of the death of Arcite with
Chaucer's profound pathos. The following is one of his
closest imitations of the original:-

> Yet could he not his closing eyes withdraw,
> Though less and less of Emily he saw;
> So, speechless, for a little space he lay;
> Then grasp'd the hand he held, and sigh'd his soul away.
>
> *Dryden*

> Duskéd his eyen two, and faill'd his breth,
> But on his ladie yet cast he his eye;
> His last-é word was 'Mercy, Emelie!'
> His spirit changéd house -
>
> *Chaucer*

   The fact is, Dryden's version of the 'Knight's Tale'
would be most appropriately read by the towering shade of
one of Virgil's heroes, walking up and down a battlement
and waving a long gleaming spear to the roll and sweep of
his sonorous numbers.
   Of the highly finished paraphrase, by Mr. Pope, of the
'Wife of Bath's Prologue', and the 'Merchant's Tale,' suffice it to say that the licentious humour of the original
being divested of its quaintness and obscurity, becomes
yet more licentious in proportion to the fine touches of
skill with which it is brought into the light. Spontaneous coarseness is made revolting by meretricious artifice.
Instead of keeping in the distance that which was objectionable by such shades in the modernizing as should have
answered to the hazy appearance of the original, it receives a clear outline, and is brought close to us. An
Ancient Briton, with his long rough hair and painted body,
laughing and singing half naked under a tree, may be
coarse, yet innocent of all intention to offend; but if
the imagination, (absorbing the anachronism,) can conceive
him shorn of his falling hair, his paint washed off, and
in this uncovered state introduced into a drawing-room
full of ladies in rouge and diamonds, hoops and hair-
powder, no one can doubt the injury thus done to the ancient Briton. This is no unfair illustration of what was
done in the time of Pope, and by these editions of Ogle
and Lipscombe. They are *not* modernized versions - which
implies modern delicacy, as well as modern language - they
are vulgarized versions. The public of the present day
would certainly never tolerate any similar proceeding,
even were it likely to be attempted.
   But if such poets and artists as Dryden and Pope are

open to objections for their unceremonious paraphrases,
what shall be said of the presumption of Messrs. Ogle,
Lipscombe, and others, in following their example. Perhaps the worst of these specimens are from the pens of Mr.
Betterton and Mr. Cobb. Their modern grossness and vulgarity are astonishing. In their execution of the finest
passages of pathos or of humour there is, at best, only
such a vestige remaining of the original as serves to show
the difference of men's minds in contemplating the same
objects.

Let the reader, who is not familiar with the portrait
and character of *Absolon,* in the 'Miller's Tale,' imagine
a jolly parish clerk of these olden times - with a ruddy
complexion, and thick golden locks 'strouting' out behind,
like a 'broad fan' - his dress neat and close, with red
stockings, and 'St. Paul's windows carved upon his shoes;'
a kirtle thick with points and tags; and a 'gay surplice'
over all, as 'white as is the blossom upon the thorn.'
This jolly parish clerk, smitten with the charms of the
wife of a carpenter, sends her all sorts of presents, and
serenades her continually with voice and instrument. But
finding all his efforts to attract her love or admiration
ineffectual, he has recourse to a more dignified proceeding. He brings a small scaffolding or stage (probably
drawn by a mule) before her window, - mounts it, and
enacts the part of *Herod* in one of the Miracle plays!
This most ludicrous and matchless climax is vulgarized by
Mr. Cobb in these lines; not one word of which belongs to
Chaucer any more than the sense of them, -

> Sometimes he *scaramouch'd* it all on hie,
> And *harlequin'd* it with activity:
> Betrays the lightness of his empty head,
> And how he could cut capers * * * .

But it is not only the loss of this unexampled picture,
as a piece of rich graphic humour, that constitutes the
ground of complaint, but the loss of the *historical* information involved in the original description. This performance of the part of *Herod* by the jolly parish clerk is a
proof of the kind of plays that were acted in the reigns
of Edward III. and Richard II., *viz.* Miracle Plays; since
called, erroneously, Mysteries and Moralities.

When the Pardoner is describing how he stands up 'like
a clerk in his pulpit,' to preach the money out of the
pockets of his deluded audience, by 'an hundred japes' or
knaveries, the following most graphic picture is given:-

Then paine I me to stretchen forth my necke,
And east and west *upon the people I beck*
As doth a dove, sitting upon a barn!
Chaucer

Then forth with painful *toil* my neck I stretch,
And east and west *my arms* extended reach.
So on a barn's long roof you might have seen
A *pouting* pigeon *woo his feather'd queen!*
Lipscombe

In the quotation from Chaucer, be it observed, all the
words are his own, and only one spelt differently. An old
man, (who is Death in disguise) tired of life through decrepitude and loss of his faculties, is thus described:-

And on the ground, which is my mother's gate,
I knock-e with my staff, early and late,
And say to her, 'Leave, mother! - let me in!'
Chaucer

Here at my mother earth's *deaf sullen* gate,
My staff, *sad sole support*, early and late
Knocks *with incessant stroke, but knocks in vain,*
For nought she hears though sadly I complain.
Lipscombe

And on this principle are heaps of common-place epithets and expletives employed throughout these editions,
in order to evade taking the incomparable original, even
where it needs but the most trifling assistance. The
idea of any one re-writing or paraphrasing such passages!
What would become of the finest things in Spenser and
Shakespeare by this process? And yet Mr. Lipscombe seems
to endeavour to keep closer upon the borders of his author
than most of the others, though he takes equal care never
to touch upon his domains. Perhaps the best in execution
of these paraphrases (of course excepting those of Dryden
and Pope), are the tales furnished by Mr. Boyce: at all
events, they are the most ambitious. He renders the
'Squire's Tale' in stanzas. The opening, it must be
acknowledged, is high and imposing:-

Where peopled Scythia's verdant plains extend
    East in that sea, in whose unfathom'd flood
Long-winding Volga's rapid streams descend
    On Oxus bank, an ancient city stood;
Then Sarra - but to later ages known
    By rising Samarcand's imperial name,
There, held a potent prince his honour'd throne, &c.

Many readers may perhaps admire the lofty tone of this opening stanza - but why associate it with the name of Chaucer? The whole of the above is thus simply given in the original:-

At Sarra, in the land of Tartarie,
There dwelt a king, &c.

When the wounded falcon, in the same tale, perceives the sympathy with her distress which is felt by the king's daughter Canace, a part of the passage is thus rendered by Mr. Boyce, -

So may the sad reflection be believ'd
   Which from experience deeply wounded flows,
That *thy superior virtue* undeceiv'd
   May *scorn the semblance faithless manhood shows* -
Their vows, their sighs, and all the flatt'ring arts
By which (*they skill'd*) betray deluded virgin hearts.

Here is the original, without a word altered, even in the spelling:-

I see well, that ye have on my distresse
Compassion, my faire Canace,
Of veray *womanly benignitee*
That nature in your principles hath set.

And where the falcon begins to tell her story by saying that she was bred, -

And fostered in a rock of marble gray,
So tenderly that nothing ailéd me, &c.,

Mr. Boyce commences it with his sounding geographicals, -

Where rapid Niester rolls his noisy wave
   High in a marble cliff that brow'd the flood,
My peaceful birth indulgent nature gave;
   Securely there our nest paternal stood, &c.

The following are specimens from the versions of Mr. Ogle, (the projector and editor, I believe, of the first edition,) and of Mr. Betterton, previously mentioned in no terms of admiration. The latter opens the description of the Prioress, in the Prologue, in a style which bears a striking resemblance to that of Sternhold and Hopkins:-

There was with these a Nun, a Prioress;
A lady of no ord'nary address, &c.

For reasons which will hereafter appear, the reader is
requested to observe the barbarous effect of the contrac-
tion, by syncope, of the word 'ordinary' - being evidently
done to preserve a mechanical adherence to ten syllables
instead of softly sounding the eleventh.   In the portraiture of the Friar, in the Prologue, he interpolates some
gratuitous indecencies, and omits the finest original
lines, even the one which says the friar's neck was 'white
as is the fleur de lis.'   At the close, where Chaucer
shows us the quaint begging rogue, playing his harp among
a crowd of admiring auditors, and turning up his eyes,
with an attempted expressing of religious enthusiasm
through which the humorous sense of his knavery forces its
way, till his eyes 'twinkle in his head, aright, as do the
stars upon a frosty night' - the whole of this is lost in
the vulgar association of 'little pigs' eyes,' and 'small
stars' to match, foisted in by the ingenious Mr. Betterton.
    In Mr. Ogle's labours there are few specimens approach-
ing more closely to the original than the following.   The
grammar is peculiar.

> For he, nor benefice had got, nor cure,
> No patron, yet so worldly, to insure!
> So dextrous yet, of body, or of face,
> To circumvent no chaplain, with his Grace:
> Nor fulsome Dedication could he write,
> Drudge for a dame or pander for a knight.
> Much rather had he range, beside his bed,
> A score of authors unadorn'd in red,
> With Aristotle, champion of the schools,
> To mend his ways, by philosophic rules;
> Than basely to a *vic'rage* owe his rise,
> By courting folly, or by flatt'ring vice,
> Than flourish like a prebend in his stall:
> That way, he held, was not to rise, but fall,
> Nor would he be the man, for all his rent,
> Nam'd you the priest of Bray, or priest of Trent.
>
> > *Ogle*

None of the common-place venalities particularized in
the first six lines are to be found in the original, nor
is the bad grammar.   Chaucer simply says that the poor
scholar had as yet got no benefice, nor had any worldly
anxiety to hold an office, -

> For him was lever han at his beddes hed,
> A twenty book-es clothed in black or red,
> Of Aristotle and his philosophie,
> Than rob-es rich, fiddle, or psaltery.

For all that follows, in the paraphrase, there is no further authority in Chaucer than just shown.

Whenever a difficulty occurred in the original - and it
is certain there are many - or a peculiar touch of pathos
or humour which they did not understand, these gentlemen
either said just what they pleased instead, or omitted the
passage. In the 'Frere's Tale,' when the Sompnour meets
the Devil in the shape of a forester, and asks him where
he lives, the Devil replies *in a soft voice* - 'Far in the
north countree!' This is totally omitted by Mr. Markland.
The Sompnour perseveres in asking the supposed forester so
many questions, that the poet compares his incessant prat-
ing and fidgetting to a woodpecker who is 'ever *enquiring
upon* every thing.' The idea thus presented to the imagination of the busy creature passing from branch to branch,
with his tapping inquiry, and curious prying bill, is certainly one of those wonderfully happy thoughts seldom
found in any other writer, except Shakspeare.

> This Sompnour which that was as full of jangles,
> As full of venime ben thise wariangles,
> And ever enquering upon every thing, &c.

But Mr. Markland, being indisposed to take the trouble
of studying the passage, passes over it without the most
distant allusion. It is proper to mention the names of
all these gentlemen who have had the presumption to 'throw
clean overboard' such a writer as Chaucer, in order to
place themselves at the helm of his vessel. The commonplace paraphrase of Mr. Grosvenor should not, therefore,
be omitted, but that he displays no new features in his
method. It only remains to mention one more. Here is a
specimen from Mr. Brooke's 'Man of Law's Tale,' - and very
like pantomime poetry it is.

> Hence, Want! ungrateful visitant, adieu,
> Pale empress, hence, with all thy meagre crew;
> Sour discontent, and mortify'd chagrin;
> Lean hollow care, and self-corroding spleen;
> Distress and woe, sad parents of despair,
> With wringing hands, and ever rueful air;
> The tread of *dun*, and *bum's* alarming hand,
> *Dire as the touch of Circe's circling wand,* &c.

It will readily be apprehended, that for all this
modern low wit and trite verbiage there is no fraction of
authority in the original. That the circulation of such
trash from 'bum's alarming hand,' pretending to be versions of the best songs of a poet imprisoned in an

obsolete dialect, may have contributed, in some degree, to
make the public indifferent to their first great author,
is not unlikely.   Believing these versions to be 'Chaucer'
refined,' what must they have conceived of the original?

But whatever injury to the reputation of Chaucer these
productions may, or may not, have occasioned, there can be
no doubt of the mischief done by Mr. Pope's obscene specimen, placed at the head of his list of 'Imitations of
English Poets.'   It is an imitation of those passages which
we should only regard as the rank offal of a great feast
in the olden time.   The better taste and feeling of Pope
should have imitated the noble *poetry* of Chaucer.   He
avoided this 'for sundry weighty reasons.'   But if this
so-called imitation by Pope was 'done in his youth,' he
should have burnt it in his age.   Its publication at the
present day among his elegant works, is a disgrace to
modern times, and to his high reputation.

The version given by Lord Thurlow of the 'Flower and
the Leaf' is such, in its execution and fine appreciation,
as might be expected of a true poet.   He has, however,
interpolated several lines in almost every stanza.   His
translation of the 'Knight's Tale' is admirable for its
fidelity, generally, and for its versification, - not on
the model of that uniformity of syllables and position of
accents which may be regarded as the school of Pope; but
he has quite given up the peculiar harmonies of the rhythm
of Chaucer.   On the latter subject it will be necessary to
offer some remarks in the course of the present inquiry.

Concerning the 'Prioress's Tale,' with which the public
have become acquainted in the works of Mr. Wordsworth, it
cannot be requisite to make any comments, as the severe
poetical fidelity of its execution has long since been
recognized by all true lovers of Chaucer.   A free version
of the 'Squire's Tale' was published by Mr. Leigh Hunt
some years since; the translation, however, of that tale
which appears in the present volume is an entirely new
production.

It only remains to mention the name of one more gentleman, whose 'loving labours' to make the public of this day
acquainted with the riches of Chaucer are well known, but
have been appreciated by far too small a number of readers.
About five years ago Mr. Cowden Clarke produced a volume
of selections from Chaucer's poems, in which every objectionable passage was omitted, and the greatest beauties retained.   The text was carefully collated; many of the
words spelt as now in use; a current glossary and notes
were given at the bottom of each page, to save the trouble
of continual reference and correcting, and the words were
accented, so as to enable the general reader to get some

notion of Chaucer's quantity and rhythm. But the public
recoiled, as heretofore, from the obsolete dialect. The
labours of this amiable author, and the cordial co-
operation of his publisher, received no adequate encour-
agement.

Since therefore it appears manifest that the modern
public will not undertake the task of mastering the dialect of the Father of English Poetry, and that the pleasure derived from the original seems likely to continue
the exclusive possession of a small class of readers, the
projectors of the present undertaking are anxious to adopt
such means as may be in their power of diffusing a portion
of this pleasure. They venture to hope that, while their
labours may not be unacceptable to the million, this publication may also lead to an increase in the numbers of
those who read the noble original.

There may be several methods of rendering Chaucer in
modern English. It will be sufficient, however, to mention the two extremes. The advocates of the one argue -
that in order to render Chaucer truly, it must be done in
the spirit rather than the letter; simply because so much
of the letter, or words, of his period differ both in
sound and sense from those now in use; and that while
everything is retained from the original which can be regarded as an exception, the large mass of the obsolete
remainder must be re-written, i.e. supplied by corresponding words and rhythm to the best of the writer's ability. Hence, the spiritual sense of the author is the
ruling principle. The advocates of the opposite method
argue, that all the substantial material and various
rhythm of Chaucer should be adopted as far as possible;
his obsolete phrases, words, terminations, and grammatical construction, translated, modernized, and humoured,
to the best of the writer's ability. To retain or preserve the existing substance is the rule; to rewrite and
paraphrase is the exception. The first method, were its
highest degree of success attainable, would present little
or none of the original material, yet contain the essence
of the whole: the greatest success of the other method
would be, that on comparing it with the original there
should appear to have been very little done, and yet the
version be not unacceptable to a modern reader. The first
method has its dangers; the latter its disadvantages. But,
inasmuch as there is a large portion of the original which
needs but little alteration, (except in the opinion of
those who may consider they best render Chaucer by merging
his identity in their own,) while at the same time there
is so large a portion which requires to be entirely re-
modelled, it seems plain that the greatest amount of the

original will be obtained from between these two extremes;
the only distinguishing marks of the different methods
being a general predominance of this or that principle.
What merits they may individually possess it does not rest
with us to determine; but it is only fair to state that no
one among the contributors to the present volume has
attempted the first method.

The safest method, as the most becoming, is manifestly
that of preserving as much of the original substance as
can be rendered available, 'that which appears quaint (1),
as well as that which is more modern; in short as much of
the author - his nature - his own mode of speaking and
describing, as possible. By thus preserving his best
parts we should keep the model of Nature, his own model,
before us, and make modern things bend to her, - not her,
as is the custom of our self-love, bend to every thing
which happens to be modern. It is possible, that something of a vapour, at least to common eyes, might be thus
removed from *his* glorious face; but to venture further, we
are afraid, would be to attempt to improve the sun itself,
or to go and recolour the grass it looks upon.'

With reference, however, to the omission of certain
objectionable passages, and the interpolation of a few
lines to connect the thread of the interest, it is presumed that this licence will be readily permitted, on all
sides, to the exigencies of the case. Another reason for
sundry omissions may *occasionally* exist. Chaucer sometimes becomes very prolix, and disposed to lengthy digressions. They are generally excellent when humorous;
when learned and grave, they are apt to become very tedious. He sometimes pauses on the threshold of the highest
interest to give a long list of not very similar cases
from history or scholastic lore. On one of these occasions he makes his heroine in her great anguish recount
some eighteen tragic stories, taken from 'Hieronymus
contra Jovinianum', l. i. c. 39. 'In the Troilus and
Cressida,' observes Mr. Clarke, 'there constantly inter-
vene long see-saws of argumentative dialogue; and, above
all things in such a narrative, a discourse extending to
upwards of a hundred lines upon the doctrine of *Predestination* is put into the mouth of Troilus! The same defect
of tediousness applies to some of the other extended compositions.' Chaucer is also very fond of repeating the
same things upon different occasions - and upon the same
occasion. Whenever he alludes to a recent event in his
narrative, he either tells it nearly all over again, or
apologizes for not doing so, pleading that there is 'no
need.' Sometimes with humorous petulancy he abruptly
announces that he will *not* repeat the matter any more - as

though he considered the reader wished to exact it from
him. This peculiarity is solely attributable to the
period at which Chaucer wrote - a period of religious and
political controversies, while knowledge was so new that
the difficulty of acquiring suggested proportionate fears
of inability to communicate it efficiently, and induced
all sorts of repetitions in order to prevent misunderstan-
dings. This is why Chaucer's poetry often reminds us of
remote times, and even suggests old age in the writer: in
every other respect he is the most invariably fresh and
youthful poet ever given to the world. His poetry not
only has the freshness of morning in it, but gives the
impression of the youngest heart enjoying that freshness....

   (p. xcv) Of the ludicrous anachronisms in Chaucer, it
will be sufficient to say that they by no means resulted
from want of knowledge. It was a habit of the old imaginative writers; and all writers of imagination have a
strong tendency to the same merging of time, place, and
circumstance, in universal truth. He grafts the age of
chivalry on the antique tree of time. It is therefore
presumed that the reader will be wisely pleased on his
first introduction to Mars the *knight*; Phoebus the *chivalrous bachelor; Saint* Venus, &c.

   Extraordinary as were the comic and humorous powers of
Chaucer, hsi pathos is his greatest characteristic. In
this respect he has no equal except Shakspeare; while
for the frequency of his recurrence to such emotions, and
their long sustained and unmitigated anguish - the woes
of years eating into the heart - several of Chaucer's
stories are without any parallel, - even in the great
Boccaccio, who furnished the deep ground-work of several
of them. Few, if any, of Chaucer's stories are his own
invention; many of his poems are free translations. In
comparing them with the sources of their origin - as in
the case also of Shakspeare - one of the greatest proofs
of his genius is made apparent by what he has *not* borrowed.
As an historian of the characters, manners, and habits of
his countrymen during his age, he stands alone for comprehensiveness and fidelity.

   In Chaucer's descriptions - whether of men or things -
he is so graphic, so sure of eye and hand, so rich in the
power of conveying objects of sense to the imaginations of
others, that his words have almost the effect of subs-
tances and colours, so that you seem to feel and see the
things rather than have the idea of them, which is all you
get from most other writers....

   (p. civ) As every true poet 'has a song in his mind,'
yet more certainly has every great poet a religious

passion in his soul. The emotion he derives from the
thing created, is often too strong to dwell upon its imperfections, or rest satisfied in its beauty, and impels
his imagination at once to ascend to the creative Principle, wherein alone it can find relief and repose. With
this feeling doth the profoundly simple-hearted old poet
call upon God, and upon Christ, through the voices of
earth's many happy and many suffering children; with this
thought doth he seek with aching eye to look through the
darkness of forbidden knowledge, at the Tree that burns
impalpably beyond; with this yearning doth his soul spring
upward in divine rhythmic harmony with those spheres which
are ever working while they sing.

  Scattered, neglected, overgrown with weeds, and the
dust of ignorance and olden time; thy page oft illegible
as the pale cobweb, or the tattered banner whereon the
name of the victor is confused with that of the vanquished,
and the rest all faded, - Father of English Poetry, thy
hand-writing and the writing of the hands guided by thee,
have found but a careless preservation among after generations. Somewhat of these primitive inspirations have been
mutilated; many damaged by errors of omission and intrusion; many lost. Yet from the fulness and vitality of
that genius once breathed over the lost prototypes, - the
worm, the moth, and the mouldering years, have lived their
lives and done their work upon *them,* without conveying the
records into the all-compounding earth; nor hath the silence of progressive ages been unbroken by a strange cry,
at intervals, which told that Chaucer was not gone into
ultimate oblivion, but only sleeping till the modern world
awoke. Sleeping, indeed, the deep sleep which follows
great labours and long neglect, but, by those who were
gazing with reverent love, still seen as of yore; - by
those who were listening, still heard, -

  Singing with voice memorial - in the shade.

Note

1 Polish away all the quaintness, and you erase a portion
   of *the historical* from the portraiture. It is very curious, and not a little amusing, that this word *quaint*
   should have been a term of some reproach in Chaucer's
   time. He occasionally uses it in that sense himself:

      Colours of rhetorike ben to me *queinte:*
      My spirit feleth not of swiche matere!'
                    The Franklin's Prologue

Chaucer himself is now considered quaint beyond measure. The old dramatists are called quaint. At present, the word is sometimes used with us, in the best
sense, to express the struggles of genius with an un-
formed language; sometimes as the quiet humour of our
ancestors; sometimes it means an obsolete form of expression; sometimes it expresses the resentments of a
modern ear; sometimes it means nothing - which is rather
worse than the thing complained of. All the best writers of the present age will become quaint; and as only
the best will live to enjoy the necessary odium, it
would perhaps be but reasonable in future to attach a
more charitable meaning to this unavoidable infirmity
of old age.

3. HENRY DAVID THOREAU, HOMELY, INNOCENT, CHILDISH CHAUCER

1843 (1849)

Thoreau (1817-62), lover of woods and hater of taxes, an
early example of the true American writer's characteristic
rejection of society, sees in Chaucer his own attractive
character, divided between books and Nature. The suggestion of Chaucer's childlike quality becomes, variously expressed, a commonplace of the mid- and later-nineteenth
century, and the general tone of Thoreau's comments finds
its most famous expression in Arnold (cf. No. 23); but
Thoreau also genuinely captures, in his own idiom, the un-
pretentious 'Gothic' self-presentation of the poet as a
'homely Englishman', not a dignified and sacred bard.
Thoreau's comments, first a lecture given in 1843, then
printed in 'The Dial' (Boston) IV (January 1844), pp. 297-
303, eventually helped, in expanded form, to fill out the
Friday of 'A Week on the Concord and Merrimack Rivers'
(1849), whence comes this extract.

What a contrast between the stern and desolate poetry of
Ossian and that of Chaucer, and even of Shakespeare and
Milton, much more of Dryden, and Pope, and Gray! Our
summer of English poetry, like the Greek and Latin before
it, seems well advanced toward its fall, and laden with

the fruit and foliage of the season, with bright autumnal
tints; but soon the winter will scatter its myriad clustering and shading leaves, and leave only a few desolate and
fibrous boughs to sustain the snow and rime, and creak in
the blasts of ages. We cannot escape the impression that
the Muse has stooped a little in her flight when we come
to the literature of civilised eras. Now first we hear of
various ages and styles of poetry; it is pastoral, and
lyric, and narrative, and didactic; but the poetry of
runic monuments is of one style, and for every age. The
bard has in a great measure lost the dignity and sacred-
ness of his office. Formerly he was called a *seer*, but
now it is thought that one man sees as much as another.
He has no longer the bardic rage, and only conceives the
deed, which he formerly stood ready to perform. Hosts of
warriors earnest for battle could not mistake nor dispense
with the ancient bard. His lays were heard in the pauses
of the fight. There was no danger of his being overlooked
by his contemporaries. But now the hero and the bard are
of different professions. When we come to the pleasant
English verse, the storms have all cleared away and it
will never thunder and lighten more. The poet has come
within doors, and exchanged the forest and crag for the
fireside, the hut of the Gael, and Stonehenge with its
circles of stones, for the house of the Englishman. No
hero stands at the door prepared to break forth into song
or heroic action, but a homely Englishman, who cultivates
the art of poetry. We see the comfortable fireside, and
hear the crackling fagots in all the verse.

Notwithstanding the broad humanity of Chaucer, and the
many social and domestic comforts which we meet with in
his verse, we have to narrow our vision somewhat to consider him, as if he occupied less space in the landscape,
and did not stretch over hill and valley as Ossian does.
Yet, seen from the side of posterity, as the father of
English poetry, preceded by a long silence or confusion in
history, unenlivened by any strain of pure melody, we
easily come to reverence him. Passing over the earlier
continental poets, since we are bound to the pleasant
archipelago of English poetry, Chaucer's is the first name
after that misty weather in which Ossian lived which can
detain us long. Indeed, though he represents so different
a culture and society, he may be regarded as in many respects the Homer of the English poets. Perhaps he is the
youthfullest of them all. We return to him as to the
purest well, the fountain farthest removed from the high-
way of desultory life. He is so natural and cheerful,
compared with later poets, that we might almost regard him
as a personification of spring. To the faithful reader

his muse has even given an aspect to his times, and when
he is fresh from perusing him they seem related to the
golden age.   It is still the poetry of youth and life
rather than of thought; and though the moral vein is obvious and constant, it has not yet banished the sun and daylight from his verse.   The loftiest strains of the muse
are, for the most part, sublimely plaintive, and not a
carol as free as nature's.   The content which the sun
shines to celebrate from morning to evening is unsung.
The muse solaces herself, and is not ravished but consoled.
There is a catastrophe implied, and a tragic element in all
our verse, and less of the lark and morning dews than of
the nightingale and evening shades.   But in Homer and Chaucer there is more of the innocence and serenity of youth
than in the more modern and moral poets.   The Iliad is not
Sabbath but morning reading, and men cling to this old song
because they still have moments of unbaptised and uncommit-
ted life, which give them an appetite for more.   To the innocent there are neither cherubim nor angels.   At rare
intervals we rise above the necessity of virtue into an unchangeable morning light, in which we have only to live
right on and breathe the ambrosial air.   The Iliad represents no creed nor opinion, and we read it with a rare
sense of freedom and irresponsibility, as if we trod on
native ground and were autochthones of the soil.

Chaucer had eminently the habits of a literary man and
a scholar.   There were never any times so stirring that
there were not to be found some sedentary still.   He was
surrounded by the din of arms.   The battles of Hallidon
Hill and Neville's Cross, and the still more memorable
battles of Cressy and Poictiers, were fought in his youth;
but these did not concern our poet much, Wickliffe and his
reform much more.   He regarded himself always as one pri-
vileged to sit and converse with books.   He helped to establish the literary class.   His character as one of the
fathers of the English language would alone make his works
important, even those which have little poetical merit.
He was as simple as Wordsworth in preferring his homely
but vigorous Saxon tongue when it was neglected by the
court and had not yet attained to the dignity of a literature, and rendered a similar service to his country to
that which Dante rendered to Italy.   If Greek sufficeth for
Greek, and Arabic for Arabian, and Hebrew for Jew, and
Latin for Latin, then English shall suffice for him, for
any of these will serve to teach truth 'right as divers
pathes leaden divers folke the right waye to Rome.'   In the
Testament of Love he writes, 'Let then clerkes enditen in
Latin, for they have the propertie of science, and the
knowinge in that facultie, and lette Frenchmen in their

Frenche also enditen their queinte termes, for it is kyn-
dely to their mouthes, and let us shewe our fantasies in
soche wordes as we lerneden of our dames tonge.'
    He will know how to appreciate Chaucer best who has
come down to him the natural way, through the meagre pas-
tures of Saxon and ante-Chaucerian poetry; and yet, so human and wise he appears after such diet, that we are
liable to misjudge him still. In the Saxon poetry extant,
in the earliest English, and the contemporary Scottish
poetry, there is less to remind the reader of the rudeness
and vigour of youth than of the feebleness of a declining
age. It is for the most part translation of imitation
merely, with only an occasional and slight tinge of poetry,
oftentimes the falsehood and exaggeration of fable without
its imagination to redeem it, and we look in vain to find
antiquity restored, humanised, and made blithe again by
some natural sympathy between it and the present. But
Chaucer is fresh and modern still, and no dust settles on
his true passages. It lightens along the line, and we are
reminded that flowers have bloomed, and birds sung, and
hearts beaten in England. Before the earnest gaze of the
reader the rust and moss of time gradually drop off, and
the original green life is revealed. He was a homely and
domestic man, and did breathe quite as modern men do.
    There is no wisdom that can take place of humanity, and
we find *that* in Chaucer. We can expand at last in his
breadth, and we think that we could have been that man's
acquaintance. He was worthy to be a citizen of England,
while Petrarch and Boccacio lived in Italy, and Tell and
Tamerlane in Switzerland and Asia, and Bruce in Scotland,
and Wickliffe, and Gower, and Edward the Third, and John
of Gaunt, and the Black Prince were his own countrymen as
well as contemporaries; all stout and stirring names. The
fame of Roger Bacon came down from the preceding century,
and the name of Dante still possessed the influence of a
living presence. On the whole, Chaucer impresses us as
greater than his reputation, and not a little like Homer
and Shakespeare, for he would have held up his head in
their company. Among early English poets he is the land-
lord and host, and has the authority of such. The affectionate mention which succeeding early poets make of him,
coupling him with Homer and Virgil, is to be taken into
the account in estimating his character and influence.
King James and Dunbar of Scotland speak of him with more
love and reverence than any modern author of his predecessors of the last century. The same childlike relation is
without a parallel now. For the most part we read him
without criticism, for he does not plead his own cause,
but speaks for his readers, and has that greatness of

trust and reliance which compels popularity. He confides
in the reader, and speaks privily with him, keeping nothing back. And in return the reader has great confidence
in him, that he tells no lies, and reads his story with
indulgence, as if it were the circumlocution of a child,
but often discovers afterwards that he has spoken with
more directness and economy of words than a sage. He is
never heartless,

> For first the thing is thought within the hart,
> Er any word out from the mouth astart.

And so new was all his theme in those days, that he did
not have to invent, but only to tell.
   We admire Chaucer for his sturdy English wit. The easy
height he speaks from in his Prologue to the Canterbury
Tales, as if he were equal to any of the company there
assembled, is as good as any particular excellence in it.
But though it is full of good sense and humanity, it is
not transcendent poetry. For picturesque description of
persons it is, perhaps, without a parallel in English
poetry; yet it is essentially humorous, as the loftiest
genius never is. Humour, however broad and genial, takes
a narrower view than enthusiasm. To his own finer vein he
added all the common wit and wisdom of his time, and
everywhere in his works his remarkable knowledge of the
world, and nice perception of character, his rare common
sense and proverbial wisdom, are apparent. His genius
does not soar like Milton's, but is genial and familiar.
It shows great tenderness and delicacy, but not the
heroic sentiment. It is only a greater portion of humanity with all its weakness. He is not heroic, as Raleigh,
nor pious, as Herbert, nor philosophical, as Shakespeare;
but he is the child of the English muse, that child which
is the father of the man. The charm of his poetry consists often only in an exceeding naturalness, perfect sincerity, with the behaviour of a child rather than of a
man.
   Gentleness and delicacy of character are everywhere
apparent in his verse. The simplest and humblest words
come readily to his lips. No one can read the Prioress's
tale, understanding the spirit in which it was written,
and in which the child sings *O alma redemptoris mater,* or
the account of the departure of Constance with her child
upon the sea, in the Man of Lawe's tale, without feeling
the native innocence and refinement of the author. Nor
can we be mistaken respecting the essential purity of his
character, disregarding the apology of the manners of the
age. A simple pathos and feminine gentleness, which

Wordsworth only occasionally approaches, but does not
equal, are peculiar to him. We are tempted to say that
his genius was feminine not masculine. It was such a
feminineness, however, as is rarest to find in woman,
though not the appreciation of it; perhaps it is not to be
found at all in woman, but is only the feminine in man.

Such pure and genuine and childlike love of Nature is
hardly to be found in any poet.

Chaucer's remarkably trustful and affectionate character appears in his familiar, yet innocent and reverent,
manner of speaking of his God. He comes into his thought
without any false reverence, and with no more parade than
the zephyr to his ear. If Nature is our mother, then God
is our father. There is less love and simple, practical
trust in Shakespeare and Milton. How rarely in our
English tongue do we find expressed any affection for God!
Certainly, there is no sentiment so rare, as the love of
God. Herbert almost alone expresses it, 'Ah, my dear
God!' Our poet uses similar words with propriety; and
whenever he sees a beautiful person, or other object,
prides himself on the 'maistry' of his God. He even re-
commends Dido to be his bride -

> if that God that heaven and yearth made,
> Would have a love for beauty and goodness,
> And womanhede, trouth, and semeliness.

But in justification of our praise, we must refer to
his works themselves, to the Prologue to the Canterbury
Tales, the account of Gentilesse, the Flower and the
Leaf, the stories of Griselda, Virginia, Ariadne, and
Blanche the Dutchesse, and much more of less distinguished merit. There are many poets of more taste, and
better manners, who knew how to leave out their dulness;
but such negative genius cannot detain us long; we shall
return to Chaucer still with love. Some natures, which
are really rude and ill-developed, have yet a higher standard of perfection than others which are refined and well
balanced. Even the clown has taste, whose dictates,
though he disregards them, are higher and purer than
those which the artist obeys. If we have to wander
through many dull and prosaic passages in Chaucer, we have
at least the satisfaction of knowing that it is not an
artificial dulness, but too easily matched by many passages in life. We confess that we feel a disposition commonly to concentrate sweets, and accumulate pleasures; but
the poet may be presumed always to speak as a traveller,
who leads us through a varied scenery, from one eminence
to another, and it is, perhaps, more pleasing, after all,

to meet with a fine thought in its natural setting.
Surely fate has enshrined it in these circumstances for
some end. Nature strews her nuts and flowers broadcast,
and never collects them into heaps. This was the soil it
grew in, and this the hour it bloomed in; if sun, wind,
and rain came here to cherish and expand the flower, shall
not we come here to pluck it?

A true poem is distinguished not so much by a felicitous expression, or any thought it suggests, as by the
atmosphere which surrounds it. Most have beauty of outline merely, and are striking as the form and bearing of
a stranger; but true verses come toward us indistinctly,
as the very breath of all friendliness, and envelop us in
their spirit and fragrance. Much of our poetry has the
very best manners, but no character. It is only an unusual precision and elasticity of speech, as if its author
had taken, not an intoxicating draught, but an electuary.
It has the distinct outline of sculpture, and chronicles
an early hour. Under the influence of passion all men
speak thus distinctly, but wrath is not always divine.
There are two classes of men called poets. The one
cultivates life, the other art - one seeks food for nut-
riment, the other for flavour; one satisfies hunger, the
other gratifies the palate. There are two kinds of writing, both great and rare: one that of genius, or the inspired, the other of intellect and taste, in the intervals of inspiration. The former is above criticism,
always correct, giving the law to criticism. It vibrates
and pulsates with life for ever. It is sacred, and to be
read with reverence, as the works of nature are studied.
There are few instances of a sustained style of this kind;
perhaps every man has spoken words, but the speaker is
then careless of the record. Such a style removes us out
of personal relations with its author; we do not take his
words on our lips, but his sense into our hearts. It is
the stream of inspiration, which bubbles out, now here,
now there, now in this man, now in that. It matters not
through what ice-crystals it is seen, now a fountain, now
the ocean stream running under ground. It is in Shakespeare, Alpheus, in Burns, Arethuse; but ever the same.
The other is self-possessed and wise. It is reverent of
genius and greedy of inspiration. It is conscious in the
highest and the least degree. It consists with the most
perfect command of the faculties. It dwells in a repose
as of the desert, and objects are as distinct in it as
oases or palms in the horizon of sand. The train of
thought moves with subdued and measured step, like a car-
avan. But the pen is only an instrument in its hand, and

not instinct with life, like a longer arm. It leaves a
thin varnish or glaze over all its work. The works of
Goethe furnish remarkable instances of the latter.

There is no just and serene criticism as yet. Nothing
is considered simply as it lies in the lap of eternal
beauty, but our thoughts, as well as our bodies, must be
dressed after the latest fashions. Our taste is too delicate and particular. It says nay to the poet's work, but
never yea to his hope. It invites him to adorn his def-
ormities, and not to cast them off by expansion, as the
tree its bark. We are a people who live in a bright
light, in houses of pearl and porcelain, and drink only
light wines, whose teeth are easily set on edge by the
least natural sour. If we had been consulted, the backbone of the earth would have been made, not of granite,
but of Bristol spar. A modern author would have died in
infancy in a ruder age. But the poet is something more
than a scald, 'a smoother and polisher of language'; he
is a Cincinnatus in literature, and occupies no west end
of the world. Like the sun, he will indifferently select
his rhymes, and with a liberal taste weave into his verse
the planet and the stubble.

In these old books the stucco has long since crumbled
away, and we read what was sculptured in the granite.
They are rude and massive in their proportions, rather
than smooth and delicate in their finish. The workers
in stone polish only their chimney ornaments, but their
pyramids are roughly done. There is a soberness in a
rough aspect, as of unhewn granite, which addresses a
depth in us, but a polished surface hits only the ball of
the eye. The true finish is the work of time, and the
use to which a thing is put. The elements are still pol-
ishing the pyramids. Art may varnish and gild, but it
can do no more. A work of genius is rough-hewn from the
first, because it anticipates the lapse of time, and has
an ingrained polish, which still appears when fragments
are broken off, and essential quality of its substance.
Its beauty is at the same time its strength, and it breaks
with a lustre.

The great poem must have the stamp of greatness as well
as its essence. The reader easily goes within the shal-
lowest contemporary poetry, and informs it with all the
life and promise of the day, as the pilgrim goes within
the temple, and hears the faintest strains of the wor-
shippers; but it will have to speak to posterity, traver-
sing these deserts, through the ruins of its outmost
walls, by the grandeur and beauty of its proportions.

4. 'CHRISTOPHER NORTH' (JOHN WILSON), THE ALLEGORY OF
LOVE

1845

Wilson (1785-1854), educated at Glasgow University and
Oxford, a critic and professor of moral philosophy at
Edinburgh, writes an intelligent and very full commentary
on Chaucer's poetry in a discussion of Dryden's criticism
in 'Blackwood's Edinburgh Magazine', LVII (May 1845), pp.
617ff. He expresses a preference for Chaucer's 'real and
human' poems, but is one of the earliest critics to note
the new feeling of - or about - love that began in medieval Europe, the 'religion of love'; and is apparently the
first to think of Chaucer as an allegorical writer. Here
seems to be the origin of the 'allegory of love'.

Nothing is gained by attempting to deny or to disguise a
known and plain fact, simply because it happens to be a
distasteful one - Time has estranged us from Chaucer.
Dryden and Pope we read with easy, unearned pleasure.
Their speech, their manner of mind, and their facile
verse, are of our age, almost of our own day. The two
excellent, graceful, and masterly poets belong, both of
them, to THIS NEW WORLD. Go back a little, step over an
imperceptible line, to the contemporary of Dryden, Milton,
and you seem to have overleaped some great chronological
boundary; you have transported yourself into THAT OLD
WORLD. Whether the historical date, or the gigantic soul,
or the learned art, make the separation, the fact is
clear, that the poet of the 'Paradise Lost' stands decidedly further off; and, more or less, you must acquire
the taste and intelligence of the poem. Why, up to this
hour, probably, there are three-fifths of the poem that
you have not read; or, if you have read all, and go along
with all, you have yourself had experience of the progress, and have felt your capacity of Milton grow and
dilate. So has it been with your capacity for Shakspeare,
or you are a truant and an idler. To comprehend with
delight Milton and Shakspeare as poets, you need, from
the beginning, a soul otherwise touched, and gifted for
poesy, than Pope claims of you, or Dryden. The great
elder masters, being original, require of you springs of
poesy welling in your own spirit; while the two latter,

imitative artists of luxury, exact from you nothing more,
in the way of poetical endowment, than the gusto of ease
and luxurious enchantment. To prefer, for some intellectual journey, the smooth wafture of an air-gliding ear -
to look with pleasure upon a dance of bright-hued images -
to hear more sweetness in Philomela's descant than in a
Turkish concert - to be ever so little sensible to the
bliss of dreams - ever so little sick of reality, and
ever so little glad to be rid of it for an hour - is
qualification enough to make you a willing and able reader of verse in the latter school. But if you are to
prefer the style of the antecessors, other conditions
must come in. It is, then, not a question merely whether
you see and love in Imogen the ideal of a wife in love
with her husband, or take to the surpassing and inimitable portraiture of the 'lost archangel' in Satan; but
whether you feel the sweetness of Imogen's soul in the
music of her expressions - whether you hear the tones of
the Will that not the thunder has quelled, in that voice
to which all 'the hollow deep of hell resounded.' If you
do, assuredly you will perceive in yourself that these are
discernments of a higher cast, and that place you upon a
higher degree when critics on poetry come to be ranked,
than when you had nothing better to say for yourself than
that your bosom bled at the Elegy on an Unfortunate Young
Lady, or that you varied with with Alexander to the varying current of the Ode of St Cecilia's Day.

We call Chaucer the Father of our Poetry, or its Morning Star. The poetical memory of the country stretches
up to him, and not beyond. The commanding impression
which he has made upon the minds of his people dates from
his own day. The old poets of England and Scotland constantly and unanimously acknowledge him for their master.
Greatest names, Dunbar, Douglas, Spenser, Milton, carry
on the tradition of his renown and his reign.

In part he belongs to, and in part he lifts himself
out of, his age. The vernacular poetry of reviving
Europe took a strong stamp from one principal feature in
the manners of the times. The wonderful political institution of Chivalry - turned into a romance in the minds
of those in whose persons the thing itself subsisted -
raised up a fanciful adoration of women into a law of
courtly life; or, at the least, of courtly verse, to
which there was nothing answerable in the annals of the
old world. For though the chief and most potent of human
passions has never lacked its place at the side of war in
the song that spoke of heroes - though two beautiful cap-
tives, and a runaway wife bestowed by the Goddess of
Beauty, and herself the paragon of beauty to all tongues

and ages, have grounded the 'Iliad' - though the Scaean
gate, from which Hector began to flee his inevitable foe,
and where that goddess-born foe himself stooped to destiny, be also remembered for the last parting of a husband
and a wife - though Circe and Calypso have hindered home-
bound Ulysses from the longing arms of Penelope - and
Jason, leading the flower of a prior and yet more heroic
generation, must first win the heart of Medea before he
may attain the Golden Fleece - though the veritable
nature of the human being have ever thus, through its
strongest passion, imaged itself in its most exquisite
mirror, Poetry - yet there did, in reawaking Europe, a
new love-poetry arise, distinctively characterised by the
omnipotence which it ascribed to the Love-god, legitimat-
ing in him an usurped supremacy, and exhibiting, in artificial and wilful excess, that passion which the older
poets drew in its powerful but unexaggerated and natural
proportions.

Thenceforwards the verse of the South and of the North,
and alike the forgotten and the imperishable, all attest
the predominancy of the same star. Diamond eyes and ruby
lips stir into sound the lute of the Troubadours and the
Minnesingers. Famous bearers of either name were knights
distinguished in the lists and in the field. And who is
it that stole from heaven the immortal fire of genius for
Petrarch? Laura. Who is the guide of Dante through Paradise? Beatrice. In our own language, the spirit of love
breathes, more than in any other poet, in Spenser. His
great poem is one Lay of Love, embodying and associating
that idealized, chivalrous, and romantic union of 'fierce
warres and faithful loves.' It hovers above the earth in
some region exempt from mortal footing - wars such as
never were, loves such as never were - and all - Allegory!
One ethereal extravagance! A motto may be taken from him
to describe that ascendency of the love-planet in the poetical sky of renewed Europe. It alludes to the love-
freaks of the old Pagan deities upon earth, in which the
King of the Gods excelled, as might be supposed, all the
others.

> While thus on earth great Jove these pageants play'd,
> *The winged boy did thrust into his throne;*
> And scoffing thus, unto his mother sayde,
> *'Lo! now the heavens obey to me alone*
> *And take me for their Jove, now Jove to earth is gone.'*

The pure truth of the poetical inspiration which rests
upon Spenser's poems, when compared to the absolute departure from reality apparent in the manners of his heroes

and heroines, and in the physical world which they inha-
bit, is a phenomenon which may well perplex the philosophical critic. You will hardly dare to refuse to any true
poet the self-election of his materials. Grant, therefore, to Spenser knight-errantry - grant him dragons, and
enchanters, and enchanted gardens, satyrs, and the goddess
Night on her chariot - grant him love as the single purpose of human life - a faery power, leading with a faery
band his faery world! But while you accept this Poem as
the lawful consummation and ending of that fabulous intellectual system or dream which had subsisted with authority
for centuries, it is wonderful to see how, in the very day
of Spenser, the STAGE recovers humanity and nature to
poetry - recalls poetry to nature and humanity! Shakspeare and Spenser, what contemporaries! The world that
is, and the world that *is not*, twinned in time and in
power!

This exaggeration of an immense natural power, Love -
making, one might almost say, man's worship of woman the
great religion of the universe, and which was the 'amabil-
is insania' of the new poetry - long exercised an unlimi-
ted monarchy in the poetical mind of the reasonable Chaucer. See the longest and most desperate of his Translations - which Tyrwhitt supposes him to have completed,
though we have only two fragments - seven thousand verses
in place of twenty-two thousand - the 'Romaunt of the
Rose,' otherwise entitled the 'Art of Love,' 'wherein are
shewed the helps and furtherances, as also the lets and
impediments, that lovers have in their suits.' Then
comes the work upon which Sir Philip Sydney seems to rest
the right of Chaucer to the renown of an excellent poet
having the insight of his art - the five long books which
celebrate the type of all true lovers, Troilus, and of
all false traitresses, Creseide. Then there is 'The Legende of Goode Women,' the loving heroines, fabulous and
historical, of Lemprière's dictionary. The first name is
decisive upon the signification of *goode* - Cleopatras,
Queene of Egypt - Tisbe of Babylon - Dido, Queene of Car-
thage - Hipsiphile and Medea, betrayed both by the same
'root of false lovers, Duk Jason' - Lucrece of Rome -
Ariadne of Athens - Philomen - Phillis - Hypermnestra.

The 'Assemblee of Foules' is all for love and allegory....

(p. 620) We cannot help feeling how much nearer Chaucer
was to the riddling days of poetry than we are. Did the
old Poet translate from plain English into the language of
Birds, and expect us to re-translate? Or are these blushes and this knighthood amongst birds merely regular ad-
juncts in any fable that attributes to the inferior

creation human powers of reason and speech? It is curious
that the *rapacious* fowls are presented as excelling in
high and delicate sentiment! They are the aristocracy of
the birds, plainly; yet an aristocracy described as of
'ravine' seems to receive but an equivocal compliment.

The 'House of Fame' is in Three Books. The title bespeaks Allegory; and the machinery which justifies the
allegory, as usual is a Dream. But the title does not
be-speak, what is nevertheless true, that here, too, love
steals in. During the entire First Book, the poet dreams
himself to be in the temple of Venus, all graven over with
Aeneas's history, taken point by point from the Mantuan.
The history belongs properly to its place; not because
Aeneas is the son of Venus, but because the course of
events is conducted by Jupiter consonantly to the prayer
of Venus. Why the House of Venus takes up a third part of
the poem to be devoted to the House of Fame is less apparent. Is the poet crazed with love? and so driven against
method to dream perforce of the divinity who rules over
his destiny, as she did over her son's? Or does the *fame*
conferred by Virgil upon Aeneas make it reasonable that
the dream should proceed by the House of one goddess to
that of the other?...

(p. 621) The criticism of so strange a composition is
hardly to be attempted. It shows a bold and free spirit
of invention, and some great and poetical conceiving. The
wilful, now just, now perverse, dispensing of fame, belongs to a mind that has meditated upon the human world.
The poem is one of the smaller number, which seems hitherto to stand free from the suspicion of having been taken
from other poets. For Chaucer helped himself to every
thing worth using that came to hand.

The earlier writings of Chaucer have several marks that
belong to the literature of the time.

First, an excessive and critical self-dedication of the
writer to the service of Love, this power being for the
most part arrayed as a sovereign divinity, now in the
person of the classical goddess Venus, and now of her son,
the god Cupid. Secondly, an ungovernable propensity to
allegorical fiction. The scheme of innumerable poems is
merely allegorical. In others, the allegorical vein
breaks in from time to time. Thirdly, a Dream was a
vehicle much in use for effecting the transit of the
fancy from the real to the poetical world. Chaucer has
many dreams. Fourthly, interminable delight in expatia-
ting upon the simplest sights and sounds of the natural
world. This overflows all Chaucer's earlier poems. In
some, he largely describes the scene of adventure - in
some, the desire of solace in field and wood leads him

into the scene. Fifthly, a truly magnanimous indifference
to the flight of time and to the cost of parchment, expressed in the dilatation of a slender matter through an
infinite series of verses. You wonder at the facility of
writing in the infancy of art. It seems to resemble the
exuberant, untiring activity of children, prompted by a
vital delight which overflows into the readiest utterance;
and, in proportion to its display, achieving the less that
is referable to any purpose of enduring use. Even the
admired and elaborately-written *Troilus* and *Creseide* is a
great specimen. The action is nearly null; the discoursing of the persons and of the poet endless. It is not,
then, simply the facility of the eight-syllabled couplet,
as in that interminable *Chaucer's Dreme,* that betrays;
there is a dogged purpose of going on for ever....

There must be something like thirty thousand verses,
long, short, in couplets or stanzas, which may be said to
be dedicated to love!

And of them all, only the four following Poems tread
the plain ground - have their footing upon the same earth
that we walk - Troilus and Creseide, The Legende of Goode
Women, Queen Annelida and False Arcita, the Complaint of
the Blacke Knight. We grant them for human and real, notwithstanding that most of the persons are of a very romantic and apocryphal stamp - because they are not presented
in dreams or visions, and are not allegorical creations of
beings out of the air, Impersonations of Ideas. They are
offered as men and women, downright flesh and blood, and so
are to be understood. Nevertheless even here, when Chaucer is nearest home, taking his subject in his own day, and
putting his own friend and patron in verse, there is a
trick of the riddling faculty, since the Blacke Knight lodging, during the love-month of May, in the greenwood, and
bemoaning all day long his hard love-hap, represents, it
is presumed, old stout John of Gaunt in love, who might
utter his passion, uncertain of requital,

In groans that thunder love, in sighs
of fire;

but who, most assuredly, did not build himself a forest
bower, and annually retire from court and castle, to spend
there a lovesick May.

Of absolutely fanciful creations are, as we have seen,
the 'Assemblee of Foules,' and the 'Complaint of Mars and
Venus,' which the poet overhears a fowl singing on St.
Valentine's Day ere sunrise. 'Of the Cuckou and Nightingale:' the poet, between waking and sleeping, hears the
bird of hate and the bird of music dispute against and for

love. When the nightingale takes leave of him, he wakes.
'The Court of Love:' The poet, at the age of eighteen, is
summoned by Mercury to do his obeisance at the Court of
Love, 'a lite before the Mount of Citheree,' called further on Citheron. He is, on this occasion, not asleep at
all, but dreams away like any other poet, with his eyes
open, in broad daylight.

In Chaucer thus we find every kind of possible allegory. There is the thoroughly *creative* allegory, when
thoughts are turned into beings, and impersonated abstract
ideas appear as deities, and as attendants on deities.
This is the unsubstantial allegory, which has, it must be
owned, a different meaning to different climes and times.
For example, to the belief of the old Greeks, Aphrodite
and Eros, albeit essentially thoughts, had flesh that
could be touched, wounded even, and veins, in which for
blood ran ichor. In the verses of our old poet and his
contemporaries, Venus and Cupid are as active as they were
with Homer and Anacreon; only, that now their substance
has imperceptibly grown attenuate. So that in the 'Assemblee of Foules,' for example, these two celestial poten-
tates are upon an equal footing, for subsistency and
reality, with the great goddess Dame Nature, who seems to
be more of modern than of ancient invention, and with
Plesaunce, Arrai, Beautee, Courtesie, Craft, Delite,
Gentlenesse, and others enow, whom the poet found in
attendance upon the Love-god and his mother. With or
without belief, this belongs to all the ages of poetry,
from the beginning to the consummation of the world.

Then there is the *disguising* allegory - for by no
other appellation can it be described - which may be of
a substantial kind. For example, the Black Knight, as we
have seen, forlorn in love, builds himself a lodge in the
wild-wood, to which he resorts during the month of May,
and mourns the livelong day under the green boughs. If
the conjecture which Tyrwhitt throws out, but without much
insisting upon it, that John of Gaunt, wooing his Duchess
Blanche, is here figured, this is a *disguising* allegory of
the lowest ideal idealization. The conjecture of Tyrwhitt,
whether exact or not, quite agrees to the art of poetical
invention in that age.

That old and deeply-rooted species of fable, which as-
cribes to the inferior animals human mind and manners, was
another prevalent allegory. Usually, the picture of humanity so conveyed is of a general nature. But if, as has
been guessed, the first and noblest of the Three Tercels
that woo the 'formell eagle,' in the Assemblee of Foules,
be the same John of Gaunt wooing the same Blanche, here
would be two varieties of allegory - the disguising of

particular persons and events, and the veiling of human
actions and passions, under the semblance of the inferior
kinds - mixed in this part of the poem, which, in as much
as it also introduces wholly ideal personages, would, if
the key to the enigma has been truly found, very fully
exemplify the allegorizing genius of the old poetry.

Certainly, many of the old poems, unless they are interpreted to allude, in this manner, to particular persons
and occurrences, appear to want due meaning, such as this
Complaint of the nameless Black Knight, this Wooing of the
Three Tercels, and the faithless Hawk whom Canace hears.
We may often feel ourselves justified in presuming an
allusion, although in regard to the true import of the
allusion it may be that Time has first locked the door,
and then thrown the key over the wall.

Of one Poem, to which we have hitherto but alluded, we
feel ourselves now called on to give an analysis, both for
sake of its own exquisite beauty and surpassing loveli-
ness, and for sake of Dryden's immortal paraphrase - 'The
Floure and the Leaf.'

There is in the plan of 'The Floure and the Leaf,' a
peculiarity which is not easily accounted for. In the
other poems of Chaucer, which are thrown into the form of
an adventure or occurrence personal to the relater, he
relates in person his own experience. Here the parts of
experiencing, and of relating an adventure, are both
transferred to an unknown person of the other sex. It is
also remarkable that this difference in the personality
of the relater does not appear until the very close of
the poem, and then incidentally, one of the imaginary
persons addressing the relater as 'Daughter.' In the adventure, which is simply the witnessing a Vision, there
is nothing that might not as well have happened to Chaucer himself as to dame or damsel....

(p. 645) Shakspeare commingles widely divided times;
and why, two hundred years before him, shall not Chaucer?
It requires practice to read Chaucer. Not only do you
need familiarizing to a form of the language, which is not
your own, but much more to a simplicity of style, which at
first appears to you like barenness and poverty. It seems
meagre. You miss too much the rich and lavish colours of
the later time. Your eye is used to gorgeousness and
gaudiness. The severe plainness of the old manner wants
zest for you. But, when you are used to Chaucer, can
accept his expression, and think and feel with him, this
hinderance wears off. You find a strong imagination - a
gentle pathos - no lack of accumulation, where needed -
but the crowding is always of effective circumstances or
images - a playfulness, upon occasion, even in serious

writing - but the special characteristic of the style is,
that the word is always to the purpose. He amply possesses his language, and his sparing expression is chosen,
and never inadequate - never indigent. His rule is, that
for every phrase there be matter; and narrative or argument is thus constantly progressive. He does not appear
to be hurried out of himself by the heat of composition.
His good understanding completely goes along with him, and
weighs every word.

5. SIR NICHOLAS HARRIS NICOLAS, A LIFE FOUNDED ON
EVIDENCE

1845

Nicolas (1799-1848), who was educated as a midshipman and
at the Inner Temple, was noted for his genealogical and
antiquarian research, and the reforms he agitated for in
facilities for the study of records. He was a prolific
researcher, editor, biographer, annotator and parent, and
for the first time established a sound documentary basis
for the life of Chaucer in his memoir that precedes the
edition of 1845, from which the following extracts are
taken.

(p. 1) Although great trouble was taken to illustrate the
life of CHAUCER by his former biographers, the yield of
research was but imperfectly gleaned. Many material facts
in his history have been very recently brought to light,
and are now, for the first time, published; but it is not
from these discoveries only that this account of the Poet
will derive its claim to attention. An erroneous construction has been given to much of what was before known
of him; and absurd inferences have, in some cases, been
drawn from supposed allusions to himself in his writings.
A Life of the Poet, founded on documentary evidence instead of imagination, was much wanted; and this, it is
hoped, the present Memoir will supply.
    CHAUCER'S parentage is unknown, and the conjectures
that have been hazarded on the subject are too vague to
justify the adoption of any of them. His name, which was

of some antiquity, was borne by persons in a respectable
station of society; and it is likely that some of them
were connected with the city of London. That he was of a
gentleman's, though not of a noble or distinguished
family, can scarcely be doubted; but the frequent occurrence of passages in his writings, wherein he insists that
conduct is the only proof of gentility, that he alone is
truly noble who acts nobly, with others of a similar
import, may possibly be ascribed to his desire to level
the artificial distinctions of birth, from the consciousness of being, in that respect, inferior to those of whom
his talents had rendered him the associate. Upon a supposed reference to himself in one of his works, he is considered to have been born in London; but, as will afterwards appear, no reliance can be placed on that passage....
    (p. 4) Some of Chaucer's biographers suppose that he
was educated at Oxford, and some again, at Cambridge;
while others solve the doubt, more ingeniously than probably, by concluding that he was at both Universities; but
there is no proof, however likely it may be, that he belonged to either.
    It has been said that Chaucer was originally intended
for the law, and that from some cause which has not reached
us, and on which it would be idle to speculate, the design
was abandoned. The acquaintance he possessed with the
classics, with divinity, with astronomy, with so much as
was then known of chemistry, and indeed with every other
branch of the scholastic learning of the age, proves that
his education had been particularly attended to: and his
attainments render it impossible to believe that he quit-
ted college at the early period at which persons destined
for a military life usually began their career. It was
not then the custom for men to pursue learning for its
own sake; and the most rational manner of accounting for
the extent of Chaucer's acquirements is to suppose that he
was educated for a learned profession. The knowledge he
displays of divinity would make it more likely that he was
intended for the Church than for the Bar, were it not that
the writings of the Fathers were generally read by all
classes of students. One writer says that Chaucer was a
member of the Inner Temple, and that while there he was
fined two shillings for beating a Franciscan friar in
Fleet Street, and another observes, that after he had
travelled in France, 'collegia leguleiorum frequentavit.'
Nothing, however, is positively known of Chaucer until
the autumn of 1359, when he himself says he was in the
army with which Edward the Third invaded France, and that
he served for the first time on that occasion. He was, he
adds, made prisoner by the French during the expedition,

which terminated with the peace of Chartres in May 1360.
Between 1360 and 1367 no notice has been found of him, so
that it is alike uncertain if he was ransomed, and when he
returned to England....

(p. 8) It is a natural and generous wish that illustrious men, the ornaments of their several ages and countries, whom Nature, by endowing with kindred minds and her
highest intellectual gifts, would seem to have destined
for friends, should have been acquainted with each other;
and that the admiration inspired by their respective Works
should have been warmed and strengthened by personal affection. This universal feeling justifies more attention to
the supposed friendship of Chaucer and Petrarch than a
merely speculative question would otherwise deserve.

Tyrwhitt, after alluding to Speght's inaccurate statement, that 'some write' that Chaucer and Petrarch were
present at the marriage of Lionel Duke of Clarence with
Violenta, daughter of Galeazzo Lord of Milan, at that city
in 1369, as one occasion when he might have become known
to the Italian Poet, proceeds to notice his mission to
Genoa in 1372 as having afforded him another opportunity
of seeing Petrarch. He briefly discusses the point; but
it is evident that he had not formed a conclusive opinion
upon it, his doubts being founded on the distance of Genoa
from Padua, and on the interview not having been mentioned
by Petrarch himself, nor by his biographers. Godwin, however, after answering this objection, vehemently insists
that Chaucer did actually visit Petrarch at Padua in 1373,
and that he then obtained from him the Tale of Griselda.

In his ardour, Godwin has however both overlooked and
mistaken some material circumstances; and his confidence
in the fact not only induced him to cast unmerited re-
proaches upon the learned Tyrwhitt for merely presuming to
express a doubt on the subject, but to give the reins to
his own imagination by describing Chaucer's motives for
seeking the interview, the interview itself, the feelings
of the two Poets, and the very tone and substance of their
conversation! This interesting question will now, it is
hoped, be investigated on more rational grounds....

(p. 16) It is in his own character only, that Chaucer
appears in the Pilgrimage, in the General Prologue, the
Rime of Sir Thopas, and in the prose tale of Melibeus; and
each of the other personages is individually described,
and has a distinct existence.

Their knowledge of the world, their wit and learning,
and the skill with which their narratives are written must
of course be attributed to the Author; and some of their
feelings, thoughts, and passions may have had their prototype in his own bosom. But the creator of an imaginary

hero can never be safely identified with his creation; and
when from a numerous group, a writer singles out himself
in his own individual person, acts in his own corporeal
capacity, pourtrays his own physical peculiarities, and
clearly and intentionally describes his own conduct, nay,
when he even designates himself by name, it seems unreasonable that he should be supposed to relate a circumstance of his own life by any other mouth than his own.
If, therefore, Chaucer had stated in the Rime of Sir
Thopas, or in the Tale of Melibeus, where he appears in
his own person, that he had learnt either of those Tales
from any other writer, some faith would unquestionably be
due to the statement. But the Clerk of Oxford, and others
of the Pilgrims, may have been the portraits of original
personages, and the Clerk might have learnt Griselda's
history from Petrarch at Padua; or, far more likely, both
the Clerk and the immediate source of the Tale were purely
fictitious. Godwin's argument that Chaucer could have had
no other motive for making those lines proceed from the
Clerk's lips than an 'eager desire to commemorate his interview with Petrarch,' is fairly met, even if it be not
destroyed, by the suggestion, that such an object would
have been much more effectually attained, had he himself
recited the Tale of Griselda, and given to the Clerk (by
whom it would have been both more properly and characteristically related) so moral and grave a story as that of
Melibeus. Moreover, the lines on which Godwin's theory
rests are scarcely consistent with the passage towards
the conclusion of the Clerk's Tale, where he speaks of
Petrarch's having 'written and indited' it, in a very
different manner from his previous statement that he had
'learned it at Padua' from Petrarch:-

> Every wight in his degré
> Schulde be constant in adversité,
> As was Grisild, therfore Petrark *writeth*
> *This story, which with high stile he enditeth.*
>   (II. ll. 207-210.)

Until however accident brings some hitherto undiscovered
document to light, Chaucer's visit to Petrarch and its
attendant circumstances must remain among the many doubtful circumstances in the lives of eminent men, which their
admirers wish to believe true, but for which their biographers ought to require surer evidence than what Godwin
calls 'coincidences which furnish a basis of historical
probability.'...
    (p. 54) [Chaucer's] writings must be closely studied to
form a proper estimate of the magnitude of his genius, the

extent and variety of his information, his wonderful knowledge of human nature, the boldness with which he attacked
clerical abuses, and advocated the interests of honour and
virtue, and more than all, of that philosophical construction of mind, which rendered him superior to the prejudices of his time, and placed him far in advance of the
wisest of his contemporaries.

6.   JOHN HENRY LEIGH HUNT, GENIALITY, SINGING

1846, 1855

Leigh Hunt (1784-1859), genial and prolific essayist,
editor, poet and family man, was educated at Christ's
Hospital. He edited various magazines of liberal views
and was imprisoned on one occasion. He was the friend of
many of the greatest Romantic writers and for a while particularly influential over Keats, whom he seems to have
introduced to Chaucer's works. His shrewd and copious
comments embody a fellow-practitioner's intelligent and
generous appreciation. He attempts to analyse irony,
narrative techniques and humour, and is early in his
association of poetry with the idea of music. The
extracts are taken (a) from 'Wit and Humour, Selected
from the English Poets' (1846), and (b) from 'Stories in
Verse' (1855).

(a)

(p. 18) 4th, *Irony*, (Ειρωνεια, *Talk*, in a sense of Dissi-
mulation) or *Saying one thing and Meaning another,* is a
mode of speech generally adopted for purposes of satire,
but may be made the vehicle of the most exquisite compliment. On the other hand, Chaucer, with a delightful impu-
dence, has drawn a pretended compliment out of a satire
the most outrageous. He makes the Cock say to the Hen, in
the fable told by the Nun's Priest, that 'the female is
the confusion of the male;' but then he says it in *Latin*,
gravely quoting from a Latin author a sentence to that
effect about womankind. This insult he proceeds to translate into an eulogy:-

But let us speak of mirth, and stint all this.
Madàmĕ Pèrtĕlote, so have I bliss,
Of one thing God hath sent me largè grace;
For when I see the beauty of your face,
Ye ben so scarlet red about your eyen,
It maketh all my drĕdĕ for to dyen;
For all so siker [so surely] as *In principio*
Mulier est hominis confusio;

(That is, 'for as it was in the beginning of the world,
woman is the confusion of man.')

Madam, the sentence of this Latin is,
'Woman is mànnĕs joy and mànnĕs bliss.'
                    Canterbury Tales, v. 15,163.

(p. 73) The graver portion of the genius of this great
poet will be more fitly noticed in the volume to be entitled 'Action and Passion'. He is here only in his gayer
mood.

I retain the old spelling for three reasons; - first,
because it is pleasant to know the actual words of such a
writer, as far as they can be ascertained; second, because
the antiquity is part of the costume; and third, because I
have added a modern prose version, which removes all difficulty in the perusal. I should rather say I have added
the version for the purpose of retaining the immortal
man's own words, besides being able to show perhaps how
strongly every word of a great poet tells in the most
modern prose version, provided his ideas are not absolutely misrepresented. At all events, the reader may go
uninterruptedly, if he pleases, through the version, and
then turn to the original for the finer traits, and for a
music equally correct and beautiful.

I wish I could have given more than one comic story out
of Chaucer; but the change of manners renders it difficult
at any time, and impossible in a book like the present.
The subjects with which the court and gentry of the times
of the Henrys and Edwards could be entertained, are sometimes not only indecorous but revolting. It is a thousand
pities that the unbounded sympathy of the poet with everything that interested his fellow-creatures did not know,
in this instance, where to stop. Yet we must be cautious
how we take upon ourselves to blame him. Even Shakspeare
did not quite escape the infection of indecency in a much
later and highly refined age; and it may startle us to
suspect, that what is readable in the gravest and even the
most scrupulous circles in our own day, may not be altogether so a hundred years hence. Allusions and phrases

which are thought harmless now, and that from habit really are so, may then appear in as different a light as those which we are astonished to think our ancestors could endure. Nay, opinions and daily practices exist, and are treated with respect, which may be regarded by our posterity as the grossest and cruellest barbarisms. We may, therefore, cease to wonder at the apparently unaccountable spectacle presented by such writers as Chaucer, who combine a licence the most indelicate with the utmost refinements of thought and feeling.

When Chaucer is free from this taint of his age, his humour is of a description the most thoroughly delightful; for it is at once entertaining, profound, and good-natured. If this last quality be thought a drawback by some, as wanting the relish of personality, they may supply even that (as some have supplied it) by supposing that he drew his characters from individuals, and that the individuals were very uncomfortable accordingly. I confess I see no ground for the supposition beyond what the nature of the case demands. Classes must of course be drawn, more or less, from the individuals composing them; but the un-professional particulars added by Chaucer to his charac-ters (such as the Merchant's uneasy marriage, and the Franklin's prodigal son) are only such as render the por-traits more true, by including them in the general categ-ory of human kind. The gangrene which the Cook had on his shin, and which has been considered as a remarkable in-stance of the gratuitous, is, on the contrary (besides its masterly intimation of the perils of luxury in general), painfully in character with a man accustomed to breathe an unhealthy atmosphere, and to be encouraging bad humours with tasting sauces and syrups. Besides, the Cook turns out to be a drunkard.

Chaucer's comic genius is so perfect, that it may be said to include prophetic intimations of all that followed it. The liberal-thinking joviality of Rabelais is there; the portraiture of Cervantes, moral and external; the poetry of Shakspeare; the learning of Ben Jonson; the man-ners of the wits of Charles the Second, the *bonhomie* of Sterne; and the insidiousness, without the malice, of Voltaire. One of its characteristics is a certain tran-quil detection of particulars, expressive of generals; as in the instance just mentioned of the secret infirmity of the Cook. Thus the Prioress speaks French; but it is 'after the school of Stratford at Bow.' Her education was altogether more showy than substantial. The Lawyer was the busiest man in the world, and yet he 'seemed busier than he was.' He made something out of nothing, even in appearances.

Another characteristic is his fondness for seeing the
spiritual in the material; the mind in the man's aspect.
He is as studious of physiognomy as Lavater, and far
truer. Observe, too, the poetry that accompanies it, -
the imaginative sympathy in the matter of fact. His Yeoman, who is a forester, has a head 'like a nut.' His
Miller is as brisk and healthy as the air of the hill on
which he lives, and as hardy and as coarse-grained as his
conscience. We know, as well as if we had ridden with
them, his oily-faced Monk; his lisping Friar (who was to
make confession easy to the ladies); his carbuncled
Summoner or Church-Bailiff, the grossest form of ecclesiastical sensuality; and his irritable money-getting Reve
or Steward, with his cropped head and calf-less legs, who
shaves his beard as closely as he reckons with his master's tenants.

The third great quality of Chaucer's humour is its fair
play; - the truth and humanity which induces him to see
justice done to good and bad, to the circumstances which
make men what they are, and the mixture of right and
wrong, of wisdom and of folly, which they consequently
exhibit. His worst characters have some little saving
grace of good-nature, or at least of joviality and candour.
Even the Pardoner, however impudently, acknowledges himself to be a 'vicious man.' His best people, with one
exception, betray some infirmity. The good Clerk of
Oxford, for all his simplicity and singleness of heart,
has not escaped the pedantry and pretension of the college. The Good Parson seems without a blemish, even in
his wisdom; yet when it comes to his turn to relate a
story, he announces it as a 'little' tale, and then tells
the longest and most prosing in the book, - a whole ser-
monizing volume. This, however, might be an expression of
modesty; since Chaucer uses the same epithet for a similar
story of his own telling. But the Good Parson also treats
poetry and fiction with contempt. His understanding is
narrower than his motives. The only character in Chaucer
which seems faultless, is that of the Knight; and he is a
man who has been all over the world, and bought experience
with hard blows. The poet does not spare his own person.
He describes himself as a fat, heavy man, with an 'elvish'
(wildish?) countenance, shy, and always 'staring on the
ground.' Perhaps he paid for his genius and knowledge
with the consequences of habits too sedentary, and a vein,
in his otherwise cheerful wisdom, of hypochondriacal
wonder. He also puts in his own mouth a fairy-tale of
chivalry, which the Host interrupts with contempt, as a
tiresome commonplace. I take it to have been a production
of the modest poet's when he was young; for in the midst

of what looks like intentional burlesque, are expressions
of considerable force and beauty.

This self-knowledge is a part of Chaucer's greatness;
and these modest proofs of it distinguish him from every
other poet in the language. Shakspeare may have had as
much, or more. It is difficult to suppose otherwise.
And yet there is no knowing what qualities, less desirable,
might have hindered even his mighty insight into his
fellow-creatures from choosing to look so closely into
himself. His sonnets are not without intimations of personal and other defects; but they contain no such candid
talking as Chaucer.

The father of English poetry was essentially a modest
man. He sits quietly in a corner, looking down for the
most part, and meditating; at other times eyeing everything that passes, and sympathizing with everything; -
chuckling heartily at a jest, feeling his eyes fill with
tears at sorrow, reverencing virtue, and not out of
charity with vice. When he ventures to tell a story himself, it is as much under correction of the Host as the
humblest man in the company; and it is no sooner objected
to, than he drops it for one of a different description.

I have retained the grave character of the Knight in
the selection, because he is the leader of the cavalcade.

The syllables that are to be retained in reading the
verses are marked with the brief accent ˘. The terminating vowels thus distinguished were certainly pronounced
during one period of our language, otherwise they would
not have been written; though, by degrees, the comparative faintness of their utterance, and disuse of them in
some instances, enabled writers to use them as they
pleased; just as poets in our own day retain or not, as
it suits them, the *e's* in the final syllable of parti-
ciples and past tenses; - such as *belov'd, belovèd;
swerv'd, swervèd,* &. The French, in their verses use
their terminating vowels at this moment precisely as
Chaucer did; though they drop them in conversation. I
have no living Frenchman at hand to quote, but he writes
in this respect as Boileau did: -

Ellĕ dit; et du vent de sa bouchĕ profanĕ
Lui souffle avec ces mots l'ardeur de la chicanĕ;
Le Prélat se reveillĕ; et, plein d'émotion,
Lui donnĕ toutĕfois la benediction.
            (Discord waking the Dean in the *Lutrin*).

'*Radix malorum est cupiditas.*' - Covetousness is the
root of all evil. - Those critics who supposed that Chaucer, notwithstanding his intimacy with the Latin and

Italian poets, and his own hatred of 'mis-metre,' had no
settled rules of versification, would have done well to
consider the rhythmical exactitude with which he fits
Latin quotations into his lines.... He is far more particular in this respect than versifiers of later ages.

(b)

(p. 1)   PREFACE,

CONTAINING REMARKS ON THE FATHER OF ENGLISH NARRATIVE
POETRY; ON THE ILL-UNDERSTOOD NATURE OF HEROIC VERSE; ON
THE NECESSITY, EQUALLY ILL-UNDERSTOOD, OF THE MUSICAL
ELEMENT IN POETRY TO POETRY IN GENERAL; AND ON THE ABSUR-
DITY OF CONFINING THE NAME OF POETRY TO ANY ONE SPECIES OF
IT IN PARTICULAR.

As this book, in issuing from the house of Messrs.
Routledge, acquires a special chance of coming under the
cognizance of travellers by the railway, I have pleased
myself with fancying, that it gives me a kind of new link,
however remote like the rest, with my great master in the
art of poetry; that is to say, with the great master of
English narrative in verse, the Father of our Poetry itself, Chaucer.
    Nay, it gives me two links, one general, and one par-
ticular; for as Chaucer's stories, in default of there
being any printed books and travelling carriages in those
days, were related by travellers to one another, and as
these stories will be read, and (I hope) shown to one
another, by travellers who are descendants of those travellers (see how the links thicken as we advance!), so
one of Chaucer's stories concerned a wonderful Magic
Horse; and now, one of the most wonderful of all such
horses will be speeding my readers and me together to all
parts of the kingdom, with a fire hitherto unknown to any
horse whatsoever.
    How would the great poet have been delighted to see
the creature! - and what would he not have said of it!
    I say 'creature,' because though your fiery Locomotive
is a creation of man's, as that of the poet was, yet as
the poet's 'wondrous Horse of Brass' was formed out of
ideas furnished him by Nature, so, out of elements no less
furnished by Nature, and the first secrets of which are no
less amazing, has been formed this wonderful Magic Horse
of Iron and Steam, which, with vitals of fire, clouds literally flowing from its nostrils, and a bulk, a rushing,
and a panting like that of some huge antediluvian wild

beast, is now heard and seen in all parts of the country,
and in most parts of civilized Europe, breaking up the old
grounds of alienation, and carrying with it the seeds of
universal brotherhood.

Verily, something even of another, but most grating
link, starts up out of that reflection upon the poet's
miracle; for the hero who rode his horse of brass made war
with Russia; and we Englishmen, the creators of the Horse
of Iron, are warring with the despot of the same barbarous country, pitting the indignant genius of civilization
against his ruffianly multitudes.

> At Sarra, in the land of Tartariè,
> There dwelt a king that warriëd Russiè,
> Through which there diëd many a doughty man.

Many a doughty man, many a noble heart of captain and of
common soldier, has perished in this new war against the
old ignorance; - an ignorance, that by its sullen persistence in rejecting the kindly advice of governments brave
and great enough to be peaceful, forced the very enthusi-
asts of peace (myself among the number) into the conviction, that out of hatred and loathing of war itself, war
must be made upon him....

(p. 5) Let me take this opportunity of recommending
such readers as are not yet acquainted with Chaucer, to
make up for their lost time. The advice is not to my
benefit, but it is greatly to theirs, and loyalty to him
forces me to speak. The poet's 'old English' is no difficulty, if they will but believe it. A little study
would soon make them understand it as easily as that of
most provincial dialects. Chaucer is the greatest narrative poet in the language; that is to say, the greatest
and best teller of stories, in the understood sense of
that term. He is greatest in every respect, and in the
most opposite qualifications; greatest in pathos, greatest
in pleasantry, greatest in character, greatest in plot,
greatest even in versification, if the unsettled state of
the language in his time, and the want of all native precursors in the art, be considered; for his verse is anything but the rugged and formless thing it has been supposed to be; and if Dryden surpassed him in it, not only
was the superiority owing to the master's help, but there
were delicate and noble turns and cadences in the old
poet, which the poet of the age of Charles the Second
wanted spirituality enough to appreciate.

There have been several Chaucers, and Helps to Chaucer,
published of late years. Mr. Moxon has printed his entire
works in one double-columned large octavo volume; Messrs.

Routledge have published the 'Canterbury Tales' in a
smaller volume, with delicate illustrations by Mr. Cor-
bould, the best (as far as I am aware) that ever came from
his pencil; and there is a set of the poet's works now
going through the press, more abundant than has yet appeared in commentary and dissertation, in Robert Bell's
"Annotated Edition of the English Poets,' - the only collection of the kind in the language, though it has so long
been a desideratum. Chaucer's country disgraced itself
for upwards of a century by considering the Father of its
Poetry as nothing but an obsolete jester. Even poets
thought so, in consequence of a prevailing ignorance of
nine-tenths of his writings, originating in the gross
tastes of the age of Charles the Second. There are passages, it is true, in Chaucer, which for the sake of all
parties, persons of thorough delicacy will never read
twice; for they were compliances with the licence of an
age, in which the court itself, his sphere, was as clown-
ish in some of its tastes as the unqualified admirers of
Swift and Prior are now; and the great poet lamented that
he had condescended to write them. But by far the greatest portion of his works is full of delicacies of every
kind, of the noblest sentiment, of the purest, most various, and most profound entertainment.

Postponing, however, what I have to say further on the
subject of Chaucer, it becomes, I am afraid, a little too
obviously proper, as well as more politic, to return, in
this Preface, to the book of the humblest of his followers....

(p. 9) When I wrote the 'Story of Rimini' which was
between the years 1812 and 1815, I was studying versification in the school of Dryden. Masterly as my teacher
was, I felt, without knowing it, that there was a want in
him, even in versification; and the supply of this want,
later in life, I found in his far greater master, Chaucer;
for though Dryden's versification is noble, beautiful, and
so complete of its kind, that to an ear uninstructed in
the metre of the old poet, all comparison between the two
in this respect seems out of the question, and even ludicrous, yet the measure in which Dryden wrote not only originated, but attained to a considerable degree of its
beauty, in Chaucer; and the old poet's immeasurable superiority in sentiment and imagination, not only to Dryden,
but to all, up to a very late period, who have written in
the same form of verse, left him in possession of beauties, even in versification, which it remains for some
future poet to amalgamate with Dryden's in a manner worthy
of both, and so carry England's noble heroic rhyme to its
pitch of perfection.

Critics, and poets too, have greatly misconceived the rank and requirements of this form of verse, who have judged it from the smoothness and monotony which it died of towards the close of the last century, and from which nothing was thought necessary for its resuscitation but an opposite unsystematic extreme. A doubt, indeed, of a very curious and hitherto unsuspected, or at least unnoticed nature, may be entertained by inquirers into the musical portion of the art of poetry (for poetry is an art as well as a gift); namely, whether, since the time of Dryden, any poets whatsoever, up to the period above alluded to (and very few indeed have done otherwise since then), thought of versification as a thing necessary to be studied at all, with the exceptions of Gray and Coleridge.

The case remains the same at present; but such assuredly was not the case either with Dryden himself, or with any of the greater poets before him, the scholarly ones in particular, such as Spenser, Milton, and their father Chaucer, who was as learned as any of them for the time in which he lived, and well acquainted with metres, French, Latin, and Italian.

Poets less reverent to their art, out of a notion that the gift, in their instance, is of itself sufficient for all its purposes, (which is much as if a musician should think he could do without studying thorough-bass, or a painter without studying drawing and colours,) trust to an ear which is often not good enough to do justice to the amount of gift which they really possess; and hence comes a loss, for several generations together, of the whole musical portion of poetry, to the destruction of its beauty in tone and in movement, and the peril of much good vitality in new writers. For proportions, like all other good things, hold together; and he that is wanting in musical feeling where music is required, is in danger of being discordant and disproportionate in sentiment, of not perceiving the difference between thoughts worthy and unworthy of utterance. It is for this reason among others, that he pours forth "crotchets" in abundance, not in unison with his theme, and wanting in harmony with one another.

There is sometimes a kind of vague and (to the apprehension of the unmusical) senseless melody, which in lyrical compositions, the song in particular, really constitutes, in the genuine poetical sense of the beautiful, what the scorner of it says it falsely and foolishly constitutes - namely, a good half of its merit. It answers to variety and expression of tone in a beautiful voice, and to 'air,' grace, and freedom in the movements of a charming person. The Italians, in their various terms for the

beautiful, have a word for it precisely answering to the
first feeling one has in attempting to express it -
vago, - vague; something wandering, fluctuating, undefinable, undetainable, moving hither and thither at its own
sweet will and pleasure, in accordance with what it feels.
It overdoes nothing and falls short of nothing; for itself is nothing but the outward expression of an inward
grace. You perceive it in all genuine lyrical compositions, of whatever degree, and indeed in all compositions
that sing or speak with true musical impulse, in whatsoever measure, in the effusions of Burns, of Ben Jonson,
of Beaumont and Fletcher, of Allan Ramsay, of Metastasio,
of Coleridge; and again in those of Dryden, of Spenser, of
Chaucer, of Ariosto; in poems however long, and in passages however seemingly unlyrical; for it is one of the
popular, and I am afraid, generally speaking, critical
mistakes, in regard to rhymed verse, that in narrative and
heroic poems there is nothing wanting to the music, provided the line or the couplet be flowing, and the general
impression not rude or weak; whereas the best couplet,
however admirable in itself and worthy of quotation, forms
but one link in the chain of the music to which it belongs. Poems of any length must consist of whole strains
of couplets, whole sections and successions of them, brief
or prolonged, all as distinct from one another and complete in themselves, as the *adagios* and *andantes* of sym-
phonies and sonatas, each commencing in the tone and obvious spirit of commencement, proceeding through as great a
variety of accents, stops, and pauses, as the notes and
phrases of any other musical composition, and coming at
an equally fit moment to a close.
    Enough stress has never yet been laid on the analogies
between musical and poetical composition. All poetry
used formerly to be sung; and poets still speak of 'singing' what they write. Petrarch used to 'try his sonnets
on the lute;' that is to say, to examine them in their
musical relations, in order to see how they and musical
requirement went together; and a chapter of poetical narrative is called to this day a canto, or chant. Every
distinct section or paragraph of a long poem ought to
form a separate, interwoven, and varied melody; and every
very short poem should, to a fine ear, be a still more
obvious melody of the same sort, in order that its brevity
may contain as much worth as is possible, and show that
the poet never forgets the reverence due to his art.
    I have sometimes thought that if Chaucer could have
heard compositions like those of Coleridge's 'Christabel,'
he might have doubted whether theirs was not the best of
all modes and measures for reducing a narrative to its

most poetic element, and so producing the quintessence of
a story.   And for stories not very long, not very substantial in their adventures, and of a nature more imaginary
than credible, so they might be.   But for narrative
poetry in general, for epic in particular, and for stories
of any kind that are deeply to affect us as creatures of
flesh and blood and human experience, there is nothing for
a sustained and serious interest comparable with our old
heroic measure, whether in blank verse or rhyme, in couplet or in stanza.   An epic poem written in the 'Christabel,' or any other brief lyrical measure, would acquire,
in the course of perusal, a comparative tone of levity, an
air of too great an airiness.   The manner would turn to
something like not being in earnest, and the matter resemble a diet made all of essences.   We should miss *pièces
de resistance*, and the homely, but sacred pabulum of 'our
daily bread.'   You could as soon fancy a guitar put in
place of a church organ, as an 'Iliad' or 'Paradise Lost'
written in that manner.   You would associate with it no
tone of Scripture, nothing of the religious solemnity
which Chaucer has so justly been said to impart to his
pathetic stories.   When poor Griselda, repudiated by her
husband, and about to return to her father's cottage,
puts off the clothes which she had worn as the consort of
a great noble, she says, -

[Quotes 'Clerk's Tale', 'C.T.', IV, 862-72.]

   This quotation from the Bible would have been injured
by a shorter measure.
   Griselda, in words most proper and affecting, but
which cannot so well be quoted, apart from the entire
story, goes on to say, that she must not deprive of every
one of its clothes the body which had been made sacred by
motherhood.   She tells the father of her children, that
it is not fit she should be seen by the people in that
condition.

   - 'Wherefore I you pray,
   Let me not like a worm go by the way.'

This is one of the most imploring and affecting lines that
ever were written.   It is also most beautifully modulated,
though not at all after the fashion of the once all in all
'smooth' couplet.   But the masterly accents throughout it,
particularly the emphasis on 'worm,' would have wanted
room, and could have made no such earnest appeal, in a
measure of less length and solemnity.
   Irony itself gains by this measure.   There is no

sarcasm in 'Hudibras', exquisite as its sarcasm is, comparable for energy of tone and manner with Dryden's denunciation (I do not say just denunciation) of every species of priest....

(p. 19) I have dwelt more than is customary on this musical portion of the subject of poetry, for two reasons: first, because, as I have before intimated, it has a greater connexion than is commonly thought, both with the spiritual and with the substantial portions of the art; and second, because, as I have asserted, and am prepared to show, versification, or the various mode of uttering that music, has been neglected among us to a degree which is not a little remarkable, considering what an abundance of poets this country has produced.

England, it is true, is not a musical country; at any rate not yet, whatever its new trainers may do for it. But it is a very poetical country, *minus* this requisite of poetry; and it seems strange that the deficit should be corporately, as well as nationally characteristic. It might have been imagined, that superiority in the one respect would have been accompanied by superiority in the other; - that they who excelled the majority of their countrymen in poetical perception, would have excelled them in musical. Is the want the same as that which has made us inferior to other great nations in the art of painting? Are we geographically, commercially, statistically, or how is it, that we are less gifted than other nations with those perceptions of the pleasurable, which qualify people to excel as painters and musicians? It is observable, that our poetry, compared with that of other countries, is deficient in animal spirits.

At all events, it is this ignorance of the necessity of the whole round of the elements of poetry for the production of a perfect poetical work, and the non-perception, at the same time, of the two-fold fact, that there is no such work in existence, and that the absence of no single element of poetry hinders the other elements from compounding a work truly poetical of its kind, which at different periods of literature produce so many defective and peremptory judgments respecting the exclusive right of this or that species of poetry to be called poetry. In Chaucer's time, there were probably Chaucerophilists who would see no poetry in any other man's writing. Sir Walter Raleigh, nevertheless, who, it might be supposed, would have been an enthusiastic admirer of the Knight's and Squire's Tales, openly said, that he counted no English poetry of any value but that of Spenser. In Cowley's time, 'thinking' was held to be the all in all of poetry: poems were to be crammed full of thoughts,

otherwise intellectual activity was wanting; and hence,
nothing was considered poetry, in the highest sense of
the term, that did not resemble the metaphysics of
Cowley. His 'language of the heart,' which has survived
them, went comparatively for nothing. When the Puritans
brought sentiment into discredit, nothing was considered
comparable, in any species of poetry, with the noble
music and robust sensuous perception of Dryden. Admirable poet as he was, he was thought then, and long afterwards, to be far more admirable, - indeed, the sole

> Great high-priest of all the Nine.

Then 'sense' became the all in all; and because Pope wrote
a great deal of exquisite sense, adorned with wit and
fancy, he was pronounced, and long considered, literally,
the greatest poet that England had seen. A healthy breeze
from the unsophisticate region of the Old English Ballads
suddenly roused the whole poetical elements into play, re-
storing a sense of the combined requisites of imagination,
of passion, of simple speaking, of music, of animal
spirits, &c., not omitting, of course, the true thinking
which all sound feeling implies; and though, with the prevailing grave tendency of the English muse, some portions
of these poetical requisites came more into play than
others, and none of our poets, either since or before,
have combined them all as Chaucer and Shakspeare did, yet
it would as ill become poets or critics to ignore any one
of them in favour of exclusive pretensions on the part of
any others, as it would to say, that all the music, and
animal spirits, and comprehensiveness might be taken out
of those two wonderful men, and they remain just what they
were.
    To think that there can be no poetry, properly so
called, where there is anything 'artificial,' where there
are conventionalisms of style, where facts are simply related without obviously imaginative treatment, or where
manner, for its own sake, is held to be a thing of any
account in its presentation of matter, is showing as limited a state of critical perception as that of the opposite
conventional faction, who can see no poetry out of the
pale of received forms, classical associations, or total
subjections of spiritual to material treatment. It is a
case of imperfect sympathy on both sides; - of incompet-
ency to discern and enjoy in another what they have no
corresponding tendency to in themselves. It is often a
complexional case; perhaps always so, more or less: for
writers and critics, like all other human creatures, are
physically as well as morally disposed to be what they

become. It is the entire man that writes and thinks, and
not merely the head. His leg has often as much to do with
it as his head; - the state of his calves, his vitals, and
his nerves.
There is a charming line in Chaucer: -

Uprose the sun, and uprose Emily.

Now here are two simple matters of fact, which happen to
occur simultaneously. The sun rises, and the lady rises
at the same time. Well, what is there in that, some demanders of imaginative illustration will say? Nothing,
answers one, but an hyperbole. Nothing, says another,
but a conceit. It is a mere commonplace turn of gallantry, says a third. On the contrary, it is the reverse of
all this. It is pure morning freshness, enthusiasm, and
music. Writers, no doubt, may repeat it till it becomes
a commonplace, but that is another matter. Its first
sayer, the great poet, sees the brightest of material
creatures, and the beautifulest of human creatures, rising at dawn at the same time. He feels the impulse
strong upon him to do justice to the appearance of both;
and with gladness in his face, and music on his tongue,
repeating the accent on a repeated syllable, and dividing
the *rhythm* into two equal parts, in order to leave nothing undone to show the merit on both sides, and the rapture of his impartiality, he utters, for all time, his
enchanting record.
Now it requires animal spirits, or a thoroughly loving
nature, to enjoy that line completely; and yet, on looking well into it, it will be found to contain (by implication) simile, analogy, and, indeed, every other form of
imaginative expression, apart from that of direct illus-
trative words; which, in such cases, may be called needless commentary. The poet lets nature speak for herself.
He points to the two beautiful objects before us, and is
content with simply hailing them in their combination.
In all cases where Nature should thus be left to speak
for herself (and they are neither mean nor few cases, but
many and great) the imaginative faculty, which some think
to be totally suspended at such times, is, on the contrary, in full activity, keeping aloof all irrelevancies
and impertinence, and thus showing how well it understands
its great mistress. When Lady Macbeth says she should
have murdered Duncan herself,

Had he not resembled
Her father as he slept,

she said neither more nor less than what a poor criminal
said long afterwards, and quite unaware of the passage,
when brought before a magistrate from a midnight scuffle
in a barge on the Thames; - 'I should have killed him, if
he had not looked so like my father while he was sleeping.' Shakspeare made poetry of the thought by putting it
into verse, - into modulation; but he would not touch it
otherwise. He reverenced Nature's own simple, awful, and
sufficing suggestion too much, to add a syllable to it for
the purpose of showing off his subtle powers of imaginative illustration. And with no want of due reverence to
Shakspeare be it said, that it is a pity he did not act
invariably with the like judgment; - that he suffered
thought to crowd upon thought, where the first feeling was
enough. So, what can possibly be imagined simpler, finer,
completer, less wanting anything beyond itself, than the
line in which poor old Lear, unable to relieve himself
with his own trembling fingers, asks the byestander to
open his waistcoat for him, - not forgetting, in the
midst of his anguish, to return him thanks for so doing,
like a gentleman:

Pray you undo this button. - Thank you, Sir.

The poet here presents us with two matters of fact, in
their simplest and apparently most prosaical form; yet,
when did ever passion or imagination speak more intensely? and this, purely because he has let them alone?
There is another line in Chaucer, which seems to be
still plainer matter of fact, with no imagination in it
of any kind, apart from the simple necessity of imagining
the fact itself. It is in the story of the Tartar king,
which Milton wished to have had completed. The king has
been feasting, and is moving from the feast to a ball-
room:

Before him goeth the loud minstrelsy.

Now, what is there in this line (it might be asked) which
might not have been said in plain prose? which indeed is
not prose? The king is preceded by his musicians, playing
loudly. What is there in that?
Well, there is something even in that, if the prosers
who demand so much help to their perceptions could but see
it. But verse fetches it out and puts it in its proper
state of movement. The line itself, being a line of
verse, and therefore a musical movement, becomes process-
ional, and represents the royal train in action. The word
'goeth,' which a less imaginative writer would have

rejected in favour of something which he took to be more
spiritual and uncommon, is the soul of the continuity of
the movement. It is put, accordingly, in its most emphatic place. And the word 'loud' is suggestive at once of
royal power, and of the mute and dignified serenity, superior to that manifestation of it, with which the king
follows.

> *Before* him goeth the loud minstrelsy.

Any reader who does not recognise the stately 'go,' and
altogether noble sufficingness of that line, may rest
assured that thousands of the beauties of poetry will
remain for ever undiscovered by him, let him be helped by
as many thoughts and images as he may.
So in a preceding passage where the same musicians
are mentioned.

> And so befell, that after the third course,
> While that this King sat thus in his nobley, - [*noble-*
> > *ness*]
>
> Hearing his minstrallés their thingés play
> Before him at his board deliciously,
> In at the hallé-door all suddenly
> There came a knight upon a steed of brass,
> And in his hand a broad mirror of glass;
> Upon his thumb he had of gold a ring,
> And by his side a naked sword hanging,
> And up he rideth to the highé board. -
> In all the hallé n'as there spoke a word [*was not*]
> For marvel of this knight. - Him to behold
> Full busily they waited, young and old.

In some of these lines, what would otherwise be prose,
becomes, by the musical feeling, poetry. The king,
'sitting in his nobleness,' is an imaginative picture.
The word 'deliciously' is a venture of animal spirits,
which, in a modern writer, some critics would pronounce to
be affected, or too familiar; but the enjoyment, and even
incidental appropriateness and *relish* of it, will be obvious to finer senses. And in the pause in the middle of
the last couplet but one, and that in the course of the
first line of its successor, examples were given by this
supposed unmusical old poet, of some of the highest refinements of versification.
The secret of musical, as of all other feeling, lies in
the depths of the harmonious adjustments of our nature;
and a chord touched in any one of them, vibrates with the
rest. In the Queen's beautiful letter to Mr. Sidney

Herbert, about the sufferers in the Crimea, the touching
words, 'those poor noble wounded and sick men,' would
easily, and with perfectly poetical sufficiency, flow into
verse. Chaucer, with his old English dissyllable, *poorĕ*,
(more piteous, because lingering in the sound,) would have
found in them a verse ready made to his hand -

Those poorĕ noble wounded and sick men.

The passage is in fact just like one of his own verses,
sensitive, earnest, strong, simple, full of truth, full of
harmonious sympathy. Many a manly eye will it moisten;
many a poor soldier, thus acknowledged to be a 'noble,'
will it pay for many a pang. What, if transferred to
verse, would it need from any other kind of imaginative
treatment? What, indeed, could it receive but injury?
And yet, to see what is said by the demanders, on every
possible poetical occasion, of perpetual commentating
thoughts and imaginative analogies, one must conclude that
they would pronounce it to be wholly unfit for poetry, unless something very fine were added about 'poor,' something very fine about 'noble,' something very fine about
'wounded,' and something very fine about 'sick;' a process
by which our sympathy with the suffering heroes would come
to nothing, in comparison with our astonishment at the
rhetoric of the eulogizers, - which, indeed, is a 'consummation' that writers of this description would seem to
desire.
    Of all the definitions which have been given of poetry,
the best is that which pronounces it to be 'geniality,
singing.' I think, but am not sure, that it is Lamb's;
perhaps it is Coleridge's. I had not seen it, or, if I
had, had lost all recollection of it, when I wrote the
book called 'Imagination and Fancy'; otherwise I would
have substituted it for the definition given in that book;
for it comprehends, by implication, all which is there
said respecting the different classes and degrees of
poetry, and excludes, at the same time, whatsoever does
not properly come within the limits of the thing defined.
    Geniality, thus considered, is not to be understood in
its common limited acceptation of a warm and flowing spirit
of companionship. It includes that and every other motive
to poetic utterance; but it resumes its great primal meaning of the power of productiveness; that power from which
the word Genius is derived, and which falls in so completely with the meaning of the word Poet itself, which is
Maker. The poet makes, or produces, because he has a
desire to do so; and what he produces is found to be
worthy, in proportion as time shows a desire to retain it.

As all trees are trees, whatever be the different degrees
of their importance, so all poets are poets whose productions have a character of their own, and take root in the
ground of national acceptance. The poet sings, because he
is excited, and because whatsoever he does must be moulded
into a shape of beauty. If imagination predominates in
him, and it is of the true kind, and he loves the exercise
of it better than the fame, he stands a chance of being a
poet of the highest order, but not of the only order. If
fancy predominates, and the fancy is of the true kind, he
is no less a poet in kind, though inferior in degree. If
thought predominate, he is a contemplative poet: if a
variety of these faculties in combination, he is various
accordingly; less great, perhaps, in each individually,
owing to the divided interest which he takes in the claim
upon his attention; but far greater, if equally great in
all. Nevertheless, he does not hinder his less accomplished brethren from being poets. There is a talk of
confining the appellation poet, to the inspired poet. But
who and what is the inspired poet? Inspired means 'breathed into;' that is to say, by some superior influence.
But how is not Dryden breathed into as well as Chaucer?
Milton as well as Shakspeare? or Pope as well as Milton?
The flute, though out of all comparison with the organ, is
still an instrument 'breathed into.' The only question
is, whether it is breathed into finely, and so as to render it a flute extraordinary; whether the player is a man
of genius after his kind, not to be mechanically made.
You can no more make a Burns than a Homer; no more the
author of a 'Rape of the Lock' than the author of 'Paradise Lost.' If you could, you would have Burnses as plen-
tiful as blackberries and as many 'Rapes of the Lock' as
books of mightier pretension, that are for ever coming
out and going into oblivion. Meantime, the 'Rape of the
Lock' remains, and why? Because it is an inspired poem; a
poem as truly inspired by the genius of wit and fancy, as
the gravest and grandest that ever was written was inspired by passion and imagination.
    This is the secret of a great, national, book-reading
fact, the existence of which has long puzzled exclusives
in poetry; to wit, the never-failing demand in all civilized countries for successive publications of bodies of
collected verse, called English or British Poets, Italian
Poets, French Poets, Spanish Poets, &c. - collections
which stand upon no ceremony whatever with exclusive pre-
dilections, but tend to include every thing that has
attained poetical repute, and are generally considered to
be what they ought to be in proportion as they are copious. Poetasters are sometimes admitted for poets; and

poets are sometimes missed, because they have been taken
for poetasters. But, upon the whole, the chance of excess
is preferred: and the preference is well founded; for the
whole system is founded on a judicious instinct. Feelings
are nature's reasons; communities often feel better than
individuals reason; and they feel better in this instance.

7.   JAMES LORIMER, CHAUCER IS OUR GOETHE

1849

James Lorimer (1818-90), writer and professor, was educated at the universities of Edinburgh, Berlin, Bonn, and
the academy of Geneva. He wrote many books on law and
political philosophy. He was appointed to the Chair of
the Law of Nature and of Nations at Edinburgh in 1865 and
advocated many admirable reforms. In this anonymous contribution (identified in 'The Wellesley Index of Nineteenth Century Periodicals') he gives a lengthy review of
editions of and books about Chaucer in 'The North British
Review', X (1849) and emphasises Chaucer's resemblances
to later times, concluding with the novel but valuable
comparison with Goethe.

(p. 294) In order to deal with the utilitarian spirit
which perhaps not improperly influences the choice of the
many, in literature as in more vulgar matters, and to fix,
as it were, the marketable value of Chaucer, the first
question, as it seems to us, which we are bound at once
to ask and to answer, is - belongs he to the living or to
the dead; does he or does he not speak words of living interest to living men; is he or is he not an integral part
of our existing civilisation?
     The world is old enough to have seen many intellectual
as well as political revolutions, and there are eras which
boasted probably of no mean culture, irrevocably lost in
the darkness of time. They are past, dead even in their
effects - at least we can trace no influence which they
exercise over our present life. Mediately they may work,
as the civilisation of Egypt through that of Greece, and
it is nothing more than reasonable to suppose that by

unseen links the earliest and the latest efforts of intelligence may be bound together; but the Pyramids teach no
audible lesson except that of the mutability of human affairs, and the vast Sphinx is as silent as the sand at its
base. These, for the present, we may not unfittingly hand
over to the investigations of the curious; for although it
were rashness to set limits to what learning and industry
may yet effect in these darker regions, the popular reader
may well be excused from intrusting himself to the laby-
rinth, till the clew has been found by more adventurous
spirits.

But do the sayings and doings of Chaucer thus fall
beyond the pale of general interest; does his image thus
shrink into the shadowy past? Nothing can be more erroneous than such a supposition, and indeed, so far is his
story from being strange and distant to us, that we believe every one who investigates it for the first time will
feel astonished that it should have been possible for any
one, in the times of Cressy and of Poictiers, to lead a
life in all respects so nearly resembling that of an
accomplished and successful civilian at the present day.
It may make us think better of the liberality of our
ancestors also, when we find that among iron-coated warriors and hooded monks, there was one who was neither a
soldier nor a priest who advanced himself to celebrity and
fortune, and during a long life under three monarchs enjoyed both honour and wealth by dint of his intellectual
gifts and graces alone.

It is an extremely common error, both with vulgar narrators and careless readers, to lay hold of the points of
dissimilarity between distant ages and those in which they
live, to the almost total exclusion of the often much more
important features of resemblance, and this error it is
which has so singularly estranged us from the early history of our country. We are told, for instance, that
Chaucer lived before the invention of printing, in times of
the darkest Popish superstition, when men believed in alchemy and astrology, wore armour, and fought for the most
part with bows and arrows; and we immediately form to ourselves the picture of a barbarous and benighted age, and
of a quaint and curious, but ignorant and bigoted old man,
with whom we of this generation of light can have no species of sympathy or fellowship. We forget, however, that
by drawing the picture a little nearer to us we should
probably have discovered many objects of far more interesting contemplation in the features of resemblance which
lie hidden behind the few fantastic forms of unlikeness
which have attracted our eye in the foreground, and that
in short, our superficial glance has been resting upon the

rude and barren crags which jut up prominently in the distance, instead of luxuriating in the fertile valleys and
sunny fields, which a closer inspection would have revealed to our view. Now, if we would approach the father
of our poetry in a spirit of erect and manly, but of respectful inquiry - if we would set about investigating his
life and his writings, with the view of discovering not
wherein he, in common with every man in Europe of his day,
differed from the men of modern times, but wherein he resembled us, not in the unchangeable features of humanity
alone, but in the peculiar characteristics of race and of
nation - if we would compare with our own the manners and
feelings of our own ancestors, as they move before us in
their domestic and familiar intercourse in his graphic delineations, we should not only become reconciled to the
character of the poet himself, but we should discover that
he lived among a people possessing in the highest degree
those distinctive features, that sharp and prominent
nationality which distinguishes the present inhabitants of
England from every other people. We should discover that
same joyous and exuberant reality, that hatred of 'humbug'
which distinguishes us now, existing alongside of those
superstitious observances which we rightly attribute to
that distant age, and exhibiting itself as it has ever
since done in England, in a tendency, on the part of all
classes of the people, to attack falsehood by the arms of
argument and ridicule, rather than by an ebullition of
sudden violence, which should peril the advantages of
their present position, to risk a positive good for a
possible better. We should meet, in the morning of our
English life, with that same spirit which now sneers in
Punch and wrestles in the Times, awake and busy with Pardoner, and monk, and mendicant, and with all that then was
vicious and absurd, and we should perceive, moreover, that
then, as now, it was no spirit of indiscriminate destruction - that though it was revolutionary in appearance, it
was conservative at heart, and that it consequently acted
with perfect consistency in permitting to stand, as we
know that it did for two centuries longer, a religious
system of the imperfections of which it was perfectly conscious, but the uses of which it also recognised.

Much has been done in later times to approach us to our
ancestors, and the gulf which threatened to separate us
from them for ever, has been bridged over by the adoption
of a principle little regarded by the writers of history
of the last age. It has come to be perceived that the importance of an historical fact is often by no means in
proportion to its apparent magnitude, and that the trivial
occurrences of domestic life, and the usages of familiar

intercourse, form very frequently a more accurate measure, both of the genius and culture of a people, than their great public events. It was long forgotten, that although trying situations may call forth striking manifestations of individual or of national peculiarities, it is in the peaceful and normal condition alone that we can hope to analyze that infinitely complex idea which corresponds to the character of a man or of an age; and that it is only when we behold it at rest and examine it in detail, that we can detect the individual colours which compose the variegated web of human life. In the hurry of a battle, or the confusion of a political revolution, in the panic of a pestilence, or the depression of a famine, men of all races, and in all ages, must manifest many features of re- semblance, for this simple reason, that their actions are for the time under the dominion of necessity, or at all events of a few simple and overwhelming emotions; and to prove that their conduct had been similar in such circum- stances, would be but to prove that they belonged to the common family of mankind. If their courage or their pusi- llanimity, their clemency or their cruelty, had been very remarkable, we should then indeed have the broad and gen- eral ideas that they were heroes or cowards, that they were men of mercy or men of blood; but as to their posi- tion on the intellectual or social scale, we should still be utterly at sea, since a barbarian may be generous, and poets and philosophers have been known who were no heroes. So long as the conduct of an individual is very power- fully influenced by the external circumstances which sur- round him at the time, it forms but a rude and general index to his character; and it is only when his actions proceed from the unfettered dictates of his reason or of his caprice, that its light becomes a clear and trusty guide. If we had heard the orders of Harold to his nobles, and known every circumstance of his conduct, and even every thought which passed through his mind during the battle of Hastings, we might have judged perhaps of the talents of the General, or even of the determination and energy of the man, but we should have known less of the civilisation either of him or of his age, than if we had conversed with him, as he buckled on his spurs for the battle, or had played the eves-dropper, when, in days of careless joy, he lingered by the side of the swan-necked Edith. Of all the days of Harold's life, perhaps the least instructive in this respect would have been that of the battle of Hastings.

Since the days of the learned and laborious Tyrwhitt, and the loving and enthusiastic but injudicious Godwin, numerous have been the attempts to bring us once again

face to face with the father of our poetry. We have had
'Chaucer Modernized,' 'Tales from Chaucer,' 'Riches of
Chaucer,' 'Selections from Chaucer,' with notes and illustrations and biographies without end, and to little good
end or purpose either, so far as we can judge. They have
failed one and all, for this good and simple reason, that
they satisfied the requirements of no class of readers.
Tiresome to the indolent for whom they were intended, they
in vain endeavoured to rival with them the attractions of
the slightest novel of the day; useless to the vainglorious, for it was impossible to boast of such an
acquaintance with the poet as they conveyed, and to the
better class of readers, the learned and serious, not
holding out even the promise of satisfaction, they fell,
as might have been anticipated, nearly still-born from the
press. Possessing neither brilliancy nor depth, they came
within the category of that species of easy writing which,
according to Sheridan, is hard reading....
     (Of his later life; pp. 310-11) For a short time he
seems to have had no other pension than that which he derived from the Duke of Lancaster, and his wages as one of
the King's Esquires. But on the 28th February 1394, he
again obtained a grant from the King of £20 for life; and
this fact, taken in connexion with the powerful friend-
ships which we know he possessed, and the very recent
period at which, as Clerk of the Works, he must have been
very well off, renders it, to our thinking, rather a hasty
conclusion on the part of his biographers, that he must
have been in great want of money, merely because he seems,
once or twice, to have anticipated his pension at the Exchequer. The truth of the matter probably is, that he
made the Exchequer serve him in some measure as a banker
- that he treated his pension as an account-current, upon
which he drew as he found occasion for his ordinary ex-
penses; and this view we think is confirmed by the fact,
that he allowed it to lie after the term of payment,
nearly as often as he drew it in advance. On the whole,
we conceive that the attempt to make Chaucer a martyr to
the world's forgetfulness of men of genius, has not very
well prospered in the hands of his biographers; and we
think it not unlikely, that the phantom of poverty with
which they have insisted on marring his fortunes, may have
been conjured up by that which overshadowed their own.
On this subject Sir Harris Nicolas is quite as pathetic as
Godwin; and the similarity of his fate, which we have recently had occasion to deplore, with that which so long
pressed upon the indiscreet but gifted author of Caleb
Williams, may not improbably have brought about this solitary coincidence. Nor are we at all shaken in our opinion

on this subject by Chaucer's address 'to his Emptie Purse,'
which has been relied on as an additional proof of his
poverty. It is manifestly a sportive production, written
for the purpose of bringing his claims for an increase to
his pensions in a light and graceful manner before the
young king, Henry IV, the son of his patron, John of
Gaunt, and with whom, be it remembered, he was then nearly
connected by marriage, and in these circumstances the expressions, 'I am sorrie now that ye be light,' 'be heavy
againe,' &c., seem to us nothing more than what we daily
hear from persons in very easy circumstances. They might
be brought forward as a proof of his avarice, quite as
well as of his poverty. But if he was a needy, he seems
not to have been an unsuccessful suitor, for we know that
within four days after Henry came to the throne, and probably the very day that he received the verses in question,
he doubled the poet's pension, and on the 15th of October
of the preceding year, just at the time when his supposed
penury must have been at its height, he obtained in addition to his daily pitcher, another grant of a tun of wine
every year during his life, 'in the port of London, from
the King's chief butler or his deputy.' If he had been
so 'rascally poor' as his biographers would make him, one
would think that the *pitcher* daily ought to have been sufficient for his consumption in the article of wine. That
Chaucer was extravagant, or at least that he possessed
those expensive tastes which so frequently accompany
intellectual refinement, is extremely probable, and if
such were the case it is not unlikely that his purse was
occasionally 'lighter' than was consistent with his habits;
but we rejoice to think that there is no reason for quar-
relling with the buxom age in which he lived, on the score
of his having been subjected to actual want, and so far
are we from wishing to claim for him the glories of pecu-
niary martyrdom, that we confess to regarding with some
degree of pleasure, the many indications of wealth and
comfort with which at every stage of his life we find him
surrounded. We remember that Knox had 'his pipe of Bor-
deaux in that old Edinburgh house of his,' and we remember
also the flagon of Einbecker beer, which the kind hands of
Duke Erich proffered to Doctor Martin Luther, on his exit
from the *Saale* at Worms, and the gratitude with which he
drank it; and neither the one nor the other of these hero-
priests is one whit the less heroic in our eyes from his
hearty enjoyment of the good things which Providence sent
him. We have every reason to believe that the father of
our poets was considerably more fortunate in external circumstances than either of the Reformers, and we have no
reason to doubt that his enjoyments were tempered with the

same kindly and pious spirit....

(p. 314) We have now concluded what we conceived it
needful to say of the external position of Chaucer, and
of his varied career, and it will probably be admitted
that we have in some measure fulfilled the promise with
which we commenced the recital. We have called from the
fourteenth century as a witness to its manners, one who
neither in his occupations, nor in his fortunes, differed
greatly from hundreds of the best class of Englishmen of
the present time, and whose story, in its external aspect,
might be told of many under the reign of Queen Victoria,
as well as under that of King Edward III. Are we to conclude from this, that Chaucer was a solitary and isolated
character, plucked as it were by anticipation from the
realm of the future, and sent as a spectator for our
behoof into the halls of our ancestors? or are we to
accept him as a specimen of the man of his time, at the
expense of foregoing all our preconceived opinions with
reference to the character of the fourteenth century? On
either hypothesis we should be equally in error; solitary
and isolated he certainly was not, for with all that was
acted, and all that was thought, he was entwined; in his
life and in his character he was the expression of his
time; but neither was he an average specimen, for he was
its highest expression; we do not say that he was before
his time, for though the phrase is often used with reference to those whose development surpasses that of their
contemporaries not in kind but in degree, we do not think
that it is rightly so used, and if there was any one of
that day to whom in its proper signification we might
apply it, it would be to Wycliffe, and not to Chaucer.
Chaucer did not anticipate the future, but he comprehended the present, he was a 'seer' of what was - not of
what was to be. He was the 'clear and conscious' man of
his time. In his opinions there was nothing which others
did not feel, but what they felt unconsciously he thought
and expressed, and what to them was a vapour, to him was
a form. There was no antagonism between him and his age,
and hence the popularity which we know that he enjoyed.
In taking this view of the matter, it may be thought that
we give up all pretension on the part of our poet, to the
highest - the prophetic part of the poetic character. We
answer that we are not here to discuss the question, as
to whether the proper function of the poet is to express
the age in which he lives, or to shadow forth an age which
is to follow. We state the fact as we conceive it to be,
and so important do we regard it in order to a just appreciation of the character and influence of Chaucer, that we
shall take the liberty of illustrating it by tracing it

out as well as we may, first in his philosophy, and then
in his religion.

For this purpose it is not necessary that we should
speak at length of his metaphysical creed, for the philosophy of Aristotle was still all-prevalent; and there is
abundant proof in many parts of his writings that Chaucer,
like the rest of the learned of his day, was brought up at
the feet of the Stagyrite, and that he read it with the
light which the Schoolmen afforded. It is probable also
that the study was a very favourite one with him, that he
'hadde unto logic long ygo,' and that in this, as in many
other respects, he painted his own character in that of
the Clerk of Oxenford, when he says, that

> him was liever han at his bed's head
> A twenty bookes cloth'd in black or red
> Of Aristotle and his philosophy
> Than robès rich, or fiddle, or psaltry.

But there is no reason to think that in this department
Chaucer ever assumed a higher position than that of a re-
cipient. In none of his works that have come down to us
does he deal with the pure intelligence; and, indeed,
from his whole character, it is obvious that his interest
in the concrete was so intense as scarcely to admit of
his lingering long in the regions of metaphysical or logical abstraction. The part of our nature with which he
was concerned, and upon which it was his vocation to act,
was precisely that which the logician excludes from his
view; as a poet, he had to deal with man not as he thinks
merely, but as he feels and acts - with his passions and
affections even more than with his intelligence, and hence
his devotion to ethical studies.

Of the manner in which he studied, and endeavoured to
elaborate this latter department of mental philosophy, we
are fortunately enabled to judge with considerable precision. In early life he translated the celebrated work of
Boethius 'De Consolatione Philosophiae;' a book more remarkable for its fortunes than even for its merits....

(p. 324) Chaucer's language was therefore the language
of his time. Of all the errors into which Godwin and his
school have fallen, the most absurd is that of asserting
that Chaucer at the age of eighteen, when a student at
Cambridge, having maturely considered the prospects of
his own future celebrity, coolly set himself down to compose his 'Court of Love' in English, as the language which
was most likely in future to be that of his country, and
in order to the proper accomplishment of his task, that he
vigorously applied himself to purify and refine that

hitherto barbarous tongue. However it may tell for the
glory of Chaucer, the truth of the matter unquestionably
is, that he took the language as he found it, in its most
modern form of course; for he was in this as in other respects of the progressive party of his day, and insensibly
he contributed what one mind might do in one generation
towards its development. As to his merit in preferring
it to the Norman French, all that we have to say is, that
though it is highly probable that he knew that language
sufficiently to have used it for the purposes of poetical
composition if he had chosen, that fact is by no means
certain, and that he regarded it at all events in the
light of a foreign tongue, is clear on his own showing.
'Let then clerkes enditen in Latin, for they have the
propertie of science, and the knowing of that facultie;
and *lette Frenchmen in their French also enditen their
queint termes, for it is kindely to their mouthes, and
let us shewe our fantasies in such wordes as we learneden
of our dames tongue.'*
   It were needless to occupy the small space which remains to us by insisting further on this point. The
theory of that sorrowful interregnum between Anglo-Saxon
and English, when our ancestors are said to have spoken a
chaotic and Babylonish jargon, incapable of being turned
to intellectual uses, is now happily abandoned by all our
scholars, and we have the Anglo-Saxon, the semi-Saxon,
the old, the middle, and the modern English, each shading
gradually and naturally into the other. From the reign
of Henry III up to Chaucer's time, we have a series of
political and satirical songs and poems in the vernacular
tongue; and so far from the native language having been
prohibited by the earlier Norman kings, we know that from
the Conquest till the reign of Henry II, it was invariably
employed by them in their charters, when it made way, not
for French, but for Latin. We have thus at last recovered
the missing link, and we have now to thank modern industry
for the unbroken chain which binds together our speech and
that of our ancestors.
   Our space does not permit us to dwell at any length on
the poetical merits of Chaucer, and, indeed, our intention
from the first has been to supply our readers with such
information as might induce them to peruse his works,
rather than to save them the trouble of perusal, by furnishing them with opinions ready made. But a few observations before parting, for the purpose of fixing, in some
measure, the rank that he is entitled to hold among our
poets, we cannot deny ourselves. We do not venture to
equal him to the two greatest of them. With Milton,
indeed, he can in nowise be compared, for the difference

in kind is so absolute as to render it impossible to measure the degree; and by Shakspeare he is unquestionably
surpassed in his own walk. The divine instinct of the
Swan of Avon he did not possess, and hence his characterization is broad and common as compared with his. But
here our admission of inferiority must end. As a poet of
character - and as such chiefly he must be viewed, we believe him to come nearer to Shakspeare than any other
writer in our language. There is the same vigour in all
that he pourtrays, the same tone of health belongs to it.
When Carlyle said that Sir Walter Scott was the healthiest
man that ever was, he ought to have added, 'after Chaucer.'
We believe that no writer ever was so healthy as Chaucer;
and we dwell on this characteristic with the greater pleasure that it seems to us a proof of the thoroughly good
constitution with which our English life began. Even
where he comes in contact with grossness and immorality,
they never seem to taint him, or to jaundice his vision.
They are ludicrous or hateful, and as such he represents
them freely and unshrinkingly; but there is no morbid
gloating over impurity, or lingering around vice. There
is nothing French about him, neither has he any kindred
with such writers as those of Charles the Second's time,
or with the Swifts, and Sternes, and Byrons of later days.
He is not very scrupulous about words, but there is no
mistaking his opinion; and the question as to whether his
weight is to be thrown into the balance in behalf of
virtue or of vice is never doubtful. 'If he is a coarse
moralist,' said Mr. Wordsworth, 'he is still a great one.'
    Chaucer is essentially the poet of man. Brought up
from the first among his fellows, and discharging to the
last the duties of a citizen, he wandered not, - nor
wished to wander in solitary places. His poetry is that
of reality, and an Elysium which he sought not in the
clouds, he found abundantly in human sympathies. We have
spoken of his cheerfulness, and the best description which
we can give of him, as he appears in his works, is, that
in all respects he is a cheerful, gregarious being, not
ashamed to confess himself satisfied with the world in
which God has placed him, and with those with whom he has
seen fit to people it. There is no affectation of *taedium
vitae* about him; he does not think himself too good for
the world, not the world too bad for him. Though there is
much that he fain would mend, he is still by no means dis-
gusted with matters as they stand, and gladly and thank-
fully extracts the sweets of a present existence.
    The masculine air of his delineations is what strikes
us most. His characters are large and strong, and stand
out with an almost superfluous fulness of form, which

often reminds us of Rubens' pictures; but he is more
tender, he has more feeling, and his gentler characters
are touched with exquisite delicacy. The 'Chapeau de
Paille' will bear no comparison with the tender Prioresse
that 'was cleped Madame Eglantine,' of whose womanly heart
we have the following picture: -

> She was so charitable and so pitous
> She wolde wepe if that she saw a mous
> Caught in a trappe, if it were ded or bledde.

The Prioresse's Tale is one of the happiest examples of
the pathetic, in which Chaucer was so great a master, and
there is a depth and earnestness of feeling about it, and
others of the class to which it belongs, which we should
scarcely expect in the writings of one usually so gay as
Chaucer. There is so much gentle grief which pervades
every part of it, that the reader is insensibly led into
the feelings of the poor widow who

> Waileth al that night
> After hire litel childe, and he came nought;

and if we compare it with the common version of the story
which appears in the Percy Reliques, under the title of
the 'Jew's Daughter,' we shall see to how great an extent
it is indebted for its beauty to Chaucer's genius. If any
one should doubt the versatility of Chaucer, and should
be tempted to regard him in the light of a mere humorist,
let him peruse the Prioresse's Tale, and consider her
character along with those of Constance, the patient
Grisilde, and others of the same class in the serious
tales. In these touching delineations, the poet whom we
had known, the man of mirth, vanishes from our sight, and
in his place we have a character made up of the finest
sympathies, and regulated by sincere and humble piety.
  Another characteristic of Chaucer as a poet, is his
love for external nature. His poems seem everywhere
strewed with flowers, and wherever we go we encounter the
breezes of spring. The image of 'Freshe May' is continually recurring, the very word has a charm for him, and in
the Shipman's Tale we find it used as a woman's name. The
description of Emilie in the garden, in the commencement
of the Knight's Tale, though probably familiar to many of
our readers, is so beautiful in itself, and so completely
illustrates Chaucer's best style as a poet, that we shall
insert it at length....
  (p. 328) In many respects it seems to us that Chaucer
resembles Goethe more than any of the poets of our own

country. He has the same mental completeness and consequent versatility which distinguish the German; the same
love of reality; the same clearness and cheerfulness; and,
in seeming contradiction to this latter characteristic,
the same preference for grief over the other passions, in
his poetical delineations. In minor respects, he also resembles him; and in one, not unimportant, as marking a
similarity of mental organization, that, namely, of be-
taking himself at the close of a long life spent in literature and affairs, to the study of the physical sciences,
as if here alone the mental craving for the positive could
find satisfaction.

8. WILLIAM WATKISS LLOYD, CHAUCER'S IRONY

1856

Lloyd (1813-93), businessman and spare-time archaeologist,
classical and Shakespearian scholar, is one of the first
explicitly to emphasise Chaucer's irony. He comments in
his Critical Essay on [Shakespeare's] 'Troilus and Cressida', in 'Dramatic Works of Shakespeare', ed. S.W.
Singer, 10 vols, Vol. VII, pp. 316-19 (reprinted in
'Critical Essays', 1875).

[Of Dares Phrygius's 'De Excidio Troiae':] This, far more
than Homer, was the great authority in the middle ages for
the incidents of the Trojan war, and largely was it drawn
upon and liberally expanded in the wild and weedy literature of the semi-barbarous centuries which we perhaps
fondly flatter ourselves we have escaped from. It is very
difficult to say how much of what is most at variance with
Homer in this story may not have been derived from other
Greek sources - so multifarious, so everchanging - besides
those that we can actually trace. From Dares Phrygius
descended with other streams, the Troy-boke of Lydgate and
the Destruction of Troy of Caxton, both probably known to
Shakespeare, and thus the general circumstances of the war
as well as many of the particular are recognized as the
same in the play before us. Hence came the importance
assigned to the Trojan relationship of Ajax and that of
Calchas, the valour of Troilus as survivor and successor

of Hector, the intrigue of Achilles and Polyxena, and the
origin of the Rape of Helen in retaliation for that of
Hesione. The scene of Hector arming notwithstanding the
boding of his family, follows the description of Dares
Phrygius exactly.

Upon this stock which roots at least in classical
times, the love intrigue of Troilus and Cressida was a
true mediaeval graft; it was of course received by Shakespeare from Chaucer, probably the next in succession to
Boccaccio, whose poem of Filostrato he follows as closely
as he liberally expands, for as to his professed authority
'mine auctor Lollius,' I find none who know anything of
him; he is indeed as mere a fiction as Bishop Turpin,
whose veracity was always appealed to by the minstrels of
the Paladins, when it suited them to give forth a palpable
invention as a fact....

Chaucer's Troilus and Cressida, in five long books, is
a work remarkable for more than its length; it is exceedingly full and diffuse, a mere modicum of incident furnishes the simplest skeleton to the large bulk, yet slowly
as the story moves it is always moving, minute as are its
details they are ever touched with liveliness; and archness and mock simplicity, irony most delicate in grain is
thrown over the whole, and gives a fanciful glow to descriptions of otherwise literal nature. It is here we
recognize the inspiration of much of the texture and
treatment, thought not of the tone, of the Venus and
Adonis and the Rape of Lucrece, but Chaucer's poem, I
confess, despite its length and thinner imaginative colouring, is more readable, indeed is pleasantly and easily
to be read from beginning to end by those to whom leisure
and long summer days permit amusement not impatient for
its end.

The Cressida of Chaucer is the same dame as the heroine of Shakespeare, though he spares to give her the
terms that she deserves. He leaves her words and actions
to tell for themselves, and they are consistent enough to
assign her true place and niche in the descending line of
troth and constancy and feminine reserve. The poet is
plaintive on his own ill-luck in a theme unfriendly to
the feminine audience he stands in awe of, he would willingly have told a tale of Penelope or Alcestis, even
offers a faint defence and affects to retort pettishly on
the men as causers of all the mischief, soberly warning
'every gentilwoman' to beware of deceivers just as he
closes a tale of female art and deception that should make
the whole sex blush and cry shame upon him.

Shakespeare, who has otherwise scarcely strengthened
the leading lines of the characters, alters one

circumstance in this direction, for his Cressid is not
like Chaucer's, a widow, and she thus loses an apology,
fictitious though it be, from the latitude of allurement,
the privilege of the fair guild that wedded once is permitted censureless in compliment to former nuptials to
indicate by cabalism of its own a not unwillingness to wed
again.

Chaucer has been no more exempt than others from the
hap of having his irony taken for earnest, but a few stanzas from the courtship of Diomed suffice to show that he
designed her coyness as enacted and artifice - direct suggestion of the corresponding scene in the play....

There is some flatness perhaps in the last book both of
Chaucer and Boccaccio, from the falsehood of Cressida
being conveyed to Troilus at second-hand, by hearsay, cold
letters, and conclusively only by his love tokens being
captured with the equipments of Diomed. Shakespeare relieved this by carrying him personally to the Greek tents.

The actual conclusion of Chaucer's poem is replete
with spirit generally in both conception and execution, but
in no point more so than in the compensation allotted to
Troilus, less it must be said for his merit, than for his
simplicity and suffering. It is after his troubles are
over with his life that he rises superior to the false
loves and poor passions and pride of a low world, and
beholds the better end of existence....

Troilus is the youngest of Priam's numerous sons, and
the passion of which he is the victim is the bare instinctive impulse of the teens, the form that first love takes
when crossed by an unworthy object, which might have been
that of Romeo had Rosalind not overstood her opportunity.
It is his age that explains how, notwithstanding his high
mental endowments, he is so infatuated as to mistake the
planned provocation of Cressida's coyness for stubborn
chastity, and to allow himself to be played with and in-
flamed by her concerted airs of surprise and confusion
when at last they are brought together. He is quite as
dull in apprehending the character of Pandarus, and complains of his tetchiness to be wooed to woo, when in fact
he is but holding off in the very spirit of his niece and
affecting reluctance in order to excite solicitation.
Boccaccio furnished some of the lines of this characterization to Chaucer, but Chaucer gave them great development in handing them down to Shakespeare.

9.   JOHN RUSKIN, FIMESIS AND OTHER MATTERS

1856, 1865, 1870, 1873, 1876

John Ruskin (1819-1900), artist, art-critic, moralist,
social reformer, passionate Victorian sage and prophet,
was educated privately and at King's College, London. In
his extremely popular, influential, voluminous, digres-
sive and varied writings he frequently refers to Chaucer,
usually to make incidental points. But the relation of
coarseness to idealism, the concept of the 'national
mind', the educative and purifying power of the imagination, and the best way to manage both mental and physical
nourishment, are all topics which Chaucer's writings
either illustrate or into which they are fitted, in a
stimulating and unusual way. Life and literature are one.
Extract (a) is from 'The Harbours of England' (1856) (ed.
E.T. Cook and A.D.O. Wedderburn, 'Works' (1902-12) XIII,
pp. 20-3); (b) from The Cestus of Aglaia, 'Art Journal',
N.S. IV ('Works' XIX, pp. 82-5); (c) 'Lectures on Art'
(1870), pp. 15-16; (d) 'Fors Clavigera' (1873), Letter 34,
pp. 8-9; (e) 'Fors Clavigera', (1876), Letter 61, pp. 21-
2.

(a)

It is very interesting to note how repugnant every oceanic
idea appears to be to the whole nature of our principal
English mediaeval poet, Chaucer. Read first the Man of
Lawe's Tale, in which the Lady Constance is continually
floated up and down the Mediterranean, and the German
Ocean, in a ship by herself; carried from Syria all the
way to Northumberland, and there wrecked upon the coast;
thence yet again driven up and down among the waves for
five years, she and her child; and yet, all this while,
Chaucer does not let fall a single word descriptive of
the sea, or express any emotion whatever about it, or
about the ship. He simply tells us the lady sailed here
and was wrecked there; but neither he nor his audience
appear to be capable of receiving any sensation, but one
of simple aversion, from waves, ships, or sands. Compare
with his absolutely apathetic recital, the description by
a modern poet of the sailing of a vessel, charged with the
fate of another Constance:

It curled not Tweed alone, that breeze -
For far upon Northumbrian seas
   It freshly blew, and strong;
Where from high Whitby's cloistered pile,
Bound to St. Cuthbert's holy isle,
   It bore a bark along.
Upon the gale she stooped her side,
And bounded o'er the swelling tide
   As she were dancing home.
The merry seamen laughed to see
Their gallent ship so lustily
   Furrow the green sea foam. ['Marmion', ii.1.]

Now just as Scott enjoys this sea breeze, so does
Chaucer the soft air of the woods; the moment the older
poet lands, he is himself again, his poverty of language
in speaking of the ship is not because he despises description, but because he has nothing to describe. Hear
him upon the ground in Spring:

These woodes else recoveren greene,
That drie in winter ben to sene,

[Quotes 'Romaunt', pp. 57-70.]

In like manner, wherever throughout his poems we find
Chaucer enthusiastic, it is on a sunny day in the 'good
greenwood,' but the slightest approach to the seashore
makes him shiver; and his antipathy finds at last positive expression, and becomes the principal foundation of
the Frankeleine's Tale, in which a lady, waiting for her
husband's return in a castle by the sea, behaves and expresses herself as follows:-

   Another time wold she sit and thinke,
And cast her eyen dounward fro the brinke;
But whan she saw the grisly rockes blake,
For veray fere so wold hire herte quake
That on hire feet she might hire not sustene
Than wold she sit adoun upon the grene,
And pitously into the sea behold,
And say right thus, with careful sighes cold.
   'Eterne God, that thurgh thy purveance
Ledest this world by certain governance,
In idel, as men sein, ye nothing make.
But, lord, thise grisly fendly rockes blake,
That semen rather a foule confusion
Of werk, than any faire creation
Of swiche a parfit wise God and stable,
Why han ye wrought this werk unresonable?'

The desire to have the rocks out of her way is indeed
severely punished in the sequel of the tale; but it is
not the less characteristic of the age, and well worth
meditating upon, in comparison with the feelings of an
unsophisticated modern French or English girl among the
black rocks of Dieppe or Ramsgate.

On the other hand, much might be said about that peculiar love of *green fields and birds* in the Middle Ages; and
of all with which it is connected, purity and health in
manners and heart, as opposed to the too frequent condition of the modern mind -

> As for the birds in the thicket,
> Thrush or ousel in leafy niche,
> Linnet or finch - she was far too rich
> To care for a morning concert to which
> She was welcome, without a ticket.   (Thomas Hood)

But this would lead us far afield, and the main fact I
have to point out to the reader is the transition of
human grace and strength from the exercises of the land to
those of the sea in the course of the last three centuries.

Down to Elizabeth's time chivalry lasted; and grace of
dress and mien, and all else that was connected with
chivalry. Then came the ages which, when they have taken
their due place in the depths of the past, will be, by a
wise and clear-sighted futurity, perhaps well comprehended
under a common name, as the ages of Starch....

(b)

> Dame Paciencë sitting there I fonde,
> With facë pale, upon an hill of sonde.

As I try to summon this vision of Chaucer's into definiteness, and as it fades before me, and reappears, like the
image of Piccarda in the moon, there mingles with it
another; - the image of an Italian child, lying, she also,
upon a hill of sand, by Eridanus' side; a vision which has
never quite left me since I saw it. A girl of ten or
twelve, it might be; one of the children to whom there has
never been any other lesson taught than that of patience:
- patience of famine and thirst; patience of heat and
cold; patience of fierce word and sullen blow; patience of
changeless fate and giftless time. She was lying with her
arms thrown back over her head, all languid and lax, on an
earth-heap by the river side (the softness of the dust
being the only softness she had ever known), in the

southern suburb of Turin, one golden afternoon in August,
years ago....

But it is provoking to me that the image of this child
mingles itself now with Chaucer's; for I should like truly
to know what Chaucer means by his sand-hill. Not but that
this is just one of those enigmatical pieces of teaching
which we have made up our minds not to be troubled with,
since it may evidently mean just what we like. Sometimes
I would fain have it to mean the ghostly sand of the horo-
loge of the world: and I think that the pale figure is
seated on the recording heap, which rises slowly, and ebbs
in giddiness, and flows again, and rises, tottering; and
still she sees, falling beside her, the never-ending
stream of phantom sand. Sometimes I like to think that
she is seated on the sand because she is herself the
Spirit of Staying, and victor over all things that pass
and change; - quicksand of the desert in moving pillar;
quicksand of the sea in moving floor; roofless all, and un-
abiding, but she abiding; - to herself, her home. And
sometimes I think, though I do not like to think (neither
did Chaucer mean this, for he always meant the lovely
thing first, not the low one), that she is seated on her
sand-heap as the only treasure to be gained by human toil;
and that the little ant-hill, where the best of us creep
to and fro, bears to angelic eyes, in the patientest
gathering of its galleries, only the aspect of a little
heap of dust; while for the worst of us, the heap, still
lower by the levelling of those winged surveyors, is high
enough, nevertheless, to overhang, and at last to close in
judgment, on the seventh day, over the journeys to the
fortunate Islands; while to their dying eyes, through the
mirage, 'the city sparkles like a grain of salt.'

But of course it does not in the least matter what it
means. All that matters specially to us in Chaucer's
vision, is that, next to Patience (as the reader will find
by looking at the context in the 'Assembly of Foules'),
were 'Beheste' and 'Art'; - Promise, that is, and Art: and
that, although these visionary powers are here waiting
only in one of the outer courts of Love, and the intended
patience is here only the long-suffering of love; and the
intended beheste, its promise; and the intended art, its
cunning, - the same powers companion each other necessarily in the courts and ante-chambers of every triumphal
home of man.

(c)

[Of limitations in English artists]   Secondly - and this

is an incapacity of a graver kind, yet having its own good
in it also - we [the English] shall never be successful in
the highest fields of ideal or theological art. For there
is one strange, but quite essential character in us: ever
since the Conquest, if not earlier: - a delight in the
forms of burlesque which are connected in some degree with
the foulness of evil. I think the most perfect type of a
true English mind in its best possible temper, is that of
Chaucer; and you will find that, while it is for the most
part full of things of beauty, pure and wild like that of
an April morning, there are even in the midst of this
sometimes momentarily jesting passages which stoop to play
with evil - while the power of listening to and enjoying
the jesting of entirely gross persons, whatever the feeling may be which permits it, afterwards degenerates into
forms of humour which render some of quite the greatest,
wisest, and most moral of English writers now almost useless for our youth. And yet you find that whenever
Englishmen are wholly without this instinct, their genius
is comparatively weak and restricted.

(d)

The imaginative power always purifies; the want of it
therefore as essentially defiles; and as the wit-power is
apt to develope itself through absence of imagination, it
seems as if wit itself had a defiling tendency. In
Pindar, Homer, Virgil, Dante, and Scott, the colossal
powers of imagination result in absolute virginal purity
of thought. The defect of imagination and the splendid
rational power in Pope and Horace associate themselves -
it is difficult to say in what decided measures - with
foulness of thought. The Candide of Voltaire, in its
gratuitous filth, its acute reasoning, and its entire
vacuity of imagination, is a standard of what may perhaps
be generally and fitly termed 'fimetic literature,' still
capable, by its wit, and partial truth, of a certain service in its way. But lower forms of modern literature and
art - Gustave Doré's paintings, for instance, - are the
corruption, in national decrepitude, of this pessimist
method of thought; and of these, the final condemnation is
true - they are neither fit for the land, nor yet for the
dunghill.
    It is one of the most curious problems respecting
mental government to determine how far this fimetic taint
must necessarily affect intellects in which the reasoning
and imaginative powers are equally balanced, and both of
them at high level, - as in Aristophanes, Shakespeare,

Chaucer, Molière, Cervantes, and Fielding; but it always
indicates the side of character which is unsympathetic,
and therefore unkind; (thus Shakespeare makes Iago the
foulest in thought, as cruelest in design, of all his
villains,) but which, in men of noble nature, is their
safeguard against weak enthusiasms and ideals. It is
impossible, however, that the highest conditions of tenderness in affectionate conception can be reached except
by the absolutely virginal intellect. Shakespeare and
Chaucer throw off, at noble work, the lower part of their
natures as they would a rough dress; and you may also
notice this, that the power of conceiving personal, as
opposed to general, character, depends on this purity of
heart and sentiment. The men who cannot quit themselves
of the impure taint, never invent character, properly so
called; they only invent symbols of common humanity.

(e)

And for the standard theological writings which are
ultimately to be the foundation of this body of secular
literature, [the projected St George's library] I have
chosen seven authors, whose lives and works, so far as
the one can be traced or the other certified, shall be,
with the best help I can obtain from the good scholars
of Oxford, prepared one by one in perfect editions for
the St. George's schools. These seven books will contain, in as many volumes as may be needful, the lives
and writings of the men who have taught the purest theological truth hitherto known to the Jews, Greeks, Latins,
Italians, and English; namely, Moses, David, Hesiod,
Virgil, Dante, Chaucer, and, for seventh, summing the
whole with vision of judgment, St. John the Divine.
  The Hesiod I purpose, if my life is spared, to translate myself (into prose), and to give in complete form.
Of Virgil I shall only take the two first Georgics, and
the sixth book of the Aeneid, but with the Douglas translation; adding the two first books of Livy, for completion
of the image of Roman life. Of Chaucer, I take the authentic poems, except the Canterbury Tales; together with,
be they authentic or not, the Dream, and the fragment of
the translation of the Romance of the Rose, adding some
French chivalrous literature of the same date. I shall so
order this work, that, in such measure as it may be possible to me, it shall be in a constantly progressive relation to the granted years of my life. The plan of it
I give now, and will explain in full detail, that my
scholars may carry it out, if I cannot.

And now let my general readers observe, finally, about all reading, - You must read, for the nourishment of your mind, precisely under the moral laws which regulate your eating for the nourishment of the body. That is to say, you must not eat for the pleasure of eating, nor read for the pleasure of reading. But, if you manage yourself rightly, you will intensely enjoy your dinner, and your book. If you have any sense, you can easily follow out this analogy: I have not time at present to do it for you; only be sure it holds, to the minutest particular, with this difference only, that the vices and virtues of reading are more harmful on the one side, and higher on the other, as the soul is more precious than the body. Gluttonous reading is a worse vice than gluttonous eating; filthy and foul reading, a much more loathsome habit than filthy eating. Epicurism in books is much more difficult of attainment than epicurism in meat, but plain and virtuous feeding the most entirely pleasurable.

And now, one step of farther thought will enable you to settle a great many questions with one answer.

As you may neither eat, nor read, for the pleasure of eating or reading, so you may do *nothing else* for the pleasure of it, but for the use. The moral difference between a man and a beast is, that the one acts primarily for use, the other for pleasure. And all acting for pleasure before use, or instead of use, is, in one word, 'Fornication.'

10.   WALTER BAGEHOT, A HEALTHY SAGACIOUS MAN OF THE WORLD WITH A SYMMETRICAL MIND

1858

Bagehot (1826-77), educated at London University, was a financial and constitutional authority, banker, editor and a wide-ranging literary journalist. He makes an original and characteristic formulation of some accepted qualities of Chaucer. The extract is from the essay on Charles Dickens, first printed in 'The National Review', October 1858, reprinted from 'Literary Studies,' ed. R.H. Hutton (1895), pp. 188-9.

Possibly it may be laid down that one of two elements is
essential to a symmetrical mind. It is evident that such
mind must either apply itself to that which is theoretical
or that which is practical, to the world of abstraction or
to the world of objects and realities. In the former case
the deductive understanding, which masters first principles, and makes deductions from them, the thin ether of
the intellect, - the 'mind itself by itself,' - must evidently assume a great prominence. To attempt to comprehend principles without it, is to try to swim without
arms, or to fly without wings. Accordingly, in the mind
of Plato, and in others like him, the abstract and deduc-
ing understanding fills a great place; the imagination
seems a kind of eye to descry its data; the artistic instinct an arranging impulse, which sets in order its inferences and conclusions. On the other hand, if a symmetrical mind busy itself with the active side of human
life, with the world of concrete men and real things, its
principal quality will be a practical sagacity, which
forms with ease a distinct view and just appreciation of
all the mingled objects that the world presents, - which
allots to each its own place, and its intrinsic and appropriate rank. Possibly no mind gives such an idea of this
sort of symmetry as Chaucer's. Every thing in it seems
in its place. A healthy sagacious man of the world has
gone through the world; he loves it, and knows it; he
dwells on it with a fond appreciation; every object of
the old life of 'merry England' seems to fall into its
precise niche in his ordered and symmetrical comprehension. The 'Prologue to the Canterbury Tales' is in itself
a series of memorial tablets to mediaeval society; each
class has its tomb, and each its apt inscription. A man
without such an apprehensive and broad sagacity must fail
in every extensive delineation of various life; he might
attempt to describe what he did not penetrate, or if by a
rare discretion he avoided that mistake, his works would
want the *binding element*; he would be deficient in that
distinct sense of relation and combination which is necessary for the depiction of the whole of life, which gives
to it unity at first, and imparts to it a mass in the
memory ever afterwards. And eminence in one or other of
these marking faculties, - either in the deductive abstract intellect, or the practical seeing sagacity, - seems
essential to the mental constitution of a symmetrical
genius, at least in man. There are, after all, but two
principal all-important spheres in human life - thought
and action; and we can hardly conceive of a masculine mind
symmetrically developed, which did not evince its symmetry
by an evident perfection in one or other of those pursuits,

which did not leave the trace of its distinct reflection
upon the one, or of its large insight upon the other of
them. Possibly it may be thought that in the sphere of
pure art there may be room for a symmetrical development
different from these; but it will perhaps be found, on
examination of such cases, either that under peculiar and
appropriate disguises one of these great qualities is
present, or that the apparent symmetry is the narrow
perfection of a limited nature, which may be most excellent in itself, as in the stricter form of sacred art, but
which, as we explained, is quite opposed to that broad
perfection of the thinking being, to which we have applied
the name of the symmetry of genius.

If this classification of men of genius be admitted,
there can be no hesitation in assigning to Mr. Dickens his
place in it. His genius is essentially irregular and un-
symmetrical.

11. UNKNOWN, STORY, SITUATION AND BEAUTY

1859

A perceptive, if prolix, unknown reviewer in 'The London
Review'(later 'The London Quarterly Review') XII (1859),
pp. 285ff. comments on the essentially narrative base of
any widely accepted literary art; on the importance of
situation (as opposed to individualised character) in
Chaucer's poetry; on the importance of knowledge and the
love of things known, and of beauty in medieval literature.

(p. 290) Thus year by year was his song poured forth,
sweet and full beyond the compass of all other men. He
sang of human life in all its varieties; he never wrote a
line but with the fullest power, most abundant mastery,
and completest extrication of his subject from all en-
tanglements, his touch being as firm as granite and soft
as marble. He never failed to say at once whatever he
wished. In the abundance and joy of his genius he sometimes transgressed against the laws of delicacy, but never
against the truth of human nature, to which he was always
faithful and kind. For many long years he seems to have
made a religion of his art. Then came the change, which

must come to all such, since it came to him; the cold
wind of doubt in art - doubt whether art is religion after
all - sweeps, like breath, across that wondrous soul, and
at the end of his 'Canterbury Tales' he writes thus in
penitence, proposing to himself retractation: -

[Quotes the Retracciouns at the end of 'The Canterbury
Tales' in full.]

   (p. 292) All that is peculiar, all that seems now so
distant and unattainable, in the poetry of Chaucer, arises
from the one great typical fact, that it is always nothing
more nor less than the telling of a story. It is this in
whatever form it occurs, as well that of the small didactic verses, then called Ballads, of which the verses just
given afford a specimen, as in that of the professed tale
or legend, of which the major part of his works consists.
The people of that age were fond of hearing things; they
wanted all kinds of things to be told to them, and were
always intensely struck with what was told. There was no
art of method or settled rules, in accordance with which
things were habitually accepted or rejected. Everything
was believed intensely, and everything to their minds
took the form of a story. A sermon to them was a tale
about their moral nature; and impersonation was a truth;
and a poet was well termed a clerke or cleric. The inspiration of the poet was a thing believed in with reality
and seriousness, and his words were accepted as oracles
and discoveries of truth.
   Many indications are to be met with in Chaucer of this
kind of feeling. We must conceive of the people of the
Middle Ages as children in their love of stories, and in
their adoration of those who could tell them. Books then,
of course, were very scarce, and the reading of a new book
would be a real epoch in a person's life. In every case
to read a book was to read a tale, - to become acquainted
with something both new and strange, whatever it might be.
Hence originated a poetical complexion or turn, which
everything seems to have assumed, and the passionate cultivation of poetry by all classes. It seems incredible to
us, but it was undoubtedly the case, that in the Middle
Ages poetry formed the chief delight of the people. A
nation that read poetry deliberately, seriously, and constantly, with actual delight in it, actually living in it,
is a spectacle so strange that our minds, so long used to
the antipoetical and often base and abject things in which
people have grown accustomed to delight themselves, refuse
to credit it, and regard it rather as a theory of what
should be. Yet proofs of this prevailing love of poetry

may be found abundantly in Chaucer, whose poems always
represent the characteristics of his own age....
    (p. 293) This habit - so memorable both in the age and
the poet - of regarding everything as a story, of looking
at everything in a poetical light, is the key to the
peculiar character of Chaucer's poetry; it is to be
regarded as the reason of all that strangely true,
strangely simple, strangely sweet, life that is in him.
It was a habit which turned everything that came to his
notice into an aliment of poetry; insomuch that the comparatively dry and lifeless fables of classical mythology
take new form and beauty from his hand, and the sayings of
the philosophers are quaintly intermingled with the talk
of knights and lovers. It rendered him entirely careless
of fame, and thus gave him his envied simplicity. He is
really anxious to do nothing except tell a good story. He
cares not at all for the praise of originality or invention - probably the meaning of such terms in criticism
would have been unknown to him: he cares for nothing but
his story. Hence he is quite content to become a translator, if he has seen a good story in a foreign tongue;
and his Troilus and Cresseyde, the most perfect love-poem
in the language, is in great part a translation from the
'Filostrato' of Boccaccio; whilst his obligations to the
ancients, to Ovid (or rather Ovid's to him) in especial,
are absolutely innumerable. He cared not what material
he found to his hand, all was freely welcomed, used,
transformed, and ennobled.
    This Chaucer had in common with his age - and in common
with all great periods - a tendency to rest content with
the stories and legends already in the world, without
taxing the invention in the way of digging out fresh ones.
It was so with the cyclic poets of Greece, it was so with
the poets of Rome from Virgil to Statius, it was so with
the romances of the Middle Ages. It is singular to reflect that in the ages which have most loved poetry so few
new stories were invented; while in our own age, which
emphatically does not love poetry, so many new stories are
invented. The new characters, new catastrophes, new situations, which have been invented in the present generation, would suffice to supply all the great poets of the
world with a lifetime of reproduction. And yet the present age is not poetical. It is not so, because there
must, it would seem, be a common ground-work of legend - a
cycle - upon which to go; just as, if men are to be religious, they must consent in a certain rudimental creed.
There must be an acknowledgment of certain things as
delightful, as interesting, as containing in themselves
what is necessary, in order that poetry - or the narrating

of them - should evolve, and that we may make the true
progress of a return to the art of our forefathers. We
have the same sort of need of a poetical creed that we
have of a religious. We should not be for ever to seek
for our first principles. At present almost every new
poem that appears is an experiment in a new direction.
We lose ourselves and the finest part of us in morbid
straining after effects and novelties; we become spasmo-
dic, and are deservedly laughed at; we become self-
conscious, and are deservedly mistrusted. We are children
no longer, we delight not any more in twice-told, nay,
hundred-times told, tales. As in the lost art of architecture, so justly deplored by Mr. Ruskin, so it is in the
art of poetry. Our poets are at a loss what style they
shall write in: - shall the objective or the reflective
predominate? shall they this time be pure or naturalistic?
As if there were in reality more than one style possible,
- the story-telling style, that is, the style of saying
what you have to say, in as natural, straightforward,
workman-like, and simple a manner as possible. There is
in this age no lack of power; but there is a fearful want
of direction: we have all the eclectic scepticism without
much of the eclectic instinct. It is a common cry among
those who perceive something to be wrong with us, without
knowing what it may be, that we are deficient in originality. We are, on the contrary, painfully, agonizingly
original. We are original in deserting what has been the
way of the world since the siege of Troy. More original
directions have been opened out in the last fifty years
than ever before. If the poetically disposed amongst us,
who consume themselves in producing the modern novel (O
name well chosen!) would either relapse into silence, or
spend their genius legitimately in the only true poetical
way, then we might hope that poetry would resume her
throne in the hearts of men, noble, temperate, majestic,
like the influence of one who is both a lady and a Queen.
     Chaucer's poetry, then, like all the greatest poetry,
may be called that of situation. Chivalry supplied him
with what we may call an atmosphere, - a measure of
poetical sympathy passing current in the world, - to
which he could at once address himself; and the world's
old heritage of legend he found sufficient for his own
wants, without the necessity of taxing his invention to
make new ones. Did he wish to sing of true heroic love?
What type of it could be found to surpass the Trojan
Troilus? Or of the truth of woman? How could he hope to
invent names and stories that recalled this with the same
variety and power of association as those nine of Greece
and of Ovid, who reappear in the 'Legende of Good Women'?

The old world-histories of love and war have reappeared
in every age, dressed in its own fashion. So they would
in ours, if we had but something better to put them in
than a suit of our modern tailoring.

These things, then, concerning the age of Chaucer, and
what he got from it, are carefully to be gathered up, and
put into contrast with the tenor of the present age. We
pause for an instant to exhibit even more fully the
contrast irresistibly forced upon us by the subject, between the age of Chaucer and our own. The difference, we
repeat, is not in power: for the present age is as full
of power as any previous. But every thinker upon the
enormously important subject of the state of art will at
once admit the truth, that an indefinable difference does
exist, and that our forefathers, with a tythe of our
knowledge and experience, effected in art what lies
beyond our power. The preceding observations will have
thrown some light upon what the age of Chaucer possessed
which we have lost, viz., a common poetical atmosphere, a
common love of poetry, and desire to be instructed in a
true way, that is, to be told of things by poets, and a
common consent in the sort of thing that was to be looked
for at their hands. It remains to inquire into the cause
of this strange, sad change, which has passed like a
blight upon the love and interest which all men ought to
feel concerning poetry, and has displaced the poet from
the high eminence which no other is fitted to hold.

How are we to explain what we mean? The difference
between a poetical and an unpoetical age is the difference there was between Heathcliff, when he was preparing
the way for his great revenge, and Heathcliff, when, all
things being ready now, he found that he no longer cared
to drive down the long-impending blow. It amounts, in one
word, to loss of enjoyment. It is the difference between
acquisition and possession, between process and result.
To our forefathers every old thing was really a new thing:
every new thing is an old thing to us. Our forefathers
delighted in processes, in the realizing of what was told
them: we, on the contrary, rest content with the acceptance of results, which we do not for the most part realize. Hence, whatever knowledge was in the hands of a man
of the old time, was his real possession and delight,
thoroughly impressed upon him, and a part of what he himself was; not half-forgotten, little cared for. And if he
chose to impart it to another, he was listened to,
delighted in, and respected. For example, *logic* was
believed in, and the logical forms had a real significance
in the olden time: there is a good deal of logic - formal
dialectical reasoning - in Chaucer. We now know more of

logic than was known in Chaucer's time; but we know it
rather as a science than a process; we fancy we know its
actual value in relation to other sciences, rather than
attach an unknown value to its actual contents; our
delight in logical processes has ceased; their power over
us is gone.

Now this seems to lead to an explanation of those wants
which we all deplore in our age and in ourselves. A perception of these wants lies at the bottom of the common
and erroneous saying, that poetry flourishes better in a
barbarous than a civilized age. This is not true, but
there is a truth in it. The two requisites in a great
poetical age are - *knowledge, and the love of things
known*. The actual amount of knowledge is immaterial, and
so likewise is its nature, in itself; but that there
should be knowledge, more or less scientifically recorded,
is essential; and that whatever is known should be loved
and cared for, is co-essential. In a great poetical age
all objects of knowledge are equally objects of love, and
therefore equally objects of poetry. And the great poem
is no mere puristic abstraction; but takes hold of the
whole of human life with the widest grasp, its plan being
to embrace all - 'The Canterbury Tales' are our present
instance - with the arm of its love, to recreate all with
the arm of its power. Yet it must and does happen that
the relation between knowledge and the love of the things
known becomes in the course of time disturbed. Knowledge
increases and opens wider the eyes to see; things known
become too numerous, and the heart is not opened to
receive: and exactly as this is the case, so does the
poetical capacity recede and disappear. Knowledge, in
its progress, begets a knowledge of the value of things;
and exactly as things begin to be compared with one
another, whether the standard of value be true or false,
so do they lose the love that once environed them with the
poetical. This might be expressed as tersely and exactly
as an algebraic formula. When this is the case, we have
soon a general unsettlement, attended with continual re-
adjustments of the standards of value, and occasionally a
total perversion of them. We are now speaking strictly of
the influence of the age upon the poet, in what it puts
before him, independently of individual genius. He finds
himself compelled to accept and reject, to a very considerable extent, in deference to other men; the objects of
his knowledge cease to be all things, - whatever God presents, - and are confided to what the fashion of men
approves. Then follows his own struggle to regain a state
from which he feels that he has fallen, and which his predecessors enjoyed: and so originate those peculiarly

modern phases of mind, unnatural purism, the plaintive
feeling of regret with which past ages are regarded, the
despicable spirit of romance, the desperate efforts to
create an atmosphere in which poetry is possible. This is
an extreme picture, and is meant for one. It is the foundation - yea, so sadly rotten - upon which the gleaming,
glorious edifice of modern poetry has been built by a few
of everlasting genius. The great poets of modern times
have our deepest worship and the innermost reverence of
the hearts of all wise men: but they dwell alone, they
work unregarded, or scorned; and their individual position
is what has never as yet fallen to the lot of a poet. And
not only so, but, as we see, their work must needs be
affected by the thoughts and intents of the age; the age
does not care for poetry, and it becomes impossible to
'sing the Lord's song in a strange land.' The song raised
once and again so strong and clear, is it always of God
and the truths of His heaven and earth?

Were it not well, before proceeding further in this so
proud eclecticism, to inquire what we gain in proportion
to what we lose by it; and whither upon the whole it is
leading us? Instead of accepting everything, we make it
our privilege to choose unhesitatingly, and without
scruple, to which of the truths that surrounds us we shall
attend, and from which we shall turn our attention. The
standard fixing our choice is also itself arbitrary. Now
consider these two things, - the assumed right of choosing,
and the standard of choice. The assumed right of choosing
is in itself anti-poetical, for it involves rejection; and
the poet is commissioned to know and to love all. His
innocence cannot be guilty of profanity in ignorance, nor
of disdain in rejection. Then, the standard of choice: is
not this lowered and raised in compliance with the tastes
and fashions of common men, and not in obedience to the
deep instincts of the poet? In history, has not the false
taste of a frivolous age, or the false pride of a corrupt
age, or the false shame of an impure age, or the false
faith of a sordid age sometimes interposed to chill the
ardour, curtail the amplitude, quell the simplicity of
the poet; keeping things out of sight that should be
known, and dwindling utterances which should be hallowed
by the poet's faith to human nature, into a conventional-
ism current for the hour?

If we can by any means abandon this pride of our knowledge, and go back to the old reverence for all that God
teaches, for all the knowledge of each thing good in its
kind which He sets before us, it would be well for us.
There must eventually be a limit to it, by reason, as we
shall presently observe, of the increasingly *intellectual*

character which it is assuming. We long to mark in poetry
also the retrograde movement which has been already commenced in the other arts. At present we live in an age
which cares as little for poetry as is possible; which is
attended upon by poetry as the sensualist is by a mistress, who has denied him nothing, and is rejected and
cast off for ever at his whim. Poetry has of necessity
adapted itself to the tastes and position of the age, has
lost much savour thereby, and is cared for not at all.
Meanwhile, the whole wondrous life of man upon the earth,
the mystery that darkens it, the alternating want and fulness which play like light and shade within it, the solem-
nities which environ it, the natural analogies which
illustrate it, the rushing passions which are its changes,
the unknown unity that pervades it, stilly with an expectation beyond its restlessness, and pausing on its long-
stretched hopes as a vessel rides upon its anchor over the
swell of the waters that change beneath it, - this remains
for ever to be grasped by the God-given poetic power, and
steadied into a substance that may meet the eye of man,
and struck into a form which may do him true service and
delight.
    One main method by which we may fit ourselves for this
knowledge, this result, is the careful study of those who
by patience and faithfulness have attained it. And such
an one especially was Chaucer. We now proceed to examine
more fully what we conceive to be the great distinguishing
traits of this poet, without inquiring very much more what
share his own genius has in these, and how far they were
indebted to his age. We have arrived at this point naturally. We have seen the growth of knowledge to be incompatible with the full maintenance of that spirit of reverence for things known which is essential to poetry. We
shall now find that in several important poetical qualities of a positive nature the growth of knowledge has
marked a decline, and the diffusion of knowledge has created a vacillation of a strange character.
    We come then to discuss the great distinguishing marks
of the mind and power of Chaucer. They seem to be four in
number: dramatic fearlessness and breadth, workmanlike
directness, comparatively non-intellectual character, and
sense of beauty. These are the four facts of Chaucer to
which we wish as briefly as possible to invite attention;
and we are of opinion that they will be sufficient, when
thoroughly apprehended, to present the great poet before
our minds, and to instruct us in several things which it
is necessary we should have the knowledge of. In discussing them we shall be gradually proceeding from what he
possesses in common with many others, to what he possesses

along with fewer still, and from that to what is conspicuously his own characteristic, and shared by scarce
another.

Concerning the first, the 'dramatic breadth and fearlessness' of Chaucer, we have already said much. It is
sufficient here to observe that he possesses these qualities in a pre-eminent degree; in a degree almost equal to
Shakspeare, although they are more subordinate in him than
in Shakspeare to the other essential great poetical qualities. To represent what men and women would actually say
to one another is Shakspeare's aim: to write poems is
Chaucer's. That is the difference between them. But
Chaucer can always have whatever dramatic breadth he wants
consistently with his poetical purpose. And in dramatic
breadth and fearlessness we know no name in English that
competes with him except Shakspeare himself. It is impossible for a moment not to compare the two in the subject
upon which they have both exercised themselves, the story
of Troilus and Cressida. The play of Shakspeare so named
is amongst his best; it contains some of the most marvellous speeches in dramatic literature. The poem of Chaucer
is the most finished love story in our language; it is as
long as the 'Aeneid.' Now take the character of Pandarus
according to each of them. The Pandarus of Shakspeare is
a coarse, not altogether disinterested, bawd. The Pandarus
of Chaucer is a gentleman of loose principles, but quite
disinterested, and acting purely from good nature. This
will illustrate our meaning. Chaucer puts more nobility,
that is, more poetry, into this secondary character;
acting from poetical reasons. Shakspeare is less careful
about his secondary character, from dramatic reasons.

Concerning the second quality, 'workmanlike directness,' we shall find it difficult to express our full
meaning. Whatever Chaucer attempted was done at once, at
a stroke. His power, as compared to that of later poets,
is like the sheer cleavage of a sword compared with the
slow reduplicated work of the hammer, and chisel, and
file. Whatever it may be, high or low, it is done at once
and for ever, and leaves the feeling that it could not
possibly be otherwise. It stands out for ever with its
one effect upon it, suggestive of nothing but itself.
This quality proceeds of course in great measure from what
we have seen of the intense credence of the age in everything that came before it. Chaucer does not appear in the
least desirous of saying poetical things, and producing
poetical effects. One thing is to him equally poetical
with another. All things are equally poetical - or
equally not poetical. He did not know the distinction
between things that are 'fit subjects for poetry,' and

things that are not. But he could, for this very reason,
treat everything poetically in an unexampled degree. He
is not anxious to be poetical; but only to say whatever
is set before him. Hence he shuns not 'the moral tale
virtuous,' as Erasmus calls it, which in his day formed
part of the stock of the professional gestour, - as in
the 'Tale', or allegory, 'of Meliboeus'; nor the theological tract, - as in the 'Personne's Tale', which is a
treatise on penitence; nor indeed the absolute sermon, -
as in the 'Testament of Love'. All subjects are equally
proper to him; he is anxious to build (the true poetic
instinct) out of whatever materials come to hand. The
prose works which we have just mentioned, were probably
each a translation of some theological tract - 'Summa
Theologiae' - in use at the time, worked up by Chaucer in
his own peculiar manner. Observe how zealously he maintains, while he superadds and ornaments. Every one of
the divisions and impersonations which he found would be
to him a real thing. It would never strike him that a
division was cross, or an impersonation clumsy, or that
the whole work was rendered unnecessary by something else
on the same subject existing in the world. The book, the
work in hand was to him for the time the only thing that
the world contained. In all this he unconsciously acted
upon the great poetical law, - too often lost sight of
even by artists of no mean power, - that it is impossible
to have all beauties at once in a single work; that one
effect is to be produced, and every word ought to aid in
producing that one and no other. There is no crowding,
no hurry, and therefore no confusion or vacillation,
through all Chaucer's work. With workmanlike singleness
of eye he beholds his object, with workmanlike love he
compasses it, and with workmanlike power he accomplishes
that and no other. There is not an accident through all
his writings.

   The third of the qualities which we enumerated was
'comparatively non-intellectual character.' We do not
mean to deny that Chaucer had high intellect, and took
delight in the severest intellectual exercises. The
contrary of this is the case. Chaucer was educated most
carefully, and held acquaintance with all the sciences of
his time. His logical and astronomical acquisitions are
especially remarkable. But there is a distinction to be
drawn between intellect and genius, between the intellectual temperament and the temperament of genius. The
intellectual has a tendency to abstraction and the
abstract. It deals with pure thought. The temperament
of genius is the temperament of action, and deals with
the occurrent in life. The one strikes out thought, the

other tells stories. Now to the one there is obviously
and necessarily a limit, sooner or later. Pure thought
must sooner or later exhaust itself. The other has no
necessary limit whatever. The possible variations in a
story are infinite as the phases of the life, human and
natural, which the story arrests and describes for the
delight of mankind. Chaucer gives free play to the genial
vein, in the way of story-telling; and this is the secret
of his inexhaustible fecundity and freshness. It is only
now and then that a glimpse of pure intellectual treatment
appears, - as if to show what he could have done in that
way. In modern poetry, as a rule, the intellectual predominates; and this is sufficient to account for the
exhausted appearance of most of it, the sort of aridity
which belongs to it. The distinction between intellect
and genius, between thinking and action, is ineffaceable,
and must needs be borne well in mind. The more intellectual a poet permits himself to become, the more abstracted
does he become, and removed from living life; the more
severe, arid, and liable to the great poetical fault of
falsity, the more prone to conceits, trickery of language,
and the 'dulcia vitia' which Quintilian lamented in the
later Roman poets. It is a desolation to behold poetry
made no more than 'a well-constructed language;' in which
the care is less about facts than ideas, and, ultimately,
less about ideas than about expressions. Yet this danger
is constantly increasing, the more that poetry deserts
God's ways for man's ways; the universe of facts, the vast
region of the apparent, and the sort of truth which is
apparent, for the intellectual process which abstracts,
and, whilst it abstracts, cancels.

We come now to the final typical quality of Chaucer,
'the sense of beauty,' which is at once the sequence and
the crown of all the others. Much has been said about
the comparative claims of truth and of beauty upon the
attention of the poet. We think that the following statement will commend itself to our readers. The greatest man
will always seek for truth, independently of all other
considerations. But the greatest man will for this very
reason always be led eventually to beauty, because the
highest truth is always beautiful, and, generally, beauty
is that which gives value to truth. Now the preceding
observations will have made it plain that Chaucer's primary aim was truth; but the very appetite and instinct
which led him to pursue truth brought him into the presence of beauty. And it is impossible to read him without being struck by the clear perfection of his sense and
knowledge of what is truly beautiful. Everything that is
well defined, sharply cut, strongly outlined, instantly

comprehended; everything which has a distinctive use and
office, which nothing else could in anywise fulfil, -
everything of this kind is seized and loved by Chaucer as,
so far forth, beautiful. The rule and law according to
which a thing is beautiful is with him just this, - sharp
definition, and prominent use or service. Under the
former head would be included all clearly defined shapes,
such as those of leaves and birds, of which he was the
greatest lover ever known; all enclosed spaces, easily
taken in by the eye, such as 'sanded courts,' 'parks,' and
chambers, which he revels in describing; and the real features of the beauty of women, of which he knew more than
any of the countless poets who have written about them.
Under the latter head comes all that man devises or con-
structs for his own use, which never fails of beauty and
real satisfaction to the intellect. There is in Chaucer
nothing of set and elaborate description, though much of
recounting. His imagery is chosen in the way we have
indicated; it is always definite, and always has some reference to human uses. For instance, he introduces a
forest, in the 'Assembly of Foules'. It is a celebrated
passage, and Spenser has closely imitated it. Chaucer
does not describe the mass of trees, with the blue shadows
dwelling about the cones of their foliage, and the innum-
erous stems beneath, like colonnades leading into long-
withdrawing glades: he never gives the effect of a mass;
but he enumerates each of the kinds of trees in it, distinctly and severally, each with an epithet expressive of
the use to which it can be put by man. Indeed, the assertion of the human prerogative in everything is as characteristic of him as it is of Homer. He never cares for
the distant or vague. His trees, for example, are numerous, but not indefinite. This limitation seems to be a
very admirable and healthy thing. It at least affords a
rule to determine what is beautiful. If things are definite, they satisfy the intellect; we feel the action of
some poetic rule of selection; and if things are subordinated to the wants of humanity, we feel a human interest
and pleasure in them. There ought not to be such a thing
in poetry as elaborate, unsubordinated description.

Here we leave Chaucer. We have seen his majestic
countenance, full of brooding light; his long life and
ceaseless energy. His influence for centuries was unbounded, and probably wider than even that of Shakspeare.
He created a language and a method of versification which
was followed by the poets both of England and Scotland.
We have seen how exhaustless was his genius; how great his
love and fixed his faith in human nature; how firm, and
true, and fearless his dealing with all things. We have

seen how much of this was owing to the age which nurtured
and understood the poet. Also, we have not failed to see
how different, strangely different, the condition of
poetry in an essentially scientific age has now become.
Instead of breadth we have height, instead of definiteness
vagueness, instead of multitude mass, instead of simplicity complexity, instead of joy sorrow. It is as if the
spirit of humanity, in seeking to work out its own objective existence, had lost the old instinctive knowledge of
what was to be done and how to do it; and had started
again with a wider problem and uncertain appliances.
There is ever a dissatisfaction and sadness in modern
poetry, a loss of the old simple joy and power of doing
a thing at once and for ever. The course of poetry is
in this analogous almost to that of philosophy. Philosophy has long ceased to inquire after the nature of happiness, and seeks more temperately, but more sadly, after
that of duty. Her object is no longer *the good*, but *the
right*. What is next?

12. FRANCIS JAMES CHILD, FINAL -*E*

1863 (1869)

The great American scholar Child (1825-96), the son of a
sailmaker, educated at Harvard and in Germany, became
professor of English at Harvard. He analysed Chaucer's
language and laid the foundation stone of modern understanding in Observations on the Language of Chaucer, in
'Memoirs of the American Academy', N.S. VIII (1863),
pp. 445-502. A splendidly judicious extract from this,
re-arranged and incorporated in A.J. Ellis, 'Early English
Pronunciation', Part I, 1869, Chapter IV, p. 360, is a
token representation of his work, and remains admirable
guidance.

ELISION OF FINAL VOWELS

Even if Chaucer followed invariable rules with regard to
the pronouncing or suppressing of the final *e*, it cannot
be expected that they should be entirely made out by

examining one single text of the Canterbury Tales, which, though relatively a good one, is manifestly full of errors. A comparison of several of the better manuscripts would enable us to speak with much more accuracy and confidence. Tyrwhitt's arbitrary text may very frequently be used to clear up, both in this and in other particulars, the much superior manuscript published by Wright. Still the question whether an *e* was pronounced would often be one of much delicacy (as the previous question whether it actually existed is sometimes one of great difficulty), and not to be determined by counting syllables on the fingers. No supposition is indeed more absurd than that Chaucer, a master poet for any time, could write awkward, halting, or even unharmonious verses. It is to be held, therefore, that when a verse is bad, and cannot be made good anyway as it stands, then we have not the verse that Chaucer wrote. But with regard to the particular point upon which we are now engaged, it would often be indifferent, or nearly so, whether a final *e* is absolutely dropped, or lightly glided over. Then again, as not a few grammatical forms were most certainly written both with and without this termination, the fuller form would often slip in where the other would be preferable or necessary, much depending on the care, the intelligence, or the good ear of the scribe. Very often the concurrence of an initial vowel, justifying elision, with a doubtful final *e*, renders it possible to read a verse in two ways or more; and lastly, hundreds of verses are so mutilated or corrupted that no safe opinion can be based upon them. Such verses as these ought plainly not to be used either to support or impugn a conclusion; neither ought the general rules which seem to be authorized by the majority of instances be too rigorously applied to the emendation of verses that cannot be made, as they stand, to come under these rules.

13. WALTER SAVAGE LANDOR, CREATURES LIKE OURSELVES

1863

Walter Landor (1775-1864), poet in Latin and English, miscellaneous writer and quarreller, was educated at Trinity College, Oxford. He expresses clearly a

representative view of Chaucer as unmysterious, 'realistic' and childlike, in 'Heroic Idylls' (1863), pp. 142-3.

TO CHAUCER

Chaucer, O how I wish thou wert
Alive and, as of yore, alert!
Then, after bandied tales, what fun
Would we two have with monk and nun.
Ah, surely verse was never meant
To render mortals somnolent.
In Spenser's labyrinthine rhymes
I throw my arms o'erhead at times,
Opening sonorous mouth as wide
As oystershells at ebb of tide.
Mistake me not: I honour him
Whose magic made the Muses dream
Of things they never knew before,
And scenes they never wandered o'er.
I dare not follow, nor again
Be wafted with the wizard train.
No bodyless and soulless elves
I seek, but creatures like ourselves.
If any poet now runs after
The Faeries, they will split with laughter,
Leaving him in the desert, where
Dry grass is emblematic fare.
Thou wast content to act the squire
Becomingly, and mount no higher,
Nay, at fit season to descend
Into the poet with a friend,
Then ride with him about thy land
In lithesome nutbrown boots well-tann'd,
With lordly greyhound, who would dare
Course against law the summer hare,
Nor takes to heart the frequent crack
Of whip, with curse that calls him back.
   The lesser Angels now have smiled
To see thee frolic like a child,
And hear thee, innocent as they,
Provoke them to come down and play.

14.   ALEXANDER SMITH, CHAUCER THE ENGLISH CONSERVATIVE

1863

Alexander Smith (1830-67), Scottish man of letters and
university administrator, gives Chaucer somewhat equivocal
praise as English, in an essay on William Dunbar, 'Dream-
thorp', 1863 (text from edition of 1906, ed. J. Hogben,
pp. 66-7).

[Smith comments on the fancifulness of Chaucer's early
poems, then his varied experience of life.] And so it was
that, after mixing in kings' courts and sitting with
friars in taverns, and talking with people on country
roads, and travelling in France and Italy, and making
himself master of the literature, science, and theology
of his time, and when perhaps touched with misfortune
and sorrow, he came to see the depth of interest that
resides in actual life, - that the rudest clown even,
with his sordid humours and coarse speech, is intrinsically more valuable than a whole forest full of goddes-
ses, or innumerable processions of cardinal virtues,
however well mounted and splendidly attired.
It was in some such mood of mind that Chaucer penned
those unparalleled pictures of contemporary life that
delight yet, after five centuries have come and gone.
It is difficult to define Chaucer's charm. He does not
indulge in fine sentiment; he has no bravura passages;
he is ever master of himself and of his subject.   The
light upon his page is the light of common day.
Although powerful delineations of passion may be found in
his 'Tales' and wonderful descriptions of nature, and
although certain of the passages relating to Constance and
Griselda in their deep distresses are unrivalled in tenderness, neither passion, nor natural description, nor
pathos, are his striking characteristics. It is his
shrewdness, his conciseness, his ever-present humour, his
frequent irony, and his short, homely line - effective
as the play of the short Roman sword - which strikes the
reader most. In the 'Prologue to the Canterbury Tales' -
by far the ripest thing he has done - he seems to be
writing the easiest, most idiomatic prose, but it is
poetry all the while. He is a poet of natural manner,
dealing with outdoor life. Perhaps, on the whole, the

writer who most resembles him - superficial differences
apart - is Fielding. In both there is constant shrewdness
and common sense, a constant feeling of the comic side of
things, a moral instinct which escapes in irony, never in
denunciation or fanaticism; no remarkable spirituality of
feeling, an acceptance of the world as a pleasant enough
place, provided good dinners and a sufficiency of cash are
to be had, and that healthy relish for fact and reality,
and scorn of humbug of all kinds, especially of that
particular phase of it which makes one appear better than
one is, which - for want of a better term - we are accustomed to call *English*. Chaucer was a Conservative in all
his feelings; he liked to poke his fun at the clergy, but
he was not of the stuff of which martyrs are made. He
loved good eating and drinking, and studious leisure and
peace; and although in his ordinary moods shrewd, and
observant, and satirical, his higher genius would now and
then splendidly assert itself - and behold the tournament
at Athens, where kings are combatants and Emily the prize;
or the little boat, containing the brain-bewildered
Constance and her child, wandering hither and thither on
the friendly sea.

15. FREDERICK DENISON MAURICE, CORDIAL AFFECTION FOR MEN
AND FOR NATURE

1865 (1874)

F.D. Maurice (1805-72), educated at the dissenting Hackney
Academy and at both Oxford and Cambridge, was a clergyman,
theologian, Christian Socialist, voluminous writer and
controversialist, of great sweetness and sensibility of
character. His view of Chaucer is not particularly original, but succinctly gathers up several nineteenth-
century themes. The extract is from a lecture, 'On
Books', given in November 1865, printed in 'The Friendship
of Books and other Lectures' (1874), pp. 76-7.

The earliest poetry belongs to the same age with Wycliffe's
Bible. Chaucer was possibly the friend of Wycliffe - certainly shared many of his sympathies and antipathies. He

loved the priest, or, as he was called, the secular
priest, who went among the people, and cared for them
as his fellow-countrymen; he intensely disliked the
friars, who flattered them and cursed them, and in both
ways governed them and degraded them. His education had
been different from Wycliffe's, his early poetical powers
had been called forth by the ladies and gentlemen of the
court. He mingled much French with his speech, as they
did; he acquired from them a kind of acquaintance with
life which Wycliffe could not obtain in the Oxford
schools. Had he remained under their influence he might
have been merely a very musical court singer; but he
entered into fellowship with common citizens. He became
a keen observer of all the different forms of life and
society in his time - a keen observer, and, as all such
are, genial, friendly, humorous, able to understand men
about him by sympathising with them, able to understand
the stories of the past by his experience of the present.
Without being a reformer like Wycliffe, he helped forward
the Reformation by making men acquainted with themselves
and their fellows, by stripping off disguises, and by
teaching them to open their eyes to the beautiful world
which lay about them. Chaucer is the genuine specimen of
an English poet - a type of the best who were to come
after him; with cordial affection for men and for nature;
often tempted to coarseness, often yielding to his baser
nature in his desire to enter into all the different
experiences of men; apt through this desire, and through
his hatred of what was insincere, to say many things of
which he had need to repent, and of which he did repent;
but never losing his loyalty to what was pure, his reverence for what was divine. He is an illustration of the
text from which I started. The English books which live
through ages are those which connect themselves with
human life and action. His other poems, though graceful
and harmonious, are only remembered, because in his
'Canterbury Tales' he has come directly into contact with
the hearts and thoughts, the sufferings and sins, of men
and women, and has given the clearest pictures we possess
of all the distinctions and occupations in his own day.

16.   'MATTHEW BROWNE' (WILLIAM BRIGHTLY RANDS), CHAUCER
THE LAODICEAN

1869

Rands (1823-82) an amiable and eccentric man who wrote
under the pseudonyms of Henry Holbeach and Matthew Browne,
educated himself chiefly at second-hand bookstalls, and
after various occupations became a reporter in the House
of Commons. He wrote prolifically, especially for children, but his 'Chaucer's England', 2 vols (1869), has much
penetrating observation, though discursive and sometimes
slapdash. He uses his knowledge of the world, wide reading, and independent turn of mind, to make an interest-
ingly modern, sceptical assessment of some aspects of
Chaucer.

(II, 147-8) It has been said that this [*description of
the Parson*] is a portrait of Wickliffe, and Chaucer has
himself been called a Wickliffite; but there is no proof
that he was entitled to bear that name. There is, in the
meanwhile, every reason that the nature of the case admits
of, for judging Chaucer to have been a man incapable of
such high degrees of faith and moral steadfastness as we
must inevitably associate with the work and career of
Wickliffe. Is it conceivable that the author of the
Canterbury Tales could, under any circumstances, have
become a martyr? Could Shakspeare? I confess, I cannot
conceive it of either. But the moral intensity of men
like Wickliffe, and still more their *faith* (i.e. their
reliance, avouched by their conduct, upon unseen aid),
are essentially heroic; their whole meaning is, 'This
course of conduct upon which I have entered is dictated to
me by the Divine Spirit; its consequences are no concern
of mine; and, if death awaits me, I am ready to die.'
This is not a spirit which finds a welcome in the most
cultivated circles of modern times; but it is undeniably
the spirit of the Founder of Christianity, and of all the
martyrs and heroes that ever lived. I certainly do not
believe that the man who wrote the slippery prologue to
the Canterbury Tales was capable even of sympathising with
the high heroic spirit, much less of sharing it.
Assuredly, he could only have had a superficial understanding of the man Wickliffe, and there is, in reality,

not much reason for raising the question at all; for
there is nothing particularly Wickliffian in any portion
of his works. As for the Poor Parson standing for
Wickliffe himself, - it is just possible, of course: only
Wickliffe was an Oxford Professor, and not a poor priest,
but Rector of Lutterworth; a man quite capable of holding
his own; occupying a distinguished position in his day;
befriended by John of Gaunt; and with all the instincts,
not of a quiet country parson, but of a moral and theological polemic....
(II 234-41) There was no city in England, it need
hardly be said, so large, so thickly built, or so exclusive of field and garden, that the contrast between
'nature' and 'the city' could exist, with its modern
intensity of signification. Nature, in the Wordsworthian
sense, plays no part in Chaucer. The bent of his genius
was objective of course, and he was only meditative as
every poet must be. The great spectacle had sunk into
his heart; and, being touched and awed by it, he could
not but be meditative in a sense, and at times, as if a
field in autumn were *conscious* of the lights and shades
cast upon its bosom by the clear blue sky and the blown
clouds between. But the key-note of his poetry is, no
doubt, a joyous, homely intimacy with life in house and
field, castle and garden, forest and river-side, with no
conscious divarication of the scene into that which is
nature and that which is not nature. The colours, and
sounds, and odours, the fires, the roof-trees, the
millers, the pretty buxom women, the gentle knights, the
millers, and the friars, are all parts of the same picture. One mirror receives the entire scene: -

> There the river eddy whirls,
> And there the surly village churls,
> And the red cloaks of market girls . . .

And no voice of revelation comes from Nature. The poet
loves natural objects of course, and makes them live, and
have wills and passions of their own; but the life he puts
into them is only an infusion of his own homely vitality.
Let us take, as an instance, a passage in the Knight's
Tale: -

> The busy larke, messager of daye,
> Salueth in hire song the morwe gray,
> And fyry Phoebus ryseth up so bright
> That all the orient laugheth of the light,
> And with his stremes dryeth in the greves,
> The silver dropes, hongyng on the leeves.

This is beautiful; the laughing of the earth at sunrise
is a favourite quotation with us all, I suppose; but it is
all homely; it is all the *face* of nature; it is buxom,
brisk, and glad, but there is no undercurrent; the happy
verse moves on like a palfrey, and we move with it,
aroused to the action of the story. Thought of an inner
secret or soul in nature there is none, - even if there is
of a heart. My readers will not for a moment imagine that
I am making any complaint, as of a deficiency in the poet;
far otherwise, and I wish more poets were like him; but
the fact is what I now say. What Chaucer meant by Nature
we may gather from a passage of much beauty ... [quotes
beginning of Physician's Tale]. A mind trained in the
modern school, and always ready to slide into a Wordsworthian mood, may possibly - though scarcely with entire
honesty - *read into* what Chaucer says here, a meaning or a
suggestion which Chaucer himself had not.(1) But the
writing is here strictly objective. Nature is the bounti-
ful vicar-general of God, joyful, liberal, asking nothing,
and an obedient worker. The whole passage is more like a
speech in a Morality Play than anything else; only it is
the work of a poet. As a simple objective statement,
truly given, it *covers* much that is profoundly true, but
which never entered the head of Chaucer, and would not be
understood by him if he were raised from the grave to
hear it proposed by a disciple of Wordsworth. It is
Chaucer's way of saying what a modern poet of the meditative school would have said very differently....
As far as I can make out, the modern sentiment for
Nature, though its germ must of course have existed always
in the human heart, is a very remote consequence of the
increased civification of life as one factor, and of the
tendency of the religious ideas to take wide counsel with
the facts of life in proportion as the reliance on set
creeds grows less and less. However, this is too much
upon a collateral aspect of the idea with which the chapter
opens, and we must pass on. It will be noted, meanwhile,
that the modern feeling with respect to Nature is conspicuous by its absence in the two portraits which we are now
approaching. So inveterate are our *own* feelings in the
matter, that these types bring Nature by main force upon
the page, because they live always in her very eye, - you
smell the 'ay, as Carolina Wilhelmina Amelia Skeggs (?)
said, - but Chaucer does not try, in his verse, to bring
the sights, and sounds, and odours of the country upon the
scene when he introduces two countrymen. There was no
reason why he should; his portraits are rapid sketches
painted in upon a ground of good fellowship; but then a
modern poet would not have been able to help doing something of the kind....

Why is it that the cultivated Englishman, in particular
the man of letters, has usually cherished a weakness for
the country gentleman which he has never felt for the town
gentleman? Bourgeois is a term of dislike, which has
found a modern equivalent in Philistine, and we can hardly
set-off bumpkin against it on the other side of the case.
I think the reason, or great part of the reason, is that
the man of letters, being usually a man of the city, has
a peculiar relish of the *bonhomie* of the country gentleman
or Franklin, which presents itself to his mind softened
by the distance which lends enchantment. There is *bonhomie* in town as well as in country, and John Gilpin is as
simple-hearted as Sir Roger de Coverley; but it is difficult to pick him out of Cheapside or Ludgate, while Sir
Roger stands conspicuous in his manor-house in the midst
of his acres and his tenantry, like a tree that stands by
a hedge-row. The originalities of his character are innocent and pleasant, like gables on a roof that let light
into bed-rooms.

Note

1 This practice is far too common in criticism of all
   kinds, including criticism of the Bible. I wish those
   who indulge in it would think, among other things, of
   the harm they do to themselves, since every act of
   insincerity tends permanently to cloud the mind. The
   error I am condemning is often excused upon the ground
   that the poet and the prophet are the subjects of an
   inspiration, and do not always know the whole meaning
   of their own words. And this is true, but it is not
   an excuse which fits the case. The question - what do
   certain words cover? is quite distinct from the question - what did the writer of them mean? What crude-
   ness there was underneath Chaucer's phrase of vicar-
   general of God may be guessed by comparing this passage
   with a verse of two in his Assembly of Foules.

17. JAMES RUSSELL LOWELL, SINCERE, TENDER, HUMANE

1870 (1871)

Lowell (1819-91), member of a famous American family,

educated at Harvard, professor of belles-lettres there,
and foremost American man of letters of his day, wrote a
sentimental account of the childishly sincere and
emotional Chaucer in 1845, but deserves better to be
remembered by his rightly famous essay on Chaucer (in
origin a review of several books) published in the 'North
American Review' for July 1870, and thence in enlarged
form in 'My Study Windows' (1871). The picture of a calm,
genial, sympathetic, worldly-wise Chaucer is conveyed in
the civilised well-read prose of an affectionate Romantic
American account, with a typical emphasis on 'sincerity'
and 'the thing itself'. For Sir Harris Nicolas, see above
(No. 5). Reprinted here from 'The Writings of J.R. Lowell',
Riverside Edition, 1890, Vol. III.

(p. 291) Will it *do* to say anything more about Chaucer?
Can anyone hope to say anything, not new, but even fresh,
on a topic so well worn? It may well be doubted; and yet
one is always the better for a walk in the morning air,
- a medicine which may be taken over and over again without any sense of sameness, or any failure of its invigorating quality. There is a pervading wholesomeness in the
writings of this man, - a vernal property that soothes and
refreshes in a way of which no other has ever found the
secret. I repeat to myself a thousand times -

> Whan that Aprilë with his showrës sotë
> The droughte of March hath percëd to the rote,
> And bathëd every veine in swich licour
> Of which vertue engendered is the flour, -
> When Zephyrus eek with his swetë breth
> Enspirëd hath in every holt and heth
> The tender croppës, and the yongë sonne
> Hath in the ram his halfë cors yronne,
> And smalë foulës maken melodië, -

and still at the thousandth time a breath of uncontaminate
springtide seems to lift the hair upon my forehead. If
here be not the *largior ether,* the serene and motionless
atmosphere of classical antiquity, we find at least the
seclusum nemus, the *domos placidas,* and the *oubliance,* as
Froissart so sweetly calls it, that persuade us we are in
an Elysium none the less sweet that it appeals to our more
purely human, one might almost say domestic, sympathies.
We may say of Chaucer's muse, as Overbury of his milkmaid,
'her breath is her own, which scents all the year long of
June like a new-made haycock.' The most hardened *roué* of

literature can scarce confront these simple and winning
graces without feeling somewhat of the unworn sentiment of
his youth revive in him. Modern imaginative literature
has become so self-conscious, and therefore so melancholy,
that Art, which should be 'the world's sweet inn,' whither
we repair for refreshment and repose, has become rather a
watering-place, where one's own private touch of the
liver-complaint is exasperated by the affluence of other
sufferers whose talk is a narrative of morbid symptoms.'
Poets have forgotten that the first lesson of literature,
no less than of life, is the learning how to burn your own
smoke; that the way to be original is to be healthy; that
the fresh color, so delightful in all good writing, is won
by escaping from the fixed air of self into the brisk
atmosphere of universal sentiments; and that to make the
common marvellous, as if it were a revelation, is the test
of genius. It is good to retreat now and then beyond ear-
shot of the introspective confidences of modern literature, and to lose ourselves in the gracious worldiness of
Chaucer. Here was a healthy and hearty man, so genuine
that he need not ask whether he was genuine or no, so
sincere as quite to forget his own sincerity, so truly
pious that he could be happy in the best world that God
chose to make, so humane that he loved even the foibles of
his kind. Here was a truly epic poet, without knowing it,
who did not waste time in considering whether his age were
good or bad, but quietly taking it for granted as the best
that ever was or ever could be for *him*, has left us such a
picture of contemporary life as no man ever painted. 'A
perpetual founatin of good-sense,' Dryden calls him, yes,
and of good-humor, too, and wholesome thought. He was one
of those rare authors whom, if we had met him under a
porch in a shower, we should have preferred to the rain.
He could be happy with a crust and spring-water, and could
see the shadow of his benign face in a flagon of Gascon
wine without fancying Death sitting opposite to cry *Super-
naculum!* when he had drained it. He could look to God
without abjectness, and on man without contempt. The
pupil of manifold experience, - scholar, courtier, soldier, ambassador, who had known poverty as a housemate and
been the companion of princes, - his was one of those
happy temperaments that could equally enjoy both halves of
culture, - the world of books and the world of men.

> Unto this day it doth mine hertë boote,
> That I have had my world as in my time!

The portrait of Chaucer, which we owe to the loving regret
of his disciple Occleve, confirms the judgment of him

which we make from his works. It is, I think, more engaging than that of any other poet. The downcast eyes, half
sly, half meditative, the sensuous mouth, the broad brow,
drooping with weight of thought, and yet with an inexpug-
nable youth shining out of it as from the morning forehead
of a boy, are all noticeable, and not less so their harmony of placid tenderness. We are struck, too, with the
smoothness of the face as of one who thought easily, whose
phrase flowed naturally, and who had never puckered his
brow over an unmanageable verse.

Nothing has been added to our knowledge of Chaucer's
life since Sir Harris Nicolas, with the help of original
records, weeded away the fictions by which the few facts
were choked and overshadowed. We might be sorry that no
confirmation has been found for the story, fathered on a
certain phantasmal Mr. Buckley, that Chaucer was 'fined
two shillings for beating a Franciscan friar in Fleet
Street,' if it were only for the alliteration; but we
refuse to give up the meeting with Petrarch....

(p. 295) Our chief debt to Sir Harris Nicolas is for
having disproved the story that Chaucer, imprisoned for
complicity in the insurrection of John of Northampton,
had set himself free by betraying his accomplices. That
a poet, one of whose leading qualities is his good sense
and moderation, and who should seem to have practised his
own rule, to

> Fly from the press and dwell with soothfastness;
> Suffice̎ thee thy good though it be small,

should have been concerned in any such political excesses,
was improbable enough; but that he should add to this the
baseness of broken faith was incredible except to such as
in a doubtful story

> Demen gladly to the badder end.

Sir Harris Nicolas has proved by the records that the
fabric is baseless, and we may now read the poet's fine
verse,

> Truth is the highest thing a man may keep,

without a pang. We are thankful that Chaucer's shoulders
are finally discharged of that weary load, 'The Testament
of Love.'(1) The later biographers seem inclined to make
Chaucer a younger man at his death in 1400 than has
hitherto been supposed. Herr Hertzberg even puts his
birth so late as 1340. But, till more conclusive evidence

is produced, we shall adhere to the received dates as on
the whole more consonant with the probabilities of the
case. The monument is clearly right as to the year of his
death, and the chances are at least even that both this
and the date of birth were copied from an older inscription. The only counter-argument that has much force is
the manifestly unfinished condition of the 'Canterbury
Tales.' That a man of seventy odd could have put such a
spirit of youth into those matchless prologues will not,
however, surprise those who remember Dryden's second
spring-time. It is plain that the notion of giving unity
to a number of disconnected stories by the device which
Chaucer adopted was an afterthought. These stories had
been written, and some of them even published, at periods
far asunder, and without any reference to connection among
themselves. The prologues, and those parts which internal
evidence justifies us in taking them to have been written
after the thread of plan to string them on was conceived,
are in every way more mature, - in knowledge of the world,
in easy mastery of verse and language, and in the over-
poise of sentiment by judgment. They may with as much
probability be referred to a green old age as to the
middle-life of a man who, upon any theory of the dates,
was certainly slow in ripening....

(p. 298) The first question we put to any poet, nay,
to any so-called national literature, is that which Fari-
nata addressed to Dante - *Chi fur li maggior tui?* Here is
no question of plagiarism, for poems are not made of words
and thoughts and images, but of that something in the poet
himself which can compel them to obey him and move to the
rhythm of his nature. Thus it is that the new poet, however late he come, can never be forestalled, and the ship-
builder who built the pinnace of Columbus has as much
claim to the discovery of America as he who suggests a
thought by which some other man opens new worlds to us has
to a share in that achievement by him unconceived and in-
conceivable. Chaucer undoubtedly began as an imitator,
perhaps as mere translator, serving the needful apprenticeship in the use of his tools. Children learn to speak
by watching the lips and catching the words of those who
know how already, and poets learn in the same way from
their elders....

(p. 321) Chaucer, to whom French must have been almost
as truly a mother tongue as English, was familiar with all
that had been done by Troubadour or Trouvère. In him we
see the first result of the Norman yeast upon the home-
baked Saxon loaf. The flour had been honest, the paste
well kneaded, but the inspiring leaven was wanting till
the Norman brought it over. Chaucer works still in the

solid material of his race, but with what airy lightness
has he not infused it? Without ceasing to be English, he
has escaped from being insular. But he was something more
than this; he was a scholar, a thinker, and a critic. He
had studied the *Divina Commedia* of Dante, he had read
Petrarca and Boccaccio, and some of the Latin poets. He
calls Dante the great poet of Italy, and Petrarch a
learned clerk. It is plain that he knew very well the
truer purpose of poetry, and had even arrived at the
higher wisdom of comprehending the aptitudes and limitations of his own genius. He saw clearly and felt keenly
what were the faults and what the wants of the prevailing
literature of his country. In the 'Monk's Tale' he slily
satirises the long-winded morality of Gower, as his prose
antitype, Fielding, was to satirise the prolix sentimentality of Richardson. In the rhyme of Sir Thopas he
gives the *coup de grace* to the romances of Chivalry, and
in his own choice of a subject he heralds that new world
in which the actual and the popular were to supplant the
fantastic and the heroic.

Before Chaucer, modern Europe had given birth to one
great poet, Dante; and contemporary with him was one
supremely elegant one, Petrarch. Dante died only seven
years before Chaucer was born, and, so far as culture is
derived from books, the moral and intellectual influences
to which they had been subjected, the speculative stimulus that may have given an impulse to their minds, - there
could have been no essential difference between them. Yet
there are certain points of resemblance and of contrast,
and those not entirely fanciful, which seem to me of considerable interest. Both were of mixed race, Dante certainly, Chaucer presumably so. Dante seems to have inherited on the Teutonic side the strong moral sense, the
almost nervous irritability of conscience, and the tendency to mysticism which made him the first of Christian
poets, - first in point of time and first in point of
greatness. From the other side he seems to have received
almost in overplus a feeling of order and proportion,
sometimes wellnigh hardening into mathematical precision
and formalism, - a tendency which at last brought the
poetry of the Romanic races to a dead-lock of artifice and
decorum. Chaucer, on the other hand, drew from the South
a certain airiness of sentiment and expression, a felicity
of phrase and an elegance of turn, hitherto unprecedented
and hardly yet matched in our literature, but all the
while kept firm hold of his native soundness of understanding, and that genial humor which seems to be the
proper element of worldly wisdom. With Dante, life represented the passage of the soul from a state of nature to

a state of grace; and there would have been almost an even
chance whether (as Burns says) the *Divina Commedia* had
turned out a song or a sermon, but for the wonderful
genius of its author, which has compelled the sermon to
sing and the song to preach, whether they would or no.
With Chaucer, life is a pilgrimage, but only that his eye
may be delighted with the varieties of costume and character. There are good morals to be found in Chaucer, but
they are always incidental. With Dante the main question
is the saving of the soul, with Chaucer it is the conduct
of life. The distance between them is almost that between
holiness and prudence. Dante applies himself to the
realities, Chaucer to the scenery of life, and the former
is consequently the more universal poet, as the latter is
the more truly national one. Dante represents the justice
of God, and Chaucer his loving-kindness. If there is anything that may properly be called satire in the one, it is
like a blast of the divine wrath, before which the
wretches cower and tremble, which rends away their cloaks
of hypocrisy and their masks of worldly propriety, and
leaves them shivering in the cruel nakedness of their
shame. The satire of the other is genial with the broad
sunshine of humor, into which the victims walk forth with
a delightful unconcern, laying aside of themselves the
disguises that seem to make them uncomfortably warm, till
they have made a thorough betrayal of themselves so
unconsciously that we almost pity while we laugh. Dante
shows us the punishment of sins against God and one's
neighbor, in order that we may shun them, and so escape
the doom that awaits them in the other world. Chaucer
exposes the cheats of the transmuter of metals, of the
begging friars, and of the pedlers of indulgences, in
order that we may be on our guard against them in this
world. If we are to judge of what is national only by the
highest and most characteristic types, surely we cannot
fail to see in Chaucer the true forerunner and prototype
of Shakspeare, who, with an imagination of far deeper
grasp, a far wider reach of thought, yet took the same
delight in the pageantry of the actual world, and whose
moral is the moral of worldly wisdom only heightened to
the level of his wide-viewing mind, and made typical by
the dramatic energy of his plastic nature.
　　Yet if Chaucer had little of that organic force of life
which so inspires the poem of Dante that, as he himself
says of the heavens, part answers to part with mutual
interchange of light, he had a structural faculty which
distinguishes him from all other English poets, his contemporaries, and which indeed is the primary distinction
of poets properly so called. There is, to be sure, only

one other English writer coeval with himself who deserves
in any way to be compared with him, and that rather for
contrast than for likeness.

With the single exception of Langland, the English
poets, his contemporaries, were little else than bad
versifiers of legends classic or mediaeval, as it might
happen, without selection and without art. Chaucer is
the first who broke away from the dreary traditional
style, and gave not merely stories, but lively *pictures*
of real life as the ever-renewed substance or poetry. He
was a reformer, too, not only in literature, but in
morals. But as in the former his exquisite tact saved
him from all eccentricity, so in the latter the pervading
sweetness of his nature could never be betrayed into
harshness and invective. He seems incapable of indignation. He mused good-naturedly over the vices and follies
of men, and, never forgetting that he was fashioned of the
same clay, is rather apt to pity than condemn. There is
no touch of cynicism in all he wrote. Dante's brush
seems sometimes to have been smeared with the burning
pitch of his own fiery lake. Chaucer's pencil is dipped
in the cheerful color-box of the old illuminators, and he
has their patient delicacy of touch, with a freedom far
beyond their somewhat mechanic brilliancy....

(p. 334) 'Piers Ploughman' is the best example I know
of what is called popular poetry, - of compositions, that
is, which contain all the simpler elements of poetry, but
still in solution, not crystallised around any thread of
artistic purpose. In it appears at her best the Anglo-
Saxon Muse, a first cousin of Poor Richard, full of proverbial wisdom, who always brings her knitting in her
pocket, and seems most at home in the chimney-corner. It
is genial; it plants itself firmly on human nature with
its rights and wrongs; it has a surly honesty, prefers the
downright to the gracious, and conceives of speech as a
tool rather than a musical instrument. If we should seek
for a single word that would define it most precisely, we
should not choose simplicity, but homeliness. There is
more or less of this in all early poetry, to be sure; but
I think it especially proper to English poets, and to the
most English among them, like Cowper, Crabbe, and one is
tempted to add Wordsworth, - where he forgets Coleridge's
private lectures. In reading such poets as Langland, also
we are not to forget a certain charm of distance in the
very language they use, making it unhackneyed without
being alien. As it is the chief function of the poet to
make the familiar novel, these fortunate early risers of
literature, who gather phrases with the dew still on
them, have their poetry done for them, as it were, by

their vocabulary. But in Chaucer, as in all great poets,
the language gets its charm from him. The force and
sweetness of his genius kneaded more kindly together the
Latin and Teutonic elements of our mother tongue, and made
something better than either. The necessity of writing
poetry, and not mere verse, made him a reformer whether he
would or no; and the instinct of his finer ear was a guide
such as none before him or contemporary with him, nor
indeed any that came after him, till Spenser, could
command. Gower had no notion of the uses of rhyme except
as a kind of crease at the end of every eighth syllable,
where the verse was to be folded over again into another
layer. He says, for example,

> This maiden Canacee was hight,
> Both in the day and eke by night,

as if people commonly changed their names at dark. And he
could not even contrive to say this without the clumsy
pleonasm of *both* and *eke*. Chaucer was put to no such
shifts of piecing out his metre with loose-woven bits of
baser stuff. He himself says, in the 'Man of Law's Tale,'

> Me lists not of the chaff nor of the straw
> To make so long a tale as of the corn.

One of the world's three or four great story-tellers, he
was also one of the best versifiers that ever made English
trip and sing with a gayety that seems careless, but where
every foot beats time to the tune of the thought. By the
skilful arrangement of his pauses he evaded the monotony
of the couplet, and gave to the rhymed pentameter, which he
made our heroic measure, something of the architectural
repose of blank verse. He found our language lumpish,
stiff, unwilling, too apt to speak Saxonly in grouty mono-
syllables; he left it enriched with the longer measure of
the Italian and Provençal poets. He reconciled, in the
harmony of his verse, the English bluntness with the dignity and elegance of the less homely Southern speech.
Though he did not and could not create our language (for
he who writes to be read does not write for linguisters),
yet it is true that he first made it easy, and to that
extent modern, so that Spenser, two hundred years later,
studied his method and called him master. He first wrote
English; and it was a feeling of this, I suspect, that made
it fashionable in Elizabeth's day to 'talk pure
Chaucer.'...
    (p. 350) [Of Chaucer's metre: after quoting stanzas by
Chaucer and Boccaccio:] If the Italian were read with the

same ignorance that has wreaked itself on Chaucer, the riding-rhyme would be on its high horse in almost every line of Boccaccio's stanza. The same might be said of many a verse in Donne's satires. Spenser in his eclogues for February, May, and September evidently took it for granted that he had caught the measure of Chaucer, and it would be rather amusing, as well as instructive, to hear the maintainers of the hop-skip-and-jump theory of versification attempt to make the elder poet's verses dance to the tune for which one of our greatest metrists (in his philological deafness) supposed their feet to be trained....

(p. 351) Chaucer is a great narrative poet; and, in this species of poetry, though the author's personality should never be obtruded, it yet unconsciously pervades the whole, and communicates an individual quality, - a kind of flavor of its own. This very quality, and it is one of the highest in its way and place, would be fatal to all dramatic force. The narrative poet is occupied with his characters as a picture, with their grouping, even their costume, it may be, and he feels for and with them instead of being they for the moment, as the dramatist must always be. The story-teller must possess the situation perfectly in all its details, while the imagination of the dramatist must be possessed and mastered by it. The latter puts before us the very passion or emotion itself in its utmost intensity; the former gives them, not in their primary form, but in that derivative one which they have acquired by passing through his own mind and being modified by his reflection. The deepest pathos of the drama, like the quiet 'no more but so?' with which Shakespeare tells us that Ophelia's heart is bursting, is sudden as a stab, while in narrative it is more or less suffused with pity, - a feeling capable of prolonged sustention. This presence of the author's own sympathy is noticeable in all Chaucer's pathetic passages, as, for instance, in the lamentation of Constance over her child in the 'Man of Law's Tale.' When he comes to the sorrow of his story, he seems to croon over his thoughts, to soothe them and dwell upon them with a kind of pleased compassion, as a child treats a wounded bird which he fears to grasp too tightly, and yet cannot make up his heart wholly to let go. It is true also of his humor that it pervades his comic tales like sunshine, and never dazzles the attention by a sudden flash. Sometimes he brings it in parenthetically, and insinuates a sarcasm so slyly as almost to slip by without our notice, as where he satirises provincialism by the cock who

> By nature knew ech ascensioun
> Of equinoxial in thilke toun.

Sometimes he turns round upon himself and smiles at a trip
he has made into fine writing: -

> Till that the brightë sun had lost his hue,
> For th'orisont has reft the sun his light,
> (This is as much to sayen as 'it was night.')

Nay, sometimes it twinkels roguishly through his very
tears, as in the

> 'Why wouldest thou be dead,' these women cry,
> 'Thou haddest gold enough - and Emily?'

that follows so close upon the profoundly tender despair
of Arcite's farewell: -

> What is this world? What asken men to have?
> Now with his love now in the coldë grave
> Alone withouten any company!

The power of diffusion without being diffuse would seem
to be the highest merit of narration, giving it that easy
flow which is so delightful. Chaucer's descriptive style
is remarkable for its lowness of tone, - for that combination of energy with simplicity which is among the rarest
gifts in literature. Perhaps all is said in saying that
he has style at all, for that consists mainly in the
absence of undue emphasis and exaggeration, in the clear
uniform pitch which penetrates out interest and retains
it, where mere loudness would only disturb and irritate.
    Not that Chaucer cannot be intense, too, on occasion;
but it is with a quiet intensity of hiw own, that comes in
as it were by accident.

> Upon a thickë palfrey, paper-white,
> With saddle red embroidered with delight,
> Sits Dido:
> And she is fair as is the brightë morrow
> That healeth sickë folk of nightës sorrow.
> Upon a courser startling as the fire,
> Aeneas sits.

Pandarus, looking at Troilus,

> Took up a light and found his countenance
> As for to look upon an old romance.

With Chaucer it is always the thing itself and not the description of it that is the main object. His picturesque bits are incidental to the story, glimpsed in passing; they never stop the way. His key is so low that his high lights are never obtrusive. His imitators, like Leigh Hunt, and Keats in his 'Endymion,' missing the nice gradation with which the master toned everything down, become streaky. Hogarth, who reminds one of him in the variety and natural action of his figures, is like him also in the subdued brilliancy of his coloring. When Chaucer condenses, it is because his conception is vivid. He does not need to personify Revenge, for personification is but the subterfuge of unimaginative and professional poets; but he embodies the very passion itself in a verse that makes us glance over our shoulder as if we heard a stealthy tread behind us: -

The smiler with the knife hid under the cloak (2)

And yet how unlike is the operation of the imaginative faculty in him and Shakespeare! When the latter describes his epithets imply always an impression on the moral sense (so to speak) of the person who hears or sees. The sun 'flatters the mountain-tops with sovereign eye;' the bending 'weeds lacquey the dull stream;' the shadow of the falcon 'coucheth the fowl below;' the smoke is 'helpless;' when Tarquin enters the chamber of Lucrece 'the threshold grates the door to have him heard.' His outward sense is merely a window through which the metaphysical eye looks forth, and his mind passes over at once from the simple sensation to the complex *meaning* of it, - feels *with* the object instead of merely feeling it. His imagination is for ever dramatising. Chaucer gives only the direct impression made on the eye or ear. He was the first great poet who really loved outward nature as the source of conscious pleasurable emotion. The Troubadour hailed the return of spring; but with him it was a piece of empty ritualism. Chaucer took a true delight in the new green of the leaves and the return of singing birds, - a delight as simple as that of Robin Hood: -

In summer when the shaws be seen,
    And leaves be large and long,
It is full merry in fair forest
    To hear the small birds' song.

He has never so much as heard of the 'burthen and the mystery of all this unintelligible world.' His flowers and trees and birds have never bothered themselves with

Spinoza. He himself sings more like a bird than any other
poet, because it never occurred to him, as to Goethe, that
he ought to do so. He pours himself out in sincere joy
and thankfulness. When we compare Spenser's imitations
of him with the original passages, we feel that the
delight of the later poet was more in the expression than
in the thing itself. Nature with him is only good to be
transfigured by art. We walk among Chaucer's sights and
sounds; we listen to Spenser's musical reproduction of
them. In the same way, the pleasure which Chaucer takes
in telling his stories has in itself the effect of consummate skill, and makes us follow all the windings of his
fancy with sympathetic interest. His best tales run on
like one of our inland rivers, sometimes hastening a
little and turning upon themselves in eddies that dimple
without retarding the current; sometimes loitering
smoothly, while here and there a quiet thought, a tender
feeling, a pleasant image, a golden-hearted verse, opens
quietly as a water-lily, to float on the surface without
breaking it into ripple. The vulgar intellectual palate
hankers after the titillation of foaming phrase, and
thinks nothing good for much that does not go off with a
pop like a champagne cork. The mellow suavity of more
previous vintages seems insipid: but the taste, in proportion as it refines, learns to appreciate the indefinable flavor, too subtle for analysis. A manner has
prevailed of late in which every other word seems to be
underscored as in a school-girl's letter. The poet seems
intent on showing his sinew, as if the power of the slim
Apollo lay in the girth of his biceps. Force for the
mere sake of force ends like Milo, caught and held mock-
ingly fast by the recoil of the log he undertook to rive.
In the race of fame, there are a score capable of brilliant *spurts* for one who comes in winner after a steady
pull with wind and muscle to spare. Chaucer never shows
any signs of effort, and it is a main proof of his excellence that he can be so inadequately sampled by detached
passages, - by single lines taken away from the connection
in which they contribute to the general effect. He has
that continuity of thought, that evenly prolonged power,
and that delightful equanimity, which characterize the
higher orders of mind. There is something in him of the
disinterestedness that made the Greeks masters in art.
His phrase is never importunate. His simplicity is that
of elegance, not of poverty. The quiet unconcern with
which he says his best things is peculiar to him among
English poets, though Goldsmith, Addison, and Thackeray
have approached it in prose. He prattles inadvertently
away, and all the while, like the princess in the story,

lets fall a pearl at every other word. It is such a piece
of good luck to be natural! It is the good gift which the
fairy godmother brings to her prime favorites in the
cradle. If not genius, it alone is what makes genius
amiable in the arts. If a man have it not, he will never
find it, for when it is sought it is gone.

When Chaucer describes anything, it is commonly by one
of those simple and obvious epithets or qualities that
are so easy to miss. Is it a woman? He tells us she is
fresh; that she has *glad* eyes; that 'every day her beauty
newed:' that

> Methought all fellowship as naked
> Withouten her that I saw once,
> As a coróne without the stones.

Sometimes he describes amply by the merest hint, as where
the Friar, before setting himself softly down, drives away
the cat. We know without need of more words that he has
chosen the snuggest corner. In some of his early poems he
sometimes, it is true, falls into the catalogue style of
his contemporaries; but after he had found his genius he
never particularises too much, - a process as deadly to
all effect as an explanation to a pun. The first stanza
of the 'Clerk's Tale' gives us a landscape whose stately
choice of objects shows a skill in composition worthy of
Claude, the last artist who painted nature epically: -

> There is at the west endë of Itaile,
> Down at the foot of Vesulus the cold,
> A lusty plain abundant of vitaile,
> Where many a tower and town thou may'st behold
> That founded were in time of fathers old,
> And many another delítable sight;
> And Sàlucës this noble country hight.

The Pre-Raphaelite style of landscape entangles the eye
among the obtrusive weeds and grass-blades of the foreground which, in looking at a real bit of scenery, we
overlook; but what a sweep of vision is here! and what
happy generalisation in the sixth verse as the poet turns
away to the business of his story! The whole is full of
open air.

But it is in his characters, especially, that his
manner is large and free; for he is painting history,
though with the fidelity of portrait. He brings out
strongly the essential traits, characteristic of the genus
rather than of the individual. The Merchant who keeps so
steady a countenance that

There wist no wight that he was e'er in debt,

the Sergeant at Law, 'who seemed busier than he was,' the
Doctor of Medicine, whose 'study was but little on the
Bible,' - in all these cases it is the type and not the
personage that fixes his attention. William Blake says
truly, though he expresses his meaning somewhat clumsily,
'the characters of Chaucer's Pilgrims are the characters
which compose all ages and nations. Some of the names and
titles are altered by time, but the characters remain for
ever unaltered, and consequently they are the physiogno-
mies and lineaments of universal human life, beyond which
Nature never steps. Names alter, things never alter. As
Newton numbered the stars, and as Linnaeus numbered the
plants, so Chaucer numbered the classes of men.' In his
outside accessaries, it is true, he sometimes seems as
minute as if he were illuminating a missal. Nothing
escapes his sure eye for the picturesque, - the cut of the
beard, the soil of armor on the buff jerkin, the rust on
the sword, the expression of the eye. But in this he has
an artistic purpose. It is here that he individualizes,
and, while every touch harmonizes with and seems to complete the moral features of the character, makes us feel
that we are among living men, and not the abstracted images
of men. Crabbe adds particular to particular, scattering
rather than deepening the impression of reality, and
making us feel as if every man were a species by himself;
but Chaucer, never forgetting the essential sameness of
human nature, makes it possible, and even probable, that
his motley characters should meet on a common footing,
while he gives to each the *expression* that belongs to him,
the result of special circumstance or training. Indeed,
the absence of any suggestion of *caste* cannot fail to
strike any reader familiar with the literature on which
he is supposed to have formed himself. No characters are
at once so broadly human and so definitely outlined as
his. Belonging, some of them, to extinct types, they
continue contemporary and familiar for ever. So wide is
the difference between knowing a great many men and that
knowledge of human nature which comes of sympathetic
insight and not of observation alone.

It is this power of sympathy which makes Chaucer's
satire so kindly, - more so, one is tempted to say, than
the panegyric of Pope. Intellectual satire gets its
force from personal or moral antipathy, and measures
offences by some rigid conventional standard. Its mouth
waters over a galling word, and it loves to say *Thou*,
pointing out its victim to public scorn. *Indignatio
facit versus*, it boasts, though they might as often be

fathered on envy or hatred. But imaginative satire,
warmed through and through with the genial leaven of
humor, smiles half sadly and murmurs *We*. Chaucer either
makes one knave betray another, through a natural jealousy of competition, or else expose himself with a
naïveté of good-humored cynicism which amuses rather than
disgusts. In the former case the butt has a kind of claim
on our sympathy; in the latter, it seems nothing strange,
as I have already said, if the sunny atmosphere which
floods that road to Canterbury should tempt anybody to
throw off one disguise after another without suspicion.
With perfect tact, too, the Host is made the *choragus* in
this diverse company, and the coarse jollity of his temperament explains, if it does not excuse, much that would
otherwise seem out of keeping. Surely nobody need have
any scruples with *him*.

Chaucer seems to me to have been one of the most purely
original of poets, as much so in respect of the world that
is about us as Dante in respect of that which is within
us. There had been nothing like him before, there has
been nothing since. He is original, not in the sense that
he thinks and says what nobody ever thought and said
before, and what nobody can ever think and say again, but
because he is always natural, because, if not always absolutely new, he is always delightfully fresh, because he
sets before us the world as it honestly appeared to
Geoffrey Chaucer, and not a world as it seemed proper to
certain people that it ought to appear. He found that
the poetry which had preceded him had been first the expression of individual feeling, then of class feeling as
the vehicle of legend and history, and at last had well-
nigh lost itself in chasing the mirage of allegory.
Literature seemed to have passed through the natural
stages which at regular intervals bring it to decline.
Even the lyrics of the *jongleurs* were all run in one
mould, and the Pastourelles of Northern France had become
as artificial as the Pastorals of Pope. The Romances of
chivalry had been made over into prose, and the 'Melus-
ine' of his contemporary Jehan d'Arras is the forlorn hope
of the modern novel. Arrived thus far in their decrepitude, the monks endeavoured to give them a religious and
moral turn by allegorising them....

(p. 362) But with all secondary poets, as with Spenser
for example, the allegory does not become of one substance
with the poetry, but is a kind of carven frame for it,
whose figures lose their meaning, as they cease to be contemporary. It was not a style that could have much
attraction for a nature so sensitive to the actual, so
observant of it, so interested by it, as that of Chaucer.

He seems to have tried his hand at all the forms in vogue,
and to have arrived in his old age at the truth, essential
to all really great poetry, that his own instincts were
his safest guides, that there is nothing deeper in life
than life itself, and that to conjure an allegorical significance into it was to lose sight of its real meaning.
He of all men could not say one thing and mean another,
unless by way of humorous contrast.

In thus turning frankly and gayly to the actual world,
and drinking inspiration from sources open to all; in
turning away from a colorless abstraction to the solid
earth and to emotions common to every pulse; in discovering that to make the best of nature, and not to grope
vaguely after something better than nature, was the true
office of Art; in insisting on a definite purpose, on
veracity, cheerfulness, and simplicity, Chaucer shows
himself the true father and founder of what is characteristically *English* literature. He has a hatred of cant as
hearty as Dr. Johnson's, though he has a slier way of
showing it; he has the placid commonsense of Franklin,
the sweet, grave humor of Addison, the exquisite taste
of Gray; but the whole texture of his mind, thought its
substance seem plain and grave, shows itself at every
turn iridescent with poetic feeling like shot silk.
Above all, he has an eye for character that seems to have
caught at once not only its mental and physical features,
but even its expression in variety of costume, - an eye,
indeed, second only, if it should be called second in
some respects, to that of Shakespeare.

I know of nothing that may be compared with the prologue to the 'Canterbury Tales,' and with that to the
story of the 'Chanon's Yeoman,' before Chaucer. Characters and portraits from real life had never been drawn
with such discrimination, or with such variety, never
with such bold precision of outline, and with such a
lively sense of the picturesque. His Parson is still un-
matched, though Dryden and Goldsmith have both tried their
hands in emulation of him. And the humor also in its
suavity, its perpetual presence and its shy unobtrusive-
ness, is something wholly new in literature. For anything
that deserves to be called like it in English we must wait
for Henry Fielding.

Chaucer is the first great poet who has treated To-day
as if it were as good as Yesterday, the first who held up
a mirror to contemporary life in its infinite variety of
high and low, of humor and pathos. But he reflected life
in its large sense as the life of *men*, from the knight to
the ploughman, - the life of every day as it is made up
of that curious compound of human nature with manners.

The very form of the 'Canterbury Tales' was imaginative.
The garden of Boccaccio, the supper-party of Grazzini, and
the voyage of Giraldi make a good enough thread for their
stories, but exclude all save equals and friends, exclude
consequently human nature in its wider meaning. But by
choosing a pilgrimage, Chaucer puts us on a plane where
all men are equal, with souls to be saved, and with
another world in view that abolishes all distinctions.
By this choice, and by making the Host of the Tabard
always the central figure, he has happily united the two
most familiar emblems of life, - the short journey and
the inn. We find more and more as we study him that he
rises quietly from the conventional to the universal, and
may fairly take his place with Homer in virtue of the
breadth of his humanity.

In spite of some external stains, which those who have
studied the influence of manners will easily account for
without imputing them to any moral depravity, we feel that
we can join the pure-minded Spenser in calling him 'most
sacred, happy spirit.' If character may be divined from
works, he was a good man, genial, sincere, hearty, temperate of mind, more wise, perhaps, for this world than the
next, but thoroughly humane, and friendly with God and
men. I know not how to sum up what we feel about him
better than by saying (what would have pleased most one
who was indifferent to fame) that we love him more even
than we admire.

Notes

1 Tyrwhitt doubted the authenticity of 'The Flower and
   the Leaf' and 'The Cuckoo and the Nightingale.' To
   these Mr. Bradshaw (and there can be no higher authority) would add 'The Court of Love,' 'The Dream,' 'The
   Praise of Woman,' 'The Romaunt of the Rose,' and several of the shorter poems. To these doubtful productions there is strong ground, both moral and aesthetic,
   for adding 'The Parson's Tale.'
2 Compare this with the Mumbo-Jumbo Revenge in Collins's
   Ode.

18.   STOPFORD A. BROOKE, NATURAL BEAUTY

1871

The Rev. Stopford A. Brooke (1832-1916), cleric and man of
letters, in an essay on The Descriptive Poetry of Chaucer,
'Macmillan's Magazine', XXIV (1871), pp. 268-79, makes a
fresh analysis of a characteristic nineteenth-century
interest in Chaucer, promoting comparison with painting.
Unluckily, he has a genius for selecting for discussion
poems which in many cases we now know are not by
Chaucer.

The greatest world of Poetry and the most varied has been
built up by the English nation. It began with Caedmon
long ago on the wild headland of Whitby, and was 'of the
grace of God,' and the first song it sung was of things
divine. Then it sang of battles and the wrath of men, of
old romance, of monkish evils, and by and by of the social
and political movements, 'of the passions and feelings of
rural and provincial England,' by a voice which came, not
like that of Chaucer, from the court and castle, but from
the rude villages which clustered round the Malvern Hills.
At last in Chaucer it came to sing of men.
    The first excellence of Chaucer, an excellence un-
approached save by Shakespeare, and in Shakespeare different in kind, was the immense range of his human interest
and his power of expressing with simplicity and directness the life of man. His second excellence, and it was
an excellence new to English poetry, was his exquisite
appreciation and description of certain phases of natural
beauty. With him began that descriptive poetry of England, which, passing through many stages, has reached in
our century its most manifold development. For as the
English Painters have created the art of landscape, so
have its Poets more than those of all other nations described the beauty of the natural world. No work, by any
people, has ever been done so well. We have passed from
the conventional landscape of Chaucer to the allegorical
landscape of Spenser. The epic landscape of Milton,
varied with ease into lighter forms in the Pastoral and
the Lyric, was followed by the landscape of Gray and
Collins, a landscape where nature was subordinated to man
and to morality. Beattie, Logan, and others infused a

somewhat sickly sentiment into their natural description,
and nature was still unhonoured by a special worship till
Cowper began to speak his simple words about her, and
Burns, though with a limited range, described her glory
in the lover's eye. Then arose the great natural school,
which loved Nature for her own sake. One after another,
with unparalleled swiftness of production and variety of
imagery, with astonishing individuality, Scott, Coleridge,
Byron, Wordsworth, Shelley, and Keats sang of the mountains and skies, of the sea and woods, of streams and
moor and flowers. The landscape of Scott was accurate,
rich in colour, and romantic in note; the landscape of
Coleridge, few as were its pictures, was conceived with
passion and of a great range; the landscape of Byron was
largely composed and of delightful clearness and force;
the landscape of Shelley was transcendental, and he alone
finds an analogy in the ideal pictures of Turner; but
none have grasped with so much realism and yet with so
much spirituality, with such clearness and with such passion, as Wordsworth and Keats - Keats in this point being
only inferior as an undeveloped artist - the aspects and
the beauty of the natural world.

The subject of this paper is the rise of this descriptive poetry in the poems of Chaucer. I shall leave out,
in discussing his work, that which is best in it: the
delineation of human character; the close way in which
passion is grasped; the tender, yet sometimes broad
humour - broad from very healthiness of nature - which
makes his pages so delightful and so human.

I shall confine myself to those portions of his
poems which are directly descriptive of natural scenery,
or of such additions to the landscape as the scent of
flowers, the song of birds, and the pleasant noise of
streams, things which appeal to other senses than the
eye, and form part of a poetical - though not of a
painted - landscape.

The landscape of Chaucer is sometimes taken from the
Italian and sometimes from the French landscape. It
possesses almost always the same elements, differently
mixed up in different poems: a May morning - the greenwood, or a garden - some clear running water - meadows
covered with flowers - some delectable place or other
with an arbour laid down with soft and fresh-cut turf.
There is no sky, except in such rapid allusions as this,
'Bright was the day and blue the firmament;' no cloud
studies; no conception of the beauty of wild nature.

His range, therefore, is extremely limited, but within
the limits his landscape is exquisitely fresh, natural,
and true in spite of its being conventional. The fact is,

though the elements of the scenery were ready made, the
composition of them gave great scope to originality, and
Chaucer being a man of unique individuality, could not
adopt the landscape even of those poems which he translated without making alterations; and being an Englishman,
could not write about the May morning without introducing
its English peculiarities. Moreoever, the delightful and
simple familiarity of the poet with the meadows, brooks,
and birds, and his love of them, has the effect of making
every common aspect of nature new; the May morning is
transfigured by his enjoyment of it; the grass of the
field is seen as those in Paradise beheld it; the dew lies
on our heart as we go forth with the poet in the dawning,
and the wind blows past our ear like the music of an old
song heard in the days of childhood. Half this power lies
in the sweet simplicity of the words and in the pleasant
flowing of the metre.

'The Romaunt of the Rose' will give us the favourite
landscape of French mediaeval poetry. The poem was written by two men, William of Lorris, and John of Meun, the
latter carrying on the task of the former. Chaucer translated all the work done by William, and a sixth part of
the additional work. With the poem itself we have nothing to do, but it opens with the accredited French landscape. One morning in May, the month of love, the lover
dreams that he rises early and goes out of the town to
hear the song of the birds in 'the fair blossomed boughs.'

He begins with a delightful burst of joy in the coming
of the May, the time of love and jollity, when the earth
waxeth proud with the sweet dews that on it fall, and the
birds escaped from winter are so glad for the brightness
of the sun that they must show the blitheness of their
hearts in singing.

> Hard is his hert that loveth nought
> In May, when al this mirth is wrought;
> When he may on these braunches hear
> The smale briddes syngen clere
> Her blesful swete song pitous
> And in this season delytous
> When Love affraieth al thing.

He rises in his dream, and listening to the birds, comes
to a river, swiftly running -

> For from an hille that stood ther nere,
> Came down the streme full stiff and bold,
> Cleer was the water and as cold
> As any well is.

He is 'wonder glad' to see this lusty place and the river,
and stoops down to wash his face in the clear running
water. He sees the bottom paved with gravel, full of
beautiful stones. The meadow comes right down to the
waterside, soft, sweet, and green. The morning tide is
clear, and the air temperate, and he begins to walk
through the mead, along the river bank. By and by he
comes to a garden, long and broad, and everywhere enclosed
with embattled walls, which are painted from end to end
with symbolic pictures. This is the mediaeval conception
of a wild landscape, in which men could take pleasure. It
is delicious from its simplicity and quaint order, mixed
with enough of natural freedom to distinguish it from the
garden. But it is chiefly delightful for its cool morning
atmosphere, and the impression one receives of being
bathed in fresh water and 'attempred' air. Nothing is
permitted in the landscape which could suggest distress or
difficulty. The trees are in full leaf, and each has wide
room to grow; the grass is smooth as in a pleasaunce; the
meadow slopes gradually to the stream. The only thing
which rushes is the river, which comes down stiff and bold
from the hill, but it is still a hill stream, not a mountain torrent capable of devastation.

   This peacefulness of temper, this soothing character of
natural beauty, combined with pleasure in cool wells and
clear water, and green meadows and the shade of trees,
mark all the mediaeval landscapes in which poet or painter
took delight. One cannot help feeling that the life of
the men and women of those times, being, as it was, much
coarser and ruder at home than ours, demanded as refreshment this softness and sweetness in nature, just as our
over-refined home-life drives us to find refreshment in
Alpine scenery, the gloom and danger of which would have
horrified the mediaeval poet. It is impossible, without
smiling, to picture Chaucer or Boccacio in the middle of
a pine forest on the slopes of Chamouni, or left alone
with Tyndall on the glaciers of Monte Rosa. Both of them
would have been exhausted with terror.

   But the author of the Romaunt cannot take full pleasure even in this delightful nook of earth. It is too wild
for him: it is not till he enters the garden that he is
completely happy.

> The garden was by mesuryng,
> Right evene and square in compassing,
> It as long was as it was large,
> Of fruyt hadde every tree his charge,

and all the fruit was good for the service of man. There

were pomegranates, nutmegs, almonds, figs, dates, cloves,
cinnamon: -

> And many a spice delitable,
> To eten whan men rise fro table.

Among these were the homelier trees, bearing peaches,
apples, medlars, plums, pears, and other fruits. Then
also the great trees for beauty - pine, olives, elms great
and strong -

> Maples, asshe, oke, aspe, planes longe
> Fyne ew, popler and lyndes faire,
> And othere trees fulle many a payre.
> These trees were setts, that I devise
> One from another in assise
> Five fadme or sixe.

Their branches are knit together and full of green leaves,
so that no sun can burn up the tender grass. Doves wander
under the leafy roof, squirrels leap upon the boughs, and
the conies come out upon the grass and tourney together.
In certain places, fair in shadow, are wells, and he
cannot tell the number of small streams which mirth had
'by devise' conducted in conduits all over the garden,
and which made a delightful noise in running. About the
brink of these wells, and by the streams, sprung up the
grass, as thick-set and soft as any velvet, and wet
through the moisture of the place. And it much amended
all, that the earth was of such a grace that it had plenty
of flowers.

> There sprang the violete alle newe
> And fressche pervinke riche of hewe
> And floures yelowe, white and rede;
> Sic plenty grewe there never in mede.
> Ful gay was alle the ground, and queynt,
> And poudred, as men had it peynt
> With many a fressh and sondry flour;
> That casten up ful good savour.

This then is his perfect landscape. 'I must needs stop my
tongue,' he says, 'for I may not without dread tell you
all the beauty nor half the goodness of this place.'
    One marks in all this the subordination of nature to
man. The garden is arrayed for his delight, trees for his
shade, grass soft for his repose, all the fruits and herbs
necessary for his sickness and health, for his pleasure in
sweet scents and delicate tastes.

I have no doubt that the idea of this submission of
nature to man, which is so constant in the poems of this
time, arose out of the account of Paradise in the Book of
Genesis, where not only the rivers water the garden but
the herbs and fruits are specially set for the service of
man, and man is placed in the garden to dress and keep it.
Eden was much more of a rich kitchen garden than one
thinks, and so is the garden here, till we come to the
rosary surrounded by the hedge, where the God of Love,
hiding behind a fig-tree, shoots the poet to the heart.

But we ought especially to observe the order and definite arrangement of the whole, so different from our
actual dislike of nature defrauded of her own wild will.
The garden is even and square by measure; the trees are
planted in pairs, and are set five or six fathoms apart;
the small streams are led over the garden in conduits, so
as to make an ordered network in the grass.

Even in the pleasant grove which Chaucer describes in
the 'Flower and the Leaf,' there is the same delight in
this arrangement: -

In which were okes great, streight as a line
Under the which the gras, so freshe of hewe
Was newly sprong, and an eight foot or nine
Every tree well fro his fellowe grewe.

Observe also the definiteness of the description. We are
given the number of the feet between tree and tree.
Wordsworth tried the same sort of thing in 'The Thorn,'
when he described the pool -

I've measured it from side to side,
'Tis three feet long and two feet wide;

only that in Chaucer the definiteness belongs to the whole
landscape, and arises out of the distinctness with which
his imagination saw the grove, while in Wordsworth, the
poem being one of human feeling, not of natural description, is spoiled by the revolting prosaism of these two
lines. Nothing can be worse than Wordsworth's introduction of himself into the midst of the passion of the poem;
we think at once of a surveyor with a two-foot rule in his
pocket.

With regard to the whole, it is worth observing that
the woods we get into in Chaucer are not the wild greenwood of the ballads, but the pleasant woods full of glades
which were near many of the English towns. They have
nothing to do with the forest-land of England, nor is
there any savage wood in Chaucer's poetry. The place

Canace goes to is a grove in her father's park at no distance from the palace. The woodland Chaucer wanders in is
such as we have seen close to inhabited spaces, and itself
in lovely order. Palaemon and Arcite get into a forest,
it is true, but it is also close to the hunting lodge of
Theseus, and is traversed with broad green paths, a forest
as well cared for as that of Compiegne, and of the same
character.

The only description of a savage wood in Chaucer is of
that which is painted on the walls of the House of Fame: -

> First on the wall was painted a forest
> In which there dwelled neither man nor beaste.
> With knotty, knarry barren trées old
> With stubbes sharp and hideous to behold,
> In which there ran a swimble in a swough.

And this is in reality not the description of what we call
a forest, but of a savage part of the Foresta of England.
In Chaucer's time, both in England and France, the forest
was any wild land over which the people were not permitted
to hunt. Hence it came to mean uncultivated land as
opposed to cultivated. It might even mean, as it did
sometimes in France, the fisheries of the king. At any
rate it had not necessarily anything to do with woods,
though woods were included under the term. It was used to
describe open commons, like Wimbledon Common, with furze
and clumps of wild briars. It was used to describe the
chalk downs. Chaucer's woods are, however, real woods.
He lived for the most part in London. Highgate, Hampstead,
and all the hills on the north and northwest were then
clothed with great trees; and exactly such a landscape as
we find him describing, with the soft sward and the
sparsely-planted trees, and the fresh river running near,
he could see any morning he pleased by walking up the
valley of the Fleet towards the present ridge of the City
Road.

Once more, with regard to this poem, - the 'Romaunt
of the Rose' and its landscape - we observe what is
strange in mediaeval work, and which certainly could not
have been the case had the poem been an Italian and not a
French one, that there is in it no delight in colour.
The leaves are said to be green, the flowers yellow, white,
and red; but there is no distinctiveness in these expressions, and it is always the power of distinctive allotment
of colours, and the choice of such expressions as mark
minute shades of them, which proves love of colour in a
poet.

The question is, had Chaucer this love of colour? We

can fortunately answer that question with particular
accuracy. One of his poems - 'The Complaynte of a
Lovere's Lyfe' - opens with an exact imitation of the
'Romaunt of the Rose' - the walk through the wood by the
meadows along the river, and the entrance into the garden.
A peculiar English landscape touch is inserted, which is
not found in the French poem - the lifting of the misty
vapour; but it is the glow of colour which is so remarkable. The dew he describes as like silver in shining upon
the green mead; flowers of every hue open out their leaves
against the sun, which, gold-burnished in his sphere,
pours down on them his beams; the river runs clear as
beryl - that is, of a bright sea-green, reflecting probably the grass. The great stones of the encircling wall
are green. Within the garden, where the birds in plain
and vale were singing so loudly that all the wood rung

    Like as it should shiver in pieces small -

a wonderful piece of descriptive audacity - and where the
nightingale was wresting out her voice with so great might
as if her heart would burst for love, Nature had tapes-
tried the soil with colour; the wind blew through white
blossoms; the hawthorn wore her white mantle; and the well
in the centre, surrounded with velvet grass, has all its
sands gold colour seen through the water pure as glass.
He has departed from the whole of his model chiefly by
insertion of colour; and he is as minute and delicate in
its finish as he is large in his broad sketches of its
distribution over a landscape. When the eagle blushes -
and the absurdity of this does not spoil the lovely piece
of colour which follows - it is

    Right as the freshe redde rose newe
    Against the summer sun coloured is.

When he watches the fish glancing through the brilliant
stream, he tells us that their fins are red and the scales
silver bright. Speaking of the oak leaves in spring, he
distinguishes, with great delicacy of observation, the
colour of the leaves when they first burst from the bud,
which are of a red cinereous colour, from that of the
fully expanded foliage.

    Some very redde, and some a glad light grene.

When Canace, 'bright as the young sun,' rises very
early in the morning and walks to the dell in her father's
park, she sees the sun rising ruddy and broad through the

vapour which glides upward from the earth, and passes on
to rest beneath a tree white as chalk for dryness, a sharp
description of the gaunt white look of a blasted tree seen
in the midst of a green wood.

But of all the colours which Chaucer loved in nature,
he loved best the harmony of white and green in one of his
favourite daisied meadows. In the 'Cuckoo and the Nightingale' he holds his way down by a brook-side -

> Til I came to a laund of white and green,
> So faire one hadde I never in been:
> The ground was greene, ypoudred with daisie,
> The flowers and the greves like hie
> All greene and white, was nothing elles seen.

It may be, in an age when colours in art had each their
peculiar religious significance, that Chaucer, a man who
had travelled in Italy and who had himself the instinct of
symbolism, had some spiritual meaning in the constant
association of these two colours of white and green.
Green, the hue of spring, signified hope, and particularly
the hope of Immortality; white was the emblem, among other
things, of light and joy, and was always in pictures the
colour of the robe worn by the Saviour at and immediately
after His Resurrection, especially when in that touching
legend, He goes to visit His Mother first in her own
house. So that, if this conjecture be true, the whole
delight and rapture of Chaucer in a spring morning as he
lay in a daisied meadow and heard the birds chaunt their
service of praise to God, had a further sentiment to his
heart - the sentiment of religious victory, the hope and
joy of the resurrection to immortality.

Still dwelling on Chaucer's colour, it is curious the
number of concentrated pictures which are to be found in
his poems, pictures so sharply drawn in colour that they
might be at once painted from the description. Here is
one which Burne Jones might put down in colour on the
canvas. The poet, in the conventional May morning, comes
to a green arbour in a delectable place, benched with new
and clean turf. On either side of the door a holly and a
woodbine grow. One can imagine the exquisite way these
two plants would mingle their leaves in glossy and dead
colour, the flowers of the woodbine running through both,
like one thought drifting hither and thither through
dreams; and how Chaucer must have smiled with pleasant joy
when he saw them in his vision. He looks in and the
arbour is full of scarlet flowers, and down among them,
sore wounded, 'a man in black and white colour, pale and
wan,' is lying, bitterly complaining. Scarlet, black,

white, one sees that, 'flashing upon the inward eye,' not
in outline, nor in detail, but in colour, and that is the
test whether a poet is a good colourist or not. It is no
common excellence. Our mind's eye, which as we read
creates the landscape before it, demands harmony of colour
in the poetical as much as in the actual landscape. On
the other hand, to give no colour in a landscape which we
know must have colour, or to insist on one colour till the
eve of the imagination is dazzled by it, is equally bad in
poetical work.

There is a splendid study of colour, unequalled in its
way in our literature, in Chaucer's picture of the cock in
the 'Nun's Priests Tale,' The widow keeps in her yard a
famous stock of poultry -

> In which she had a cock, hight Chaunteclere,
> In al the lond of crowyng was noon his peere.
> His vois was merier than the mery orgon,
> On masse dayes that in the chirche goon;
> Well sikerer was his crowyng in his logge
> Than is a clok or abay orologge.
> His comb was redder than the fine coral,
> And battayld, as it were a castel wal.
> His bile was blak, and as the geet it schon;
> Like asur were his legges and his ton;
> His nayles whitter than the lily flour,
> And lik the burnischt gold was his colour.

It is as forcible and as brilliant as a picture of Honde-
coeter, whose cock, a glorious bird, used to sit to him
like a human being.

It is plain that a special study like this of an ani-
animal is not unfitting in the sphere of poetry, but one
may doubt whether a poetical description of a landscape,
even of so centralized a piece of landscape as that of the
arbour, ought to be so given as to be capable of being
rendered at once by the sister art of painting. It is a
well-known critical rule, that the arts ought never to
travel out of their own sphere - that no landscape in
poetry should be conceived, as it were, from a painting,
nor capable of being painted, and that no landscape picture should be capable of being described in words. In
both the poetical and the pictorial landscape there ought
to be elements above and beyond the power of the other art
to render, and if Chaucer's landscapes were always the
same as that of the arbour, and the black and white man
among the scarlet flowers, he would have been justly
called an inferior artist. But this is by no means the
case; the direct contrary is the case.

The influence of the landscape on the senses and on
the heart is almost always clearly marked, especially the
glow and joy which the resurrection of the earth in Spring
imparts to mind and body. He cannot restrain his delight
in the colour of the trees. He breaks out: -

> But Lord, so I was glad and wel begone,
> For over all where I mine eyen caste
> Were trees clad with leaves that aie shal last
> Eche in his kind, with colour freshe and grene
> As emeraude, that joy it was to sene.

He has 'inly so great pleasure in sweet scents that he
thinks he is ravished into paradise,' The song of the
nightingale enchants him into such an ecstasy that he does
not know, he says, 'where he was.' Wherever he goes, by
brook or through meadow, he throws himself with simple
but passionate feeling into the life of all things; never,
as our modern poets do, confusing himself with nature, or
imputing to her his feelings; but always humbly and naturally receiving without a thought of himself, almost
devotionally, impressions of sensible and spiritual
beauty from the natural world. There is nothing more
beautiful in Chaucer's landscapes than our own vision of
the child-like man moving about in them in happy 'ravish-
ment.' We must conceive him as painted by the host in the
prologue to the tale of 'Sir Thopas' -

> Thou lokest as thou woldest fynde a hare,
> For ever on the ground I see thee stare -

large-bodied, for the host jokes with him on his being as
round in the waist as himself -

> He in the wast is schape as well as I,

but with features small and fair -

> He seemeth elvisch by his countenance.

The word 'elvisch,' both in its then and later meaning,
touches the poetic quality of some of Chaucer's poetry,
and the innocent mischief of his humour is elfish enough
at times. But Chaucer used the word to express nothing
more than that his features were small and delicate.
    This simple childlikeness and intensity of Chaucer, two
qualities which, when they do not exclude, exalt each
other, and which, when combined in harmonious proportions,
are the first necessity of a poetic nature, flow over all

his landscapes like the rejoicing, enchanting light of
dawn. This is the first of those elements of his poetry
which makes his landscapes impossible to be painted.

Of two other unpaintable things the landscape is also
full - of the scent of flowers, and the songs of birds,
and now and then of the noise of water.

In the 'Flower and the Leaf,' after describing one of
his favourite arbours and the pleasant sight of the corn-
fields and the meadows, he suddenly feels so sweet an air
of the 'eglantere' that no heart, however overlaid with
froward thoughts but would have relief if it had once
felt this savour sweet. An additional delicacy is given
to the whole landscape by this sudden rich appeal to
another sense. The delight of a sweet smell enhances all
his pleasure. But he is not content with this alone, and
here comes in that law of harmony of which I have spoken
as marking the great artist's work - there must be a
melody of scents, a chord of odour as a chord of colour.
So further on, as he is searching for the nightingale,
he finds her in a fresh green laurel tree,

> That gave so passing a delicious smell
> *According* to the eglantere full well.

In another poem the same thought occurs of all things in
nature, however different, being in musical accord.

> And the river that I sat upon,
> It made such a noise as it ron
> Accordant with the bridde's harmony;
> Methought it was the best melody
> That might been yheard of any mon.

Again, the whole of Chaucer's landscapes is ringing with
the notes of birds. The woods seem to him to be breaking
to pieces with the shrill and joyous sound. He enters
into the whole of their life. He sees them tripping out
of their bowers, rejoicing in the new day. He watches
them pruning themselves, making themselves gay, and dancing and leaping on the spray, and singing loud their morning service to the May. He is lured into a trance by the
ravishing sweetness of the nightingale, and in the trance
he hears a battle royal between the nightingale and the
cuckoo.

At another time he sees all the small fowls, as he
calls them, clustering on the trees and of the season
fain, and he cannot help translating their song for them.
Some of them, delighted to escape the sophistries of the
fowler employed against them all the winter, sing loudly,

'The fowler we defy, and all his craft.' Others, full of
the summer, worship and praise love, and in their pleasure
turn often upon the branches full of soft blossoms crying,
'Blessed be St. Valentine.' At another time, they wake
him as he lies in bed through the noise and sweetness of
their song, sitting on his chamber roof and on the tiles,
and sing the most solemn service by note that ever man had
heard. And some sang low and some high, but all of one
accord. None of them fained to sing. Each of them pained
herself to find out the merriest and craftiest notes, and
not one of them spared her little throat.

They are the priests of Love in Chaucer, and they offer
up the adoration of universal nature - 'Nature the vicar
of the Almighty Lord' - to God. At the end of the 'Court
of Love,' all the birds meet to sing matins to Love. The
poem itself is an allegorical paraphrase of the matins for
Trinity Sunday and has been objected to as impious, but
this would be impossible in so religious a mind as
Chaucer's, and when he makes them sing their naive matins
to the King of Love, he has the thought of Love as the law
of God's government of the universe in his mind. Nothing
can be fresher and more charming than the poem. The birds
cluster round the desk in a temple shapen hawthorn-wise.
Each of them takes part in the service. They praise the
past season of May, and bid the flowers all hail at the
lectern. The goldfinch, fresh and gay, declares that Love
has earth in governance; the wren begins to skip and dance
with joy when she hears that pleasant tale; the throstle-
cock sings so sweet a tune that Tubal himself (for Chaucer
confuses him with Jubal), the first musician, could not
equal; the peacock, the linnet take up the service, and
the owl awaked starts out and blesses them: 'What meaneth
all this merry fare, quoth he;' the lark and kite join in;
and last the cuckoo comes to thank God for the joyous May,
but so heartily and so gladly that he bursts out into a
fit of laughter, Chaucer's way of describing that redupli-
cation of his note when he takes to flight, cuck-cuck-ooo.
Having done, the Court of Love rushes out into the meadows
to fetch flowers fresh, and branch and bloom, hawthorn
garlands, blue and white; with these they pelt one
another, flinging primroses and violets and gold, and the
royal feast is over.

Once more, flowers form a part of the landscape of
Chaucer. They were part of nearly all the mediaeval landscapes of the fourteenth and fifteenth centuries, and were
sometimes painted with exquisite skill and tenderness. In
some instances they had a definite religious significance.
Roses, as in that wonderful trellised hedge of roses in
Veronese's picture at Venice, symbolize the Virgin as the

Rose of Sharon. Lilies, of course, represent purity. But
when flowers and fruits are symbolical, they are generally
placed in the hands or on the head of the saints, and do
not properly form part of the landscape.

There is a very charming instance of their religious
use in a picture of Benozzo Gozzoli in the National Gallery. St. Jerome and St. Francis kneel at the feet of the
Virgin. A red rose-bush, full of flowers, has sprung out
of the earth at the knees of St. Jerome, a clustered plant
of the large white lily at the knees of St. Francis. The
meadow is full of wild flowers; these two alone are
flowers of culture, and they represent that the two saints
offer to the Virgin her own qualities of love and purity,
and strive to imitate them in their lives.

Sometimes flowers enter the mediaeval landscape as
objects of mere pleasure, for the delight which the artist
had in their colour, not with any distinct meaning. In
the picture of the Battle of Sant' Egidio, in the National
Gallery, Paulo Uccello has filled the whole middle distance with a hedge of red and white roses. At one end an
orange-tree, laden with golden globes of fruit, rises
beyond the hedge; at the other end is a pomegranate,
breaking open its fruits with ripeness. The picture has
been cited as a type of the neglect of the earth's beauty
by reason of the passions of men. It may seem that to us,
but Paulo Uccello, one is sure, had no such meaning. He
brought in the roses and fruits as an ornamental background, and if he had any further thought it was that he
wished to send Carlo Malatesta to his fate in the midst of
the flowers and fruits among which he was pleased to sit
in his garden when his guests were singing and dancing on
the grass of his rosery.

But on the whole, the Tuscan or other Italian schools
before Raphael do not take pleasure in cultivated flowers
so much as in meadows and the common wild flowers. The
grass is almost always the grass of Chaucer, soft and
sweet and moist; the meadows are generally water meadows,
and one either receives the impression of water being near
at hand from the richness of the grass, or sees the river
winding away in the distance. I take a few instances from
the National Gallery of the treatment of meadow land and
flowers by the earlier artists. They are all coincident
in feeling with Chaucer's rapture in grass, and they
illustrate his love of wild flowers.

Perugino's great St. Michael stands in a rich green
mead, with one or two wild flowers; but Raphael, being the
gentler angel and the angel of the earth, is walking with
Tobit through an exquisite field where the grass is short,
like smooth turf, and full of small and brilliant flowers

of the field, blue, white, crimson, and gold, each growing
separately, like the trees in Chaucer's grove, in lovely
order, so that, even in the open meadow, the impression of
definite arrangement and culture is given, only it is not
the culture of the garden, for the angel of the earth
loves the fields.

Filippino Lippi, in our picture, places his saints in
wild grass land, and the only flowers he admits are the
commonest, such as the flowering nettle. Piero di Cosimo,
in that strange picture of his of the Death of Procris,
places the dying maiden in a deep meadow, starred all over
with the large and small daisy, and the wild anemone. Two
tall reed-grass clusters, with flowers, shoot up on either
side of the group. Raphael's St. Catherine stands among
marshy meadows, lush and soft, with scarcely any flowers,
not one of the garden character.

It is curious that in all these there is pleasure, not
in flowers by themselves, but in flowers and grass, and
the flowers more for the sake of the grass than the grass
for the flowers. Even in the 'Bacchus and Ariadne,'
painted when the love of flowers had increased, and where
one would think that Titian would have made nature lavish
of her beauty, we have only the columbine, the great blue
iris, which grows wild, the lupine, and the rude equise-
tum - the horse-grass which in our country springs up in
rough moorland beside the pools. Marco Basaiti, another
Venetian artist, whose landscape is not Venetian, but
almost always laid among such scenes as one sees in travelling between Verona and Padua - terraced hills with
castles and walls running down to the plain, stone-
strewed fields, over which oxen are ploughing, a city in
the distance, a few scattered trees, a rude well and
clover meadows - gives all his strength to the clover, and
almost omits the flowers in his foreground. In that picture of the Death of St. Peter Martyr, which Lady Eastlake
has presented to the National Gallery, the carefulness and
delight with which the clover-field and the woodland grass
are painted are as remarkable as the absence of flowers.

When cultured flowers are introduced it is either for
ornament or religion's sake. There a most enchanting
little group of cut flowers in a glass, standing on a
ledge, in a picture by Lorenzo di Credi. They are there
purely for the sake of their beauty, but it is the only
instance of this in the Gallery among the pictures of the
fifteenth century. All the rest - I do not speak of
trees such as the citron and pomegranate - with the omission of Paulo Uccello's picture, are devoted to grass and
its flowers.

I have discussed this at length that we may come with

more comprehension to the grassy landscape of Chaucer. It
forms the greater·part of all his natural description, and
his delight in it is unbounded. The flowers he mentions,
roses being excepted, are all grass flowers, or flowers of
the wild hedges, woodbine, hawthorn, the *Agnus Castus,* the
last a shrub of the verbena family, growing in marshy
places to the height of five and ten feet. The crown of
all is the daisy, the simplest and the commonest. The
Queen of the Leaf, in the 'Flower and the Leaf,' comes in
chaunting its praise - 'Si douce est la Margarete.'

His green mead, with flowers white, blue, yellow, and
red, is exactly the meadow of the fifteenth-century art.
As to the grass, he never can say enough about it, but it
is never coarse. It is turf such as grows in mossy
glades; it is small, and sweet, and soft. It is, again,
so small, so thick, so short, so fresh of hue, 'that most
like unto grene wool, I wot, it was.' It is often newly
sprung, as in May. It is like velvet, it is embroidered
with its own flowers. Nothing can compare with it when it
shines like silver with the dew of morning; and of all its
flowers the daisy, as I said, is the queen. The prologue
of the 'Legend of Good Women' is entirely taken up with the
the praises of this flower. It is true he impersonates
his lady in the daisy, but the fine touches of observation, and the enthusiasm with which he speaks, mark his
love of the flower itself. As the whole piece is characteristic, I give an abstract of it, using Chaucer's own
words as much as possible. He begins by describing his
delight in books - and we must remember we have here the
pleasures of his later years, for this poem is one of his
last.

'In mine heart,' he says, 'I have books in such reverence that there is no game could make me leave them, save
only when the month of May is come, and the birds begin to
sing and the flowers to spring; then - farewell my book
and my devotion!'

I cannot help quoting Wordsworth in comparison: -

Books, 'tis a dull and endless strife,
    Come hear the woodland linnet;
How sweet his music - on my life
    There's more of wisdom in it.
And hark! how blithe the throstle sings,
    He too is no mean preacher;
Come forth into the light of things,
    Let Nature be your teacher.

Chaucer goes on: 'Of all the flowers in the mead I love
most those flowers white and red, such as men call daisies

in our town. When the May comes, no day dawneth, but I am
up and walking in the meadow to see this flower spreading
in the sun when it riseth early in the morning. That
blissful sight softeneth all my sorrow. So glad am I to
do it reverence, for it is the flower of all flowers fulfilled of all virtue and honour, fair and fresh of hue,
that I love it, and ever shall until my heart die. And
when it is eve, I run quickly, as soon as ever the sun
begin to west, to see this flower how it will go to rest
for fear of night, so hateth it darkness.' We see at once
where Wordsworth borrowed his thoughts: -

> When smitten by the morning ray
> I see thee rise, alert and gay,
> Then, cheerful flower, my spirits play
>   With kindred gladness:
> And when at dusk my dews oppressed
> Thou sink'st, the image of thy rest
> Hath often eased my pensive breast
>   Of careful sadness.

Then Chaucer turns and identifies it with his lady, and
after some lovely lines proceeds to describe the fire in
his heart which drove him forth at the dawn to be at the
resurrection of the daisy when it uncloses against the
sun. He sets himself right down upon his knees to greet
it. Kneeling alway until it was unclosed upon the small,
soft, sweet grass, soon 'full softly he begins to sink,'
and leaning on his elbow and his side, settles himself to
spend the whole day for nothing else but to look upon the
daisy, or else the eye of day, as he prettily turns its
name. When night falls he goes home and has his bed made
in an arbour strewn with flowers. He dreams a dream, and
sees the God of Love coming through a meadow, and 'in his
hande a queen.' She is the incarnation of the daisy. Her
habit is of green, and above the habit, which represents
the leaves, rose the flower of her head, crowned with a
crown of pearls, like the white petals of the flower, and
in the midst a fret or band of gold, the cluster of yellow
stamens. One compares this at once with Wordsworth's 'A
queen in crown of rubies drest.' This is Chaucer's hymn
of praise to the daisy, half in love of his lady, half in
real honour of the flower. It is a charming picture of
the simple and happy scholar, now verging into years;
devoted all the winter to his books, but in the spring
changing from the scholar to the poet - feeling still the
secret of the May moving in the chambers of his blood, and
dawn and evening worshipping the daisy.
    Love of this flower is found again in England the

moment the more natural school of poetry arose. In a
certain degree it has always kept its place in poetry as
the representative flower of the fields and hills; but
when the fields and hills were little looked at in England
for their own sake, the daisy drops out of our poetry as a
direct subject for song. The allusions to it are many,
but it is only when we get to Burns and Wordsworth - and
Wordsworth, at least, drew the beginnings of his ardour
for this flower from Chaucer - that the worship of this
little fairy of the field begins again.

Wordsworth has consecrated three poems to its honour.
In one he lets his busy fancy weave round it a web of
similes, quaint and far-fetched, the lawful work of fancy,
which is in poetry what wit is in prose. In another the
imagination, which is related to humour, follows the daisy
from field to mountain side and forest brook, and marks
its varied relations to sudden moods of human feeling. In
another, he carries it into a higher but a less poetical
region, dwelling on the concord of its daily life with
that of humanity, and turning it into a moral lesson.

The poem of Burns is an elegy over the fate of one of
these flowers done to death by his ploughshare. It is
exquisitely tender, less loaded with thought than Wordsworth's poems, but coming home with more poetic intensity
to the nature of the flower. Can anything be happier than
this?

Cauld blew the bitter-biting North
Upon thy early humble birth,
Yet cheerfully thou glinted forth
        Amid the storm,
Scarce reared above the parent earth
        Thy humble form.

There in the scanty mantle clad,
Thy snowy bosom sunward spread,
Thou lift's thy unassuming head
        In humble guise.

But Chaucer's delight in the daisy is more natural,
less mixed up with reflection, more direct, and when he
does mingle its image with that of Alcestis or of his wife,
the two are more completely fused together by imagination
than is the case with Wordsworth or Burns. The flower is
first in Chaucer. In Wordsworth one thinks more of the
thoughts than of the flower. In Burns we pity the flower,
and its fate is woven in with the fate of luckless bard
and artless maid. But Chaucer would not have considered
the ruin which befell the daisy at the hands of Burns a

fit subject for poetry. He would have shrunk from it as
a sacrilege. Agricultural work on his meadows would have
been abominable. They were to be kept soft, and smooth,
and sweet, for poets, and knights, and ladies to walk on
and to meditate. If daisies had to be destroyed by the
plough, let the fact be ignored by the poet.

Mr. Ruskin, dwelling on this sentimental view of nature
- looked on no longer with the eye of the farmer, for use,
but with the eye of the gentleman, for beauty - thinks
that the mediaeval pleasure in flowers became connected
with less definite gratitude to God for the produce of the
earth.

This, at least, is not true of Chaucer. Through a
great part of his descriptions there exhales an indefinite
incense of reverence and thankfulness to God for the
beauty of the fields. The religious tone is marked. Even
in the more humorous poems, such as the 'Assembly of
Foules,' where Nature, the goddess, is enthroned on a hill
enriched with grass and daisies, we are made to feel that
Nature is of God, and that the beauty and perfection of
the queen is not intrinsic but delegated beauty; and when
the daisy is identified with his lady, the wife he loved
so well, and made the mistress of all the flowers, we know
from many an allusion, that in Chaucer's reverential
thought the grace of his lady is derived from the grace of
God.

19.   FREDERICK JAMES FURNIVALL, WORK AT CHAUCER

1873

F.J. Furnivall (1825-1910), educated at London University
and Trinity Hall, Cambridge, was the dominant figure in
the discovery and scholarship of earlier English literature in the nineteenth century. His personality was
lively and genial and among many interests in social and
educational reform he founded a number of literary societies including the Early English Text Society (1864) and
the Chaucer Society (1868). He printed transcriptions of
many early texts, and inspired much work in others. The
following extract from 'Macmillan's Magazine', March 1873
(XXVII), pp. 383-93, is representative of his attitudes,
style and interests, and suggests something of the foundation of scholarship being laid. Henry Bradshaw (1831-86)

was Librarian of the University Library, Cambridge, where
many of his working papers on Chaucer remain.

RECENT WORK AT CHAUCER

Following the revival of Gothicism in architecture and of
Pre-Raphaelism in painting, has come (says a critic) a
revival of Antiquarianism in literature, a conviction that
it is the duty of cultured Englishmen to study the early
records of their language and social history, and, in
order that they may study these, first to print the manuscripts containing them. That this conviction is not yet
widely spread is evidenced by the state of the subscrip-
tion-lists of some of the printing societies that have of
late years sprung into existence. The Chaucer Society,
for instance, has, out of the millions of Great Britain,
found just sixty men in England and Wales, five in Scotland, and one in Ireland, to support it; and, but for the
help of Professor Child and his friends in the United
States, could never have crept into being. - Still, it is
something to have a Chaucer Society alive; and it is more
to have grounds for hope that the pitiable indifference
(due to pure ignorance) shown by the classically-trained
men of the present generation to the second greatest
English poet - which Chaucer incontestably is - will not
be shared by their successors, the youths and boys now
training at college and school....
   Taking therefore for granted that the study of Early
English has revived and is spreading, though miserably
slowly, in England and elsewhere, let us ask what that
study has done for CHAUCER, that tenderest, brightest,
most humourful sweet soul, of all the great poets of the
world, whom a thousand Englishmen out of every thousand
and one are content to pass by with a shrug and a sneer:
'How can one find time to read a man who makes "poore"
two syllables? Life is not long enough for that.'
   To his successors Chaucer was the sun in the firmament
of poetry....
   The first man to try and get rid of some of the rubbish
that had been piled round Chaucer's name was the first
real editor of the 'Canterbury Tales,' Thomas Tyrwhitt.
He unluckily did not follow up his edition of Chaucer's
great work by an edition of the 'Minor Poems;' but in his
Glossary to the Tales, publisht in 1778, he gave a list
of those works attributed to Chaucer which he considered
genuine, and another list of those that he thought spurious. With his judgment subsequent editors, reprinters,

and biographers, have been content, and have presented to
us as genuine Chaucer - besides the works named above -
the following poems, together with the prose 'Testament of
Love.'

The Court of Love;
The Cuckoo and the Nightingale;
The Flower and the Leaf;
Chaucer's Dream (or Isle of Ladies);
The Romaunt of the Rose;
The Complaint of the Black Knight;
A Goodly Ballade of Chaucer;
A Praise of Women;
A Roundel, Virelai, and Prophecy.

Now most of these poems, as well as the prose 'Testament,'
contain biographical details as to their several writers;
and Chaucer's biographers, with a boldness to be wondered
at, and a want of caution to be condemned, quietly mixt up
all these details with the known events of Chaucer's life,
and vowed that their hodge-podge was pure flour, their
medley all one hue. They made Chaucer write poems before
he was born, married him to one or two other men's wives,
banished him from England, put him in prison, gave him
somebody else's son, and generally danced him about on
the top of his head.
    The ways taken to quiet these antics were, for one man
to search the Issue Rolls of the Exchequer, and find out
from them where Chaucer was when the half-yearly payments
of his pension were made to him - whether in Zealand, in
prison, or quietly at home - and for other men to settle
the much more important question of what were Chaucer's
genuine works, so that the life details in these alone
might be set down to him, and also his genius cleared from
the reproach of having written much poor stuff attributed
to it. The first part of this work was undertaken by Sir
Harris Nicolas, who in 1845 wrote a Life of Chaucer for
Pickering's reprint of Chaucer's Poetical Works, and for
it ransackt the Patent and Issue Rolls, which Godwin had
used but sparingly. He showed that while Chaucer was said
to have been in banishment and in great distress, he was
quietly doing the duties of his two offices in the Customs
in London, and 'that at the very moment when he is supposed to have been a prisoner in the Tower, he was sitting
in Parliament as a Knight of the Shire for one of the
largest counties in England.' Another most important
addition to the external evidence as to the life of Chaucer was made in 1866 by Mr. Edward A. Bond, the present
Keeper of the Manuscripts in the British Museum - for

whose class catalogue thereof may his memory be blesst! -
who got out of an old book-cover some bits of the household book for 1356-9 of the wife of Prince Lionel,
Edward III's third son, which bits contained three entries
of payments for clothes for 'Geoffrey Chaucer,' probably
her page. The finding of these entries rendered almost
certain the fact that when Chaucer swore in 1386 that he
was fourty years old and upwards, he did not mean fifty-
eight, but, say, fourty-six, which would make his birth
year 1340, a date with which the internal evidence from
his poems harmonizes. The investigation of this internal
evidence, or the second part of the work mentioned above,
was undertaken independently by two men unknown to each
other; first in England, by Mr. Henry Bradshaw, Fellow of
King's and Librarian of the University of Cambridge - who,
unluckily for all English students, has persistently
refused to print any account of his process and his
results - and Professor Bernhard ten Brink, Professor of
the Neo-Latin Languages at Marburg in Cassel, and Profes-
sor-elect of English at the re-founded University of
Strassburg, who, like a true German uhlan, suddenly and
most unexpectedly made his appearance one morning by his
'Chaucer: Studien zur Geschichte seiner Entwicklung und
zur Chronologie Seiner Schriften, erster Theil, 1870,'
and carried off from England the main credit of the
reform or re-creation of Chaucer.

The chief test with which these two scholars workt was
the rymes of Chaucer, similar ryme-solvents having been
long used on the Continent with great effect, though
never applied to an English poet here before....

The authenticity of Chaucer's chief poems being thus
confirmed, lists of the rymes in them were made independently by Mr. Bradshaw and Professor ten Brink, and these
were then applied as a test - first to the 'Death of
Blaunche' and the 'Romance of the Rose,' and then to all
the other poems named in the list on p.[169], which had
been attributed to Chaucer by old printers, &c., and even
by Tyrwhitt.

The 'Death of Blaunche' stood the test, and was therefore set down as genuine; the 'Romance of the Rose'
unexpectedly failed, and Mr. Bradshaw at once unhesitatingly said - 'This cannot be Chaucer's version. The one
he wrote must be lost, or hasn't yet been found.' Professor ten Brink and I argued for the known version for a
time: that it might have been Chaucer's earliest piece of
work; that in it he might have followed his less careful
predecessors, Minot, Shoreham, Robert of Brunne, &c.- but
we were obliged to acknowledge that the claim of the present version to be Chaucer's could not be establisht, and

we now almost share Mr. Bradshaw's opinion that this
'Rose' is not Chaucer's.

The ryme-test was then applied to the list of poems on
p.[169] above, together with the manuscript 'Balade,'
'Cronicle,' and continuation of the 'Pity,' and every one
of them broke down under it; every one sinned against
Chaucer's laws of ryme. These poems were accordingly all
labelled 'spurious;' and they must remain so ticketed till
any critic can establish their genuineness - a hard task,
for every one of them contains further internal evidence
showing its spuriousness. - The 'Testament of Love' being
prose, the ryme test could not be applied to it; but the
mere reading of its confusion and straggling, the mere
noting of its writer's strong praise of Chaucer, and the
absolute inconsistency of its biographical details with
the known facts of Chaucer's life, made one set it aside
at once as never written by him. The supposition of its
genuineness is preposterous.

With the ground thus cleared from the sham works,
Chaucer's real ones could be approacht with a certainty
that trustworthy information about him could be got from
them, that their order of writing could be found out, and
thus the great poet's development of mind and life made
clear. This was the object of, and justification for, all
the previous work....

[Professor ten Brink] was the first man to throw a real
light on the distinction between genuine and spurious in
Chaucer's works, and the true order of succession in those
works. Single-handed he did it without ever having seen a
Chaucer manuscript, or heard of a Chaucer Society, and
with no better books at hand than hundreds of Englishmen
had had on their shelves for many years past. Alone he
beat us, and beat us well, on our own ground. All honour
to him for it! He is well worthy to be one of those who
are to lay anew the foundations of a great University of
Strassburg.

Professor ten Brink showed that the first great distinction between Chaucer's works was to be made between the
early and poorer ones when he was under French influence,
and the later and finer poems written after he had come
under Italian influence, had read Dante, Boccaccio, Petrarca, had visited Italy in 1372. Before this year, in
Chaucer's first period, the Professor put the 'Romance of
the Rose,' and 'The Death of Blaunche,' In the second
period, 1372-84, he put the 'Life of St. Cecile,' 'Parlament of Fowles,' 'Palamon and Arcite,' 'Boece,' 'Troylus,'
and 'Hous of Fame,' all of which he treated at length; and
then promist to deal in his Second Part with the works of
the third and greatest period of Chaucer's life, 1385-1400,

to which belonged, at least, the Legende of Good Women,
Astrolabe, Anelida and Arcite, Canterbury Tales, and Mars
and Venus.

This arrangement made clear the process of Chaucer's
development, and was an immense gain to students; but it
did not disclose the secret of Chaucer's early life.   The
short poems were not workt in with the longer ones; the
'Compleynte to Pity' was not noticed; and yet in it lay
the explanation of the sadness of all Chaucer's early
work, his sympathy with the mourning Duke of Lancaster,
the forsaken Mars, the abandoned Anelida, the deserted
Troylus, the lovelorn Dido.   For, in truth, he himself had
begun his life with bitterly disappointed love, and its
pangs shot through him for many a year before he could
write the merry lines which laugh with gladness still.
Most happily for us, Chaucer has himself identified himself with the suffering lover of the 'Pity' by an after-
allusion which is indisputable.   In his 'Death of Blaunche
the Duchesse (of Lancaster)' - she died September 12, 1369
- Chaucer tells us that he cannot sleep at night because
'he has been ill for eight years, and yet his cure is no
nearer, for there is but one physician who can heal him.
But that is done. Pass on. What will not be, must needs
be left.' Thus quietly does he then speak of his disappointed love. But if we turn to his 'Compleynte to
Pity' of a year or two earlier, when his rejection was
fresh in his mind, we there find the passionate sad
pleadings of his early love. He tells us that when after
the lapse of 'certeyne yeres' - seven must he have served
in vain, like Jacob, for his desire - during which he had
sought to speak to his love, at last, even before he
could speak, he saw all pity for him dead in her heart;
and down he fell, dead as a stone while his swoon lasted.
Then he arose; and to her, in all her beauty, he still
prayed for mercy and for love....A touching poem it is,
and a touching story it tells, to those who read it
aright: the poet's young love crusht in the bud, and he,
who has been the comfort and joy of many souls, left to
say of himself, as he does of Troylus: -

But forthe hire cours Fortune ay gan to holde:
Criseyde loveth the sonne of Tydeus;
And Troilus mot wepe in cares colde.
Suich is this worlde, who so kan it beholde!
  In ech estat is litel hertes reste!
  God leve us for to take it for the beste!
          (Troylus, Bk. V., st. ccli., 1759-64)

This is the key to Chaucer's early life; and the man

who would understand him must start with him in his
sorrow, walk with him through it into the fresh sunshine
of his later life, and then down to the chill and poverty
of his old age. 'Out of the bitter cometh the sweet,' and
never was the adage better verified than in Chaucer, whose
early sadness produced his joyous prime.

Want of space prevents my following up here the tracks
of disappointed love through Chaucer's other early minor
poems, or dwelling on the most interesting revival of it -
seemingly after a reconciliation - as seen in the standard
version of his Prologue to the 'Legende of Good Women,'
when compared with the unique version printed in the Chaucer Society's 'Odd Texts,' from MS. Gg. 4. 27 in the Cambridge University Library. But one cannot insist too
strongly on the fact that Chaucer's works, like those of
every other writer, must be studied chronologically by the
man who wants to understand fully them and their writer;
and in the following order should they be read: -

	FIRST PERIOD
?	A B C.
1367—8.	Pity
1369.	Death of Blaunche.

	SECOND PERIOD
1373?	St. Cecile (Second Nun's Tale).
	Parlament of Fowles.
	Compleynte of Mars.
	Anelida and Arcite.
	Boece. ?Former Age.
	Troylus.
	Adam Scrivener.
1384.	Hous of Fame.

	THIRD PERIOD (*greatest*)
1386.	Legende of Good Women.
	Canterbury Tales (1373-1400;
	Prologue, 1388).
	Truth.
?	Mother of God.

	FOURTH PERIOD (*decline*)
1391.	Astrolabe.
	Compleynt of Venus.
1393?	Envoy to Skogan.
	Marriage.
	Gentleness.
1397?	Lack of Stedfastness.
1398?	Fortune.
1399, Sept.	Purse (to Henry IV).

The order of dates of the 'Canterbury Tales' is not
yet quite workt out; but clearly the following are late: -
The Canon's, Yeoman's, Manciple's (note the moralizing at
the end of both), Monk's, Parson's. As clearly these,
with the general Prologue, belong to Chaucer's best time:
The Miller's, Reeve's, Cook's, Wife's Preamble (and the
Tale too), Merchant's, Friar's, Nun's, Priest's, Pardoner's, and perhaps the Sompnour's. No doubt these are
before the Third Period: Second Nun's (the earliest),
Doctor's, Man of Law's, Clerk's, Prioress's, Squire's,. and
Franklin's, ?Thopas, and Melibe, with The Knight's Tale,
in its first cast. Thus far had one got, when Mr. Hales
supplied the generalization wanted - 'Power of characterization is the true test. Where you know the people in
the Tales, as you do those in the Prologue, there you have
work of Chaucer's best time, say 1386-90. Who knows which
is Palamon and which is Arcite? The Knight's Tale *must* be
comparatively early, though a few late lines that imply
1387 may have been put into it. The Tales, too, that take
half-views of life, like the Clerk's, Grisilde, the Man of
Law's, and Constance, must be before the best time too.'
   With this guide every reader can work out the succession of the Tales for himself, and mix them in proper
order with the Minor Poems as ranged above. He will then
see Chaucer, not only outwardly as he was in the flesh -
page, soldier, squire, diplomatist, Customhouse officer,
Member of Parliament, then a suppliant for protection and
favour, a beggar for money; but inwardly as he was in the
spirit - clear of all nonsense of Courts of Love, &c. -
gentle and loving, early timid and in despair, sharing
others' sorrow, and by comforting them, losing part of
his own; yet long dwelling on the sadness of forsaken
love, seeking the 'consolalation of philosophy,' watching
the stars, praying to the 'Mother of God;' studying books,
and, more still, woman's nature; his eye open to all the
beauties of the world around him, his ear to the 'heavenly
harmony' of birds' song; at length becoming the most gracious and tender spirit, the sweetest singer, the best
pourtrayer, the most pathetic, and withal the most genial
and humourful healthy-souled man that England had ever
seen. Still, after 500 years, he is bright and fresh as
the glad light green of the May he so much loved; he is
still second only to Shakespeare in England, and fourth
only to him and Dante and Homer in the world. When will
our Victorian time love and honour him as it should?
Surely, of all our poets he is the one to come *home* to us
most.
   We have hitherto dwelt together mainly on the most
overlookt of Chaucer's works, his Minor Poems, those

produced in the first of the two great divisions of his
life, the pathetic and romantic period, and we may now
turn to his great work, the 'Canterbury Tales,' in its
best-known parts the production of his later and finer
period, the humorous and contemporary-life one. For Chaucer was not like Tennyson. The cloud of his early loss
was not on him to the end; his temperament was cheerier,
his time perchance less 'real,' less 'earnest'; the burden
of the years perhaps was less. So the earlier poet passt
from sadness into joy, or at least to mirth, while the
Victorian one sings still in age the grave and purposeful
notes of his youth. What a contrast, too, these two poets
are in other respects! Set side by side the strenuous
wrestling of Tennyson with the deepest problems of his
age, and the sunny sketches by Chaucer of the surface of
his; compare the finisht art and tenacity of subject of the
modern with the careless ease(1) and quick-tiring of the
old one. Alike in perfection of metre, alike in love of
women fair and good, how different are they in freshness
and grace, how far apart in humour and moral intensity.
Put Tennyson judging Guinevere beside Chaucer sparing
Cressid 'for very routhe:' set the 'Northern Farmer' by
the 'Miller,' or any like character in the Canterbury Prologue, and the difference between poet and poet, as well
as age and age, will be felt; just as when one takes up
'Middlemarch,' or Mrs. Browning's poems, after reading
Chaucer's 'Wife of Bath,' his 'Constance,' or 'Grisilde,'
one feels the wondrous change that five hundred years
have wrought in English women and women's nature. When
has the world matcht ours, of this Victorian time?

   But to return to Chaucer. His Canterbury Prologue and
humorous Tales show us a new man - a man whose existence
indeed was indicated before by that most comical bird-jury
scene in the 'Parlament of Fowles,' and by the creation of
Pandarus in the 'Troylus,' but a man so different from the
sad lover of the 'Pity,' the 'Anelida,' the 'Troylus,'
that but for the music of his verse, his love of women and
his insight into them, one might be excused for asking, Is
this Chaucer still? A change has come over him. As
Claude among painters first set the sun in the heavens, so
now into his own heart Chaucer first let sunshine come,
and thence reflect, gilding all on whom it shone. His
humour glanced over all the England he could see, and he
has left us such photographs of the folk that rode with
him, that dwelt about him - pictures aglow with life's own
hues - as, I dare say, no other poet ever left of any land
to after times. Who can look at them now, who can read
the oft-conned lines, without his heart opening, his hand
stretching out, to greet the sunny soul that penned them?

I do not, however, propose to discuss here Chaucer's
place as a poet, or the value and meaning of his 'Canterbury Tales,' or even the light they throw on his character
or life. My business is with the Chaucer Society's work
on the Tales, in order to show what has been lately done
for the clearing-up of the structure, and improvement of
the text, of our poet's greatest work. The Chaucer
Society was founded in 1868, first, from the conviction
that it was a mean and unpatriotic thing of Englishmen to
have done so little as they had for their great poet's
memory; and, secondly, from the wish to supplement Mr.
Bradshaw's work, and prepare for his projected edition,
and for all future students of Chaucer, material not
easily accessible to them. For this purpose the six
finest and oldest unprinted vellum manuscripts of the
'Canterbury Tales,' all copied within from twenty to
fourty years of Chaucer's death, were chosen from public
and private collections to be printed in parallel columns,
so that their various readings and spellings might be at
once apparent. With the exception of Lord Ashburnham -
who refused to allow his MSS. to be even seen - all the
noblemen and gentlemen in England who owned Chaucer MSS.
readily granted the use of their treasures to the Society;
and the private MSS. at last selected were, first, the
magnificent illustrated MS. of Lord Ellesmere, the
choicest Chaucer MS. in the world; second, the rat-gnawed
and ill-used but excellent MS. of the old Hengwrt collection, belonging to Mr. William W.E. Wynne of Peniarth, a
most interesting MS. for its type; and thirdly, the spot-
less and gorgeously-clad MS. of Lord Leconfield at Pet-
worth House, an old Percy treasure which has been in the
possession of the family for at least four hundred years,
when the fourth Earl's arms were blazoned at its end.
The public MSS. chosen were, first, the oldest and most
curious one at Cambridge, in the University Library,
remarkable not only from its dialectal peculiarities
and its having been largely corrected by a contemporary
reviser, but also for its containing the best copies
extant of many of Chaucer's minor poems (including his
'Troilus'), and also the unique version of the first cast
of his 'Prologue to the Legende of Good Women;' secondly,
the earliest and best MS. at Oxford, that in Corpus
Christi College, a good representative of the second or
B type of MSS.; and thirdly, from the British Museum, the
probably second-best complete MS., Lansdowne 851, because
the best, Harl. 7334, had already been edited and printed
three times - by Mr. Thomas Wright, Mr. Jephson (for
R. Bell's annotated edition), and Dr. Richard Morris (for
G. Bell's Aldine edition).

Now, these manuscripts varied greatly in their arrangements of the Tales; and the question was, which was right, or whether they all were wrong. Previous editors, knowing no better, had followed the order of the MS. they printed, and had patcht up the bad joins in it with dabs of spurious putty. The consequence was, a regular muddle as to the journey and geography; places on the road to Canterbuty, like Rochester, thirty miles from town, being made to come after Sittingbourne, which is forty miles from it, &c. As Dean Stanley said in his interesting 'Historical Memorials of Canterbury': -

Not only are the stages of the route indistinctly marked, but the distances are so roughly calculated as to introduce into the geography, though on a small scale, incongruities almost as great as those which disfigure the 'Winter's Tale' and 'The Two Gentlemen of Verona.' The journey, although at that time usually occupying three or four days, is compressed into the hours between sunset and sunrise on an April day; an additional pilgrim is made to overtake them within seven miles of Canterbury, 'by galloping hard for three miles,' and the tales of the last two miles occupy a space equal to an eighth part of the whole journey of fifty miles.

It is, perhaps, needless to say that Chaucer was not such a muddler or goose as the scribes, editors, and critics had made him for five hundred years; but no one could prove it till Mr. Bradshaw, who had carefully separated the Tales into their constituent fragments or groups, one day quietly lifted up his tenth fragment (containing the Tales of the Shipman, Prioress, Sir Thopas, Melibe, Monk, and Nun's Priest) to its right place as fragment 3, or the second part of Group B, for which Chaucer wrote it, when at once the whole scheme came right. Rochester got into its proper place, the journey turned into the regular three or four days' one, and all the allusions to time, place, former tales &c., at once harmonized. The Chaucer Columbus had made his egg stand.

Note

1 The outcome of a supreme artistic nature.

20.   JOHN WESLEY HALES, PITY AND IRONY

1873

Hales (1836-1914), educated at Glasgow University and
Christ's College, Cambridge, became Professor of English
Literature at King's College, London. In an essay on
Chaucer and Shakespeare in 'The Quarterly Review',
CXXXIV (1873), pp. 225-55, after an account of the recent
founding of the Chaucer Society, he presents Chaucer as
unsentimental and ironic, as well as sympathetic.

(p. 236) Assuredly Chaucer was endowed in a very high
degree with what we may call the pathetic sense. It would
seem to have been a favourite truth with him that

    Pite renneth sone in gentil herte.

It ran 'sone' and abundantly in his own most tender bosom.
But he is never merely sentimental or maudlin. We can
believe that the Levite of the Parable shed a tear or two
as he crossed over to the 'other side' from where that
robbed and wounded traveller lay, and perhaps subsequently
drew a moving picture of the sad spectacle he had so carefully avoided. Chaucer's pity is of no such quality. It
springs from the depths of his nature; nay, from the
depths of Nature herself moving in and through her interpreter.
    Another respect in which Chaucer is not unworthy of
some comparison with his greater successor is his irony.
We use the word in the sense in which Dr. Thirlwall uses
it of Sophocles in his excellent paper printed in the
'Philological Museum' some forty years ago, and in which
Schlegel, in his 'Lectures on Dramatic Literature,' uses
it of Shakespeare, to denote that dissembling, so to
speak, that self-retention and reticence, or at least,
indirect presentment, that is a frequent characteristic of
the consummate dramatist, or the consummate writer of any
kind who aims at portraying life in all its breadth. We
are told often enough of the universal sympathy that
inspires the greatest souls, and it is well; but let us
consider that universal sympathy does not mean blind,
undiscriminating, wholesale sympathy, but precisely the
opposite. Only that sympathy can be all-inclusive that is

profoundly intelligent as well as intense; and this profound intelligence is incompatible with any complete and
unmitigated adoration. The eyes that scrutinise the world
most keenly, though they may see infinite noblenesses that
escape a coarser vision, yet certainly see also much mean-
ness and pravity. Hence, to speak generally, for exceptions do not concern us, there is no such thing amongst
the deep-seeing and really man-learned as unqualified and
absolute admiration. And thus the supremest writers have
no heroes in the ordinary acceptation of that term. There
is not a hero in all Shakespeare; not even Harry the Fifth
is absolutely so. For a like reason, there is no quite
perfect villain. Neither monsters of perfection nor of
inperfection find favour with them that really know mankind. Thus a real master never completely identifies himself with any one of his characters. To say that he does
so is merely a *façon de parler*. They are all his children,
and it cannot but be that some are dearer to him than
others, but not one, if he is wise, is an idol unto him.
His irony consists in the earnest, heartfelt, profound
representation of them, while yet he is fully alive to
their failings and failures. It is observable only in
the supremest geniuses. Men of inferior knowledge and
dimmer light are more easily satisfied. They make golden
images for themselves and fall down and worship them.
Shakespeare stands outside each one of his plays, a
little apart and above the fervent figures that move in
them, like some Homeric god that from the skies watches
the furious struggle, whose issue is irreversibly ordered
by Μοῖρα κραταιή - that cannot save Sarpedon or prolong
the days of Achilles. Chaucer, too, in a similar way
abounds in secondary meanings. What he teaches does not
lie on the surface. He never resigns his judgment or
ceases to be a free agent in honour of any of the characters he draws. He never turns fanatic. He hates without
bigotry; he loves without folly; he worships without
idolatry. This excellent temper of his mind displays
itself strikingly in the Prologue, which, with all its
ardour, is wholly free from extravagance or self-aban-
donment.

It is because his spirit enjoyed and retained this
lofty freedom that it was so tolerant and capacious. He,
like Shakespeare, was eminently a Human Catholic, no mere
sectary. He refused to no man an acknowledgment of kindred; for him there were no poor relations whom he forbade his house, or neighbours so fallen and debased that
in their faces the image of God in which man was made was
wholly obliterated. And it is because his understanding
is thus wide and deep, and his sympathies commensurate

with that understanding, that his ethical teaching is,
for all time, sound and true. He is no formal or formulating moralist; he never adds his voice to the mere party
cries of his day, or concentrates his energies on any
dogma. To speak of him as a zealous religious reformer is
ridiculous; far other was his business. But yet he was a
great moral teacher, one of our greatest - μετ'ἀμύμονα
Πηλεΐωνα. All the world's a school, if we may adapt
Jaques' words, and all the men and women merely school-
children. Chaucer is a teacher in this great-world-school,
and in no lesser or special seminary; and the lessons he
gives are 'exceeding broad.' They are such as life itself
gives. They breathe out of his works in a natural stream,
no mere accidents, but the essential spirit of them, to be
discovered not by the labels but in the works themselves....

There is just one point of personal likeness between
Chaucer and Shakespeare that we wish to notice. Of each
man, as his contemporaries knew him, the chief characteristic was a wonderful loveableness of nature.

21. WILLIAM MINTO, THE SPIRIT OF CHIVALRY

1876

Minto (1845-93), Professor of Logic and English at Aber-
deen University, in his article for the ninth edition of
the 'Encyclopaedia Britannica', vol. 5, gives a sensible
account of the then state of knowledge, though his scepticism about the value of mechanistic rhyme-tests in
making and denying attributions, and his fondness for his
own productions, lead him into some critical folly. But
his general view of Chaucer's relation to society and to
literary tradition is fresh and penetrating.

(p. 451) ...inelasticity of conjecture appears in the
grounds on which certain of the works commonly attributed
to Chaucer are rejected as spurious. The 'Testament of
Love', the 'Assembly of Ladies', and the 'Lamentation of
Mary Magdalene' bear no internal marks of being Chaucer's,
and are now universally rejected; but of late some commentators have adopted a test of genuineness which would

deprive us of several works which are in no respect unworthy of Chaucer's genius. It is known from Chaucer's
own statement in the undisputed 'Legend of Good Women'
that he translated the 'Roman de la Rose', but Mr Bradshaw
refuses to believe that the extant translation, of which
we have only one 15th century manuscript, can be his,
because its rhymes do not conform to a rhyme-test which
Chaucer observed in works which are undoubtedly his. The
extant 'Romance of the Rose' admits the adverbial _ly_ to
rhyme with the adjectival or infinitival _ye_, and it cannot
be Chaucer's because _y_ is never allowed to rhyme with _ye_
in the 'House of Fame' and the 'Canterbury Tales'. For
the same reason - no other of any shadow of validity has
yet been adduced - the 'Court of Love,' which Mr Swinburne
calls 'that most beautiful of young poems,' and the
'Flower and the Leaf', which Dryden and Hazlitt have
praised and quoted as a choice example of the poet's
genius, have also been pronounced to be spurious. We
cannot give up such poems unless more urgent reasons are
advanced for their confiscation. They cannot be set aside
as spurious so long as their variation from the rhyming
rule, which the commentators have shown much ingenuity in
detecting, can be explained in any reasonable way. There
is no getting over the plain question which every one asks
when first told that they are not Chaucer's. If they are
not his, who else could have written them? Is it conceivable that the name of the writer of such works could have
been utterly unknown in his own generation, or if known
could have been by accident or design so completely sup-
pressed? If he deliberately tried to palm them off as
Chaucer's upon the transcribers, would not this rule of
rhyme have been precisely the sort of mechanical likeness
which he would have tried to preserve? The 'Court of
Love' we have special reasons for declining to give up.
It might be argued that, though the 'Flower and the Leaf'
bears internal marks of being Chaucer's, although its picturesque richness, its tender atmosphere, and the soft
fall of its words are like his, yet it is easy to grow the
plant once you have the seed, and it may be the work of an
imitator. The 'Flower and the Leaf' professes to be
written by a lady, and there may have been at the court
some wonderful lady capable of it, although it passed in
the monkish scriptorium as Chaucer's. But there is some
external evidence for the authenticity of the 'Court of
Love', which also contains traces of Chaucer's most inimitable quality, his humour. Mr Minto has put forward some
minor considerations for believing this to be Chaucer's
('Characteristics of English Poets', p. 22), but the
strongest fact in its favour is that the 'Court of Love'

was imitated by James I of Scotland in the 'King's
Quhair', and that in paying the customary compliment to
his poetical masters, he mentions no names but Lydgate and
Gower, who were clearly incapable of writing the poem, and
Chaucer....

At what periods of his life Chaucer wrote his poetry,
we have no means of ascertaining. There are no manuscripts of any of his works that can be referred to his
own time; the earliest of them in existence are not supposed to have been written till several years after his
death. The only one of his works of which the date is
fixed by an external circumstance is the 'Book of the
Duchess'; if, as is taken for granted, this was written to
commemorate the death of the wife of his patron, John of
Gaunt, its date is 1369. Chaucer, if born in 1340,
would then have been twenty-nine, and there is none of his
extant works, except the translation of the 'Romance of
the Rose', and the 'Dream' (which we hold to be Chaucer's,
though its authenticity is not worth contending for),
which can be confidently assigned to an earlier period.
Philogenet, in the 'Court of Love', professes to be eighteen, but this is not the slightest reason for concluding
that Chaucer was that age when he wrote it. The 'Book of
the Duchess' is certainly not very mature work for a poet
of twenty-nine, and it is probable that Chaucer did not
cultivate the art, as he certainly did not develop the
faculty, till comparatively late in life. The translation
of the 'Romance of the Rose' is to all appearance the
earliest of his surviving compositions. If we may judge
from his evident acquaintance with dry studies, and his
capacity for hard business work, the vintner's son received a scholastic training in the *trivium* and *quadrivium*
which then formed the higher education. If he had been
nurtured on troubadour love from his youth up, it is
exceedingly unlikely that he would afterwards have been
able to apply himself to less fascinating labours. His
study of mathematics and astronomy in his old age for the
benefit of 'little Lewis, his son,' looks like a return
such as we often see in age to the studies of youth. But,
indeed, he can hardly be said ever to have lost his interest in such studies, for in his theory of sound in the
'House of Fame' and his description of alchemical processes in the Canon's Yeoman's Prologue he shows a genuine
scholar's interest in the dry details of learning. His
knowledge of the Trouvere and Troubadour poetry, from
which his genius received its impulse, probably began
with his introduction, however, that was brought about, to
court society. He was about seventeen at the date of the
first mention of his name as attached to the household of

Prince Lionel. It is permissible to conjecture that he
had French poets to beguile his captivity in France a few
years afterwards.

Professor Ten Brink divides Chaucer's work into three
periods: - a period of French influence, lasting up to
1372-3, the date of his visit to Italy; after that a
period of Italian influence, lasting up to 1387, the supposed date of his 'House of Fame'; finally, a period of
mature strength and originality, in which he pursued the
bent of his own genius. Not much is gained by this division into strict periods. It is obvious enough that, in
the 'House of Fame', the 'Legend of Good Wcmen', and the
general plan of the 'Canterbury Tales', Chaucer strikes
out more unmistakably a path for himself, and exhibits a
maturer power, a more masterly freedom of movement than in
his earlier works, but there profitable division ends. To
erect a period of Italian influence, implying that at any
time the stimulus that Chaucer received from Italian
sources was at all comparable to the stimulus he received
from French sources, is most misleading. The difference
between the 'Book of the Duchess' and the 'House of Fame',
or between the 'Court of Love' and 'Troilus and Cresside'
is not to be explained by an influx of Italian influence;
it is part of the self-governed development, the spontaneous expansion of his own mind. As he went on writing,
his powers continued to expand, and to take in materials
and suggestions from all quarters open to him, French,
Italian, or Latin. Comparing the 'Troilus', the raw
material of which is taken from Boccaccio's 'Filostrato',
with his 'Romance of the Rose', we can trace no change in
method or in spirit fairly attributable to Italian influence. In both translations he shows a bold independence
of his originals- they are not so much translations as
adaptations. He does not imbibe the spirit of Guillaume
de Lorris or Jean de Meun in the one and the spirit of
Boccaccio in the other; he boldly modifies all three to
bring them into harmony with his own conceptions of love's
laws, and in both his so-called translations there is the
same high spirit of chivalry and the same tender worship
and kindly mockery of woman. Where he chiefly shows
advance of strength, apart from the mere technical workmanship, is in his grasp of character; and that is a clear
development on the lines of his earlier conceptions and
not a new acquisition. His Cresside and his Pandarus were
not the Cresside and Pandarus of Boccaccio; they are re-
generated by him and developed till they become figures
that might have moved in his own 'Court of Love'. He held
the knightly and 'gentle' character too high to adopt
Boccaccio's conceptions. In the method also, 'Troilus'

has a close affinity with Chaucer's earlier work and his first models. Troilus' pursuit of Cresside is the pursuit of the Rose over again in the concrete. The greater subtilty of the stages is due to the increased strength of the narrator's faculty.

M. Sandras is in the main right as to the extent of Chaucer's obligations to French sources, although he fails to recognize the forceful individuality of the man. Chaucer was really an English *trouvère*, thoroughly national, English in the whole texture of his being, but a *trouvère*. We must not allow our conviction of his loyalty to his own English nature to blind us to the fact that he was a poet in the school of Guillaume de Lorris; nor on the other hand must we allow the peculiar extent of his obligations to his predecessors in the school to obscure the fact that he was an original poet. M. Sandras is a special pleader for one side of the case, and naturally presses unfairly against the other. Chaucer, writing in a different language from his masters, was at liberty to borrow from them more literally than he could have done if he had written in their language; but though M. Sandras proves with superfluous completeness that he freely appropriated from them not merely stories and hints of stories, but narrative methods, phrases, images, maxims, reflections, - not only treated their works as quarries of raw material, but adopted their architectural plans, and even made no scruple of seizing for his own purposes the stones which they had polished, still he so transmuted the borrowed plans and materials that his works are original wholes unmistakably stamped with his own individuality. Whatever he appropriated, whether ore or wrought metal, all passed through his own alembic, and his moulds were his own, though shaped according to the fashion of the school. The very affluence of Chaucer's pages, their wealth of colour, of tender and humorous incident, of worldly wisdom, is due to his peculiar relations to his predecessors, to the circumstance which enabled him to lay them so royally under tribute. He was not the architect of his own fortune, but the son and heir of a family which for generations had been accumulating wealth. Edward III's spoliation of the French was nothing to Chaucer's, and the poet had this advantage, that his appropriations neither left the spoiled country desolate nor corrupted the spoiler.

'The ground-work of literary genius,' Mr Matthew Arnold says, 'is a work of synthesis and exposition, not of analysis and discovery; its gift lies in the faculty of being happily inspired by a certain intellectual and spiritual atmosphere, by a certain order of ideas, when it finds itself in them, of dealing divinely with these

ideas, presenting them in the most effective and attractive combinations - making beautiful works with them, in
short.' The poet's constructive power must have materials, and ideas round which materials accumulate. The
secret of the richness and enduring character of Chaucer's
work is that he had a fruitful idea ready to his hand, an
idea which had been flowering and bearing fruit in the
minds of two centuries, which had inspired some later
songs and tales, which had been illustrated, expounded,
formulated by every variety of native invention and critical ingenuity. Chivalrous love had been the presiding
genius, the inspiring spirit of several generations of
poets and critics when Chaucer began to write. Open any
of his works, from the 'Court of Love' down to the 'Canterbury Tales', and you find that the central idea of it
is to expound this chivalrous sentiment, either directly
by tracing its operation or formulating its laws, or indirectly by setting it off dramatically against its
counterpart, the sentiment of the villain or churl.
Gradually as years grew upon him, and his mind assumed
more and more its natural attitude of descriptive impartiality, he became less a partizan of the sentiment, more
inclined to view it as one among the varieties of human
manifestation, but never to the last does he become wholly
impartial. Not even in the 'Canterbury Tales' does he set
the churl on a level with 'the gentles.' Thoroughly as
he enjoyed the humour of the churl, freely as his mind
unbent itself to sympathize with his unrestrained animal
delights, he always remembers, when he comes forward in
his own person, to apologize for this departure from the
restraints of chivalry.

The very opposite of this is so often asserted about
the 'Canterbury Tales' that it almost has a paradoxical
air, although nothing can be more plain to any one who
takes the trouble to read the tales observantly. It has
been said to be the crowning merit of Chaucer that he
ignores distinctions of caste, and that his pilgrims
associate on equal terms. It should be noticed, however,
in the first place, that in the Prologue, he finds it
necessary to apologize for not 'setting folk in their
degree,' 'as that they shouldé stand;' and, in the second
place, that although he does not separate the pilgrims
according to their degrees in the procession, yet he
draws a very clear line of separation between them in the
spirit of their behaviour. At the outset of the pilgrimage the gentles are distinctly so mentioned as taking a
sort of corporate action, though in vain, to give a more
decorous aspect to the pilgrimage. When the Knight tells
his tale, it is loudly applauded by the whole company, but

the poet does not record their verdict indiscriminately;
he is careful to add, particularly by 'the *gentles* every
one.' And though all applauded the tale, the more vulgar
and uproarious spirits were somewhat restive under its
gravity: the host called for a merry tale, and the Pardoner eagerly stepped forward to comply with his request.
But 'the gentles' interposed, and began to cry that they
must have no ribaldry; 'tell us,' they said, 'some moral
tale that we may learn.' And the gentles would have
carried their point if the Miller, as the poet is most
careful to ma're clear, had not been so drunk that he insisted upon telling a noble tale that he knew, and would
forbear for no man. Chaucer is profuse in his apologies
for introducing such a tale; it was a churlish tale, he
admits, told in a churlish manner, and he does not wish
to be responsible for it.

> Every gentle wight I pray
> For Goddès love, deemeth not that I say
> Of evil intent; but for I must rehearse
> Their talès all, be they better or worse,
> Or ellès falsen some of my matter.

If gentle readers do not like it, they may turn over the
leaf, and choose another tale; there is plenty 'of
storial thing that toucheth gentillesse.' They must not
blame him for repeating this churlish tale; 'the Miller
is a churl, ye know well this,' and such tales are in his
way. Gentle readers must not take it too seriously; 'men
should not make earnest of game;' it is, after all, only
for their amusement that he thus exhibits to them the
humours of the lower orders.

Such is the elaborate apology that Chaucer makes for
introducing into his verse anything inconsistent with the
sentiments of chivalry. It may be said that it is all a
humorous pretence; and so no doubt it is, still it is
characteristic that the pretence should be of so courtly
a tone. All through the 'Canterbury Tales' Chaucer is
very careful to remember that he was writing for a courtly
audience, studious to guard against giving offence to the
chivalrous mind. He contrives that the gentles shall mix
with the churls without sustaining any loss of dignity;
they give the churls their company, and with polite compliance let them have their own gross will, but they
never lay aside the restraints of their own order. Every
here and there is some trace of deference to them, to show
that their ribald companions have not wholly forgotten
themselves, and are only receiving a saturnalian licence
for the time. Nothing is done to throw any disrespect on

the gentle order; its members - the Knight, the Squire,
the Monk, the Prioress, the Second Nun; and the professional men - the Lawyer, the Doctor, the Clerk - admit no
ribaldry into their tales, and no ribald tales are told
about them.   The ribaldry is confined to the meaner members of the company, - the Reeve, the Miller, the Friar,
the Summoner, the Wife of Bath; the narrators as well as
the subjects of the ribald tales are of churlish and not
of gentle position.

The 'Canterbury Tales' are really in their underlying
design an exposition of chivalrous sentiment, thrown into
relief by contrast with its opposite.   The spirit of chivalry is the vital air of all Chaucer's creations, the rain,
the wind, and the sun which have quickened their germ and
fostered their growth.   We to whom the chivalrous spirit,
at least in the fantastic developments of its vigorous
mediaeval youth, is an historical thing are apt to overlook this.   There is so much on the surface of Chaucer's
poems, such vivacity of movement, such tender play of
feeling, such humour, such delight in nature, in green
leaves and sweet air, sunshine and bird singing, that few
of us care to look beneath.   The open air, on the breezy
hillside or by the murmuring brook, seems the only proper
atmosphere for such a poet.   There, no doubt, with sun and
wind contending playfully to divert us from the printed
pages, there perhaps more than anywhere else, Chaucer is a
delightful companion; but it is the duty of the dry-as-
dust critic to remind us that Chaucer's sweet verses were
first read under wholly different conditions, in tapest-
ried chambers, to the gracious ear of embroidered lords
and ladies.   It was from such an audience that Chaucer
received in a vapour what he poured back in a flood.
This is the secret of his exquisite courtliness of phrase,
his unfailing tone of graceful deference, his protesta-
tions of ignorance and lack of cunning, his tender handling of woeful love-cases, the gentle playfulness of his
satire, the apologetic skill with which he introduces a
broader and more robust humanity into his verse.   If you
place yourself within the circle for which the poet wrote,
you see the smile play on sweet lips as he proceeds; you
see the tear gather in the eye; you see the needle laid
aside, as the mind of the fair listener is transported to
the poet's flowery mead, or plied more briskly as she
bends over her work to conceal her laughter at his more
vulgar adventures.   It was because Chaucer wrote for such
an audience that his picture of the life of the time,
various and moving as it is, is so incomplete on one side.

There was more than romancing in green fields and Canterbury pilgriming in the travelled times in which Chaucer

lived; there were wars, plagues, insurrections, much misery and discontent. But for the disagreeable side of the 14th century we must go to the writer of Piers the Plowman; we find little trace of it in Chaucer. The outside of the walls of the Garden of Mirth is painted with horrible and squalid figures, - Ire, Envy, Covetice, Avarice, Felony, Villany, Sorrow, Eld, and Poverty; but no such figures are admitted within the gates; the concierge is Idleness; the chief inmates are Love, Sweetlooking, Beauty, Richesse, Largesse, Franchise, and Courtesy; and Mirth and Gladness are the master and mistress of the ceremonies.

22. WILLIAM CYPLES, INCREDIBLE SENTIMENTALITY, AND THE OLD WONDER OF SEX

1877

William Cyples (1831-82), a journalist born in the Potteries, was self-educated with the help of his working mother. He also wrote a philosophical work and a novel called 'Hearts of Gold'. In this anonymous essay (identified in 'The Wellesley Index of Nineteenth Century Periodicals'), in 'The Cornhill Magazine', XXXV (1877), pp. 280-97, entitled Chaucer's Love Poetry, he claims that nine-tenths of Chaucer is unread, unknown, outlandish 'erotics', most of it sentimental and melancholy.
Cyples could hardly be more mistaken in thinking that general interest in sex was waning, but his historical and psychological observations have value. The embarrassing coyness at the beginning of the essay has historical interest in itself, but the whole essay, however mistaken or remote from modern thought and feeling, is full of sense. It makes an interesting analysis of literary love, though confusion about the Chaucerian canon affects it. He introduces the notion of the code of love.

Chaucer's Love-Poetry

Whenever Chaucer is spoken of, every English face within sight brightens. A special, very oddly-mixed, but, on the

whole, a highly pleasant literary sensation is stirred.
The chiefest outward sign is a twinkling of the eyes.
With the men, the look instantly becomes very knowing, and
there is a quick impulse to laughter, more-or-less broad;
in the best instances among the women, just a little
stiffening of carriage sets in, with the beginning of a
blush. After five centuries, the sex in those ways
recognises the poet as its great critic. In neither case
is the effect bad. An Englishman in the first stage of
enjoying a sly joke, and an Englishwoman sedately flushing
in the cheeks at the apprehension of it, are seen at an
advantage. The two aspects form our best national presentment. What is really at the bottom of the provocation
is a knowledge that Chaucer, amidst all his merits of keen
comic wit, high poetic fancy, and love of some scenes of
nature, is improper.

If ever there was any chance of the fact being forgotten, Pope, and before him Dryden in a lesser degree, did
it away, by fastening upon some of the worst passages,
doing all that was possible to modernise the scandal.
Luckily, the gross incidents themselves have an incurable
clumsy antiqueness; the jokes are a good deal too broad to
be made quite fresh and very injurious. But, in the meantime, the popular recollection of the love-poetry of
Chaucer has dwindled down to little but these obscenities;
'The Wife of Bath' and 'January and May' being only miti-
gated and purified in part by the immortal sketch of the
Prioress of the Prologue to the 'Tales'. The fact seems
nearly to have dropped out of sight, that he has a quite
different set of erotics - one so high-flown, so sentimental, as not merely not to be wicked, but to be childishly
good. For the injustice, he has himself to thank more
than his too fragmentary, unsavoury modernisers. He has
hidden away in sheer overwhelming prolixity some of the
sweetest female characterisations in the world. What his
amazing multiplication of words did not quite fully do,
he finished by the unhappy association of the passion with
a bad choice of main theme. Literature shows miracles of
want of sense in picking topics, but, for us, Chaucer must
ever remain the worst example. It is hard to forgive him
at even this distance. His sublime folly in selecting
'The Romaunt of the Rose' and 'Troilus and Creseide' was
the precedent in our own literature of Shakespeare's
exactly similar preposterousness in meddling with 'Venus
and Adonis' and 'The Rape of Lucrece'. If the two men had
not lived to do other work, our two greatest, sweetest
literary names would have sunk to the bottom of the list,
drawing the eyes of posterity thither by a shameful glit-
ter of phrase.

Before going further, it may be as well to point out
how very small a portion of Chaucer's work decides the
special impression of him which now is historically trans-
mitted from generation to generation.

If it were possible to take away only little more than
a tenth part of the poet's voluminous writings, there
would be left a mass of outlandish recital having nothing
whatever to do with anything we now know of English
tastes. Instead of appearing a broad humourist, with an
overpowering love of nature, painting persons and scenes
with exact reality, there would then seem to be no English
poet so artificial, so romantic, so lackadaisical as
Chaucer. The truth is, that the literary associations for
which the mention of his name is the cue, belong to the
'Canterbury Tales' only. Even this is too large a statement. The 'Tales themselves, for the greater part, are as
outlandish as anything else in the works, although, speaking generally, they have some activity, some incident,
and, in so far, appeal to common sympathy. But if the
matchless Introduction had not been written, or had been
different, and if he had not included in the list two or
three of the stories, or not given prologues to the others,
Chaucer could not have survived in our literature. Of
course, there is a historical explanation for it all, only
it would be tedious to give it here in detail. Nor is it
wholly without honour for Chaucer. Put at its briefest,
the explanation is this: his object was to give Englishmen
a literature bodily, instantly as it were, by transferring
into our tongue, such as he found it and made it, the
famous achievements of the great foreign writers. The
upper circles of those he wrote for, though forming the
Court of England, could hardly be described as other than
foreigners; at any rate, they were of most artificial
tastes, and the highly-spiced borrowings from France and
Italy were meant for that class in the first place. What
is most wonderful is, that in spite of this endless translating, Chaucer could still keep for a part of his other
work the homelier but keener vein of English thinking so
pure. For in the prefatory portion of 'The Canterbury
Tales' are the roots of what is special in our literature.
If anyone was asked to describe that specialty, he would
very likely say - It is a robust kind of humour eager to
note failure, doing this originally in a spirit of fun,
but rising, ever-and-again, into short flights of pathos;
the opposite feelings being so truly mixed as to answer to
a perfect pictorial characterisation of human life from a
point of critical superiority, but of a resigned acceptance of it as good enough, or nearly so, when recognised
to be imperfect. The kind criticism is, at bottom, so

wide and liberal that it is a sort of natural religion, a
mild sympathy being taught in the very midst of the
laughter, out of which a large forgiving goodness is to
grow without much effort. This spirit of English literature is now called Shakespearian, and it must be so by
reason of Shakespeare sharing its impulses more largely
still. But with strict historical accuracy it might for
a moment be styled Chaucerian; and, indeed, if there had
been exact criticism in Shakespeare's lifetime, his work
at the first must have been christened after Chaucer.
Both by bulk and fineness the later poet in the end makes
good his superiority, for the quantity of this excellence
in Chaucer is not great. His best things, however, are
the most English things yet written in our language.
The point need not be dwelt on further. Our business
here is instantly to narrow all we have been saying into
the statement, that, with the above exceptions, Chaucer's
writings are a lackadaisical exaggeration of one feeling -
Love, and that in them the passion is taken in its weakest, vainest form of sentimentality. He is, and for ever
will remain, the chief erotic poet of our language.
Simply from the growing multiplicity of motives in human
life, and the increase in the general business of existence, the sexual instinct must lose part of its sway in
literature. It had far fewer competitors in the days of
Chaucer, but he availed himself of it to the very utmost.
Tom Moore's very modern treatment of love was only
meagre and occasional alongside Chaucer's use of the
topic; Herrick's lyrics, in comparison, could only be
called the merest momentary snatches; Byron's ostenta-
tious dark dallying with the theme was only desultory
trifling contrasted with Chaucer's industry in celebrat-
ing the relations of the sexes. This is the true description he gives of himself(1) to Rosiall in 'The Court
of Love': -

> In art of love I write, and songes make
> That may be sung in honour of the king
> And queue of love.
> Lines 898-900.

His surviving stock of versification reckons up to
nearly 48,000 lines - a long day's labour, especially if
we take into account the small stock of words there then
was for rhyming. Out of this grand total 'The Romaunt of
the Rose' and 'Troilus and Creseide' make 16,000 lines.
These are the only objectionable writings of the sentimental kind; the wrong-doing in 'The Canterbury Tales' is
simple rough indecency - a scandalous use of low comic

incident for the sake of broad merriment. In these other
highly ornate translations, the spirit is that of the
Italian and French erotics. The former poem, 'The Romaunt
of the Rose', taken, as everybody knows, from the French,
admits, it has been hinted, of being moralised; but for
this you would have to treat it as a fable twice symbo-
lised, and it labours under the drawback that the first
interpretation would be indecent. One is glad to mention
that, as Chaucer's imperfect version now stands, some of
the worst passages are left out. But the fact remains
that he allotted to this task the spinning of 7,700 lines;
that is, it stands for more than an eighth part of all his
rhythmical doings. When every mitigation has been urged,
surprise is still left. The marvel increases on turning
to the second of these his two great achievements.
'Troilus and Creseide' is a poem of which nobody has yet
ventured to hint that it is a sermon in disguise. The
moral is more completely hidden than in 'The Romaunt of
the Rose'; in fact, everybody knows that it has none. It
is a poem having to do with wantons, bad being made worse
by the interposition of Pandarus, whose name furnishes
the most disgraceful christening of human works. In this
piece Chaucer had Boccace for his master, but he so dwelt
upon his work that his variations and additions make the
poem longer than the original by above 2,700 lines. It
was a subject which could not be either varied or amplified into morality, and, fortunately, there could scarcely
be any adding to its badness. Chaucer simply made it
more, without making it any worse or any better. The
five cantos contain 8,193 lines. The giving of 16,000
lines to such topics as these is amazing, not to say preposterous. But this, luckily, does not nearly exhaust
Chaucer's love-poetry. The rest, if anyone had the rough
unfeelingness to say it, might be said to be sillier than
what we have been speaking of, since from it the politico-
ecclesiastical satire, which is the one redeeming feature
of 'The Romaunt of the Rose', has nearly quite vanished,
while the hard philosophy of worldly wisdom sprinkled
liberally throughout 'Troilus and Creseide', has dis-
appeared wholly. In their stead, Chaucer's own pieces
offer only the vainest exaggeration of a natural personal
liking of a man for a woman, or a woman for a man, refined
by a meditative contemplation of a general inscrutable
excellence in the idol, until not a trace of the scent of
flesh remains in the passion; the words simply from pointing to nothing to be done, save an aimless impractical
worship of sex on either side, giving off, from mere
excess of feeling purely heated, a perfume as sound and
sweet and keen as cedar. But that is a point to be made

clear later. First, let us run over the list without much
heeding this inner quality.

Of not a few of the pieces, the title sufficiently
tells the tale. The 'Court of Love', which makes 1,400
lines, is an imitation of 'The Romaunt of the Rose'. It
is absolutely decent, which, in the circumstances, is a
great merit; but, if we except a fine thin vein of humour
in it, and pass by all its passages of delicate poetry, it
might be said to be as unreal as its model. 'The Complaint of Pity', in so far as it now has any intelligi-
bility, is an appeal against the cruelty of love refused;
the only subject being a fanciful conceit, which was sufficient for literature in those days, though far from
being so now, to the effect that Pity is dead and buried
in a gentle heart. The piece headed 'Of Queen Annelida and
and False Arcite' is a very sentimental ditty; it being
the lady this time, and not, as in 'Troilus and Creseide',
the gentleman, who is the victim. The description of
Queen Annelida, 'Queen of Ermony,' is not without some
artful strokes. But her woeful epistle may be put as a
companion piece to the 'Letter of Troilus'; they both are
exemplifications of that astounding maudlin air of which we
shall have to speak again. In the 'Assembly of Fowles' we
have a parable about St. Valentine's Day, and the choosing
of mates. 'The Complaint of the Black Knight' is all that
he cannot win his lady's grace. In 'The Booke of the
Dutchesse' the woe arises in a way a little more natural,
since the mourner has lost his idol by death, but his own
feelings had already nearly killed him in the wooing of
her. 'Chaucer's Dream' comes to him while

In May, I lay upon a night
Alone, and on my lady thought. - Lines 8-9.

Within the marvellous isle to which he goes in sleep, the
adventures and the catastrophe all relate to love. 'The
Flower and the Leaf,' whatever be its intended moral, has
for its obvious theme the sexual relation. A sufficient
explanation is given of 'The Complaint of Mars and Venus',
by the names brought together in the title. 'The Cuckoo
and the Nightingale' is another bird fable, of which the
first phrase is that well-worn one - 'The God of Love.'

In this hurried mention we have nearly got through the
list of the works; but, if in what remains, the monotonous
topic varies a little, there is still much of the old
vein. 'The Legend of Good Women' seems to be meant to
supply the defect pointed out by 'The Wife of Bath'. That
merry lady says, with a strength of phrase not too small
for a gentleman -

By God, if wimmen hadden written stories,
As clerkes han, within hir oratories,
They wold have writ of men more wikkednesse
Than all the merke of Adam may redresse. - Lines 6275-8.

Chaucer, in the prologue to the 'Legend', is ordered by
the god himself -

Thou shalt while that thou livest, yere by yere,
The most partie of thy time spende
In making of a glorious legende
Of good women, maidenes and wives,
That weren trewe in loving all hir lives,
And tell of false men that hem betraien. - Lines 481-6.

It is still love, though only the sadness of it in its
catastrophes.

If we now turn back for a moment to 'The Canterbury
Tales', we have only to put aside 'The Knighte's Tale',
'The Man of Lawe's Tale', and 'The Clerke's Tale', the
stories meant to be utterly tragic, and we shall find the
very opposite aspect of the passion given. In the place
of the sentimentality, there is hard realism of the coar-
sest, commonest kind in literature. Out of the twenty-
two pieces, nine have love in some sort for their direct
theme - sad, wicked, or farcical; and 'The Coke's Tale',
if it had not been cut short, promised to make a bad
tenth. To complete our rough survey (leaving out the
prose piece, 'The Tale of Melibeus'), we have to add to
the other twelve tales, which may be classed as stories
of adventure, 'The House of Fame', which, however, is
not wholly without allusions to love; 'Chaucer's A.B.C.';
and the half-score trifles of the minor poems. That is
absolutely all, out of the marvellous mass of Chaucer's
work, which escapes the monotony of this one feeling. At
least, two-thirds of his life-long labours were about
love, having no other motive or inspiration whatever. He
was himself fully aware of this, for the *Man of Lawe,* in
the prologue, speaking of Chaucer by name, says -

For he hath told of lovers up and down,
Mo than Ovide made of mentioun. - Lines 4473-4.

So far as to the quantity of the love-poetry; the
quality, however, is of more significance and interest
still. Later we will show that there is a faint play of
comic wit throughout the sad treatment of the topic; but
for every satirical or droll line Chaucer wrote of love,
he penned fifty of the most artificial melancholy which

English words, with a good eking out of French, Italian,
and Latin phrases, could take on. It is this incredible
sentimentality of Chaucer we are seeking for a moment
again to bring into remembrance.

A vague notion exists, that as love is a fixed fact of
human nature, its mode is also fixed, with only, in each
community, some little peculiarity arising from difference of race. Nothing can be further from the truth of
history. At present, in European society, love's ceremonial has dwindled to nothing; though it is, perhaps, in
England that it has most utterly lost all regulative etiquette. The one lingering formality of being closeted for
ten painful moments with the lady's papa in a room called
his own, is no longer absolutely required. What has to be
said has been known to be blurted out in riding to-or-from
the meet of hounds, or when sitting on the lawn in front
of the house, or in walking in the garden. A word with
mamma, in some cases which require to be made very easy,
will even substitute the set interview with the male head
of the family altogether. The elder gentleman afterwards
makes a joke to the younger about it, and all is considered settled. At the actual, critical, decisive scene
between the young people there is still, in most instances, a specialty of manner - something of the nervousness
of prior generations of ancestral wooers yet lingeringly
survives in a womanly blush on one side, a passing pallor
on the other. But as soon as the indispensable question
has been asked and aswered, the diffidence tumbles into
the blankest familiarity. That antique exaggeration of
the sexual feeling which made distant approaches, gradual
advances, and long-sustained suspense, natural and necessary, is gone; no longer is a sigh an incident, a glance
an episode, the touch of two hands fate, and a spoken
refusal a life's catastrophe. It has all shrunk into the
buying and giving of an engaged ring, worn with bold ost-
entatiousness. The old highly elaborated organisation of
the feeling is thought nonsense by those who would be
none the worse for a little of its emotional heightening.
But between that stately ceremonial and the present bald-
ness of manner, there have been all intermediate degrees
of decay and lessening. Now we are arrived at this point,
that the distinction of the sexes can scarcely any longer
be said to have a sentimental value; a physiological difference is, perforce, recognised; but it is a politico-
economical arrangement, which counts for nothing further.
Chaucer knew nothing of this. In the greater part of his
poetry, love is at its most picturesque height; the inter-
communication of men and women is of the style of romance;
wooing has a set ritual. We do not say that the mode of

the passion he pictures was really in full English use
at any time - rather, we confess, that there is a good
deal about it of a foreign air. But, at least, the style
was sufficiently domesticated here to be popularly available for literature. Amazing as it is, we have to suppose that this meditative, do-nothing fashion of love, at
one time had a real interest for our ancestors.

Chaucer's presentation of it may be hastily given
thus: - Love is a fatal necessity. In 'The Knighte's
Tale', at the first dispute between Palamon and Arcite
over Emelie in the garden, the point is stated by Arcite -

> A man moste nedes love maugre his hed,
> He may not fleen it, though he shuld be ded.
> > - Lines 1171-2.

No detailed explanation is given of the cause of this portentous obligation, further than a general mythological
celebration of the power of the god of love. In a later
passage of the same tale, he makes Duke Theseus say, in
amazement -

> The god of love, a! *benedicite,*
> How mighty and how grete a lord is he? - Lines 1788-9.

And, in a still more lengthy eulogy, with which 'The
Cuckow and the Nightingale' opens, it is affirmed -

> Shortly, all that ever he woll he may. - Line 16.

This is all we are told. The passion is left as a large
natural excitement; it is somehow part of the world's
great agitations; but, as in the birds and other creatures, it has a special reference to the almanack. An
access of it comes in the month of May. From 'The Cuckow
and the Nightingale' we take this passage -

> For every true gentle herte free

> *   *   *   *   *   *

> Againe May now shall have some stering,
> Or to joy, or els to some mourning. - Lines 21-24.

A great modern poet has somewhat revived this rustic tradition. Mr. Tennyson says it is in spring that young
men's thoughts most lightly turn to love. But we believe
that these calendar appointments no longer strictly hold
good.

The excitement, whenever or however it comes, is so
natural that a personal selection is not needed to inspire
it.   In 'The Court of Love', where he makes himself the
exemplar, Chaucer, on arriving before the Queen, simply
prays her -

> Of thy grace,
> Me to bestow now in some blessed place. - Lines 636-7.

Directly, he adds -

> For hote I love, determine in no place. - Line 646.

And although he goes on to mention a vision of a lady in a
dream, saying -

> Might iche her know, her would I faine, God wot,
> Serve and obey with all benignitie. - Lines 660-1,

he winds up with, if -

> that no wise I shall her never see,
> Than graunt me her that best may liken me.
>   - Lines 662-3.

He adds, despite this indeterminateness -

> Great is the paine which at mine herte doth sticke,
> Till I be sped by thine election. - Lines 673-4.

Indeed, in some places, yet more mysterious hints are
scattered.   At the beginning of Canto V. of 'Troilus and
Creseide', Diomede tells the frail Creseide -

> For I have heard or this of many a wight,
> Hath loved thing he never saw his live. - Lines 164-5.

At 'Love's Court' there was a crowd of unallotted persons
suffering these vague pangs.   They are, in these terms,
bid to seek the temple of the goddess: -

> And ye that ben unpurveyed, pray her eke
> Comfort you soon. - Lines 561-62.

But the whole case is still better stated by the Black
Knight in 'The Booke of the Dutchesse'.   He says he did
'homage' to love -

>   Long, and many a yere
>   (Ere that my herte was set o' where)
>   That I did thus and n'ist why,
>   I trowe it came me kindely. - Lines 774-7.

He even regrets that he, in some way, came short of the
requirements -

>   Full little good I couth,
>   For all my werkes were flitting
>   That time, and all my thought varying,
>   All were to me ylicke good. - Lines 800-3.

There is something in this, we doubt, which does not
sound like perfect innocence. It looks very real.
     But the vagueness only holds good of the preliminary
period and stage. Once the true selection is made, it is
always fatal - at least, on one side. The general predis-
position does not lessen the shock of the falling in love
in the final instance in any degree. When it comes, it
occurs with such precipitation as makes it done certainly
once for all. A single look is enough. No sooner does
Philobene lead Chaucer into 'that chamber gay' of Love's
Court where Rosiall was, than the -

>   sotell piercing of her eye,
>   Mine herte gan thrill for beauty in the stound,
>   'Alas' (quod I), 'who hath me yeve this wound?'
>   - Lines 768-71.

But bad as this is, the case of Palamon, in 'The Knighte's
Tale', is almost more suddenly worse. Looking out of his
prison in the tower, he catches a glimpse of Emelie walking in the garden, instantly -

>   He blent and cried, a!
>   As though he stongen were unto the herte.
>   - Lines 1079-80.

Palamon's companion fares no better. He looks on the same
fatal lady -

>   And with a sigh, he saide pitously,
>   The fresshe beautee sleth me sodenly. - Lines 1118-19.

The like thing happens to the knight in 'The Booke of the
Dutchesse'. No other words than 'wounds,' 'stinging,' and
'slaying,' would do; even these fail to give the whole
disaster. For if we go now to the effects of the passion

on the male lover, they are awful. The first symptom is
thus described in 'The Court of Love', as felt by Chaucer
himself -

I drede to speak. - Line 771.

So with the lover in 'The Booke of the Dutchesse' -

> She wist it nought,
> Ne tell her durst I not my thought. - Lines 1186-7.

The very first effect of the passion, so soon as it becomes actual in a real confronting of the parties, might
be described in the male as a glorification of a great new
sense of shame, arising from unworthiness. The misery
into which the man is plunged is complete; perfect,
unmitigated woe is the only account which can be given of
the matter. For a male human being to fall in love is
instantly to become wretched in a very vague but absolutely undefective way. The calamity is, at the same time,
swift and lingering....
   (p. 289) The fuller consequences are given in 'The
Knighte's Tale', when speaking of Arcite: -

> His slepe, his mete, his drinke is him byraft,
> That lene he wex, and drie as is a shaft,
> His eyen holwe, and grisly to behold,
> His hewe falwe, and pale as ashen cold. - Lines 1363-6.

A briefer summary occurs in 'The Romaunt of the Rose' -

> Certes, no woe ne may attaine
> Unto the sore of love's pain. - Lines 2744-5.

The account of Arcite, in 'The Knight's Tale', goes on -

> Whan he endured had a yere or two,
> This cruel torment, and this peine and wo.
> > - Lines 1383-4.

For, again, it must be noted that, no matter how irres-
pective and general the feeling was in the preliminary
stage, no sooner is the allotted person met than it turns
into the utmost particularity. Only the special lady who
gave the dreadful wound can heal it. The third statute of
love's code, as given in 'The Court of Love', runs -

Withouten chaunge to live and die the same,
None other love to take for wele ne wo,
For blind delite, for ernest, nor for game;
Without repent for laughing or for grame,
To bidden still in full perseveraunce. - Lines 317-21.

In a word, the position held by the woman in this
incredible style of love seems at first sight to be one of
utter advantage. 'The Legend of Good Women' sadly gives
the other aspect of their fortune, but the tragedy arises
later than this stage. In these earliest moments the
worship to be rendered by the male would be excessive if
offered to a goddess. To the woman, merely as such, is
ascribed an ideal superiority which is in no way
explained; it comes to her naturally, from sex. Her
great all-sufficiency of merit is, that she fixes love.
Eventually, she is herself involved, but during the preliminary period she is almighty. Not that anything like
coquetry is brought into play; her maintenance of reserve
is enough. It is not quite easy to say whether this is
instigated by a doubt of the continuance of power, or if
it arises from a naturally instinctive hesitation of
modesty. The woman does not seem to enjoy any intense
gratification from her power; only in one case is there
rejoicing in the cruelty. In 'The Complaint of the Black
Knight', one of the moanings of that prodigy of sentimentality very rightly is -

And most of all I me complaine,
That she hath joy to laugh at my paine. - Lines 427-8.

But, though that is a wholly exceptional instance, the
man must always be abject in his suit to the lady. Not
only has he to lose self-possession, he must abandon all
self-respect; his humiliation is condemned to sink as low
as wretchedness. He has to ask for 'mercy;' or rather, as
the Black Knight puts it, for 'grace, mercie, and pity.'
Troilus, when Creseide visits him -

Lo, the alderfirst word that him astart,
Was twice, 'Mercy, mercy, O, my sweet herte.'
          'T. and C.,' B. III., lines 97-8.

Chaucer himself, in 'The Court of Love,' appeals to
Rosiall -

Ah mercy herte, my lady and my love! - Line 967.

Indeed, the whole code of laws set forth in 'The Court of

Love', if a suspicion of intended burlesque were not suggested by the vein of comic humour in some of the statutes,
prescribes a manner of behaviour for a male wooer which
would be a trifle too humble in a beaten spaniel. Fortunately, for our interest in the heroines, they do not
themselves seem to be aware of this unintelligible natural
worth in the woman, which makes it a high offence, to be
expiated by sighs and dread, for a man to lift his eyes
to her....

(p. 291) It hardly needs pointing out that the style of
love here is as far as possible removed from chivalry.
Actual achievement in some real way for the purpose of
showing manly worth is not dreamt of. On the contrary,
it is deliberately put aside. In 'The Booke of the Dutchesse', the asking for feats to be performed is simply
ridiculed. One trait in the description of the peerless
lady is that -

She ne used no soch knackes smale. - Line 1030.

In place of anything of this sort, a new proof is asked,
that of experiencing wretchedness of heart for the lady,
without (if we except 'The Knighte's Tale' in 'The Canterbury Tales') any attempt at action. So soon as the man
swoons from the sheer stress of his own feelings, that is
enough; but swoon he must. Nearly all Chaucer's heroes
faint. The black knight in the poem with that title
swoons; so does the other knight in 'The Booke of the
Dutchesse'; so does Chaucer himself in 'The Court of
Love'; so does the prince in 'Chaucer's Dream'.

There is, indeed, a suggestion that some moral quality
which the women greatly admire, is brought to light by
this test of woe. Creseide says -

Ne pompe, array, nobley, or eke richesse,
Ne made me to rue on your distresse,
But moral virtue, grounded upon trouth.
    'T. and C., ' B. IV., lines 1668-70.

But the metaphysical morality is rather high for this
light lady. The fact of sufficient distress, however,
always tells....

Still, if there is this silly, sentimental excess in
the passion on both sides, there is not a trace of
immorality. This is the specific characteristic of the
true Chaucerian erotics. If we except 'Troilus and
Creseide', there is in all these poems outside 'The Canterbury Tales' no wrongdoing whatever. The feeling is
left without any practical motive of the ordinary kind.

This superfine style of wooing has no necessary reference
to marriage; there is not a hint given anywhere of the
common family relations; no children are seen in all this
world or romance. The connection is rather an affair to
be kept secret; that, in fact, is one of the set duties
which are prescribed....
       The one capital crime is to be an 'avaunter.' Against
that chiefest vice, Pandarus himself piously utters denunciations. The matter so excites him that he hotly
exclaims -

    Avauntour and a lier, all is one. - Line 309, B.III.

But the aimless, inexplicable morals most pretentiously
enforced amidst it all need more fully bringing into view.
The original doctrine on which everything rests is, that
it is a state of wickedness not to pay service to Love.
How queer the thing is will be seen, when we say that
Pandarus may be taken as the faith's prophet. This is how
he addresses Troilus, in Book I. of 'Troilus and Creseide'
Creseide': -

            Sith Love of his goodnesse
    Hath thee converted out of wickednesse.
                - Lines 999, 1000.

The very greatest things are said of Love continually. In
'The Court of Love' this is part of a ritual which is
chanted -

    Love is exiler aye of vice and sinne. - Line 598.

At the commencement of 'The Cuckow and the Nightingale',
it is claimed for Love, among many other things, that he
'destroyes vice'. And later in the same poem, in opposing
the cuckoo's ribald version of the matter, the nightingale
gives full details -

            thereof truly commeth all goddnesse,
    All honour, and all gentleness. - Lines 151-2.

Nor is it only mere theorising; personal exemplars are
given. Even in the queer case of Troilus, the influence
works in the following way:

            his manner tho forth aye
    So goodly was, and gat him so in grace,
    That eche him loved that looked in his face,
    For he became the friendliest wight,

> The gentilest, and eke the most free,
> The thriftiest *   *   *   *
> Dead were his japes and his cruelte,
> His high port and his manner straunge,
> And eche of hem gan for a vertue chaunge.
>   'T. and C.', B.I., lines 1075-85.

In Book III., when his desires had full prosperity, he, in self-wonder at this process, says -

> I n'ot myself not wisely, what it is,
> But nowe I feele a new quality,
> Ye all another than I did er this.
>   B. III., lines 1654-7.

The second Book has what is called 'A Trojan Song', which Antigone sings; its burden is the same.
The proem to Book III. puts the matter still more generally. It is there asserted of Love that his function is -

>   Ye maken hertes digne:
> Algates hem that ye woll set a fire,
> They dreden shame and vices they resigne,
> Ye doen him curteis be, fresh, and benigne.
>   - Lines 23-6.

In the stanzas coming just before, as previously in 'The Knighte's Tale', and in a number of other places, the office of Love is enlarged till it stands for everything else. A scheme of natural physics, as well as a moral philosophy, is got from it, Love having an empire given it over beast, fish, and green tree, besides over man; it being, in fact, made to do for gravitation, chemical affinity, and we know not what. By an anticipation of a rather modern theory, it holds together all that is. Into this mysticism we need not go. We have only to do with the plain ethical part of the subject. Love himself, in 'The Romaunt of the Rose', gives up a whole day to teaching systematic rules of conduct. We can only give a few sentences; the first can be made comprehensive.

> 'Villanie at the beginning,
> I woll,' sayd Love, 'over all things
> Thou leave.'   - Lines 2175-7.

> For nothing eke thy tongue applie
> To speke words of ribauldrie.
>   *   *   *   *   *

> Looke fro pride thou keepes thee wele,
>
> *   *   *   *   *   *
>
> Alway with good chere
> Thou yeve, if thou have richesse,
> And if thou have nought spend the lesse.
>
> - Lines 2223-74.

Perhaps we had better skip some very homely particulars
which follow. The wooer is not only bid wear the best of
clothing 'his rent affordeth,' but he is told how points
and sleeves should be shaped, how boots and gloves should
fit. The prescriptions even descend to such details as
the washing of hands, the paring of nails, the cleansing
of teeth, the combing of the hair - all excellent advice
if it was really needed, but still not tragical. It goes
to present the woman under a fastidious, if not a trivial,
aspect. Still worse remains. Counsels are given how the
lady, instead of being won by the mysterious inner moral
worth of the male, is to be influenced by accomplishments
in him, by his good riding and sweet singing. Reference
is even made to the wisdom of his offering presents, not
only to the idol herself, but also to the maid. This is a
sad falling away from the high sentimental ideal. After
such worldly wisdom has been brought in, it only half
affects us when the lover is again warned of his woe in
weighty words....

(p. 295) If all these requirements, conditions, and
prescriptions be taken together, the scheme which they
make up certainly has to be pronounced moral. They are
not the erotics of self-indulgence in any way, but of
self-denial. The adherence to a single choice, and this
industry of observance towards a woman, form one of the
most perfect tests of male character conceivable. There
is as much talk about 'diligence' and 'business' in this
love-making as if it was by it men saved their souls.
Nobody, indeed, would have had to go further than 'The
Romaunt of the Rose' itself to find in the long dialogue
between 'Raison' and 'L'Amant' the most perfect discipline of temperance taught.

This, then, is Chaucer's higher literary presentation
of love - that which purports to be his poetical version
of it. Everybody will see that light and darkness are not
much further apart than it is from the coarse humour of
'The Canterbury Tales', where the married man is always
made sport of. Nor does it any better agree with the rendering given of love in the 'Minor Poems', for love is
incidentally discussed there. Strangely enough, marriage
is treated worse there than in the 'Tales', since what is
said pretends to be said a little more seriously.

'L'Envoy de Chaucer à Bukton' puts into rhyme St. Paul's
advice upon the subject. Alongside those hard-headed
views, the huge weak sentimentality of these other poems
grows more-and-more amazing. It is true that, if it
should be asked whether this artificiality in the delineation of the feeling is always consistently maintained at
its full height, we must answer - no. The answer was
hinted beforehand, some pages back. Not only does it
break down by an unskilful mingling with the sad heroics
of some incongruous advice of craft in wooing, but, in
Chaucer's own compositions especially, the beautiful folly
of it all is adulterated by flashes of common sense,
enlivened by a perpetual recurrence of gay wit, which,
although for most readers it may be greatly hidden by the
awful prolixity, is still there. The irresistible
sprightliness, now-and-again, so soon as it busies itself
really with details, tends even towards wantonness. It
was part of our plan to show that Chaucer's comic muse
swayed him in those ways in the most artificial parts of
his work. But we have not space left for it. If we
meddled with that aspect of the matter, then, after the
fun, it would be needed, in order to bring back this
paper to its proper and natural sentimental key, that we
should give, as a full and final example of the higher
Chaucerian erotics, the account in 'The Booke of the
Dutchesse' of the mournful Knight's wooing and winning of
the sweetest lady ever talked of in English words - she
in whom

Every day her beauty newed,

and who

             List so well to live
    That *dulness was of her afrade,*
    She n'as to sobre ne to glad.

Let the reader turn for himself to the splendid sketch.
It is to the surprising fact of male maudlin having so
well satisfied our oldest popular poet for a literary
subject, that we must come back for a moment.

What is the deliberate judgment to be given of the
value of this treatment of the topic of love? A good many
qualifications and deductions would have to be made before
we got to what would at last be left for Chaucer in the
way of clear merit. Obviously it is not any more in
spirit than in form a lyrical dealing with the subject.
For though the feeling is often highly-wrought, there are
no sufficiently short issues of success or failure, nor

any defined connections with locally marked-off scenes or
occasions, requiring or admitting of brief triumphal or
pathetic celebrations. On the other hand, it is not a
dramatic mode of treatment. There is no progressive
action, no interposition of any third person, no compli-
cating by mistake or malice. Two individuals only are
confronted with one another, there being nothing in the
way of incident beyond the postponement on one side or
the other of personal liking. This has never been found
enough of tragedy to satisfy a public. All the poesy in
the pieces arises from an excited meditation on an inscrutable superiority really referable to nothing but difference of sex, this excellence instantly appearing in the
idol so soon as she specially challenges the male's attention, her only but incalculable merit being that she fixes
liking. It is the old wonder of sex, not admitting of
more explanation. But Chaucer took the fact at its cru-
dest and its narrowest, and so exaggerated it that every
man brought by him into these love-poems abjectly breaks
down under its weight. His delineation answers to only a
short part of the passion's career. Really, it is a
glorification of a few of the physiological phenomena of
the first stage of a first juvenile excitement, and the
transfer of them to adults has, to adult men, a childish
air. For Chaucer's characters do not give the impression
of juvenility; they are grown-up people, the males among
them behaving like moon-calfs. And here we come upon the
one excellence of Chaucer in these sentimental pieces -
that which redeems all, saving them from insipidity and
idleness. It is only the men who are noodles. The
women not only are not girls, but they do not behave as
such. They are perfectly able to take care of themselves.
Not one of them is pictured as having a mother to look
after her; not one of them needs any such guardianship.
The personal descriptions given of them are not those of
sylphs, or supernatural beings, of any kind. They are
sound-hearted, clear-headed, lovely English maidens, who,
if ever the matter went as far as marriage, would make
admirable wives, and soon cure their males of maudlin, by
requiring in its stead manly respect as shown in the full
discharge of family duties. It is the utter absence of
domesticity, and of everything pointing clearly towards
it, which makes this class of the Chaucerian poems
unreal. But the women themselves are the very ladies
whom Shakespeare met long after, and happily matched with
more reasonable and bolder lovers. The perfume sound,
and sweet, and keen as that of cedar, which we earlier
spoke of as being given forth from these poems, is from
the breathing of these noble maidens, the poetic types of

the women of our race.

The silly presentation of men in the poems must have had something to do with the great neglect into which the pieces have undoubtedly fallen, in spite of their merits. Men could not for ever go on reading what made them ridiculous. How it is that the women have not kept the compositions more in vogue, rests on reasons of other kinds. Chaucer has scared them with other parts of his work very different in style. But though they can never forgive him for having placed them under suspicion, that does not do away the fact that nothing was ever written so complimentary to the sex as the poems we have been dealing with. It is even doubtful whether his substitution of the suffering by the males of misery on mere sexual grounds will not secretly commend itself more to many women than the opposite chivalric spirit of being won by the men through the men doing something. The sense of being able to give pain and pleasure for no reason save that of being what you are - a woman, and fair, - inspiring liking without effort, so being worshipped in any case, could not be other than dear to the female heart. Males find gratification in it whenever the fatal faculty happens to be allotted the other way. In not a little of our very successful literature to-day, traces of the Chaucerian erotics give what seems to be the only possible explanation of the popularity with feminine readers. Nobody, however, could now venture on Chaucer's exaggeration of the fact of sex. His use of it has to be left an antique silliness to be wondered at for ever, because of the priceless beauty of its setting. The historical value of the pieces should increase, since there is no doubt that, in modern Christianised civilisation, the influence of sex is waning. Fade past a certain limit it, of course, cannot, or the race must pass with it. There can never come a time when the young man will not foolishly but sweetly ascribe boundless desert to some fair girl simply for not being another youth like himself, but a different creature, longer-haired, finer-limbed, and sweeter-faced, with a gentler heart. But if the maiden herself could have acquaintance with these parts of the oldest of the great poets of her language, she might sigh in thinking that she could not now make the young man so miserable through his liking as it was poetically pretended women could make men in Chaucer's time.

Note

1 The Chaucer critics reject this poem, but as we are not writing a *critical* paper we cannot afford to forego so much good material.

23.   ADOLPHUS WILLIAM WARD, DRAMATIST AND NOVELIST

1879

Sir Adolphus William Ward (1837-1924), educated at Peter-
house, Cambridge, famous for its interest in Chaucer in
the sixteenth century, was a distinguished academic, and
scholar of English and of European history, at Manchester
and Cambridge. His view of Chaucer as dramatist and novelist sums up the emphasis developed since Dryden, and is
frequently repeated in the twentieth century. The extract
is from pp. 146ff. of 'Chaucer' (1879), in the series
English Men of Letters.

(p. 146) One very pleasing quality in Chaucer must have
been his modesty. In the course of his life this may have
helped to recommend him to patrons so many and so various,
and to make him the useful and trustworthy agent that he
evidently became for confidential missions abroad. Physically, as has been seen, he represents himself as prone to
the habit of casting his eyes on the ground; and we may
feel tolerably sure that to this external manner corres-
ponded a quiet, observant disposition, such as that which
may be held to have distinguished the greatest of Chaucer's successors among English poets. To us, of course,
this quality of modesty in Chaucer makes itself princi-
pally manifest in the opinion which he incidentally shows
himself to entertain concerning his own rank and claims
as an author. Herein, as in many other points, a contrast
is noticeable between him and the great Italian masters,
who were so sensitive as to the esteem in which they and
their poetry were held. Who could fancy Chaucer crowned
with laurel, like Petrarch, or even, like Dante, speaking
with proud humility of 'the beautiful style that has done
honour to him,' while acknowledging his obligation for it
to a great predecessor? Chaucer again and again disclaims all boasts of perfection, or pretensions to pre-
eminence, as a poet. His Canterbury Pilgrims have in his
name to disavow, like Persius, having slept on Mount Par-
nassus, or possessing 'rhetoric' enough to describe a
heroine's beauty; and he openly allows that his spirit
grows dull as he grows older, and that he finds a difficulty as a translator in matching his rhymes to his French
original. He acknowledges as incontestable the

superiority of the poets of classical antiquity: -

>   - Little book, no writing thou envý,
>   But subject be to all true poësy,
>   And kiss the steps, where'er thou seest space
>   Of Virgil, Ovid, Homer, Lucan, Stace.

But more than this. In the 'House of Fame' he expressly
disclaims having in his light and imperfect verse sought
to pretend to 'mastery' in the art poetical; and in a
charmingly expressed passage of the 'Prologue' to the
'Legend of Good Women' he describes himself as merely
following in the wake of those who have already reaped
the harvest of amorous song, and have carried away the
corn: -

>   And I come after, gleaning here and there,
>   And am full glad if I can find an ear
>   Of any goodly word that ye have left.

Modesty of this stamp is perfectly compatible with a
certain self-consciousness which is hardly ever absent
from greatness, and which at all events supplies a stimulus not easily dispensed with except by sustained effort
on the part of a poet. The two qualities seem naturally
to combine into that self-containedness (very different
from self-contentedness) which distinguishes Chaucer, and
which helps to give to his writings a manliness of tone,
the direct opposite of the irretentive querulousness
found in so great a number of poets in all times. He
cannot indeed be said to maintain an asbolute reserve
concerning himself and his affairs in his writings; but
as he grows older, he seems to become less and less
inclined to take the public into his confidence, or to
speak of himself except in a pleasantly light and incidental fashion. And in the same spirit he seems, without
ever folding his hands in his lap, or ceasing to be a busy
man and an assiduous author to have grown indifferent to
the lack of brilliant success in life, whether as a man of
letters or otherwise. So at least one seems justified in
interpreting a remarkable passage in the 'House of Fame',
the poem in which perhaps Chaucer allows us to see more
deeply into his mind than in any other.

[Quotes lines 1871-82.]

With this modest but manly self-possession we shall not
go far wrong in connecting what seems another very distinctly marked feature of Chaucer's inner nature. He

seems to have arrived at a clear recognition of the truth
with which Goethe humorously comforted Eckermann in the
shape of the proverbial saying, 'Care has been taken that
the trees shall not grow into the sky.' Chaucer's, there
is every reason to believe, was a contented faith, as far
removed from self-torturing unrest as from childish credu-
lity. Hence his refusal to trouble himself, now that he
has arrived at a good age, with original research as to
the constellations. (The passage is all the more significant since Chaucer, as has been seen, actually possessed
a very respectable knowledge of astronomy.) That winged
encyclopaedia, the Eagle, has just been regretting the
poet's unwillingness to learn the position of the Great
and the Little Bear, Castor and Pollux, and the rest,
concerning which at present he does not know where they
stand. But he replies, 'No matter,'

> - It is no need;
> I trust as well (so God me speed!)
> Them that write of this matter,
> As though I knew their places there.

Moreover, as he says (probably without implying any special allegorical meaning), they seem so bright that it
would destroy my eyes to look upon them. Personal inspection, in his opinion, was not necessary for a faith which
at some times may, and at others must, take the place of
knowledge....
   (p. 152) If he had strong political opinions of his
own, or strong personal views on questions either of
ecclesiastical policy or of religious doctrine - in which
assumptions there seems nothing probable - he at all
events did not wear his heart on his sleeve, or use his
poetry, allegorical or otherwise, as a vehicle of his
wishes, hopes, or fears on these heads. The true breath
of freedom could hardly be expected to blow through the
precincts of a Plantagenet court. If Chaucer could write
the pretty lines in the 'Manciple's Tale' about the caged
bird and its uncontrollable desire for liberty, his contemporary Barbour could apostrophise Freedom itself as a
noble thing, in words the simple manliness of which stirs
the blood after a very different fashion. Concerning his
domestic relations, we may regard it as virtually certain
that he was unhappy as a husband, though tender and
affectionate as a father. Considering how vast a proportion of the satire of all times - but more especially that
of the Middle Ages, and in these again pre-eminently of
the period of European literature which took its tone from
Jean de Meung - is directed against woman and against

married life, it would be difficult to decide how much of
the irony, sarcasm, and fun lavished by Chaucer on these
themes is due to a fashion with which he readily fell in,
and how much to the impulse of personal feeling. A perfect anthology, or perhaps one should rather say a complete herbarium, might be collected from his works of
samples of these attacks on women. He has manifestly
made a careful study of their ways, with which he now and
then betrays that curiously intimate acquaintance to which
we are accustomed in a Richardson or a Balzac. How accurate are such incidental remarks as this, that women are
'full measurable' in such matters as sleep - not caring
for so much of it at a time as men do! How wonderfully
natural is the description of Cressid's bevy of lady-
visitors, attracted by the news that she is shortly to be
surrendered to the Greeks, and of the 'nice vanity' -
i.e. foolish emptiness - of their consolatory gossip....
    (p. 154) But his satire against women is rarely so
innocent as this; and though several ladies take part in
the Canterbury Pilgrimage, yet pilgrim after pilgrim has
his saw or jest against their sex. The courteous *Knight*
cannot refrain from the generalisation that women all
follow the favour of fortune. The *Summoner*, who is of a
less scrupulous sort, introduces a diatribe against
women's passionate love of vengeance; and the *Shipman*
seasons a story which requires no such addition by an
enumeration of their favourite foibles. But the climax
is reached in the confessions of the *Wife of Bath*, who
quite unhesitatingly says that women are best won by
flattery and busy attentions; that when won they desire
to have the sovereignty over their husbands, and that
they tell untruths and swear to them with twice the
boldness of men; - while as to the power of their tongue,
she quotes the second-hand authority of her fifth husband
for the saying that it is better to dwell with a lion or
a foul dragon, than with a woman accustomed to chide. It
is true that this same *Wife of Bath* also observes with an
effective *tu quoque*: -

> By God, if women had but written stories,
> As clerkès have within their oratòries,
> They would have writ of men more wickednéss
> Than all the race of Adam may redress;

and the '*Legend of Good Women*' seems, in point of fact, to
have been intended to offer some such kind of amends as is
here declared to be called for. But the balance still
remains heavy against the poet's sentiments of gallantry
and respect for women. It should at the same time be

remembered that among the 'Canterbury Tales' the two which
are of their kind the most effective, constitute tributes
to the most distinctively feminine and wifely virtue of
fidelity. Moreover, when coming from such personages as
the pilgrims who narrate the 'Tales' in question, the
praise of women has special significance and value. The
Merchant and the *Shipman* may indulge in facetious or
coarse jibes against wives and their behaviour, but the
Man of Law, full of grave experience of the world, is a
witness above suspicion to the womanly virtue of which
his narrative celebrates to illustrious an example, while
the *Clerk of Oxford* has in his cloistered solitude, where
all womanly blandishments are unknown, come to the conclusion that

> Men speak of Job, most for his humbleness,
> As clerkës, when they list, can well indite,
> Of men in special; but, in truthfulness,
> Though praise by clerks of women be but slight,
> No man in humbleness can him acquit
> As women can, nor can be half so true
> As women are, unless all things be new.

As to marriage, Chaucer may be said generally to treat it
in that style of laughing with a wry mouth, which has
from time immemorial been affected both in comic writing
and on the comic stage, but which, in the end, even the
most determined old bachelor feels an occasional inclination to consider monotonous....

(p. 165) It may be said, without presumption, that such
a general view as this leaves ample room for all reasonable
theories as to the chronology and sequence, where these
remain more or less unsettled, of Chaucer's indisputably
genuine works. In any case, there is no poet whom, if
only as an exercise in critical analysis, it is more
interesting to study and re-study in connexion with the
circumstances of his literary progress. He still, as has
been seen, belongs to the Middle Ages, but to a period in
which the noblest ideals of these Middle Ages are already
beginning to pale and their mightiest institutions to
quake around him; in which learning continues to be in the
main scholasticism, the linking of argument with argument,
and the accumulation of authority upon authority, and
poetry remains to a great extent the crabbedness of clerks
or the formality of courts. Again, Chaucer is mediaeval
in tricks of style and turns of phrase; he often contents
himself with the tritest of figures and the most unre-
freshing of ancient devices, and freely resorts to a mixture of names and associations belonging to his own times

with others derived from other ages. This want of
literary perspective is a sure sign of mediaevalism, and
one which has amused the world, or has jarred upon it,
since the Renascence taught men to study both classical
and biblical antiquity as realities, and not merely as a
succession of pictures or of tapestries on a wall.
Chaucer mingles things mediaeval and things classical as
freely as he brackets King David with the philosopher
Seneca, or Judas Iscariot with the Greek 'dissimulator'
Sinon. His Dido, mounted on a stout palfrey paper white
of hue, with a red-and-gold saddle embroidered and
embossed, resembles Alice Perrers in all her pomp rather
than the Virgilian queen. Jupiter's eagle, the poet's
guide and instructor in the allegory of the 'House of
Fame', invokes 'Saint Mary, Saint James,' and 'Saint
Clare' all at once; and the pair of lovers at Troy sign
their letters '*la vostre T.*' and '*la vostre C.*' Anachronisms of this kind (of the danger of which, by the
way, to judge from a passage in the 'Prologue' to the
'Legend of Good Women', Chaucer would not appear to have
been wholly unconscious) are intrinsically of very slight
importance. But the morality of Chaucer's narratives is
at times the artificial and overstrained morality of the
Middle Ages, which, as it were, clutches hold of a single
idea to the exclusion of all others - a morality which,
when carried to its extreme consequences, makes mono-
maniacs as well as martyrs, in both of which species,
occasionally perhaps combined in the same persons, the
Middle Ages abound. The fidelity of Griseldis under the
trials imposed upon her by her, in point of fact, brutal
husband is the fidelity of a martyr to unreason. The
story was afterwards put on the stage in the Elizabethan
age; and though even in the play of 'Patient Grissil' (by
Chettle and others), it is not easy to reconcile the husband's proceedings with the promptings of common sense,
yet the playwrights, with the instinct of their craft,
contrived to introduce some element of humanity into his
character and of probability into his conduct. Again,
the supra-chivalrous respect paid by Arviragus, the Breton
knight of the 'Franklin's Tale', to the sanctity of his
wife's word, seriously to the peril of his own and his
wife's honour, is an effort to which probably even the
Knight of La Mancha himself would have proved unequal. It
is not to be expected that Chaucer should have failed to
share some of the prejudices of his times as well as to
fall in with their ways of thought and sentiment; and
though it is the *Prioress* who tells a story against the
Jews which passes the legend of Hugh of Lincoln, yet it
would be very hazardous to seek any irony in this legend

of bigotry. In general, much of that naïveté which to
modern readers seems Chaucer's most obvious literary
quality must be ascribed to the times in which he lived
and wrote. This quality is in truth by no means that
which most deeply impresses itself upon the observation
of any one able to compare Chaucer's writings with those
of his more immediate predecessors and successors. But
the sense in which the term naïf should be understood in
literary criticism is so imperfectly agreed upon among us,
that we have not yet even found an English equivalent for
the word.

To Chaucer's times, then, belongs much of what may at
first sight seem to include itself among the characteristics of his genius; while, on the other hand, there are
to be distinguished from these the influences due to his
training and studies in two literatures - the French and
the Italian. In the former of these he must have felt at
home, if not by birth and descent, at all events by social
connexion, habits of life, and ways of thought, while in
the latter he, whose own country's was still a half-
fledged literary life, found ready to his hand masterpieces of artistic maturity, lofty in conception, broad
in bearing, finished in form. There still remain, for
summary review, the elements proper to his own poetic
individuality - those which mark him out not only as the
first great poet of his own nation, but as a great poet
for all times.

The poet must please; if he wishes to be successful
and popular, he must suit himself to the tastes of his
public; and even if he be indifferent to immediate fame,
he must, as belonging to one of the most impressionable,
the most receptive species of humankind, live in a sense
with and for his generation....

(p. 169) The vividness with which Chaucer describes
scenes and events as if he had them before his own eyes,
was no doubt, in the first instance, a result of his own
imaginative temperament; but one would probably not go
wrong in attributing the fulness of the use which he made
of this gift to the influence of his Italian studies -
more especially to those which led him to Dante, whose
multitudinous characters and scenes impress themselves
with so singular and immediate a definiteness upon the
imagination. At the same time, Chaucer's resources seem
inexhaustible for filling up or rounding off his narratives with the aid of chivalrous love or religious legend,
by the introduction of samples of scholastic discourse or
devices of personal or general allegory. He commands,
where necessary, a rhetorician's readiness of illustration, and a masque-writer's inventiveness, as to machinery;

he can even (in the 'House of Fame') conjure up an elaborate but self-consistent phantasmagory of his own, and
continue it with a fulness proving that his fancy would
not be at a loss for supplying even more materials than
he cares to employ....

(p. 183) It was by virtue of his power of observing and
drawing character, above all, that Chaucer became the true
predecessor of two several growths in our literature, in
both of which characterisation forms a most important
element, - it might perhaps be truly said, the element
which surpasses all others in importance. From this point
of view the dramatic poets of the Elizabethan age remain
unequalled by any other school or group of dramatists and
the English novelists of the eighteenth and nineteenth
centuries by the representatives of any other development
of prose-fiction. In the art of construction, in the
invention and the arrangement of incident, these dramatists and novelists may have been left behind by others;
in the creation of character they are on the whole without
rivals in their respective branches of literature. To the
earlier at least of these growths Chaucer may be said to
have pointed the way. His personages, more especially of
course, as has been seen, those who are assembled together
in the 'Prologue' to the 'Canterbury Tales', are not mere
phantasms of the brain, or even mere actual possibilities,
but real human beings, and types true to the likeness of
whole classes of men and women, or to the mould in which
all human nature is cast. This is upon the whole the most
wonderful, as it is perhaps the most generally recognised,
of Chaucer's gifts. It would not of itself have sufficed
to make him a great dramatist, had the drama stood ready
for him as a literary form into which to pour the inspiration of his genius, as it afterwards stood ready for our
great Elizabethans. But to it were added in him that perception of a strong dramatic situation, and that power of
finding the right words for it, which have determined the
success of many plays, and the absence of which materially
detracts from the completeness of the effect of others,
high as their merits may be in other respects. How
thrilling, for instance, is that rapid passage across the
stage, as one might almost call it, of the unhappy Dorigen
in the 'Franklin's Tale'! The antecedents of the situation, to be sure, are, as has been elsewhere suggested,
absurd enough; but who can fail to feel that spasm of
anxious sympathy with which a powerful dramatic situation
in itself affects us, when the wife, whom for truth's sake
her husband has bidden be untrue to him, goes forth on her
unholy errand of duty?

24. MATTHEW ARNOLD, CHAUCER LACKS SERIOUSNESS

1880

Arnold (1822-88), educated at Balliol College, Oxford,
poet, critic and schools-inspector, emphasises and overemphasises Chaucer's debt to the French, and expresses
again the strong nineteenth-century feeling for Chaucer's
genial worldliness and humanity. With more originality he
has good things to say about Chaucer's metre and diction.
In a famous judgment he denies him 'high and excellent
seriousness'; perhaps by this he meant to imply the lack
of some sense of passionate commitment. It is curious to
note how Arnold's quotation from Dante, and his reference
to Villon, were taken up for independent use by Ezra
Pound and T.S. Eliot. The extract is from the General
Introduction to 'The English Poets', ed. T.H. Ward (1880),
reprinted in 'Essays in Criticism', 2nd series (1888),
pp. xxx-xxxvi.

The predominance of French poetry in Europe, during the
twelfth and thirteenth centuries, is due to its poetry of
the *langue d'oil*, the poetry of northern France and of
the tongue which is now the French language. In the
twelfth century the bloom of this romance-poetry was
earlier and stronger in England, at the court of our
Anglo-Norman kings, than in France itself. But it was a
bloom of French poetry; and as our native poetry formed
itself, it formed itself out of this. The romance-poems
which took possession of the heart and imagination of
Europe in the twelfth and thirteenth centuries are French;
'they are,' as Southey justly says, 'the pride of French
literature, nor have we anything which can be placed in
competition with them.' Themes were supplied from all
quarters; but the romance-setting which was common to them
all, and which gained the ear of Europe, was French. This
constituted for the French poetry, literature, and language, at the height of the Middle Age, an unchallenged
predominance. The Italian Brunetto Latini, the master of
Dante, wrote his 'Treasure' in French because, he says,

'la parleure en est plus delitable et plus commune a
toutes gens.'...

Yet it is now all gone, this French romance-poetry, of
which the weight of substance and the power of style are
not unfairly represented by this extract from Christian of
Troyes. Only by means of the historic estimate can we
persuade ourselves now to think that any of it is of
poetical importance.

But in the fourteenth century there comes an Englishman nourished on this poetry, taught his trade by this
poetry, getting words, rhyme, metre from this poetry; for
even of that stanza which the Italians used, and which
Chaucer derived immediately from the Italians, the basis
and suggestion was probably given in France. Chaucer (I
have already named him) fascinated his contemporaries, but
so too did Christian of Troyes and Wolfram of Eschenbach.
Chaucer's power of fascination, however, is enduring; his
poetical importance does not need the assistance of the
historic estimate; it is real. He is a genuine source of
joy and strength, which is flowing still for us and will
flow always. He will be read, as time goes on, far more
generally than he is read now. His language is a cause of
difficulty for us; but so also, and I think in quite as
great a degree, is the language of Burns. In Chaucer's
case, as in that of Burns, it is a difficulty to be
unhesitatingly accepted and overcome.

If we ask ourselves wherein consists the immense
superiority of Chaucer's poetry over the romance-poetry -
why it is that in passing from this to Chaucer we suddenly
feel ourselves to be in another world, we shall find that
his superiority is both in the substance of his poetry and
in the style of his poetry. His superiority in substance
is given by his large, free, simple, clear yet kindly
view of human life, - so unlike the total want, in the
romance-poets, of all intelligent command of it. Chaucer
has not their helplessness; he has gained the power to
survey the world from a central, a truly human point of
view. We have only to call to mind the Prologue to 'The
Canterbury Tales'. The right comment upon it is Dryden's:
'It is sufficient to say, according to the proverb, that
here is God's plenty.' And again: 'He is a perpetual
fountain of good sense.' It is by a large, free, sound
representation of things, that poetry, this high criticism
of life, has truth of substance; and Chaucer's poetry has
truth of substance.

Of his style and manner, if we think first of the
romance-poetry and then of Chaucer's divine liquidness of
diction, his divine fluidity of movement, it is difficult

to speak temperately. They are irresistible, and justify
all the rapture with which his successors speak of his
'gold dew-drops of speech.' Johnson misses the point
entirely when he finds fault with Dryden for ascribing to
Chaucer the first refinement of our numbers, and says that
Gower also can show smooth numbers and easy rhymes. The
refinement of our numbers means something far more than
this. A nation may have versifiers with smooth numbers
and easy rhymes, and yet may have no real poetry at all.
Chaucer is the father of our splendid English poetry; he
is our 'well of English undefiled,' because by the lovely
charm of his diction, the lovely charm of his movement, he
makes an epoch and founds a tradition. In Spenser,
Shakespeare, Milton, Keats, we can follow the tradition of
the liquid diction, the fluid movement, of Chaucer; at one
time it is his liquid diction of which in these poets we
feel the virtue, and at another time it is his fluid
movement. And the virtue is irresistible.

Bounded as is my space, I must yet find room for an
example of Chaucer's virtue, as I have given examples to
show the virtue of the great classics. I feel disposed to
say that a single line is enough to show the charm of
Chaucer's verse; that merely one line like this -

O martyr souded in virginitee!

has a virtue of manner and movement such as we shall not
find in all the verse of romance-poetry; - but this is
saying nothing. The virtue is such as we shall not find,
perhaps, in all English poetry, outside the poets whom I
have named as the special inheritors of Chaucer's tradition. A single line, however, is too little if we have
not the strain of Chaucer's verse well in our memory; let
us take a stanza. It is from 'The Prioress's Tale', the
story of the Christian child murdered in a Jewry -

My throte is cut unto my nekke-bone
Saidè this child, and as by way of kinde
I should have deyd, yea, longè time agone;
But Jesu Christ, as ye in bookès finde,
Will that his glory last and be in minde,
And for the worship of his mother dere
Yet may I sing O Alma loud and clere.

Wordsworth has modernised this Tale, and to feel how delicate and evanescent is the charm of verse, we have only to
read Wordsworth's first three lines of this stanza after
Chaucer's -

> My throat is cut unto the bone, I trow,
> Said this young child, and by the law of kind
> I should have died, yea, many hours ago.

The charm is departed. It is often said that the power of
liquidness and fluidity in Chaucer's verse was dependent
upon a free, a licentious dealing with language, such as
is now impossible; upon a liberty, such as Burns too
enjoyed, of making words like *neck, bird,* into a dissyllable by adding to them, and words like *cause, rhyme,* into
a dissyllable by sounding the *e* mute. It is true that
Chaucer's fluidity is conjoined with this liberty, and is
admirably served by it; but we ought not to say that it
was dependent upon it. It was dependent upon his talent.
Other poets with a like liberty do not attain to the
fluidity of Chaucer; Burns himself does not attain to it.
Poets, again, who have a talent akin to Chaucer's, such as
Shakespeare or Keats, have known how to attain to his
fluidity without the like liberty.

  And yet Chaucer is not one of the great classics. His
poetry transcends and effaces, easily and without effort,
all the romance-poetry of Catholic Christendom; it transcends and effaces all the English poetry contemporary with
it, it transcends and effaces all the English poetry subsequent to it down to the age of Elizabeth. Of such avail
is poetic truth of substance, in its natural and necessary
union with poetic truth of style. And yet, I say, Chaucer
is not one of the great classics. He has not their
accent. What is wanting to him is suggested by the mere
mention of the name of the first great classic of Christendom, the immortal poet who died eighty years before
Chaucer, - Dante. The accent of such verse as

    In la sua volontade è nostra pace . . .

is altogether beyond Chaucer's reach; we praise him, but
we feel that this accent is out of the question for him.
It may be said that it was necessarily out of the reach
of any poet in the England of that stage of growth.
Possibly; but we are to adopt a real, not a historic,
estimate of poetry. However we may account for its
absence, something is wanting, then, to the poetry of
Chaucer, which poetry must have before it can be placed
in the glorious class of the best. And there is no doubt
what that something is. It is the σπουδαιότης, the high
and excellent seriousness, which Aristotle assigns as one
of the grand virtues of poetry. The substance of Chaucer's poetry, his view of things and his criticism of
life, has largeness, freedom, shrewdness, benignity; but

it has not this high seriousness. Homer's criticism of
life has it, Dante's has it, Shakespeare's has it. It is
this chiefly which gives to our spirits what they can
rest upon; and with the increasing demands of our modern
ages upon poetry, this virtue of giving us what we can
rest upon will be more and more highly esteemed. A voice
from the slums of Paris, fifty or sixty years after Chaucer, the voice of poor Villon out of his life of riot and
crime, has at its happy moments (as, for instance, in the
last stanza of 'La Belle Heaulmière') more of this important poetic virtue of seriousness than all the productions
of Chaucer. But its apparition in Villon, and in men like
Villon, is fitful; the greatness of the great poets, the
power of their criticism of life, is that their virtue is
sustained.

   To our praise, therefore, of Chaucer as a poet there
must be this limitation; he lacks the high seriousness of
the great classics, and therewith an important part of
their virtue. Still, the main fact for us to bear in mind
about Chaucer is his sterling value according to that real
estimate which we firmly adopt for all poets. He has
poetic truth of substance, though he has not high poetic
seriousness, and corresponding to his truth of substance
he has an exquisite virtue of style and manner. With him
is born our real poetry.

25. GERARD MANLEY HOPKINS, CHAUCER'S SCANNING

1880, 1881

In the year 1880 yet another remarkable Balliol poet commented on Chaucer. Hopkins (1844-89), Jesuit priest and
tormented poet, educated at Balliol College, Oxford,
spent much time and thought on the techniques of scansion.
In extract (a) the mention of Wyatt and Surrey, and of
'rhythm' leads one to suspect that his remarks are based
consciously or unconsciously on Nott (Vol. 1, No. 94).
Hopkins, though a great poet, was eccentric in matters of
scholarship ('The Letters of G.M. Hopkins to Robert
Bridges', ed. C.C. Abbott, 1935, 5 September 1880,
pp. 106-7). Extract (b) appears to take a different line
('The Correspondence of G.M. Hopkins and R.W. Dixon', ed.
C.C. Abbott, 1935; 3 October 1881, pp. 66-7).

(a)

I have not studied Wyatt, but Surrey I used to read: he, I
think, is a greater man. He was an accomplished rhythmist,
not that the experiments in couplets of long twelves and
thirteens are pleasing, though this is better than couplets both twelves or both thirteens. He has a very fine
style free from Euphuism. However, to speak of the
sample you send, I must say that I think you have missed
the clue. You take the rhythm for free triple time,
iambs and anapaests say, and four feet to a line (except
the refrain). But to get this you have to skip, in two
lines out of these few, a whole foot as marked and stressy
as any other foot. This is a licence unpardonable by the
reader and incredible in the writer.
     Before offering my own thoughts I must premise some-
thing. So far as I know triple time is in English verse
a shy and late thing. I have not studied 'Piers Ploughman' and so cannot pronounce how far triple time is boldly
employed in it; at least it must have been suggested. But
on the Romance side of our versification triple time
appeared, I think, late. It may have been suggested by
'Piers Ploughman's' rhythm, as I have said, but partly I
conjecture it arose from a simple misunderstanding or
misreading of Chaucer and the verse of that date and
thereabouts. Chaucer and his contemporaries wrote for a
pronunciation fast changing (everybody knows that final
e for instance has often to be sounded in Chaucer, but
everybody does not know that mostly it is *not* to be
sounded and that the line which scans by its aid is really
to be scanned another way). Their versification was popular and hit the mark in its time, but soon, as far as I
can see, became obsolete, and they being much read and not
rightly scanned thus came to suggest rhythms which they
never thought of. The same sort of thing has, I think,
happened often in the history of verse. And so far,
Wyatt's piece might be scanned as you scan it - but for
the two lines with a foot too much.
     Now in particular I suppose that the verse called
doggrel (in which the play of 'Royster Doyster' is written
and parts of 'Love's Labour', the 'Shrew' etc) arose in
this way: I do not know how else such a shapeless thing
can have arisen. If it were a spontaneous popular growth
it wd. [be] simpler and stronger. It must be the corruption or degeneration of something literary misunderstood
or disfigured. Its rule is: couplets, with a pause dividing each line and on either side of this either two or
three (perhaps sometimes even more) stresses, so that the
line may range from four to six feet, and the rhythm
variable too, iambic or anapaestic.

This wretched doggrel I think Surrey was sytematising
and raising in that couplet of his of which I spoke above
and, to come to the point, I conjecture that Wyatt is
dealing with the same thing here. The main point is the
pause or caesura; on that the line turns. The notion of
pause or caesura had come to English versification from
two different quarters ; from 'Piers Ploughman' and the
older native poetry on the one hand, where it is marked
by a sort of Greek colon or by a stroke, and from France
on the other, where it is essential both to the Alexan-
drine and to the old ten-syllable or five-foot line of
the Chansons and is marked after the fourth syllable, I
find.

(b)

I have found that Chaucer's scanning, once understood, is
extremely smooth and regular, much more so than is thought
by Mr. Skeat and other modern Chaucerists, and they think
it regularity itself compared to what Dryden and older
critics thought of it.

26. ALGERNON CHARLES SWINBURNE, THE MIDDLE CLASS

1880, 1886

The poet and critic Swinburne (1837-1909), educated at
Balliol College, Oxford, after some commonplace remarks
about humour and pathos, asserts class to be more divisive
than country, and accepts a characteristically late-
nineteenth-century and misguided threefold social scheme
of upper, middle and lower classes for placing Chaucer in
the poet's own class, from which it has been hard for
Chaucer to escape. Extract (a) is from Short Notes on
English Poets, 'The Fortnightly Review' (1880), pp. 708-13
(a comment on W.M. Rossetti, 'Short Lives of English
Poets', 1878); (b) Chaucer Lacks Sublimity, 'Miscel-
lanies' (1886), p. 152.

(a)

It is through no lack of love and reverence for the name
of Chaucer that I must question his right, though the
first narrative poet of England, to stand on that account
beside her first dramatic, her first epic, or her first
lyric poet. But, being certainly unprepared to admit his
equality with Shakespeare, with Milton, and with Shelley,
I would reduce Mr. Rossetti's mystic four to the old
sacred number of three. Pure or mere narrative is a form
essentially and avowedly inferior to the lyrical or the
dramatic form of poetry; and the finer line of distinction
which marks it off from the epic marks it also thereby as
inferior.

Of all whose names may claim anything like equality of
rank on the roll of national poets - not even excepting
Virgil - we may say that Chaucer borrowed most from
abroad, and did most to improve whatever he borrowed. I
believe it would be but accurate to admit that in all his
poems of serious or tragic narrative we hear a French or
Italian tongue speaking with a Teutonic accent through
English lips. It has utterly unlearnt the native tone and
cadence of its natural inflections; it has perfectly put
on the native tone and cadence of a stranger's; yet is it
always what it was at first - *lingua romana in bocca
tedesca*. It speaks not only with more vigour but actually
with more sweetness than the tongues of its teachers; but
it speaks after its own fashion no other than the lesson
they have taught. Chaucer was in the main a French or
Italian poet, lined thoroughly and warmly throughout with
the substance of an English humourist. And with this
great gift of specially English humour he combined, naturally as it were and inevitably, the inseparable twin-born
gift of peculiarly English pathos. In the figures of
Arcite and Grisilde, he has actually outdone Boccaccio's
very self for pathos: as far almost as Keats was afterwards to fall short of the same great model in the same
great quality. And but for the instinctive distaste and
congenital repugnance of his composed and comfortable
genius from its accompanying horror, he might haply have
come nearer than he has cared or dared to come even to the
unapproachable pathos of Dante. But it was only in the
world of one who stands far higher above Dante than even
Dante can on the whole be justly held to stand above
Chaucer, that figures as heavenly as the figures of
Beatrice and Matilda could move unspotted and undegraded
among figures as earthly as those of the Reve, the Miller,
and the Wife of Bath: that a wider if not keener pathos
than Ugolino's or Francesca's could alternate with a

deeper if not richer humour than that of Absolon and
Nicholas.

It is a notable dispensation of chance - one which a
writer who might happen to be almost a theist might desig-
nate in the deliciously comical phrase of certain ambiguous pietists as 'almost providential' - that the three
great typical poets of the three great representative
nations of Europe during the dark and lurid lapse of the
Middle Ages should each afford as complete and profound
a type of a different and alien class as of a different
and alien people. Vast as are the diversities of their
national and personal characters, these are yet less
radical than the divergences between class and class which
mark off each from either of his fellows in nothing but in
fame. Dante represents, at its best and highest, the
upper class of the dark ages not less than he represents
their Italy; Chaucer represents their middle class at its
best and wisest, not less than he represents their
England; Villon represents their lower class at its worst
and its best alike, even more than he represents their
France. And of these three the English middle class,
being incomparably the happiest and the wisest, is indisputably, considering the common circumstances of their
successive times, the least likely to have left us the
highest example of all poetry then possible to men. And
of their three legacies, precious and wonderful as it is,
the Englishman's is accordingly the least wonderful and
the least precious. The poet of the sensible and prosperous middle class in England had less to suffer and to sing
than the theosophic aristocrat of Italy, or the hunted and
hungry vagabond who first found articulate voice for the
dumb longing and the blind love as well as for the reck-
less appetites and riotous agonies of the miserable and
terrible multitude in whose darkness lay dormant, as in a
cerecloth which was also a chrysalid, the debased and
disfigured godhead which was one day to exchange the de-
gradation of the lowest populace for the revelation of
the highest people - for the world-wide apocalypse of
France. The golden-tongued gallows-bird of Paris is distinguished from his two more dignified compeers by a
deeper difference yet - a difference, we might say, of
office and of mission no less than of genius and of gift.
Dante and Chaucer are wholly and solely poets of the past
or present - singers indeed for all time, but only singers
of their own: Villon, in an equivocal and unconscious
fashion, was a singer also of the future; he was the first
modern and the last mediaeval poet. He is of us, in a
sense in which it cannot be said that either Chaucer or
Dante is of us, or even could have been; a man of a

changing and self-transforming time, not utterly held
fast, thought still sorely struggling, in the jaws of
hell and the ages of faith.

But in happy perfection of manhood the great and fortunate Englishman almost more exceeds his great and unfortunate fellow-singers than he is exceeded by them in
depth of passion and height of rapture, in ardour and
intensity of vision or of sense. With the single and
sublimer exception of Sophocles, he seems to me the happiest of all great poets on record; their standing type
and sovereign example of noble and manly happiness. As
prosperous indeed in their several ages and lines of life
were Petrarch and Ariosto, Horace and Virgil; but one only
of these impresses us in every lineament of his work with
the same masculine power of enjoyment. And when Ariosto
threw across the windy sea of glittering legend and fluc-
tuant romance the broad summer lightnings of his large
and jocund genius, the dark ages had already returned into
the outer darkness where there is weeping and gnashing of
teeth - the tears of Dante Alighieri and the laughter of
François Villon. But the wide warm harvest-field of Chaucer's husbandry was all glorious with gold of ripening
sunshine while all the world beside lay in blackness and
bonds, throughout all those ages of death called ages of
faith by men who can believe in nothing beyond a building
or a book, outside the codified creeds of a Bible or the
oecumenical structures of a Church.

(b)

On all other points Chaucer is of course almost immeasur-
ably the superior of Wordsworth; in breadth of human
interest, in simplicity of varied sympathies, in straightforward and superb command of his materials as an artist,
the inspired man of the world as much excels the slow-
thoughted and self-studious recluse as in warmth and
wealth of humour, in consummate power of narrative, and
in childlike manfulness of compassionate or joyous emotion; but their usual relations are reversed when the subject treated by Wordsworth exacts a deeper and intenser
expression of feeling, or when his thought takes wing for
higher flights of keener speculation, than the strong,
elastic, equable movement of Chaucer's thought and verse
could be expected to achieve or to attain. In a word,
the elder singer has a thousand advantages over the later,
but the one point on which the later has the advantage is
worth all the rest put together: he is the sublimer poet
of the two.

27. WILLIAM MORRIS, GENTLEMAN AND HAPPY CHILD

1888

William Morris (1834-96), poet, artist, and socialist, was
educated at Exeter College, Oxford. Love of his idea of
the Middle Ages and of fourteenth-century England was a
mainspring of his multifarious activity and almost universal genius. Chaucer, however, does not appear greatly to
interest him, and his only substantial comment is in a
popular summary, Feudal England, 'Signs of Change' (1888),
pp. 73-5.

The successor of the deposed king, the third Edward,
ushers in the complete and central period of the Middle
Ages in England. The feudal system is complete: the life
and spirit of the country has developed into a condition
if not quite independent, yet quite forgetful, on the one
hand of the ideas and customs of the Celtic and Teutonic
tribes, and on the other of the authority of the Roman
Empire. The Middle Ages have grown into manhood; that
manhood has an art of its own, which, though developed
step by step from that of Old Rome and New Rome, and
embracing the strange mysticism and dreamy beauty of the
East, has forgotten both its father and its mother, and
stands alone triumphant, the loveliest, brightest, and
gayest of all the creations of the human mind and hand.
    It has a literature of its own too, somewhat akin to
its art, yet inferior to it, and lacking its unity,
since there is a double stream in it. On the one hand is
the court poet, the gentleman, Chaucer, with his Italian-
izing metres, and his formal recognition of the classical
stories; on which, indeed, he builds a superstructure of
the quaintest and most unadulterated mediaevalism, as gay
and bright as the architecture which his eyes beheld and
his pen pictured for us, so clear, defined, and elegant
it is; a sunny world even amidst its violence and passing
troubles, like those of a happy child, the worst of them
an amusement rather than a grief to the onlookers; a world
that scarcely needed hope in its eager life of adventure
and love, amidst the sunlit blossoming meadows, and green
woods, and white begilded manor-houses. A kindly and
human muse is Chaucer's, nevertheless, interested in and
amused by all life, but of her very nature devoid of

strong aspirations for the future; and that all the more,
since, though the strong devotion and fierce piety of the
ruder Middle Ages had by this time waned, and the Church
was more often lightly mocked at than either feared or
loved, still the *habit* of looking on this life as part of
another yet remained: the world is fair and full of adventure; kind men and true and noble are in it to make one
happy; fools also to laugh at, and rascals to be resisted,
yet not wholly condemned; and when this world is over we
shall still go on living in another which is a part of
this. Look at all the picture, note all and live in all,
and be as merry as you may, never forgetting that you are
alive and that it is good to live.
     That is the spirit of Chaucer's poetry; but alongside
of it existed yet the ballad poetry of the people, wholly
untouched by courtly elegance and classical pedantry; rude
in art but never coarse, true to the backbone; instinct
with indignation against wrong, and thereby expressing the
hope that was in it; a protest of the poor against the
rich, especially in those songs of the Foresters, which
have been called the mediaeval epic of revolt; no more
gloomy than the gentleman's poetry, yet cheerful from
courage, and not content. Half a dozen stanzas of it are
worth a cartload of the whining introspective lyrics of
to-day; and he who, when he has mastered the slight differences of language from our own daily speech, is not
moved by it, does not understand what true poetry means
nor what its aim is.
     There is a third element in the literature of this time
which you may call Lollard poetry, the great example of
which is William Langland's 'Piers Plowman.' It is no bad
corrective to Chaucer, and in *form* at least belongs wholly
to the popular side; but it seems to me to show symptoms
of the spirit of the rising middle class, and casts before
it the shadow of the new master that was coming forward
for the workman's oppression.

28. THOMAS RAYNSFORD LOUNSBURY, CHAUCER AVOIDS DULL
ENGLISH SERIOUSNESS

1891

Lounsbury (1838-1915), professor of English literature at

Yale University, wrote a massive and learned three-volume
work, 'Studies in Chaucer' (1891 in the USA, 1892 in the
UK), which cleared away much rubbish and established much
useful fact. His admirable essay on the Learning of
Chaucer is still useful. His final critical summary of
which an extract follows, is judicious if not original,
and the comment on English heaviness is worthy to be set
against Arnold (No. 24). The extract is from 'Studies in
Chaucer', III, pp. 438-45.

There is satisfactory evidence that the perfection his
work attained was the result of patient labor. It would,
accordingly, be no wonder if there should be found some
places which his ultimate revision never reached. Yet
there is a difficulty about even this view from the way
Chaucer himself speaks of his own productions. No other
inference could well be drawn from the language he uses
than that he regarded the 'House of Fame,' for instance,
as perfectly complete. If so, that completed form of it
has certainly perished. But it has too many companions
of the same kind for us to entertain confidence that it
ever existed.   It is impossible now to discover what were
the causes which brought about the results that have been
described. The unfinished condition in which so much of
Chaucer's work was left may have been due to the pressure
of duties from which he could not escape. His life was a
busy one, and literature during much of it could only have
been an occasional avocation. It may have been due to a
sanguine disposition which led him to project undertakings
which he had neither the requisite leisure nor strength to
accomplish, or to a procrastinating habit of mind and that
submitted easily to the necessity or desirability of
deferring the performance of a duty to a time that never
came. Or, finally, it may have been due to weariness of
his subject, and even to positive disgust with it.
Whether due to one of these causes or to all of them, or
to some cause not as yet pointed out, the fragmentary
state in which many of the works of Chaucer have come down
is an undeniable fact. It is a result there is every
reason to deplore. Had the 'Canterbury Tales', in particular, been completed on the scale on which they were projected, we should have had a picture of the entire social
and religious life of the fourteenth century, and to some
extent of its political life, such as has never been
drawn of any century before or since in the history of
the world.
    In the foregoing pages I have sought to show that

Chaucer was not only a great artist, but that he became
so at the cost of time and labor; that in him, standing at
the fountain-head of English literature, the critical
spirit was as highly developed as the creative; that the
course he pursued in any given case was no accident of
momentary impulse, nor was it due to unquestioning acquiescence in what was then generally accepted; that, on the
contrary, it was the fruit of ripened reflection and
deliberate choice; that it caused him in consequence to
censure in some cases what his contemporaries approved,
and continued to approve; that it led him in other cases
to condemn at last what he had at first been disposed to
deem praiseworthy. Contrary as are these views to those
once universally held, the evidence presented hardly permits us even to doubt their truth. If we need further
confirmation, we can find it in one marked change that
took place in his literary methods. In his earlier work
he introduces constantly characters that are merely per-
sonifications of qualities or acts or sentiments. In so
doing he followed the practice of his immediate predecessors. As he advanced in knowledge and judgment and taste
he shook himself free from the trammels of this temporary
fashion. He abandoned almost entirely the field of
abstractions in which the men of his time delighted, and
in which his contemporary Langland was contented to
remain. For the shadowy beings who dwell in the land of
types he substituted living men and women; for the allegorical representation of feelings and beliefs, the
direct outpourings of passion. Changes of method such as
these are not the result of freak or accident. Chaucer,
accordingly, must stand or fall not merely by our opinion
of what he did, but by our knowledge that what he did was
done consciously. The responsibility for his words and
acts cannot be shifted from him to his age. We can
accept the convictions he entertained or we can reject
them; but we can never dismiss them as not being in a
genuine sense his convictions. He is not merely a man
of genius acting under the influence of an inspiration
to which he commits himself blindly and unreservedly. He
is a force that must be reckoned with in all critical
discussions of the art he practised.
    It is impossible to take final leave of the poet with-
out some notice of what is on the whole the most pronounced characteristic of his style. This is the uni-
formly low level upon which he moves. There is no other
author in our tongue who has clung so closely and so persistently to the language of common life. Such a characteristic appealed strongly to the men who led the revolt
against the artificial diction that prevailed in the

poetry of the last century. It attracted in particular
the attention of Wordsworth. The course of his predecessor he cited as an authority for the one which he himself
adopted. He cannot, it is true, be always congratulated
upon the way in which he himself carried his theories in
practice. The invariable felicity of Chaucer in treating
the simplest themes is made especially noteworthy by the
frequent failures that attended the similar efforts of one
of the greatest of his successors. For the acknowledged
mastery which is conceded in this particular to the early
poet means much more than at first sight it seems. It is
difficult, says Horace, in a passage the precise purport
of which has been much disputed, to say common things with
propriety. In a sense which has frequently been given to
these words there is no question as to the unrivalled
skill displayed by Chaucer. There have been many men of
genius who have been able to say grand things grandly. To
the fewest of the few is reserved the achievement of the
far harder task of discoursing of mean things without discoursing meanly; of recounting the prosaic events of life
without becoming prosaic one's self; of narrating them in
the plainest terms, and yet investing them with poetic
charm. It is in the power of genius only to accomplish
this at all; but it is by no means in the power of all
genius.

It is because he stayed so persistently on these low
levels that Chaucer was enabled to combine with apparent
ease characteristics and methods that are often deemed
incompatible. His words are the more effective because
their very simplicity makes upon the mind the impression
of understatement. The imagination of the reader fills in
and exaggerates the details which have been left half-
told. It is owing to this restraint of expression that
whatever he says is not only at all times and in all
places free from literary vulgarity, it never loses the
dignity that belongs, as well in letters as in life, to
consummate high-breeding. There is an exquisite urbanity
in his manner which gives it an attractiveness as perva-
sive and yet as undefinable as that which the subtle
evanescent flavor of arch allusion imparts to his matter.
I do not mean by this to convey the idea that Chaucer
abounds in ornate and brilliant passages, or that he is
constantly saying remarkable things in a remarkable way.
It is simply that in dealing with the common he is never
commonplace. However trivial may be the theme upon which
he is discoursing, his language always retains the air of
distinction. As a further result of this absolute
naturalness, he is enabled to pass from the gravest to the
lightest topics without giving the reader the slightest

sensation of shock. The border-land between simplicity
and silliness is both a narrow and a dangerous one. It
is beset with pitfalls for the unwary, and it is only the
greatest masters that can traverse it with impunity. Chaucer treads its limited confines with a liberty which few,
even of men of loftiest genius, have ventured to take.
His freedom, indeed, verges at times upon audacity. In the
Knight's tale, for illustration, following close upon the
high-wrought description of the great tournament comes the
recital of the methods taken by the physicians to save the
life of the victor in the struggle. The failure they meet
with is told in the simplest terms. Their efforts were
fruitless because they received no help from nature. Suddenly the poet interposes his own comment on the useless-
ness, under such conditions, of the medical art in words
like these:

> And certainly there nature will not wirche,
> Farewell physíc! Go bear the man to church!

With this quaint expression of personal opinion, he passes
at once to the pathetic parting-scene between the dying
lover and the woman for whom he is about to die. Yet
these rapid transitions do not produce upon the mind any
effect of inappropriateness or incongruity. Tears and
laughter stand side by side in Chaucer's verse as they do
in life. The gay, and at times almost comic, element that
appears in the midst of exciting and even sorrowful scenes
never jars upon the feelings. It seems to us no more out
of place than the figures on the exteriors of stately
cathedrals, where antic forms grin from every gargoyle,
and imps are perched upon every coign of vantage, as if to
impress upon the beholder how near the comedy of life
stands to its tragedy; how inextricably involved is the
tie between its lightest and most mocking moods and its
profoundest mysteries.

   I am not claiming for Chaucer that he is one of the
few supremest poets of the race. His station is near
them, but he is not of them. Yet, whatever may be the
rank we accord him among the writers of the world's chief
literatures, the position he holds in his own literature
is one that can no longer be shaken by criticism or disturbed by denial. Time has set its final seal upon the
verdict of his own age, and the refusal to acknowledge
his greatness has now no effect upon the opinion we have
of the poet himself, but upon our opinion of those who are
unable to appreciate his poetry. To one alone among the
writers of our own literature is he inferior. Nor even by
him has he been surpassed in every way. There are

characteristics in which he has no superior, and, it may
be right to add, in which he has no equal. Nor is the
supremacy accorded him in these respects due to any consideration of his antiquity; though it can be easily
admitted that to appreciate fully what Chaucer did for
English literature we must first read the works of his
predecessors and contemporaries. It might not be altogether amiss to add to the list several of his successors.
There is one particular in which his merits in reference
to the literature are simply transcendent. He overcame
its natural tendencies to a dull seriousness which could
sometimes be wrought into vigorous invective, but had
little power to fuse the spiritual element of poetry with
the purely intellectual. Into the stolid English nature,
which may be earnest, but evinces an almost irresistible
inclination towards heaviness, he brought a lightness, a
grace, a delicacy of fancy, a refined sportiveness even
upon the most unrefined themes, which had never been known
before save on the most infinitesimal scale, and has not
been known too much since.

Nor is this the only distinctive characteristic in
which Chaucer excels. There is no other English author so
absolutely free, not merely from effort, but from the
remotest suggestion of effort. Shakespeare mounts far
higher; yet with him there are times when we seem to hear
the flapping of the wings, to be vaguely conscious that
he is lashing his imagination to put forth increased
exertions. But in Chaucer no slightest trace of strain
is to be detected. As on the lower levels the line never
labors, so on the higher he never makes the impression
that he is trying to make an impression. It is the absolute ease with which he rises that often prevents our
perceiving how rapidly he has risen. We have suddenly
been transported into another atmosphere without the
least consciousness on our part of the extent of the distance traversed. In this the poet is like his own picture
of Fame. At one moment the goddess seems to the visitor
at her temple to be hardly the length of a cubit. In an
instant, and almost before he is aware of what has taken
place, she stands before his wondering eyes with her feet
resting upon the earth and her head touching the heights
of highest heaven. Nor is it alone for the naturalness
and ease which results from this union of strength and
simplicity that the greatest of his successors have
delighted to honor the poet. Full as willingly have they
paid homage to the qualities of character displayed in his
works as to those of intellect.

29. WILLIAM PATON KER, THE COMMONPLACE TRANSFORMED

1895

Ker (1855-1923), educated at Glasgow University and
Balliol College, Oxford, professor of English at London
University, united immense scholarly knowledge with richly
thoughtful critical appreciation, expressed in prose
whose learning and intelligence is matched by its wit and
elegance. This example is taken from The Poetry of
Chaucer, a very long and full review of 'The Complete
Works of Chaucer', 6 vols (1894), edited by W.W. Skeat,
in 'The Quarterly Review', CLXXX (April 1895), pp. 521-48.

(p. 522) There is a place for biographical particulars,
and there is a place for commentaries and glossaries; but
the first and most necessary thing for every reader of
Chaucer is that he should be allowed to read the poems for
himself in something like peace of mind. It may be at
times amusing to make one's own emendations, but not in
the middle of Chaucer's story of 'Troilus.' Mr. Skeat's
edition has removed these offences, and in it the writings
of the great master of verse may be read without the
impertinences of 'Adam Scriveyn' and his successors.
     The art of Chaucer in some of its qualities was as
fully recognised two hundred years ago as it can be at
the present day. With regard to some of the strongest
parts of Chaucer's poetry, no later writer has been able
to add anything essentially new to the estimate given by
Dryden. 'Here is God's plenty' is still the best criticism ever uttered on the 'Canterbury Tales'; and Dryden's
comparison of Chaucer and Ovid, with his preference of
the English author's sanity and right proportions over the
Latin poet's ornamental epigrams, is to this day a summary
of the whole matter, and enough in itself to give liveliness and meaning even to such a battered critical phrase
as the 'following of Nature'; a phrase which is so
employed by Dryden in this context as almost to look like
a new idea.
     In other respects, however, there is a defect in
Dryden's criticism; and, in spite of the exertions of many
scholars, his failure to appreciate Chaucer's versification has been very generally repeated since his time. It
is possible that, even at the present day, Dryden's estimate of the laxity of Chaucer's verse may still represent

the common opinion. That Chaucer's verse is irregular, though it may have 'the rude sweetness of a Scotch tune,' is possibly even now a fallacy not too extravagant to be entertained. If it is anywhere to be found, this error is a natural and pardonable result of the old uncritical editions. Mr. Skeat, in one place, shows himself aggrieved with Dryden's opinion, and taxes Dryden with arrogance for overlooking the beauties of Chaucer's verse. Perhaps Mr. Skeat will come to admit that he has in this case allowed himself to be drawn too far by zeal for his author. Dryden, who in criticising Chaucer explains that 'it is an easy matter for a man of ordinary parts to find a fault in one of greater,' and who protests with emphasis against the common patronising view of Chaucer, was plainly speaking his mind without any trace of disparagement when he confessed himself unable to find correctness in Chaucer's verse. For this censure he had every justification in the text of the edition that he read, and in the traditional way of reading Chaucer. But whatever may have been his justification, the censure was wrong, and it is in this respect that Dryden's criticism of Chaucer has become antiquated. The poetical imagination of Chaucer and the general virtues of his thought and manner are recognised by Dryden: the delicacy and beauty of his verse have had to wait longer for acknowledgment, and can hardly be said to be rightly estimated even now. The ways of Chaucer's verse and the laws of his rhymes have been studied and ascertained by many critics: by Mr. Skeat himself, by Dr. Bernhard ten Brink, by Mr. Henry Bradshaw. But after all their work, it still remained to carry out consistently, in a critical edition of the text, the principles which had been detected in the study of the documents. This is what Mr. Skeat has done, and this is the chief part of his credit.

The text of Chaucer as here printed will no doubt be made to pass under examination by the specialists in that branch of learning, and will not be allowed to go altogether without criticism. In many places there is room for argument about the readings preferred by the editor, and in some there may appear to be good ground, in the materials afforded by the editor himself, for disputing his decision. But while it may be left to time and to the minute investigation of critics to prove the validity of certain of Mr. Skeat's readings, there can be little question as to the soundness of his method and the success with which he has applied his principles to the separate problems as they rose in the course of his labours.

It cannot be said that the text of Chaucer has been ill-preserved, on the whole, in manuscripts. The

materials for a critical text of Chaucer are rich enough,
if they are compared with the foundations of the text of
Shakespeare. There are, however, certain unfortunate
circumstances by which the manuscripts of Chaucer are
commonly affected. These are indicated not obscurely by
Chaucer himself in more places than one: his appeal to
the conscience of Adam, the ready writer, is the cry of
an injured man who had suffered much and long without protest; and 'Troilus' ends with a prayer for the preservation of his book: -

> that noon miswryte thee
> Ne thee mysmetre for defaute of tonge.

This anxiety and this grievance of Chaucer were caused
by something more than the ordinary and universal inaccuracy of mankind in dealing with other people's copy, and
with their own when it has to be corrected. Whatever may
be the explanation of the fact, the fact is too certain,
that after Chaucer for nearly a hundred and fifty years
there was a general decay in England, in English writers
and readers, of the sense of metre and rhythm. Nothing
more abject and decrepit ever passed for English verse
than some of the things produced by English poets in the
fifteenth century, and by poets who boasted themselves
the followers of Chaucer. The best manuscripts of Chaucer were written by and for people who found music in
Lydgate; and it is only by some standard of the difference between Chaucer's verse and Lydgate's that the
readings of Chaucerian manuscripts can be tested and
controlled. It seems impossible to believe that the
melody of Chaucer's verse was ignored by his contemporaries; but the practice of his chief imitators is enough
to prove that the secret of his verse was very generally
lost even in the lifetime of some of his contemporaries.
Adam Scriveyn, at his worst, could hardly make more discord out of his 'mismetring' of Chaucer than Lydgate was
capable of producing out of his own head on any provocation. Where Lydgate was an honoured poet, it is no
wonder that the copiers of books were occasionally indifferent to Chaucer's accuracy of verse.
  This common condition of English literary taste in the
fifteenth century must be the justification of an editor
when he prefers one manuscript reading to another for the
sake of the metres of Chaucer. The difficulty is to prove
that the principles on which the text is chosen are the
same as the principles of Chaucer's versification. Whatever may be thought cf Mr. Skeat's theoretic prosody, and
there is some reason to think it questionable in many

points of detail, his practice in the comparison of alternative readings appears to be guided by a sound instinct.
He does not trust the manuscripts for readings that are
plainly unmetrical and discordant; at the same time the
accuracy for which he contends is not the accuracy of an
a priori system or a modern theory. It is not forced upon
the text by an editor contending for his own private ideal
of style, 'like slashing Bentley with his desperate hook.'
The reading of Chaucer's verse and the rules of Chaucer's
practice are learned by comparison of the texts, and by
induction from the evidence they present. The texts of
Chaucer in the manuscripts, with all their imperfections,
are good enough to prove that Chaucer was an artist. The
corruptions are not enough to hide or distort the beauty
of his verse, and a fair amount of certainty is attainable
in respect of his usage and his variations of usage. The
principles of Chaucer's verse may be discovered and demonstrated, and Mr. Skeat has done nothing immoderate in his
practical application of them.

There is not very much conjectural emendation in the
text. There are, however, some happy restorations which
have all the charm of infallible conjectures. In the case
of Chaucer at any rate, however it may be with other difficult and hazardous authors, there seems to be required
almost as rare a gift to detect and read aright the right
reading of the manuscript, as to invent a plausible new
reading to take its place. There are in Mr. Skeat's text
some admirable and memorable examples of safe and decisive
criticism, where the result is produced, not by conjecture,
but by discrimination of the meaning of the extant version.
One or two of these may be quoted, to prove what sort of
things have been done by Mr. Skeat, and on what sort of
ground the reputation of his great work may be based. In
'Troilus and Criseyde,' B. iii., 673, Dr. Morris's text
reads:

> Ther nys no more, but here efter soone
> Thei voide, dronke, and traveres drawe anon;
> Gan every wyghte that hadde nought to done
> More in the place, oute of the chaumber gone.

Mr. Skeat's text and the notes thereto pertaining are as
follows: -

> (Text:)
> Ther nis no more, but here-after sone,
> The voydè dronke, and travers drawe anon,
> Gan every wight, that hadde nought to done
> More in that place, out of the chamber gon.

(Various readings:)
674.   Cl. Cp. H. The voyde; Cm. they voydyn; Ed. They
voyde; H. 2. They voydid, &c.

(Commentary:)
'The voidè being drunk, and the cross-curtain drawn
immediately afterwards.' The best reading is voyde or
voydee. This seems to be here used as a name for the
'loving-cup' or 'grace-cup,' which was drunk after the
table had been cleared or voided. Properly it was a
slight dessert of 'spices' and wine; where spices meant
sweetmeats, dried fruits, &c. See Notes and Queries,
2 S. xi. 508. The traverse was a screen or curtain drawn
across the room; cf. Cant. Ta. E 1817, King's Quair,
st. 90.

An 'additional note' at the end of the volume gives
further instances of the word, including one from the
account of the 'Dethe of James Stewarde, Kyng of Scotys,'
and one from Mr. Rossetti's poem on this same subject,
the 'King's Tragedy': 'then he called for the voidee-cup.'
In this case the manuscript authority, which is good,
has been commonly neglected in the editions of Chaucer
for the sake of a gloss which looks easy, but which really
makes nonsense of the sense and dislocates the syntax.
Mr. Skeat has invented nothing: he has merely read the
text aright, and understood the words before him.
Another instance from the same book is equally satisfactory. The reading 'gofish people,' in 'Troilus,' iii.
584, has amused and perplexed many etymologists. Mr.
Skeat spoils the fun by reading the manuscripts with
attention; he finds the word there to be really goosish,'
a word equally expressive and more intelligible, which,
it may be remarked, had to be reinvented by Mrs. Carlyle
in her correspondence: 'the goosish man, my quondam
lover.'
It would not be difficult to find many similar cases,
where the text is made sound and good by the editor's
industry, erudition, and sense, without any need of the
more dangerous and showy expedients of criticism, and at
the same time with all the exhilarating effect of a good
game well played according to the rules and conventions.
The six volumes of the book are disposed in the following order. The first contains the 'Romaunt of the Rose'
and the minor poems, with their commentaries and elaborate
introductions: a Life of Chaucer stands at the beginning
of the volume. The second contains 'Boethius' and
'Troilus'; the third, 'The House of Fame,' the 'Legend of
Good Women,' and the 'Treatise on the Astrolabe,' each

with its accompaniment of notes: the latter part of the
volume is taken up by the essay on the sources of the
'Canterbury Tales.' The 'Canterbury Tales' themselves are
the contents of the fourth volume; the notes are in the
fifth. The sixth is made up of the general Introduction,
together with the glossary to the whole of Chaucer. There
are also many additional short essays and passages of commentary. Of works doubtfully or wrongly attributed to
Chaucer, Mr. Skeat has admitted the 'Romaunt of the Rose'
and the 'Tale of Gamelyn,' besides some short pieces, of
little importance. The Apocrypha, one is glad to know,
are to be collected, later, in a volume by themselves.

The commentary in this edition is throughout intended
to be positive and substantial. It may be confessed that
it gives the impression of weight and bulk, and that the
Clarendon Press has done little to relieve the general
aspect of sobriety, much at variance with the demeanour of
the contents, and very unlike the appearance of the illu-
minated books from which the poems are copied. Something
of this is inevitable. There must be commentaries and
explanations; the 'old fields' of poetry cannot be left
to themselves, and the machinery by which they are re-
freshed is not to be set going without some amount of
strain and noise. It may not be out of place to hope that
the editor and the Delegates of the Press may see good to
publish some day a text of Chaucer by itself, in something
like the form of Dr. Morris's six volumes in the Aldine
series. Chaucer will still be read by idle people, and
some of his light poems are rather heavily weighted in
this edition. 'Boece' and the 'Astrolabe' are good in
their way, but it is too much to be asked to carry them
everywhere for the sake of the poems that are here bound
up along with them.

And was it necessary to give such prominence in the
'Canterbury Tales' to Dr. Furnivall's distinguishing
labels, from 'Group A' to 'Group H'? To enumerate the
separate blocks in which the uncompleted last work of
Chaucer was left, and to mark the separate bales for reference in an inventory, was a useful piece of business.
Dr. Furnivall, as a factor on Chaucer's estate, was able
to make out the condition in which it had been left, and
no reader can afford to neglect his description of it, his
enumeration of the different sections of the Tales, groups
beginning and ending abruptly, without prologues or interludes to make a connexion with the rest. But these
'groups' are accidental; the line of division between them
is drawn by the mere chance that prevented Chaucer from
completing his interludes between all the Tales, from
carrying out his great design, from finishing the

composition with a story and a prologue for each of the
pilgrims. The order of the groups is open to question:
Mr. Skeat, while using Dr. Furnivall's arrangement, does
not accept it as authoritative. Are the faces of the
Tales to be blackened for ever with Dr. Furnivall's A's
and B's? Is the gentle reader to have these imposed on
him in the headline of every page? Is he nowhere to be
allowed to escape from the machinery, and are all future
generations to quote the Tales according to these super-
scriptions? This may seem a trivial matter, but it is
really of some importance that the implements of the commentator should be kept in their own place, and not be
left lying about when their work is done. As a historical
fact, it is true that a 'group' of the Tales is begun by
the Prologue of the Wife of Bath, that no introduction
connects this group with any previous group, that Chaucer
had in this place left something to be finished later when
he should have time, and that he never found time to
supply what was wanting. It does not however seem expedient or necessary on this account that the lines of the
Wife of Bath's Prologue should be quoted for ever as
beloning to 'Group D,' nor that every page of this group
should be stamped with a black D in the headline. It is
for the interest of the whole world that Chaucer's writings should possess their most appropriate and most adequate commentary; and, on the other hand, that the commentary should be restrained from intrusion into the text.
These irrelevant earmarks of the groups are the only blemish on pages that are otherwise clear and pleasant to
read.

Mr. Skeat's introductions and annotations have in part
been anticipated in his earlier editions of separate works
of Chaucer: the minor poems, the 'House of Fame,' the
'Legend of Good Women,' the 'Astrolabe,' and various selections from the Tales. If in this way some of the commentary may be wanting in novelty, on the other hand the
editor's clients have been educated in the meantime, and
the reception of the book has been made easier. Further,
the editor has been making fresh improvements at all
points of his ground, and each division of his book shows
that his study of Chaucer is continually bringing in new
discoveries. There is no suggestion or trace of a belief
that the work of interpreting Chaucer has been brought to
a close in these six volumes. The reader is kept inspiri-
ted by the thought that there is more to be reaped, or at
any rate to be gleaned, in these old fields of poetry;
while it is manifest at the same time that the editor
intends to secure what he can out of the things that still
remain to be discovered.

It is occasionally, by some writers and disputants,
taken for granted that the scientific study of the old
forms of English is in some mysterious way incompatible
with any knowledge or appreciation of the beauties of
literature. Into the grounds of this prejudice it is not
necessary to enquire. Mr. Skeat has proved in this book,
as often before in others, that a knowledge of the language in which an author wrote need be no hindrance to a
comprehension of his meaning. It is time that this, which
'was some time a paradox,' should come to be more generally recognised. There are one or two places in particular which may be selected from the notes to stand as
examples at once of method and of the results of method.
The best of these perhaps is presented by sections 25 to
51 of the general Introduction (vol. 6, p. xxxi.), in
which there is a discussion of the vowels of Chaucer's
rhymes, with the most satisfactory and clear conclusions
in regard to a great number of textual problems. The
seventeenth section also, on Chaucer's occasional use of
Kentish forms, is a demonstration well conducted to a
profitable end. There is no need to quote or to repeat
the argument of these passages. It may be permissible,
however, to refer to them as instances of discrimination
and sound reasoning rightly applied, and of the scholarly use of scientific grammar in the foundation of a
text.
    With respect to some other parts of the grammatical
Introduction, it is not possible to feel quite the same
confidence: more especially in the section on Chaucer's
forms of verse there appears to be room for some amend-
ment. Mr. Skeat has invented a metrical notation of his
own, and has gone somewhat elaborately into the difficulties of scansion. Every writer on English verse has his
own metrical symbols, and no one appears to pay any
attention to any other theorist, except in occasional
intervals for depreciation. It is dangerous to have an
opinion on this subject, which seems to exasperate the
mind and diction of most of its professors. Yet it may be
submitted, though without any pretension of authority,
that to scan a verse is not, as Mr. Skeat and some other
writers seem to hold, the same thing as to recite it.
The scansion or measurement or analysis of a verse is not
intended to show how a verse should be read or chanted.
The method of some writers on English versification is to
take a line and read it with what appears to them to be
the just accent and the right pauses; then to try to represent their own ideas of time and emphasis in notes of
their own invention. But as a matter of theory there may
be many right ways of chanting a verse, while as a matter

of fact the opinions of one man with regard to just accent
and right pauses are generally detestable to other men; so
that this form of measurement is illusory, because it
satisfies only its own author and no one else. It is not
the pulse of a verse, but the skeleton, that has to be
measured by metrical theory. It is hard to believe that
Mr. Skeat's symbolic pictures of Chaucer's rhythms can
possibly make anything clear that might not have been
explained without them. That they may produce confusion
and distress among innocent people is perhaps only one of
the jealous suspicions that are too frequent in this
region of speculation. It is beyond contest that the
effect of this part of the Introduction is far short of
the lucidity and security attained by the dissertation on
Chaucer's use of the vowels.

Mr. Skeat in this connexion refers to the varieties of
French verse known to Chaucer, and especially to the varieties of the French decasyllable, and its analogous measure the hendecasyllable in Italian. Here the ground is
surer; but unfortunately Mr. Skeat appears to have stopped
too soon in his consultation of the authorities. He takes
from Mr. Paget Toynbee's 'Specimens of Old French' a summary description of the four varieties of the Old French
decasyllable. This is perfectly satisfactory and clear,
and gives the right beginning. The French line, with its
sharp division after the fourth syllable, is more primitive than the Italian or the English line, with its
greater freedom; the French line deserves to be considered first, even apart from any claim it may derive from
its place in the French poems that Chaucer knew and
admired. But Mr. Skeat goes on from this point in a way
that can hardly fail to be confusing; and this is the
more to be regretted because it is just at this point
that he approaches one of the difficult metrical questions in Chaucer, namely, the dropping of a syllable at
the beginning of a line.

For to delen with no swich poraille

is, according to ordinary notions, an heroic line short of
one syllable. The licence is common enough in the shorter
couplets, and that Chaucer thought such a variety good
enough for his longer verse need not be doubted; it shall
not, at any rate, be disputed here. The care that Mr.
Skeat gave many years ago to this point of Chaucerian
scholarship is one of the innumerable grounds of obligation to him. Unfortunately he appears to have done something to spoil his treatment of this subject in his
Introduction, by a somewhat inconsiderate use of other

people's theories, and by a reference to analogies and
precedents that will not stand enquiry. There is nothing
to be gained from French verse in this connexion. If
Chaucer used this exceptional rhythm in his heroic lines,
it was by following the common practice of the shorter
octosyllabic verse and of early English verse generally in
its treatment of foreign rhyming measures. There is
nothing like it to be found among the decasyllables of
Chaucer's French poets.

It is peculiarly difficult to follow Mr. Skeat in his
description of the French decasyllabic line. After a sufficient account of the 'epic caesura' and the feminine
rhyme, he continues, in a passage which is surely more
than disputable: -

> But the fact is that Old French verse admits of more
> licences than the above. It was also permissible for
> the poet, besides adding to the line at the end [i.e.,
> in the feminine rhyme, by the addition of an eleventh
> syllable], to subtract from it at the beginning, viz.
> by omitting the first weak syllable at the beginning,
> or the first weak syllable in the second half line;
> i.e., after the caesura.

Mr. Skeat appears to imply in this (besides some other
questionable things which may be neglected) that Chaucer
had before him, in the French poets whom he read, examples
of lines analogous to his own shortened form, as represented in the line 'Til wel ny / the day began to springe.'
This is a point that requires to be proved by citation;
it can hardly be proved in any other way. Mr. Skeat has
not presented any such form of verse as a variation
allowed to French decasyllables. That such a monstrosity
may exist in some Old French verse written in England,
appears to be confessed, although with pain and reluctance,
by the masters of French prosody. That it occurs anywhere
in the myriads of decasyllables in French of France is a
discovery that has yet to be made; a prodigy which, in the
minds of some scholars, would call for something like a
ceremony of expiation. But though this part of the Introduction may appear to be somewhat hasty in its conclusions
and in its employment of evidence, it ought to be remarked
that these defects, if admitted to exist, are yet nothing
like an equivalent on the negative side, to the solid
excellences of the grammatical survey. Mr. Skeat's theoretical prosody, if it is wrong, can be altered, without
injury to the rest of the book.

If there is weakness in the description of Chaucer's
verse, it is a weakness that does not affect the editor's

reading of his texts. Its influence does not extend
beyond the few pages of the Introduction in which the
subject of prosody is considered, while, on the other
hand, the goodness of the strong part of the Introduction
is felt and proved in every line and page of the text.
The grammatical Introduction gives the principles by which
the text is rendered secure. The description of Chaucer's
vowels, the notes on his Kentish variations, are of some
importance, it may be surmised, to students of philology,
if that be the right name for the province of natural
history to which such things belong. But the importance of
this section of Mr. Skeat's work is not limited to that
study; it declares itself in the whole process by which
the manuscripts are compared and scrutinised; it is part of
the code of the editor's critical scholarship. These two
portions of the Introduction - one certainly strong, the
other apparently weak - ought to be compared: the result of
the comparison must be, for every candid reader, an
increased admiration of the way in which the editor has
worked. There are not many books of equal compass in which
the faults are of so little account. They are all far
removed from the vital centres; a caviller with the worst
imaginable will could hardly do more damage in this rich
ground than might be repaired by the editor in a morning's
labour.

It is hardly necessary or expedient to go over Mr.
Skeat's commentary and describe what will be plain enough
to any one who makes a trial of it. There are, however,
three pieces of editing which it would be unjust to pass
over without acknowledgment and praise. These are, the
text of the 'Romaunt of the Rose,' the text of 'Troilus,'
and the text of the 'Legend of Good Women.'

The text of the 'Romaunt of the Rose' has been studied
by many scholars since Mr. Henry Bradshaw made it the
ground of his demonstration of Chaucer's usage in rhymes.
In Mr. Skeat's Preface the evidence on this question is
given clearly in a summary form. It is not, perhaps, to
this that the chief interest will belong, but rather to
the text, particularly to the text of the first fragment,
which is here for the first time printed on the same page
with the French original, and emended by comparison with
it.

The poem of 'Troilus' has never before been edited with
any care, though it is long since the ground was broken by
the parallel texts of the Chaucer Society. As it is dem-
onstrably the largest in scale of all the poet's compositions, while it is plausibly maintained by some to be his
greatest poem, there is reason to be glad that it has at
last received the attention of an editor, and at last been

freed from the impossible readings that disgraced it in the older editions.

The double version of the Prologue to the 'Legend of Good Women' has been published already in Mr. Skeat's small edition of that poem; but the discovery of it is still recent enough to be a novelty, and its appearance here, in its proper place among the collected works of Chaucer, is an event to be respectfully chronicled.

Mr. Skeat has deliberately left out of account, in his prefaces and commentaries, the question of the value of Chaucer's writings. This is the great omission in the book. The case must have been fully considered, and it is possible to accept the reasons that have prevailed. A commentary exact and positive, a record of ascertainable facts about the poems, a carefully edited text of Chaucer's writings, these are the things that are given in this book; they are left to be used as may be thought fit by those who have wit enough to read them. It is a good example to all editors who may be less temperately inclined; and the austerity and parsimony of the design must be refreshing and stimulating to any one of the many who are exhausted and cloyed by too much effusive criticism.

In the case of Chaucer it is peculiarly difficult to draw any line between criticism which is historical and positive, and criticism which is purely aesthetic. The distinction is always an elusive one. The criticism that deals in historical facts, that traces origins, that investigates old debts of poet to poet and pupil to master, is a different process, no doubt, from that which calculates the present value, the immediate effect, of a passage of verse. But in reality those distinct processes are seldom found apart. They may be distinguished logically and in the abstract, but they are always together in real life if either of them is to be worth anything. It is impossible to trace the history of a poem which you do not understand, and it is impossible to understand a poem if you understand nothing else. The 'Book of the Duchess,' for instance, may be worth something at a first reading to one who has never before read anything of Chaucer, or anything of Chaucer's date; but it is hardly to be estimated how large a part of its meaning is kept back when there is no association in the reader's mind with the great host of earlier and later similar poems on similar motives, when the poem of the Duchess Blanche is separated from all its companions in that masque of shadows, the old courtly poetry of France.

It is possible that Mr. Skeat may have been led too far in his abstinence from literary criticism. Some of the

subjects which he has left out might very well have been
admitted, as positive matter of history, without tres-
passing too far on any debatable ground. It is necessary
to know a good deal about French poetry before one can
rightly appreciate the difference, the individual and
indefinable grace, which was added by Chaucer to the
inheritance received by him from Machault and the other
poets of that school. There is plenty of room in Mr.
Skeat's edition for something more than he has thought fit
to say about the authors whom Chaucer read, and the
character of the literature in which he was educated. Mr.
Skeat, for instance, in his renunciation of the task of
literary criticism, refers to Mr. Lowell's essay on Chaucer to make good his defection. But he gives no indication that in Mr. Lowell's essay, apart from his criticism
and praise of Chaucer, there is much that is questionable
or plainly erroneous in his historical opening. Mr.
Lowell reiterates the old historical theory which Dryden
learned from Rymer, and Pope from Dryden, and which may be
traced down through Warton to many later essayists, that
Chaucer knew the poetry of Provence as well as that of
France, or, in Mr. Lowell's language, 'was familiar with
all that had been done by Troubadour or Trovère.' This is
an historical question, belonging closely indeed to the
literary criticism of Chaucer, but not to be decided out
of hand by any critic without some careful enquiry. Mr.
Skeat, in referring to Mr. Lowell's essay, might have
drawn attention to this point, and might have indicated
whether there is or is not any evidence for a statement
which seems to have been repeated by English critics for
two centuries on the inauspicious authority of Thomas
Rymer, and without any other or better evidence whatsoever. It would be easy to find other and more important
examples of the questions that arise in connexion with
Chaucer, where the historical record of his poetical education is inextricably mixed with the problems of his own
individual genius and his own poetical imagination.

There is hardly any author of whom so many commonplaces
are true, and by whom so many commonplaces are proved to
be inept and ridiculous. The commonplaces of historical
origin and environment, of the conditions of literary production, of the evolution of literary forms, and all the
rest of them, are verified and illustrated in the life of
Chaucer. 'The poet as representative of his age' is made
ready for the preacher in the volumes of Chaucer. The
author of 'Typical Developments' might find his booty in
those early poems of Chaucer that seem at first to be the
product wholly of some 'tendency,' some 'spirit of the
age,' without any admixture of any particular character

from the man who took the trouble to write them. And it
is not one tendency only, or one taste or study, that is
embodied in Chaucer's writings, but all the ideas, all
the prepossessions, all the fashions, all the vanities of
the world, from courtly rhyming to importunate moralities;
all the learning, from the trivial arts to the heights of
Astronomy, and beyond the *primum mobile*. He comes out of
the Middle Ages like Glaucus from the sea, in the tenth
book of the 'Republic, where the real man, or god, is
unrecognisable in the overgrowth of shells and tangle.
The rich chaotic and formless life, the ooze and wrack of
the mediaeval depths, are indeed left behind and cleared
away when Chaucer comes to his own. But no great poet has
retained in so large a part of his extant work the common
'form and pressure' of his own time and the generation
immediately before his own.

Dante had as large a share of mediaeval learning, and
in his earlier writings is almost as much subject as
Chaucer was to the prevalent fashions. There is not, however, in the progress of Dante from the earlier poetical
conventions and from the learning of the schools, the same
paradoxical element as in the history of Chaucer's poetry.
Dante in one way is a 'representative' of mediaeval habits
of thought and imagination, shared by him with unnumbered
nameless scholars and metaphysical poets. But he always
wears the common habit with some difference of his own,
and, more than that, he carries up all the commonplaces of
his reading and his early experiments into the 'heaven of
his invention,' in the 'Divine Comedy.' Whereas Chaucer
is again and again content to remain simply on the level
of his contemporaries: one large fragment of the 'Canterbury Tales' is an undistinguished and unmanageable block
of the most hopeless commonplace: the 'Tale of Melibeus'
is a thing incapable of life, under any process of interpretation, a lump of the most inert 'first matter' of
mediaeval pedantry, which is yet introduced by Chaucer in
his own person, in company with his latest and finest
work, for the entertainment of the Canterbury Pilgrims.
In many of his poems, though in these always with some
grace of form and never with anything like the oppression
of Melibeus, Chaucer repeats the common tunes, the idle
sequences of phrases and rhymes in fashion among the most
abstract and most unsubstantial of all the schools of
poetry. In his great poems, in 'Troilus,' in the 'Legend
of Good Women,' in the most notable parts of the 'Canterbury Tales,' he has carried on the commonplace matter to
a higher form, and has given individuality to the commonplace without destroying its generic character altogether;
as, in his own way, Dante always, in the most exalted

parts of his poetry in the 'Commedia,' retains some of the
features of the 'Vita Nuova' and the 'Convito.' Chaucer,
however, in his collected writings is encumbered, unlike
Dante, with a crowd of miscellaneous pieces of work;
sketches, fragments, translations, exercises, the product
of hours in which he had no call to do anything else or
anything better than a journalist or an ordinary person
might do. He could escape, when he thought good, from the
restrictions of the mediaeval habit; he could turn the
mediaeval fashion into something incomparably bright and
lively; he could give body and strength to the dreams and
the echoes of the garden of the Rose. But very often, and
that to the very end of his life, he found it easier and
more comfortable to take the traditional conventions as he
found them, and to use them as they were used by people of
no importance, and no remarkable power of their own.

It is this relation of Chaucer to the mediaeval commonplaces that gives room for any amount of historical commentary. Mr. Lowell asks, at the beginning of his essay,
'Will it *do* to say anything more about Chaucer? Can any
one hope to say anything, not new, but even fresh, on a
topic so well-worn?' It is no less fair a problem to
enquire whether there can ever be any end to the illustration of a writer who is in such sympathy with the common
moods of his contemporaries and his predecessors that
every new discovery or new opinion about the literary
wealth of the Middle Ages must inevitable have some bearing, more or less direct, on the study of his writings.
It is still a long way to the end, and not so very far
from the beginning of the criticism of the French poets
whom Chaucer read. It is only the other day that the
poems of Oton de Granson were discovered - 'Graunson flour
of hem that maken in France,' - and among them the original
of Chaucer's 'Complaint of Venus.' There is not yet any
good edition of Machault, and the edition of Eustache
Deschamps is not yet completed for the *Société des anciens
Textes*. It is still open to any one to make his own critical judgment of the works of those authors; there has
been little dictation of any formal or established opinion
on the subject. Those authors are included in the great
host of amatory poets whose common qualities are so common,
and whose distinctive characters are so hard to fix and to
describe. Little has yet been done to seize the volatile
essence of that courtly poetry which takes so many forms
in different countries, and all of them so shadowy. So
long as the spirit of those French poets is still undetec-
ted and undescribed, except in the most general terms, by
the literary historian, it cannot be said that the criticism of Chaucer is exhausted.

It is easily possible to be tired of the historical
criticism that plies its formulas over the sources and
origins of poetry, and attempts to work out the spiritual
pedigree of a genius. It cannot, however, be seriously
argued that enquiries of this sort are inept in the case
of Chaucer, whose obligations to his ancestors are manifest
in every page, not to speak of those debts that are less
obvious. If the result, in most instances, is to bring
out Chaucer's independence more in relief by the subtraction of his loans, and to prove the limitations of this
historical method when it is made to confront the problems
of original and underived imagination, there is no great
harm done, but the contrary. It is the result to be
looked for.

These volumes of Chaucer present one interesting case
where the enquiry into origins has scored one conspicuous
success, and in an equal degree has found its limits and
proved its inability, after all, to analyse the inexplicable. The 'House of Fame' has been subjected to laborious
study, and one important set of facts has been brought to
evidence about it. The relation of the poem to the 'Divine Comedy' has been considered and discussed by Sandras,
Ten Brink, and other scholars, and is here explained by
Mr. Skeat. The proof is decisive. There is no remnant of
doubt that Chaucer had been reading Dante when he wrote
the 'House of Fame'; that he derived from the suggestions
of Dante the images and the pageants of his dream, and
many of the phrases in which it is narrated. Here, however, the proof comes to an end. The historical enquiry
can do no more. And when all is said and done, the 'House
of Fame' still stands where it stood - a poem inexplicable
by any references to the poem from which it was borrowed,
a poem as different from the 'Divine Comedy' as it is possible to find in any Christian tongue. The true criticism
of the poem has to begin where the historical apparatus
leaves off. If its quiddity is to be extracted, the
'House of Fame' must be taken, first of all, as the poem
it is, not as the poem from which it is derived.

It is in this way that the works of Chaucer afford the
most delightful tests of ingenuity and of the validity
and right use of the methods of criticism. No task is
more dangerous for a critic who has his own private device for the solution of all problems. The problems in
Chaucer are continually altering, and the ground is one
that calls for all varieties of skill if it is to be
tracked out and surveyed in all its changes of level.

The appearance of Chaucer's works at last in this satisfactory and convenient form, with the blemishes of the
vulgate texts removed, and everything made easy for every

one who is not too anxious about his ease, can hardly fail
to call out some new devotion to the great master of
stories. Chaucer is always being discovered, like Homer,
Shakespeare, and the book of Baruch; and his discoverers
are not to be pitied, though one may be inclined to ask
them to deal gently with their ignorant friends, and not
to be vexed because of the obdurate who say that Chaucer
was a hack and a translator.

After the first discovery of all, there is none more
pleasant than the discovery how little Chaucer's genius is
exhausted in the 'Canterbury Tales,' and how far his
great book is from being his greatest poem, or from representing his genius to the full. It is only by looking at
the 'Canterbury Tales' from the vantage-ground of the
other works that the magnitude of Chaucer can be in any
way estimated aright.

The 'Canterbury Tales,' which include so much, do not
include the whole of Chaucer. Some of his masterpieces
are there, and there is nothing like the Prologue anywhere else; but outside of the group of the Tales is to be
found the finest work of Chaucer in the more abstract and
delicate kind of poetry 'Anelida'; the most massive and
the richest of his compositions, which is 'Troilus'; and
the most enthralling and most musical of all his idylls,
in the Prologue to the 'Legend of Good Women,' with the
balade of Alcestis, 'sung in carolwise':

Hyd, Absolon, thy gilte tresses clere.

The poem of 'Anelida and the false Arcite,' it may be
suspected, is too often and too rashly passed over. It
has a good deal of the artificial and exquisite qualities
of the court poetry; it appears to be wanting in substance.
Yet for that very reason the fineness of the style in this
unfinished poetical essay gives it rank among the greater
poems, to prove what elegance might be attained by the
strong hand of the artist, when he chose to work in a
small scale. Further, and apart from the elaboration of
the style, the poem is Chaucer's example of the abstract
way of story telling. It is the light ghost of a story,
the antenatal soul of a substantial poem. The characters
are merely types, the situation is a mathematical theorem;
yet this abstract dama, of the faithless knight who leaves
his true love for the sake of a wanton shrew, is played as
admirably, in its own way, as the history of the two Noble
Kinsmen, or the still nobler Troilus.

It is difficult to speak moderately of Chaucer's
'Troilus.' It is the first great modern book in that kind
where the most characteristic modern triumphs of the

literary art have been won; in the kind to which belong
the great books of Cervantes, of Fielding, and of their
later pupils, - that form of story which is not restricted
in its matter in any way, but is capable of taking in
comprehensively all or any part of the aspects and humours
of life. No other mediaeval poem is rich and full in the
same way as 'Troilus' is full of varieties of character
and mood. It is a tragic novel, and it is also strong
enough to pass the scrutiny of that Comic Muse who detects
the impostures of inflated heroic and romantic poetry.
More than this, it has the effective aid of the Comic
Muse in that alliance of tragedy and comedy which makes an
end of all the old distinctions and limitations of narrative and drama.

The original of 'Troilus,' the 'Filostrato' of Boccaccio, is scarcely more substantial in its dramatic part,
though it is longer and has a more elaborate plot, than
Chaucer's 'Anelida.' The three personages of the one poem
are not more definite than the three of the other. The
'Filostrato' is not merely 'done into English' in Chaucer's 'Troilus and Criseyde.' Chaucer has done much more
than that for the original poem; he has translated it from
one form of art into another, - from the form of a light
romantic melody, vague and graceful, into the form of a
story of human characters, and of characters strongly contrasted and subtly understood by the author. The difference is hardly less than that between the Italian novels
and the English tragedies of 'Romeo' or 'Othello,' as far
at least as the representation of character is concerned.
Chaucer learned from Boccaccio the art of construction:
the design of the 'Filostrato' is, in the main outline,
the design of Chaucer's 'Troilus and Criseyde'; but in
working out his story of these 'tragic comedians,' the
English poet has taken his own way, a way in which he had
no forerunners that he knew of, and for successors all
the dramatists and novelists of all the modern tongues.

No other work of Chaucer's has the same dignity or the
same commanding beauty. It would be difficult to find in
any language, in any of the thousand experiments of the
modern schools of novelists, a story so perfectly propor-
tioned and composed, a method of narrative so completely
adequate. Of the dramatic capacities of the original
plot, considering the use made of it in Shakespeare's
'Troilus and Cressida,' there is little need to say anything. Boccaccio chose and shaped the plot of his story
with absolute confidence and success; there is nothing to
break the outline. The general outline is kept by Chaucer, who thus obtains for his story a plan compared with
which the plan of Fielding's greatest novel is ill-

devised, awkward, and irregular; while the symmetry and
unity of Chaucer's story is compatible with a leisure and
a profusion in the details not less than Shakespeare's,
and in this case more suitably bestowed than in Shakespeare's 'Troilus.' There is nothing in the art of any
narrative more beautiful than Chaucer's rendering of the
uncertain faltering and transient moods that go to make
the graceful and mutable soul of Cressida; nothing more
perfect in its conception and its style than his way of
rendering the suspense of Troilus; the slowly-rising doubt
and despair keeping pace in the mind of Troilus with the
equally gradual and inevitable withdrawal and alteration
of love in the mind of his lady, till he comes to the end
of his love-story in Cressida's weak and helpless letter
of defence and deprecation.

Besides the triumph of art in the representation of the
characters, there are more subsidiary beauties in 'Troilus' than anywhere else in Chaucer; as in the effective
details of the less important scenes, the ladies reading
the romance of Thebes together, the amateur medical advice
for the fever of Troilus, the visit of Helen the queen,
the very Helen of the Odyssey, to show kindness to Troilus
in his sickness. There are other poems of Chaucer, the
'Knight's Tale' for instance, in which Chaucer relies more
consistently throughout on the spell of pure romance,
without much effort at strong dramatic composition. But
it is in 'Troilus,' where the art of Chaucer was set to do
all its utmost in the fuller dramatic form of story, that
the finest passages of pure romance are also to be found;
in 'Troilus,' and not in the story of Palamon and Arcite,
or of Constance, or of Cambuscan, or any other. At least
it may be imagined that few readers who remember the most
memorable passage of pure narrative in 'Troilus,' his
entrance into Troy from the battle without, will be
inclined to dispute the place of honour given to it by
Chaucer's last disciple, in his profession of allegiance
in the 'Life and Death of Jason.' The 'tragedie' of the
lovers is embellished with single jewels more than can be
easily reckoned; with scenes and pictures of pure romance;
with the humours and the 'ensamples' and opinions of Pandarus; with verses of pure melody, that seem to have
caught beforehand all the music of Spenser:

And as the newe abaysshed nightingale
That stinteth first whan she biginnith singe;

with many other passages from which the reader receives
the indefinable surprise that is never exhausted by long
acquaintance, and that makes the reader know he is in the

presence of one of the adepts. But all these single and
separable beauties are nothing in comparison with the
organic and structural beauty of the poem, in the order of
its story, and in the life of its personages.

Chaucer is always at his best when he is put on his
mettle by Boccaccio. He is well enough content in other
instances to borrow a story ready made. In his appropriation of Boccaccio he is compelled by his sense of honour
to make something as good if he can, in a way of his own.
He learns from the Italian the lesson of sure and definite
exposition; he does not copy the Italian details or the
special rhetorical prescriptions. The story of 'Palamon
and Arcite,' on which Chaucer appears to have spent so
much of his time, is a different sort of thing from
'Troilus'; the problems are different; the result is no
less fortunate in its own way. The 'Teseide,' the original of the 'Knight's Tale,' is reduced in compass under
Chaucer's treatment, as much as the 'Filostrato' is
strengthened and enlarged. The 'Teseide,' unlike the
'Filostrato,' is an ambitious experiment, no less than the
first poem in the solemn procession of modern epics according to the rules of the ancients; an epic poem written
correctly, in twelve books, with epic similes. Olympian
machinery, funeral games, and a catalogue of the forces
sent into the field, all according to the best examples.
Chaucer brings it down to the form of a romance, restor-
ing it, no doubt, to the form of Boccaccio's lost original, whatever that may have been; at any rate to the
common scale of the less involved and less extravagant
among the French romances of the twelfth or thirteenth
century. For Boccaccio's 'Theseid,' with all its bril-
liance, is somewhat tedious, as an epic poem may be; it
is obviously out of condition, and overburdened in its
heroic accoutrements. The 'Knight's Tale' is well designed, and nothing in it is superfluous. There are some
well-known instances in it of the success with which
Chaucer has changed the original design: reducing the pompous and unwieldy epic catalogue of heroes to the two
famous contrasted pictures 'in the Gothic manner,' the
descriptions of Lycurgus and Emetreus, and rejecting
Boccaccio's awkward fiction in the account of the prayers
of Palamon, Arcita, and Emilia. But the most significant
part of Chaucer's work in this story is the deliberate
evasion of anything like the drama of 'Troilus and Cressida.'

The 'Knight's Tale' is a romance and nothing more; a
poem, a story, in which the story and the melody of the
poem are more than the personages. Chaucer saw that the
story would not bear a strong dramatic treatment. The

Comic Muse was not to be bribed: neither then, nor later,
when the rash experiment of Fletcher in the 'Two Noble
Kinsmen' proved how well the elder poet was justified in
refusing to give this story anything like the burden of
'Troilus.' The Lady Emilia, most worshipful and most
shadowy lady in the romance, is too cruelly put to the
ordeal of tragedy: the story is refuted as soon at it is
made to bear the weight of tragic passion or thought.
Chaucer, who found the story of 'Troilus' capable of
bearing the whole strength of his genius, deals gently
with the fable of the 'Theseid'; the characters are not
brought forward; instead of the drama of 'Troilus,' there
is a sequence of pictures; the landscapes of romance, the
castles and the gardens, are more than the figures that
seem to move about among them. There is pathos in the
'Knight's Tale,' but there is no true tragedy. How
admirably Chaucer tells the pathetic story may be seen at
once by comparing the meeting of Palamon and Arcita in the
wood with the corresponding scene in Fletcher's play: -

> Ther nas no good day, ne no saluing;
> But streight, withouten word or rehersing,
> Everich of hem halp for to armen other,
> As freendly as he were his owne brother.

This simplicity of style is the perfection of mere narrative, as distinguished from the higher and more elaborate forms of epic poetry or prose. The situation here
rendered is one that does not call for any dramatic fulness or particularity: the characters of Palamon and
Arcite in any case are little qualified for impressive
drama. But the pathos of the meeting, and of the courtesy rendered to one another by the two friends in their
estrangement, is a pathos almost wholly independent of
any delineation of their characters. The characters are
nothing: it is 'any friend to any friend,' an abstract
formula, used by Chaucer in this place with an art for
which he found no suggestion in Boccaccio, nor obtained
any recognition from Fletcher. In the 'Teseide' the
rivals meet and argue with one another before the duel in
which they are interrupted by Theseus; in the play of the
'Two Noble Kinsmen' they converse without any apparent
strain. In Chaucer's poem the division between them is
made deeper, and indicated with greater effect in four
lines, than in the eloquence of his Italian master or his
English pupil.
    Such is the art of Chaucer in the 'Knight's Tale': per-
fect in its own kind, but that kind not the greatest. It
needs the infinitely stronger fable of his 'Troilus and

Criseyde' to bring out the strength of his imagination.
'Troilus,' to use a familiar term of Chaucer's own, cannot
but 'distain' by comparison the best of the 'Canterbury
Tales.' 'Troilus' is not a romance, but a dramatic story,
in which the characters speak for themselves, in which the
elements that in the 'Canterbury Tales' are dissipated or
distributed among a number of tales and interludes are all
brought together and made to contribute in due proportion
to the total effect of the poem. In the 'Canterbury
Tales' the comic drama is to be found at its best outside
of the stories, best of all in the dramatic monologues of
the 'Wife of Bath' and the 'Pardoner.' It takes nothing
away from the glory of those dramatic idylls to maintain
that Chaucer's Pandarus belongs to a higher and more difficult form of comic imagination. The 'Wife of Bath' and
the 'Pardoner' are left to themselves as much, or very
nearly as much, as the 'Northern Farmer' or 'Mr. Sludge
the Medium.' Pandarus has to acquit himself as well as he
may on the same stage as other and more tragic personages,
in a story where there are other interests besides that of
his humour and his proverbial philosophy. This is not a
question of tastes and preferences; but a question of the
distinction between different kinds and varieties of narrative poetry. It is open to any one to have any opinion
he pleases about the value of Chaucer's poetry. But the
question of value is one thing; the question of kinds is
another. The value may be disputed indefinitely; the kind
may be ascertained and proved. The kind of poetry to
which 'Troilus' belongs is manifestly different from that
of each and all of the 'Canterbury Tales,' and manifestly
a richer and more fruitful kind; and for this reason alone
the poem of 'Troilus' would stand out from among all the
other poems of its author.

The problems regarding Chaucer's methods of composition
are inexhaustible. They are forced on the attention,
naturally, by this collected edition of his writings,
which makes the contradictions and paradoxes of Chaucer's
life more obvious and striking than they ever were before.
'Boece' and 'Troilus,' which are mentioned together by
Chaucer himself, are here associated in the same volume:
the 'Treatise on the Astrolabe' goes along with the
'Legend of Good Women.' Of all the critical problems
offered by this great collection of the works of a great
master there is none more fascinating and none more hopeless than the task of following his changes of mood and
his changes of handling. 'Troilus' is followed by the
'House of Fame,' a caprice, a fantasy, the poet's compensation to himself for the restraint and the application
bestowed on his greater poem. 'Ne jompre eek no

discordant thing yfere,' is the advice of a literary
critic in the book of 'Troilus' itself: the critic knew
the mediaeval temptation to drag in 'termes of physik'
and other natural sciences, whether they were required or
not. The 'House of Fame' is an indulgence, after 'Troilus,' in all the mediaeval vanities that had been dis-
couraged by the ambitious and lordly design of that poem.
Allegory, description, painted walls, irrelevant science,
pageants and processions of different kinds, everything
that the average mediaeval book makes play with, - these
are the furniture of the 'House of Fame'; and, in addition
to these and through all these, there is the irony of the
dream, and the humorous self-depreciation which gives to
the 'House of Fame' the character of a personal confession.
It is one of the most intimate as well as one of the most
casual of all his works; a rambling essay in which all the
author's weaknesses of taste are revealed, all his fondness for conformity with his age and its manners, while at
the same time there is no other poem of Chaucer's so clear
and so ironical in its expression of his own view of himself. On the one hand, it is related to all the dreariest
and stalest mediaeval fashions; on the other, to the
liveliest moods of humorous literature. The temper of
Chaucer in his tedious description of the pictures from
the 'Aeneid,' in the first book, is in concord with all
the most monotonous and drawling poets of the mediaeval
schools; his wit in the colloquy with the eagle in the
second book is something hardly to be matched except in
literature outside the mediaeval conventions altogether.
The disillusion of the poet, when he imagines that he is
going to heaven to be 'stellified,' and is undeceived by
his guide, is like nothing in the world so much as the
conversation with Poseidon in Heine's 'Nordsee,' where
the voyager has his fears removed in a manner equally
patronising and uncomplimentary.
　　The contradictions and the problems of the 'House of
Fame,' in respect of its composition and its poetical
elements, are merely those that are found still more pro-
fusely and more obviously in the 'Canterbury Tales.'
There is little need for any one to say more than Dryden
has said, or to repeat what every reader can find out for
himself, about the liveliness of the livelier parts of
the collection. The Prologue, the Interludes of conversation and debate, the Host's too masterful good humour,
the considerate and gentle demeanour of the Monk, the
Shipman's defence of true religion, the confessions of
the Wife of Bath and the Pardoner, the opinions of the
Canon's Yeoman, - of all this, and of everything of this
sort in the book, it is hopeless to look for any terms of

praise that will not sound superfluous to people with eyes
and wits of their own. It is not quite so irrelevant to
enquire into the nature of the separate tales, and to ask
how it is that so many of them have so little of the character of Chaucer, if Chaucer is to be judged by the Prologue and the Interludes.

Some of the Tales are early works, and that explains
something of the mystery. Still the fact remains that
those early works were adopted and ratified by Chaucer in
the composition of his great work, when he made room for
the Life of St. Cecilia, and expressly set himself to be-
speak an audience for the gravity of 'Melibeus.' Here
again, though on a still larger scale, is the contradiction of the elements of the 'House of Fame,' the discord
between the outword garment of the Middle Ages and the new
web from which it is patched.

There is nothing in all the 'Canterbury Tales' to set
against the richly varied story of 'Troilus and Cressida.'
There are, however, certain of the 'Canterbury Tales'
which are not less admirable in respect of mere technical
beauty of construction, though the artistic skill is not
shown in the same material as in 'Troilus.' The 'Knight's
Tale' preserves the epic, or rather the romantic unities
of narrative, as admirably as the greater poem. The
'Nun's Priest's Tale' is equally perfect in its own way,
and that way is one in which Chaucer has no rival. The
story of Virginia, the story of the fairy bride, the
story of the revellers who went to look for Death, and
many others, are planned without weakness or faltering in
the design. There are others which have an incurable
fault in the construction, a congenital weakness,
utterly at variance from the habit of Chaucer as shown
elsewhere, and from the critical principles which he had
clearly mastered for his own guidance in his study of
Boccaccio.

The 'Man of Law's Tale,' the story of Constance, is a
comparatively early work, which Chaucer apparently did not
choose to alter as he altered his first version of 'Palamon and Arcite.' At any rate, the story declares itself
as part of a different literary tradition from those in
which Chaucer has taken his own way with the proportions
of the narrative. The story of Constance has hardly its
equal anywhere for nobility of temper; but in respect of
unity and harmony of design it is as weak and uncertain
as the 'Knight's Tale' is complete, continuous, and
strong. Chaucer, whose modifications of Boccaccio are
proof of intense critical study and calculation of the
dimensions of his stories, here admits, to rank with his
finished work, a poem beautiful for everything except

those constructive excellences on which he had come to
set so much account in other cases. The story of Constance follows the lines of a dull original. It has the
defects, or rather the excesses, of most popular traditional fairy-tales. Chaucer, who afterwards refused to
translate Boccaccio literally, here follows closely the
ill-designed plot of a writer who was not in the least
like Boccaccio. The story repeats twice over, with variations in detail, the adventure of the princess suffering
from the treacherous malice of a wicked mother-in-law;
and, also twice over, her voyage in a rudderless boat;
the incident of her deliverance from a villain, the
Northumbrian caitiff in the first instance, the heathen
lord's steward in the second, is also repeated; while the
machinery of the first false charge made against Constance
by the Northumbrian adversary goes some way to spoil the
effect of the subsequent false charge made by the queen-
mother, Donegild. The poem has beauties enough to make
any one ashamed of criticism; yet it cannot be denied that
its beauties are often the exact opposite of the virtues
of Chaucer's finished work, being beauties of detail and
not beauties of principle and design. The 'Man of Law's
Tale' with all the grace of Chaucer's style has also the
characteristic unwieldiness of the common mediaeval
romance; while the 'Knight's Tale,' which is no finer in
details, is as a composition finished and coherent, with
no unnecessary or irrelevant passages.

Besides the anomalies of construction in the 'Canterbury Tales,' and not less remarkable than the difference
between the neatness and symmetry of the 'Knight's Tale'
and the flaccidity of the 'Man of Law's,' there is an ano-
maly of sentiment and of mood. 'Melibeus' may be left
out of account, as a portent too wonderful for mortal
commentary: there are other problems and distresses in
the 'Canterbury Tales,' and they are singular enough,
though not altogether inexplicable or 'out of all
whooping,' like that insinuating 'little thing in prose'
by which Sir Thopas was avenged on his detractors.

The 'Knight's Tale' is an artifíce, wholly successful,
but not to be tampered with in any way, and above all
things not to be made into a drama, except for the theatre of the mind. Chaucer refused to give to Emilie and
her rival lovers one single spark of that imaginative
life which makes his story of 'Troilus' one of the great
narrative poems of the world, without fear of comparison
with the greatest stories in verse or prose. By the original conception of the 'Knight's Tale,' the Lady Emilie
is forbidden to take any principal part in the story.
This is an initial fallacy, a want of dramatic proportion,

which renders the plot impossible for the strongest forms
of novel or of tragedy. But Chaucer saw that the fable,
too weak, too false for the stronger kind, was exactly
right when treated in the fainter kind of narrative which
may be called romance, or by any other name that will distinguish it from the order of 'Troilus,' from the stronger
kind of story in which the characters are true.

In some of the other Tales the experiment is more hazardous, the success not quite so admirable. What is to be
said of the 'Clerk's Tale'? what of the Franklin's? That
the story of Griselda should have been chosen by the
author of 'Troilus' for an honourable place in his 'Canterbury Tales' is almost as pleasant as the publication
of 'Persiles and Sigismunda' by the author of 'Don Quix-
ote.' Chaucer had good authority for the patience of
Griselda; by no author has the old story been more beautifully and pathetically rendered, and his 'Envoy' saves him
from the suspicion of too great solemnity: but no consideration will ever make up for the disparity between the
monotonous theme and the variety of Chaucer's greater
work, between this formal virtue of the pulpit and the
humanities outside. In the 'Franklin's Tale' again, in a
different way, Chaucer has committed himself to superstitions of which there is no vestige in the more complex
parts of his poetry. As Griselda represents the abstract
and rectilinear virtue of mediaeval homilists, the 'Franklin's Tale' revolves about the point of honour, no less
gallantly than Prince Prettyman in the 'Rehearsal.' The
virtue of patience, the virtue of truth, are there
impaled, crying out for some gentle casuist to come and
put them out of their torment. Many are the similar victims, from Sir Amadace to Hernani: 'the horn of the old
Gentleman' has compelled innumerable romantic heroes to
take unpleasant resolutions for the sake of a theatrical
effect. That the point of honour, the romantic tension
between two abstract opposites, should appear in Chaucer,
the first of modern poets to give a large, complete, and
humorous representation of human action, is merely one of
the many surprises which his readers have to accept as
best they may. It is only one of his thousand and one
caprices: the only dangerous mistake to which it could
possibly lead, would be an assumption that the 'Franklin's Tale' can stand as a sample of Chaucer's art in its
fullest expression; and the danger of such an error is
small. The beginning of right acquaintance with Chaucer
is the conviction that nothing represents him except the
whole body of his writings. So one is brought round to
Dryden's comfortable and sufficient formula: 'Here is
God's plenty.' From the energy and the volume of his

Trojan story, as glorious as his Trojan river:

> And thou, Simoys, that as an arwe clere
> Through Troie rennest ay downward to the se;

from the passion and the music of that 'tragedie' to the
doleful voices of 'Melibeus,' there is no form or mood, no
fashion of all the vanities, that is not in some way or
other represented there.   The variety of the matter of
Chaucer may possibly to some extent have hindered a full
and general recognition of the extraordinary variety in
his poetical and imaginative art.   It may be doubted
whether there is any general appreciation of the height
attained by Chaucer in the graver tragic form of story,
or of the perfection of his style in all the manifold
forms in which he made experiments.   If there be any such
established injustice in the common estimate of Chaucer
as makes it possible for reasonable but misguided people
to think of him as merely a 'great translator,' then the
refutation will come best of all, without clamour or heat,
from the book in which Chaucer's work is presented in the
most adequate way.   Mr. Skeat in his edition has excluded
a number of critical questions which might be maintained
to be as capable of argument as the subject of Chaucer's
dialect and his practice in the composition of English
verse.   But although the problems of Chaucer's poetry are
not exhausted, and many of them untouched, in this edition,
it is still to this edition that appeal will be made for
many a year to come.   Its value as the first critical text
of the whole of Chaucer will scarcely be much impaired by
the future edition of a hundred years hence, which shall
stand in the same relation to this edition as this to
Tyrwhitt's, not to disparage its work, but to complement
it.   The spirit of the editor is fortunately such as to
make him disinclined to rest on his accomplishments.   It
is evident from many signs that these six volumes are not
yet the end of his studies, and that it will probably be
something even more strongly equipped than these six
volumes which will be left by him to the next age as the
final version of his work.

30.   F.J. SNELL, CHAUCER IS THE MOST IRRESPONSIBLE OF MEN

1901

F.J. Snell (1863-?), scholar and man of letters, who was
educated at Balliol College, Oxford, recognises Chaucer's
humanity without feeling obliged to insist that all he
writes is uplifting. The passage is reprinted from the
general summary that concludes a sensible and fairly detailed account of Chaucer and his contemporaries, 'The Age
of Chaucer', pp. 231-4 (omitting a long quotation from
Emerson, above, No. 1 (b)), Bell (1901), by permission of
the publisher.

In estimating Chaucer's position as a writer, the first
point with which it seems necessary to deal is the charge
many entertain, if they do not openly allege - that, after
all, he is a mere imitator, that he has no true gift of
originality. The frequent references we have been compelled to make, and they are by no means exhaustive, to
Chaucer's sources, cannot but raise the problem to what
extent such obligations are admissible, and how far they
may consist with practical independence. Here, then, it is
requisite to distinguish between mechanical appropriation
and spiritual assimilation involving, it may be, verbal
reminiscence. That Chaucer was never guilty of mechanical appropriation we dare not aver, but the ratio between
slavish imitation and free reproduction, or masterly re-
casting, was constantly varying, and always in favour of
the latter....
     In his discourse at the unveiling of the Chaucer window
at Southwark Church, Mr. Alfred Austin seemed to advocate
the theory that Chaucer, holding a brief for conduct, made
of his poetry a handmaid of virtue, a nurse of good
morals. This doctrine conflicts with the present writer's
opinion, according to which Chaucer never grasped the
idea of duty, as the stern, perhaps solitary, fulfilling
of what is right. Virtue to him was not something binding
on the conscience, but that which was socially convenient
and attractive - the 'good fair White' - in other words,
a sort of higher etiquette accepted by a few. How else
explain the composition of poems, the tendency of which is
the reverse of edifying? The truth is, Chaucer had a
taste and relish, an eye and understanding for many things
in human nature, from which the ideal moralist turns away

with horror and indignation. Chaucer, on the contrary, with perfect complacency, takes the world as he finds it, and, like a practised harmonist, extracts from its jarring discords an infinity of pleasing strains. Even this hardly states the case. Chaucer is the most irresponsible of men. The obligations of morality sit so lightly on him that they have become a theory of which he sometimes reminds himself, but which has no real influence on his poetical procedure. In his capacity as poet he is a mirror, an Aeolian harp, a faithful amanuensis of Phoebus, who tweaks his ear and bids him write for the diversion of a weary world.

One of the first essentials for such a mission was the conquest of rhythm. The lay or casual reader will entirely fail to comprehend Chaucer's mastery of verse, for the simple reason that Time has wrought the same havoc on his writings as on the statuary of our old cathedrals. Patience and study, however, not necessarily prolonged, will bring their reward in appreciation of one of the most tunable of bards, who, singing in an age when English was not so poor in inflexions, could smooth and sweeten his verse with the aid of end-vowels. Rhyming also, in spite of his confessions, appears to have been no great trouble to him.

But the supreme charm of Chaucer's poetry, after all, is the revelation it affords of a gracious personality that shines through and suffuses every line. The mild yet manly note, the transforming sympathy, the signal absence of bigotry and partisanship make up a pattern of courtesy, of humanity never more needed than in that brutal, cynical, and ignorant age, and not superfluous to-day. It is this warmth of feeling, this wealth of observation that furnish Chaucer with what was long since recognized as his dominant characteristic - namely, his dramatic quality. That Chaucer did not adopt the form of the drama is an accident that may be safely attributed to temporal conditions. Born in the fourteenth century, when the drama signified the buffoonery of the miracle plays, the fashion of his youth led him away from his true *milieu*. But the shrewdness, the knowledge of the world, the knowledge of the human heart, the power of realizing and depicting feelings the most various, the most opposed, that constitute the play - these high and happy gifts were united in Chaucer as in none of his contemporaries, and lie at the root of the perennial freshness, the undying popularity of the 'Canterbury Tales.'

31.   SIR WALTER RALEIGH, IRONY AND SIMPLE GOOD ENGLISH

1905 (1926)

Sir Walter Raleigh (1861-1922), Merton Professor of
English in the University of Oxford, in lectures given in
1905, posthumously published in 1926, emphasises, besides
irony and dramatic quality, how frequently Chaucer breaks
his own 'tone'. Raleigh overemphasises Chaucer's simplicity of diction while recognising the social basis of
speech. Reprinted from 'On Writers and Writing', ed.
G. Gordon, pp. 108-19, Edward Arnold (1926), by permission of the publisher.

Chaucer's strong sanity and critical commonsense, his
quick power of observation, and his distaste for all
extravagances and follies helped to make him a great
comic poet. But he is not a railing wit, or a bitter
satirist. His broad and calm philosophy of life, his
delight in diversities of character, his sympathy with
all kinds of people, and his zest in all varieties of
experience - these are the qualities of a humorist.

Charles Lamb thought with misgiving of a heaven in
which all irony and ironical modes of expression should
be lacking. Certainly it would be no heaven for Chaucer. The all-pervading essence of his work is humour.
Sometimes it breaks out in boisterous and rollicking
laughter at the drunken and unseemly exploits of churls;
sometimes it is so delicate and evanescent that you can
hardly detect its existence. But it is everywhere, even
in places where it has no right to be. The intellectual
pleasure of standing aside and seeing things against an
incongruous background was a pleasure he could not long
forgo.

In this matter, and in this alone, Chaucer is sometimes guilty of what I shall call 'literary bad manners.'
It is like the fault of distracted attention. Even at a
funeral he must insinuate his jest. Now, it is quite
excusable to jest at a funeral so long as it is regarded
as a formal, official function; or if it is merely matter
for thought. The suit of clay as the dwelling-house made
for this creature a little lower than the angels is a
jest of the Gods. But Chaucer will arouse deep feelings
of pathos and sympathy, and in the atmosphere thus created, he will let off a little crackling penny jest, from

pure love of mischief. This spirit of witty mischief is
always breaking out.
Chaucer has the true humorist's gift - the gift of the
wooden face. He utters a truism ('Honesty is the best
policy') with a solemn air; and only the faintest twinkle
in the eye makes one hesitate in believing him serious.
Chaucer's self-consciousness is of a piece with his
critical art. Sometimes (as in 'Troilus' and the
'Knight's Tale') he is fairly caught in the web of his own
imagination, and forgets himself. Far more frequently he
reminds you of his presence by some sly allusion to himself, or some ironical piece of self-depreciation. Then
the tale becomes a mere tale again, and we come back into
the company of the teller,
This is a common trait of the humorist. He sees much
that is ridiculous in human life; what if he himself is
ridiculous? So he anticipates criticism, and discounts
the retort, by laughing at himself.
You will find this in Falstaff ('I do here walk before
thee like a sow that hath overwhelmed all her litter but
one.') You may find it in all the jackanapes tricks of
Sterne, his posturings and grimaces. You will find it in
Mr. Bernard Shaw, who cannot forget that laughter is
generally a hostile weapon, and is unwilling to stand the
push of it in championing his ideas. Being skilled with
it, he over-values it and over-fears it. So, like Bob
Acres, he stands edgeways, or turns his weapon against
himself, that he may still be on the side of the
laughers.
This furnishes excellent wit and comedy, but is not
consistent with good epical work. The man who is afraid
of being caught in a serious sentiment lest others should
find it ridiculous, cannot tell a moving tale in a forth-
right, wholehearted way. His mind is a kingdom divided
against itself, - under two kings, a warrior and a clown.
A cavalry charge cannot be led by one who is thinking of
the figure he cuts in the eyes of a bystander. The professions of reformer and humorist have never been successfully combined. A reformer does not care who laughs.
The escape from this sort of self-consciousness - the
besetting sin of the professed humorist - is in the drama;
and all Chaucer's best and deepest humour occurs in parts
of his work that are dramatic in everything but form.
The dramatist stands aside and has not to defend himself.
He speaks through many voices, and is himself unseen.
He looks at human life and portrays it, and smiles.
All profound dramatic humour depends on sympathy and
breadth of view, that keeps sight of the whole even while
it spends delighted attention on a part. A wit or a

satirist can be angry and laugh; he can laugh at what he
misunderstands and misrepresents. The dramatic humorist
laughs because he understands and enjoys. Now there
never was a poet whose zest and delight in life was fuller
and broader thatn Chaucer's. He hates nothing that he has
made; in the realms of his creation the sun shines upon
the evil and the good. His characters, as they come
alive, almost always find in him an admirer and abetter.
Pandarus, it is to be supposed, was originally designed to
be a base, broken lackey, just as Falstaff may have been
designed for a shallow, vainglorious, lying heartless
rascal. But Pandarus, like Falstaff, comes alive, and we
end by almost loving him. He has the worldly wisdom, the
shrewd humour, the tender affections, and the philosophic
outlook of his creator. He is a good friend, and, like
Falstaff, he too is a poet.

Anything fair to see or hear awakes Chaucer's enthusiasm. Of Troilus riding into Troy he says: -

It was an hevene upon him for to see!

When the people applaud, Troilus blushes: -

That to biholde it was a noble game.

When Antigone sings in the garden: -

It an heven was hir voys to here.

Anything on a large and generous scale, such as the house-
keeping of the Franklin ('It snewed in his hous of mete
and drinke'), or the marriages of the Wife of Bath,
arouses Chaucer's sympathy. He loves a rogue, so that the
rogue be high-spirited and clever at his trade, and not a
whey-faced, bloodless rascal. The Pardoner, in describing
his own preaching, says: -

Myn hondes and my tonge goon so yerne,
That it is joye to see my bisiness,

and so Chaucer felt it. His joy is chronic and irrepressible.

Chaucer makes the most enormous claim on the sound
sense and quick intelligence of his readers. He assumes
that they are at one with him, and that it is unnecessary
for him to expound his point of view. The natural form
for the dramatic sense of humour is irony. Often enough
Chaucer's irony is dramatic, as when the Carpenter, in the
very act of being befooled by Nicholas the clerk,

congratulates himself that he is a plain, unlearned man.
But the best of Chaucer's irony is found in his own interpolated utterances. He seems to be telling the story
simply and directly. Suspect him! He is conveying his
own criticisms, expressing his own amusement, in touches
- a word here and a word there - so subtle and delicate
that eleven out of twelve men in any jury would acquit
him of any comic intent. These quiet smiles that flicker
over his face are so characteristic that I have ventured
to call the passages where we can detect them *Chaucerisms*.
Take the 'Shipman's Tale': -

> A Marchant whylom dwelled at Seint Denys,
> That riche was, for which men helde him wys.

Chaucer is at his work already.
When the merchant returns from abroad,

> His wyf ful redy mette him atte gate
> As she was wont of olde usage algate.

How quietly, almost inaudibly, Chaucer indicates that
she had no very lively affection for her husband!
It is impossible to overpraise Chaucer's mastery of
language. Here at the beginning, as it is commonly
reckoned, of Modern English literature, is a treasury of
perfect speech. We can trace his themes, and tell something of the events of his life. But where did he get
his style - from which it may be said that English literature has been (in some respects) a long falling away?
What is the ordinary account? I do not wish to cite
individual scholars, and there is no need. Take what can
be gathered from the ordinary text-books - what are the
current ideas? Is not this a fair statement of them?

> English was a despised language little used by the
> upper classes. A certain number of dreary works
> written chiefly for homiletic purposes, or in order to
> appeal to the humble people, are to be found in the
> half century before Chaucer. They are poor and flat
> and feeble, giving no promise of the new dawn. Then
> arose the morning star! Chaucer adopted the despised
> English tongue and set himself to modify it, to shape
> it, to polish it, to render it fit for his purpose.
> He imported words from the French; he purified the
> English of his time from its dross; he shaped it into
> a fit instrument for his use.

Now I have no doubt that a competent philologist

examining the facts could easily show that this account *must be* nonsense, from beginning to end. But even a literary critic can say something certain on the point - perhaps can even give aid by divination to the philologists, and tell them where it will best repay them to ply their pickaxes and spades.

No poet makes his own language. No poet introduces serious or numerous modifications into the language that he uses. Some, no doubt, coin words and revive them, like Spenser or Keats in verse, Carlyle or Sir Thomas Browne in prose. But least of all great English poets did Chaucer mould and modify the speech he found. The poets who take liberties with speech are either prophets or eccentrics. From either of these characters Chaucer was far removed. He held fast by communal and social standards for literary speech. He desired to be understood of the people. His English is plain, terse, homely, colloquial English, taken alive out of daily speech. He expresses his ideal again and again, as when the Host asks what is the use of telling a tale that sends the hearers to sleep: -

> For certeinly, as that thise clerkes seyn,
> Where-as a man may have noon audience,
> Noght helpeth it to tellen his sentence.

The same admirable literary critic repeats Chaucer's creed when he instructs the Clerk: -

> Your termes, your colours, and your figures,
> Kepe hem in stoor till so be ye endite
> Heigh style, as whan that men to kinges write,
> Speketh so pleyn at this tyme, I yow preye,
> That we may understonde what ye seye.

Chaucer has expressed his views on the model literary style so clearly and so often, and has illustrated them so well in his practice, that no mistake is possible. His style is the perfect courtly style: it has all the qualities of ease, directness, simplicity, of the best colloquial English, in short, which Chaucer recognised, three centuries before the French Academy, as the English spoken by cultivated women in society. His 'facound,' like Virginia's, 'is ful womanly and pleyn.' He avoids all 'counterfeted terms,' all subtleties of rhetoric, and addresses himself to the 'commune intente.'

Examples of his plain, terse brevity are easy to find. Take one, from the 'Monk's Tale' - of Hugelin of Pisa. (The imprisoned father bites his hands for grief; his young sons think it is for hunger): -

> His children wende that it for hunger was
> That he his armes gnew, and not for wo,
> And seyde, 'Fader, do not so, allas!
> But rather ete the flessh upon us two;
> Our flesh thou yaf us, take our flesh us fro,
> And ete y-nough': right thus they to him seyde,
> And after that, with-in a day or two,
> They leyde hem in his lappe adoun, and deyde.

Now a style like this, and in this perfection, implies a society at the back of it. If we are told that educated people at the Court of Edward III spoke French and that English was a despised tongue, we could deny it on the evidence of Chaucer alone. His language was shaped for him, and it cannot have been shaped by rustics. No English style draws so much as Chaucer's from the communal and colloquial elements of the language. And his poems make it certain that from his youth up he had heard much admirable, witty talk in the English tongue.

The conclusion is that Chaucer's language is the language of his own day, like Gower's, but used by a quicker intelligence, and freer from repetition, artificial tags, flatnesses, etc. It was his good fortune to live at a time when bookish learning had not yet severed classes. He broke loose from the literary fashions which at all time affect the 'educated classes,' and wrote the good English of peers and peasants. In this respect he comes near to the poets of Dryden's age.

This language was his own, not painfully acquired. Ease and skill of this kind is not attainable save in the birth tongue. Too much has been made of French; and of the dates of the 'adoption' of English for public documents, law courts, schools. The English language had throughout a healthy, full-blooded existence. Chaucer had no adequate *literary* predecessors in English. But how partial and poor a thing the manuscript literature of the time compared with the riches of spoken lore, proverb, tale and romance! As Chaucer helps us, by his portrait of the age, to correct the formal annalists, so he helps us, by his writing, to a truer appreciation of literary history.

If there is to be any profitable investigation of Chaucer's language it must be remembered that he is at the *end* of an age, not at the beginning. His pupils could make nothing of him, and the Renaissance brought in ideals which made him unintelligible. Like Burns, Chaucer is a culmination and a close. We can understand Burns only by remembering his debts to Fergusson, Ramsay, and scores of nameless poets. If we are to understand Chaucer, it must be by reference to a tribe of story-tellers, songsters, traffickers in popular lore and moral maxims who, because they did not relate themselves to paper, have almost passed, except by inference, from our ken.

32. W.M. HART, REALISM, UNITY AND COMIC POETIC JUSTICE

1908

W.M. Hart, while remaining in the tradition of a general humane criticism, was the first American scholar to give serious extended attention to Chaucer's specifically comic poems on indecent subjects, which he derived from the somewhat similar earlier French comic poems known as *fabliaux*. Hart makes a detailed comparison between 'The Reeve's Tale' and the French poem 'Le Meunier et les II Clers', which both tell the same international popular tale. Hart makes the working hypothesis, without completely committing himself, that 'Le Meunier' was the direct source of 'The Reeve's Tale'. Hart's work laid down the future lines of criticism of what it is now usual to call Chaucer's own *fabliaux*, with emphasis on realistic description of place and person, unity of time, place and action, poetic justice - in short, the full apparatus of Neoclassical criticism. Hart's article is very full and long, and it has been necessary to abridge it severely, omitting many examples and footnotes, but retaining the line of argument. Excerpts reprinted by permission of the Modern Language Association of America from The Reeve's Tale, 'Publications of the Modern Language Association' XXIII (1908), pp. 1-44.

THE REEVE'S TALE

(p. 10) The fabliaux were 'destinés à la récitation publique,'(1) and in the 'Reeve's Tale', thanks to its dramatic setting,(2) we seem to have the actual public recitation of a fabliau by one who, though not, indeed, a professional trouvère, is a master of the art of

narration. It is effective not merely because it is well
told, however, but also because it is opportune. It is
inspired by the Reeve's desire for revenge upon the Miller,
in whose tale, just told, the victim is, like the Reeve, a
carpenter. He is stupid and superstitious, the old husband of a young wife, and the Reeve's senile melancholy in
his own prologue, shows that the cap has fitted. The
victim of the 'Reeve's Tale' is inevitably, then, a miller,
and in describing him the Reeve draws a portrait which
skilfully suggests, yet does not reproduce, the miller of
the 'General Prologue'.

As in the fabliau, the persons of the tale are the two
clerks, the miller, his wife and daughter. But we know
more about them; they seem to us real people, in a real
world, with a place in actual society....

(p. 12) To the *dramatis personae* of his source Chaucer
adds characters which, though they remain in the background, contribute something to the verisimilitude of
the tale. In addition to the parson, there is the maunciple, whose sudden illness leads to the outrageous
thefts of the miller. The warden's permission must be
secured before the clerks may undertake the adventure.
The mention of the nunnery, of Soler-halle at Cambridge,
of the effect upon observers of Simkin and his dame, and
even phrases like 'he was a market-beter atte fulle'
(v. 3936), all contribute to the impression of a complex
social setting which stands in sharp contrast to the sense
of isolation produced by Chaucer's original. Even the
mare of the fabliau, who does not differ essentially from
the sack of grain, is transformed, and becomes Bayard, a
horse with volition, if not personality, who leads the
clerks a merry chase:

> Toward the fen, ther wilde mares renne,
> Forth with wehee, thurgh thikke and thurgh thenne (vv.
> 4065f.).

Of the scene of the action Chaucer tells us rather more
than does his source; he names and locates it, carrying
out, perhaps, the suggestion of the 'molin à choisel' of
the fabliau:

> At Trumpington, nat fer fro Cantebrigge,
> Ther goth(3) a brook and over that a brigge,
> Up-on the whiche brook ther stant a melle;
> And this is verray soth that I yow telle (vv. 3921ff.).

Nearby is the fen:(4) behind the mill an arbor (v. 4061),
and a barn (v. 4088). Within the mill are hopper and

trough (vv. 4036ff.). The miller's house is 'streit,'
'twenty foot of space' (vv. 4122ff.), but has evidently
more than one room, for Simkin

> in his owne chambre hem made a bed
> With shetes and with chalons faire y-spred,
> Noght from his owne bed ten foot or twelve.
> His doghter hadde a bed, al by hir-selve,
> Right in the same chambre, by and by;
> It mighte be no bet, and cause why,
> Ther was no roumer herberwe in the place (vv. 4139ff.).

Through a hole in the wall of this room the moonlight fell
upon Simkin's bald head, and at a critical moment he
tripped over a stone in the floor, - if there was a floor?
The clerks, returning from the pursuit of their horse,
found Simkin sitting by the fire. By this same fire, no
doubt, Simkin's wife baked the cake made of the clerks'
flour.

The time of the action seems to be the not very distant
past: 'a Miller was ther dwelling many a day' (v. 3925).
'On a day it happed, in a stounde, sik lay the maunciple'
(vv. 3992f.). When the clerks returned with the horse it
was night (v. 4117). 'Aboute midnight wente they to
reste' (v. 4148), an unusually late hour.(5) 'Hem nedede
no dwale' (v. 4161), Chaucer says, implying the custom of
the 'night-cap.'

> This Ioly lyf han thise two clerkes lad
> Til that the thridde cok bigan to singe.
> Aleyn wax wery in the daweninge (vv. 4232ff.).

Chaucer is, then, somewhat more careful than the trouvère
to indicate the time of the action.

The action is more closely unified than is that of the
fabliau. From beginning to end its mainspring is the contest of clerks and miller. Simkin's thefts, opportunely
increased by the sudden illness of the maunciple, react
upon the clerks:

> Testif they were, and lusty for to pleye,
> And, only for hir mirthe and revelrye,
> Up-on the wardeyn bisily they crye,
> To yeve hem leve but a litel stounde
> To goon to mille and seen hir corn y-grounde;
> And hardily, they dorste leye hir nekke,
> The miller shold nat stele hem half a pekke
> Of corn by sleighte, ne by force hem reve (vv. 4004ff.).

This exposition of character and mental states, of a situation very different from that at the beginning of the fabliau, prepares us at once, and paves the way, for all that is to come. Carrying out their purpose, the clerks set out to watch hopper and trough, - clearly *two* clerks are necessary, if the miller is to be circumvented, and they do not seem, as they do in the fabliau, to be present in the cheating-miller story simply for the sake of the cradle story which follows. Simkin gets rid of them easily enough by turning their horse loose, and the long and exasperating pursuit is followed by contrasting situations, which form exceedingly effective transition to the clerks' revenge. They return, 'wery and weet, as beste is in the reyn' (v. 4107), to find the miller sitting comfortably by the fire. John's state of mind is significant:

> 'Now are we drive til hething and til scorn.
> Our corn is stole, men wil us foles calle,
> Bathe the wardeyn and our felawes alle,
> And namely the miller; weylawey!' (vv. 4110ff.).

Although the 'streitness' of his house necessitates all sleeping in the same room, Simkin agrees to put them up for the night, and indulges freely and until a late hour in the ale, which the clerks, he supposes, will pay for. (One must contrast the frugal 'viande de bochage' of the fabliau.) The result is sleep, not merely, as Varnhagen points out,(6) oblivious, but audible (v. 4163), with what effect upon the nerves of the wakeful clerks no human being need be told. Yet the story demands that it be emphasized. Says Aleyn:

> 'This lange night ther tydes me na reste;
> But yet, na fors; al sal be for the beste.
> For Iohn,' seyde he, 'als ever moot I thryve,
> If that I may, yon wenche wil I swyve.
> Som esement has lawe y-shapen us;
> For Iohn, ther is a lawe that says thus,
> That gif a man in a point be y-greved,
> That in another he sal be releved' (vv. 4175ff.).

One does not suppose, of course, that this morality seemed wholly satisfactory to Chaucer, or that Aleyn himself could have taken it very seriously. Nevertheless we have here something more than the mere animalism of the fabliau. Though they had sworn to get the better of the miller, the clerks had been cheated; they were weary and wet from pursuing Bayard while Simkin sat comfortably by

the fire; and now their vexation, and, thanks to their own
ale, the snoring chorus, promised them a sleepless night.
The situation cried aloud for revenge, and to Aleyn, whom
one cannot pretend to regard as more than one remove from
the typical clerk of the fabliaux, - to Aleyn, who had
seen the highly sexed Malin, and who was, of course, perfectly familiar with Simkin's weakest point, one particular
form of wild justice would inevitably suggest itself....
   (p. 17) One gets from the whole an impression of an
action well-knit, carefully constructed, foreseen, and,
granting but a little of that play of chance which the
comic muse may always demand, inevitable. The central
motive has become the contest of clerks and miller; mere
animalism is a secondary matter; the form of the clerks'
revenge is the inevitable result of the characters of all
concerned....
   (p. 20) While, by means of detailed action and dialogue, Chaucer, as we have seen, retards the movement of
his story, he attempts no suspense of the sort that con-
ceals the outcome. The Reeve is telling the tale and
the miller is sure to be worsted in the end....
   (p. 21) Chaucer suppresses the dualogue of John and the
miller's wife, and substitutes for the preliminary talk of
clerk and daughter the farewell and confession; otherwise
he follows the fabliau in the use of the dialogic form.
He adds, however, the monologues and soliloquies, notably
those of Simkin's wife and Aleyn, when they go astray in
the dark, Simkin's reflections upon his own cleverness,
and his wrathful outburst in reply to Aleyn's tale of his
adventures. Chaucer's method is, then, strictly speaking,
less dramatic than that of the fabliau; he is less likely
to use dialogue in those parts of his story where one
character affects the actions of another; he is more
likely to use it to express thought or emotion, and, in
the group-conversations,'to give brilliant pictures of
human life and picturesque scenes of nature.' It does not,
however, lack vividness or liveliness and vigor. It has,
too, in high degree the dramatic quality of suggested exposition:

   Aleyn spak first, 'al hayl, Symond, y-fayth;
   How fares thy faire doghter and thy wyf?'
   'Aleyn! welcome,' quod Simkin, 'by my lyf,
   And Iohn also, how now, what do ye heer?' (vv. 4022ff.).

From this passage and John's reply in the lines that
follow we might infer enough to make the preliminary exposition unnecessary, yet the story moves steadily forward.
   The Chaucer of the 'Reeve's Tale' is manifestly the

Chaucer of the 'General Prologue', with the same interest
in character and the same skill in portraying it. Aleyn
and John are perhaps a little cleverer than the French
clerks, but they carry on the fabliau tradition, Chaucer,
however, not taking the type for granted, but describing
them as 'testif' and 'lusty for to pleye' (v. 4004).
Similarly, he is not content with the conventional description of the miller's daughter as 'bele et cointe';
Malin

> thikke and wel y-growen was,
> With camuse nose and yën greye as glas:
> With buttokes brode and brestes rounde and hye,
> But right fair was hir heer, I wol nat lye (vv.
>   3973ff.).

Chaucer, however, is chiefly interested in Simkin and his
wife, and upon them he depends for comic effects quite
distinct from those which have their source in the intrigue....
     (p.23) In the portrait of Simkin Chaucer, as has been
said, follows the familiar methods of the 'General Prologue.' There is the same effective absence of system,
the order of items in the little catalogue determined,
perhaps, wholly by the exigencies of rhyme. There is,
too, the same skill in the selection of characteristic
detail, the same harmony, the same final unity in the
portrait. In this topsy-turvy order the well-known
methods are combined: epithet and dress, accomplishment,
equipment, effect upon others, physiognomy, habits,
effect, habits, and epithets. Other methods, elsewhere
in the tale, deepen the impression of the characters,
and sometimes increase our knowledge of them. Thus Simkin's slyness is expressed by pantomime:

> Out at the dore he gooth ful prively,
> Whan that he saugh his tyme, softely;
> He loketh up and doun til he hath founde
> The clerkes hors . . . (vv. 4057ff.).

It is expressed by self-description: 'Yet can a miller
make a clerkes berd'(v. 4096). We should not know, however, that John was swift of foot but for his 'I is ful
wight, god waat, as is a raa' (v. 4086). The Northern
dialect of the clerks is the most notable piece of
characterization by utterance; their exclamations upon the
discovery of the loss of the horse, together with the
pantomime, are revelation of the 'testif' quality, of
their excitability....

(p. 26) Character, as has been said, is a matter of interest in the 'Reeve's Tale' and an important source of comic effect. There is similar contrast with the fabliau in style: Chaucer puts into the mouth of the Reeve epigram, irony, play upon words, clever turns of expression not to be paralleled in the fabliau. It is superfluous to point them out....

(p. 27) Emphasis of comic effects in character and style does not prevent Chaucer from working out the comic possibilities of plot; he follows, indeed, the fabliau traditions, and makes this the matter of first importance. By minor changes he makes the same intrigues more effective and preserves a better proportion between them. The cheating of the clerks becomes a less serious affair, but much more is made of their expectation, as well as of their vexation and physical pain, when it is not fulfilled, so that the comic incongruity between expectation and fulfilment is far more pronounced. In the Aleyn and Malin intrigue Malin, unlike her French prototype, is not deceived, but joins with Aleyn in disappointing the family hopes of a great marriage, and further aids in victimizing the miller by telling of his theft of corn. Aleyn, unlike the French clerk, meets more than his match in the miller, and thus becomes temporarily the victim in this by-product of John's intrigue. Chaucer adds a new 'incongruity,' adding mockery to physical pain, in the beating of Simkin by his own wife, but wisely refrains from all reference to her feelings when she discovers how she had been duped by means of the misplaced cradle. On the whole, then, Chaucer multiplies and sharpens the comic contrasts, largely because he gives us a story in which we have always, or nearly always, aggressor *versus* aggressor, each with an expectation doomed to a comic disappointment. Chaucer's tale is better than the fabliau in much the same way that tennis is a better game than golf; in the first there is a real clash of skill and cunning; in the second each plays his own game, neither necessarily conscious of the other.

Chaucer not only makes more of the comic possibilities of his story, but he leaves the reader, largely by the same means, with his desire for poetic justice more completely satisfied. The same criminal is overtaken by much the same 'questionable ruse.' The punishment of the miller seems poetically just, not because of its perfect equality with his crime, - though it is to be remembered that his Catastrophe is the result of many years of thieving, - not because of its suddenness, but because it comes in part from an unlooked-for source, - his own wife and daughter; because it is combined with mockery, in that it

is his own act that has compelled the benighting of the
clerks; because it is delayed by his temporary success;
because it is emphasized by repetition and multiplication,
taking effect in the persons of his wife and daughter as
well as in his own, and in his loss of the cake and the
cost of the supper. The reader, moreover, sympathizes
with the clerks in their attempt to prevent a theft, and
is antagonistic to the miller, who, unlike his French prototype, has no redeeming quality, and to his wife. The
neutral daughter, who promptly conspires with the clerk
against the miller, is a happy substitute for the girl
betrayed by the iron ring. Her mother's origin and education similarly modify the effect of the catastrophe.

Chaucer takes special pains to emphasize poetic justice: the miller is a swaggerer who goes heavily armed,
that he may get the worst of an encounter; he and his wife
are foolishly proud of her lineage and breeding, that
their pride may have a fall; the parson has plans for a
great marriage for Malin, only that they may be disappointed. That mother and daughter are 'difficult' heightens
the effect of the clerks' conquest. The unusual thefts
of the miller, - his taking advantage of the illness of
the maunciple, - demand unusual punishment. His delight
in the success of his own cunning directly paves the way
for his downfall. Chaucer, as we have seen, even formu-
lates the principle upon which the clerks act.

Chaucer carries on the fabliau tendency to indulge in
proverbial comment upon life. John has a good memory for
sayings of this sort, and they are peculiarly effective in
his dialect:

'Symond,' quod Iohn, 'by god, nede has na peer;
Him boës serve him-selve that has na swayn'
                                        (vv. 4026f.).

'I have herd seyd, man sal taa of twa thinges
Slyk as he fyndes, or taa slyk as he bringes'
                                        (vv. 4129f.).

'With empty hand men may na haukes tulle;
Lo here our silver, redy for to spende'
                                        (vv. 4134f.).

THE REEVE'S TALE AND THE FABLIAUX

Comparing the results of the foregoing analyses, one finds
that Chaucer may have learned, not only his story, but
also some important elements of his technique, from the

fabliau. The interest in the everyday life of bourgeois
or peasant society, seen in its commonplace surroundings,
in its local color, is already there: so that Chaucer, in
one of the most English tales of his English period, may
have imitated (as genius imitates) a French interest, a
French point of view. The strict unity of time, and the
virtue of brevity, rare in medieval literature, are
already there. Neatness of structure, too, clear relation
of part to part, excellent proportion and emphasis, skilful handling of synchronous events, Chaucer may have
learned from the fabliau. The fabliau is not without evidence that the author grasped the story as a whole, saw
the end and prepared for it from the beginning. And it
may have taught Chaucer something in the way of rapid,
realistic, and vigorous dialogue. It may have taught him
dramatic impersonality, objectivity, absence of attitude
toward his characters. It may have taught him the comic
possibilities of intrigue. And he may have learned from
it the tendency toward proverbial comment upon life. In
both Chaucer's tale and the fabliau, finally, we have the
same perfect fitness of style to subject-matter; in
coarseness of expression there is nothing to choose between them.

So much Chaucer may have learned from his source; but
if he knew one fabliau he must have known others, and it
is rather to be expected that he was influenced by the
technique of the whole body of this literature; that if
he elaborated his source, he elaborated it along the
lines of fabliau tradition. An examination of the
Montaiglon-Raynaud collection shows that many of the Chaucerian characteristics, which a comparison with his source
alone would lead one to regard as peculiar to him, are to
be found there. While, manifestly, many fabliaux have
been lost, and while this collection no doubt contains
some that Chaucer never saw or heard, yet we may safely
assume that the fabliaux which have come down to us are
typical of the whole body.

Chaucer does not isolate his characters, differs from
his source in placing them in a setting, social and geo-
graphical. In this respect his changes are in keeping
with the spirit of the fabliaux. The miller's wife becomes a priest's daughter: the 'priestess,' mistress, possibly in some cases actual wife, of the priest, is not an
uncommon figure in the fabliaux, and she is drawn, like
all the persons of the fabliaux, from life. Not much is
said, naturally, of the offspring of these wild marriages,
yet they are occasionally mentioned....

(p. 34) The action of most of the fabliaux occurs
within twenty-four hours.

A majority of the fabliaux probably contain but a
single intrigue. When two intrigues are combined, as in
the 'Reeve's Tale' and its source, the two are closely
related, usually as cause and effect. Unity of action is
thus as inevitable as unity of time. Ordinarily, too,
just as in Chaucer, the action is set in motion by adequate motivation; poverty compels a clerk to give up his
studies, to leave Paris, and on his way home, tired,
thirsty, and hungry, to beg a lodging for the night at the
house of a peasant (132); marriage parts two friends,
leads to groundless jealousy and suspicion whereby the
innocent become guilty, in 'Le lay l'espervier' (115).
Action springs from character, too, and of this there is
no better illustration than the story of a jongleur, an
inveterate gambler, who, left in charge of the lost souls
during the absence of the Devil, shook dice for them and
lost them all to St. Peter (117). This fabliau opens with
a fairly careful description of the hero's character and
way of life, and it is of course the saint's knowledge of
his weakness that leads him to take this method of winning
back lost souls.

While in many of the fabliaux we find but a single
intriguer, whose victim is as passive, as stupid and
superstitious, as the carpenter in the 'Miller's Tale',
there are still some where there is a contest of intri-
guers like that in the 'Reeve's Tale.'...

(p. 36) The use of concrete detail, the complete real-
ization of the action, while it distinguishes the
'Reeve's Tale' from its source, is yet common enough in
the fabliaux....

(p. 37) The fabliau plots are commonly of such a
nature as to require foresight and hindsight, grasp of
the story as a whole, and in this respect, also, Chaucer's
advance beyond his source can be paralleled from the
fabliaux....

CONCLUSION. THE REEVE'S TALE AS A SHORT STORY

(p. 42) Chaucer, we may say then, perfected a type that
had already run its course in France, reaching there a
state of high development. It is therefore not surprising
that he was technically at his best in tales like the
Miller's and the Reeve's. He was at his best, not because
he found stories of this type more interesting than
others, nor merely because he had reached the zenith of
his development as an artist, but because he was here
writing under the influence of the best narrative art
known to the Middle Ages.

Professor Kittredge defines (7) the fabliaux as 'short
stories in verse,' and it is perhaps from this point of
view that we may best sum up whatever differencing characteristics of the type have come under our observation.
The 'Reeve's Tale' possesses unity of time: all the action
of the story proper occurs within twenty-four hours. It
has unity of place: the scene of the whole is laid in or
about the mill. The action consists of a single episode,
made up of events or scenes organically related. The
whole is firmly knit by the single central motive. The
end is seen from the beginning. The persons are few in
number, yet they seem to be placed in a social setting.
The clerks' motives and fortunes are so nearly identical
that they produce the effect of a single hero. Unity of
impression or effect is preserved; technique and style are
in perfect accord with the narrator and with the events
which he sets forth. One has only to change the time to a
distant or romantic past, the scene to Brittany, or
Athens, or to the foot of Vesulus the cold; to introduce
descriptions of all the emotions involved; or to imagine
in the mouth of Simkin's wife the 'complaints' and *exempla*
of Dorigen; or to imagine the clerks, like the Wife of
Bath's hero, condemned to die and saved by supernatural
means; or to endow them with personalities like that of
the Prioress's little clergeon, or like that of the
threadbare student who told the story of Grisildis; or to
confront them with a figure like the Pardoner's mysterious old man; or to give them a glimpse of Malin walking,
like Emilia, in a garden; or to substitute for Simkin a
Summoner or a Friar; or even to put a John the carpenter
in the miller's place; one has, in short, only to imagine
any one of these changes in the story, to see how clearly
Chaucer distinguished fabliau from lay, from fairy tale,
from saint's legend, from *exemplum,* or from romance;
intrigue fabliau from satirical fabliau, 'Reeve's Tale'
from 'Miller's Tale'.
Not only in its unity, - of time, of place, of action,
of plot, of characters, of impression, - but also in its
concreteness, does the 'Reeve's Tale' anticipate the
modern short story. It is dramatic in its use of dialogue
to carry on the action, to suggest character or past
events; in its wealth of vivid and concrete incident and
detail; in its tendency to avoid analysis or epithet, to
depend rather upon words, actions, dress, effect upon
others, to indicate character or emotion.
It differs from the modern short story chiefly in its
lack of unity of point of view. It should be the clerks'
story, yet the action is not always seen through their
eyes, but often through the eyes of Simkin, or of his

wife. Yet one can imagine Chaucer working deliberately in
this respect also, following fabliau tradition, yet at the
same time consciously preferring the dramatic point of
view, the point of view of an audience watching the action
on the stage, by whatever persons it might be carried on.
Again, it should be the clerks' story, but it is their
victims, not they, that Chaucer delights to describe.
This may be due to the fact that two clerks had just been
described in the 'Miller's Tale'; to differentiate two
others from these would have led to descriptions of character inappropriately subtle. Or it may be due to the
fact that the Reeve, replying to the Miller, would naturally shift the emphasis to the clerks' victim. Contrasting characters, moreover, are not required, as they are in
the 'Miller's Tale', to motive contrasting actions.
And, after all, unity of point of view is an academic
requirement, sometimes effectively neglected by the modern
short story. The remarkable thing is that Chaucer elaborated and developed in the 'Reeve's Tale' the already
excellent technique of the Old French fabliaux, and, in so
doing, anticipated the typical unity and concreteness, the
(to make use of Professor Baldwin's admirable phrase)
'dramatic concentration' of the modern short story.

Notes

1 Bédier, 'Les Fabliaux', Paris (1895), p. 37.
2 The fabliau does not 'former de suite ni de série'
   (Montaiglon-Raynaud, 'Recueil Général et Complet des
   Fabliaux' I, viii.)   But the fact that the story of
   the Miller of Trumpington is one of the 'Canterbury
   Tales', heightens its effect, without in any way
   changing its form. Though one of a series of tales,
   it is none the less a fabliau.
3 The peculiar vividness of the present tense *in descriptions* is noteworthy. In the present instance it
   implies that skeptical readers may verify the tale by
   examination of brook and bridge and mill. In narration, on the other hand, the present tense is less
   vivid, perhaps because it is, necessarily, artificial.
   For the modern reader it is associated with second-
   hand summaries and abstracts. Cf. 'A microscopic boy
   upon a cosmic horse *came* slowly down the road leading
   to the town watering trough.... The watering trough *is*
   at the curb line of the street, in front of the post-
   office' - 'Atlantic Monthly', 88, 409.
4 See Skeat's identification of the scene, 'Chaucer's
   Works' (1899) V, 116.

5   Dead sleep fell upon the carpenter, in the 'Miller's
    Tale', 'aboute corfew-tyme, or litel more' (v. 3645),
    - 8 or 9 p.m., 'People invariably went to bed very
    early.' - Skeat, V. 108.
6   H.E. Varnhagen, 'Englische Studien' IX (1886), p. 262.
7   In the Universal Cyclopaedia.

33.   GEORGE SAINTSBURY, CHAUCER'S HUMOUR

1908

Saintsbury (1845-1933) was educated at Merton College,
Oxford, became a journalist, then Professor of Rhetoric
and English Literature in the University of Edinburgh,
1895-1915. In the tradition of general criticism Saintsbury examines with discrimination the all-pervading
quality of Chaucer's humour, which unifies his miscellaneity and does not nullify pathos, learning, or high
poetry. Reprinted by permission from an article on
Chaucer in 'The Cambridge History of English Literature',
ed. A.W. Ward and A.R. Waller, Cambridge University Press
(1908), pp. 189-93.

Of the matter, as well as of the languages, forms and
sources of his knowledge, a little more should, perhaps,
be said. It has been by turns exalted and decried, and
the manner of its exhibition has not always been wisely
considered. It has been observed above, and the point is
important enough for emphasis, that we must not look in
Chaucer for anything but the indiscriminateness and, from
a strictly scholarly point of view, the inaccuracy, which
were bred in the very bone of medieval study; and that it
would be hardly less of a mistake to expect him not to
show what seems to us a singular promiscuousness and irre-
levancy in his display of it. But, in this display, and
possibly, also, in some of the inaccuracies, there is a
very subtle and personal agency which has sometimes been
ignored altogether, while it has seldom been fully allowed
for. This is the intense, all-pervading and all but incalculable presence of Chaucer's *humour* - a quality which
some, even of those who enjoy it heartily and extol it

generously, do not quite invariably seem to comprehend.
Indeed, it may be said that even among those who are not
destitute of the sense itself, such an ubiquitous, sub-
terranean accompaniment of it would seem to be regarded
as an impossible or an uncanny thing. As a matter of fact,
however, it 'works i' the earth so fast' that you never
can tell at what moment it will find utterance. Many of
the instances of this are familiar, and some, at least,
could hardly fail to be recognised except by portentous
dulness. But it may be questioned whether it is ever far
off; and whether, as is so often the case in that true
English variety of the quality of which it is the first
and one of the most consummate representatives, it is not
mixed and streaked with seriousness and tenderness in an
almost inextricable manner. 'Il se moque,' says Taine of
another person, 'de ses émotions au moment même où il s'y
livre.' In the same way, Chaucer is perpetually seeing
the humorous side, not merely of his emotions but of his
interests, his knowledge, his beliefs, his everything. It
is by no means certain that in his displays of learning he
is not mocking or parodying others as well as relieving
himself. It is by no means certain that, seriously as we
know him to have been interested in astronomy, his frequent astronomical or astrological lucubrations are not
partly ironical. Once and once only, by a triumph of
artistic self-restraint, he has kept the ludicrous out
altogether - in the exquisite 'Prioress's Tale', and even
there we have a sort of suggestion of the forbidden but
irrepressible thing in

As monkes been, *or elles oghten be.*

Of this humour, indeed, it is not too much to say
(borrowing Coleridge's dictum about Fuller and the analogous but very different quality of wit) that it is the
'stuff and substance,' not merely of Chaucer's intellect,
but of his entire mental constitution. He can, as has
been said, repress it when art absolutely requires that he
should do so; but, even then, he gives himself compensations. He has kept it out of 'The Prioress's Tale'; but
he has indemnified himself by a more than double allowance
of it in his description of the prioress's person in 'The
Prologue'. On the other hand, it would have been quite
out of place in the description of the knight, for whom
nothing but respectful admiration is solicited; and there
is no need to suspect irony even in

And though that he were worthy, he was wys.

But in 'The Knight's Tale' - which is so long that the
personage of the supposed teller, never obtruded, may be
reasonably supposed forgotten, and where the poet almost
speaks in his own person - the same writ does not run;
and, towards the end especially, we get the famous touches
of ironic comment on life and thought, which, though they
have been unduly dwelt upon as indicating a Voltairian
tone in Chaucer, certainly are ironical in their treatment
of the riddles of the painful earth.

Further, it is desirable to notice that this humour is
employed with a remarkable difference. In most great English humorists, humour sets the picture with a sort of
vignetting or arabesquing fringe and atmosphere of exaggeration and fantasy. By Chaucer it is almost invariably
used to bring a higher but a quite clear and achromatic
light on the picture itself or parts of it. The stuff is
turned rapidly the other way to show its real texture; the
jest is perhaps a burning, but also a magnifying and illuminating, glass, to bring out a special trait more definitely. It is safe to say that a great deal of the combination of vivacity and veracity in Chaucer's portraits
and sketches of all kinds is due to this all-pervading
humour; indeed, it is not very likely that any one would
deny this. What seems, for some commentators, harder to
keep in mind is that it may be, and probably is, equally
present in other places where the effect is less immediately rejoicing to the modern reader; and that medieval
pedantry, medieval catalogue-making, medieval digression
and irrelevance are at once exemplified and satirised by
the operation of this extraordinary faculty.

That the possession of such a faculty almost necessarily implies command of pathos is, by this time, almost
a truism, though it was not always recognised. That
Chaucer is an instance of it, as well as of a third quality, *good* humour, which does not invariably accompany the
other two, will hardly be disputed. He is not a sentimen-
talist; he does not go out of his way for pathetic effect;
but, in the leading instances above noted of 'The Clerk's'
and 'Prioress's Tales', supplemented by many slighter
touches of the same kind, he shows an immediate, unforced,
unfaltering sympathy which can hardly be paralleled. His
good humour is even more pervading. It gives a memorable
distinction of kindliness between 'The Wife of Bath's Prologue' and the brilliant following of it by Dunbar in 'The
Tua Mariit Wemen and the Wedo'; and it even separates
Chaucer from such later humorists as Addison and Jane
Austen, who, though never savage, can be politely cruel.
Cruelty and Chaucer are absolute strangers; indeed, the
absence of it has brought upon him from rather short-

sighted persons the charge of pococurantism, which has
sometimes been translated (still more purblindly) into one
of mere courtliness - of a Froissart-like indifference to
anything but 'the quality,' 'the worth,' as he might have
put it himself. Because there is indignation in 'Piers
the Plowman', it is thought that Chaucer does not well *not*
to be angry: which is uncritical.

This curious, tolerant, not in the least cynical,
observation and relish of humanity gave him a power of representing it, which has been rarely surpassed in any respect save depth. It has been disputed whether this power
is rather that of the dramatist or that of the novelist -
a dispute perhaps arguing a lack of the historic sense.
In the late sixteenth or early seventeenth century, Chaucer would certainly have been the one, and in the mid-
nineteenth the other. It would be most satisfactory could
we have his work in both avatars. But what we have contains the special qualities of both craftsmen in a certain
stage of development, after a fashion which certainly
leaves no room for grumbling. The author has, in fact,
set himself a high task by adopting the double system
above specified, and by giving elaborate descriptions of
his personages before he sets them to act and speak up to
these descriptions. It is a plan which, in the actual
drama and the actual novel, has been found rather a dangerous one. But Chaucer discharges himself victoriously
of his liabilities. And the picture of life which he has
left us has captivated all good judges who have given
themselves the very slight trouble necessary to attain
the right point of view, from his own day to this.

Something has been said of the poetic means which he
used to work this picture out. They were, practically,
those which English poetry had been elaborating for itself during the preceding two or three centuries, since
the indrafts of Latin or Romance vocabulary, and the
gradual disuse of inflection, had revolutionised the language. But he perfected them, to, probably, their utmost
possible point at the time, by study of French and Italian
models as regards arrangement of lines in groups, and by
selecting a diction which, even in his own time, was recognised as something quite extraordinary. The old delu-
sion that he 'Frenchified' the language has been nearly
dispelled as regards actual vocabulary; and, in points
which touch grammar, the minute investigations undertaken
in the case of the doubtful works have shown that he was
somewhat more scrupulous than were his contemporaries in
observing formal correctness, as it is inferred to have
been. The principal instance of this scrupulousness - the
management of the valued final -*e*, which represented a

crowd of vanished or vanishing peculiarities of accidence
- was, by a curious consequence, the main cause of the
mistakes about his verse which prevailed for some three
centuries; while the almost necessarily greater abundance
of unusual words in 'The Prologue', with its varied subjects, probably had something to do with the concurrent
notion that his language was obsolete to the point of difficulty, if not to that of unintelligibility. As a matter
of fact, his verse (with the exception of one or two
doubtful experiments, such as the nine-syllabled line
where ten should be) is among the smoothest in English;
and there are entire pages where, putting trifling differences of spelling aside, hardly a single word will offer
difficulties to any person of tolerable reading in the
modern tongue.

It is sometimes complained by those who admit some, if
not all, of these merits in him that he rarely - a few
would say never - rises to the level of the highest
poetry. Before admitting, before even seriously contest-
ing, this we must have a definition of the highest poetry
which will unite the suffrages of the competent, and this,
in the last two thousand years and more, has not been
attained. It will, perhaps, be enough to say that any
such definition which excludes the finest things in
'Troilus and Criseyde', in 'The Knight's' and 'Prioress's
Tales' and in some other places, will run the risk of
suggesting itself as a mere shibboleth. That Chaucer is
not always at these heights may be granted: who is? That
he is less often at them than some other poets need not
be denied; that he has access to them must be maintained.
While as to his power to communicate poetic grace and
charm to innumerable other things less high, perhaps, but
certainly not always low; as to the abounding interest of
his matter; as to the astonishing vividness in line and
idiom of his character-drawing and manners-painting; and,
above all, as to the wonderful service which he did to the
forms and stuff of English verse and of English prose,
there should be no controversy; at least the issue of any
such controversy should not be doubtful.

34.   JOHN WILLIAM MACKAIL, DAYLIGHT AND ROMANCE

1909

J.W. Mackail (1859-1945), educated at Balliol College,
Oxford, was a man of letters and civil servant, who wrote
on Classical and English Literature.   Though slightly ham-
pered by the implicit nineteenth-century theory of poetry
represented by Mill and Arnold, and repeating commonplaces
about childishness and dramatic quality, he nevertheless
achieves an independent rich multiplicity of response to
both romance and realism, praises the fabliaux, and with
some originality identifies Chaucer's highest achievement
as the mingling of romance and realism in 'Troilus and
Cryseyde'.   Reprinted from 'The Springs of Helicon',
Longmans Green & Co. (1909), pp. 6-7, 49-69, by permission
of Longman Group Ltd.

(p. 6) He has much of the spirit of the child, easily
pleased and easily fatigued, prone to follow the suggestions of an alert but vagrant fancy.

> Love is too young to know what conscience is;
> Yet who knows not conscience is born of love?

And so we may see Chaucer writing sometimes with a grace
and charm that are quite idle and irresponsible, and then
kindling to some piteous or tragic motive, some beauty of
situation or splendour of passion, until the bird-note
thrills us by turning into the song of an angel.
      Hence, in a world which always tends to be obtuse to-
wards poetry, to feel safe with dulness and to take kindly
to the second-best, it is not surprising that Chaucer's
fame as a poet has been much confused with false issues.
It rests, or has rested, in great part on work which is
not his best, or which is not his at all.   To the normal
modern reader he is known mainly through extracts; and it
is singular how often these extracts seem chosen to miss
his highest poetry, his specific greatness as a poet.   We
may be pretty sure to find among them the description of
the Squire or the Miller, the Clerk of Oxford or the
Parson - admirable sketches of character, terse, lifelike,
humorous, executed in quite fluent and workmanlike verse,
but not exactly poetry, or if so, only poetry with a

difference. We may very probably find the Prioress' Tale,
a legend gracefully told, with a sort of thin elegance,
suited admirably and with perfect dramatic instinct to the
person of its narrator, but not poetry of the first excellence. We may find a few vignettes of landscape, or
highly wrought descriptive passages like that of the
temple of Mars in the Knight's Tale. But we shall seldom
find anything that really shows to what a height Chaucer's
poetry can rise. We shall not find the Complaint of Queen
Anelida, nor the exquisite narratives in the 'Legend of
Good Women', nor anything to give a notion of the sustained magnificence and mastery of the 'Book of Troilus
and Creseide'. Even for those who know their Chaucer more
fully, emphasis has to be laid on the first-rate work to
disengage it from the work that is short of first-rate,
from the work that is the poetry of his time and surroundings rather than of his own essential genius.

  With Chaucer, too, as with some few others among the
great poets, it is necessary to draw a distinction between
the poet and the story-teller. His narrative gift is
probably unsurpassed; it has not been equalled except by
one or two in England, by a very small number anywhere.
It is a gift of immense value to a poet, but it is not the
gift of poetry....

  (p. 49) The narrators [of 'The Canterbury Tales'] are a
mixed company of men and women, mostly belonging to the
bourgeoisie, and not conversant with high thoughts or profound emotions. Throughout we must always remember who it
is that is telling the story. While the accent of Chaucer
himself is clear through all the tales, while they are all
informed by his sweetness of temper, his humour, his keen
observation and quick sympathy, each of them bears also
the personality of the narrator in whose mouth it is
placed. No greater triumph of dramatic art has been
achieved, so far as dramatic art consists in creating
people and making them live and act from within.

  Without at present raising the whole formidable question of what poetry is, we may say that in any case it
must fulfil two conditions; that it was worth writing in
verse, and that it could not have been written but in
verse. The first condition would exclude a great deal
of the metrical output of Chaucer's contemporaries, and
perhaps some of his own. The second excludes almost nothing that ranks as literature during times earlier than the
period at which a language has developed the art of prose
composition. This in Chaucer's England was just beginning
to be the case, but only just beginning. Wiclif was
founding English prose; but it is a long step from Wiclif
to Coverdale, or from the so-called Mandevile to Malory.

Such prose as had been created for Italy by Boccaccio, supple, succinct, lucid, was not yet available in English. It would be very odd, if we were not so much accustomed to it, that a volume or volumes entitled 'The Poetical Works of Chaucer' should include 'Melibeus' and the Parson's Tale. In the latter, Chaucer has carried his dramatic sympathy to the point where poetry is rejected as a sort of invention of the devil. In the former ('a little thing in prose,' as he calls it in one of those delicious touches of his that often lie too deep for laughter - it is enormously long besides being portentously dull, and would take about two hours and a half in the telling) he is making fun of the contention of the romantic school that their poetry is the only genuine thing, and that if we will not have 'Sir Thopas', we shall have 'Melibeus' - certainly an awful alternative either way. We may be thankful to Chaucer for this among his many mercies, that his humour took this particular line, and that he did not waste his time, and probably mislead many generations of critics, by going through the more elaborate jest of giving us the whole of 'Melibeus' in verse, even had the verse been as smooth and as workmanlike as that of the 'Confessio Amantis'.

If we set aside the little thing in prose, the wild burlesque of 'Sir Thopas', and the Parson's sermon, twenty-one tales in verse are left. In estimating the effective poetical value of the whole work, we have to consider partly what I have already hinted at, the entire construction in which the tales are set, and the dramatic fitness of each story to the occasion of the telling and the person of the teller; and partly, the poetic quality and excellence of the stories themselves. The former criterion is strictly relevant to our judgment of Chaucer as a creative artist. But this kind of creative art may exist in its highest perfection - as it does in Scott for instance, or in Dickens - without entering the sphere of poetry at all. In 'David Copperfield' or the 'Antiquary' we have a little world of people as living, as interesting, as distinct and various as the God's plenty of the Canterbury Pilgrims. In the main framework of the 'Canterbury Tales' - the prologues and interstitial verse - there is little that could not be done in prose, at all events in the prose of a more mature accomplishment. For poetry, in the sense of high poetry, we must look mainly to the tales themselves.

The twenty-one which we have to consider fall naturally into three divisions. Seven are serious in subject and treatment; those of Palamon and Arcite, of Custance, of Griselda, of Cambuscan, of Dorigen, of Appius and Virginia,

and of the little Christian boy in Asia. Seven are what
Chaucer himself very aptly calls harlotry; those told by
the Miller and Reeve, the Friar and Sompnour, the Merchant and Shipman, and the fragment which is all we are
allowed to hear - though it has perhaps already gone quite
far enough - of the life of Perkin Reveller, the Idle
Apprentice. Seven are in an intermediate or mixed manner.
Of these last, two are hardly poems at all, so much as
versified material for sermons, tales told for edification, not for delight. The Legend of Saint Cecilia puts
into verse, with considerable dexterity but with little
beauty or imagination, the prose of the Golden Legend
with all its prosaic details even down to the absurd
etymologies. The Monk's Tale, while it contains passages
of fine rhetoric, has no unity of construction, no organic quality. A string of instances chosen out of a stock
such as, ever since Lactantius wrote the 'De Mortibus
Persecutorum', formed a regular part of every churchman's
library, is sufficient material for a sermon, but hardly
for a poem. Both of these pieces seem clearly to be
early work, retouched and inserted here. The other five
differ from these two in constructive quality; but they
also differ from the first group of seven in not treating
the story with high poetic seriousness. They do not
stand out against the general narrative framework of the
tales as against a background of lower tone; in some cases
they rise out of it, or fade into it, almost insensibly.
As stories indeed, while the Canon's Yeoman's Tale and
the Manciple's Tale are trivial, and the Wife of Bath's
Tale a slight thing pleasantly told, it would be difficult
to beat the Pardoner's Tale of the three thieves for grim
strength, or the Nun's Priest's Tale of the cock and fox
for humour and light grace. But one does not look in
them for really great poetry.

Even in the seven serious tales, the poetry seldom
rises to a high tension. To the Knight's Tale I will
return in a moment. In the rest we may notice the relaxation of a genius which had ascended in its central period
to poetry, not of greater or sunnier charm, but of more
ardent imagination, of a loftier purpose and movement.
The Clerk's Tale of Griselda is interesting as showing a
wavering between romantic and humanistic treatment. It
is because the difference is never adjusted that, with
all its many beauties, it is on the whole a failure as a
poem. When he wrote it, Chaucer was clearly not at the
stage, or in the mood, where he could treat it in the
spirit of the *fabliau*. He had passed out of the romantic
atmosphere into the open air. But in cool daylight the
whole story of Griselda is either preposterous or

shocking; in either case not fit material for high art.
That it made a great impression on Petrarch from whom
Chaucer took it, is matter of known fact. But Petrarch
in his whole life seems never once to have come into contact with real things.

This relaxation has its degree of seriousness. In the
stories of Custance and of Dorigen Chaucer finds ample
scope for beauty, imagination, pity, as well as for the
special graces of romance. The former rises more than
once to a splendid eloquence.

> Paraventure in thilke large book
> Which that men clepe the heaven, ywritten was
> With sterres, when that he his birthe took,
> That he for love should han his death, alas!
> For in the sterres, clearer than in glass,
> Is written, God wot, whoso could it read,
> The death of every man, withouten dread.

This is noble poetry at high tension; and as noble, and
more piercingly vivid, is another famous stanza:

> Have ye nat seen sometime a pale face
> Among a press, of him that hath be lad
> Toward his death, whereas him gat no grace,
> And such a colour in his face hath had,
> Men mighte know his face that was bestad,
> Amonges all the faces in that rout?
> So stant Custance, and looketh her about.

But the essential difference between the tale of Custance
and the 'Book of Troilus and Creseide' is that the one is
but a tale, told gracefully and movingly to pass the time
away, and the other a creative masterpiece going to the
heart of life.

Even the Knight's Tale, with its stately movement and
lavish richness of ornament, does not bring us into the
heart of things. It is no derogation from a poem which
is one of the chief splendours of our literature to say
this. The same might be said of another poem which on
its smaller scale much resembles it, Keats 'Lamia'. It
is arguable that 'Lamia' is Keats' finest poem; and the
Knight's Tale is, I suppose, the single poem which represents Chaucer most fully. In it the pictorial or decorative value of his poetry is at its maximum. It is all
beautiful, all dexterous and masterly, all Chaucer at a
high level that only comes short of his highest. It has
more range than any other single poem of his; it supplies
more memorable phrases and lovely lines. It ranges from

the sweet garrulous manner of the romance-writer, to a
loftiness and incisiveness that are almost Homeric,
almost Virgilian.

> Alas, why pleynen folk so in commune
> Of purveyance of God, or of fortune,
> That giveth them full oft in many a guise
> Well better than they can themself devise?

These lines recall the great words of Zeus at the opening
of the 'Odyssey' -

> Alas, how idly do these mortals blame
> The Gods, as though by our devising came
> The evil that in spite of ordinance
> By their own folly for themselves they frame!

The words of Arcite -

> So stood the heaven when that we were born:
> We must endure: this is the short and plain -

seem to echo some stately cadence of the 'Aeneid' like
the 'Stat sua cuique dies' or the 'superanda omnis fortuna
ferendo est'. Now we come on a fully elaborated epic
simile -

> Right as the hunter in the regne of Thrace
> That standeth at the gappe with a spear,
> Whan hunted is the lion or the bear,
> And heareth him come rushing in the greaves
> And breaketh both the boughes and the leaves,
> And thinketh, *Here cometh my mortal enemy*,
> *Withoute fail he mote be dead, or I:*
> *For either I mote slay him at the gap,*
> *Or he mote slain me, if that me mishap:*
> So fareden they:

and again, on a line of Greek simplicity like that of
Palamon's -

> For since the day is come that I shall die -

the sort of line in which the art is so consummate that
it looks like accident. We have passages of light speed,
those lovely lines for instance beginning -

> The busy lark, the messenger of day,

that read like a piece of early Shakespeare; and concentrated couplets, now smooth and weighty like the comment
of Theseus,

> Then is it wisdom, as it thinketh me,
> To make a virtue of necessity;

now filled with lyric air and fire, as in the lamentation
of the Athenian women over Arcite's body (like the weeping in Troy over Hector, Chaucer is bold enough to say) -

> Why woldestow be dead, these women cry,
> And haddest gold enough, and Emily?

In the Knight's Tale Chaucer (again like Keats in
'Lamia') was trying to write as well as he could. If a
fault in it is to be hinted at, it is that now and then
(but here again we must remember that the tale is told
not in his own person, but in the Knight's) he seems to
pay a little too much attention to the writing, and does
not give quite free play to his humour or to his power of
dramatic imagination. With Chaucer, indeed, as with that
college friend of Johnson's who has made himself immortal
by a single thoughtless phrase, 'I don't know how, cheerfulness was always breaking in.' When he says of the
portraits in the temple of Mars -

> All be that thilke time they were unborn,
> Yet was their death depeinted therebeforne:

when, in the highly wrought and noble description
of Arcite's death, he says -

> His spirit changed house, and wente there,
> As I came never, I cannot tellen where:

it is with the flicker of a smile, checked as soon as it
appears. The two passages are in singular likeness and
contrast to two others of the same purport in Shakespeare, where the lightning of a grimmer laughter flashes
across a situation of tragic horror. 'This prophecy
Merlin shall make; for I live before his time,' says the
Fool in 'Lear', in a passage which is vainly rejected as
an interpolation by some editors. 'In heaven; send thither to see: if your messenger find him not there, seek
him i' the other place yourself,' is the sinister sarcasm
of Hamlet. But here, as even in the dying words of
Arcite with all their unsurpassable grace and tenderness,
the strange sob of their cadences -

> What is this world? what asketh men to have?
> Now with his love, now in his colde grave
> Alone, withouten any company -

we are in the faint world of romance, among dreams that
linger a moment, retreating in the dawn.

But in their main structure and substance, even where
they deal with romantic stories and episodes, the 'Canterbury Tales' represent the reaction from romance.
Chaucer brought poetry into the open air, just when the
romantic atmosphere was beginning to be oppressive. It
was not before this, it was more likely a little later,
that the English metrical romance reached its last and
perhaps its greatest success in 'Sir Degrevaunt'. But
over Degrevaunt and all his kin rests henceforth the
mocking note of 'Sir Thopas'. Their feet move in an
elderly morning dew; their sentiment begins to look
tawdry under the daylight. Yet on the other hand in contrast with the author of 'Piers Ploughman' Chaucer is the
head of the romantic school, as Homer is romantic in contrast with Hesiod. He carries romance even into his
comedy, as he carries his comedy even into romance. This
is what gives his work so complex and intricate a fascination. I have already spoken of the Nun's Priest's Tale
as a masterpiece in his lighter style of poetry; airy,
delicate, exquisitely humorous, with a light silvery
grace about it, although it is only silver and not gold.
It is in this poem that he makes his most direct attack
on the romances -

> This story is all so true, I undertake,
> As is the book of Lancelot de Lake.

In a way too, it is all so poetical, all so romantic. He
is a poet making fun of poetry, just as, being an accomplished and sensitive stylist, he is so fond of parodying
style, even his own. Unless we realise how continually
he is doing this, we miss half his meaning. Sometimes it
is done quite broadly, oftener with so demure an air as
almost to escape notice.

> For the orizont had reft the sunne's light
> (This is as much to sayn as it was night):

it may be suspected that here he is making fun of Dante.

> And in his ire he hath his wife yslayn:
> This is th' effect, there is no more to sayn:

this is a parody of his own epic manner. May's visit to
the sick-bed of Damian in the Merchant's Tale is a conscious parody of Cressida's visit to the sick-bed of
Troilus. It is audaciously introduced by the very phrase,
'pity runneth soon in gentle heart,' used with such serious beauty in 'Palamon and Arcite' and used again with a
slighter and subtler touch of comedy in the proem of the
falcon's speech to Canace; that speech itself being a
parody from beginning to end of Chaucer's own seriously
romantic manner as we see it in the 'Legend of Good Women'.
Indeed, except where Chaucer is at his very highest ele-
vation, or where, as in the Prioress' Tale, he suppresses
it for dramatic purposes, the suspicion of parody, the
lurking instinct of making fun, is never far round the
corner. It glances and sparkles through the Knight's
Tale; it gives added breadth and charm to the earlier
books of 'Troilus and Creseide'. It keeps his tenderness
from becoming sentimental, as his sentiment keeps it in
turn from becoming heartless.

This comes out most vividly in his treatment of the
feathered things, the 'smale foules,' of which he was so
loving and so keen an observer. With his romantic passion for birds, he is full of their comic aspect. He is
alike responsive to the magic of the nightingale and to
the absurdity of the dove sitting upon a barn-roof. The
'Parliament of Fowls' is a sort of epitome of his own
poetical genius on all its sides: the romantic sensibility of the turtle -

For though she died, I would none other make;
I will be hers till that the death me take:

the reaction from romance in the duck -

Who can a reason find or wit in that?
Yea, quek! yit quod the duck: full well and fair!
There be mo sterres, God wot, than a pair:

the high seriousness with which that Canterbury pilgrim
is checked by the tercelet -

Thy kind is of so low a wretchedness
That what love is thou canst not see ne guess.

And so also with his loving and humorous view of other
animals, like cats and dogs, as in the lines -

> And if the cattes skin be sleek and gay,
> She wol nat dwell in house half a day;
> But forth she wol, ere any day be dawed,
> To show her skin, and gone a-caterwawed:

or in a passage about dogs' manners in the Parson's Tale
which can hardly be quoted with decorum, but which is
even more intensely funny and true to life than Launce's
lecture to Crab in the 'Two Gentlemen of Verona'.

Seldom for very long together does Chaucer keep perfectly serious. But the world itself is not constantly
serious; and when it is, it is often with the seriousness,
not of a great art that sweeps by with sceptred pall, but
of a Puritanism that renounces art altogether. Of Chaucer's Muse, both in her more impassioned and in her
lighter vein, it may well be said -

> By her attire so bright and shene,
> Men might perceive well and seen
> She was not of religioun.

Yet in this bright secular world we may see, towards the
end, the spirit of Puritanism rising and casting a shadow
over his work; not merely in the recantation at the conclusion of the 'Canterbury Tales', but in the grave
impressive moralisations with which the Doctor's and the
Manciple's Tales end - though here, once more, we must not
forget the dramatic element. Even the light-hearted Pag-
anism of Boccaccio had ended thus; as did, a century
later, the splendid humanistic art of Botticelli; as did
the whole Renaissance movement by the end of the sixteenth
century. In Chaucer's own age and country, which were
also the age and country of Wiclif and of John Ball, Langland gives us a criticism of life deeper than Chaucer's,
though narrower. As responsive to the wretchedness of
this world as Chaucer was to its variety and beauty, he
dreams, not of a House of Fame, not of ladies dead and
lovely knights, but of heaven opened, of Mercy and Truth
meeting, of Righteousness and Peace kissing one another.
When the vision comes on him -

> Into the land of longing · alone she me brought,
> And in a mirror that hight middle-earth · she made to
>   behold.
> *Son*, she said to me - *here might thou see wonders*.

But they are not the wonders of Chaucer; and in that
mirror the world is seen, full indeed of sharp colour and
life, but without romance, without joy, without pity.

This seriousness is quite a different thing from the
high seriousness of art. In its eyes, 'Troilus and Creseide' falls under the same condemnation with the Miller's
Tale; both are mere worldly vanity. But as poetry, the
distinction between the two is evidently profound. We can
hardly ignore, or leave unanswered, the question whether
the Miller's Tale, and that whole body of brilliant work
to which it belongs, be poetry at all, and if so, in what
sense. To reduce the matter to a concrete instance, let
me take two passages which are closely alike in substance
and handling. In the Sompnour's Tale the friar responds
to the invitation to order his own dinner as follows: -

> Now dame, quod he, je vous dy sanz doute,
> Have I not of a capon but the liver,
> And of your softe bread not but a shiver,
> And after that a roasted pigges head
> (But that I wold no beast for me were dead)
> Than had I with you homely suffisance.
> I am a man of little sustenance.
> My spirit hath his fostering in the Bible;
> The body is aye so ready and penible
> To wake, that my stomach is destroyed.

The other passage is from an author who is like Chaucer in
many qualities, in a combination of humour and sentiment,
in creative fertility, and in the breadth of his outlook
on human life.

> 'I think, young woman,' said Mrs. Gamp, in a tone ex-
> pressive of weakness, 'that I could pick a little bit
> of pickled salmon, with a nice little sprig of fennel
> and a sprinkling of white pepper. I takes new bread,
> my dear, with jest a little pat of fresh butter, and a
> mossel of cheese. In case there should be such a
> thing as a cowcumber in the 'ouse, will you be so kind
> as bring it, for I'm rather partial to 'em, and they
> does a world of good in a sickroom. If they draws the
> Brighton Tipper here, I takes that ale at night, my
> love: it bein' considered wakeful by the doctors. And
> whatever you do, young woman, don't bring more than a
> shilling's worth of gin and water when I rings the
> bell a second time; for that is always my allowance,
> and I never takes a drop beyond.'

This last passage is of course not poetry; what is it,
if anything, beyond the mere absence of metrical form, in
which it differs from the other? There are two things to
say about this: first, that the matter of metrical form

is not accidental but essential; secondly, that a poet
working in a medium which is the medium of poetry is producing potential poetry, and that this potential poetry is
to some extent, which may be greater or less, converted
into actual poetry in the process of production. He may
let it run at low pressure; he may reduce the elements of
beauty, of construction and imagination; but the interac-
tion of the mind of a poet and the forms of poetry is so
close that he cannot, nor would he if he could, wholly
shut these elements off. Even where the verse seems to
run automatically off the machine, to be at low pressure
or at none, the artist's hand is on the lever, and able at
any moment to fill and flood the verse with the quality of
essential poetry. The Pardoner's Tale is a *fabliau* which
is entirely suited to prose treatment, and has in fact
made its impression on Europe through prose versions, from
the 'Gesta Romanorum' to the 'Jungle Book'. But it rises
without effort in Chaucer's hands to such grave rhythmic
rhetoric as this:

> And on the ground, which is my mother's gate,
> I knocke with my staff both early and late
> And saye: *Leve mother, let me in!*
> *Lo how I vanish, flesh and blood and skin!*
> *Alas, when shall my bones been at rest,*

And in the opening lines of the Wife of Bath's Tale -

> In the olde dayes of the King Arthour
> Of which that Britons speaken great honour,
> All was this land fulfilled of fayerie:
> The Elf-Queen, with her jolly company,
> Danced full oft in many a greene mead -

we have the note that, at a higher imaginative pressure,
but hardly with more melodious grace, comes back in the
splendid prologue to 'Lamia':

> Upon a time, before the faery broods
> Drove Nymph and Satyr from the prosperous woods,
> Before King Oberon's bright diadem,
> Sceptre, and mantle clasp'd with dewy gem,
> Frighted away the Dryads and the Fauns
> From rushes green, and brakes, and cowslipp'd lawns.

The difficulty disappears if we take larger views.
For poetry, like all real art, is a function of life, and
its province is as wide as that of life itself. The har-
lotries of the 'Canterbury Tales' have qualities other

than those of poetry; but even of them it may be said that
the thing could not be done in prose, or at least that in
prose it would lose a specific charm, a definite artistic
quality. It comes of his width of outlook, his large sane
handling of life, that Chaucer, while at his slackest he
never loses touch of beauty, at his highest never loses
his sunlit charm and brilliant speed. He says of the
Duchess Blanch:

> Her list so well to live
> That dulness was of her adrad.

Chaucer is never dull; except where he means to be dull,
and is so dramatically. It is far otherwise with his
successors. 'Chaucer fain would have me taught, but I
was dull,' says Occleve; and all his readers - they are
not many - answer fervently, 'Indeed you were.' The
Chaucerians are always being dull. Even their best work
lacks the ripple and sparkle that never deserts that of
their master. It is for this that even the high Muse is
indulgent to him when, in the not unkindly phrase of
Dryden, he mingles trivial things with those of deeper
moment, and forgets that an author is not to write all he
can, but only all he ought.

But Chaucer's supreme work is neither his earliest nor
his latest; it is the work of that central period where
his field first broadens, and the enchanted atmosphere of
romance begins to melt into the open day. Such is the
law of progress in poetry. We may long to fix that brief
perfection; but we might as well attempt to stay the sun.
It is there that we find his largest and firmest handling
of beauty. In his earlier and wholly romantic work we

> may on these branches hear
> The smale birdes singen clear
> Their blissful sweete song pitous,

in a world of garden-closes where the grass is powdered
with daisies, where the railed alleys are 'shadowed well
with blosmy boughes green, and benched new and sanded all
the ways'; the beauty is small and intricate, like that
of pictures in a painted book. From that lovely babble
of birds -

> Layes of love full well souning
> They sungen in their jargoning -

he rises to a freer handling, at once more natural and
more impassioned:

> A nightingale upon a cedar green
> Under the chamber wall thereas she lay,
> Full loude sang again the moone sheen,
> Paraunture in his birdes wise a lay
> Of love.

Just so likewise from his romantic descriptions of summer dawns he rises to this picture in the large epic manner:

> On heaven yet the sterres weren seen
> Although full pale ywaxen was the moon,
> And whiten gan the orizonte sheen
> All eastward.

In both of these passages we hear the great note of classical romance which is poetry consummate.

It is by virtue of his high poetry that Chaucer takes his rank as a poet.

> Sometimes a-dropping from the sky
> I heard the skylark sing;
> Sometimes all little birds that are,
> How they seemed to fill the sea and air
> With their sweet jargoning!

(with what a beautiful instinct Coleridge uses the Chaucerian word!)

> And now 'twas like all instruments;
> Now like a lonely flute;
> And now it is an angel's song
> That makes the heavens be mute.

To this angel's song he rises. It ceased; and it is elsewhere, in a later day, that Chapman heard, and we hear now

> the music of the spheres
> And all the angels singing out of heaven.

As the daylight broadens, the enchantment slowly fades away. Once the sun has climbed high, we must needs look back wistfully, not only to that magnificence of the *splendori antelucani,* but even beyond it to the magic of dusk, to the world of enclosed gardens, of cool green rooms, of lit chapels and shadowy halls. For poetry must perpetually return to the romance that again and again she seems to have outgrown. 'He seeth well,' says the author of the 'High History of the Holy Grail', 'that albeit the

night were dark, within was so great brightness of light
without candles that it was marvel; and it seemed him the
sun shone there. With that he issueth forth and betaketh
him to the way he had abandoned, and prayeth God grant he
may find Lancelot of the Lake.'

35. WILLIAM WITHERLE LAWRENCE, TO SHOW IT AS IT WAS

1911

W.W. Lawrence (1876-1958), educated at Leipzig and Harvard, was Professor of English at Columbia University, New
York, 1916-36. He begins to develop a social theory of
literature, based on an underlying concept of the primarily mimetic function of literature (a 'mirror'). Chaucer
is denied sublimity and, more surprisingly, pathos, but
the critic observes the significant diversity of Chaucer's
work, concentrating on 'The Canterbury Tales'. Reprinted
from 'Medieval Story', Columbia University Press (1911),
pp. 211-20.

The tales of the common folk contain many a caustic comment on the aristocratic manners of the day. We have
already seen two separate tendencies in the literature of
the middle classes, - the one satirical, mocking with
bitter laughter at Church and State through the mouth of
Reynard the Fox; the other a more dignified and good-
humored protest uttered by Robin Hood. In the 'Canterbury
Tales' the bitter and cynical tone is very noticeable in
the criticism of life which comes from the commons. These
folk have sharp tongues; they love to ridicule the errors
of churchmen and the frailties of women. Chivalry had insisted on blind devotion to the gentler sex and to the
majesty of religion; these people answer, with a sneer,
that neither women nor clerics are any better than they
should be. Most of their stories will not bear repeating.
The closest modern analogues of these *fabliaux,* told among
men in the ale-house and tavern, are our smoking-room
stories, indefensibly coarse, even though indisputably
humorous. The grossness of Chaucer's tales is well-known,
but they have some redeeming qualities. They differ from

their descendants of the smoking-room in that they are
really artistic in their narrative method, the precursors
of the modern short-story, and that they contain, under
their broad jesting, mordant social satire. The knight
tells a tale of two lovesick young warriors, Palamon and
Arcite, who woo a pink and white beauty named Emily with
all the elaborate mannerisms of romance. Hardly has the
knight finished, when the drunken miller steps in and
shows what the common people made of the airs and graces
of aristocracy. His heroes are two rascally young
'clerks'; his heroine a carpenter's wife of doubtful
virtue. The extravagant way in which these two knaves
make love to the lady is no less than a parody of the sentimentality of the knight's tale. One of them sings love-
songs and sighs under her window: -

> The mone, whan it was night, ful brighte shoon,
> And Absolon his giterne hath y-take,
> For paramours, he thoughte for to wake.
> And forth he gooth, Iolif and amorous,
> Til he cam to the carpenteres hous
> A little after cokkes hadde y-crowe;
> And dressed hym up by a shot-windowe
> That was upon the carpenteres wal.
> He singeth in his vois gentil and smal,
> 'Now, dere lady, if thy wille be,
> I preye yow that ye wol rewe on me,'
> Ful wel acordaunt to his giterninge.

This is the final outcome of the absurdities of the system
of chivalry in the minds of the sharp-witted common folk;
caricature of its elaborate manners, and satire of its
immorality, which permitted a married woman to encourage
the love of other men than her husband.

We must be careful not to take all that is said in the
'Canterbury Tales' about the faults and failings of women
too seriously. It represents truly neither Chaucer's
feelings nor those of his age. The frailty of women
formed one of the stock subjects for medieval satire, just
as her peerless perfection served as the corner-stone of
the system of chivalry. Both of these artificial literary
fashions affect the spontaneity of the sentiments of the
pilgrims. Again, some other tales, like that of the
lawyer, are not intended to be taken seriously at all;
they exaggerate the virtue of woman out of all reason for
a moral purpose. The young Oxford student tells of the
patient Griselda, who was so obedient to her husband that
she was willing to let him kill her children and put her
aside for another wife, and yet make no complaint. This

represents the ideals of no class of society; Chaucer himself says that the tale is not told because wives ought to
imitate the humility of Griselda, for that would be un-
bearable, even if they were willing to try, but because
every one ought to be constant in adversity, as she was.
We may fancy the disgust of the wife of Bath at this
story! And then, by way of antidote, Chaucer tells of the
lean cow which fed on patient wives, and the fat cow which
fed on patient husbands, showing, just as in the wife of
Bath's tale, that the moral must be taken with a grain of
salt. We must surely disregard such evidence as this in
studying Chaucer's work as an indication of social ideals.
It is the expression of individuals, it smells of the
lamp, it is little connected with that literature which
rises spontaneously from the thoughts and feelings of any
great class of society; or, if it was once the property of
the people, it has been so altered in learned hands as to
be completely changed in spirit. The 'Canterbury Tales,'
it will be observed, are not like the great poetry which
we have considered in the earlier lectures, - they are a
collection of diverse material, some of it popular, some
of it aristocratic, some of it learned and 'literary.' In
so far as these stories mark the emergence of the individual, or the narrow interests of the moralist, they are a
less trustworthy guide to social progress.

Yet this very diversity is itself significant. We have
now, at the end of the fourteenth century, reached a time
when story-telling no longer reflects the ideals of a few
sharply defined social orders, but when it is complicated
in a thousand ways by the more elaborate structure of the
English nation. It is more difficult to see English life
clearly because it is no longer simple. Its confusion
appeared so great to the author of 'Piers Plowman' - if
we may speak of him as one man - that he represented it
as a field full of folk of the most diverse habits and
occupations, a motley throng indeed. Despite his vivid
characterizations, he did not succeed in interpreting the
true spirit of the time as Chaucer did. Chaucer's vision
is wider; he sees virtue in many classes of society,
while Langland is so intent on remedying social abuses
that he has little sympathy for any one but his plowman
hero. Langland shows us many vividly contrasted types,
but Chaucer introduces us more intimately to the people
themselves. He makes them speak, sometimes formally,
when they are entertaining the rest of the pilgrims, sometimes informally, but always naturally. What any group
of persons say is quite as important for an understanding
of their true character as how they look. There is no one
figure in the Field of Folk so complex and at the same

time so human as the wife of Bath, but if Chaucer had contented himself with mere description, her personality
would have been far less vivid. The same is true of many
of the other characters. And Chaucer had a sympathetic
understanding of them all. It is indeed rare in any age
to find an author with interests so wide as to embrace all
classes of people, acquainted with all kinds of story-
telling, from saints' lives to the coarse jests of the
tavern, and with the power to put before us a human comedy
perfectly representative of his age, making his men and
women reveal, by means of narratives told by themselves,
their own thoughts and ideals.

For such a task as this Chaucer was particularly fitted
by his experience with all sorts and conditions of men.
He lived in London, then, as now, the heart of England.
He was born a commoner, but he spent his earlier years at
the royal court. He was thrown on terms of intimacy with
the greatest in the land, he was an active man of business, he was a traveler in foreign countries, he was a
soldier who saw active service in the field, he was a
member of Parliament, and the holder of various public
offices, and he was a diplomatist, engaged in important
and confidential negotiations. His career was far more
varied than Shakspere's, it will be observed. Shakspere
was, indeed, a shrewd man of business, he lived in London
in a most picturesque and active era, and he was on intimate terms with persons of distinguished birth and superior breeding. But that he was ever more than an actor
and a sharer in theatrical enterprises there is nothing
to show. His life was passed in the midst of most interesting scenes, but he took only a restricted share in the
manifold activities of his day. He was able to devote
his full energies to the drama, while with Chaucer literary work was of necessity subordinated to business.
Shakspere passed the best years of his life in the atmosphere of the theater; Chaucer was constantly obliged to
give up his books and his writing in order to discharge
faithfully the duties which had been laid upon him.
Charles Lamb used to assert that his real 'works' were in
the rolls of the East India Office; Chaucer might have
said that his own were in the ledgers of the Customs
Office for the Port of London. For a considerable time
he was obliged to fill in these ledgers with entries in
his own handwriting. In this work many hours were con-
sumed which might have given classics to the world. His
public occupations claimed so much of his time through
the prime of his life that it seems a marvel that he produced as much as he did. But all this activity among many
classes of men, in swarming London, in Italy in the

springtime of the Renaissance, in France and in Flanders,
gave him the breadth of view, the insight into human
nature, the poise of judgment, which make his work so
perfect a mirror of his own day. Had he spent more time
among his books, and less in the great world, he might
have been less representative of his age. The imprisonment of his gay spirit behind the bars of routine may perhaps have even given his song an added freshness when once
the doors of his cage were opened.

He viewed the human comedy with a certain detachment.
As a man of the world, he was interested in a great
variety of things, but, like Horace, without the deepest
feeling. He never quite lets himself go; if he becomes
tragic or tender, he is likely to turn aside with a shrug
and a smile, and to deny his own emotion. He identifies
himself with no one class of society; he stands apart, and
views them all from his own point of vantage. When he
exposes the abuses of the times, he is rather amused than
indignant. If monks and friars steal from the poor, and
meanwhile line their own pockets, he has more real delight
in seeing through their hypocritical pretenses than he
has righteous anger at their villainy. Nothing pleases
him more than to set two of them against each other, to
make the summoner and the friar expose each other's
tricks. He is no particular friend of the commons. He
hates shams and hypocrisies, in whatever station. The
miller who steals corn, or the sailor who is sometimes
dishonest and cruel, are treated with as little mercy as
the lawyer or the doctor. Chaucer does not lift up his
voice in favor of the lower classes, like Langland or
Gower. In fact he seems, like Shakspere, to have been
rather impatient of the multitude. He is no brother of
the men who gave final form to the stories of Reynard
the Fox. Probably he had seen enough of the turbulent
commons of his day to despise their instability and treachery. 'O stormy people,' he exclaims, 'so little serious, so little true to what you say! Ever indiscreet,
changing like a weathercock, delighting in rumor, waxing
and waning like the moon, full of gabble, your judgments
are false, your constancy is vain, the man who believes in
you is a great fool!' This is what differentiates Chaucer
from many other great literary men of his day. He had no
desire to reform the world, he merely strove to show it as
it was. His attitude was akin to that of Shakspere and
of Molière. We have long since abandoned the absurd
notion that a definite didactic purpose was the control-
ling force in the composition of the plays of Shakspere.
We know, too, that while Molière doubtless produced
'Tartuffe' partly in order to strike at hypocrisy, and

'L'Avare' partly to expose avarice, his genius was not
confined with limits so narrow; his ultimate object was
not to fulfil the functions of a Bossuet or of a La
Rochefoucauld, but to show life in the large as he saw it
in the brilliant and varied society of his day.

On the other hand, the personality of the author is far
more in evidence in the work of Chaucer than in the plays
of these great dramatists. In this respect, Chaucer is
more like Thackeray, who constantly interrupts his narrative in order to interject remarks in his own person.
Chaucer rides with his pilgrims, he is one of their company, he tells two of the stories himself. But he is not
content to appear merely as a character, he speaks out as
author too. Sometimes he gets so much interested in his
tale that he forgets that one of his characters is telling
it. Suddenly the mask drops, and it is Chaucer who
addresses us straight from the desk where he is writing,
and not even from his place in the procession on the road
to Canterbury. It is surely not the shy and serious
Oxford student who finishes the tale of the patient Griselda. At the end of the story, after the irritating patience of the virtuous wife has been finally rewarded, a
half-waggish, half-cynical epilog follows, at which we
have already glanced. Every reader must feel that the
clerk of Oxford has faded out of the picture completely,
and that Chaucer has usurped his place. Rightly enough
the scribe has written above the lines, 'L'Envoy de
Chaucer:'

> Griselda is dead, and her patience too! And I warn all
> married men not to try the patience of their wives in
> the hopes of finding a Griselda, for they'll surely
> fail! ... Stand at your defense, ye arch-wives, I
> counsel you! Since you are as strong as camels, don't
> suffer men to offend you! And ye slender wives,
> feeble in fighting, be savage as Indian tigers, keep on
> gabbling as fast as a mill, I counsel you! ... Make
> your husbands jealous, and you shall make them couch
> like quails.... Be light as leaf on linden tree, and
> let your husbands have sorrow and weeping, wailing and
> wringing of hands!

Chaucer was not, of course, the originator of his
tales; he borrowed them from whatever sources he chose,
and in many cases these sources were truly popular - as
much so as those of the Robin Hood ballads or of the
stories of Reynard the Fox. But in placing them in a distinctive and picturesque framework, in which he himself
appeared, Chaucer emphasized the personal note almost as

much as he did by his comments delivered in his capacity as author. His great contemporary and master in story-telling, Boccaccio, does not appear among the noble company in the 'Decameron,' nor does he express his own ideas about their conduct. Chaucer's friend and fellow-towns-man, Gower, speaks in his own person in his collection of tales, the 'Confessio Amantis,' but only as a sort of lay-figure, conversing with an impossible half-mythological, half-allegorical figure, the Priest of Venus. But Chaucer moves among the pilgrims a live and breathing man, full of spirit and humor. He was medieval in his willingness to tell absurd and archaic stories, full of the artificial conventions of chivalry or the exaggerations of morality and religion common to his day, but he was modern in his fresh and common-sense outlook upon life, and in his willingness to let this influence his work. Even when he is not speaking, we constantly feel his presence. He takes us into his confidence; he draws us aside and laughs with us at the merry jest of life. By a supreme stroke of genius, he reveals to us a personality more fascinating and more complex than that of any of his pilgrims, - his own.

We cannot delay over an analysis of his genius; our main emphasis must be on his stories and their significance for the social conditions of his age. But this may be said ere we take leave of him: he was as great a poet as a man can be who rarely achieves pathos and who never attains sublimity.

36. GEORGE LYMAN KITTREDGE, A CONNECTED HUMAN COMEDY

1912

G.L. Kittredge (1860-1941), educated at Harvard University, was Professor of English in Harvard University, 1894-1936. His criticism of Chaucer is learned, sympathetic, historically informed, sensitive, and immensely influential. Taking up a well-established tradition he argues for an underlying structural principle for 'The Canterbury Tales' as a 'Human Comedy', and by means of what he calls 'straightforward interpretation' reads 'The Canterbury Tales' as a fully dramatic piece of a realistic kind, a self-enclosed fiction like a novel. Kittredge

sees the Wife of Bath as a central figure in a series of
connected dramatic outbursts by various pilgrims on the
subject of marriage in what is probably the most characteristic and influential of all his numerous writings on
Chaucer: Chaucer's Discussion of Marriage, 'Modern Philosophy' IX (1912), pp. 435-67. Reprinted here are pp. 435-
51, 452-4, 461-4, 466-7, by permission of the University
of Chicago Press.

CHAUCER'S DISCUSSION OF MARRIAGE

We are prone to read and study the 'Canterbury Tales' as
if each tale were an isolated unit and to pay scant attention to what we call the connecting links, - those bits of
lively narrative and dialogue that bind the whole
together. Yet Chaucer's plan is clear enough. Structurally regarded, the 'Canterbury Tales' is a kind of Human
Comedy. From this point of view, the Pilgrims are the
dramatis personae, and their stories are only speeches
that are somewhat longer than common, entertaining in and
for themselves (to be sure), but primarily significant,
in each case, because they illustrate the speaker's character and opinions, or show the relations of the travelers
to one another in the progressive action of the Pilgrimage. In other words, we ought not merely to consider the
general appropriateness of each tale to the character of
the teller: we should also inquire whether the tale is not
determined, to some extent, by the circumstances, - by the
situation at the moment, by something that another Pilgrim
has said or done, by the turn of a discussion already
under way.

Now and then, to be sure, this point is too obvious to
be overlooked, as in the squabble between the Summoner and
the Friar and that between the Reeve and the Miller, in
the Shipman's intervening to check the Parson, and in the
way in which the gentles head off the Pardoner when he is
about to tell a ribald anecdote. But, despite these unes-
capable instances, the general principle is too often
blinked or ignored. Yet its temperate application should
clear up a number of things which are traditionally regarded as difficulties, or as examples of heedlessness on
Chaucer's part.(1)

Without attempting to deny or abridge the right to
study and criticize each tale in and for itself, - as
legend, romance, *exemplum,* fabliau, or what-not, - and
without extenuating the results that this method has

achieved, let us consider certain tales in their relation
to Chaucer's structural plan, - with reference, that is
to say, to the Pilgrims who tell them and to the Pilgrimage to which their telling is incidental. We may begin
with the story of Griselda.

This is a plain and straightforward piece of edification, and nobody has ever questioned its appropriateness
to the Clerk, who, as he says himself, had traveled in
Italy and had heard it from the lips of the laureate Petrarch. The Clerk's 'speech,' according to the General
Prologue, was 'sowning in moral vertu,' so that this
story is precisely the kind of thing which we should
expect from his lips. True, we moderns sometimes feel
shocked or offended at what we style the immorality of
Griselda's unvarying submission. But this feeling is no
ground of objection to the appropriateness of the tale to
the Clerk. The Middle Ages delighted (as children still
delight) in stories that exemplify a single human quality,
like valor, or tyranny, or fortitude. In such cases, the
settled rule (for which neither Chaucer nor the Clerk was
responsible) was to show to what lengths this quality may
conceivably go. Hence, in tales of this kind, there can
be no question of conflict of duties, no problem as to
the point at which excess of goodness becomes evil. It
is, then, absurd to censure a fourteenth-century Clerk
for telling (or Chaucer for making him tell) a story
which exemplifies in this hyperbolical way the virtue of
fortitude under affliction. Whether Griselda could have
put an end to her woes, or ought to have put an end to
them, by refusing to obey her husband's commands is *parum
ad rem*. We are to look at her trials as inevitable, and
to pity her accordingly, and wonder at her endurance. If
we refuse to accept the tale in this spirit, we are ourselves the losers. We miss the pathos because we are
aridly intent on discussing an ethical question that has
no status in this particular court, however pertinent it
may be in the general forum of morals.

Furthermore, in thus focusing attention on the morality
or immorality of Griselda's submissiveness, we overlook
what the Clerk takes pains to make as clear as possible,
- the real lesson that the story is meant to convey, - and
thus we do grave injustice to that austere but amiable
moralist. The Clerk, a student of 'Aristotle and his
philosophye,' knew as well as any of us that every virtue
may be conceived as a mean between two extremes. Even
the Canon's Yeoman, an ignorant man, was aware of this
principle:

That that is overdoon, it wol nat preve
Aright, as clerkes seyn, - it is a vyce. [G. 645-6]

Chaucer has too firm a grasp on his *dramatis personae* to
allow the Clerk to leave the true purport of his parable
undefined. 'This story is not told,' says the Clerk in
substance, 'to exhort wives to imitate Griselda's humility, for *that* would be beyond the capacity of human
nature. It is told in order that every man or woman, in
whatever condition of life, may learn fortitude in adversity. For, since a woman once exhibited such endurance
under trials inflicted on her by a mortal man, a fortiori
ought *we* to accept patiently whatever tribulation God may
send us. For God is not like Griselda's husband. He does
not wantonly experiment with us, out of inhuman scientific
curiosity. God *tests* us, as it is reasonable that our
Maker should test his handiwork, but he does not *tempt* us.
He allows us to be beaten with sharp scourges of adversity, not, like the Marquis Walter, to see if we can stand
it, for he knoweth our frame, he remembereth that we are
dust: all *his* affliction is for our better grace. Let us
live, therefore, in manly endurance of the visitations of
Providence.'

And then, at verse 1163, comes that matchless passage
in which the Clerk (having explained the *universal* application of his parable, - having provided with scrupulous
care against any misinterpretation of its serious purport)
turns with gravely satiric courtesy to the Wife of Bath
and makes the *particular* application of the story to her
'life' and 'all her sect.'

Here one may appreciate the vital importance of considering the 'Canterbury Tales' as a connected Human
Comedy, - of taking into account the Pilgrims in their
relations to one another in the great drama to which the
several narratives are structurally incidental. For it
is precisely at this point that Professor Skeat notes a
difficulty. 'From this point to the end,' he remarks, 'is
the work of a later period, and in Chaucer's best manner,
though unsuited *to the coy Clerk*.' (2) This is as much as to
say that, in the remaining stanzas of the Clerk's Tale
and in the Envoy, Chaucer has violated dramatic propriety.
And, indeed, many readers have detected in these concluding portions Chaucer's own personal revulsion of feeling
against the tale that he had suffered the Clerk to
tell. (3)

Now the supposed difficulty vanishes as soon as we
study vss. 1163-212, not as an isolated phenomenon, but in
their relation to the great drama of the Canterbury Pilgrimage. It disappears when we consider the lines in what

we may call their dramatic context, that is (to be specific), when we inquire what there was in the situation to
prompt the Clerk, after emphasizing the serious and universal moral of Griselda's story, to give his tale a
special and peculiar application by annexing an ironical
tribute to the Wife of Bath, her life, her 'sect,' and
her principles. To answer this question we must go back
to the Wife of Bath's Prologue.

The Wife of Bath's Prologue begins a Group in the
'Canterbury Tales,' or, as one may say, a new act in the
drama. It is not connected with anything that precedes.
Let us trace the action from this point down to the moment
when the Clerk turns upon the Wife with his satirical
compliments.

The Wife had expounded her views at great length and
with all imaginable zest. Virginity, which the Church
glorifies, is not required of us. Our bodies are given
us to use. Let saints be continent if they will. She
has no wish to emulate them. Nor does she accept the
doctrine that a widow or a widower must not marry again.
Where is bigamy forbidden in the Bible, or octogamy
either? She has warmed both hands before the fire of
life, and she exults in the recollection of her fleshly
delights:

> But lord Crist! whan that it remembreth me
> Upon my youthe and on my iolitee,
> It tikleth me aboute myn herte rote;
> Unto this day it doth myn herte bote
> That I have had my world as in my time! [D. 469-73]

True, she is willing to admit, for convention's sake,
that chastity is the ideal state. But it is not *her*
ideal. On the contrary, her admission is only for appearances. In her heart she despises virginity. Her contempt
for it is thinly veiled, or rather, not veiled at all.
Her discourse is marked by frank and almost obstreperous
animalism. Her whole attitude is that of scornful, though
good-humored, repudiation of what the Church teaches in
that regard.

Nor is the Wife content with this single heresy. She
maintains also that wives should rule their husbands, and
she enforces this doctrine by an account of her own life,
and further illustrates it by her tale of the knight of
King Arthur who learned that

> Wommen desiren to have sovereyntee
> As wel over hir housband as hir love,
> And for to been in maistrie him above,

and who accepted the lesson as sound doctrine. Then, at
the end of her discourse, she sums up in no uncertain
words:

> And Iesu Crist us sende
> Housbandes meke, yonge, and fresshe abedde,
> And grace to overbyde hem that we wedde;
> And eek I preye Iesu shorte her lyves
> That wol nat be governed by her wyves. [D. 1258-62]

Now the Wife of Bath is not *bombinans in vacuo*. She
addresses her heresies not to *us* or to the world at large,
but to her fellow-pilgrims. Chaucer has made this point
perfectly clear. The words of the Wife were of a kind to
provoke comment, - and we have the comment. The Pardoner
interrupts her with praise of her noble preaching:

> 'Now, dame,' quod he, 'by God and by seint Iohn,
> Ye been a noble prechour in this cas!' [D. 164-5]

The adjective is not accidental. The Pardoner was a judge
of good preaching: the General Prologue describes him as
'a noble ecclesiaste' (A. 708) and he shows his ability in
his own sermon on Covetousness. Furthermore, it is the
Friar's comment on the Wife's preamble that provokes the
offensive words of the Summoner, and that becomes thereby
the occasion for the two tales that immediately follow in
the series. It is manifest, then, that Chaucer meant us
to imagine the *dramatis personae* as taking a lively interest in whatever the Wife says. This being so, we ought
to inquire what effect her Prologue and Tale would have
upon the Clerk.
  Of course the Clerk was scandalized. He was unworldly
and an ascetic, - he 'looked holwe and therto sobrely.'
Moral virtue was his special study. He had embraced the
celibate life. He was grave, devout, and unflinchingly
orthodox. And now he was confronted by the lust of the
flesh and the pride of life in the person of a woman who
flouted chastity and exulted that she had 'had her world
as in her time.' Nor was this all. The woman was an
heresiarch, or at best a schismatic. She set up, and
aimed to establish, a new and dangerous sect, whose principle was that the wife should rule the husband. The
Clerk kept silence for the moment. Indeed, he had no
chance to utter his sentiments, unless he interrupted, -
something not to be expected of his quiet ('coy') and
sober temperament. But it is not to be imagined that his
thoughts were idle. He could be trusted to speak to the
purpose whenever his opportunity should come.

Now the substance of the Wife's false doctrines was not
the only thing that must have roused the Clerk to protest-
ing answer. The very manner of her discourse was a direct
challenge to him.(4) She had garnished her sermon with
scraps of Holy Writ and rags and tatters of erudition,
caught up, we may infer, from her last husband. Thus she
had put herself into open competition with the guild of
scholars and theologians, to which the Clerk belonged.
Further, with her eye manifestly upon this sedate philosopher, she had taken pains to gird at him and his fellows. At first she pretends to be modest and apologetic,
- 'so that the clerkes be nat with me wrothe' (vs. 125),
- but later she abandons all pretense and makes an open
attack:

> For trusteth wel, it is an impossible
> That any clerk wol speken good of wyves,
> But-if it be of holy seintes lyves,
> Ne of noon other womman never the mo....
> The clerk, whan he is old, and may noght do
> Of Venus werkes worth his olde sho,
> Than sit he doun, and writ in his dotage
> That wommen can nat kepe hir mariage. [D. 688-91,
> 707-10]

And there was more still that the Wife made our Clerk
endure. Her fifth husband was, like him, a 'clerk of
Oxenford' - surely this is no accidental coincidence on
Chaucer's part. He had abandoned his studies ('had left
scole'), and had given up all thought of taking priest's
orders. The Wife narrates, with uncommon zest, how she
intrigued with him, and cajoled him, and married him
(though he was twenty and she was forty), and how finally
she made him utterly subservient to her will, - how she
got 'by maistrie al the soveraynetee.' This was gall and
wormwood to our Clerk. The Wife not only trampled on his
principles in her theory and practice, but she pointed
her attack by describing how she had subdued to her heretical sect a clerk of Oxenford, an alumnus of our Clerk's
own university. The Wife's discourse is not malicious.
She is too jovial to be ill-natured, and she protests that
she speaks in jest ('For myn entente nis but for to
pleye,' vs. 192). But it none the less embodies a rude
personal assault upon the Clerk, whose quiet mien and
habitual reticence made him seem a safe person to attack.
She had done her best to make the Clerk ridiculous. He
saw it; the company saw it. He kept silent, biding his
time.
     All this is not speculation. It is nothing but

straightforward interpretation of the text in the light
of the circumstances and the situation. We can reject it
only by insisting on the manifest absurdity (shown to be
such in every headlink and endlink) that Chaucer did not
visualize the Pilgrims whom he had been at such pains to
describe in the Prologue, and that he never regarded them
as associating, as looking at each other and thinking of
each other, as becoming better and better acquainted as
they jogged along the Canterbury road.

Chaucer might have given the Clerk a chance to reply to
the wife immediately. But he was too good an artist. The
drama of the Pilgrimage is too natural and unforced in its
development under the master's hand to admit of anything
so frigidly schematic. The very liveliness with which he
conceived his individual *dramatis personae* forbade. The
Pilgrims were interested in the Wife's harangue, but it
was for the talkative members of the company to thrust
themselves forward. The Pardoner had already interrupted
her with humorous comments before she was fully under way
[D. 169] and had exhorted her to continue her account of
the 'praktike' of marriage. The Friar, we may be confi-
dent, was on good terms with her before she began: she
was one of those 'worthy wommen of the toun' whom he
especially cultivated.(5) He, too, could not refrain
from comment:

> The Frere lough, whan he had herd al this:
> 'Now, dame,' quod he, 'so have I ioye or blis,
> This is a long preamble of a tale!' [D. 829-31]

The Summoner reproved him, in words that show not only
his professional enmity but also the amusement that the
Pilgrims in general were deriving from the Wife's dis-
closures.(6) They quarreled, and each threatened to
tell a story at the other's expense. Then the Host
intervened roughly, calling for silence and bidding the
Wife go ahead with her story. She assented, but not
without a word of good-humored, though ironical, deference to the Friar:

> 'Al redy, sir,' quod she, 'right as yow lest,
> If I have licence of this worthy Frere.' [854-5]

And, at the very beginning of her tale, she took humorous
vengeance for his interruption in a characteristic bit of
satire at the expense of 'limitours and other holy
freres' [D. 864-81]. This passage, we note, has nothing
whatever to do with her tale. It is a side-remark in
which she is talking at the Friar, precisely as she has

talked at the Clerk in her prologue.

The quarrel between the Summoner and the Friar was in
abeyance until the Wife finished her tale. They let her
end her story and proclaim her moral in peace, - the same
heretical doctrine that we have already noted, that the
wife should be the head of the house. [D. 1258-62] Then
the Friar spoke, and his words are very much to our present purpose. He adverts in significant terms both to the
subject and to the manner of the Wife's discourse, - a
discourse, we should observe, that was in effect a doctrinal sermon illustrated (as the fashion of preachers was)
by a pertinent *exemplum:*(7)

> Ye have here touched, al-so moot I thee,
> In scole-matere greet difficultee. [D. 1271-2]

She has handled a hard subject that properly belongs to
scholars. She has quoted authorities, too, like a clerk.
Such things, he says, are best left to ecclesiastics:

> But, dame, here as we ryden by the weye,
> Us nedeth nat to speken but of game,
> And lete auctoritees, on Goddes name,
> To preching and to scole eek of clergye. [D. 1274-7]

This, to be sure, is but a device to 'conveyen his
matere,' - to lead up to his proposal to 'telle a game'
about a summoner. But it serves to recall our minds to
the Wife's usurpation of clerkly functions. If we think
of the Clerk at all at this point (and assuredly Chaucer
had not forgotten him), we must feel that here is another
prompting (undesigned though it be on the Friar's part)
to take up the subject which the Wife has (in the Clerk's
eyes) so shockingly maltreated.

Then follows the comic interlude of the Friar and the
Summoner,(8) in the course of which we may perhaps lose
sight of the serious subject which the Wife had set
abroach, - the status of husband and wife in the marriage
relation. But Chaucer did not lose sight of it. It was
a part of his design that the Host should call on the
Clerk for the first story of the next day.

This is the opportunity for which the Clerk has been
waiting. He has not said a word in reply to the Wife's
heresies or to her personal attack on him and his order.
Seemingly she has triumphed. The subject has apparently
been dismissed with the Friar's words about leaving such
matters to sermons and to school debates. The Host,
indeed, has no idea that the Clerk purposes to revive the
discussion; he does not even think of the Wife in calling

upon the representative of that order which has fared so
ill at her hands.

> 'Sir clerk of Oxenford,' our hoste sayde,
> 'Ye ryde as coy and stille as doth a mayde
> Were newe spoused, sitting at the bord;
> This day ne herde I of your tonge a word.
> I trowe ye studie aboute som sophyme.' [E. 1-5]

Even here there is a suggestion (casual, to be sure, and,
so far as the Host is concerned, quite unintentional) of
marriage, the subject which is occupying the Clerk's mind.
For the Host is mistaken. The Clerk's abstraction is only
apparent. He is not pondering syllogisms; he is biding
his time.
    'Tell us a tale,' the unconscious Host goes on, 'but
don't preach us a Lenten sermon - tell us som mery thing
of aventures.' 'Gladly,' replies the demure scholar.
'I will tell you a story that a worthy *clerk* once told me
at Padua - Francis Petrarch, God rest his soul!'
    At this word *clerk*, pronounced with grave and inscrut-
able emphasis, the Wife of Bath must have pricked up her
ears. But she has no inkling of what is in store, nor is
the Clerk in any hurry to enlighten her. He opens with
tantalizing deliberation, and it is not until he has
spoken more than sixty lines that he mentions marriage.
'The Marquis Walter,' says the Clerk, 'lived only for the
present and lived for pleasure only' -

> As for to hauke and hunte on every syde, -
> Wel ny al othere cures leet he slyde;
> And eek he nolde, and that was worst of alle,
> Wedde no wyf, for noght that may bifalle.

These words may or may not have appeared significant to
the company at large. To the Wife of Bath, at all
events, they must have sounded interesting. And when, in
a few moments, the Clerk made Walter's subjects speak of
'soveraynetee,' the least alert of the Pilgrims can hardly
have missed the point:

> Boweth your nekke under that blisful yok
> Of soveraynetee, noght of servyse,
> Which that men clepeth spousaille or wedlok.
>   [E. 113-15](9)

'Sovereignty' had been the Wife's own word:

And whan that I hadde geten unto me
By maistrie al the soveraynetee (D. 817-18);

Wommen desyren to have sovereyntee
As wel over hir housband as hir love,
And for to been in maistrie him above (D. 1038-40).

Clearly the Clerk is catching up the subject proposed by
the Wife. The discussion is under way again.

Yet, despite the cheerful view that Walter's subjects
take of the marriage yoke, it is by no means yet clear to
the Wife of Bath and the other Pilgrims what the Clerk is
driving at. For he soon makes Walter declare that 'liberty is seldom found in marriage,' and that, if he weds a
wife, he must exchange freedom for servitude.(10) Indeed,
it is not until vss. 351-7 are reached that Walter reveals
himself as a man who is determined to rule his wife absolutely. From that point to the end there is no room for
doubt in any Pilgrim's mind: *the Clerk is answering the
Wife of Bath;* he is telling of a woman whose principles in
marriage were the antithesis of hers; he is reasserting
the orthodox view in opposition to the heresy which she
had expounded with such zest and with so many flings and
jeers at the clerkly profession and character.

What is the tale of Griselda? Several things, no
doubt - an old *märchen,* an *exemplum,* a *novella,* what you
will. Our present concern, however, is primarily with
the question what it seemed to be to the Canterbury Pilgrims, told as it was by an individual Clerk of Oxford
at a particular moment and under the special circumstances. The answer is plain. To them it was a retort (indirect, impersonal, masterly) to the Wife of Bath's heretical doctrine that the woman should be the head of the
man. It told them of a wife who had no such views, - who
promised ungrudging obedience and kept her vow. The Wife
of Bath had railed at her husbands and badgered them and
cajoled them: Griselda never lost her patience or her
serenity. On its face, then, the tale appeared to the
Pilgrims to be a dignified and scholarly narrative, derived
from a great Italian clerk who was dead, and now utilized
by their fellow-pilgrim, the Clerk of Oxford, to demolish
the heretical structure so boisterously reared by the Wife
of Bath in her prologue and her tale.

But Chaucer's Clerk was a logician - 'unto logik hadde
he longe ygo.' He knew perfectly well that the real moral
of his story was not that which his hearers would gather.
He was aware that Griselda was no model for literal imitation by ordinary womankind. If so taken, his tale proved
too much; it reduced his argument *ad absurdum.* If he let

it go at that, he was playing into his opponent's hands.
Besides, he was a conscientious man. He could not mis-
represent the lesson which Petrarch had meant to teach and
had so clearly expressed, - the lesson of submissive fortitude under tribulation sent by God. Hence he does not
fail to explain this moral fully and in unmistakable
terms, and to refer distinctly to Petrarch as authority
for it:

> And herkeneth what this auctor seith therfore.
>
> This storie is seyd, nat for that wyves sholde
> Folwen Griselde as in humilitee,
> For it were importable, though they wolde;
> But for that every wight, in his degree,
> Sholde be constant in adversitee
> As was Grisilde; therfor Petrark wryteth
> This storie, which with heigh style he endyteth.
>
> For, sith a womman was so pacient
> Un-to a mortal man, wel more us oghte
> Receyven al in gree that God us sent;
> For greet skile is, he preve that he wroghte.
> But he ne tempteth no man that he boghte,
> As seith seint Iame, if ye his pistel rede;
> He preveth folk al day, it is no drede,
>
> And suffreth us, as for our exercyse,
> With sharpe scourges of adversitee
> Ful ofte to be bete in sondry wyse;
> Nat for to knowe our wil, for certes he,
> Er we were born, knew al our freletee;
> And for our beste is al his governaunce:
> Lat us than live in vertuous suffrance. [E. 1141-62]

Yet the Clerk has no idea of failing to make his point
against the Wife of Bath. And so, when the tale is finished and the proper Petrarchan moral has been duly elaborated, he turns to the Wife (whom he has thus far sedu-
lously refrained from addressing) and distinctly applies
the material to the purpose of an ironical answer, of
crushing force, to her whole heresy. There is nothing inappropriate to his character in this procedure. Quite the
contrary. Clerks were always satirizing women - the Wife
had said so herself - and this particular Clerk had, of
course, no scruples against using the powerful weapon of
irony in the service of religion and 'moral vertu.' In
this instance, the satire is peculiarly poignant for two
reasons: first, because it comes with all the suddenness

of a complete change of tone (from high seriousness to
biting irony, and from the impersonal to the personal);
and secondly, because, in the tale which he has told, the
Clerk has incidentally refuted a false statement of the
Wife's, to the effect that

> It is an impossible
> That any clerk wol speke good of wyves,
> But if it be of holy seintes lyves,
> Ne of noon other womman never the mo. [D. 688-91](11)

Clerks *can* 'speak well' of women (as our Clerk has shown),
when women deserve it; and he now proceeds to show that
they can likewise speak well (with biting irony) of womèn
who do *not* deserve it - such women as the Wife of Bath
and all her sect of domestic revolutionists.

It now appears that the form and spirit of the conclusion and the Envoy [E. 1163-1212] are not only appropriate
to clerks in general, but peculiarly and exquisitely
appropriate to this particular clerk under these particular circumstances and with this particular task in hand, -
the duty of defending the orthodox view of the relations
between husband and wife against the heretical opinions
of the Wife of Bath: 'One word in conclusion,(12) gentlemen. There are few Griseldas now-a-days. Most women will
break before they will bend. Our companion, the Wife of
Bath, is an example, as she has told us herself. Therefore, though I cannot sing, I will recite a song in
honor, not of Griselda (as you might perhaps expect)´, but
of the Wife of Bath, of the sect of which she aspires to
be a doctor, and of the life which she exemplifies in
practice -

> For the wyves love of Bathe,
> Whos lif and al hir secte God mayntene
> In high maistrye, and elles were it scathe. [E. 1170-2]

Her *way of life* - she had set it forth with incomparable
zest. Her *sect* - she was an heresiarch or at least a
schismatic. The terms are not accidental: they are chosen
with all the discrimination that befits a scholar and a
rhetorician. They refer us back (as definitely as the
words 'Wife of Bath' themselves) to that prologue in which
the Wife had stood forth as an opponent of the orthodox
view of subordination in marriage, as the upholder of an
heretical doctrine, and as the exultant practicer of what
she preached.(13)

And then comes the Clerk's Envoy,(14) the song that he
recites in honor of the Wife and her life and her sect,

with its polished lines, its ingenious rhyming, and its
utter felicity of scholarly diction. Nothing could be
more in character. To whom in all the world should such
a masterpiece of rhetoric be appropriate if not to the
Clerk of Oxenford? It is a mock encomium, a sustained
ironical commendation of what the Wife has taught:

'O noble wives, let no clerk ever have occasion to
write such a story of you as Petrarch once told me about
Griselda. Follow your great leader, the Wife of Bath.
Rule your husbands as she did; rail at them, as she did;
make them jealous, as she did; exert yourselves to get
lovers, as she did. And all this you must do whether you
are fair or foul [with manifest allusion to the problem
of beauty or ugliness presented in the Wife's story]. Do
this, I say, and you will fulfil the precepts that she has
set forth and achieve the great end which she has pro-
claimed as the object of marriage: that is, *you will make
your husbands miserable, as she did!*'

> Be ay of chere as light as leef on linde,
> And lat him care and wepe and wringe and waille!
>   [E. 1211-12]

And the Merchant (hitherto silent, but not from inat-
tention) catches up the closing words in a gust of bitter
passion:

> 'Weping and wayling, care and other sorwe
> *I* know ynough on even and amorwe,'
> Quod the Merchant, 'and so don othere mo
> That wedded ben.' [E. 1213-16]

The Clerk's Envoy, then, is not only appropriate to
his character and to the situation: it has also a marked
dynamic value. For it is this ironical tribute to the
Wife of Bath and her dogmas that, with complete dramatic
inevitability, calls out the Merchant's *cri du coeur*.
The Merchant has no thought of telling a tale at this
moment. He is a stately and imposing person in his
degree, by no means prone (so the Prologue informs us) to
expose any holes there may be in his coat. But he is suffering a kind of emotional crisis. The poignant irony of
the Clerk, following hard upon the moving story of a patient and devoted wife, is too much for him. He has just
passed through his honeymoon (but two months wed!) and he
has sought a respite from his thraldom under color of a
pilgrimage to St. Thomas.

> I have a wyf, the worste that may be! [E. 1218]

She would be an overmatch for the devil himself. He need
not specify her evil traits: she is bad in every respect.(15)

> There is a long and large difference
> Bitwix Grisildis grete pacience
> And of my wyf the passing crueltee. [E. 1223-5]

The Host, as ever, is on the alert. He scents a good
story:

> Sin ye so muchel knowen of that art,
> Ful hertely I pray yow telle us part. [E. 1241-2]

The Merchant agrees, as in duty bound, for all the Pilgrims take care never to oppose the Host, lest he exact
the heavy forfeit established as the penalty for rebel-
lion.(16) But he declines to relate his own experiences,
thus leaving us to infer, if we choose, - for nowhere is
Chaucer's artistic reticence more effective, - that his
bride has proved false to him, like the wife of the worthy
Knight of Lombardy.
     And so the discussion of marriage is once more in full
swing. The Wife of Bath, without intending it, has
opened a debate in which the Pilgrims have become so
absorbed that they will not leave it till the subject is
'bolted to the bran.'
     The Merchant's Tale presents very noteworthy features,
and has been much canvassed, though never (it seems) with
due attention to its plain significance in the Human
Comedy of the Canterbury Pilgrimage. In substance, it is
nothing but a tale of bawdry, one of the most familiar of
its class. There is nothing novel about it except its
setting, but that is sufficiently remarkable. Compare
the tale with any other version of the Pear-Tree Story, -
their name is legion, - and its true significance comes
out in striking fashion. The simple fabliau devised by
its first author merely to make those laugh whose lungs
are tickle o' the sere, is so expanded and overlaid with
savage satire that it becomes a complete disquisition on
marriage from the only point of view which is possible
for the disenchanted Merchant. Thus considered, the cynicism of the Merchant's Tale is seen to be in no way surprising, and (to answer another kind of comment which
this piece has evoked) in no sense expressive of Chaucer's
own sentiments, or even of Chaucer's momentary mood. The
cynicism is the Merchant's. It is no more Chaucer's than
Iago's cynicism about love is Shakspere's....
     (p. 452) So far, in this act of Chaucer's Human Comedy,

we have found that the Wife of Bath is, in a very real
sense, the dominant figure. She has dictated the theme
and inspired or instigated the actors; and she has always
been at or near the center of the stage. It was a quarrel
over her prologue that elicited the tale of the Friar and
that of the Summoner. It was she who caused the Clerk to
tell of Griselda - and the Clerk satirizes her in his
Envoy. 'The art' of which the Host begs the Merchant to
tell is *her* art, the art of marriage on which she has dis-
coursed so learnedly. That the Merchant, therefore,
should allude to her, quote her words, and finally mention
her in plain terms is precisely what was to be expected.

The order and method of these approaches on the Merchant's part are exquisitely natural and dramatic. First
there are touches, more or less palpable, when he describes the harmony of wedded life in terms so different
from the Wife's account of what her husbands had to
endure. Then - after a little - comes a plain enough
allusion (put into January's mouth) to the Wife's character, to her frequent marriages, and to her inclination to
marry again, old as she is:

> And eek thise olde widwes, God it wot,
> They conne so muchel craft on Wades boot,
> So muchel broken harm, whan that hem leste,
> That with hem sholde I never live in reste!
> For sondry scoles maken sotil clerkis:
> Wommen of many scoles half a clerk is. [E. 1423-8]

Surely the Wife of Bath was a woman of many schools, and
her emulation of clerkly discussion had already been commented on by the Pardoner [D. 165] and the Friar.
[D. 1270-7] Next, the Merchant lets Justinus quote some
of the Wife's very words - though without naming her: 'God
may apply the trials of marriage, my dear January, to your
salvation. Your wife may make you go straight to heaven
without passing through purgatory.'

> Paraunter she may be your purgatorie!
> She may be Goddes mene, and Goddes whippe;
> Than shal your soule up to hevene skippe
> Swifter than doth an arwe out of the bowe. [E. 1670-3]

This is merely an adaptation of the Wife of Bath's own language in speaking of her fourth husband:

> By God, in erthe I was his purgatorie,
> For which I hope his soule be in glorie. [D. 489-90]

Compare also another phrase of hers, which Justinus
echoes: 'Myself have been the whippe.' [D. 175] And
finally, when all the Pilgrims are quite prepared for
such a thing, there is a frank citation of the Wife of
Bath by name, with a reference to her exposition of
marriage:

> My tale is doon: - for my wit is thinne.
> Beth not agast herof, my brother dere.
> *But lat us waden out of this matere:*
> *The Wyf of Bathe, if ye han understonde,*
> *Of marriage, which we have on honde,*
> *Declared hath ful wel in litel space.*
> Fareth now wel, God have yow in his grace. [E. 1682-8]

Are the italicized lines a part of the speech of Justinus, or are they interpolated by the Merchant, in his
own person, in order to shorten Justinus' harangue?
Here is Professor Skeat's comment: 'These four paren-
thetical lines interrupt the story rather awkwardly.
They obviously belong to the narrator, the Merchant, as
it is out of the question that Justinus had heard of the
Wife of Bath. Perhaps it is an oversight.' Now it makes
no difference whether we assign these lines to Justinus
or to the Merchant, for Justinus, as we have seen, has
immediately before quoted the Wife's very words, and he
may as well mention her as repeat her language. Either
way, the lines are exquisitely in place. *Chaucer* is not
speaking, and there is no violation of dramatic propriety
on *his* part. It is not Chaucer who is telling the story.
It is the Merchant. And the Merchant is telling it as a
part of the discussion which the Wife has started. It is
dramatically proper, then, that the Merchant should quote
the Wife of Bath and that he should refer to her. And it
is equally proper, from the dramatic point of view, for
Chaucer to let the Merchant make Justinus mention the
Wife. In that case it is the Merchant - *not Chaucer* -
who chooses to have one of his characters fall out of his
part for a moment and make a 'local allusion.' Chaucer
is responsible for making the *Merchant* speak in character;
the Merchant, in his turn, is responsible for *Justinus*.
That the Merchant should put into the mouth of Justinus
a remark that Justinus could never have made is, then, not
a slip on Chaucer's part. On the contrary, it is a first-
rate dramatic touch, for it is precisely what the Merchant
might well have done under the circumstances....
   (p. 461) Thus it appears that the dramatic impulse to
the telling of the Franklin's Tale is to be found in the
relations among the Pilgrims and in the effect that they

have upon each other, - in other words, in the circumstances, the situation, and the interplay of character.

It has sometimes been thought that the story, either in
subject or in style, is too fine for the Franklin to tell.
But this objection Chaucer foresaw and forestalled. The
question is not whether this tale, thus told, would be
appropriate to a typical or 'average' fourteenth-century
franklin. The question is whether it is appropriate to
this particular Franklin, under these particular circumstances, and at this particular juncture. And to this
question there can be but one answer. Chaucer's Franklin
is an individual, not a mere type-specimen. He is rich,
ambitious socially, and profoundly interested in the
matter of *gentillesse* for personal and family reasons. He
is trying to bring up his son as a gentleman, and his position as 'St. Julian in his country' has brought him into
intimate association with first-rate models. He has,
under the special circumstances, every motive to tell a
gentleman's story and to tell it like a gentleman. He is
speaking under the immediate influence of his admiration
for the Squire and of his sense of the inferiority of his
own son. If we choose to conceive the Franklin as a mediaeval Squire Western and then to allege that he could not
possibly have told such a story, we are making the difficulty for ourselves. We are considering - not Chaucer's
Franklin (whose character is to be inferred not merely
from the description in the General Prologue but from all
the other evidence that the poet provides) - not Chaucer's
Franklin, but somebody quite different, somebody for whom
Chaucer has no kind of responsibility.

In considering the immediate occasion of the Franklin's
Tale, we have lost sight for a moment of the Wife of Bath.
But she was not absent from the mind of the Franklin. The
proper subject of his tale, as we have seen, is *gentillesse*. Now that (as well as marriage) was a subject on
which the Wife of Bath had descanted at some length. Her
views are contained in the famous harangue delivered by
the lady to her husband on the wedding night: 'But for ye
spoken of swich gentillesse,' etc (D. 1109-76). Many
readers have perceived that this portentous curtain-
lecture clogs the story, and some have perhaps wished it
away, good as it is in itself. For it certainly seems to
be out of place on lips of the *fée*. But its insertion is
(as usual in such cases) exquisitely appropriate to the
teller of the tale, the Wife of Bath, who cannot help
dilating on subjects which interest her, and who has had
the advantage of learned society in the person of her
fifth husband. Perhaps no *fée* would have talked thus to
her knightly bridegroom on such an occasion; but it is

quite in character for the Wife of Bath to use the *fée*
(or anybody else) as a mouthpiece for her own ideas, as
the Merchant had used Proserpine to point his satire.
Thus the references to Dante, Valerius, Seneca, Boethius,
and Juvenal - so deliciously absurd on the lips of a *fée*
of King Arthur's time - are perfectly in place when we
remember who it is that is reporting the monologue. The
Wife was a citer of authorities - she makes the *fée* cite
authorities. How comical this is the Wife did not know,
but Chaucer knew, and if we think he did not, it is our
own fault for not observing how dramatic in spirit is the
'Canterbury Tales'.
   A considerable passage in the curtain-lecture is given
to the proposition that 'such gentillesse as is descended
out of old richesse' is of no value: 'Swich arrogance is
not worth an hen.'[D. 1109ff.] These sentiments the
Franklin echoes:

>   Fy on possessioun
> But-if a man be vertuous withal! [F. 686-7]

But, whether or not the Wife's digression on *gentillesse*
is lingering in the Franklin's mind (as I am sure it is),
one thing is perfectly clear: the Franklin's utterances
on marriage are spoken under the influence of the discussion which the Wife has precipitated. In other words,
though everybody else imagines that the subject has been
finally dismissed by the Host when he calls on the Squire
for a tale of *love*, it has no more been dismissed in fact
than when the Friar attempted to dismiss it at the beginning of his tale. For the Franklin has views, and he
means to set them forth. He possesses, as he thinks, the
true solution of the whole difficult problem. And that
solution he embodies in his tale of *gentillesse*.
   The introductory part of the Franklin's Tale sets
forth a theory of the marriage relation quite different
from anything that has so far emerged in the debate. And
this theory the Franklin arrives at by taking into consideration both *love* (which, as we remember, was the subject that the Host had bidden the Squire treat of) and
gentillesse (which is to be the subject of his own story).
   Arveragus had of course been obedient to his lady
during the period of courtship, for obedience was well
understood to be the duty of a lover. Finally, she con-
sented to marry him -

> To take him for hir housbande and hir lord,
> Of swich lordshipe as men han over her wyves.

Marriage, then, according to the orthodox doctrine (as held by Walter and Griselda) was to change Arveragus from the lady's servant to her master. But Arveragus was an enlightened and chivalric gentleman, and he promised the lady that he would never assert his marital authority, but would content himself with the mere name of sovereignty, continuing to be her servant and lover as before. This he did because he thought it would ensure the happiness of their wedded life....

But, just as Arveragus was no disciple of the Marquis Walter, so Dorigen was not a member of the sect of the Wife of Bath. She promised her husband obedience and fidelity in return for his *gentillesse* in renouncing his sovereign rights....

This, then, is the Franklin's solution of the whole puzzle of matrimony, and it is a solution that depends upon love and *gentillesse* on both sides. But he is not content to leave the matter in this purely objective condition. He is determined that there shall be no misapprehension in the mind of any Pilgrim as to his purpose. He wishes to make it perfectly clear that he is definitely and formally offering this theory as the only satisfactory basis of happy married life. And he accordingly comments on the relations between his married lovers with fulness, and with manifest reference to certain things that the previous debaters have said.

The arrangement, he tells the Pilgrims, resulted in 'quiet and rest' for both Arveragus and Dorigen. And, he adds, it is the only arrangement which will ever enable two persons to live together in love and amity. Friends must 'obey each other if they wish to hold company long.'...

(p. 466) The Franklin's praise of marriage is sincere; the Merchant's had been savagely ironical. The Franklin, we observe, is answering the Merchant, and he answers him in the most effective way - by repeating his very words.

And just as in the Merchant's Tale we noted that the Merchant has enormously expanded the simple *fabliau* that he had to tell, inserting all manner of observations on marriage which are found in no other version of the Pear-Tree Story, so also we find that the Franklin's exposition of the ideal marriage relation (including the pact between Arveragus and Dorigen) is all his own, occurring in none of the versions that precede Chaucer.(17) These facts are of the very last significance. No argument is necessary to enforce their meaning.

It is hardly worth while to indicate the close connection between this and that detail of the Franklins' exposition and certain points that have come out in the

discussion as conducted by his predecessors in the debate.
His repudiation of the Wife of Bath's doctrine that men
should be 'governed by their wives' (D. 1261-2) is express, as well as his rejection of the opposite theory.
Neither party should lose his liberty; neither the husband
nor the wife should be a thrall. Patience (which clerks
celebrate as a high virtue) should be mutual, not, as in
the Clerk's Tale, all on one side. The husband is to be
both servant and lord - servant in love and lord in marriage. Such servitude is true lordship. Here there is a
manifest allusion to the words of Walter's subjects in the
Clerk's Tale:

> That blisful yok
> Of sovereynetee, noght of servyse   [E. 113-14]

as well as to Walter's rejoinder:

> I me reioysed of my libertee,
> That selde tyme is founde in mariage;
> Ther I was free, I moot been in servage   [E. 145-7]

It was the regular theory of the Middle Ages that the
highest type of chivalric love was incompatible with marriage, since marriage brings in mastery, and mastery and
love cannot abide together. This view the Franklin
boldly challenges. Love *can* be consistent with marriage,
he declares. Indeed, without love (and perfect, *gentle*
love) marriage is sure to be a failure. The difficulty
about mastery vanishes when mutual love and forbearance
are made the guiding principles of the relation between
husband and wife.

The soundness of the Franklin's theory, he declares,
is proved by his tale. For the marriage of Arveragus and
Dorigen was a brilliant success:

> Arveragus and Dorigene his wyf
> In sovereyn blisse leden forth hir lyf.
> Never eft ne was ther angre hem bitwene;
> He cherisseth hir as though she were a quene;
> And she was to him trewe for evermore.
> Of this two folk ye gete of me na-more. [F. 1551-62]

Thus the whole debate has been brought to a satisfactory
conclusion, and the Marriage Act of the Human Comedy ends
with the conclusion of the Franklin's Tale.

Those readers who are eager to know what Chaucer
thought about marriage may feel reasonably content with
the inference that may be drawn from his procedure. The

Marriage Group of Tales begins with the Wife of Bath's
Prologue and ends with the Franklin's Tale. There is no
connection between the Wife's Prologue and the group of
stories that precedes; there is no connection between the
Franklin's Tale and the group that follows. Within the
Marriage Group, on the contrary, there is close connection throughout. That act is a finished act. It begins
and ends an elaborate debate. We need not hesitate,
therefore, to accept the solution which the Franklin
offers as that which Geoffrey Chaucer the man accepted for
his own part. Certainly it is a solution that does him
infinite credit. A better has never been devised or
imagined.

Notes

1   Since the 'Canterbury Tales is an unfinished work, the
    drama of the Pilgrimage is of course more or less frag-
    mentary, and, furthermore, some of the stories (being
    old material, utilized for the nonce) have not been
    quite accurately fitted to their setting. Such defects,
    however, need not trouble us. They are patent enough
    whenever they occur, and we can easily allow for them.
    Indeed, the disturbance they cause is more apparent
    than real. Thus the fact that the Second Nun speaks of
    herself as a 'son of Eve' does not affect our argument.
    The contradiction would eventually have been removed by
    a stroke of Chaucer's pen, and its presence in no wise
    prevents the Legend of St. Cecilia from being exqui-
    sitely appropriate to the actual teller.
2   Whether vss. 1163-1212 are later than the bulk of the
    Clerk's Tale, when the Tale was written, and whether
    it was originally intended for the Clerk, or for the
    'Canterbury Tales' at all, are questions that do not
    here concern us, for they in no way affect the present
    investigation. It makes no difference in our argument
    whether Chaucer translated the story of Griselda in
    order to put it into the Clerk's mouth, or whether he
    created the Clerk in order to give him the story of
    Griselda, or whether, having translated the story and
    created the Clerk as independent acts, he noticed that
    the story suited the Clerk, and so brought the two
    together. It is enough for us that the Tale was sooner
    or later allotted to the Clerk and that it fits his
    character without a wrinkle.
3   Against this particular view I have nothing to object,
    for (manifestly) the theory that Chaucer relieved his
    own feelings in this fashion does not conflict at all

with my opinion that the passage is dramatically consistent with the Clerk's character and with the circumstances.

4 We may note that the tale which Chaucer first gave to
the Wife, as it seems, but afterwards transferred to
the Shipman, had also a personal application. It was
aimed more or less directly at the Monk, and its application was enforced by the Host's exhortation to the
company: 'Draweth no monkes more unto your in'
(B. 1632). And it contained also a roving shot at the
Merchant. Compare the General Prologue:

> Ther wiste no wight that he was in dette,
> So estatly was he of his governaunce,
> With his bargaynes and with his chevisaunce
> (A. 280-82).

with the words of the Merchant in the Shipman's Tale:

> For of us chapmen, also God me save,
> And by that lord that cleped is Seint Yve,
> Scarsly amonges twelve ten shul thryve
> Continuelly, lasting unto our age.
> We may wel make chere and good visage,
> And dryve forth the world as it may be,
> And kepen our estaat in privetee
> Til we be deed, or elles that we pleye
> A pilgrimage, or goon out of the weye (B. 1416-24).

5 Prologue, vs. 217. The Wife 'was a worthy woman al hir
lyve' (Prologue, vs. 459).
6 'Thou lettest our disport in this manere' (D. 839).
7 We remember that this is also the form of the Pardoner's Tale (which even included a text, 'Radix malorum
est cupiditas'), and that the Nun's Priest's Tale is
in effect but a greatly expanded *exemplum*, without a
text, to be sure, but with an appropriate moral
('taketh the moralitee,' B. 4630), an address to the
hearers ('good men'), and a formal benediction
(B. 4634-36).
8 Note also the comic interlude (Miller, Reeve, Cook)
that follows the Knight's Tale, and the dramatic
manner in which it is brought in and continued.
9 Petrarch has 'ut coniugio scilicet animum applices,
collumque non liberum modo sed imperiosum legitimo
subjicias iugo.' Chaucer may or may not have understood this Latin, but he certainly did not think that
he was translating it. He was rewriting to suit himself. It may be an accident that the ideas he

expressed and the words he chose are so extremely
apropos. If accident is to be assumed, however, the
present argument is in no way affected. Grant that
the translation was made before Chaucer had even conceived the idea of a Canterbury Pilgrimage, and it
remains true that, in utilizing this translation as
the Clerk's Tale and in putting it into its present
position, he found these words *sovereynetee* and
servyse particularly apt, and that the Pilgrims (who
were living men and women to Chaucer) found them
equally pertinent. It is Chaucer's final design, I
repeat, that we are considering, not the steps by
which he arrived at it.

10 Petrarch has 'delectabat omnimoda libertas, quae in
coniugio rara est'; but 'Ther I was free, I moot been
in servage' (E. 147) is the Clerk's own addition.

11 When the clerk is too old for Venus, says the Wife,
he sits down and writes 'that wommen can nat kepe hir
mariage.' But our Clerk is not old, and he has told
of a woman who kept her marriage under difficult conditions.

12 'Er I go' is a mere formula (derived from the technique of the wandering narrator) for 'before I finish.' Its use does not indicate that either Chaucer
or the Clerk has forgotten the situation.

13 As to the Wife's 'life' see her expressions in D.
111-12, 469-73, 615-26.

14 The scribe's rubric 'Lenvoy *de Chaucer*' should not
mislead us, any more than the word *auctor* does when
attached by the scribe to E. 995-1001 (a stanza which
is expressly ascribed by the Clerk to 'sadde folk in
that citee').

15 'She is a shrewe at al' (E. 1222). *Shrew* has, of
course, a general sense. It is not here limited to
the specific meaning of 'scold.'

16   Who-so be rebel to my iuggement
    Shal paye for al that by the weye is spent
                (Prologue, vss. 833-34).

17 The original point of the story is, of course, preserved in the question 'Which was the most free?'
(F. 1622) - the same question that occurs in other
versions. The peculiarity consists in the introduction of the pact of mutual love and forbearance and
in dwelling upon the lesson which it teaches.

37. EZRA POUND, CHAUCER SHOULD BE ON EVERY MAN'S SHELF

1914, 1918, 1927, 1934

Ezra Pound (1884-1973), poet and critic, was educated at Hamilton College in the USA, and the University of Pennsylvania. As perhaps the most important single intellectual influence in the changes in much poetic practice and theory in England and America in the early twentieth century, his scattered remarks on Chaucer have interest, though they do not amount to much more than a vague recognition of some special significance and value in Chaucer's work, which is often placed in opposition to Milton's. These extracts are reprinted by permission of Faber & Faber Ltd, and of New Directions Publishing Corporation, New York, from Ezra Pound, 'Literary Essays' (Copyright 1918, 1920, 1935, 1954). All rights reserved. Details of attribution are appended to extracts.

(a) 'Literary Essays', p. 216; from The Renaissance, 'Poetry', 1914.

Chaucer should be on every man's shelf. Milton is the worst sort of poison.

(b) 'Literary Essays', p. 235; from Elizabethan Classicists, 'The Egoist', 1917-18.

But Golding's book published before all these others will give us more matter for reverie. One wonders, in reading it, how much more of the Middle Ages was Ovid. We know well enough that they read him and loved him more than the more Tennysonian Virgil.
     Yet how great was Chaucer's debt to the Doctor Amoris? That we will never know. Was Chaucer's delectable style simply the first Ovid in English? Or, as likely, is Golding's Ovid a mirror of Chaucer? Or is a fine poet ever translated until another his equal invents a new style in a later language? Can we, for our part, know our Ovid until we find him in Golding? Is there one of us so good at his Latin, and so ready in imagination that Golding will not throw upon his mind shades and glamours

inherent in the original text which had for all that
escaped him? Is any foreign speech ever our own, ever so
full of beauty as our *lingua materna* (whatever *lingua
materna* that may be)? Or is not a new beauty created, an
old beauty doubled when the overchange is well done?

(c) 'Literary Essays', pp. 286-7, from The Hard and Soft
in French Poetry, 'Poetry XI', 1918.

We have however some hardness in English, and in Landor we
have a hardness which is not of necessity 'rugged'; as in
'Past ruin'd Ilion Helen lives'. Indeed, Gautier might
well be the logical successor to Landor, were he not in
all probability the logical co-heir with Landor of certain
traditions.
    Landor is, from poem to poem, extremely uneven. Our
feeling of him must in part rest on our admiration of his
prose. Lionel Johnson had a certain hardness and smoothness, but was more critic than poet, and not a very great
poet. There is definite statement in George Herbert, and
likewise in Christina Rossetti, but I do not feel that
they have much part in this essay. I do not feel that
their quality is really the quality I am seeking here to
define.
    We have in English a certain gamut of styles: we have
the good Chaucerian, almost the only style in English
where 'softness' is tolerable; we have the good Elizabethan; which is not wholly un-Chaucerian: and the bad, or
muzzy, Elizabethan; and the Miltonic, which is a bombastic
and rhetorical Elizabethan coming from an attempt to write
English with Latin syntax. Its other mark is that the
rich words have gone: i.e., words like *preluciand*, which
have a folk tradition and are, in feeling, germane to all
Europe: *Leuchend, luisant, lucente*; these words are
absent in Miltonism, and purely pedantic words, like
irriguous, have succeeded them....
    It is approximately true, or at least it is a formula-
tion worth talking over: that French prose is good in
proportion as it reaches a sort of norm; English prose is
good in proportion as a man makes it an individual language, one which he alone uses. This statement must not
be swallowed whole. And we must also remember that when
Italians were writing excellent and clear prose - in the
time of Henry VIII - Englishmen could scarcely make a
clear prose formulation even in documents of state and
instructions to envoys; so backward were things in this
island, so rude in prose the language which had been
exquisite in the lyrics of Chaucer.

(d) 'Literary Essays', p. 7; from A Retrospect, 'Pavannes and Divisions', 1918.

That part of your poetry which strikes upon the imaginative *eye* of the reader will lose nothing by translation into a foreign tongue; that which appeals to the ear can reach only those who take it in the original.

Consider the definiteness of Dante's presentation, as compared with Milton's rhetoric. Read as much of Wordsworth as does not seem too unutterably dull.

If you want the gist of the matter go to Sappho, Catullus, Villon, Heine when he is in the vein, Gautier when he is not too frigid; or, if you have not the tongues, seek out the leisurely Chaucer. Good prose will do you no harm, and there is good discipline to be had by trying to write it.

Translation is likewise good training, if you find that your original matter 'wobbles' when you try to rewrite it. The meaning of the poem to be translated can not 'wobble'.

(e) 'Literary Essays', pp. 28-9; from How to Read, 'New York Herald', 1927.

In Italy, around the year 1300, there were new values established, things said that had not been said in Greece, or in Rome or elsewhere.

VILLON: After Villon and for several centuries, poetry can be considered as *fioritura*, as an efflorescence, almost an effervescence, and without any new roots. Chaucer is an enrichment, one might say a more creamy version of the 'matter of France', and he in some measure preceded the verbal richness of the classic revival, but beginning with the Italians after Dante, coming through the Latin writers of the Renaissance, French, Spanish, English, Tasso, Ariosto, etc., the Italians always a little in the lead, the whole is elaboration, medieval basis, and wash after wash of Roman or Hellenic influence. I mean one need not read any particular part of it for purpose of learning one's comparative values.

If one were studying history and not poetry, one might discover the medieval mind more directly in the opening of Mussato's *Ecerinus* than even in Dante. The culture of Chaucer is the same as that which went contemporaneously into Ferrara, with the tongue called '*francoveneto*'.

One must emphasize one's contrasts in the quattrocento. One can take Villon as pivot for understanding them. After Villon, and having begun before his time, we find this *fioritura*, and for centuries we find little else.

(f) 'Literary Essays', pp. 34-5; from How to Read, 'New York Herald', 1927.

All the developments in English verse since 1910 are due almost wholly to Americans. In fact, there is no longer any reason to call it English verse, and there is no present reason to think of England at all.

We speak a language that was English. When Richard Coeur de Lion first heard Turkish he said: 'He spik lak a fole Britain.' From which orthography one judges that Richard himself probably spoke like a French-Canadian.

It is a magnificent language, and there is no need of, or advantage in, minimizing the debt we owe to Englishmen who died before 1620. Neither is there any point in studying the 'History of English Literature' as taught. Curiously enough, the histories of Spanish and Italian literature always take count of translators. Histories of English literature always slide over translation - I suppose it is inferiority complex - yet some of the best books in English are translations. This is important for two reasons. First, the reader who has been appalled by the preceding parts and said 'Oh, but I can't learn all these languages', may in some measure be comforted. He can learn the art of writing precisely where so many great local lights learned it; if not from the definite poems I have listed, at least from the men who learned it from those poems in the first place.

We may count the 'Seafarer', the 'Beowulf', and the remaining Anglo-Saxon fragments as indigenous art; at least, they dealt with a native subject, and by an art not newly borrowed. Whether alliterative metre owes anything to Latin hexameter is a question open to debate; we have no present means of tracing the debt. Landor suggests the problem in his dialogue of Ovid and the Prince of the Gaetae.

After this period English literature lives on translation, it is fed by translation; every new exuberance, every new heave is stimulated by translation, every allegedly great age is an age of translations, beginning with Geoffrey Chaucer, Le Grand Translateur, translator of the 'Romaunt of the Rose', paraphraser of Virgil and Ovid, condenser of old stories he had found in Latin, French, and Italian.

After him even the ballads that tell a local tale tell it in art indebted to Europe. It is the natural spreading ripple that moves from the civilized Mediterranean centre out through the half-civilized and into the barbarous peoples.

(g) 'Literary Essays', pp. 68-70; from Mr Housman at
Little Bethel, 'The Criterion', January 1934.

'The poetry of the eighteenth century', says Mr Housman,
'was most satisfactory when it did not try to be poetical.' And in other centuries? Again we find a curious
trilogy 'satire, controversy and burlesque'. What has
satire done, that it should be found so confounded? And
what did Hermes say to Calypso?
   Mr Housman must be being hortatory, we must indeed be
headed for the loftiest possible heights where Homer,
Ovid, Dante and Chaucer are not to be quite given the
entrée. His bethel must be contracting....
   Again the ways of Housman's mind are recondite; having
damned burlesque and disparaged Gilpin as lacking sublimity, he produces:

   Uprose the sun and up rose Emily

as Chaucerian unbetterableness. Heaven knows I don't want
to improve it, but is it the height of seriousness, here
attained, or have we Chaucerian chuckle? Or at any rate
can the reader familiar with Chaucer, but without looking
up the context, suppose this line to be any more expressive, any closer to the heart of another's dark forest,
etc., than some line of spitfire Alex?
   Heaven be my witness that I, at any rate, and of all
men, don't want Johnnie Dryden dug up again. Whether by
maturity of wit, or whether it be that from early, very
early childhood I have been protected by the association
of ideas inherent in the first syllable of John's patro-
nymic - Mr Eliot's endeavours having served only to
strengthen my resolve never, never again, to open either
John Dryden, his works or any comment upon them, but if
anything could stir an interest in that outstanding ari-
tidy it would be the isolation of some quite sensible
remark about Chaucer illustrated pro and con; con by
three brays as blatant as Milton; and pro? well, perhaps
not very successfully.
   In short, Dryden found a rather good critical term,
but being by nature a lunk-head, was unable to derive much
light from that accident. The marvel, to me, is how any
man bent on recreation 'among the best', and yet so limited a range (apparently) in his selected reading matter,
should between beer and the hedgerows have pervaded,
transgressed, wandered into, even to the extent of so many
quoted lines, Mr Dryden's plasterings upon Chaucer.

(h)   'Literary Essays', p. 181; from Cavalcanti, 'Make it New', 1934.

Whatever Dante's symboligating propensities, he was posi-
tivist on his craft, in this he was a *fabbro,* and one respecting the craft and the worker.   Italian poetry would
have gained by following his traces, and our own would be
less a mess if Chaucer had so closely considered technique
instead of uselessly treating the Astrolabe.

38.   HARRIET MONROE, CHAUCER AND LANGLAND

1915

Harriet Monroe (d. 1936), poet and editor, was educated at
Visitation Academy, Georgetown, DC, USA.   She founded in
1912 and for many years edited 'Poetry: a Magazine of
Verse', important for encouraging the modern movement in
poetry.   Chaucer and Langland are made to appear rather
as two different sides of Ezra Pound, but the appreciation, if unscholarly, is sympathetic.   It places Chaucer
firmly in a complex poetic tradition, and while expressing
a characteristic twentieth-century unease about an art
with apparently no social commitment, signalises the early
stages of a new feeling for Langland.   Reprinted by permission from 'Poetry' VI, April-September 1915.   pp. 297-
301.

CHAUCER AND LANGLAND

When the English language was in the making - the English
language, which the Germans call 'the bastard tongue,'
'the insignificant pirate dialect,' in comparison with
their own throaty and mouth-filling speech; when English
was taking unto itself Saxon strength, Norman splendor,
and a touch of the more southern Latin grace, to become
that powerful, flexible, and richly tuned organ which was
to be heard around the world: even in those half-articu-
late and illiterate centuries the shaping influences were
yet more or less conscious, and more or less incarnate in
human beings of differing minds.   The singers who wandered

from castle to castle, or from hamlet to hamlet - ambas-
sadors and newsmongers to the lords and the folk - chanted
their sagas and romances in forms derived from Norse,
Teutonic or French tradition, and fought on English soil
the war of *kultur* even then.

It was fitting, and singularly dramatic, that the final
battle of this war should have been delivered over to two
such sturdy champions as Chaucer and Langland. The time
was the militant and imaginative fourteenth century of
Edward the Third, of his knightly son the Black Prince,
and his work-hating, beauty-loving grandson Richard the
Second; the fourteenth century of amazing contrasts -
extravagance and starvation, beauty and loathsomeness,
jewelled embroideries and vermivorous rags. And the scene
was mostly London - London of the Norman court and the
Saxon people, of lords and starvelings, castles and
hovels, pageants and pests; little London, already rising
into glory out of the slime of the river Thames.

Not that the two champions consciously faced each other
in their intellectual lists. Neither may have known of
the other's existence; or, if they ever met in those
narrow mudways, no doubt the courtly Chaucer smiled when
surly 'Long Will' refused to make way for him, or take
off his ragged cap to this retainer of kings. Neither
suspected, probably, that the future of England, or at
least of English, lay between them, that one or the other
of them was molding a world-encircling language and cut-
ting the patterns of an immortal art.

Of course all the odds were with Chaucer; then, as now,
he was irresistible. Well born, well reared, learned in
three or four languages, a cosmopolite who had carried his
king's messages to Italy - Italy, then mothering the Renaissance - and withal, one of the most engaging and sympathetic beings who ever took human shape - it was no
wonder that Chaucer had it all his own way, and that
English poets have done his will for centuries. Reared
in the Norman court, chanting French romances from childhood, he naturally preferred rhyme and the three-time
iambic measure to the alliterations and assonances, and
the harsh irregularities, of the pounding four-time measure derived from that Saxon tradition which was still
dear to the hearts and sweet to the ears of the common
people. Indeed, it was a proof of Chaucer's broad sympathy, of his strong mind and big heart, that he did not
abandon English altogether, that he, like Dante, loved his
'dames tongue,' and insisted on writing his poems in it
instead of in courtly French or learned Latin. It was a
fortunate day for us all when Chaucer said:

Let clerks enditen in Latin, for they have the property
of science and the knowinge in that faculty; and let
Frenchmen in their French also endite their quaint
terms, for it is kindly to their mouths; and let us
show our fantasies in such words as we learneden of
our dames tongue.

So, while Chaucer did not introduce the French forms
into the new combination language, it is not too much to
say that he domesticated them. He made rhyme, and the
iambic measure, as much at home in English as they ever
have been in the romance tongues, and he opened the way
for some of the greatest rhythmists who ever lived -
Shakespeare, Spenser, Milton, Coleridge, Shelley, Swinburne and others - whose verse-structure, however varied,
is almost entirely based upon the three-time iambic foot
or bar, their four-time experiments being comparatively
slight and incidental.

Thus Langland was left far behind, 'Piers Plowman' was
forgotten except by scholars. From his time until
Shelley's, four-time measures were almost abandoned, being
found only in a few Elizabethan songs, in parts of Dryden's two music-praising odes, and in a few other experiments. The iambus 'reigned supreme,' usually in the five-
footed line which Chaucer's fine instinct had preferred to
the French hexameter as better suited to the genius of the
new language. And even when Coleridge - in the 'Ancient
Mariner' and a few other poems, Shelley - in 'The Cloud',
'The Skylark', and others, and Byron - in 'There be none
of beauty's daughters', and one or two other songs, began
to vary the music of English verse with four-time measures, their experiments bore little relation to Langland,
or to the earlier Saxon bards. And while Swinburne's
varied rhythms wove with infinite delicacy new renaissance
patterns, they never went back to the stern old Gothic
motive.

The first great modern poet, no doubt, to put aside
altogether the renaissance patterns was Whitman. In doing
so, he did not consciously return to the music of the
sagas - the Gothic motive, as it may be called - yet his
free verse is more allied to Langland than to Chaucer; it
has more in common with the old Anglo-Saxon bards than
with Shakespeare or Milton or Swinburne. It does, in
short, remind us once more of the older tradition - older,
that is, in English poetry - though the reminder is far-
away and indefinite, a matter of feeling and flavor and
general rhythmic pace, rather than of form or tune.

But in the impetus toward free verse which Whitman led,
and which is evident in so much modern poetry - French and

Italian as well as English - it is possible that Langland
and his Old-English predecessors will have increasing influence.   Indeed, we have evidences of this - in such
modern presentations of mediaeval music as Mr. Ezra
Pound's truly wonderful paraphrase, 'The Sea-farer', for
example.   Those old poets will be studied, not from the
point of view of academic scholarship, but from that of
immediate beauty and fecundity.   We shall have a new real-
ization of their power of imagination and of the splendor
and variety of their rhythms.

And thus Langland, after more than five centuries, may
come into his own at last.   The world may rediscover that
modern socialist, anarchist, anti-militarist, who in the
king-ruled, monk-ridden, war-lorded fourteenth century,
lifted up his prophet's voice for the brotherhood of
man, and was called crazy for his pains.   Chaucer took
his world as it was, and left us a Holbein portrait-
gallery of the people he saw around him; loving the pro-
cessional pageantry of the life of lords and commons, and
ignoring the invisible and inarticulate miseries of the
forgotten remnant - the poor who froze and starved in
hovels, and died in battles and periodic plagues.   Langland, on the contrary, felt these miseries of the poor as
the only fit subject for tragic passion: a great democrat,
he made the crowd the subject of his epic; a great seer,
he looked forward to the end of their miseries, not
through mythical compensations in heaven, but through
increase of justice on earth.

The urbane Chaucer for five centuries has led the poets
his successors: in motive as well as technique they have
been mostly of his mind, accepting his aristocratic point
of view, his delight in the upper-class pageant, and
almost entirely ignoring the burden-bearing poor.   But
perhaps Langland is like to bridge the centuries and clasp
hands with the poets of the future, the prophets of the
new era....

39.   JOHN S.P. TATLOCK, CHAUCER THE LAODICEAN

1916

J.S.P. Tatlock (1876-1948), educated at Harvard

University, was Professor of English in the University of
California, 1929-46. He made an important advance in the
study of the religious and general ideas and attitudes implicit in Chaucer's work, comparing Chaucer with his contemporary Wyclif. He saw Chaucer as having 'liberal
views', being neither a denier nor devotee nor reformer,
but something of a 'Laodicean' (as suggested by 'Browne',
No. 16 above, and an opion that R.S. Loomis attempted to
refute in 'Essays and Studies in Honor of Carleton
Brown', New York (1940), pp. 129-48). Reprinted from
'Modern Philology' XIV (1916), pp. 257-68, by permission
of the University of Chicago Press.

CHAUCER AND WYCLIF

As we look back at England of the later fourteenth century
two men stand out beyond others in the realm of mind.
Chaucer's distinction in literature is no greater than
John Wyclif's in destructive thought and practical reform.
His learning had earned him in the schools the prophetic
title of Evangelical Doctor. His itinerant preachers
carried his name and his teachings far and wide over the
kingdom; he poured out homily, exhortation, argument, invective in English and Latin. He had set the church at
odds with the state, bishops with princes, metropolitans
with universities; he had divided the reigning house
against itself; and though he had defied popes, such was
his influence that he suffered persecution chiefly in his
followers, died unmolested, and laid his bones, for a
short rest only, in the churchyard at Lutterworth.
     There was that in his teachings to commend them especi-
ally to broad men of the world. At bottom his work was a
protest against professionalism in religion, a plea that
religion should be mindful once more rather of the end
that the means, of the human soul rather than of an intricate apparatus. Ambition and convenience drive every
system toward elaboration, before which the layman has
helplessly to resort to the man of special training.
Every system may have to be brought back to simplicity,
lest its main purpose be impeded or forgotten. So much
we may have to admit, however much we may revere an imposing historic system. The church was thus brought back at
the Reformation, but Wyclif showed the way a century and
a half earlier. To this end (1) he assailed the papal
court and the hierarchy, whose interest it was to maintain
a complex professionalism; to this end he assailed the
regular orders - partly a manifestation and partly a tool

of professionalism - who he held laid more stress on their
own cramping and minute rules than on the teachings of the
Gospels; to this end he assailed those dogmas especially
on which professional power rested, the doctrine of the
Eucharist and the power of the keys.(2) It was the power
to bring God visibly to their altars, and to influence
the eternal destiny of man, which left the mediaeval world
almost helpless in the hands of the clergy, and which gave
them a sphere whence they could control but where they
could not be reached. At the voice without reply which
came from thence the flesh might repine, but as yet reason
did not chafe. Anyone with a historical imagination must
regard with veneration the stately words, 'Et ego dico
tibi quia tu es Petrus, et super hanc petram edificabo
ecclesiam meam, et porte inferi non prevalebunt adversus
eam. Et tibi dabo claves regni celorum. Et quodcumque
ligaveris super terram, erit ligatum et in celis: et
quodcumque solveris super terram, erit solutum et in
celis.' For on them is based the greatest institution
that ever existed. But Wyclif, for all his intellectual
training, was a practical man. He was the champion of
the state against the church, of the people against those
who preyed on them, of the secular clergy who were doing
(well or ill) the essential work of the church against
those who interfered with them. The remarkable thing is
that, being a highly professional man himself, he set his
face like a flint against professionalism; in him Protes-
tantism grew out of scholasticism.

Wyclif's views and activities are likely to have
appealed to Chaucer, no uncritical mystic or devotee, yet
a man interested in the essence of religion, a servant of
the state, and deeply sympathetic with humanity, with a
keen eye for inconsistency and sham. Further, it is
hardly credible that he was not very familiar with
Wyclif's views and even with the man himself, through his
own friends. Wyclif was supported by the royal family,
especially by John of Gaunt and the mother and wife of
Richard II, with some of whom Chaucer seems to have
enjoyed a certain intimacy. Numerous adherents and supporters of Wyclif were among his friends and associates;
I shall not undertake to collect all their names, but the
fact is clear.(3) The question is not of Chaucer having
been a Lollard, or of having drawn an admiring portrait
of Wyclif in the Parson of the 'Prolog';(4) he was not
such stuff as martyrs are made of, but something of a
Laodicean. But it is certain that he would know and
likely enough that he would sympathize with some of
Wyclif's views. If we find passages in the 'Canterbury
Tales' agreeing strikingly with certain of Wyclif's most

emphatic opinions not often found elsewhere, it is an acceptable conjecture that Chaucer here shows his influence.

The passages involved are few, but there is no mistaking their significance. The most important are two in the 'Prolog'. Of the Parson it is said,

Ful looth were him to cursen for his tythes [1. 486].

For non-payment or 'subtraction' of tithes a man might be excommunicated with the major sentence, though not by the parson himself;(5) the parson was to delare that the defaulter might be or *ipso facto* was excommunicated (*excommunicatio a jure, ferendae* or *latae sententiae*). Chaucer clearly felt the sordidness of using so solemn a spiritual weapon for such mundane reasons. The other passage is in the description of the Sumner (11. 653-62):

And if he fond o-wher a good felawe,
He wolde techen him to have noon awe,
In swich cas, (6) of the erchedeknes curs,
But-if a mannes soule were in his purs;
For in his purs he sholde y-punisshed be.(7)
'Purs is the erchedeknes helle,' seyde he.
But wel I woot he lyed right in dede;
Of cursing oghte ech gilty man him drede -
For curs wol slee, right as assoiling saveth -
And also war him of a *significavit*.

This sounds quite innocent. Chaucer seems to rebuke the archdeacon's official for speaking lightly of excommunication. But our suspicions are aroused, both by the ambiguity of this warning (the curse and the absolution stand or fall together, but do they stand or do they fall?) and also by the very strength of the language. Who but a narrow and ill-informed ecclesiastic would say that an archdeacon's ban for concubinage would slay a soul? Our suspicion is confirmed by the last line. *Significavit* is the first word of the writ *De excommunicato capiendo*, issued from chancery at the request of the ordinary in the king's name, directing the sheriff to enforce justice against the culprit; which meant imprisoning, till he had been absolved, anyone who had been excommunicated for forty days with the major excommunication.(8) The anticlimax, in a writer of Chaucer's sly subtlety, makes the meaning clear; however it may be with the eternal consequences of excommunication, we should look out for the temporal ones anyway. This throws us back once more to l. 661. Chaucer seems to speak lightly and skeptically

of both excommunication and absolution.(9)   Both passages
show an attitude of doubt toward the power of the keys as
commonly understood in Chaucer's day.

On no subject does Wyclif express himself with more
frequency and more intensity than on the abuses which had
grown up about the practice of excommunication. He denies
its spiritual efficacy and denounces its use, especially
as a weapon against purely worldly or financial offenses
toward the clergy, such as non-payment of tithes. 'Alle
þo þat mystiþen ony goodis ben cruely cursed foure times
in þe ȝeer'; great is the author's indignation; 'whi
cursen oure weiward curettis so many mennus soulis to
helle, and bodies to prison....for a litel muk?'(10)
'Cursing is a fendis fynding to curse men þus for worldly
godis.'(11) He constantly makes light of the general
efficacy of excommunication, and condemns its free use;
God blesses him who is cursed wrongfully.(12) He denounces the procedure of the writ *Significavit*.(13)

Chaucer's implied doubt of the value of assoiling is
fully paralleled in Wyclif, whether Chaucer means canoni-
cal or sacramental absolution. Doubt of the saving power
of the church's lifting of her ban is entirely involved
in Wyclif's doubt of the efficacy of the ban. Sacramental
absolution he constantly belittles. He discourages auricular confession, implying small regard for absolution;
it does much good and much harm and should not be compul-
sory; he declares that if the penitent is not contrite,
absolution is useless, and if he is, it is needless; God
alone absolves, the priest merely announces.(14)

Doubtless Chaucer and Wyclif were not the only men in
the fourteenth century who held liberal views as to the
power of the keys.(15) But the writer has been through a
great many literary works of Chaucer's day and somewhat
earlier without finding any parallels. The height of
Wyclif's attack on the power of the keys came only some
half-dozen years before the date when Chaucer probably
wrote the 'Prolog'. It is hard to doubt that the *obiter
dicta* of the poet reflect the loud denunciations of his
contemporary. That he does not also reflect Wyclif's
attacks on the doctrine of the Eucharist may be due to the
latent streak of mysticism in his own nature. In any case
this doctrine is more attractive to a practical and warm-
hearted man than the other.

I say little of other, less tangible, ties between
Chaucer and Wyclif, which show that they were interested
in some of the same things, and that as to opinions which
they held in common with others they shaded strongly
toward each other. Everybody assailed the clergy, but
the reformer's club and the poet's rapier made for the

same points; there is a striking resemblance in what they
say, and they clearly thought much the same, with different intensity.(16)   One other tie between the two may be
mentioned.   Chaucer was interested in certain of the theo-
logico-philosophical issues with which Wyclif had concerned himself, especially in the question of foreordination, which with Chaucer took the form of the question why
things happen - the relation between fortune, free-will
and divine foreknowledge.(17)   That he was somewhat acquainted with the later 'literature of the subject' is shown
by his reference to Archbishop Bradwardine (N.P.T.,
4432ff.), the 'Profound Doctor,' who had died as early as
1349 but influenced Wyclif's views on predestination and
antipelagianism (though Wyclif's views were less extreme).
It is not unlikely that Chaucer's deep interest and learning in astrology may have had a relation to his interest
in foreordination; the connection between the matters is
clearly recognized by St. Thomas Aquinas, John of Salisbury, Dante, and other thinkers.(18)   When we find the
concretely minded and unphilosophical Chaucer ever recurring to the subject of foreordination, we cannot but see
a connection with the fact that the subject was a very
lively one in his day.   That Chaucer was not fertile in
original thinking leads us to believe that here he reflects contemporary views, and that as to excommunication
he reflects Wyclif's.

It would be a pity to stop here without saying a little
about Chaucer's religious position in general, especially
since one or two of the passages discussed above have
been used for proof of a far greater heterodoxy than they
really show.   Chaucer students will greatly miss the late
Professor T.R. Lounsbury's learning and charm, but he mis-
took both Chaucer and his age when he represented him as
a kind of agnostic.(19)   One of the passages he mainly
relied on was the Sumner's scoff at excommunication and
absolution, in which, however, most people will be readier
to see the spirit of Wyclif than the spirit of Huxley.
Another is the opening lines of the 'Legend of Good
Women', where Chaucer avers that we know of the joy of
heaven and the pain of hell only through books, and
thereby bespeaks credence for the old stories which he is
about to extract from books; we marvel at Mr. Lounsbury's
argument when we realize that the passage makes directly
against his position.   Finally, in the 'Knight's Tale'
(ll. 2805-15), Chaucer does not know where Arcite's dep-
arting soul went, except that it was to a place where he
had never been himself.(20)   In this undoubtedly flippant
refusal of the eternal blazon to ears of flesh and blood,
there may well be nothing but flippancy; Chaucer certainly

did not know and undeniably had never been there. A
somewhat light tone is characteristic of the poem. But
more than this, he may be rejecting impatiently Boccaccio's lengthy and frigid description of Arcite's aviation
through the celestial spheres;(21) or (Dryden's interpretation in his 'Palamon and Arcite') he may be doubtful as
to the eternal destiny of such a virtuous pagan as Arcite.
No one of these three acceptable explanations implies
religious skepticism.

Certain other matters bear on Chaucer's religious position. The apparent irreverence which Mr. Lounsbury detected in Chaucer's works is not only amply paralleled in
other mediaeval writers, not always worldly ones, either;
it is largely an optical illusion. At a time when all old
women dressed as nuns do now, when people drank their wine
at dinner out of cups like chalices and lighted their
tables with high-altar candlesticks, there was not the
distinction between sacred and secular which we observe
(to the uncertain advantage of the sacred). Irreverence
is usually more of a shock to the taste than to the conscience, and no one who has lifted the choir seats in
mediaeval churches and peered at the *misereres* will deny
that mediaeval taste differed from modern in these matters. God was so sturdy a reality to our forefathers
that his name and his personality had no need to be protected from the rude world by a hedge of taboos; the conception made up in solidity what it lacked in vastness,
in comprehensibility what it lacked in adequacy. Since
any idea of the infinite is merely symbolic at best, the
mediaeval attitude may have had its advantages. As to
Chaucer's view of the clergy, that would prove little, as
Mr. Lounsbury recognized; the most earnest believers are
frequently, though not always, their severest critics. It
suffices to say that Chaucer on the whole is much more
charitable toward the clergy than most of his contemporaries are.(22) Mr. Lounsbury's belief in Chaucer's unusually skeptical habit of mind about secular things,
though an important observation, and in general well
founded, is much exaggerated.(23) He also greatly over-
estimated the danger which the poet would have incurred
had he expressed religious skepticism, especially in the
veiled and subtle way characteristic of him. This in-
clines us the less to read far-reaching meanings into the
few skeptical passages we find.

Chaucer was neither a denier nor a devotee. He mused
often on questions, such as the origin of evil and the
control of the universe over the individual's destiny,
for which the usual answer in his day was a religious
one; his musings were without result, but show what in

our day would be felt as a not irreligious nature. Toward the church he was critical, though not unusually so, and he was probably not unsympathetic to the concrete criticism directed at her by other vigorous and earnest souls of his day. We have no reason to doubt that he went to mass at least on Sundays and holy days, and to confession and communion at least once a year; and that at the hour of death he would have been disturbed if he had missed absolution, unction, and the viaticum.(24) We cannot affirm that all this is so; but it is what is to be supposed of the sort of man he appears to have been.(25)

Notes

1 The unity and far-reaching design in Wyclif's work was doubtless a growth, and less plain to him than to us. The purposefulness may have been as it were rather emotional than intellectual. He attacked what he disliked, and what he disliked was apparatus. But as we look back at his battles we see they resemble a well-planned campaign. Even Luther felt that Wyclif's teachings were practical rather than theoretical 'Wicklef und Huss haben nur das Leben des Pabstes angefochten': *Tischreden,* in *Sämmtliche Schriften* (St. Louis, 1887), XXII, 892). Much of his teaching has long been seen to follow from his theory of dominion - that the right to rule depends on a relation to God, not to an institution, an idea thoroughly moral and practical in its results.
2 In the earliest known accusation against Wyclif, in the bulls of Gregory XI (1377), eight of the eighteen or nineteen charges relate to his views on the power of the keys (Lechler, 'John Wiclif', English tr., London, 1881, p. 191; 'Dict. Nat. Biogr.'). Similarly in 1382 (Lechler, p. 420). There is a good study of the spirit of Wyclif's work in H.W. Clark's 'History of English Nonconformity', I, 23-68.
3 On some friends or associates of Chaucer's who were more or less supporters or adherents of Wyclif, cf. Kittredge in 'Mod. Phil.', I, 9, 13, 17; Tait in 'Dict. Nat. Biogr.', XLVIII, 151 (cf. 'Life Records of Chaucer', Chaucer Soc., 154, 163, 203f., 210, 283f.), XLIV, 400 (cf. 'L. Rec.' 163, 173). The men are Clifford, Latimer, Clanvowe, Sir Richard Stury, Henry Percy. Chaucer's friend Strode had been a colleague and friend, but a theological opponent, of Wyclif (Jones in 'Publ. Mod. Lang. Assoc.', XXVII 114; Kuhl, ibid., XXIX 272-73; Gollancz in 'Dict. Nat. Biogr.').

4   This notion has been disposed of, especially by Louns-
    bury, 'Studies in Chaucer', II, 459-84. Simon's
    'Chaucer a Wicliffite' (Chaucer Soc., 'Essays', III,
    227-92) has found little favor. The Shipman (if it is
    he) calling the puritanical Parson a 'loller' means no
    more than a modern fellow calling someone of dark com-
    plexion a 'Dago.' A thorough Wyclifite would hardly be
    found on a pilgrimage. But though many of the traits
    of the Parson are found elsewhere, or might spontane-
    ously embody the Christian ideal of any age, there is
    no reason to deny Simon's belief that the portrait
    reflects Chaucer's esteem for some of the virtues of
    the Wyclifites, as their emphasis on the teachings of
    the Gospels, their fearless preaching (cf. Matthew,
    'Engl. Wks. of Wiclif', E.E.T.S., p. 264), their pas-
    toral zeal and simple manners. The more human limita-
    tions which the Parson shows later might even show
    Chaucer's consciousness of a certain tendency to purit-
    anism in Wyclif's teachings. The Parson shows a narrow
    tactlessness in rebuking the Host in the 'Shipm. Prol.'
    (1171) for swearing, and in reprobating tales and rimes
    in the 'Pars. Prol.' (31-34) after three days of rimed
    tales (cf. 'De officio pastorali', Matthew, p. 438).
    Chaucer himself grew as the 'Tales' grew, and his
    liking for the ideal gave way before his love of
    truth. I should add that there is no evidence of
    Chaucer's having used the Wyclifite Bible; J.H.
    Ramsay's evidence is wholly unconvincing ('Academy',
    XXII, 435-36). Wyclifite or not, he would have stuck
    to the Vulgate. Cf. B.F. Westcott, 'Hist. of the Engl.
    Bible' (London, 1905), p. 19, note.
5   This is referred to in the 'Friar's Tale', where the
    functions of the archdeacon's court are described
    (ll. 1312-18); the last two lines mean that the bishop
    enforced by excommunication the archidiaconal court's
    sentence:

        And smale tytheres weren foule y-shent,
        If any persone wolde up-on hem pleyne.
           [I emend Skeat's punctuation.]
        Ther mighte asterte him no pecunial peyne.
        For smale tythes and for smal offringe
        He made the peple pitously to singe.
        For er the bisshop caughte hem with his hook,
        They weren in the erchedeknes book.

The bringing of suits for tithes in lay courts became
discountenanced in the twelfth century owing to ecclesiastical opposition (Selden, 'Historie of Tithes', London,

1618, pp. 421-22), though they were sometimes sued for
in the court of the exchecquer and other lay courts
(Phillimore, 'Eccl. Law of the Ch. of Engl.', London,
1873, p. 1502). The jurisdiction of the church courts
in these cases was confirmed in the reigns of Edward
I and II and Henry VIII (ibid.). Non-payers after
three warnings were to be punished with the greater
excommunication ('anathema'), according to a decree of
the Council of Rouen, held in the seventh century
(Hefele, 'Hist. of Councils', tr. Clark, V, 211-12);
see Friedberg, 'Corpus iuris canonici' (Leipzig, 1881),
II, xvi, vii, 5; and his 'Lehrbuch des Kirchenrechts'
(ibid., 1909), p. 574. There are archiepiscopal constitutions to much the same effect (1328-48) in Lyndwood, 'Provinciale', pp. 11. 187, 189. Archbishop Islip of
Canterbury decreed in 1352 that failure to pay the
greater tithes should be punished with the greater
excommunication (Wilkins, 'Concilia', III, 26); so did
William of Wykeham, bishop of Winchester (ibid., p.
390). Cf. also a decree of Archbishop Courtenay,
1393 (ibid., p. 220); also Friedberg, 'Corp. iur. can.',
lib. III, xxx, 5 (a decretal of Pope Alexander III,
1159-81); Schmalzgrueber, 'Jus eccl. univ.' (Rome,
1843-44), III, ii, 685; Stubbs, 'Const. Hist. of Engl.',
III, 345; Pollock and Maitland, 'Hist. of Engl. Law',
I, 106, 554-58. Among the fifteen excommunicable sins
'Cursor mundi' (29322ff.) puts withholding or falsification of tithes. Wyclif reprobates curates for cursing for tithes (see below). That is was the greater
excommunication which was inflicted is indicated in one
of the Wyclifite works quoted below, 'The Grete Sentence of Curs'. So difficult was the collection of
tithes, and so set was the church on getting them, that
at one time it had stigmatized as heretics those who
did not pay up (H.C. Lea, 'History of the Inquisition
of the Middle Ages', I, 26). One of the most impudent
bits of priestcraft I have found is in Robert Manning
of Bourne's 'Handlyng Synne' (9315ff.): 'to withhold
tithes is sacrilege, and to pay ensures long life,
good health, grace in the soul and forgiveness of sins.'
That is all! I have said that the tithes were to be
recovered by suit in the church courts, the decree of
which was enforced by excommunication, which in turn
was followed up by the secular authorities (cf. ...
Matthew, 'Engl. Works', p. 510; also the beginning of
this note). Though Chaucer and the 'Cursor mundi'
(e.g., 29500ff.) speak of priests cursing, the parish
priest has and had no power to inflict the greater
excommunication (St. Thomas Aquinas, 'Summa theologiae',

Pars III, Supplementum, Quaestio XXII, art. i.; Lyndwood, 'Provinciale', 196). But among the Provincial
Constitutions at the end of Lyndwood, p. 34... is one
by Archbishop Winchelsey, 1305, according to which a
parishioner who did not pay his tithes was to be
warned thrice, and then if recalcitrant to be excluded
from the church-building (which would perhaps be
equivalent to the lesser excommunication), and then
compelled to pay by ecclesiastical censure (presumably
through the courts). The Wyclifite 'Office of Curates'
(Matthew, p. 152) complains that curates will not give
communion to those who are behind on tithes. An early
printed copy of the 'Sarum Manual' directs curates four
times a year to denounce the greater excommunication
against various offenders, including non-payers of
tithes: 'Isti sunt generales articuli majoris excommu-
nicationis'...'Also men of holy chirche have leve by
Goddis lawe, for to acurse al tho by name that wyl
noght paye ther tythes, as it is writen in many places
in the lawe of holy Chirche' (Arnold, Select Engl.
Works of Wyclif', Oxford, 1871, III, 267, 269); on this
see also Arthur Ogle, 'The Canon Law in Mediaeval
England', p. 172. Obviously this does not mean that
the parson excommunicated; he merely declared that
certain persons by church law might be or already were
excommunicated (like the modern *excommunicatio a jure,
ferendae sententiae, or latae sententiae*). It may be
partly this commination that both Chaucer and Wyclif
refer to. It is doubtful if the lesser excommunication (exclusion from the sacraments) would be called
by the severe word 'cursen' (defined in the 'Prompt-
orium parvulorum', about 1440, as 'excommunico, anat-
ematizo,' which well fits the terrifying language of
the greater. What a parson could do was to exclude
from the church building, declare that a person had
made himself liable to excommunication, and bring
suit against him; this latter would result in the
greater excommunication by the ordinary (in default of
payment), and this in turn in imprisonment by the
secular authorities. Doubtless procedure was not
always uniform, or always in fact what it was by law.
This note will supplement and correct Skeat's quotation
(V, 45) from Bell that 'refusal to pay tithes was
punishable with the lesser excommunication.' See also
Myrc's 'Instructions for Parish Priests' (E.E.T.S.,
1868), pp. 21, 24, 80. The best account of excommunication in general is in H.C. Lea's 'Studies in Church
History' (Philadelphia, 1883), pp. 235-521; see especially pp. 382, 458, 479.

6   I.e., if he were caught in incontinence.

7   Strikingly paralleled in 'Piers Plowman', A-text, III,
     137-39.

8   This procedure seems to date back at least to the
     twelfth century; but later the clergy sometimes com-
     plained that it was not enforced. The writ as given
     by Bracton begins. 'Significavit nobis venerabilis
     pater N....quot talis...excommunicatus est.' See
     Bracton, 'De legibus Angliae' (Rolls Ser.), VI, 370;
     Pollock and Maitland, 'Hist. Engl. Law' (2d ed.), I,
     478; Makower, 'Const. Hist. Ch. of Engl.', p. 452;
     Maitland, 'Const. Hist. of Engl.', p. 524; 'Select
     Essays in Anglo-American Legal Hist.' (Boston, 1908),
     II, 310-11; Blackstone, 'Commentaries', III, vii
     (Philadelphia, 1875, II, 101); Wilkins, 'Concilia', I,
     749-50; Cowell's and Blount's Law Dictionaries (Lon-
     don, 1708 and 1670); 'Les Termes de la Ley' (ibid.,
     1721), p. 320; Holdsworth, 'Hist. Engl. Law', I, 433;
     Stubbs, 'Const. Hist. Of Engl.' (Oxford, 1878), III,
     357; J.F. Stephen, 'Hist. Crim. Law in Engl.' (London,
     1883), II, 412; Phillimore, 'Eccl. Law', 1263, 1404,
     1419. The law was still in force in the nineteenth
     century. In the thirteenth century one who remained
     excommunicate for forty days, the council of Béziers
     decreed, was to be punished as a heretic (Lea, 'Hist.
     of the Inquisition of the Middle Ages', I, 404).

9   This is commonly understood as referring to sacramen-
     tal absolution, as part of the sacrament of penance.
     The context favors canonical absolution, i.e., the
     removal of the sentence of excommunication. Either
     is possible.

10   'Grete Sentence of Curs' (Thomas Arnold, 'Select
     English Works of John Wyclif', Oxford, 1871, III,
     309-12). This may be by a follower, and not by
     Wyclif himself, but it reflects his views. Here and
     elsewhere I have not attempted the impossible and un-
     necessary task of distinguishing Wyclif's works from
     those of contemporary adherents; I simply follow
     Arnold and Matthew. He frequently declares also that
     tithes should be withheld from unworthy parsons, and
     over and over again even denounces tithes altogether
     (cf. such of the Latin works as 'De blasphemia', pp.
     183ff., 'De civili dominio', pp. 310ff., and 'Ser-
     mones', II, 307; the Latin works are always quoted
     here from the Wyclif Society's edition). But some-
     times he allows them ('De civili dominio', I, 317ff.).

11   'De officio pastorali', Matthew, p. 453. See also
     'How Men Ought to Obey Prelates'. 'Of Clerks Posses-
     sioners', 'The Office of Curates', 'How Satan and His

Children', 'Why Poor Priests' (Matthew, pp. 36, 132,
144-46, 150, 156, 160-61, 214, 250); also the Wyclifite 'Apology for the Lollards', pp. 13-25 (Camden
Soc., 1842). Likewise, in the Latin works, he condemns cursing 'pro temporalibus,' or 'principaliter
propter peccuniam'; one who excommunicates for tithes
excommunicates himself. See 'De blasphemia', pp. 70-
71, 103, 106, 175; 'De ecclesia', p. 154; 'Sermones',
II, 238-39, 314; III, 159; 'De officio regis', pp.
167, 171, 175, 227; 'De civili dominio', I, 277,
335ff. (but it is allowable if the motive of the ex-
communicator is not lucre but the good of the delin-
quent, pp. 353ff. Faith, here's an equivocator!) St.
Thomas Aquinas declares that excommunication may be
inflicted 'pro temporali damno' (including presumably
the withholding of tithes); 'Summa' (Rome, 1906, Vol.
XII, Suppl., p. 43), III, Supplementum, Q. XXI, art.
iii.

12 One of the views attributed to Wyclif by Benedict XI
is 'Non est possible hominem excommunicari ad sui
dampnum, nisi excommunicetur primo et principaliter a
se ipso'; another attacks the exaction of temporalities by means of ecclesiastical censures. See Arnold,
III, 218; 'Dict. Nat. Biogr.', LXIII, 208-9, 214;
'Fasciculi Zizaniorum' (Rolls Ser., 1858), pp. 250,
251, 279, 321, etc.; G.M. Trevelyan, 'Engl. in the
Age of Wyclif', p. 48. All this appears repeatedly
in the English works: 'How Men Ought to Obey Prelates', 'Of Prelates', 'Office of Curates', 'Of Poor
Preaching Priests', 'Of Dominion' (Matthew, 35-36,
75, 153, 277, 287-88); 'Sermons on the Gospels',
'Church Temporalities', 'Grete Sentence of Curs',
'Church and Her Members', 'Octo in quibus' (Arnold,
II, 159; III, 217, 328-29, 354, 450). Still oftener
the view appears in the Latin works: 'De blasphemia,
pp. 58, 70, 97, 98 (he reprobates the formal excommunication with bell and candle), 145, 173; 'De officio
regis', pp. 22, 111, 166-76, 192, 227-37; 'Sermones',
II, 183, 201, 302, 305, 313f.; III, 147-48, 264, 491;
'De ecclesia', p. 153; 'De civili dominio', pp.
274ff., 374f.; 'Dialogus', p. 56. He does admit that
excommunication may sometimes be allowable ('De
blasph.' pp. 97, 103; cf. also the Wyclifite 'Apology
for the Lollards', Camden Soc., 1842, pp. 13-25).
Thomas Aquinas says that even an unjust excommunication has its effect, since exclusion from the means of
grace deprives of grace ('Summa', III, Suppl., Q.
XXI, art. iv). This is not inconsistent with the
saying of Pope Innocent III that a man might be bound

in the sight of the church but free in the sight of
God. As one of its reforms the Council of Trent
recommended more moderation in the use of the greater
excommunication; the lesser was abolished in the nineteenth century. What Wyclif objected to was of course
the practice rather than the theory.

13 'Of Prelates', 'Office of Curates' (Matthew, pp. 74,
95, 146); 'De blasph.', pp. 108, 271; 'De ecclesia',
p. 156; 'Sermones', III, 209-10, 264; 'De officio
regis', pp. 169, 175.

14 Cf. the fifth of the articles condemned by bull in
1382 (Lechler, p. 420; 'Dict. Nat. Biogr., LXIII,
213). See also 'Of Prelates', 'Office of Curates',
'Of Confession' (Matthew, pp. 106-7, 160, 328ff.);
'Sermons on the Gospels' (over and over again), 'De
Pontificum Romanorum Schismate', 'The Church and Her
Members', 'On the Twenty-five Articles' (Arnold I, 18,
35, 47; II, 87, 100, 206; III, 252-56, 358, 461; also
'Fasc. Ziz.' 278, 321, etc.; Trevelyan, 'Engl. in the
Age of Wyclif', pp. 140-42. The Latin works are full
of such views: 'De civili dominio', pp. 259-60;
'Polemical Works', II, 622, 625; 'Sermones', I, 283,
307-10, 341; II, 62-63, 133, 138-39; III, 27, 67, 182,
261; IV, 102-3, 118, 122-23, 135, 146; 'De ecclesia',
pp. 577, 585; 'De apostasia', p. 35; 'De blasph.', pp.
58, 136, 140; 'De eucharistia et poenitentia', pp.
333 (here he is more orthodox; auricular confession is
necessary, but not absolutely necessary), and 335.
Here and elsewhere a certain amount of inconsistency
does not prove difference of authorship; what an inno-
vator says, and even what he believes, may vary from
time to time, with his audience, the development of
his principles, and the like.

15 The thirteenth-century Middle High German writer
suggestively nicknamed Freidank (possibly Walther von
der Vogelweide), belittles sacramental absolution
(Hildebrand's 'Didaktik aus der Zeit der Kreuzzüge',
in 'Deutsche National-Litteratur', IX, 336). The
Waldenses had attacked the Catholic doctrine of the
power of the keys; so had the Cathari, the Amaurians,
and other strange heretics (Lea, 'Hist. of the Inquis.
of the Middle Ages', I, 79, 93; II, 150, 320). The
large use of excommunication in the later Middle Ages
to further the political and financial interests of
the church became a burning scandal; so much so that
she had to legislate against those who settled down
to a comfortable life under her ban and made no
effort to remove it. But the loyalty of her children
is well shown by the almost universal acceptance of

her principles. For other condemnation of the excessive use of excommunication see Matthew, 'Engl. Works
of Wyclif', p. 509. Robert Manning of Bourne berates
the priest who 'for little curseth his parishioners'
('Handlyng Synne', pp. 10881ff.); but he bids the
'lewd man, þou shalt cursying doute' (p. 10921).
Both passages are in the French original. Dante
agrees pretty well with St. Thomas, as we should
expect. He sometimes seems liberal:

> Per lor maledizion sì no si perde,
> Che non possa tornar l'eterno amore,
> Mentre che la speranza ha fior del verde.-['Purg.'
> III, 133-35.]

But the contumacious toward holy church, even though
repentant at the last, must wait in Antepurgatory
thirty times as long as they resisted the church,
unless prayers shorten their suspense.

16   Many of the similar passages are cited by Skeat, but
far from all. To collect them would take too much
space, but here are a few which I might add: 'Prol.',
649-51, 'Fri. T.', 1362, Matthew, p. 249, Arnold, III,
288 (on blackmail for concubinage); 'Prol.', 259-63,
Arnold, II, 216 (on the voluminous garb of the
friars); 'Prol.', 235-37, Matthew, p. 9 (on their
singing, playing and dancing 'to get the stinking
love of damsels'); 'Summ. T.', 1832, 1840, Latin
'Sermones', III, 222 (on the affected use of French
by the friars).

17   Cf. the present writer in 'Mod. Phil.', III, 370-72.
On the prominence in the fourteenth century of the
controversy as to predestination and free-will, and
as to Bradwardine's prominence in it, and his influence on Wyclif, see Carleton Brown in 'Publ. Mod.
Lang. Assoc.', XIX, 128-30, 144. There was a great
deal of popular fatalism in the fourteenth century;
Chaucer's admiring contemporary Thomas Usk says
'Wherfore the comune sentence of the people in
opinion, that everything after destenee is ruled
false and wicked is to beleve' ('Testament of Love',
III, ix, 5-7, in Oxford 'Chaucer', VII).

18   See the writer's 'Scene of the Franklin's Tale Visited' (Chaucer Soc., 1914), chap. iii.

19   'Studies in Chaucer', II, 458-536. See the review by
Kittredge in 'The Nation', LIV, 231-32.

20   His spirit chaunged hous, and wente ther
      As I cam never, I can nat tellen wher, etc.

a passage easily misunderstood. It does not mean
'Since I was never there I cannot tell where' (*as* not
being causal in Chaucer); it means 'went to a place
where I never was, I cannot tell where.'

21   'Teseide', XI, 1ff., a passage which Chaucer had used
already in the 'Troilus', V, 1807-27. Elsewhere too
in the 'Troilus' he had adopted pagan eschatology
(IV, 789-91, 1187-88). Neither the pagan nor the
Christian other-world would have fitted the tone of
the 'Knight's Tale'. The fact that so unobvious a
thing is said at all seems to indicate a certain
levity; but levity is a totally different thing
from skepticism.

22   The chief difference is his gentleness toward the
seculars compared with the regulars, which certainly
harmonizes with Wyclif's attitude. This is mainly in
the 'Prolog', for they do not fare very well in the
'Reeve's' and the 'Canon's Yeoman's Tales'. I have
spoken already of the striking resemblances in detail
between Chaucer's and Wyclif's strictures on the
clergy, especially the regulars; Chaucer's fleers may
be paralleled again and again in Wyclif's censures.
But some of the same charges may be found elsewhere,
and of course were based on facts known to both.
There is a thesis called 'Der Klerus im mitteleng-
lischen Versroman', by Richard Kahle (Strassburg,
1906), which throws less light on the historical side
of the subject than might be anticipated.

23   For example, I have shown elsewhere that Chaucer held
much the same view as to the validity of astrology
and magic that was held by his contemporaries; and
that such doubt and distaste as he expresses is sometimes based on religious grounds. Therefore such
passages (as those in the 'Franklin's Tale') are no
better an argument for skepticism than they are for
orthodoxy. See 'The Scene of the Franklin's Tale
Visited', pp. 22-37, especially pp. 34-35. The
natural background of skepticism for an intellectually
independent Englishman of the late fourteenth century
is Wyclifism.

24   There is evidence in the Retractions at the end of
the 'Parson's Tale' (ll. 1081-92) that late in life he
was at least conventionally submissive to even the
narrower religious spirit of his time. In writing
them he was following what might almost be called a
literary-religious custom of earlier periods, and the
impulse which produced them has often been paralleled
among later literary men. See 'Publ. Mod. Lang.
Assoc.', XXVIII, 521-29.

25   Chaucer is not greatly given to ecclesiastical lan-
     guage. Occasionally the terms of theology and of the
     liturgies appear, especially in the 'Troilus' (the
     cases cited not being in its original). Pandarus
     taunts Troilus with having 'caught attrition' (the
     minimum degree of repentance in a good confession,
     opposed to contrition; 'T.C.', I, 557); twice Chaucer
     contrasts substance and accidents ('T.C.', IV, 1505;
     'Pard. T.', 539). He refers to the form of confession
     (the *Confiteor*), when Pandarus bids Troilus (I, 932)
     beat his breast and beg pardon for speaking against
     love, and when Pandarus says he overheard Troilus say,
     '"*Mea culpa, lord!* I me repente"' (II, 525). A line
     in the proem of the 'Troilus', 'For I, that god of
     Loves servaunts serve' (I, 15, *servus servorum dei
     amoris*, as it were), may be playing on the papal style
     used at the beginning of bulls and other especially
     formal missives ('Benedictus episcopus, servus servo-
     rum Dei'; Dante thus alludes to the pope, 'il servo
     de' servi.' 'Inf.', XV, 112). Skeat refers 'A B C',
     81, to the *Stabat mater dolorosa*; a little farther on
     there may be a reminiscence of the *Dies irae* if it
     was sufficiently familiar in Chaucer's day. It was
     not sung then in masses for the dead as the sequence
     (between the epistle and the gospel), as in the modern
     Roman rite, where it first appeared in the fifteenth
     century (Rock, 'Church of Our Fathers', 2d ed., IV,
     204-5; 'Missale Romanum, 1474', Bradshaw Soc., II,
     293).

> But, for your bothes peynes, I you preye,
> Lat not our alder foo make his bobaunce,
> That he hath in his listes of mischaunce
> Convict that ye bothe have bought so dere
>
> Quaerens me sedisti lassus,
> Redimisti crucem passus,
> Tantus labor non sit cassus.

The Wife of Bath at the beginning of her tale (869ff.)
ridicules friars' services of benediction (Wyclif also
speaks of such things with contempt). King Alla's
submitting himself to the pope for penance and his
going to Rome ('M.L.T.', pp. 988ff.) doubtless refers
to the practice of 'reserving' certain sins to the
pope. But this is the same in the French original of
the poem. For more on this matter see Brown in 'Mod.
Phil.', IX, 1ff., and 'Miracle of our Lady' (Chaucer
Soc., 1910), 120ff.; Tupper in 'Mod. Lang. Notes',

XXX, 9-11; Young, ibid., 97-99. The title and some of
the language (especially in the rubrics) of the
'Legend' are ecclesiastical. The *Ave Maria* is mentioned in 'ABC', 104 (not too respectfully, one would
almost fancy). The writer will shortly discuss elsewhere the marriage service in 'Merch. T.', 1701-8,
1819. The use of the opening of St. John's Gospel as
a charm, etc. ('Prol.', 254), was discussed in 'Mod.
Lang. Notes', XXIX, 140; other cases are mentioned in
Luther's 'Tischreden' (Foerstemann's ed.), II, 442;
'Lay Folk's Mass Book' (E.E.T.S., 1879), 146, 383-84;
Arderne, 'Fistula' (ibid., 1910), 104, 135; J.M.
Stone, 'History of Mary I' (London, 1901), I, 427.

40.   ALDOUS HUXLEY, IN LOVE WITH THE INEVITABLY MATERIAL

1920

Aldous Leonard Huxley (1894-1963), novelist and man of
letters, was educated at Balliol College, Oxford. He sees
a Chaucer who only recognises the material world, in which
he takes inexhaustible delight; a lover also of astronomy,
who has deep insight into human character; and a man who
is totally sceptical. The ending of 'Troilus' is thus
inevitably regarded as 'boggled'. That Chaucer finds what
is perfect of its kind to be admirable is a shrewd point:
no mention is made of Chaucer's religious works. The
essay was first printed in 'The London Mercury', II
(1920), here reprinted from 'On the Margin', Chatto &
Windus, 1923, pp. 203-27, by permission of the publisher
and Mrs Laura Huxley, and Harper & Row, Inc.

There are few things more melancholy than the spectacle
of literary fossilization. A great writer comes into
being, lives, labours and dies. Time passes; year by year
the sediment of muddy comment and criticism thickens round
the great man's bones. The sediment sets firm; what was
once a living organism becomes a thing of marble. On the
attainment of total fossilization the great man has become
a classic. It becomes increasingly difficult for the
members of each succeeding generation to remember

that the stony objects which fill the museum cases were
once alive. It is often a work of considerable labour
to reconstruct the living animal from the fossil shape.
But the trouble is generally worth taking. And in no case
is it more worth while than in Chaucer's.

With Chaucer the ordinary fossilizing process, to which
every classical author is subject, has been complicated by
the petrification of his language. Five hundred years
have almost sufficed to turn the most living of poets into
a substitute on the modern sides of schools for the mental
gymnastic of Latin and Greek. Prophetically, Chaucer saw
the fate that awaited him and appealed against his doom:

> Ye know eke that, in form of speech is change
> Within a thousand year, and wordes tho
> That hadden price, now wonder nice and strange
> Us thinketh them; and yet they spake them so,
> And sped as well in love as men now do.

The body of his poetry may have grown old, but its spirit
is still young and immortal. To know that spirit - and
not to know it is to ignore something that is of unique
importance in the history of our literature - it is necessary to make the effort of becoming familiar with the body
it informs and gives life to. The antique language and
versification, so 'wonder nice and strange' to our ears,
are obstacles in the path of most of those who read for
pleasure's sake (not that any reader worthy of the name
ever reads for anything else but pleasure); to the ped-
ants they are an end in themselves. Theirs is the car-
cass, but not the soul. Between those who are daunted
by his superficial difficulties and those who take too
much delight in them Chaucer finds but few sympathetic
readers. I hope in these pages to be able to give a few
of the reasons that make Chaucer so well worth reading.

Chaucer's art is, by its very largeness and objective-
ness, extremely difficult to subject to critical analysis.
Confronted by it, Dryden could only exclaim, 'Here is
God's plenty!' - and the exclamation proves, when all is
said, to be the most adequate and satisfying of all criticisms. All that the critic can hope to do is to expand
and to illustrate Dryden's exemplary brevity.

'God's plenty!' - the phrase is a peculiarly happy one.
It calls up a vision of the prodigal earth, of harvest
fields, of innumerable beasts and birds, of teeming life.
And it is in the heart of this living and material world
of Nature that Chaucer lives. He is the poet of earth,
supremely content to walk, desiring no wings. Many
English poets have loved the earth for the sake of

something - a dream, a reality, call it which you will - that lies behind it. But there have been few, and, except for Chaucer, no poets of greatness, who have been in love with earth for its own sake, with Nature in the sense of something inevitably material, something that is the opposite of the supernatural. Supreme over everything in this world he sees the natural order, the 'law of kind,' as he calls it. The teachings of most of the great prophets and poets are simply protests against the law of kind. Chaucer does not protest, he accepts. It is precisely this acceptance that makes him unique among English poets. He does not go to Nature as the symbol of some further spiritual reality; hills, flowers, sea, and clouds are not, for him, transparencies through which the workings of a great soul are visible. No, they are opaque; he likes them for what they are, things pleasant and beautiful, and not the less delicious because they are definitely of the earth earthy. Human beings, in the same way, he takes as he finds, noble and beastish, but, on the whole, wonderfully decent. He has none of that strong ethical bias which is usually to be found in the English mind. He is not horrified by the behaviour of his fellow-beings, and he has no desire to reform them. Their characters, their motives interest him, and he stands looking on at them, a happy spectator. This serenity of detachment, this placid acceptance of things and people as they are, is emphasized if we compare the poetry of Chaucer with that of his contemporary, Langland, or whoever it was that wrote 'Piers Plowman'.

The historians tell us that the later years of the fourteenth century were among the most disagreeable periods of our national history. English prosperity was at a very low ebb. The Black Death had exterminated nearly a third of the working population of the islands, a fact which, aggravated by the frenzied legislation of the Government, had led to the unprecedented labour troubles that culminated in the peasants' revolt. Clerical corruption and lawlessness were rife. All things considered, even our own age is preferable to that in which Chaucer lived. Langland does not spare denunciation; he is appalled by the wickedness about him, scandalized at the openly confessed vices that have almost ceased to pay to virtue the tribute of hypocrisy. Indignation is the inspiration of 'Piers Plowman', the righteous indignation of the prophet. But to read Chaucer one would imagine that there was nothing in fourteenth-century England to be indignant about. It is true that the Pardoner, the Friar, the Shipman, the Miller, and, in fact, most of the Canterbury pilgrims are rogues and scoundrels; but, then, they

are such 'merry harlots' too. It is true that the Monk
prefers hunting to praying, that, in these latter days
when fairies are no more, 'there is none other incubus'
but the friar, that 'purse is the Archdeacon's hell,' and
the Summoner a villain of the first magnitude; but Chaucer
can only regard these things as primarily humorous. The
fact of people not practising what they preach is an unfailing source of amusement to him. Where Langland cries
aloud in anger, threatening the world with hell-fire,
Chaucer looks on and smiles. To the great political
crisis of his time he makes but one reference, and that a
comic one:

> So hideous was the noyse, ah *benedicite*!
> Certes he Jakke Straw, and his meyné,
> Ne maden schoutes never half so schrille,
> Whan that they wolden eny Flemyng kille,
> As thilke day was mad upon the fox.

Peasants may revolt, priests break their vows, lawyers lie
and cheat, and the world in general indulge its sensual
appetites; why try and prevent them, why protest? After
all, they are all simply being natural, they are all
following the law of kind. A reasonable man, like himself, 'flees fro the pres and dwelles with soothfast-
nesse.' But reasonable men are few, and it is the nature
of human beings to be the unreasonable sport of instinct
and passion, just as it is the nature of the daisy to
open its eye to the sun and of the goldfinch to be a
spritely and 'gaylard' creature. The law of kind has
always and in everything domination; there is no rubbing
nature against the hair. For

> God it wot, there may no man embrace
> As to destreyne a thing, the which nature
> Hath naturelly set in a creature.
> Take any brid, and put him in a cage,
> And do all thine entent and thy corrage
> To foster it tendrely with meat and drynke,
> And with alle the deyntees thou canst bethinke,
> And keep it all so kyndly as thou may;
> Although his cage of gold be never so gay,
> Yet hath this brid, by twenty thousand fold,
> Lever in a forest, that is wyld and cold,
> Gon ete wormes, and such wrecchidnes;
> For ever this brid will doon his busynes
> To scape out of his cage when that he may;
> His liberté the brid desireth aye....
> Lo, heer hath kynd his dominacioun,

And appetyt flemeth [banishes] discrescioun.
Also a she wolf hath a vilayne kynde,
The lewideste wolf that she may fynde,
Or least of reputacioun, him will sche take,
In tyme whan hir lust to have a make.
Alle this ensaumples tell I by these men
That ben untrewe, and nothing by wommen.

(As the story from which these lines are quoted happens to
be about an unfaithful wife, it seems that, in making the
female sex immune from the action of the law of kind,
Chaucer is indulging a little in irony.)

For men han ever a licorous appetit
On lower thing to parforme her delit
Than on her wyves, ben they never so faire,
Ne never so trewe, ne so debonaire.

Nature, deplorable as some of its manifestations may be,
must always and inevitably assert itself. The law of kind
has power even over immortal souls. This fact is the
source of the poet's constantly expressed dislike of celi-
bacy and asceticism. The doctrine that upholds the superiority of the state of virginity over that of wedlock
is, to begin with (he holds), a danger to the race. It
encourages a process which we may be permitted to call
dysgenics - the carrying on of the species by the worst
members. The Host's words to the Monk are memorable:

Allas! why wearest thou so wide a cope?
God give me sorwe! and I were a pope
Nought only thou, but every mighty man,
Though he were shore brode upon his pan [head]
Should han a wife; for all this world is lorn;
Religioun hath take up all the corn
Of tredyng, and we burel [humble] men ben shrimpes;
Of feble trees there cometh wrecchid impes.
This maketh that our heires ben so sclendere
And feble, that they may not wel engendre.

But it is not merely dangerous; it is anti-natural. That
is the theme of the Wife of Bath's Prologue. Counsels of
perfection are all very well when they are given to those

That wolde lyve parfytly;
But, lordyngs, by your leve, that am not I.

The bulk of us must live as the law of kind enjoins.
It is characteristic of Chaucer's conception of the

world, that the highest praise he can bestow on anything
is to assert of it, that it possesses in the highest
degree the qualities of its own particular kind. Thus of
Cressida he says:

> She was not with the least of her stature,
> But all her limbes so well answering
> Weren to womanhood, that creature
> Nas never lesse mannish in seeming.

The horse of brass in the 'Squire's Tale' is

> So well proportioned to be strong,
> Right as it were a steed of Lombardye,
> Thereto so *horsely* and so quick of eye.

Everything that is perfect of its kind is admirable, even
though the kind may not be an exalted one. It is, for
instance, a joy to see the way in which the Canon sweats:

> A cloote-leaf [dock leaf] he had under his hood
> For sweat, and for to keep his head from heat.
> But it was joye for to see him sweat;
> His forehead dropped as a stillatorie
> Were full of plantain or of peritorie.

The Canon is supreme in the category of sweaters, the
very type and idea of perspiring humanity; therefore he is
admirable and joyous to behold, even as a horse that is
supremely horsely or a woman less mannish than anything
one could imagine. In the same way it is a delight to
behold the Pardoner preaching to the people. In its own
kind his charlatanism is perfect and deserves admiration:

> Mine handes and my tonge gon so yerne,
> That it is joye to see my busynesse.

This manner of saying of things that they are joyous,
or, very often, heavenly, is typical of Chaucer. He looks
out on the world with a delight that never grows old or
weary. The sights and sounds of daily life, all the
lavish beauty of the earth fill him with a pleasure which
he can only express by calling it a 'joy' or a 'heaven'.
It 'joye was to see' Cressida and her maidens playing together; and

> So aungellyke was her native beauté
> That like a thing immortal seemede she,
> As doth an heavenish parfit creature.

The peacock has angel's feathers; a girl's voice is heavenly to hear:

> Antigone the shene
> Gan on a Trojan song to singen clear,
> That it an heaven was her voice to hear.

One could go on indefinitely multiplying quotations that testify to Chaucer's exquisite sensibility to sensuous beauty and his immediate, almost exclamatory response to it. Above all, he is moved by the beauty of 'young, fresh folkes, he and she'; by the grace and swiftness of living things, birds and animals; by flowers and placid, luminous, park-like landscapes.

It is interesting to note how frequently Chaucer speaks of animals. Like many other sages, he perceives that an animal is, in a certain sense, more human in character than a man. For an animal bears the same relation to a man as a caricature to a portrait. In a way a caricature is truer than a portrait. It reveals all the weaknesses and absurdities that flesh is heir to. The portrait brings out the greatness and dignity of the spirit that inhabits the often ridiculous flesh. It is not merely that Chaucer has written regular fables, though the 'Nun's Priest's Tale' puts him among the great fabulists of the world, and there is also much definitely fabular matter in the 'Parliament of Fowls'. No, his references to the beasts are not confined to his animal stories alone; they are scattered broadcast throughout his works. He relies for much of his psychology and for much of his most vivid description on the comparison of man, in his character and appearance (which with Chaucer are always indissolubly blended), with the beasts. Take, for example, that enchanting simile in which Troilus, stubbornly anti-natural in refusing to love as the law of kind enjoins him, is compared to the corn-fed horse, who has to be taught good behaviour and sound philosophy under the whip:

> As proude Bayard ginneth for to skip
> Out of the way, so pricketh him his corn,
> Till he a lash have of the longe whip,
> Then thinketh he, 'Though I prance all biforn,
> First in the trace, full fat and newe shorn,
> Yet am I but an horse, and horses' law
> I must endure and with my feeres draw.'

Or, again, women with too pronounced a taste for fine apparel are likened to the cat:

> And if the cattes skin be sleek and gay,
> She will not dwell in housé half a day,
> But forth she will, ere any day be dawet
> To show her skin and gon a caterwrawet.

In his descriptions of the personal appearance of his
characters Chaucer makes constant use of animal characteristics. Human beings, both beautiful and hideous, are
largely described in terms of animals. It is interesting
to see how often in that exquisite description of Alisoun,
the carpenter's wife, Chaucer produces his clearest and
sharpest effects by a reference to some beast or bird:

> Fair was this younge wife, and therewithal
> As any weasel her body gent and small ...
> But of her song it was as loud and yern
> As is the swallow chittering on a barn.
> Thereto she coulde skip and make a game
> As any kid or calf following his dame.
> Her mouth was sweet as bragot is or meath,
> Or hoard of apples, laid in hay or heath.
> Wincing she was, as is a jolly colt,
> Long as a mast and upright as a bolt.

Again and again in Chaucer's poems do we find such simili-
tudes, and the result is always a picture of extraordinary
precision and liveliness. Here, for example, are a few:

> Gaylard he was as goldfinch in the shaw,

or,

> Such glaring eyen had he as an hare;

or,

> As piled [bald] as an ape was his skull.

The self-indulgent friars are

> Like Jovinian,
> Fat as a whale, and walken as a swan.

The Pardoner describes his own preaching in these words:

> Then pain I me to stretche forth my neck
> And east and west upon the people I beck,
> As doth a dove, sitting on a barn.

Very often, too, Chaucer derives his happiest metaphors
from birds and beasts. Of Troy in its misfortune and decline he says: Fortune

> Gan pull away the feathers bright of Troy
> From day to day.

Love-sick Troilus soliloquizes thus:

> He said: 'O fool, now art thou in the snare
> That whilom japedest at lovés pain,
> Now art thou hent, now gnaw thin owné chain.'

The metaphor of Troy's bright feathers reminds me of a
very beautiful simile borrowed from the life of the plants:

> And as in winter leavés been bereft,
> Each after other, till the tree be bare,
> So that there nis but bark and branches left,
> Lieth Troilus, bereft of each welfare,
> Ybounden in the blacke bark of care.

And this, in turn, reminds me of that couplet in which
Chaucer compares a girl to a flowering pear-tree:

> She was well more blissful on to see
> Than is the newe parjonette tree.

Chaucer is as much at home among the stars as he is among
the birds and beasts and flowers of earth. There are some
literary men of to-day who are not merely not ashamed to
confess their total ignorance of all facts of a 'scientific' order, but even make a boast of it. Chaucer would
have regarded such persons with pity and contempt. His
own knowledge of astronomy was wide and exact. Those whose
education has been as horribly imperfect as my own will
always find some difficulty in following him as he moves
with easy assurance through the heavens. Still, it is
possible without knowing any mathematics to appreciate
Chaucer's descriptions of the great pageant of the sun and
stars as they march in triumph from mansion to mansion
through the year. He does not always trouble to take out
his astrolabe and measure the progress of 'Phebus, with
his rosy cart'; he can record the god's movements in more
general terms that may be understood even by the literary
man of nineteen hundred and twenty. Here, for example, is
a description of 'the coldé frosty seisoun of Decembre,'
in which matters celestial and earthly are mingled to make
a picture of extraordinary richness:

Phebus wox old and hewed like latoun,
That in his hoté declinacioun
Shone as the burned gold, with streames bright;
But now in Capricorn adown he light,
Where as he shone full pale; I dare well sayn
The bitter frostes with the sleet and rain
Destroyed hath the green in every yerd.
Janus sit by the fire with double beard,
And drinketh of his bugle horn the wine;
Beforn him stont the brawn of tusked swine,
And 'noel' cryeth every lusty man.

In astrology he does not seem to have believed. The magnificent passage in the 'Man of Law's Tale', where it is
said that

In the starres, clearer than is glass,
Is written, God wot, whoso can it read,
The death of every man withouten drede,

is balanced by the categorical statement found in the
scientific and educational treatise on the astrolabe,
that judicial astrology is mere deceit.

His scepticism with regard to astrology is not surprising. Highly as he prizes authority, he prefers the evidence of experience, and where that evidence is lacking
he is content to profess a quiet agnosticism. His respect
for the law of kind is accompanied by a complementary mis-
trust of all that does not appear to belong to the natural
order of things. There are moments when he doubts even
the fundamental beliefs of the Church:

A thousand sythes have I herd men telle
That there is joye in heaven and peyne in helle;
And I accorde well that it be so,
But natheless, this wot I well also
That there is none that dwelleth in this countree
That either hath in helle or heaven y-be.

Of the fate of the spirit after death he speaks in much
the same style:

His spiryt changed was, and wente there
As I came never, I cannot tellen where;
Therefore I stint, I nam no divinistre;
Of soules fynde I not in this registre,
Ne me list not th' opiniouns to telle
Of hem, though that they witten where they dwelle.

He has no patience with superstitions. Belief in dreams, in auguries, fear of the 'ravenes qualm or schrychynge of thise owles' are all unbefitting to a self-respecting man:

> To trowen on it bothe false and foul is;
> Alas, alas, so noble a creature
> As is a man shall dreaden such ordure!

By an absurd pun he turns all Calchas's magic arts of prophecy to ridicule:

> So when this Calkas knew by calkulynge,
> And eke by answer of this Apollo
> That Grekes sholden such a people bringe,
> Through which that Troye muste ben fordo,
> He cast anon out of the town to go.

It would not be making a fanciful comparison to say that Chaucer in many respects resembles Anatole France. Both men possess a profound love of this world for its own sake, coupled with a profound and gentle scepticism about all that lies beyond this world. To both of them the lavish beauty of Nature is a never-failing and all-sufficient source of happiness. Neither of them are ascetics; in pain and privation they see nothing but evil. To both of them the notion that self-denial and self-mortification are necessarily righteous and productive of good is wholly alien. Both of them are apostles of sweetness and light, of humanity and reasonableness. Unbounded tolerance of human weakness and a pity, not the less sincere for being a little ironical, characterize them both. Deep knowledge of the evils and horrors of this unintelligible world makes them all the more attached to its kindly beauty. But in at least one important respect Chaucer shows himself to be the greater, the completer spirit. He possesses, what Anatole France does not, an imaginative as well as an intellectual comprehension of things. Faced by the multitudinous variety of human character, Anatole France exhibits a curious impotence of imagination. He does not understand characters in the sense that, say, Tolstoy understands them; he cannot, by the power of imagination, get inside them, become what he contemplates. None of the persons of his creation are complete characters; they cannot be looked at from every side; they are portrayed, as it were, in the flat and not in three dimensions. But Chaucer has the power of getting into someone else's character. His understanding of the men and women of whom he writes is complete; his slightest character sketches are always solid and three-dimensional. The

Prologue to the 'Canterbury Tales', in which the effects
are almost entirely produced by the description of external physical features, furnishes us with the most obvious
example of his three-dimensional drawing. Or, again,
take that description in the 'Merchant's Tale' of old
January and his young wife May after their wedding night.
It is wholly a description of external details, yet the
result is not a superficial picture. We are given a
glimpse of the characters in their entirety:

> Thus laboureth he till that the day gan dawe,
> And then he taketh a sop in fine clarré,
> And upright in his bed then sitteth he.
> And after that he sang full loud and clear,
> And kissed his wife and made wanton cheer.
> He was all coltish, full of ragerye,
> And full of jargon as a flecked pye.
> The slacké skin about his necké shaketh,
> While that he sang, so chanteth he and craketh.
> But God wot what that May thought in her Heart,
> When she him saw up sitting in his shirt,
> In his night cap and with his necke lean;
> She praiseth not his playing worth a bean.

But these are all slight sketches. For full-length portraits of character we must turn to 'Troilus and Cressida',
a work which, though it was written before the fullest
maturity of Chaucer's powers, is in many ways his most
remarkable achievement, and one, moreover, which has
never been rivalled for beauty and insight in the whole
field of English narrative poetry. When one sees with
what certainty and precision Chaucer describes every
movement of Cressida's spirit from the first movement she
hears of Troilus' love for her to the moment when she is
unfaithful to him, one can only wonder why the novel of
character should have been so slow to make its appearance.
It was not until the eighteenth century that narrative
artists, using prose as their medium instead of verse,
began to rediscover the secrets that were familiar to
Chaucer in the fourteenth.

'Troilus and Cressida' was written, as we have said,
before Chaucer had learnt to make the fullest use of his
powers. In colouring it is fainter, less sharp and brilliant than the best of the 'Canterbury Tales'. The
character studies are there, carefully and accurately
worked out; but we miss the bright vividness of presentation with which Chaucer was to endow his later art. The
characters are all alive and completely seen and understood. But they move, as it were, behind a veil - the

veil of that poetic convention which had, in the earliest
poems, almost completely shrouded Chaucer's genius, and
which, as he grew up, as he adventured and discovered,
grew thinner and thinner, and finally vanished like gauzy
mist in the sunlight. When 'Troilus and Cressida' was
written the mist had not completely dissipated, and the
figures of his creation, complete in conception and execution as they are, are seen a little dimly because of the
interposed veil.

The only moment in the poem when Chaucer's insight
seems to fail him is at the very end; he has to account
for Cressida's unfaithfulness, and he is at a loss to
know how he shall do it. Shakespeare, when he rehandled
the theme, had no such difficulty. His version of the
story, planned on much coarser lines than Chaucer's, leads
obviously and inevitably to the fore-ordained conclusion;
his Cressida is a minx who simply lives up to her character. What could be more simple? But to Chaucer the problem is not so simple. His Cressida is not a minx. From
the moment he first sets eyes on her Chaucer, like his
own unhappy Troilus, falls head over ears in love. Beautiful, gentle, gay; possessing, it is true, somewhat
'tendre wittes,' but making up for her lack of skill in
ratiocination by the 'sudden avysements' of intuition;
vain, but not disagreeably so, of her good looks and of
her power over so great and noble a knight as Troilus;
slow to feel love, but once she has yielded, rendering
back to Troilus passion for passion; in a word, the
'least mannish' of all possible creatures - she is to
Chaucer the ideal of gracious and courtly womanhood. But,
alas, the old story tells us that Cressida jilted her
Troilus for that gross prize-fighter of a man, Diomed.
The woman whom Chaucer has made his ideal proves to be no
better than she should be; there is a flaw in the crystal.
Chaucer is infinitely reluctant to admit the fact. But
the old story is specific in its statement; indeed, its
whole point consists in Cressida's infidelity. Called
upon to explain his heroine's fall, Chaucer is completely
at a loss. He makes a few half-hearted attempts to solve
the problem, and then gives it up, falling back on authority. The old clerks say it was so, therefore it must be
so, and that's that. The fact is that Chaucer pitched
his version of the story in a different key from that
which is found in the 'olde bokes,' with the result that
the note on which he is compelled by his respect for
authority to close is completely out of harmony with the
rest of the music. It is this that accounts for the
chief, and indeed the only, defect of the poem - its
hurried and boggled conclusion.

41.   CAROLINE F.E. SPURGEON, CRITICS OF CHAUCER JUDGE
THEMSELVES NOT HIM

1925

Caroline F.E. Spurgeon (1869-1942) was educated at King's
College and University College, London, and was Professor
of English Literature in the University of London, 1913-
29.   She enormously added to the collection of references
to Chaucer which was initiated by Speght in 1598 (see Vol.
1, No. 53), and which had been continued by other scholars, to create the massive and fundamental collection of
five hundred years of Chaucer criticism and allusion to
which modern scholarship and this present work in particular are so greatly indebted.   In her long Introduction her
own critical appreciations are unoriginal, but a real
sense of historical relativity is introduced into the criticism, leading to the gentle but profoundly sceptical
reflection that criticism tells us more about the critic
than about the writer he claims to discuss.   A history of
appreciation is sketched, and it is suggested that a feeling for nature and a sense of humour are modern developments.   This comment is reprinted from 'Five Hundred
Years of Chaucer Criticism and Allusion 1357-1900', 3
vols, Cambridge University Press (1925), I, cxxiv-cxxvii,
cxxix-cxxxv, cxxxviii-cxxxix, by permission of Messrs
Crofts & Ingram and Wyatt & Co.

As we watch this vast company of writers passing before
Chaucer, and leaving on record their opinion of him, it is
curious to reflect that the criticism Chaucer has received
throughout these five centuries in reality forms a measurement of judgment - not of him - but of his critics.
Just as we trace the development of the mind of an individual by studying his opinions and works at different periods of his life, so it would seem that in looking at this
ever-shifting procession of critics we can trace the
development of the mind and spirit of the nation to which
they belong.   We know that as individuals our taste
changes and fluctuates from youth to age; the favourite
authors of our youth are not, as a rule, the favourites of
middle age, or, if they are, we like them for other qualities, they make another appeal to us.   Similarly, we can
here watch the taste of a nation changing and fluctuating;
Chaucer is now liked for one quality, now for another,

while at times different ideals and interests so predominate that he makes no appeal to it at all.

Chaucer undoubtedly suffered from change in language
quite as much as from change in taste, but even making
due allowance for this, there is no question that had the
average men of letters and critics of the later seventeenth and earlier eighteenth centuries been able to read
and scan his work with perfect ease, they would yet not
have seen in him what is seen by the average literary
reader of to-day. Cowley would probably still have had
'no taste of him,' and Addison would have thought his
'wit' out of date. They had different ideals before them,
with which Chaucer did not fit in. It is for precisely
this reason that we no longer have 'a taste of' Waller,
who, to the later seventeenth century, was the most important figure in English letters.

We are so accustomed to this change of taste that we
accept as a natural condition of evolution, as a necessary
sign of growth, in nations as in individuals, this continual fluctuation, of which not the least curious quality is
that, although we are intellectually conscious of its
existence, we are as incapable of realizing it as we are
of realizing that our physical bodies are composed of
whirling and ever-changing atoms.

We all of us, individually and collectively, at any
given time, trained and guided as we are by the best
thought of our age, are inclined to feel that the way we
regard an author, a classic, for instance, like Chaucer,
is the truest and only possible way he can be regarded.
We of to-day are sure that we appreciate to the full all
his special qualities, and that his position in the history of our literature has been once and for all established. It may be so, but the experience of the past
does not confirm it. Cowley, Addison, Dr. Johnson, and
a host of minor critics, all probably felt exactly as we
do; they never doubted that their taste was true, their
attitude the only sane one, and that Chaucer's position,
in spite of Dryden's curious fancy for him, was quite
certainly and definitely settled.

To-day, with the record of the opinion of five centuries before us, we can see that the verdict of the most
competent critic cannot be wholly trusted until Time has
set his seal on it, and that much allowance must always be
made, as Hazlitt would have said, 'for the wind,' that is,
for the prevailing bias of the age, the standards, ideals
and fashions, change in which constitutes change in taste.

Some further light may be thrown on the evolution of
critical taste and method when we are able to compare
over an appreciable space of time the critical attitude of

a nation towards more than one great poet of its own race.
This is only to-day beginning to be possible. If, for
instance, we compare the movement of critical opinion and
research on Shakespeare with that on Chaucer, it is clear
that there is a certain similarity, which would appear to
indicate the existence of a definite rhythm in the evolution of taste and critical method, as there is a rhythm
in all life. The investigation in the future will be
complicated by the fact that there will be two rhythms to
follow [1] that of the development of the nation itself
and of its critical powers, and [2] that of the evolution
of its attitude towards any one given poet. Owing, however, to the literary barrenness of the fifteenth century
in England, the development of the first was not at the
outset sufficiently rapid to make any great difference in
the treatment of Chaucer and Shakespeare.

Thus, in the case of each of these poets there is a
period of early praise and personal appreciation, love
for the man, with an unquestioned recognition of his position as a great artist. This is followed by a more critical attitude, which, in Shakespeare's case, for various
fairly obvious reasons, comes about much sooner after his
death than it does with Chaucer. Then follows, for both
poets, a time of effort to make their rough and unpolished
works more acceptable to modern taste; Shakesperian revision and 'improvement' began as early as 1662 (when Daven-
ant produced his blend of 'Measure for Measure' and 'Much
Ado'), though it did not continue so late into the nineteenth century as is the case with Chaucer.

At the same time it is in the eighteenth century that
the gradual revival of real first-hand knowledge and
appreciation of both poets began, critical and scholarly
investigation was started, stupendous work on Shakespeare's text was done by the great succession of eighteenth-century editors, and Tyrwhitt brought out his monu-
mental edition of the 'Canterbury Tales'.

In the later period of 'romantic' criticism for both
poets, which began at the end of the eighteenth century
and went on all through the nineteenth century, we find
in the case of Chaucer that this romantic, psychological
and often ethical appreciation is followed and accompanied
from the eighteen sixties onwards with very close textual
work and specialised investigation of his language and
versification. This closer and specialised investigation
of Shakespeare has yet to come; it is, possibly, just
beginning. It is in fact probable that investigators to-
day, three hundred years after Shakespeare's death, may
be about to do for his text something analogous to what
Tyrwhitt, three hundred and seventy-five years after

Chaucer's death, did for him when he disposed of the persistently erroneous view of his versification and proved
that he was a far greater artist and a far more finished
literary craftsman than had up to that time been suspected....

(p. cxxix) There are certain influences, foreign
literatures, canons of criticism, indicated in every history of the subject, which we can plainly see do much to
bring about this change. But all these 'causes' only
push the question one step further back. These influences, taken singly or together, do not explain why taste
is in a state of continual flux and changes with each
generation. This flux is as mysterious as life itself;
it is in truth the fundamental characteristic of life,
and it is because taste is a living thing, because it is
the capacity for discernment of what is good, that it must
inevitably change.

Granting this, then, we see that in Chaucer's case the
change in critical attitude accounts for much. We no
longer have a definite body of poetic rules and ideals to
which all poets, however alien in kind, must conform or be
condemned; and that class of criticism is extinct, which
is so admirably exemplified in Miss Jenkyns's remark on
the author of the 'Pickwick Papers', 'Doubtless, a young
man, who might do very well if he would take Dr. Johnson
for a model.'

Our demands are different and our tests are different.
Today we prize Chaucer above all because he is a great
artist, we delight in his simplicity, his freshness, his
humanity, his humour, but it is possible that these may
not be the only or even the principal reasons why he is
liked three hundred years hence. If, as would seem to be
the case, the common consciousness of a people becomes
enriched with time and experience, enabling them to see
ever more and more in the work of a great poet, the
lovers of Chaucer three centuries hence will be capable of
seeing more in him and will be able to come actually
nearer to him than can those who love him to-day.

Three directions may be indicated in which this enrichment of consciousness is here seen. They are all exactly
parallel with what takes place in the growth and development of the individual personality. The first is the
development of self-consciousness, of the art of criticism
itself; the second is the development of a new sense, and
the third is intellectual development, as seen in accuracy and trained scholarship.

7. THE BIRTH AND GROWTH OF CRITICISM AS AN ART.

We know that in nations, as in individuals, the critical
faculty develops late, for criticism is a self-conscious
art, and cannot exist in the intellectual childhood of a
race. England, as compared with France and Italy, was
backward in this art, for the northern races mature less
quickly, and it is only necessary to cast a glance over
the tributes to Chaucer during the first 150 years after
his death, to realize why England was late in producing
criticism. Chaucer is praised mainly for two reasons,
because he settled or established the language, and because he was our first, and by far our greatest poet. We
lacked, until later than either France or Italy, a single
form of standard speech and, with one exception, we also
lacked good writers. Thus no criticism was for us possible until the pre-eminence of Chaucer's work had helped
to establish the dialect of London as the standard English speech, and until we possessed a certain body of
literary work, both in prose and verse, which could be
analyzed, commented on and compared.

We have here under our hand, and can easily trace as
we turn over the pages, the gradual change in the conception of criticism. It begins with bare classification of
the external and obvious, and the analysis of form, or,
it is concerned only with the ethics of the matter: next
it searches for the establishment of an outside fixed
standard, by the degree of conformity to which it judges
a work, and it delights in the manufacture of receipts
for poetry. With Dryden comes the dawn of the conception
of organic life and growth in matters literary - 'for we
have our Lineal Descents and Clans, as well as other Fami-
lies' - in the eighteenth century the reaction to the
judgment by fixed standard, and finally the gradual real-
ization that aesthetic is not fixed, but relative, varying
from age to age, and from country to country, and that
criticism, even as poetry, is a creative art, whose true
function lies in interpretation, in painting to the intellect what already 'lies painted to the heart and imagination.' From this point of view the remarks on Chaucer by
Ascham (1544), Gascoigne (1575), Nash (1592), Waller
(1668), Dryden (1700), Johnson (1755), Warton (1774),
Blake (1809), and Hazlitt (1817-18) would in themselves,
if rightly read, form a short illustrated History of English Criticism.

Besides the new idea of the function of criticism and
the change in the standard in critical judgment, we find
here what is really a rather startling illustration of the
curiously slow growth of any sort of critical power in

the modern sense of the word.

If we examine the comments on Chaucer which have any pretension to be called literary or aesthetic criticism, we see that up to the middle of the sixteenth century they consist purely of praise of a very simple and vague kind, the vagueness and general nature of the remarks being their most striking feature. Elizabethan criticism is either a very elementary analysis of Chaucer's metre and language, or a tribute of admiration, or a defence of the poet against certain shortcomings with which he is charged. The sixteenth-century criticisms are good illustrations of how completely literature was treated as an external phenomenon; the work was tested 'in vacuo,' the critic was concerned with its unity, regularity, harmony and so on, but never with its relation to the mind that created it, or to the age in which it was written. Of the change in this respect which gradually took place in the seventeenth century, we cannot here judge, for of seventeenth-century Chaucerian criticism there is practically none, until in the last year of the century, quite suddenly, and as it were without any preparation, we find the first aesthetic criticism of his work, which is in many respects the finest, sanest and most illuminating essay ever written concerning Chaucer's merits and position as a poet.

Nothing more astonishingly brings out Dryden's greatness as a critic, his freedom, breadth, acuteness, courage, and extraordinary independence of view, than does his treatment of Chaucer. Not only is he the first writer to give us real criticism in the modern sense of the word, but in an age which despised Chaucer, and frankly looked upon him as barbarous and obsolete,(1) Dryden calmly compares him with Ovid, and maintains that the English poet is the more classical of the two. In this surprising and ever refreshing piece of criticism, Dryden makes use, for the first time as applied to Chaucer, of the comparative and historical methods, both of which were new in English criticism. Before this time the mention of a date or of the fact that Chaucer is our first poet is the only evidence that a rudimentary historical sense existed. There is no attempt really to compare one writer with another, unless the simile 'our English Homer' is to be described as such. Dryden also shows the way to the study of poetry by definite illustration, quotation and comparison. This method was practically unknown in England until Rymer wrote his preface to Rapin in 1674, before which date, as has been pointed out,(2) 'scarcely a line of English verse had been quoted for the purpose of critical analysis or discussion.' Unfortunately,

Rymer in discussing the heroic poets of England, passes
Chaucer over, because in his time the English language was
'not capable of any Heroick character.'

   After Dryden, criticism as an art stood still for more
than a hundred years, or, indeed, it may more accurately
be said to have gone back. This is well illustrated by
the Chaucer criticism of the eighteenth century. George
Sewell, in 1720, shows acuteness in his remarks, putting
his finger on the weak points in contemporary Chaucer
criticism, and he gives two concrete illustrations of the
statement he makes as to Dryden's debt to Chaucer.
George Ogle (1739) also uses concrete illustrations, and
attempts some comparison of qualities with the classical
poets. Apart from these, which only stand out because
other criticisms are so inadequate, there is nothing of
real critical worth about Chaucer until we come to the
revival in the third quarter of the century, which shows
itself so strongly in the love for the literature of the
past. Thomas Warton, first in his observations on Spenser (1754 and 1762), and later and more fully in his
'History of English Poetry' (1774-8); Gray, in his notes
on Chaucerian metre (1760-1), and Tyrwhitt, in his edition of the 'Canterbury Tales' (1775), mark a new departure in interpretative, philological and metrical criticism. Warton is followed by Scott, Blake, Coleridge,
Hazlitt, and the early nineteenth-century reviewers, but
it was to be nearly ninety years before any worthy successor of Tyrwhitt again applied himself to the text of
Chaucer.

   It is a fact worth noting, that the earliest literary
critic, and the earliest philologist in England (in the
modern sense of the terms), were alike in their love for
Chaucer, and each of them has left as a monument to him,
a work which was not even approached in merit for a century after its appearance.

8. THE EVOLUTION OF NEW SENSES.

In addition to the evolution in taste, in critical standard, and critical faculty, we would seem also to have
evolved new senses.

   An obvious instance of this is the feeling for nature,
the development of which is so recent a feature of our
literature. Why should this sense, more especially the
appreciation of wild scenery, have lain practically dormant until the third quarter of the eighteenth century?
Why should mountains and moors until then have been
found 'sad,' 'frightful' and 'horrid'?(3)   'Who *can* like

the Highlands?' replied Dr. Johnson to an incautious
inquiry from a Southerner as to how he had liked the
North. An Englishman, describing in 1740 the beautiful
road which runs along the south-eastern shore of Loch
Ness, calls the rugged mountains 'those hideous productions of nature';(4) the poet Gray, when crossing Perth-
shire early in September (1765), when the heather must
have been a blaze of purple, describes it as 'a weird and
dismal heath, fit for an assembly of witches';(5) and a
little later (1775) we find the citizens of Edinburgh
being urged to plant trees near the town so as to purify
the air 'and dispel those putrid and noxious vapours which
are frequently wafted from the Highlands.'(6) Twenty-
three years later Wordsworth and Coleridge were writing
the Lyrical Ballads.

A similar problem as regards the evolution of a sense
meets us in respect of the subtle and well-nigh indefinable quality, which we now call humour.

This faculty, which surely must be distinctively human,
for the animals have it not, and the gods perchance trans-
cend it,(7) this consciousness of human life in relation
to its eternal environment, this quick recognition of incongruity and contrast seen in the light of a larger wisdom; this power of inverting the relative values of things
both small and great, because of an instinct that from
some point outside they would be seen to be neither small
nor great, but only deeply significant - this is a quality
which, in its literary expression, is peculiarly English.
Wit we cede to France, and philosophy to Germany, but in
humour we stand supreme.

It is an interesting, although an obviously natural
fact that seriousness and humour constantly go together;
it is the most serious nations in Europe - England and
Spain - who have on the whole been the most humorous. For
humour implies belief, deep feeling, tenderness; and the
dissonances of life stand out more apparent to eyes which
have been used 'to look on man's mortality.'(8)

That the quality of humour existed in full measure in
fourteenth-century England we know by reading Chaucer's
Prologue, but we are forced to ask whether it was less
common than now, only to be found here and there among men
of genius. If it was as general and as well recognised
as it is to-day, by what name was it called? The faculty,
it would seem, is of late growth, in the race as in the
individual, savages and children possess it very slightly
and in a very elementary form. Possibly it is only yet
in the germ. One thing is certain, that in Chaucer's
time, and for long after, it was not called 'humour,' for
it is evident that no glimmering of the modern meaning of

that word was known until the very end of the seventeenth
century. It is perhaps the most important of a number of
words - such as 'wit,' 'fancy,' 'taste' - which have so
extended their meaning as to be new creations. These all
came into being in their literary sense, as qualities of
the mind, during the seventeenth and eighteenth centuries,
and brought about practically a new terminology in criticism.

'Humour,' which is literally 'moisture,' was first used
in mediaeval physiology as a term for one of the chief
fluids of the body (blood, phlegm, choler and melancholy),
(9) and so by extension in the later sixteenth century in
England it came to mean the special singularity of disposition or character which distinguishes a man from his
fellows. Shakespeare employs it in this sense, while Ben
Jonson's use of it is characteristic.(10)...

(p.cxxxviii) There can be no question, then, that although
the quality itself is to be found as far back as Chaucer,
the people as a whole possessed it only in an elementary
and gross form, and were far less susceptible to it than
they are to-day. 'Nothing,' says Goethe, 'is more significant of men's character than what they find laugh-
able.' George Eliot, in quoting this remark, observes
that it would perhaps have been more accurate to say
'culture' instead of 'character.'(11) It is most certain
that, as men evolve, as they grow in refinement, in
quickness and delicacy of perception, in sensitiveness
and in sympathy, their conception of what is humorous
must grow proportionately.

It is only necessary to stray a little in the by-
paths, more especially of sixteenth- and seventeenth-
century literature, to realize that in no one quality of
mind is the growth of the race more marked and apparent
than in this conception. We may briefly illustrate this
point by the history of Chaucer criticism. In Chaucer we
have a poet whose distinguishing quality of mind is a
subtle, shifting, delicate and all-pervading humour, to
which full justice has not perhaps even yet been done;(12)
yet through all these years of critical remark there is
until the eighteenth century no reference to the quality
as we know it, which he so amply possessed. There is a
certain recognition among some earlier writers of his
'pleasant vayne and wit,' and his 'delightsome mirth'....
by which is probably meant his relish of a good story, his
sly sense of fun, and the general atmosphere of good-
humour which pervades his work, but there is no hint of
appreciation of that deeper and more delicate quality
alone deserving the name of 'humour,' which is insight,
sympathy and tender seriousness, all brought into play

upon the ever-present sense of the incongruous, and of
the inconsistent in character and life. Of all this, as
far as we can judge, they are unconscious.

The first mention we find of the word 'humour' as
applied to Chaucer is in some verses by John Gay in 1712,
where he speaks of Prior entertaining the admiring
reader with 'Chaucer's Humour'; but we cannot be certain
of the exact meaning here attached to the word, although
if we may judge from the coarse and vulgar comedy which
Gay in some sense founded on the Canterbury pilgrims, what
he was most aware of in Chaucer was facetiousness, jokes
and general jollity. In 1715 John Hughes clearly employs
the word in the older Jonsonian sense of the predominating characteristic, but it would seem as if Pope, in
1728, when censuring Addison, was using the word with
some approach to its modern meaning. So, surely, was
Elizabeth Cooper (1737), when she says that Chaucer
'blended the acutest Raillery, with the most insinuating
Humour.'

It is Thomas Warton who, in 1754, first uses the term
in what we can be quite sure is something near the modern
sense; moreover he lays considerable emphasis on the fact
that Chaucer was the first English writer to possess it.
After Warton, the idea began very gradually to creep in
that a sense of humour was one of the qualities of the
poet. Bishop Percy (1765), in his remarks on Sir Thopas,
and Charles Burney (1782), who speaks of Chaucer's 'wit
and humour,' are cases in point.(13) It is not, however,
until well on in the nineteenth century, not indeed until
Leigh Hunt wrote on it in 1846, that Chaucer's humour
seems to have met with any adequate recognition.

Notes

1 The general and most lenient attitude towards Chaucer
   at this time is well represented by Edward Phillips
   (1675), who says that Chaucer 'through all the neglect
   of former ag'd Poets still keeps a name, being by some
   few admir'd for his real worth, to others not unpleas-
   ing for his facetious way, which joyn'd with his old
   English intertains them with a kind of Drollery.'
2 Introduction to 'Critical Essays of the 17th Century',
   ed. Spingarn, vol. i, p. lxv.
3 See a letter from Mason to Walpole, 1773, Walpole's
   'Letters', ed. Cunningham, vol. v, p. 501, note, or
   'Life of John Buncle', by Thomas Amory, 1756, vol. i,
   p. 291, ii, p. 97; or Hutchinson's 'Excursion to the
   Lakes', 1773, pp. 11, 17.

4   'Letters from a Gentleman in the North of Scotland',
    London, 1754, vol. ii, p. 339.
5   Gray's 'Works', ed. Gosse, vol. iii, p. 214.
6   Topham's 'Letters from Edinburgh', 1776, pp. 231, 233.
7   'A sense of humour is dependent on a condition of
    partial knowledge. Complete knowledge or complete
    ignorance are fatal to it. A Mrs. Gamp is not hum-
    orous to a Betsy Prig, for both are on the same level.
    Neither could be humorous to a Power, who knows every-
    thing and can be surprised at nothing and to whom no
    one thing is more incongruous than another.' - W.H.
    Mallock.
8   See The Evolution of Humour, by S.J. Butcher, in
    'Harper's Magazine', May 1890, vol. 80, p. 906: also,
    'The Humorous in Literature', by J.H. Shorthouse, in
    'Literary Remains', 1905, vol. ii, pp. 248-280.
9   So used by Chaucer, for example, in the 'Nonne
    Preestes Tale', 4113-4128.
10 Thus, in the Induction to 'Every Man out of his
    Humour', Jonson, after explaining the medical notion
    of a humour, continues -

>   It may by metaphor apply itself
>   Unto the general disposition:
>   As when some one peculiar quality
>   Doth so possess a man, that it doth draw
>   All his effects, his spirits, and his powers,
>   In their confluctions, all to run one way
>   This may be truly said to be a Humour.

11 German Wit, Heinrich Heine, 'Westminster Review',
    1856.
12 See the excellent remarks on this by Prof. Saintsbury
    in the 'Cambridge History of English Lierature', vol.
    ii, 1908, chap. vii.
13 It is worth noting that although Gray seems to use
    the word in its modern sense in speaking of Lydgate,
    he does not apply it at all to Chaucer....

42. VIRGINIA WOOLF, THE MORALITY OF THE NOVEL

1925

Virginia Woolf (1882-1941), novelist and critic, was

educated at home. She notes, more subtly than most,
Chaucer's narrative power and 'brightness', the solidity
and breadth of his poetic world, and brings out with
especial clarity the peculiarity that Chaucer's work seems
to evade the ordinary modern critical procedure which
uses exemplary quotation as 'proof' of poetic power. Reprinted from The Pastons and Chaucer, 'The Common Reader',
The Hogarth Press (1925), pp. 24-34, by permission of
the publishers; and Harcourt Brace Jovanovich Inc.,
copyright 1925; copyright 1953 by Leonard Woolf, by permission of Harcourt Brace Jovanovich, Inc.

To learn the end of the story - Chaucer can still make us
wish to do that. He has pre-eminently that story-teller's
gift, which is almost the rarest gift among writers at
the present day. Nothing happens to us as it did to our
ancestors; events are seldom important; if we recount
them, we do not really believe in them; we have perhaps
things of greater interest to say, and for these reasons
natural story-tellers like Mr. Garnett, whom we must distinguish from self-conscious story-tellers like Mr. Mase-
field, have become rare. For the story-teller, besides
his indescribable zest for facts, must tell his story
craftily, without undue stress or excitement, or we shall
swallow it whole and jumble the parts together; he must
let us stop, give us time to think and look about us, yet
always be persuading us to move on. Chaucer was helped
to this to some extent by the time of his birth; and in
addition he had another advantage over the moderns which
will never come the way of English poets again. England
was an unspoilt country. His eyes rested on a virgin
land, all unbroken grass and wood except for the small
towns and an occasional castle in the building. No villa
roofs peered through Kentish tree-tops; no factory chimney smoked on the hill-side. The state of the country,
considering how poets go to Nature, how they use her for
their images and their contrasts even when they do not
describe her directly, is a matter of some importance.
Her cultivation or her savagery influences the poet far
more profoundly than the prose writer. To the modern
poet, with Birmingham, Manchester, and London the size
they are, the country is the sanctuary of moral excel--
lence in contrast with the town which is the sink of vice.
It is a retreat, the haunt of modesty and virtue, where
men go to hide and moralise. There is something morbid,
as if shrinking from human contact, in the nature worship
of Wordsworth, still more in the microscopic devotion

which Tennyson lavished upon the petals of roses and the
buds of lime trees. But these were great poets. In their
hands, the country was no mere jeweller's shop, or museum
of curious objects to be described, even more curiously,
in words. Poets of smaller gift, since the view is so
much spoilt, and the garden or the meadow must replace the
barren heath and the precipitous mountain-side, are now
confined to little landscapes, to birds' nests, to acorns
with every wrinkle drawn to the life. The wider landscape
is lost.

But to Chaucer the country was too large and too wild
to be altogether agreeable. He turned instinctively, as
if he had painful experience of their nature, from tem-
pests and rocks to the bright May day and the jocund
landscape, from the harsh and mysterious to the gay and
definite. Without possessing a tithe of the virtuosity
in word-painting which is the modern inheritance, he
could give, in a few words, or even, when we come to look,
without a single word of direct description, the sense of
the open air.

And se the fresshe floures how they sprynge

- that is enough.

Nature, uncompromising, untamed, was no looking-glass
for happy faces, or confessor of unhappy souls. She was
herself; sometimes, therefore, disagreeable enough and
plain, but always in Chaucer's pages with the hardness
and the freshness of an actual presence. Soon, however,
we notice something of greater importance than the gay
and picturesque appearance of the mediaeval world - the
solidity which plumps it out, the conviction which ani-
mates the characters. There is immense variety in the
'Canterbury Tales', and yet, persisting underneath, one
consistent type. Chaucer has his world; he has his young
men; he has his young women. If one met them straying in
Shakespeare's world one would know them to be Chaucer's,
not Shakespeare's. He wants to describe a girl, and
this is what she looks like:

Ful semely hir wimpel pinched was,
Hir nose tretys; hir eyen greye as glas;
Hir mouth ful smal, and ther-to soft and reed;
But sikerly she hadde a fair foreheed;
It was almost a spanne brood, I trowe;
For, hardily, she was nat undergrowe.

Then he goes on to develop her; she was a girl, a virgin,
cold in her virginity:

> I am, thou woost, yet of thy companye,
> A mayde, and love hunting and venerye,
> And for to walken in the wodes wilde,
> And noght to been a wyf and be with childe.

Next he bethinks him how

> Discreet she was in answering alway;
> And though she had been as wise as Pallas
> No countrefeted termes hadde she
> To seme wys; but after hir degree
> She spak, and alle hir wordes more and lesse
> Souninge in vertu and in gentillesse.

Each of these quotations, in fact, comes from a different
Tale, but they are parts, one feels, of the same personage, whom he had in mind, perhaps unconsciously, when he
thought of a young girl, and for this reason, as she goes
in and out of the 'Canterbury Tales' bearing different
names, she has a stability which is only to be found where
the poet has made up his mind about young women, of course,
but also about the world they live in, its end, its nature,
and his own craft and technique, so that his mind is free
to apply its force fully to its object. It does not occur
to him that his Griselda might be improved or altered.
There is no blur about her, no hesitation; she proves
nothing; she is content to be herself. Upon her, therefore, the mind can rest with that unconscious ease which
allows it, from hints and suggestions, to endow her with
many more qualities than are actually referred to. Such
is the power of conviction, a rare gift, a gift shared in
our day by Joseph Conrad in his earlier novels, and a
gift of supreme importance, for upon it the whole weight
of the building depends. Once believe in Chaucer's young
men and women and we have no need of preaching or protest.
We know what he finds good, what evil; the less said the
better. Let him get on with his story, paint knights and
squires, good women and bad, cooks, shipmen, priests, and
we will supply the landscape, give his society its belief,
its standing towards life and death, and make of the journey to Canterbury a spiritual pilgrimage.

This simple faithfulness to his own conceptions was
easier then than now in one respect at least, for Chaucer
could write frankly where we must either say nothing or
say it slyly. He could sound every note in the language
instead of finding a great many of the best gone dumb
from disuse, and thus, when struck by daring fingers,
giving off a loud discordant jangle out of keeping with
the rest. Much of Chaucer - a few lines perhaps in each

of the Tales - is improper and gives us as we read it the
strange sensation of being naked to the air after being
muffled in old clothing. And, as a certain kind of humour
depends upon being able to speak without self-consciousness of the parts and functions of the body, so with the
advent of decency literature lost the use of one of its
limbs. It lost its power to create the Wife of Bath,
Juliet's nurse, and their recognisable though already
colourless relation, Moll Flanders. Sterne, from fear of
coarseness, is forced into indecency. He must be witty,
not humorous; he must hint instead of speaking outright.
Nor can we believe, with Mr. Joyce's 'Ulysses' before us,
that laughter of the old kind will ever be heard again.

> But, lord Christ! When that it remembreth me
> Up-on my yowthe, and on my Iolitee,
> It tikleth me aboute myn herte rote.
> Unto this day it doth myn herte bote
> That I have had my world as in my tyme.

The sound of that old woman's voice is still.
But there is another and more important reason for the
surprising brightness, the still effective merriment of
the 'Canterbury Tales'. Chaucer was a poet; but he never
flinched from the life that was being lived at the moment
before his eyes. A farmyard, with its straw, its dung,
its cocks and its hens, is not (we have come to think) a
poetic subject; poets seem either to rule out the farmyard entirely or to require that it shall be a farmyard
in Thessaly and its pigs of mythological origin. But
Chaucer says outright:

> Three large sowes hadde she, and namo,
> Three kyn, and eek a sheep that highte Malle;

or again,

> A yard she hadde, enclosed al aboute
> With stikkes, and a drye ditch with-oute.

He is unabashed and unafraid. He will always get close
up to his object - an old man's chin -

> WIth thikke bristles of his berde unsofte,
> Lyk to the skin of houndfish, sharp as brere;

or an old man's neck -

> The slakke skin aboute his nekke shaketh
> Whyl that he sang;

and he will tell you what his characters wore, how they
looked, what they ate and drank, as if poetry could handle
the common facts of this very moment of Tuesday, the sixteenth day of April, 1387, without dirtying her hands. If
he withdraws to the time of the Greeks or the Romans, it
is only that his story leads him there. He has no desire
to wrap himself round in antiquity, to take refuge in age,
or to shirk the associations of common grocer's English.

   Therefore when we say that we know the end of the journey, it is hard to quote the particular lines from which
we take our knowledge. Chaucer fixed his eyes upon the
road before him, not upon the world to come. He was
little given to abstract contemplation. He deprecated,
with peculiar archness, any competition with the scholars
and divines:

> The answere of this I lete to divynis,
> But wel I woot, that in this world grey pyne is.

> What is this world? What asketh men to have?
> Now with his love, now in the colde grave
> Allone, withouten any companye.

> O cruel goddes, that governe
> This world with binding of your worde eterne,
> And wryten in the table of athamaunt
> Your parlement, and your eterne graunt,
> What is mankinde more un-to yow holde
> Than is the sheepe, that rouketh in the folde?

Questions press upon him; he asks questions, but he is
too true a poet to answer them; he leaves them unsolved,
uncramped by the solution of the moment, and thus fresh
for the generations that come after him. In his life,
too, it would be impossible to write him down a man of
this party or of that, a democrat or an aristocrat. He
was a staunch churchman, but he laughed at priests. He
was an able public servant and a courtier, but his views
upon sexual morality were extremely lax. He sympathised
with poverty, but did nothing to improve the lot of the
poor. It is safe to say that not a single law has been
framed or one stone set upon another because of anything
that Chaucer said or wrote; and yet, as we read him, we
are absorbing morality at every pore. For among writers
there are two kinds: there are the priests who take you
by the hand and lead you straight up to the mystery;
there are the laymen who imbed their doctrines in flesh
and blood and make a complete model of the world without
excluding the bad or laying stress upon the good.

Wordsworth, Coleridge, and Shelley are among the priests;
they give us text after text to be hung upon the wall,
saying after saying to be laid upon the heart like an
amulet against disaster -

Farewell, farewell, the heart that lives alone

He prayeth best that loveth best
All things both great and small

- such lines of exhortation and command spring to memory
instantly. But Chaucer lets us go our ways doing the
ordinary things with the ordinary people. His morality
lies in the way men and women behave to each other. We
see them eating, drinking, laughing, and making love, and
come to feel without a word being said what their standards are and so are steeped through and through with their
morality. There can be no more forcible preaching than
this where all actions and passions are represented, and
instead of being solemnly exhorted we are left to stray
and stare and make out a meaning for ourselves. It is
the morality of ordinary intercourse, the morality of the
novel, which parents and librarians rightly judge to be
far more persuasive than the morality of poetry.
   And so, when we shut Chaucer, we feel that without a
word being said the criticism is complete; what we are
saying, thinking, reading, doing, has been commented
upon. Nor are we left merely with the sense, powerful
though that is, of having been in good company and got
used to the ways of good society. For as we have jogged
through the real, the unadorned country-side, with first
one good fellow cracking his joke or singing his song and
then another, we know that though this world resembles,
it is not in fact our daily world. It is the world of
poetry. Everything happens here more quickly and more
intensely, and with better order than in life or in prose;
there is a formal elevated dullness which is part of the
incantation of poetry; there are lines speaking half a
second in advance what we were about to say, as if we read
our thoughts before words cumbered them; and lines which
we go back to read again with that heightened quality,
that enchantment which keeps them glittering in the mind
long afterwards. And the whole is held in its place, and
its variety and divagations ordered by the power which
is among the most impressive of all - the shaping power,
the architect's power. It is the peculiarity of Chaucer,
however, that though we feel at once this quickening, this
enchantment, we cannot prove it by quotation. From most
poets quotation is easy and obvious; some metaphor

suddenly flowers; some passage breaks off from the rest.
But Chaucer is very equal, very even-paced, very unmeta-
phorical. If we take six or seven lines in the hope that
the quality will be contained in them it has escaped.

> My lord, ye woot that in my fadres place,
> Ye dede me strepe out of my povre wede,
> And richely me cladden, o your grace
> To yow broghte I noght elles, out of drede,
> But feyth and nakedness and maydenhede.

In its place that seemed not only memorable and moving
but fit to set beside striking beauties. Cut out and
taken separately it appears ordinary and quiet. Chaucer,
it seems, has some art by which the most ordinary words
and the simplest feelings when laid side by side make
each other shine; when separated, lose their lustre.
Thus the pleasure he gives us is different from the pleasure that other poets give us, because it is more closely
connected with what we have ourselves felt or observed.
Eating, drinking, and fine weather, the May, cocks and
hens, millers, old peasant women, flowers - there is a
special stimulus in seeing all these common things so
arranged that they affect us as poetry affects us, and
are yet bright, sober, precise as we see them out of
doors. There is a pungency in this unfigurative language; a stately and memorable beauty in the undraped
sentences which follow each other like women so slightly
veiled that you see the lines of their bodies as they go -

> And she set down hir water pot anon
> Biside the threshold in an oxe's stall.

And then, as the procession takes its way, out from behind
peeps the face of Chaucer, in league with all foxes,
donkeys, and hens, to mock the pomps and ceremonies of
life - witty, intellectual, French, at the same time
based upon a broad bottom of English humour.

43.   JOHN MATTHEWS MANLEY, FROM ART TO NATURE

1926

J.M. Manly (1865-1940), educated at Harvard University,

was Professor of English in the University of Chicago,
1898-1933. In collaboration with Professor Edith Rickert,
and other helpers, he edited 'The Canterbury Tales' from
all the MSS., and published other fruitful scholarly work.
His British Academy lecture on Chaucer and the Rhetoricians was one of his most influential writings, and opened
up an important new vein in Chaucer scholarship and criticism. Manly's criticism is an essentially Romantic one
of the poet escaping from art to nature, and so echoes
the opinions of many other critics of this period, but it
brings new information and historical interest, if also
dubious statistics. The lecture is here reprinted almost
in entirety by permission of the British Academy from 'The
Proceedings of the British Academy', 1926, pp. 96-113.

Are we to infer that [Chaucer] regarded rhetorical theories in general only as objects of ridicule and, like the
author of Hudibras in a later age, held that

> All a rhetorician's rules
> Teach nothing but to name his tools?

There are a score of other passages in which he or the
characters through whom he speaks profess to care little
and know nothing about rhetoric. Says the Franklin:

> I lerned never rethoric certeyn;
> Thing that I speke, it mote be bare and pleyn.
> I sleep never on the Mount of Pernaso
> Ne lerned Marcus Tullius Scithero.
> Colours ne knowe I none, withouten drede,
> But swiche colours as growen in the mede,
> Or elles swiche as men dye or peynte.
> Colours of rethoryk been to me queynte.

In like manner the Host says contemptuously to the Clerk
of Oxenford:

> Youre termes, youre colours, and youre figures,
> Keepe hem in stoor til so be ye endite
> Heigh style, as whan that men to kynges write.

With most writers, medieval or modern, such passages would
be conclusive as to the writer's scorn of rhetoricians
and rhetorical theory, but the interpretation of Geoffrey
Chaucer is not so simple a matter. One is not always safe
in taking his words as having only their plain and obvious

meanings. When, for example, he denies the Summoner's
view that the archdeacon's curse need not be dreaded by
any one who was willing to pay, and says:

>   Of cursing oghte ech gilty man him drede,
>   For curs wol slee, right as assoillyng saveth,

many scholars think he was speaking ironically and meant
that neither curse nor absolution had any validity. And
certainly the humorous citation by Chauntecleer and Pertelote of 'Daun Catoun', and 'the hooly doctour Augustyn,
or Bocce or the bishop Bradwardyn' does not imply any
lack of respect for those eminent authorities. Moreover,
in the passages adduced above from the Host and the Franklin, it is clear that we have the views of those two
characters, not the views of Chaucer himself, for the
Clerk responds to the admonition of the Host not only by
telling a tale he had learned from that excellent rhetorician Francis Petrarch, but by delivering a panegyric on
Petrarch's 'heigh style' and 'rethoryke sweete'; and the
very terms of the Franklin's disclaimer of rhetorical
skill are derived from that most rhetorical of Latin
poets, Persius, no doubt through the medium of some
medieval treatise on rhetoric.

To any student of his technique, Chaucer's development
reveals itself unmistakably, not as progress from crude,
untrained native power to a style and method polished by
fuller acquaintance with rhetorical precepts and more
sophisticated models, but rather as a process of gradual
release from the astonishingly artificial and sophisticated art with which he began and the gradual replacement
of formal rhetorical devices by methods of composition
based upon close observation of life and the exercise of
the creative imagination. His growth in artistic methods
and in artistic power - a growth unequalled so far as I
am aware among medieval authors - seems inexplicable unless we admit that he had thought long and deeply upon
the principles of composition, the technique of diction
and phrasing, methods of narration, description, and
characterization, and numberless other details of the
writer's art. The astonishing advance from the thin
prettiness of the 'Boke of the Duchesse' to the psycho-
logic depth of 'Troilus and Criseyde', the swift tragic
power of the 'Pardoner's Tale', the rollicking exuberance
of the tales of the Miller and the Reeve, the matchless
humour of the first half of the 'Summoner's Tale', and
the incomparable portraiture of the 'Prologue' is incon-
ceivable as mere vegetative growth. The great debt of
Chaucer to the Italians - and I suspect that his debt to

Dante was as great as that to either Petrarch or Boccaccio
- was perhaps not so much because they furnished new
materials and new models for imitation, as because they
stimulated his powers of reflection by forms and ideals of
art different from those with which he was familiar.

Without arguing this point, I shall merely suggest
certain evidences of his fondness for experimentation.
Unfortunately - or perhaps fortunately - most of his early
writings have perished. The balades, roundels, virelayes,
and other hymns to the god of Love testified to in 'The
Legend of Goode Women' are gone, but two of the extant
minor poems are obviously experimental. The fragment
entitled 'A Compleynte to his Lady', possibly written when
he was in search of a suitable form for narrative verse,
preserves an experiment in *terza rima*, the measure of
Dante's great poem. The much discussed and little understood 'Anelida and the False Arcite' seems also purely an
experiment in versification and is of interest, chiefly
if not solely, because the formal Complaint is an even
more remarkable *tour de force* in rhyming than the famous
translations from Sir Otes de Granson.

In investigating the sources of Chaucer's notions of
literature and his conceptions of style, scholars have
hitherto discussed only the writings of other authors
which may have served as models for imitation. The possibility of his acquaintance with formal rhetorical
theory and the precepts of rhetoricians has not been considered, notwithstanding the hint that might have been
derived from the allusion to Gaufred de Vinsauf and the
other passages on rhetoric scattered through his works.
Even *a priori* there would seem to be a high probability
that Chaucer was familiar with the rhetorical theories of
his time, that he had studied the text-books and carefully
weighed the doctrines. Whatever modern scholars may have
said of the errors in his references and the shallowness
of his classical learning - and there are few of his
critics whose errors are less numerous than his - he was
a man of scholarly tastes and of considerable erudition.
His works bear witness to no small reading in astronomy
and astrology, in alchemy, in medicine, and in philosophy
and theology, as well as in the classical authors current
in his day. The ancient tradition that he was educated,
in part at any rate, in the law school of the Inner Temple
has recently been shown to be possible, if not highly probable. The education given by the inns of court seems to
have been remarkably liberal. What more likely than that
the formal study of rhetoric not only was included in his
academic curriculum, as one of the Seven Arts, but also
occupied much of his thought and reflection in maturer
years?

What, then, was medieval rhetoric? Who were its principal authorities in Chaucer's time? And what use did
Chaucer make of methods and doctrines unmistakably due to
the rhetoricians?

To the first two questions satisfactory answers can be
readily given. Professor Edmond Faral has recently printed the chief rhetorical texts of the thirteenth and
fourteenth centuries, with illuminating biographical and
bibliographical notes and excellent summaries of the doctrines. To answer the third question fully would require
a volume, but a provisional view of the matter can be
obtained from a rapid survey of Chaucer's best-known work.

Fortunately for our inquiry, the Middle Ages knew only
one rhetorical system and drew its precepts from few and
well-known sources. Moreover, there was little development of the doctrines or variety in the mode of presentation. The principal sources of the doctrines were three:
the two books of Cicero entitled 'De Inventione', the four
books entitled 'De Rhetorica, ad Herennium', and the
Epistle of Horace to Piso. Treatises based upon these
were not uncommon in the earlier Middle Ages, but after
the beginning of the thirteenth century the practical
spirit of the time tended in the universities to substitute instruction in letter writing and the *artes dictami-
nis* for the more theoretical and supposedly less useful
study of general rhetorical principles. It is perhaps
for this reason that the treatises of Matthieu de Vendôme
and Gaufred de Vinsauf, written early in the thirteenth
century, retained their vogue in the time of Chaucer.
These treatises are the 'Ars Versificatoria' of Matthieu,
and the 'Documentum de Arte Versificandi' and the 'Nova
Poetria' of Gaufred. The first two are prose treatises,
carefully defining and discussing all processes and terms
and illustrating them by examples, in part drawn from
earlier writers, such as Virgil, Horace, Ovid, Statius,
and Sidonius, and in part composed by the rhetorician
himself, either to show his skill or to pay off a grudge.
For example, Matthieu is tireless in the composition of
verses attacking the red-haired rival whom he calls Rufus;
Gaufred, illustrating the beauties of *circumlocutio*, says
it is of special value when we wish to praise or diffame
a person: thus if any one were speaking of William de
Guines, the disreputable butler of the king, he might,
instead of his name, more elegantly use this circumlocution, *Regis ille pincerna, pudor et opprobrium, pincern-
arum faex, et inquinamentum domus regiae.*

The doctrine taught by these two authorities, the
common medieval doctrine, falls logically and naturally
into three main divisions or heads: [1] arrangement or

organization; [2] amplification and abbreviation; [3] style
and its ornaments.

Of arrangement they had little to say, and that little
was purely formal and of small value. They treated mainly
of methods of beginning and ending, distinguishing certain
forms as natural and others as artificial. Artificial
beginnings consisted either of those which plunge *in
medias res* or set forth a final situation before narrating
the events that led up to and produced it, or of those in
which a *sententia* (that is, a generalization or a proverb)
is elaborated as an introduction, or an *exemplum* (that is,
a similar case) is briefly handled for the same purpose.
It will be readily recognized that all these varieties of
beginnings are in familiar use at the present day; and,
curiously enough, in recent years writers for the popular
magazines have shown a special fondness for beginning with
an elaborately developed *sententia*.

We have not time to-day for a detailed examination of
Chaucer's methods of beginning, but this is hardly necessary. The moment one undertakes a survey of his poetry in
the light of rhetorical theory, one is struck by the elaborate artifice of its beginnings and the closeness of
their agreement with rhetorical formulae. This artificiality has long been recognized but has been mistakenly
ascribed to the influence of the poems upon which he drew
for his materials. His French sources, however, are
hardly responsible for these elaborate beginnings; they
furnish only the raw materials which Chaucer puts together
in accordance with the instructions of his masters in
rhetoric. The apparent simplicity with which the 'Boke of
the Duchesse' begins disappears under examination: the
reader is led through several long and tortuous corri-
dors - totalling one-third of the poem - before he
arrives at the real subject, which in turn is developed
with amazing artificiality. The long failure of the
mourning knight to make clear the nature of his loss may
be regarded as an expanded form of the rhetorical figure
called *occupatio*.

The 'Parlement of Foules' admirably illustrates the
method of beginning with a *sententia*:

The lyf so short, the craft so long to lerne.

This is expanded into two seven-line stanzas. Then comes,
not the narrative itself, but a preliminary narrative,
interspersed with various rhetorical devices, including
generalizations, an apostrophe, and an outline of
Cicero's 'Somnium Scipionis', in all 119 lines, before the
story proper begins.

This method is even more elaborately developed in the 'Hous of Fame'. In fact the poet is within twenty lines of the end of Book I before he begins to tell his story. There are sixty-five lines on dreams, sixty-five more of invocation, and more than 350 telling in outline the entirely unnecessary story of Dido and Aeneas.

Even when the narrative begins in a natural manner, as in 'Anelida and Arcite', the poem is given an artificial character by prefixing an invocation or by some other rhetorical device. The beginning of the 'Legend of Goode Women' combines the methods of *sententia* and *exemplum*: our belief in the joys and pains of heaven and hell, says the poet, is based, not upon experience, but upon the acceptance of the sayings of 'these olde wise'; in like manner we must accept the testimony of books - those treasuries of wisdom - about the existence of good women, though we have never known them. A few of the separate legends begin inartificially, but it was not until late in his career that Chaucer developed the method of beginning used with such masterly skill in the tales of Miller, Reeve, Summoner, and Pardoner.

Methods of ending are treated by the rhetoricians even more summarily than beginnings, the preferred forms being the employment of a proverb or general idea, an *exemplum,* or a brief summary. Chaucer is fond of some sort of explicit application of his stories. In the 'Reeve's Tale' this takes the form of a proverb:

And therfore this proverbe is seyd ful sooth
Him thar nat wene wel that yvele dooth:
'A gylour shal hymself bigyled be.'

And the 'Manciple's Tale' ends in a stream of proverbs and proverbial sayings. But the more common form of application is a generalization or an exclamatory comment. Very common also is the ending summarizing the situation at the end of the tale. On the other hand, notwithstanding Chaucer's fondness for *exempla,* the *exemplum*-ending is very rare; perhaps the only instance, and that a doubtful one, is in the 'Friar's Tale':

Herketh this word, beth war, as in this cas:
'The leoun sit in his awayt alway
To sle the innocent, if that he may.'

Peculiar to Chaucer are the references to other writers for further information - as in several of the legends - and the triple *demande d'amours* with which the 'Franklin's Tale' ends.

The technical means of passing from the beginning to the body of the work - *prosecutio*, as it is called - are treated with much formality by Gaufred, though he remarks with great good sense that the prime requisite is to get on with the subject: *In ipsa continuatione, primum est continuare*.

In Chaucer, after a rhetorical beginning, the transition to the narrative itself is usually clearly and formally indicated; so, for example, in 'Troilus and Criseyde':

For now wol I gon streight to my matere.

The amount of attention devoted by the rhetoricians to the second main division, that of amplification, is to the modern reader surprising, but it results quite naturally from the purely mechanical character of the art of rhetoric as conceived by them. To them the problems of composition were not problems of the creative imagination but problems of 'fine writing' - *l'art de bien dire*. They had no conception of psychological processes or laws. The questions they raised were not questions of methods by which the writer might most perfectly develop his conception or of the means by which he might convey it to his audience. The elaborate system of technical devices was discussed only with reference to the form and structure of each device, never with reference to its emotional or aesthetic effects. As the rhetoricians conceived the matter, if a writer had something new to say, rhetoric was unnecessary; the novelty of the material relieved him of any concern for its form. But alas! this situation seldom arose. Practically everything had already been said. All the tales had been told, all the songs had been sung, all the thoughts of the mind and feelings of the heart had been expressed. The modern writer, they held, could only tell a thrice-told tale, only echo familiar sentiments. His whole task was one of finding means and methods of making the old seem new. He might therefore well begin his task of composition by choosing some familiar but attractive text - some tale, or poem, or oration, or treatise - or by making a patchwork of pieces selected from many sources. His problem would be that of renewing the expression and especially of making it more beautiful - *ornatior* is the common term.

Let no one scoff at this method as incapable of producing interesting and attractive writing. It has been practised very commonly by writers in all lands and epochs. It is recommended and taught in a widely used series of French text-books. It is the method recently

revealed as pursued by that most charming of stylists,
Anatole France, and is perhaps the only method by which he
or Laurence Sterne could have produced such effects as
they achieved.

Medieval rhetoricians assume that the writer, having
chosen his subject, will find his material either too
great or too small for his purpose. His problem will
almost necessarily be one of amplification or abbreviation. The methods of amplifying and abbreviating are
derived from the technique of style. They are therefore
dealt with in their proper places when style and its ornaments are under discussion, but for the sake of clearness
they are also expounded elaborately with special reference
to their uses and values as means of amplification and
abbreviation.

The principal means of amplification are six - some
writers say eight:

Description, though perhaps not the most important, may
be named first, as receiving fullest attention from both
Matthieu de Vendôme and Gaufred de Vinsauf. Elaborate
patterns and formulas are given for describing persons,
places, things, and seasons. If the description applies
to externals, the features to be described are enumerated
and the order in which they are to be taken up is strictly
specified; if it concerns a character, the characteristics
to be mentioned are listed, and those appropriate to each
sex, age, social status, employment, temperament, and
career are set forth in detail. Specimens are given to
illustrate the doctrines. These descriptions are not,
like those in Chaucer's later work, determined by the
requirements of the situation in which they occur. Their
use is purely conventional, for the purpose of amplifying
the material and their construction is purely mechanical.
They are merely opportunities for the writer to display
his rhetorical training. It is very enlightening to compare Chaucer's later descriptions - such, for example, as
those of Alysoun and Absalon in the 'Miller's Tale'- with
the early ones; for example, with that of the Duchess
Blanche, which, with the exception of one or two possibly
realistic touches, is nothing more than a free paraphrase
of lines 563-597 of the 'Nova Poetria', composed by
Gaufred de Vinsauf as a model for the description of a
beautiful woman. The features described in the two passages are the same, they are taken up in the same order,
and the same praise is given to each. The resemblance is
still further heightened by the fact that, like Chaucer,
Gaufred declines to guess at the beauties hidden by the
robe - a trait hitherto regarded as characteristically
Chaucerian.

There seems little doubt, indeed, that Chaucer's
character sketches, widely as they later depart from the
models offered by the rhetoricians, had their origins in
them. An American scholar has recently attempted to show
that Chaucer derived them from the treatises on Vices and
Virtues, with their descriptions of character types. The
possibility of an influence from this source I will neither deny nor discuss, but the specimen sketches given by
the rhetoricians seem entirely sufficient to account for
Chaucer's interest in this type of description.

The next most important device was digression, of
which two subdivisions were recognized: first, digression
to another part of the same subject, anticipating a scene
or an event which in regular course would come later;
second, digression to another subject. Digression may
obviously be made in many ways and may include many special rhetorical devices. Prominent among the special
forms are the development of a *sententia* and the introduction of *exempla,* illustrating the matter in hand.
These two devices are of the utmost importance for Chaucer
in particular and for the Middle Ages in general. The
temper of the Middle Ages being distinctly practical and
its literary valuations being determined, not by the cri-
teria of art, but by those of edification, *sententiae,*
proverbs, and *exempla* were used with an ardour now difficult to appreciate. The use of *exempla* was strongly
inculcated by the rhetoricians. Matthieu de Vendôme
urges the writer to provide an abundance of *exempla.* With
an amusing anticipation of the Wife of Bath's remark,

> I hold a mouses herte not worth a leek
> That hath but oon hole for to sterte to,

he declares: '*Etenim mus intercipitur facile muscipulae
detrimentis, cui propinat refugium crepido singularis*'.
But the precepts of the rhetoricians on this point had
already been heeded by other writers, and in Chaucer's
poems it is difficult to separate the direct influence of
rhetorical theory from that of the practice of Guillaume
de Machaut, whose first use of *exempla* was in his 'Dit de
l'Alerion' and whose later use of them gave them a vogue
attested by the imitation of all his successors. Chaucer
was unfortunately as much seduced by this astonishing fad
as was any of the French imitators of Machaut. They are
familiar from the series of twenty-one consecutive instances in the 'Franklin's Tale' and the humorous accumulation
of them in the controversy between the Cock and the Hen.

Third in importance among the devices of amplification
may be placed apostrophe, with its rhetorical colours

exclamatio, conduplicatio, subiectio, and *dubitatio.* It
would be difficult to exaggerate the importance of apostrophe in medieval literature. Addresses to persons
living or dead, present or absent, to personified abstractions, and even to inanimate objects are to be found in
almost every composition with any pretensions to style
from the eleventh century onward; and a special form, the
Complainte, developed into one of the most widely cultivated types of literature. Chaucer's use of apostrophe is
so frequent that no examples need be cited. Almost every
tale contains from one to a dozen examples of it. Among
the colours, his favourites seem to be those known as
exclamatio - simply a passionate outcry addressed to some
person or thing present or absent - and *dubitatio,* that
is, a feigned hesitation what to say, a rhetorical ques-
tioning as to which of two or more expressions is appropriate to the idea and situation. Like Wordsworth's -

> O Cuckoo, shall I call thee Bird
> Or but a wandering Voice?

Fourth in order may come *prosopopeia* or *effictio,* the
device which represents as speaking persons absent or
dead, animals, abstractions, or inanimate objects.
Widely used for purposes of amplification, this figure
often furnished forth the whole of a piece of literature.
Examples are numerous. A charming one contemporary with
Chaucer is the *débat* in which Froissart represents his
dog and horse as discussing their master and the journeys
which he compels them to make with him. Chaucer uses it
briefly many times, and elaborately in the principal
scene of the 'Parlement of Foules'.

Less important than the foregoing are the devices of
periphrasis or *circumlocutio,* and its closely related
expolitio. *Circumlocutio* was highly regarded as one of
the best means, both of amplifying discourse and of raising commonplace or low ideas to a high stylistic level.
It is too familiar to require discussion, but Master
Gaufred seems not to have distinguished clearly between a
statement expanded for the mere sake of amplification and
one which expresses some important detail or phase of an
idea. For example, he calls the opening lines of Virgil's
'Aeneid' *circumlocutio* and declares, 'This is nothing else
than to say, I will describe Aeneas'. And, after quoting
from Boethius three lines of the metre beginning,

> O qui perpetua mundum ratione gubernas,

adds,

Quod nihil aliud est quam, 'O Deus'.

These remarks and the similar ones by Matthieu de Vendôme
will doubtless recall Chaucer's sly comment in the
'Franklin's Tale' on his own rhetorical description of
the end of the day:

> Til that the brighte sonne lost his hewe,
> For thorizonte hath reft the sonne his lyght, -
> This is as much to seye as it was nyght.

The colour *expolitio* includes the repetition of the
same idea in different words (one form of *interpretatio*)
and also the elaboration of an idea by adding the reasons
or authorities, pronouncing a generalization with or without reasons, discussing the contrary, introducing a simi-
litude or an *exemplum*, and drawing a conclusion. Although
these two figures are of minor importance, they nevertheless play a considerable part in the writings of Chaucer,
as of most other medieval authors.

Other devices for amplification existed, but I will
spare you even the enumeration of them.

Abbreviation is joined by the rhetoricians with
amplification, but is obviously of much less practical
interest. The medieval writer is, as a rule, not so much
concerned to abbreviate as to amplify. Master Gaufred,
however, instructs his readers that in treating a well-
worn subject the best means of creating an appearance of
novelty is to survey the whole subject and then run
quickly over the parts that predecessors have dwelt upon
and dwell upon parts they have neglected. The principal
means of abbreviation recommended are certain of the
figures of words: asyndeton, reduction of predication,
and the like. Chaucer's favourite methods are two:

[1] The use of absolute constructions - perhaps the
most striking and beautiful example of this is the opening line of the second book of the 'Troilus':

> Out of these blake wawes for to saile,
> O wind, o wind, the weder ginneth clere!

the second line furnishing an instance of the figure
called *epizeusis*.

[2] The figure called *occupatio*, that is, the refusal
to describe or narrate - a figure used with special frequency in 'The Squire's Tale', as for example:

> But for to telle yow al hir beaute
> It lyth nat in my tonge, nyn my konnyng

and

> I wol not tellen of hir straunge sewes

or

> I wol nat taryen yow, for it is pryme

or

> Who koude tellen yow the forme of daunces
> So unkouthe, and so fresshe countenaunces?...
> No man but Launcelot, and he is deed.

Into the vast and tangled jungle of the medieval treatment of Style and its Ornaments we cannot venture now. Its extent may be inferred from the fact that, notwithstanding the inclusion of very long specimens of apostrophe, prosopopeia, and description (328 lines in all) the portion of the 'Nova Poetria' devoted to the important subjects of 'Art in General', 'Organization', and 'Amplification and Abbreviation' occupies only 674 lines, whereas that devoted to the 'Ornaments of Style' occupies 1125. The tangle is suggested by the fact that there are recognized, defined, and discussed thirty-five colours, or figures of words, twenty figures of thought, and ten varieties of tropes, with nine more sub-varieties. These figures fall into two very distinct classes: first, those in which human emotion and aesthetic feeling have always found utterance - metaphor, simile, exclamation, rhetorical question, and the like; and second, a vast mass of highly artificial and ingenious patterns of word and thought, such as using the same word at the end of a line as at the beginning, heaped-up rhymes, and alliteration.

Like other writers in all ages, Chaucer makes extensive use of the first class of figures; of the artificial patterns he makes only a limited use, and that solely in highly rhetorical passages, like the 'Monk's Tale', certain parts of the 'Boke of the Duchesse', and in the apostrophes, exclamations, and *sententiae* of other serious compositions. The humorous tales, for which the rhetoricians forbid the use of *colores*, are entirely free from special rhetorical devices, with the single and striking exception of the 'Nun's Priest's Tale', a mock-heroic composition so full of rhetoric and so amusingly parodying the style of the 'Monk's Tale', which immediately preceded it, as to invite the suggestion that the 'high style' and its parody were purposely juxtaposed. Is it possible that Chaucer's desire to carry out this amusing contrast

explains the otherwise puzzling change of the Monk from
the spectacular huntsman and hard rider of the 'Prologue'
to the bookish pedant of the hundred lamentable tragedies
who greets our astonished ears when he is called upon for
a tale?

As no one ever pays any attention to statistics and
percentages, they rest the mind. This may therefore be a
fitting time to introduce a few. If we list the 'Canterbury Tales' according to the percentages of the larger
rhetorical devices which they contain, they form an interesting descending series, ranging from nearly 100 per
cent to 0. Highest, as might be expected, stands the
'Monk's Tale', with nearly 100 per cent of rhetoric. Next
comes the 'Manciple's Tale' with 61 per cent; then the
tales of the 'Nun's Priest' and the 'Wife of Bath' with
50 per cent. The tales of the 'Pardoner' and the 'Knight'
have 40 and 35 per cent respectively; while those of the
'Man of Law', the 'Doctor', the 'Prioress', the 'Franklin', the 'Second Nun', and the 'Merchant' fall between
30 and 20 per cent. The half-told tale of the 'Squire'
stands alone with 16 per cent, and slightly below it come
the tales of the 'Clerk' and the 'Canon's Yeoman', with
10 per cent. Quite in a class by themselves stand the
tales of the 'Reeve' and the 'Shipman', with about 5 per
cent of rhetoric, and those of the 'Miller', the 'Friar',
and the 'Summoner', in which the rhetorical devices do
not occupy more than 1 per cent of the text.

Although some of these percentages are just what we
should expect from the character of the tales and their
probable dates, some are rather surprising. It is
natural enough that the 'Monk's Tale' should head the
list, for it is professedly a collection of tragedies.
But that some of Chaucer's freest and most delightful
work should contain twice as much rhetoric as some of his
least inspired compositions is a puzzle that demands
investigation.

Let us begin by examining one of the least known and
least interesting of the tales, that of the 'Manciple'.
It is in fact so insignificant and so little read that I
cannot even assume that all of you recall the plot.
'When Phebus lived here on earth, we are told, he had a
fair young wife, whom he loved dearly, and a white Crow,
whom he had taught to speak. But the wife was unfaithful
and took a lover. This was observed by the Crow, who
upon Phebus's return home told him. Phebus in sorrow
and anger slew his wife, and then, repenting of his deed
and disbelieving the charge brought against her, plucked
the white feathers from the bird and doomed all crows to
be black.'

We may note in the first place that the tale is not
particularly appropriate to the Manciple or indeed to any
other of the pilgrims, and that no effort is made to adapt
it to him. It consists of 258 lines, of which 41 are
devoted to describing Phebus, his wife, and the crow, and
50 to telling the incidents of the story. The remaining
167 lines - 61 per cent of the tale - are patches of rhetoric. Even this high percentage is perhaps too low, for
the 25 lines of description devoted to Phebus are so conventional, so much in accordance with rhetorical formulas,
that they might fairly be added to our estimate of the
percentage of rhetoric. No effort was made by the author
to conceive any of his characters as living beings or to
visualize the action of the tale. The action, to be sure,
seems in itself unpromising as the basis of a masterpiece
of the story-teller's art, but so, if we consider them
closely, are the basic narratives of the 'Nun's Priest's
Tale' and the tales of the 'Miller', the 'Reeve', and the
'Friar'. If Chaucer had been as well inspired when he
wrote this tale as when he wrote his masterpieces, Phebus
might have been as real to us as the Oxford Carpenter or
the Miller of Trumpington, his wife as brilliant a bit of
colour as the Carpenter's wife, and the Crow as interesting a bird as Chaunticleer or Pertelote. But he developed
the tale, not imaginatively, but rhetorically. Instead
of attempting to realize his characters psychologically
and conceive their actions and words as elements of a
dramatic situation, he padded the tale with rhetoric.
Thus he thrust into it and around it 32 lines of sententiae, 36 of exempla, 18 of exclamatio, 14 of sermocinatio,
3 of technical transition, 17 of demonstratio, and 63 of
applicatio - all external and mechanical additions,
clever enough as mere writing, but entirely devoid of
life. If the tale had been written as a school exercise,
to illustrate the manner in which rhetorical padding could
be introduced into a narrative framework, the process of
composition could not have been more mechanical or the
results more distressing.
   But Chaucer was endowed with the temperament, not of
the rhetorician, but of the artist; and in some way he
arrived at the memorable discovery that the task of the
artist is not to pad his tales with rhetoric, but to conceive all the events and characters in the forms and activities of life. For this he was well prepared by native
endowment and by a habit of close observation which developed early and which redeems even his earliest poems from
entire banality. Owing to the loss of so much of his
prentice work and the uncertain chronology of what has
been preserved, we cannot trace in detail the displacement

of the older rhetorical by the new psychological methods.
But certain lines in the 'Hous of Fame' indicate that
when he was writing that poem he at least had formed an
idea of the new methods, even though he may long have continued in some respects under the dominance of the old.
The lines in question are in the proems of the second and
third books:

> O thought that wroot al that I mette,
> And in the tresorie it shette
> Of my brayn, now shal men se
> If any vertu in thee be;

and more specifically:

> And if, Divyne Vertu, thou
> Wilt helpe me to shewe now
> That in myn hede y-marked is.

These passages, although the first is translated from
Dante, seem to me to express Chaucer's growing conviction
that narration and description, instead of being mere
exercises in clever phrasing, depend upon the use of the
visualizing imagination.

But in spite of this recognition of the true method,
and in spite of his ability later in the 'Nun's Priest's
Tale' to parody the whole apparatus of medieval rhetoric,
Chaucer did not free himself at once - and perhaps never
entirely - of the idea that writing which pretended to
seriousness and elevated thought was improved by the presence of apostrophes and *sententiae* and *exempla,* as he
had been taught by the rhetoricians. Nor could it be
expected that he should. The whole weight of the medieval conception of literature was against him - the conception, I mean, that literature, like history, is of
value only in so far as it can be profitably applied to
the conduct of human life, a conception which not only
remained in full vigour through the Middle Ages and the
period we are accustomed to call the Renaissance, but
even now lies at the basis of much critical theory.

Chaucer's greatness arose from his growing recognition
that for him at least the right way to amplify a story
was not to expand it by rhetorical devices, but to conceive it in terms of the life which he had observed so
closely, to imagine how each of the characters thought
and felt, and to report how in this imaginative vision
they looked and acted. And if he felt obliged, as
apparently he still did, in writings of serious and
lofty tone, to supply *sententiae,* proverbs, *exempla,* and

other fruits of erudition, he came more and more to make
only a dramatic use of these rhetorical elements, that is,
to put them into the mouths of his *dramatis personae* and
to use only such as might fittingly be uttered by them.

It is this dramatic use of rhetorical devices which we
must learn to recognize in the later and more artistic
poems, and which must be taken into account in our examination of the percentages of rhetoric in the separate tales
of the Canterbury pilgrimage. The mere fact that the
percentage in two such masterpieces of narrative art as
the tales of the 'Nun's Priest' and the 'Wife of Bath'
is nearly twice as great as in the less successful tales
of the 'Man of Law' and the 'Doctor' would be very misleading, if taken without further investigation. But the
difference in manner of introduction and use appears
immediately and is of fundamental significance. In the
tales of the 'Doctor' and the 'Man of Law' the rhetoric
is prevailingly, indeed almost exclusively, used by the
narrator; that is, it is not incorporated and used dramatically but stands apart from the tale. There is even a
difference between the 'Doctor's Tale' and that of the
'Man of Law' in manner of handling. In the 'Man of Law's
Tale' the narrative is, for the most part, broken into
comparatively brief sections and the rhetoric of the
narrator is freely interspersed in the forms of *apostrophe, exclamatio, collatio, sententiae,* and *exempla,*
with various digressions on astrology. In the 'Doctor's
Tale', on the other hand, the narrative comes in a solid
block of 172 lines, preceded by 109 lines, all but 39 of
which are purely rhetorical utterances of the narrator,
and followed by 10 lines of rhetorical application. But
both stories are, as artistic compositions, pretty crude
and show no fusion of rhetorical elements. In the tales
of the 'Nun's Priest' and the 'Wife of Bath' the situation is very different. In the 'Nun's Priest's Tale',
although the rhetoric is scattered through the narrative
as in the 'Man of Law's Tale', it is not the external
comment of the narrator but the vitally dramatized utterance of speakers whose actions, and attitudes, and sentiments we accept as belonging to a world of poetic reality.
In the 'Wife of Bath's Tale' there are two main masses of
rhetorical devices: one of them is the famous oration on
'gentilesse', poverty, and age uttered by the Fairy Wife
to her humbled husband, the other is the long *exemplum* on
woman's inability to keep a secret, uttered by the garrulous Wife of Bath herself. But in the latter instance no
less than in the former the rhetoric is dramatic, is con-
formed to the character, and is motivated.

The tales of the 'Prioress' and the 'Second Nun' differ

very slightly in percentage of rhetorical devices or in
the placing of them. If we could isolate the tales - dis-
connect them from their narrators and the circumstances of
their telling - we should probably agree that they show the
same style of workmanship and may belong to the same
period, a comparatively early one. But the difference between them in effect is very great. Why is this? Apart
from the mere difference in appeal of the material of the
two stories, is it not because in the one tale Chaucer has
failed to visualize or to make his readers see the principal characters - Cecilia, Valerian, and Pope Urban remain
to him and to us mere names - whereas both he and we have
a vivid and charming picture of the little choir boy as he
goes singing to his death? Is it not also because through
some freak of chance the Second Nun herself is a mere name
in the 'Prologue' and is not mentioned at all in the pilgrimage, whereas both by the portrait in the 'Prologue' and
by the little episode of conversation with the Host the
Prioress is endowed with lasting beauty and sympathetic
appeal? Chaucer himself seems to have felt this. When the
Prioress's tale is ended he tells us of its profound effect
upon the whole party including himself; after the other
tale he says, drily,

> When toold was al the lif of Seint Cecile
> Er we had ridden fully five mile,

we were overtaken by two men.
    The tales of the 'Franklin' and the 'Merchant' differ
only slightly in percentage of rhetorical devices from
those of the 'Prioress' and the 'Second Nun', but in the
placing and handling of these devices, as well as in other
respects, they seem to belong to a much later period of
Chaucer's workmanship. The *dramatis personae* are vividly
conceived and the action is clearly visualized. Both
tales show, however, the persistence of the rhetorical
habit and training. In the 'Merchant's Tale' most of the
rhetoric is introduced dramatically as forming the
speeches of January and his advisers, but there is a long
undramatic passage - inappropriate either to the Merchant
or to the clerical narrator for whom the tale appears to
have been originally composed. In the 'Franklin's Tale' a
fine story finely told is nearly spoiled by one hundred
lines of rhetorical *exempla*. The fact that they are put
into the mouth of Dorigen in her complaint against Fortune
indicates that Chaucer was trying to motivate them dramatically. But what reader, modern or medieval, would not have
been more powerfully and sympathetically affected if Chaucer, with the psychological insight displayed in 'Troilus

and Criseyde', had caused his distressed and desperate heroine to express the real feelings appropriate to her character and situation?

It may be noted that the tales showing a low percentage of formal rhetorical devices are, with a single exception, humorous tales and all are tales which on other grounds are regarded as of late date. The exception is the 'Clerk's Tale', a pretty close translation from Petrarch. The small amount of rhetoric added by Chaucer in making this translation from Petrarch is in curious contrast to the large amount added in translating the 'Man of Law's Tale' from Trivet. Can it be that his rivalry with Gower in the latter case was responsible for the rhetoric?

The absence of rhetorical devices from the humorous tales may be due in part to the specific declaration of the rhetoricians that rhetorical ornament of all sorts should be strictly excluded from such tales. But surely Chaucer's growing power of artistry, his vast observation of life, and his newly devised method of imaginative reconstruction of the scenes, characters, and events of his stories gave him such a wealth of significant detail that there was no need and no space for the older methods of amplification. *Sententiae* are reduced to single lines, mostly proverbs; *exempla* to passing allusions; apostrophes and exclamations to the briefest of utterances. For it is not only in the humorous tales that his advanced method is displayed. The most tragic of them, the 'Pardoner's Tale' of the three roysterers who sought Death, is as vividly imagined as the tales of the Miller and the Reeve, and the long passages of rhetoric, placed between the opening twenty lines, which so wonderfully create background and atmosphere, and the narrative itself, are thoroughly explained and justified by their function as part of the Pardoner's sermon.

The survey we have made of Chaucer's work, hasty as it has necessarily been, has, I think, shown that he began his career, not merely as a disciple and imitator of a thoroughly artificial school of writing, but as a conscious exploiter of the formal rhetoric taught by the professional rhetoricians, and that it was only gradually and as the result of much thought and experiment that he replaced the conventional methods of rhetorical elaboration by those processes of imaginative construction which give his best work so high a rank in English literature. To treat his poems as if they all belonged to the same stage of artistic development and represented the same ideals of art is to repeat the error so long perpetrated by students of Shakespeare.

44.   MARIO PRAZ, CHAUCER THE MERCHANTMAN

1927

Mario Praz (born 1896), distinguished Italian scholar and
critic of literature and art, was Professor of English
Language and Literature in the University of Rome, 1934-
66.   The valuable scholarly examination of Chaucer's debt
to the great Italian writers Dante, Boccaccio and Petrarch reveals a Chaucer already established in the tradition of English nineteenth-century criticism: a placid
bourgeois, incapable of conceiving Dante's greatness; a
simple medieval mind hungering for quotation, and incapable of presenting Criseyde with irony; but of a keen
dramatic genius.   Nevertheless Chaucer is indeed seen as
'Dante in English' - as much of Dante as English could
accommodate.   Boccaccio's influence is argued to be much
less significant than Dante's.   Chaucer's artistry is considered to be economical, concrete and domestic, though
Chaucer shows off his superficial learning; his interests
are in loyalty and morality; all very suitable to a trad-
ing nation.   The vivid spectacle of Italian life must also,
it is claimed, have sharpened Chaucer's sense of drama.
Reprinted from the 'Monthly Criterion', pp. 20-39, 131-7,
149-57 by permission of Doubleday & Co. Inc.

CHAUCER AND THE GREAT ITALIAN WRITERS
OF THE TRECENTO

(p. 20) Even among the safest Chaucerian scholars over-
subtlety proves sometimes to be a vice; we need not, then,
be surprised at the vagaries of the less safe source-
hunters.   Were the reading-public alive to a morbid curiosity about source-complexes, as it is admittedly about
sex-complexes, a publisher could find sufficient inducement to issue a selection of Chauceriana uniform with
H.L. Mencken's annual anthologies of Americana; and I am
not sure whether, after that, 'Americana' would still
bear the palm in the way of supreme nonsense writing.
      I am going to give only one instance of priceless
pettifogging interpretation, because it may serve as a
convenient introduction to my study of Italian influence
on Chaucer.   A contributor to 'The Nation' for October
20th, 1904, conjectured that the nineteen ladies following
the God of Love in the Prologue to the 'Legend of Good

Women' were suggested by the hundred and forty and four
thousand sealed out of every tribe of the children of
Israel, and the 'tras of wemen' by the great multitude
which no man could number standing before the throne and
before the Lamb in the seventh chapter of the Apocalypse!
J.L. Lowes, on the other hand, is quite justified in seeing in Chaucer's procession of ladies another instance of
the endlessly recurring convention, in the poems of the
Court of Love *genre*, of the band of lovers about the God
of Love, and proceeds to point out an accidental parallel
in Dante, ('Purgatorio', XXXII, 1, 38ff.). Now, the suggestion for the 'tras of wemen' comes actually from Dante,
as I am going to show, and it is strange that the source
should have escaped Lowes, who has gone deeper than any
one else in the study of Dante's influence on Chaucer.
The passage in the A-Prologue (1. 188ff.) of the 'Legend'
runs thus:

> And after hem [i.e., the God of Love] com of wemen
>   swich a tras
> That, sin that god Adam made of erthe,
> The thredde part of wemen, ne the ferthe,
> Ne wende I nat by possibilitee
> Hadden ever in this world y-be.

In the Ante-Hell Dante meets the spirits of the pusillani-
mous: they are preceded by a banner,

> E dietro le venia sì lunga tratta
> Di gente, ch'io non averei creduto
> Che morte tanta n'avesse disfatte. ('Inf.', III, 55-57)

> [And behind it came so long a train of people, that I
> could never have conceived that so many had been undone
> by death.]

Further on, in the same Canto, is mentioned Adam's sinful
offspring, *il mal seme d'Adamo*. The mention of Adam,
together with the use of the word *tras*, is a conclusive
test. The word *tras* is used only here by Chaucer in the
sense of 'train of people', and is obviously a close rendering of *tratta*. Moreover, the whole line 188 echoes
1. 55 in 'Inferno', III, and the word *tras*, as well as
tratta, occurs in rhyme. One could even push the investigation a little further, and guess why Chaucer was reminded of that passage in Dante. A few lines back Chaucer
describes the appearance of the God of Love (A-Prologue,
11, 163-165, 168):

> For sekirly his face shoon so brighte,
> That with the gleem a-stoned was the sighte;
> A furlong-wey I mighte him nat beholde....
> And aungellich his wenges gan he sprede.

The appearance of the God of Love has been modelled on
the appearance of the angel in the Second Canto of 'Purgatorio' (ll. 37-39, 34):

> Poi, come più e più verso noi venne
> L'uccel divino, più chiaro appariva;
> Per che l'occhio da presso nol sostenne....
> Vedi come l'ha dritte verso il cielo.

> [Anon, as the bird of heaven came ever towards us, he
> was more bright, so that, when near, mine eyes were
> overpowered....Mark how he has raised his wings towards
> heaven.]

And the skylark (l. 141ff.) had heralded the approach of
the God of Love thus:

> 'I see,' quod she, 'the mighty god of love!
> Lo! yond he cometh, I see his winges sprede!'

in the same way as Virgil had announced to Dante the
coming of the angel (l. 26ff.):

> Mentre che i primi bianchi apparser ali:
> Allor che ben conobbe il galeotto,
> Gridò: 'Fa, fa che le ginocchia cali:
> Ecco l'angel di Dio....'

> [...while the first white features revealed themselves
> as wings: when he clearly recognized the pilot, he
> cried: 'See, see thou bend thy knees, behold the angel
> of God....'](1)

Now the angel appears first to Dante and Virgil in the
form of a light approaching over the sea with such speed,
that no bird's flight could rival its motion (l. 16ff.):

> ...m'apparve...
> Un lume per lo mar venir si ratto,
> Che 'l mover suo nessun volar pareggia.

The speed of approach of the vessel of saved souls piloted
by the angel has reminded Chaucer at once of another
speedy approaching of spirits, precisely in that Canto of

the 'Inferno' which, containing the description of
Charon's boat ferrying the lost souls into Hell, is a
counterpart of the second Canto of the 'Purgatorio'. The
spirits of the cowards appear in the wake of

> ...una insegna
> Che girando correva tanto ratta,
> Che d'ogni posa mi parea indegna. ('Inf.', III, 52-54)

Possibly line 17 of 'Purgatorio', II, has brought about
the association of ideas. That line runs:

> Un lume per lo mar venir sì *ratto*.

Such a line is apt to recall instantaneously to one's
mind 'Inferno', III, 53:

> Che girando correva tanto *ratta*.

Both sense and sound are closely related in these two
lines. Finally the two 'fyry dartes, as the gledes rede',
which Love holds in hand, are his *insegna*, and they are
red as glowing embers, because the light approaching over
the sea, in the 'Purgatorio', was at first like the planet
Mars, when, at dawn, it glimmers red in the west above the
sea-level: 'Per li grossi vapor Marte rosseggia' ('Purg.',
II, 14).

The case of derivation I have just examined is safely
established, as I was saying, by the use of the word *tras*
corresponding in meaning, sound, and position to the
Dantesque word *tratta*. If one wished indeed to formulate
rules about Chaucer's borrowings, the first one should be:
in most of the cases Chaucer is following a source, he
betrays himself, so to say, by the use of some word
closely modelled on some of the foreign words of the text
he has either before his mind or before his eyes. Very
often, in 'Troilus and Criseyde', he takes his rhyme-words
over from the Italian original, the 'Filostrato'.(2)
Apart from the exceedingly frequent case of *Troie* rhyming
with either *joye* or *anoye*, in the final couplet of a
stanza, to be paralleled in Boccaccio's frequent rhyme of
Troia with *gioia* and *noia* in the same position, you find
there *descerne-eterne-werne* ('Tr.', III, st. 2), where the
'Filostrato' has, in the corresponding stanza (III, st.
75), *discerno-eterno; martire-desire* (IV, st. 117), to
reproduce *desiri-martiri* ('Fil.', IV, st. 96); *sentement-
argument* (IV, st. 169), echoing Boccaccio's *sentimento-
argomento* ('Fil.', IV, st. 119); *Diomede- (blede)* (V,
st. 3), modelled on *Diomede-(diede-vede)* ('Fil.', V, st.I);

and, most remarkable of all, *Monesteo-Rupheo* (IV, st. 8),
taken over bodily from Boccaccio's stanza 3 of Book IV.(3)
I call this last case very remarkable indeed, because one
would expect Chaucer to give to proper names the endings
used in English. But, in the field of proper names, con
sistency is the last thing to be expected from him: a
proper name, chiefly a classical one, appeals to him like
a spell, a magic formula, and apparently he does not dare
to subject it to the common laws of language. This point
ought to be kept in mind when I shall speak of Chaucer's
use of authorities. In another passage of 'Troilus' (V,
1. 1806) Chaucer spells *Achille* as he found it spelt in
the parallel Italian stanza ('Fil.', VIII, st. 27), in
the 'Hous of Fame' (1. 458) he uses the form *Lavyna*
(Lavinia), probably from Dante's *Lavina* ('Purg.', XVII,
37), and in the same poem Marsyas is spelt *Marcia*
(1. 1229) and made feminine, very likely through a confusion engendered by Dante's mention of Marcia, Cato's wife.
Apart from the borrowing of rhymes,(4) Chaucer's use of
words modelled on foreign ones he has found in his sources
could be abundantly illustrated. Sometimes his candour
goes so far as to borrow the foreign word, and then to
devote one or more lines to the explanation of it, as
when, after copying from Boccaccio the learned word *ambage*
('Fil.', VI, st. 17) he proceeds thus ('Tr.', V, st. 129):

> And but if Calkas lede us with ambages,
> That is to seyn, with double wordes slye,
> Swich as men clepe a word with two visages.

But this passage falls rather under the heading, 'display
of learning', of which I shall have to speak later on.
The word *ambages* is used only once by Chaucer, in connexion with Boccaccio's *ambage*: such is often the case of
borrowed foreign words with him. They are transferred
into English with just as much alteration in spelling as
is deemed sufficient to naturalize them; but they lack
vitality, they do not occur again, independent of their
source. Such is the case of *poeplissh (appetit)*=popular,
used in 'Tr.', IV, 1677, to translate Boccaccio's *(appet-
ito) popolesco* ('Fil.', IV, st. 165), of *palestral
(pleyes)* ('Tr.', V, 304), rendering Boccaccio's *palestral
(gioco)* ('Teseide', VII, st. 27), of *erratik (sterres)*
('Tr.', V, 1812), corresponding to *(stelle) erratiche* in
'Teseide', XI, st. 1, of *affect*, a characteristically
Dantesque word, used only in 'Troilus', III, 1393, in a
passage inspired by Dante, and of *revoken* used in the
sense of 'to recall' only in 'Troilus', III, 1118.
     As in other instances, *revoken* is here the sign-manual

of the author from whom Chaucer derives the entire passage; and the author, in the present case, which, so far
as I know, has escaped notice, is Boccaccio. The use of
that word, which is the Italian *rivocare* slightly dis-
guised, gives evidence that the episode of Troilus's
fainting at the sight of Criseyde crying, in Book Three,
is nothing else but a transferred episode of the Italian
poem, Book IV, when Troilus faints at learning that the
Trojans are willing to give up Criseyde to the Greeks. In
stanza 160 of the English poem Pandarus and Criseyde try
to revive Troilus:

> Therwith his pous and paumes of his hondes
> They gan to frote, and ek his temples tweyne;...
> Hym to *revoken* she did al hire peyne.

In stanza 19 of Book IV of the 'Filostrato', Priam and his
other sons try to recall to life Troilus:

> ...e ciascun si procaccia
> Di confortarlo, e le sue forze morte,
> Ora i polsi fragando, ed or la faccia
> Bagnandogli sovente...
> ...s'ingegnavan *rivocare*.

[And each one of them tries to comfort him, and now by
rubbing his wrists, now by wetting his face, they were
trying to *revoke* his dead spirits.]

Once the source established, it is easy to find out
other parallels in the same passage.
Of course in Book IV, when Chaucer's Troilus learns
that Criseyde must be delivered to the Greeks, he is sensible enough not to faint as in Boccaccio: he had already
made use of his fainting propensities in Book III, and he
had been left nothing to spare for the next opportunity.
Still, this is not entirely correct: something had been
spared in Book III, and now has come the moment to use it
up. Troilus at line 235 of Book IV appears:

> Ful lik a ded ymage, pale and wan

precisely as Boccaccio's fainting Troilus (IV, st. 20):

> E'l viso suo pallido, smorto...
> ...e più morta parea
> Che viva cosa.

[And his face pale, wan...seemed more a dead thing than
a living one.]

This last case illustrates well a curious practice of Chaucer's, which is usually described as his wonderful economy. Illustrations of the peculiar way Chaucer has of making use of his sources are so well-known and abundant that I must content myself with reminding you only of the most remarkable ones. So in the 'Knightes Tale' the soaring of Arcite's soul to heaven is not described, because Boccaccio's description of that journey had been already used with respect to the death of Troilus; in the 'Seconde Nonnes Tale' the *Invocatio ad Mariam* is taken from Dante, 'Paradiso', XXXIII, 1-9, but Dante's lines following the 9th, though no less worth imitating, are left out because they had already been used in 'Troilus', III, 1262ff., in a prayer to Venus, and the translation of Dante's l. 14 ('La tua benignità non pur socorre'), which occurs in both of Chaucer's passages, is differently worded in each case.(5) No doubt Chaucer must have been an excellent controller, since he knew so well how to husband his literary resources. No waste with him: to use a very homely and indecorous simile, I should say that he knew how to use the dripping, after he had roasted in an English fashion the foreign meat. Whenever, for instance, in 'Troilus' he leaves out a passage of the 'Filostrato', you may be sure that the passage will be turned to account in another connexion: you almost imagine him pronouncing Pandarus's words in Shakespeare's 'Troilus and Cressida': 'Let us cast away nothing, for we may live to have need of such a verse; we see it, we see it!' In the second book of 'Troilus' Chaucer does not relate the lovers' letters *in extenso*: is he going then to waste those letters? Not he. The time for them to be exploited comes only in Book Five, when Criseyde writes to Troilus her last letter. 'The letter of Criseyde has no counterpart in "Filostrato"' - runs the remark of the commentator. No counterpart in the corresponding passage of the story, but one has only to look up the letters in the 'Filostrato', Book Two, to recognize at once the model of Criseyde's last letter. Criseyde's beginning in 'Troilus', V (st. 228), is:

> How myght a wight in torment and in drede,
> And heleles, yow sende as yit gladnesse?

This is a close rendering of 'Filostrato', II, st. 96 (Troilus's letter):

> Come può quegli che in affanno è posto,
> In pianto grave e in istato molesto...
> Ad alcun dar salute?

[How might one who is dwelling with sorrow, heavy crying and troublesome plight...send gladness to anyone?]

And the closing line of the stanza:

Yow neyther sende ich herte may nor hele

is echoing

Qui da me salutata non sarai.

Next stanza (229) is modelled on a passage of Criseyde's
letter in Book Two of the 'Filostrato' (st. 122):

Youre lettres ful, the papir al ypleynted,
Conceyved hath myn hertes pietee;
I have ek seyn with teris al depeynted
Youre lettre.

I' ho avute....
Piene le carte della tua scrittura;
Nelle quai lessi la tua vita grama
Non senza doglia...
...e benché sian fregiate
Di lacrime, pur l'ho assai mirate.

[I have received your papers full of your writing, in
which I read of your miserable life not without compassion...and although they are decorated (*depeynted*)
with tears, still I have admired them very much.]

Finally, the conclusion of Criseyde's letter is derived
from stanza 126.
    Two other passages in 'Troilus' are of great interest
as illustrations of Chaucer's sense of economy. In the
'Filostrato', Book VII, st. 23-24, Troilus dreams of a
boar which tramples down Criseyde, then tears out her
heart with its tusks (*grifo*, i.e., snout: Root, in his
note to 'Troilus', V, 1233-43, translates it by 'claws',
obviously misled by *grifo* resembling in sound French
griffe, and entirely overlooking the fact that a boar is
not favoured with claws). Criseyde, in Boccaccio, seems
not to consider the treatment she receives at the hands
(Root's 'claws'!) of the boar as a pain, but rather as a
pleasure. Had Freud known of this dream, he would have
quoted it as a striking illustration of his theories. But
let us see now the use Chaucer has made of this dream. He
has split it up into two. On one hand he draws upon it
for Criseyde's dream in Book Two (st. 133): Criseyde

dreams that her heart is being torn out by an eagle which
replaces it in her breast with its own heart: 'of which
she nought agroos, ne no thyng smerte.' On the other
hand, in Book Five, st. 177-178, in the passage corresponding to 'Filostrato', VII, st. 23-24, Troilus dreams
of a boar 'with tuskes grete' which is kissing Criseyde.
Obviously Chaucer has distributed the different elements
of the one dream he found in Boccaccio into the two dreams
of his poem. But why an eagle in the first case? Was the
eagle suggested by *grifo*, by the same mistake into which
Root has fallen? The use by Chaucer of the word *claws*
seems to countenance this view. But another explanation
occurs to me. *Grifo*, in Italian, means not only 'snout',
but also 'griffin', and Chaucer must have been reminded of
Dante's *grifo* in the mystic pageant which takes place in
the Earthly Paradise ('Purg.', XXIX, 108, and foll.
Cantos). The griffin or *grifone* or *grifo* has a double
nature of eagle and lion: part of its limbs, in Dante, are
white. Chaucer's eagle is 'fethered whit as bon'. Moreover, in 'Purgatorio', XXXII, where the allegorical pageantry is still going on, an eagle rushes down with the
speed of a thunderbolt on the mystic tree, tears off its
bark, flowers and fresh leaves, and smites the triumphal
chariot with its full force: then it leaves the chariot
covered with its own plumage. The chariot undergoes a
wonderful transformation. Finally, in another Canto of
the 'Purgatorio' (IX) Dante dreams of another eagle,
which also comes down with the speed of a thunderbolt,
and snatches Dante up to the region of fire: an episode
Chaucer exploits in his 'Hous of Fame', as is well known.
Similar cases of associations of ideas in Chaucer seem to
point to the fact that the eagle has stolen into Criseyde's dream through a process not unlike the one here
described.

   To conclude about economy, Chaucer is so averse to
repetition that he does not even allow Boccaccio to
repeat himself. In Book Four of the 'Filostrato' (st.
120ff.), Troilus, believing Criseyde to be dead, un-
sheathes his sword in order to kill himself. In the
parallel passage in 'Troilus' (IV, st. 170) also Troilus
'his swerd anon out of his shethe he twighte, hym self to
slen'. So far, so good. But Boccaccio's Troilus is reck-
less, and in Book Seven (st. 33), on being aware of Criseyde's disloyalty, runs to a knife and tries to smite his
own breast with it. This will not do for Chaucer, and his
Troilus wisely avoids the monotony which would ensue from
attempting suicide a second time, when confronted with
Criseyde's falsehood. *Non bis in idem* seems to have been
Chaucer's motto.

The most interesting fact emerging from the study of
Chaucer's economy is the deliberate, conscious use he
makes of his sources. He succeeds in avoiding repetition
to such an extent as to lead one to postulate on his part
either a prodigious memory, or a constant consultation of
his authorities. Very likely the latter supposition hits
the mark. As in the case of the Clerk's tale, where no
doubt can be entertained, so in most of the other cases of
imitation Chaucer had the foreign text before his eyes.
To some of the foreign writers he had recourse every now
and then, but others, which were always within his reach,
supplied him with an inexhaustible mine of expressions and
suggestions. Amongst these latter, are to be ranked first
of all the two great epitomes of the poetry of the Middle
Ages: the 'Roman de la Rose' and the 'Divina Commedia'.
It is the merit of Prof. J.L. Lowes to have shown for the
first time how deep, widespread and constant has been the
influence of Dante upon Chaucer. While drawing on other
sources, Chaucer is now and then combining them with passages from those other two masterpieces of the Middle
Ages. For him, the least hint is sufficient to establish
at once a connexion between the text which forms his
immediate source and quotations from either the 'Roman de
la Rose' or the 'Divina Commedia': possibly he was so conversant with these two works, as to have them always in
the back of his mind: a fact which seems to suggest, if
not necessarily implies, that he had them by heart.

While he is imitating Boccaccio, he perceives at once
whenever the Italian author is reminiscent of Dante, and
he avails himself of the opportunity for drawing on the
better poet. Lowes has given several instances of this
proceeding, on which Ten Brink had already called attention. I will give only one example, the significance of
which reaches beyond the particular passage in question.
In the 'Filostrato', when Troilus learns that Criseyde
must be given up to the Greeks, he collapses like dead.
Boccaccio makes use of a Virgilian simile (IV, st. 18):

> Qual, poscia ch'è dall'aratro intaccato
> Ne' campi il giglio, per soverchio sole
> Casca ed appassa, e 'l bel color cangiato
> Pallido fassi....

> [As in the fields the lily, after it has been cut into
> by the plough, falls and withers through too much of
> sun, and its fair colour, changed, turns pale....]

The simile is one of the most widespread commonplaces in
western literatures: Byron also employs it when the

shipwrecked Don Juan faints on the shore of the Greek
island. Chaucer, as I have shown above, had already exploited the fainting of Troilus in Book Three, and he does
not repeat it here. Troilus here only becomes like a dead
image, pale and wan. But the floral simile, which Boccaccio has taken from Virgil, recalls to his mind another
simile derived also from decaying vegetation, a simile
used by Dante in that third Canto of the 'Inferno', on
which Chaucer has drawn several times: a Canto, moreover,
at the end of which Dante is overpowered by a sudden
earthquake and falls astounded like one mastered by sleep:
not unlike Boccaccio's Troilus. Chaucer replaces the
simile given in the 'Filostrato' by the Dantesque one:

> Come d'autonno si levan le foglie
> L'una appresso dell'altra, infin che il ramo
> Vede a la terra tutte le sue spoglie. ('Inf.', III,
> 112-14).

> And as in wynter leves ben beraft,
> Ech after other, til the tree be bare,
> So that ther nys but bark and braunche ilaft....
> ('Tr.', IV, st. 33).

Now Dante's lines, on their turn, are modelled on a
passage of Virgil's 'Aeneid'. This instance is very
characteristic of the relations between the several poets
concerned. What Virgil is to Dante, Dante is to Chaucer.
Chaucer is an individual illustration of a phenomenon
which was to become general in the Renaissance, when the
legacy of the classical world was handed over to Europe
through the medium of Italy.

My coupling the influence of the 'Roman de la Rose'
with that of the 'Divina Commedia' needs at once to be
qualified. Because, while the influence of the French
romance is not limited to scattered passages, but has born
upon the poet's frame of mind, so that his production has
appeared to a French critic to fall into two periods, controlled by the twin stars of Guillaume de Lorris and Jean
de Meun, the influence of the 'Divina Commedia' is mainly
local, it hardly informs the point of view of the poet,
the spirit of a single one of his poems, with, perhaps,
one exception, and since this exception, if admitted,
would be very striking indeed, I reserve its discussion
until further on.

This exception is not, at any rate, to be seen in
'Troilus and Criseyde', notwithstanding Ten Brink, who
described the general character of that work as more akin
to Dante's spirit than to Boccaccio's. The definition of

'litel tragedye', given by Chaucer to his poem, the
proems of the several books, modelled on Dante's proems,
and the religious conclusion, are not sufficient to stamp
a Dantean character on a work which can be called a 'Filostrato' diluted with delays and proverbs by an author who,
for all his sense of humorous and dramatic situations,
paid homage to Albertano da Brescia and Boethius.

Neither is that exception to be seen in the 'Hous of
Fame', in which critics have tried to recognize that mysterious *Dante in ynglyssh* of Lydgate's list. As a matter
of fact, one of the source-hunters, Rambeau, went so far
in the way of finding parallels between the 'Divina Commedia' and the 'Hous of Fame', that, since then, it has
been a sign of good taste among safe critics to underrate
Dante's influence on that poem. Recently, Froissart's
'Temple D'Onnour' has been set up as having stronger
claims than the 'Divina Commedia' on the paternity of the
'Hous of Fame'. Other critics, impressed by the undeniable diversity of spirit between the possibility that what
Chaucer was aiming at was some sort of a travesty, or
parody of the 'Divina Commedia'. The impression of an
ironical intent is conveyed to modern readers chiefly by
the metre of the poem, and the awkwardness of some of
Chaucer's turns of phrase. Who would recognize a serious
imitation of Virgil in the lines (143ff.): 'I wol now
singe, if that I can, the armes...' It is Virgil interpreted by a mediaeval minstrel; but Chaucer was himself
also a mediaeval minstrel, though he knew how to make fun
of minstrels, when he liked, as in 'Sir Thopas'. No,
Chaucer cannot have meant to parody Dante any more than
he did to travesty Virgil, and if he really intended to
give in the 'Hous of Fame' a humorous counterpart of the
'Divina Commedia', the less Chaucer he! Of the spirit of
Dante, nothing breathes in the lines of the 'Hous of
Fame'. But the fact of the 'Hous of Fame' being a failure
does not exclude the possibility of a serious intention on
the part of the poet. What, after all, if he really had
meant it to be a sort of Dantesque journey through the
realms of allegory? Not an actual journey, of course, as
Dante assumed his own to have been. Because one of the
great differences between Dante and the rest of mediaeval
visionaries, is that the Florentine speaks of his own
visit to the realms of eternity as of an actual visit, not
a dream. To him that journey is a reality greater than
any mundane reality. But the boldness of Dante's conception was not calculated to appeal to the bourgeois in
Chaucer:

A thousand sythes have I herd men telle
That ther is Ioye in heven and peyne in helle;
And I acorde wel that hit be so;
But natheles, this wot I wel also,
That *ther nis noon that dwelleth in this contree*
That either hath in helle or heven y-be.
                   ('Leg. of Good Women', A-Prologue, l. 1ff.).

His spirit chaunged hous, and wente ther,
As I cam never, I can nat tellen wher.
Therfor I stinte, *I nam no divinistre;*
Of soules finde I nat in this registre,
Ne me ne list thilke opiniouns to telle
Of hem, though that they wryten wher they dwelle.
                   ('Cant. Tales', A, 2809-2814).

Dante is, in a way, 'a divinistre' - and such he must have
appeared to Chaucer, at times. With all Dante's hopes of
individual and social salvation, with all his holy prophetic wrath against coward emperors and degenerated
popes, the placid London bourgeois had very little in
common. Political revolutions in England, if they disturbed now and then his welfare, were on the other hand
incapable of affecting his inspiration. In this respect
Dante and Chaucer were poles apart. All things considered, Chaucer, faced with the problem of a supernatural
journey, would have clung by instinct to the customary
dream-fiction of the 'Roman de la Rose' school, even with
Dante's poem before his eyes. Dante had rightly said:

Non è pileggio da picciola barca
Quel che fendendo va l'ardita prora,
Né da nocchier ch'a se medesmo parca. (Par., XXIII,
                                           67-69).

['Tis no fit voyage for a little boat, this which my
daring prow pursues as it cleaves the main, nor for a
pilot who spares himself.]

Of course Chaucer was no little boat: but he was a
merchantman. His attitude towards Dante's sublimity
finds an exact parallel in the position of another bourgeois poet - Horace - when confronted with Pindar:

Non hoc iocosae conveniet lyrae-
Quo, Musa, tendis? desine pervicax
Referre sermones deorum et
Magna modis tenuare parvis. ('Carm.', III, 3)

Nowhere can the difference of stature between Dante
and Chaucer be better gauged than in reading side by side
with Dante's powerful lines the English version of the
episode of Count Hugolino. Commentators point out five
lines, which are Chaucer's own, and call attention to the
tenderness of heart the poet displays in them. Hugolino's
young son is clamouring for his 'potage', and with heartrending accents complains that he cannot sleep, that it
would be much better for him to sleep always, because then
hunger would not creep into his belly; that there is
nothing he is more longing for than a piece of bread.
Very human and pathetic words indeed; but when you read
them in the light of Dante's grim account, they sound
almost idyllic. Their relation to the 'Inferno' episode
is of the same sort as the relation of the prattle of Mac-
duff's son (Act IV, Sc. 2) to the neighbouring scenes in
'Macbeth'. For Chaucer, Hugolino's tragedy is essentially
a tragedy of lack of food: his attention is concentrated
solely on the manner of death. Chaucer says that the pri-
soners had so little meat and drink, that it was hardly
sufficient, and, besides, it was very poor and bad.
Chaucer is not content with hints, as Dante; he enters
into details. After translating Dante's 'our flesh thou
yaf us, tak our flesh us fro', he adds: 'and eet y-nough'.
One feels, with Chaucer, that the poor creatures' bellies
are frightfully empty. And instead of the terrible pauses
and silences and implications of Dante, you find the wail-
ing of human beings in distress. Dante's Ugolino, when
he hears the door of the tower being locked up, gazes
speechless at his sons' faces and does not cry, but feels
petrified in his heart. Chaucer's Hugolino, also, apparently, does not speak: but only apparently, because,
immediately afterwards, upon apprehending that they are
doomed to die by hunger, says - let us hope only to himself - 'Alas! that I was born!' and then cries abundantly:
'therwith the teres fillen from his yën'. For Dante the
tragedy is not merely a tragedy inherent in a peculiar
manner of death, namely, death by hunger: its import is
much greater. The tragedy reaches such a high pitch in
Dante because it is seen against the background of public
events, because treachery, and revenge, and persecution
are there as themes of a Greek chorus. Chaucer slurs
over Ugolino's dream, in which the Count imagines himself
and his children as a wolf with its cubs, hunted down with
hue and cry, and, of course, does not translate the famous
invective against Pisa *vituperio delle genti,* with the
apocalyptic vision of divine revenge which follows. What
in Dante is a cosmic tragedy, in Chaucer is dwarfed down
to the size of a domestic tragedy of starvation.

Chaucer succeeds much better in imitating Dante's style in the brief account of the death of Peter the Cruel, where the second stanza is very Dantesque:(6) but I do not know of another passage in which he comes closer to the forceful concision of the 'grete poete of Itaille'. When he translates Dante's passage about envy ('Leg. Good Women', A-Prologue, 333ff.), he substitutes the tame equivalent, 'lavender',(7) to Dante's *meretrice,* and instead of the powerful image of her not turning away her shameless eyes, he merely says: 'ne parteth'. In the story of Custance, the Man of Law indulges an outburst of indignation against the traitor, Donegild, who, like Dante's Frate Alberico,(8) is represented as still alive, while his spirit is in hell; but that outburst of indignation sounds more like abuse than like a curse.

The instances given are sufficient to show how little Chaucer was affected by the sublimer sides of Dante's genius. We are not far from the truth, when we assume that Chaucer must have judged Dante according to the average standards of contemporary taste. To him Dante must have appealed chiefly as an immensely learned poet, 'il Savio', 'doctus'. We shall see that Chaucer's appreciation of Petrarch rests on the same point of view. Accordingly, the 'Divina Commedia' was to Chaucer primarily a mine of learned information; to use one of Dante's expressions (in the 'Convivio', I, vii, 14), he loosens Dante's lines from their *legame musaico,* sees them as units detached from the whole of the poem, inserts them as precious stones into new mosaics of his own. Dante's epos, which appears to us so all of a piece, was to him chiefly an aggregate of learned quotation, an encyclopaedia.

(p. 131) Chaucer, like most mediaeval minds, had an immoderate craving for what was deemed then the supreme achievement of learning, namely a multifarious command of quotations:

> For out of olde feldes, as men seith,
> Cometh al this newe corn fro yeer to yere;
> And out of olde bokes, in good feith,
> Cometh al this newe science that men lere. ('Parl.
>   Foules,' 22ff.).

Old books; the 'wise clerkes that ben dede' ('Tr.', III, l. 292): these he reveres in his heart, to them he gives 'lust and credence' ('Leg. Good Women', A-Prol., 31-32). They are the shrines to which Chaucer goes for worship, as soon as he is released each day from his official duties: he goes home, and there, as dumb as any stone, sits at a book, till his eyesight is fully dazed ('Hous of Fame', l. 655ff.). Dante and Petrarca were similarly keen on 'wise clerkes that ben dede', but they never fell into the grotesque, parvenu-like crudity of some of Chaucer's displays of erudition.

When Troilus gives the instructions for his funeral, he asks that his ashes be conserved

> In a vessell, that men clepeth an urne, ('Tr.', V, l. 311)

and informs Pandarus that the last two nights he has been warned of his approaching end by the owl 'which that hette Escaphilo' (ibid., 319). Criseyde swears a solemn oath (IV, st. 221) on 'Satiry and Fawny more and lesse', and very sensibly informs whoever might be ignorant of it, that those strange creatures 'halve goddes ben of wilder-nesse', as she, or rather Chaucer, had read in Boccaccio's 'Genealogia Deorum': *Faunos...et Satyros, nemorum dice-bant deos*. Despondent Troilus, in the 'Filostrato' (V, st. 17):

> ...bestemmiava il giorno che fu nato,
> E gli dei e le dee e la natura.

But Chaucer's Troilus delights in letting us know how proficient he is in classical mythology (V, st. 30):

> He corseth Jove, Appollo, and ek Cupide,
> He corseth Ceres, Bacus, and Cipride,
> His burthe, hym self, his fate, and ek nature....

Now Chaucer is in real earnest while parading such an amount of sound lore. Whenever he can supplement the source he has in hand for the moment with additional information derived from other sources, he does not let slip the opportunity. To add a new mythological name to a list, to adduce a new proverb in support of a statement are deemed by him very creditable performances indeed. He little bothered whether the mythological information was reliable or not, whether the proverb was so vulgar as to clash with the loftiness of the argument: the very fact of their being a classical name or a proverb con-ferred upon those purple patches an indisputable glamour.

When fully aware of this fact, one is apt to be very cautious before accepting modern views on Chaucer's sense of humour. In cases like the preceding ones Chau-cer appears quaint to us, but he did not mean it, not in the least. When he causes the Franklin to speak of Marcus

Tullius Ci*the*ro, he is not blundering on purpose, in
order to make the Franklin appear really ignorant, as a
benevolent critic was pleased to think. The Franklin is
a very learned person, as he is going to show further on
by his collection of stories of chaste women borrowed
from S. Jerome (one feels that Dorigen could proceed to
such didactic lengths as Dame Prudence: see 'Canterbury
Tales', F, 1457-58). Confusion between Ci*the*ro and Ci*c*ero
can be easily ascribed to phonetic influence. Chaucer
wants quotations and classical reminiscences to adorn his
sentences, and authorities to ennoble the plots of his
stories. The smile of Ariosto, referring for fun to the
authority of Turpino, does not curl the lips of Chaucer,
while he mentions Suetonius and other worthies in passages where they have no reason whatever to be produced;
not even Agaton or the fabulous Zanzis are conjured up by
the English poet as a freak of humour.

The older an authority is, the more venerable and worth
quoting: the same principle which leads Chaucer to replace
Boccaccio's lines by Dante's, when he recognizes the ultimate source, prompts him, in the Knight's tale, to attribute to Statius, rather than to Boccaccio, statements
which he actually finds made by Boccaccio, and appeal to
Livy as the author he follows for the Virginia story,
though he is really following the account in the 'Roman
de la Rose'. Occasionally, when the modernity of the
source defies direct reference, he has recourse to some
vague statement. So Dante's (since he is the authority
vainly sought after by Root):

    Né creator né creatura mai
    ...fu sanza amore,
    O naturale, o d'animo....('Purg.', XVII, 91-93)

is referred to by Pandarus as the saying of 'wyse lered'
('Tr.', I, st. 140):

    For this have I herd seyd of wyse lered:
    'Was nevere man nor womman yit bigete
    That was unapt to suffren loves hete,
    Celestial, or elles love of kynde.'

But more frequently a fictitious authority is preferred to
a vague one. So, in Book Four, (st. 60) Pandarus is prevented by obvious chronological reasons from giving Ovid
as the authority for 'the newe love out chaceth ofte the
olde', and, quite naturally, he quotes the mysterious
Zanzis as his source. Sandras's candour went so far as to
suggest to emend *Zanzis* into *Naso*, as being *certainement*

la véritable leçon! But Chaucer, for all his references
to Seint Venus, the Palladion service, and the tale of
Wade, had enough historical sense to know that a Trojan
was hardly in a position to quote Ovid, and he preferred
to refer to a precise, though unwarrantable, authority,
than to a vague one. So Froissart's *ce dist li escripture*
becomes *Agaton* in the 'Legend of Good Women' (A-Prol.,
514). Boccaccio, in the 'Teseide' (I, st. 2), is speaking of

> ...una storia antica
> Tanto negli anni riposta e nascosa
> Che latino autor non par de dica,
> Per quel ch'io sento, in libro alcuna cosa.

[An old story so hidden and concealed in the past,
that no Latin author, for what I know, seems to mention it in any book.]

But Chaucer does not like to rely solely on oral tradition, and he actually boasts to have found what Boccaccio
had been unable to find ('Anelida and Arcite', st. 2):
'This olde storie, *in Latin* which I finde.'
    Other times he invokes the support of authority for
facts he assumes gratuitously. In 'Troilus' (III, st.
172) he imagines that 'clerkes in hire bookes olde' write
that Criseyde, when her lover took her in his arms for
the first time, 'right as an aspes leef she gan to
quake', while Boccaccio's heroine behaves very differently in the heat of her juvenile enthusiasm. Root calls
Chaucer's appeal to the old books, in this case, 'delightfully ironic'. Such a contention is very misleading.
Chaucer, of course, has a delightful sense of humour, but
whenever he means to be humorous he gives unmistakable
signs of his intention. In a case like the one just
quoted, he would have kept the laughter for himself,
since, obviously, no mediaeval reader was in a position
to dispute his appeal to authority. He would have had a
sense of humour more developed and subtle than say
Ariosto or Anatole France. But his treatment of Criseyde's behaviour in the whole of the story excludes such
possibilities of irony. Criseyde is caused to appear coy
for the same reasons she is credited elsewhere with good
intentions (III, ll. 923-24; IV, ll. 1415-16). Whatever
can be said in favour of Criseyde finds in Chaucer a ready
acceptance. So he insists that she did not fall in love
'in sodeyn wyse' (II, 98), and, in order to make her fall
appear inevitable, heaps up all sorts of inducements to
love: influence of the stars (III, st. 90), alluring

songs, appeals to her womanly sense of pity; and when he
finds his authorities decidedly against Criseyde's behaviour, he sighs (IV, 19-21):

> Allas! that they sholde evere cause fynde
> To speke hire harm! and if they on hire lye,
> Iwis, hem self sholde han the vilanye.

Until, even when Criseyde's position appears indefensible,
he does not give up her defence: 'Men seyn, I not, that
she yaf hym hire herte' (V, st. 150), and seeks a last
refuge in the reticence of the old books about the period
of time which is supposed to elapse between Criseyde's
departure from Troy, and her forsaking Troilus for Diomede
(V, st. 156). In face of such overwhelming evidence of earnestness on Chaucer's part, the assumption of 'delightful
irony' can hardly be maintained.

'Mystification' is another word made use of by some
critics in connexion with Chaucer's reference to fabulous
sources. But this hypothesis also is misleading. First
of all, it is anachronistic, because in the Middle Ages
there did not exist such a duty of accuracy as in modern
times, after the method of writing history has been developed on entirely new bases. An amazing output of fungous
criticism has been the result of applying to Chaucer's
times modern ideas about historical accuracy and reference
to sources. There are still critics who rack their brains
about Lollius, and Trophe, and other imaginary problems;
some of them feel their moral sense shocked by Chaucer's
entirely failing to mention Boccaccio's name in his works.
To Boccaccio, they say, Chaucer is indebted more than to
anybody else; his silence with reference to that Italian
author is positively unfair. First of all, it ought to be
proved that Chaucer knew that Boccaccio was the author of
the works he was exploiting; but even granted, for the
moment, that he was fully aware of that authorship, we
must remember that in the 'Teseide' and the 'Filostrato',
Boccaccio, in his turn, confesses himself under obligation
to old sources. And Chaucer's practice - we have seen -
was always to have recourse to the older source as to the
more authoritative. Boccaccio acted merely as a link between Chaucer and the old source, on the authority of
which the story was ultimately relying. The artistic
merit of Boccaccio's account has nothing to do with what
was the real point with Chaucer: authority. The facts
were not Boccaccio's invention - Chaucer believed - and
the facts were everything to him, theoretically.(9) In
practice he was drawing heavily on Boccaccio's artistic
achievement, but in Chaucer's time the aesthetic truth

that 'form is everything' was far from being discovered....

(p. 149) At a given moment, Chaucer found in his stock
a plurality of short writings, his own translations and
adaptations of works of widely divergent character, in
prose and in verse: he found there a tale of womanly
loyalty such as Griselda's, a confession of feminine wantonness such as the monologue of the 'Wife of Bath', a
pious rhymed legend of Saint Cecile, a moral prose treatise on the advantages of prudence, a chivalric poem derived from Boccaccio's 'Teseide', a story of Constance's
trials adapted from Nicholas Trivet....As soon as Chaucer
began to survey these works simultaneously, as soon as he
summoned them up together before the tribunal of his mind,
his keen dramatic genius must have been aware of the amazing variety of contrasts they offered when thus envisaged
side by side. Each one of them spoke with a different
voice, with a different *tempo*. Each one possessed a character, an individuality of its own. Here was such a
romance as would have delighted a knight and a courtier;
there was a tale which had been told by a worthy clerk in
Italy; there again a chapter of the Golden Legend, fit to
be perused by a refined nun.

It is generally maintained that the tales were used by
Chaucer in such a way as to help to set off the different
characters of the pilgrims. *'Les contes dont il dispos-*
ait' - writes Legouis - *'étaient disparates. Tant mieux!*
Il en profita, grâce à une habile distribution, pour
caractériser les conteurs. Il choisit pour chacun
l'histoire qui convenait à sa caste et à son caractère.'
I think we are much nearer the truth, much more trustworthy in reconstructing what must actually have taken
place in Chaucer's mind, when we imagine that a first
group of characters sprung up from the stories themselves,
as Chaucer contemplated them with his powerful dramatic
imagination. The plan of the 'Canterbury Tales' - in my
opinion - was not brought about through a juxtaposition
of a framework - a company of story-tellers - and a body
of tales already extant, but gradually took shape as
Chaucer was envisaging his scattered writings as units
endowed each of them with a peculiar character, coloured
with a different experience; while he was contrasting them
dramatically, personifying them as so many living beings.
Such a projection of a story into the character of a
story-teller, such an embodiment of the spirit of each
work in a concrete person is the nucleus of Chaucer's masterpiece, the sudden intuition of dramatic genius bringing
light and order into a chaos of heterogeneous matter. The
characters of the story-tellers form the central feature

of Chaucer's idea. Had he taken the hint for the frame
from the 'Decameron', he would have represented his story-
tellers as people belonging to the same class, bound to
show an uniformity of taste and language, as Boccaccio's
story-tellers do only too strikingly (in Boccaccio, the
story-tellers are little more than shadows, the real speaker being always and solely Boccaccio himself).

As a next stage, we may imagine Chaucer bringing the
characters together. On what occasion people belonging
to different strata of society, 'alien of end and of aim',
were likely to be met together? It is at this point that
Italian influence may have interfered: not Boccaccio's
influence, but Dante's.

All stations of life, all kinds of character, from the
lowest to the highest, appear and talk to Dante, bent on
his pilgrimage through the realms of the dead. Loathsome,
poignant, noble, celestial apparitions, they talk to him
each one in a suitable style: demons speak the language
of demons, brutes, like Nembrot, utter mere gibberish,
angels, like Gabriel, sing with a voice sweeter than any
human melody: between these extremes, 'each from the other
heaven-high, hell-deep removed', all the modes and shades
of human souls find expression in Dante's drama. Since
the mediaeval idea of a drama, according to the definition
of Pietro di Dante, was of a poem delivered by the poet
accompanied by mummers or *joculatores carminum pronuntia-
tionem gestu corporis effigiantes per adaptationem ad
quemlibet ex cuius persona ipse poeta loquebatur.*

A pilgrimage to the other world, we have seen, was not
among Chaucer's possibilities. He clings to the dear
everyday world, and brings down to the homely plan of
common sense the situations he finds in his models. The
relation between Philosophy and Boethius, between Dame
Prudence and Melibeus, is mirrored by Chaucer in his
treatment of the relation between Pandarus and Troilus.
Though trained in the school of French allegory, the
English bourgeois poet was for the concrete, and, not
unlike Sancho Panza, he understood in terms of common
sense the quixotic visions of philosophers and divines.
'I...mervaile...that hee in that mistie time could see so
clearly' - runs Sidney's appreciation. No pilgrimage to
the kingdoms of the other world for the man who was no
'divinistre'; but an earthly pilgrimage to the shrine of
the national saint. On this pilgrimage there were no
demons or angels to be met, but all varieties of human
folk; and Chaucer cared only for the humans. There was
God's plenty for him, in a company of pilgrims. Thus, in
a far deeper and broader sense than the one meant by Lydgate, Chaucer succeeded in being 'Dante in ynglyssh', a

human instead of a divine Dante, resuming, like the
Florentine, the Middle Ages in the compass of a dramatic
epos.

Unfortunately he did not, like Dante, live long enough
to complete his 'structure brave'. Once planned the whole
along the lines suggested by the central nucleus of tales
and characters, it was left to him to expand that nucleus
with other stories and story-tellers; to alter some of the
stories already written in order to imbue them more
thoroughly with the humours of the story-tellers, to give
life to secondary figures. Traces of the unfinished condition of the extant portion of the 'Tales' abound. So
the Shipman suddenly speaks as if he were a woman; the
Second Nun calls herself 'unworthy sone of Eve', while the
Man of Law announces a story in prose and actually deliv-
ers a legend in verse.

Dante in English, then, rather than an English Boccaccio. All things considered, the numerical superiority of
the lines for which Chaucer is indebted to Boccaccio does
not blind me to the fact of the more deeply interfused and
widespread influence of Dante: an influence to which Chaucer paid due homage, mentioning the 'grete poete of
Itaille' several times in his works. Chaucer appropriated
from Dante what was within the compass of his own nature:
the Florentine poet was to him a fountain of lore, a
master of versification,(10) and, perhaps, a model of
dramatic treatment for his own 'fressh comodyes' and
'pitous tragedyes'. As Jean de Meun had been; and the
character of an abiding source, which we ascribe to both
the 'Roman de la Rose' and the 'Divina Commedia' might
point to a similar intensity of study on the part of the
English poet: a study amounting perhaps to actual translation also in the case of Dante, as Lydgate's expression
seems to imply.

The other acknowledgment of indebtedness Chaucer makes
to an Italian author concerns 'Maister Petrark', and it
seems strange indeed, if we consider how slight Petrarca's
influence was on his English admirer. Practically, none
whatever. Chaucer's acquaintance with the 'Trionfi'
cannot be demonstrated (all attempts have been so far, and
are bound to be, sterile),(11) and the insertion of a Petrarchan sonnet (12) into 'Troilus' is, in a way, a mystery. Of course, several passages in the 'Filostrato'
reproduce, more or less dilutedly, Petrarchan lines, in
the same way as one passage imitates part of a canzone by
Cino da Pistoia: so, for instance, two stanzas (V, 54-55),
which Young (p. 88) says may easily be regarded as a
development of suggestions already present in the 'Filocolo', are, instead, an almost literal imitation of a

well-known sonnet of Petrarca (*Sennuccio, io vo' che sappi*...); another passage (III, st. 84-85) derives from the still more famous *Benedetto sia 'l giorno*.... Was Chaucer aware of the relation between those passages in the 'Filostrato' and the 'Canzoniere', and did this relation prompt him to adopt a whole sonnet as Troilus's song? Obviously he did not find the sonnet in the manuscript of the 'Filostrato' he had before his eyes, because he says explicitly that Lollius writes *only* the sentence of the song.(13)   One sonnet and the Latin version of the Griselda story seem hardly sufficient to justify Chaucer's homage to Petrarca and the title of 'Maister' conferred upon him, unless Chaucer actually believed Petrarca to be the author of some of Boccaccio's works.

Chaucer's temperament - it is generally said - was much more akin to Boccaccio's than to either Dante's or Petrarca's.   No wonder - I imagine Legouis saying - since Boccaccio was of French origin, like Chaucer. Still, if we consider closely enough Chaucer's indebtedness to Boccaccio, we shall not be long in perceiving how, for all the affinities existing between the two men, there are also great differences which cause their artistic methods to be almost opposite. The relation of 'Troilus' to the 'Filostrato' is, not unfrequently, that of a drama to a story. Boccaccio is more interested in the story itself, in its development and conclusion; for Chaucer, on the other hand, the characters overgrow the story. For Boccaccio Troilus's love for Criseyde was a simile of his own love to Fiammetta: he had undergone the same experience, he had lived the story for himself. What he did, was to melt the various sources of the story into a whole, at the heat of his own love-passion. Boccaccio brought about the *mise au point* of the Troilus and Criseyde story. Chaucer *con poco moto seguitò la imprenta* (with slight motion rounded off the figure: 'Parad.', XVIII, 114). But what the Italian had *lived* from within, the English poet *saw* from without. To this difference of attitude are to be traced Chaucer's psychological superiority to Boccaccio, as well as his emotional inferiority. This latter deficiency is largely compensated by the former quality; but one cannot help regretting, sometimes, the deliberate suppression, on Chaucer's part, of those fresh, direct effusions of naive sensual love which give such a juvenile charm to Boccaccio's account:

Or foss'io teco una notte d'inverno,
Cento cinquanta poi stessi in inferno ('Fil.', II,
                                        st. 88),

...or foss'io nelle braccia
dolci di lui, stretta a faccia a faccia! (Ibid., st.
117),

...anima mia,
I' te ne prego, sì ch'io t'abbia in braccio
Ignuda sì come il mio cor disia ('Fil.', III, st. 32),

and the stanzas following this last passage, with their
sensuous insistence on *in braccio* and *l' uno all' altro,*
entirely vanished in Chaucer's translation ('Troilus',
III, st. 190-91). Modern critics are only too ready to
daub Boccaccio's Criseyde as a courtesan, and Chaucer's as
a more controlled English lady. The English Criseyde is
no more virtuous than the Italian heroine: only, the
English poet is anxious to justify her, and worries about
the question of her loyalty. Curiously enough, the
stories Chaucer borrowed from Boccaccio are all illustrations of different cases of either kept or broken loyalty.
Apart from 'Troilus', the Griselda story is a *de oboedien-
tia et fide uxoria mythologia,* as Petrarca's title runs;
Chaucer's version of the 'Teseide' is called 'The com-
pleynt of feire Anelida and fals Arcite'; and the character of Dorigen (a counterpart of Tarolfo's beloved in the
'Filocolo') is revealed in a sole heartrending cry:

Unto the gardin, as myn housbond bad,
My *trouthe* for to holde, allas! allas!
('Cant. Tales', F, 1512-13)(14)

Needless to say, this moral outlook is entirely Chaucer's;
in Boccaccio the problem of loyalty is, if at all, very
crudely formulated. The central *motif* in the 'Filostrato'
is Troilus's (i.e., Boccaccio's) pain in being far from
his beloved.
   Thus much can be said about Italian literary influence
on Chaucer. But Chaucer was not only a reader of books;
he was also a direct observer of human life. The new
spirit which breathes in his production after his first
Italian journey is, doubtless, due in part to his acquaintance with Italian authors, but in part only. There is
another kind of influence which cannot be easily defined
and still less easily gauged: an influence which, though
elusive, we find is there. Jusserand tried to specify it
by conjuring up before our eyes the spectacle of Italy all
alive with the dawn of the Renaissance, when Chaucer visited it. But it is hardly the sight of the paintings of
Giotto and Orcagna, or of the sculptures of Andrea Pisano,
or even the rediscovery of the ancient world which was

likely to impress the English envoy. We are too much inclined to think of those first steps of Renaissance as a
pageant apt to strike the eyes of contemporaries in the
same way as they strike our focussing historical outlook.
We see that distant age through the magnifying glasses of
posterity. Certainly, Chaucer must have felt the identity
of his aims with those of the Italian forerunners of the
Renaissance: he also was trying to raise the vernacular
('naked wordes in English') up to the splendour of literary language, he also was an admirer of the classics, and
saw Venus 'naked fletinge in a see', her divine head
crowned with a 'rose-garlond whyt and reed' ('Hous of Fame',
133-135). But surely, this again is literature, and what
Italy had to offer to Chaucer, beside literature, was
actual life.

I imagine Chaucer's experience to have been not unlike
that of some Elizabethan dramatist, or, to take a more
modern and clearer instance, that of Robert Browning.
The intense dramatic character of Italian life does not
escape a foreigner; and when I speak of dramatic character
I do not necessarily imply that Italian life teems with
either tragic or comic subjects. I mean that the Italians
have always appeared to foreigners as wonderfully lively
beings, giving outward expression to all shades of feeling, now wildly gesticulating, now resuming a whole philosophy in a rapid wink of the eye. The wonderful thing
Chaucer saw in Italy was the same Elizabethan dramatists
discovered two centuries later, the same Stendhal and
Browning admired in more recent times: the wonderful thing
Alfieri well expressed when he said that *la pianta uomo*
grows more vigorous in Italy than anywhere else. The
spectacle of Italian everyday life no doubt sharpened
still more in Chaucer the feeling for drama, both innate
in him and furthered by the perusal of Jean de Meun's
masterpiece, so that, coming back to his native country,
the poet was able to see life round him in the light of
his newly acquired experience, and to express that life in
words which were 'cosin to the dede'.

Notes

1 Version A of the Prologue is much closer to Dante's
   lines than B, which runs (ll. 232-233): 'Therwith me
   thoughte his face shoon so brighte That wel unnethes
   mighte I him beholde'. This divergence constitutes a
   strong evidence against the hypothesis of the priority
   of the B version. Moreover, the lines corresponding to
   188ff., in B, show signs of revision: *wemen* of (l. 190

A altered into *mankynd* (B, 287), in order to avoid the
repetition (*wemen*, A, 188=B, 285), 1. 192 A, changed
through the insertion of *wide* (B, 289) to eke out the
metre. Ll. 141-143 are left out in B. Much has been
written - most of it entirely wide of the mark - on the
relation between the two forms of the Prologue. Whoever wants to feel very pessimistic about Chaucerian
criticism ought to read Hugo Lange's 'Neue Beiträge zu
einer endgültigen Lösung der Legendenprologfrage bei
Chaucer in Anglia', Band XLIX (1926), pp. 173ff., and
the articles on the same subject by J. Koch, V. Lang-
hans, in Band L, Heft 1, of the same review, p. 62ff.

2 The borrowing of rhymes is, of course, not confined to
   'Troilus'. So for instance the rhyme, 'Anne-Osanne',
   in 'Canterbury Tales' B, 641-42, and G, 69-70, is a
   reminiscence of Dante's 'Anna-Osanna' ('Par.', XXXII,
   133-35).

3 In a few cases the Italian rhyme impresses Chaucer as
   mere spelling and sound, quite apart from the meaning.
   So in 'Troilus' V, st. 131 *pace-face-deface* is suggested by *fallace-face* (from the verb *fare*, to make)-
   piace in 'Filostrato' VI, st. 20. Perhaps Dante's
   rhyme ('Inferno', XXVIII, 119-23) *come-chiome-o me*,
   has suggested Chaucer's *Rome-tô me* ('Canterbury Tales',
   A, 671-72).

4 Even where no definite source has been traced, Chaucer's use of foreign words shows at once in what language we should expect to find his original. Thus in
   'Troilus' (II, st. 124), we find the word *verre*, used
   only here by Chaucer for 'glas', rhyming with *werre=
   war*. Such two words rhyme together only in French:
   verre-guerre. Accordingly, the version of the proverb
   Chaucer has in mind, ought to be a French one. The
   quotation occurs in Antigone's song which bears a general resemblance to Guillaume de Machaut's 'Paradis
   d'amour' (see Kittredge, 'Mod. Lang. Notes', xxv.,
   p. 158).

5 See Koeppel, 'Chauceriana', in 'Anglia' XIII, p. 229.

6 The way of hinting at Du Gueschlin through the description of his arms, and of making, so to say, a
   personification of these arms, is entirely Dantesque.
   Cf., for instance, 'Inferno', XXVII, 49ff..

7 Cf. G.P. Krapp's note in 'Mod. Lang. Notes', XVII
   (1902), pp. 204-6.

8 'Come il mio corpo stea. Nel mondo su, nulla scienza
   porto' ('Inf.', XXXIII, 122-123).

9 To become convinced of the power of authoritative tradition over the mediaeval mind one has but to think of
   the iconographical formulae which controlled the fine

arts until the Renaissance. While an artist was copying from another, for instance, the scene of the descent from the cross, he must have felt not that he was
falling under a personal obligation to his model, but
rather that he was merely accepting at the hands of
the other artist a ritual, fixed convention....

10   Brusendorff (p. 161, note) draws a parallel between
'Clerkes Tale', F, 995ff., and 'Trionfo del Tempo',
127-135. I cannot see the inevitability of this parallel, the whole passage being too much of a commonplace.

11   This point awaits still a thorough treatment.

12   To Brusendorff (p. 270) the 'Complaint of Pity'
appears strongly coloured by *il dolce stil nuovo* as
exemplified by Dante and Petrarca. He thinks he has
discovered also a close verbal parallel to Chaucer's
expression in l. 14, in Petrarca's sonnet, *Ite, caldi
sospiri*.... But Chaucer's expression is part of the
stock-in-trade of his contemporary poetry, and the
parallel which strikes Brusendorff so much, is far from
being a close one. On the strength of his arguments,
Brusendorff would move down the poem from the early
date commonly given to it at present, and date it at
least after the first Italian journey, and not improbably still later.

13   'Troilus', I, ll. 393-94. An error, often repeated,
is to suppose that the author of the sonnet is meant
by 'Lollius'. See for instance the recent 'Chaucer'
by G.M. Cowling, London (Methuen), 1927, p. 101.

14   Very much has been written about the difference of
the condition set by 'the wife' in Boccaccio's story
and in Chaucer's, but nowhere did I find stress laid
on the fact that while the wife in Boccaccio merely
mentions an arbitrary impossibility (a blossoming
garden in midwinter), in Chaucer she really utters a
sort of vow, in connexion with the return of her husband. Chaucer, similarly as in the case of Criseyde,
was here anxious to justify the woman, to conciliate
her binding herself to a - however impossible - condition, with her loyalty to her husband: her condition
will therefore be such as to lead, if fulfilled, to
the husband's safety. It is a vow. Dorigen, no less
than Alcestis, is 'of love so trewe' as to be ready to
sacrifice herself for her husband's sake. Possibly
this desire to change the capricious condition into a
logical one, led Chaucer to alter the setting of Boccaccio's tale in the 'Filocolo': hence the scene laid
on a sea-coast notoriously dangerous to sailors, hence
the fiction of a Briton lay, introduced to make the
story appear more authoritative.

45.   THOMAS FREDERICK TOUT, A PRUDENT COURTIER

1929

T.F. Tout (1855-1929), educated at Balliol College, Oxford,
was Professor of History at Manchester University, 1890-
1925. His main professional concern was the history of
medieval English administration, which enabled him to
focus on Chaucer's professional career with an historian's
appropriate scepticism. Chaucer's position as a courtier
in a relatively mobile society is emphasised. Reprinted
from 'Speculum' IV (1929), pp. 368-71, 379-88, by permission of the Editor.

(p. 368) My chief thesis to-day is that an appreciable
proportion of fourteenth-century English literature came
from the civil servants of the state. By English literature I mean books written by Englishmen, in whatever
tongue they were written, it being understood that most
books made in England were then written in Latin, some in
French, and some in English. To write good books in any
tongue involves a good education, and I may perhaps begin
with a few words about the education of the civil servant
of the Middle Ages. That he was a fairly well educated
man is clear from his works. He had, for example, to
have a reading and writing knowledge of three languages.
Assuming English to be his mother tongue (an assumption
not always warranted in the fourteenth century), his
official vernacular was certainly French until the very
end of the period, and his official communications, so
far as they were formal, were generally made in Latin,
though again, as the century grew older, the official
language became to an increasing extent French. To this
we must add a wide acquaintance with official forms and
precedents, the traditions of his office, the corresponding formalities and traditions of foreign courts and
offices, skill in the art of *dictamen* or literary composition and form, and a good knowledge of law, municipal,
civil, and ecclesiastical. How was all this knowledge
obtained? Mainly, I feel convinced, by apprenticeship
under a master, the method in which all knowledge was
acquired in the Middle Ages. The junior official copied
forms under direction, until he was skillful enough to
write them on his own responsibility. Ultimately he became in his turn, the master, that is, the instructor and

director, of his juniors. The clerk may also have gone to
a university, but a university training and degree were, I
am convinced, the exception rather than the rule. That
can be proved by the rarity with which the individual
official is designated by the coveted title of 'master,'
which, like its equivalents 'doctor' or 'professor,' then
denoted the attainment of a full university degree in any
recognised faculty.

The Chancery, whose sphere took in all administration
and the higher secretarial work, was the most learned of
the government offices, and we know that occasionally a
graduate of distinction was brought in from the outside
and given from the beginning a conspicuous post. But it
is an illusion to think that 'masters of chancery' - a
rare term before the end of the fourteenth century - were
so called because they were commonly masters of arts or
doctors of laws. They were so called because they had the
privilege of acting as masters of the junior clerks
who served under them and whom they introduced into official life. Moreover, the members of a north European university were, in the Middle Ages, clerks by the fact of
their studentship, and there was, therefore, no place in
the university for the lay element, which was now becoming
increasingly prominent in the civil service. Of course, a
university-trained clerk could easily renounce his clergy
for a lay career, culminating perhaps in knighthood.
Doutbless there were other places than the university
where a lay aspirant to the civil service might receive an
education. Perhaps already, as certainly in the fifteenth
century, he might frequent the London law schools which, I
imagine, owed their very existence to the fact that the
university had no place for the lay student or for the
student of common law. I feel fairly convinced that the
normal school of the civil servant was a sort of apprenticeship, either in the royal household or in some government office under a senior officer. We have instances of
civil servants using the standard manuals of *dictamen*, or
the art of literary composition, and themselves compiling
treatises on the common forms of documents for the use of
themselves or their office. I shall return to this question later when dealing with the concrete problem of the
education of that eminent lay civil servant, Geoffrey
Chaucer.

However this may be, it is clear from his works that
the mediaeval civil servant had somehow the opportunity of
a good education. Like most mediaeval education, its tendency was technical rather than humanistic. Its object
was not to widen the mind, but to give a man the tools of
his trade. Subject to these limitations, the mediaeval

civil servant had the training which enabled him, on occasion, to befriend literature and science and, in some cases, to make personal contributions to them. This was in the very dawn of our civil service and remains true of the present day, despite the increasing call of the exacting modern state on the services of its members.

Professor Haskins has suggested, even as regards the twelfth century, that literature, though never a department of government, has its importance to those who, like myself, are concerned with administrative history. 'It is,' he says, 'at least a phase of the larger life of the mediaeval court and thus not without its contacts with actual administration.' To see what these contacts were in the twelfth century, when administrative history as a serious study begins, I need only refer to Stubbs' two lectures on 'Learning and Literature at the Court of Henry II' and to the admirable supplement in Dr Haskins' paper on 'Henry II as a Patron of Literature,' which he contributed not long ago to a volume in which I take a particular interest.(1) It is enough to note that among the men who practised the literary craft at that great king's court, were Richard FitzNeal, the exchequer magnate, who wrote the 'Dialogus de Scaccario' and I know not what beside; the mighty justiciar, Ranulf Glanville with his famous law book; and that humbler 'clerk of chancery' (if we may anticipate a later phrase) who wrote one of the lives of the great chancellor who became St Thomas of Canterbury. If the literary stream flowed less copiously from the court during the thirteenth century, it revived after the death of Edward I. It is with this revival that we have chiefly to do.

The civil servants of the fourteenth century with direct literary interests may be divided into three classes. Firstly, there were, conspicuously and clearly, men of the academic type who had, before their entrance into state service, studied and taught at a university. There were, secondly, the men who, without being themselves profound scholars, posed as patrons of learning, friends of learned men, collectors of libraries, benefactors of universities, or pious founders of academic colleges. Thirdly, there were (most important of all) the men who themselves made solid contributions to literature. Each class shades into the other, and the line between them is hard to draw, just as it was difficult in those days to make our modern distinction between civil servant and political minister, since, as in modern imperial Germany, the minister was often the promoted civil servant, and the modern differentiation of professions had hardly begun. There is, moreover, the trouble that always besets

the mediaevalist when he finds that very different things
are being done at the same time by a person with a given
name. He is always in doubt whether these things are all
the work of the same man or whether they suggest two different persons with precisely the same name, and how,
assuming the second possibility to be true, he can divide
the acts done between these hypothetically separate individuals. Perhaps we shall clear up the ground best if we
begin with these doubtful identifications. This we can do
the more rapidly since, with one possible exception, they
concern personalities of no great importance.

   This possible exception is that of John Wycliffe. We
all know that 'John Wycliffe' appears in the later part of
Edward III's reign, doing so many different things that
many have been led to insist on there being two John
Wycliffes and some have gone so far as to believe that
only the hypothesis of three John Wycliffes will explain
all the facts. This is a problem on which I have no
views, but it is one irrelevant to our present purpose,
for the great John Wycliffe, who is undoubtedly the only
Wycliffe who was at any time in the service of the state,
cannot be regarded as, in modern speech, a member of the
permanent civil service, though he was so frequently
employed by the crown on special missions that he called
himself 'specialis regis clericus.' We may, however, dismiss him and go on to the less distinguished persons more
regularly in the royal service, whose identity is doubtful. They are all too obscure to make it worth while to
tarry long over them, but they are numerous enough to
make their cases worth consideration....

   (p. 379) Of other persons of high academic standing,
though not of learned output, who were distinguished in
the king's service, I may mention instances. Among them
were John Thoresby, doctor of laws, chancery clerk, chancellor, and archbishop of York; Walter Skirlaw, doctor of
laws, clerk of chancery, and bishop of Durham; and John
Ronhale, doctor of laws, worthy of special notice because
he went from the mastership of the King's Hall at Cambridge to serve the king as notary of chancery, thus fulfilling for once the special function of that foundation.
Ronhale is the most conspicuous instance of a Cambridge
master in Edward III's service. It is indeed sometimes
said that Robert Thorp, a common lawyer by profession, was
in earlier life master of Pembroke Hall, Cambridge, and
based his attitude as chancellor on his loyalty to the
house of Pembroke, which had founded the college of which
he was once head. However, the identity of names is not
enough, especially in the case of so common a name as his.
Robert Thorp, the chancellor, had long been a practising

lawyer. It is conceivable that he might, like other successful common lawyers, have renounced his clergy for the bar and knighthood. Yet by the end of Edward III's reign, when the common law had become substantially a lay profession, some more positive proof is needed before we can accept so improbable an identification.

I must not dwell longer on the academic personage in politics. Still less must I stress the relation to our subject of the many men of letters who were attached for a time to the courts of Edward III, his queen, his sons, and his grandson, though in the aggregate they suggest a literary atmosphere, more literary in the narrow sense than that of the shrewd worldlings and saintly recluses who fluctuated between the service of the university and the service of the crown. Yet in days when service in the household was hardly yet differentiated from the service of the state, a plausible claim might be made for their inclusion. Such were John Froissart of Valenciennes, poet, clerk, chronicler, and traveller, attached for some years to the service of his countrywoman, Queen Philippa, and upholding a very English point of view until better pay or prosepcts lured him away to serve French masters and change his attitude to politics.

In the same category as Froissart we may place the anonymous Chandos Herald, a Hainaulter like Froissart, if we may argue from his language, who chronicled in rhyme the doings of Chandos' master, the Black Prince. The presence of skilled pens about the court made easy the establishment of what we may almost call an effective publicity department, by which knowledge of the king's great doings against the French were duly reported home in despatches that had the same function of interesting and educating public opinion as was thought necessary during our most recent war. The same spirit inspired the incorporation of these despatches in the drum and trumpet history of Robert Avesbury, himself an official of the ecclesiastical courts, and in the lurid patriotism of Geoffrey Baker's 'Chronicle', and of Laurence Minot's war songs. In home affairs we have already had an instance of such appeal to public opinion in the controversy between Edward III and John Stratford, in which the frenzied denunciations of the courtiers who drew up the *libellus famosus* were countered by the dignified utterances of Stratford from his retreat at Canterbury.

These appeals to public opinion came to a head in the opposition to Richard's attempt at autocracy when Thomas Favent, the chaplain of a lord of the opposition, wrote in Latin a strongly partisan account of the acts of the Wonderful Parliament of 1387, so anti-royalist into temper

that it was disinterred and translated into English as
a weapon to fight the cause of the Long Parliament
against Charles I. It was equally conspicuous on the
king's side in the falsification of the parliament roll of
1397, worked by chancery clerks in Richard II's interests.
Finally, we see its effects in the considerable literature,
mainly of French provenance, which sought to stir up European opinion against the Lancastrian usurper by depicting
the sufferings and murder of the deposed Richard II. Even
such acts as the reconciliation of Richard II with the
Londonders in 1392 have their literary commemoration in
the person of Richard Maidstone. Long before this the
strenuous Sir Peter de la Mare's speakership of the Commons inspired popular songs in honour of the popular hero.
The remarkable account of the Good Parliament preserved in
the annals of a Yorkshire abbey, and recently published in
the 'Anonimalle Chronicle' by Mr Galbraith, shows that
there was a public for the faithful reporting of memorable
parliamentary debates. The spread of interest in current
affairs from the magnate to the simple squire and citizen
had, as one of its results, the increasing attention paid
in court circles to publicity. This had some effect in
the increasing value of the government agent who could
write.

We have still to consider the direct contribution of
the fourteenth-century official to literature, and especially to current vernacular literature. Preëminent among
these we have now to deal with two personages who were undoubtedly men of letters, and equally undoubtedly civil
servants. These were Geoffrey Chaucer and Thomas Hoccleve, respectively representing the lay and clerical
branches of that service.

No mere historian can add anything material to the biography of either Chaucer or Hoccleve. All he can hope to
do is to harp on the claims of the civil service on its
own and perhaps put into focus their professional career,
which the literary historian, too often unmindful of fourteenth-century social and political conditions, may sometimes fail to coördinate with their literary activities.
Yet their professional record cannot be overstressed; for
Chaucer, a *bona fide* layman at every stage of his career,
could not have written his poems but for the court favour
which gave him and his something approaching a sufficiency
to live upon, and even Hoccleve, the clerk, when he cut
off all chance of a career by becoming *clericus uxoratus*,
had nothing to keep him alive save his modest salary and
other occasional state bounties. And to obtain the payment of all of these he had frequent occasion to call upon
the aid of his muse. Mediaeval conditions made literature

an impossible profession.   There could hardly be publication in our sense.   There were certainly no direct profits
of authorship and no legal copyright, as long as there was
no printing or other means of rapidly multiplying copies
to meet a commercial demand.   Preferment in the church for
the clerk, offices in the state for clerk and layman alike,
the bounty of kings and magnates in all cases - such were
the only means by which the man of letters could earn his
living and that by occupations quite foreign to his literary profession.   Hence the importance of political service
for the literary aspirant of the later Middle Ages.   For
it was rarely indeed that literature was cultivated by a
man of private means, like John Gower, who seems to have
lived on his patrimony and to have written for writing's
sake.

Geoffrey Chaucer's literary primacy needs neither
statement nor demonstration.   My humbler duty to-day is to
emphasise his position as a permanent civil servant, a
position the more emphatic since it was, after a fashion,
hereditary.   His father, John Chaucer, a prosperous London
wine merchant, was attached to Edward III's household
service as deputy butler.   So intimate were the ties involved in that office that John Chaucer attended the king
in his long sojourns in the Netherlands between 1338 and
1340, his foreign service probably lasting until nearly
the period of his famous son's birth.   It was easy for a
youth, born in the atmosphere of the royal household, to
be attached from early years to the service of the court.
I am convinced that the excellent education which Geoffrey
undoubtedly received was the education which the household
of a king, or one of the greater magnates, could give to
its junior members.   How this education was conducted we
know very little, but it clearly combined that familiar
knowledge of the Latin tongue, which in the Middle Ages
was the essence of literacy, with that broader accomplishment in modern literature whose chief vehicle was still
French, the *lingua franca*, so to say, of cultivated lay
society in Western Europe.   I emphasise the point since
this part of the 'Chaucer legend' has not yet been so
decisively dissipated as the rest of it has been by the
admirable scholars who are collecting, with extraordinary
patience, every scrap of evidence from record sources.

This process of investigation is still going on, and a
notable example of the sort of picture it enables us to
build up can be found in Mr J.M. Manly's 'Some New Light
on Chaucer'.   He throws over most of the derelict planks
of the Chaucer legend.   He rightly dismisses the conjecture, with which one is still sometimes confronted, that
Chaucer might have been educated at Oxford or Cambridge.

There is not a scrap of evidence in support of these imag-
inings, and all our knowledge of fourteenth-century conditions is against them. The university legend fades away
when we remember that, north of the Alps, the mediaeval
universities were universities of clerks, and there is the
extreme unlikelihood that such a *bona fide* layman as Chaucer was at any time in his career a tonsured clerk. Moreover, we cannot find any time during which a youth, who
had been for some years a page in a subordinate royal
household, and who took arms in the campaign of 1359, before he was twenty, could have attended the courses of any
university. Unluckily, Mr Manly is still inclined to the
alternative theory that Chaucer was educated at the
Temple. His only positive reason for thinking this is a
reference in an Elizabethan writer, which, if only a
scrap of contemporary corroboration could be found, would
make the theory probable. But no such contemporary evidence exists. Mr Manly makes much of the inadequacy of
a training about the court, and considers it far more
likely that an exceptional education, such as that of
Chaucer, would have been obtained in one of the common law
schools of London, the 'Inns of Court,' for such he
assumes the Temple had already become. This assumption
may well be right, but we have no certain knowledge to
support it. Mr Manly goes further and says that a legal
training is a natural explanation of Chaucer's career.
Both these arguments, I think, are pressed too far.
Households, royal and baronial, were the usual training
ground for officials, and I see no unlikelihood whatever
in their having been responsible for the education of a
man like Chaucer. I am certain too that there is nothing
in his career which suggests that he was a trained lawyer, and we know that most of his contemporaries, who
held similar posts, were not trained lawyers either. The
whole theory remains conjectural, therefore, and I think
that our absolute lack of knowledge of the early history
of the London law schools makes it improbable that it will
ever be proved. We must guard against that subtle, but
widespread, sin of the historian, namely, the reading
back into an earlier age, for which he has no evidence,
the testimony of the documents of a later date. It is
highly dangerous to assume that Fortescue's famous account
of the education of the London law schools, nearly a hundred years later, applied to the reign of Edward III. For
Fortescue's own days it suggests just the sort of education Chaucer might well have received, including the study
of history on Sundays and saints' days, when no more serious lectures were available! But even if such schools
were in operation in the middle of the fourteenth century,

we have no evidence of Chaucer being in any sense a
lawyer. On the contrary, his whole early history centres
round the households of the king and his sons, and those
only.(2)

As a boy, Chaucer was a page in the household of the
king's son, Lionel of Antwerp. He was still in Lionel's
retinue when he made his first campaign in France in 1359,
and was already important enough for the king to contribute towards his ransom when he was taken prisoner in a
skirmish near Rethel. Geoffrey was subsequently transferred to the king's household, and to that confidential
branch of it called the king's chamber. In 1367, and
probably earlier, he was yeoman, or *valettus,* of the
king's chamber, and afterwards held the higher rank of
esquire of the chamber. Chamber office, originally the
personal service of the king's bedroom, still normally
involved close attendance at court and intimate relations
with the king. It was, however, usual to employ chamber
officers on delicate missions at home and abroad. Such
incidents of the duty of an esquire of the chamber gave
Chaucer his diplomatic experiences in France and Italy, and
perhaps, therefore, his personal acquaintance with Italian
poets. His marriage with a lady of the court not only
strengthened his position, but involved him ultimately in
a left-hand connexion with John of Gaunt. Modest pensions
and grants from both king and duke of Lancaster rewarded
the divided service to two masters which was so usual with
the officials of that age.

In 1374 Chaucer was relieved from his constant attendance at court by his appointments as controller of the
great and petty customs in the port of London. Henceforth
he was settled in a home of his own over Aldgate. He
became increasingly prosperous as a landed proprietor and
justice of the peace in Kent, and, though never knighted,
he was elected *loco militis* to represent Kent in the memorable parliament of 1386 at which the baronial opposition
began their attack upon prerogative government by the im-
peachment of the chancellor, the earl of Suffolk. I have
no doubt that Chaucer's presence in parliament was part of
a policy which Edward III and Richard II handed on to
later generations. I mean the policy of securing the complacency of the Commons by the infusion of a liberal
sprinkling of courtiers and placemen among their ranks.
In 1386, however, such precautions were to no purpose.
The lords and commons drove Suffolk from office, and it is
most unlikely that Chaucer, though he sat, or at least
drew pay, for sixty-one days' attendance at that parliament, ever raised a voice on behalf of the unpopular minister. In his 'Hous of Fame' (ll. 652-660) he has for once

deviated from the impersonal note which characterises
nearly all his writings, by describing how, indifferent to
distractions, social or political, he divided his life
between his work in his office and his literary pursuits
at home:

> For whan thy labour doon al is,
> And hast y-maad thy rekeninges,
> In stede of reste and newe thinges,
> Thou gost hoom to thy hous anoon;
> And also domb as any stoon,
> Thou sittest at another boke
> Till fully daswed is thy loke,
> And livest thus as an hermyte,
> Although thyn abstinence is lyte.

Chaucer's prudence did not, however, keep him long in
his posts. Before the end of 1386, a fresh storm burst,
provoked by the reluctance of the king to carry out the
wishes of the parliament which had driven the earl of
Suffolk from the chancery. The reforming commissioners
appointed by that parliament answered the king's action by
greater activity in purging the administration of undesir-
able elements. It was doubtless the result of their energy
that in December Chaucer lost his two posts in the customs
and was reduced to such financial straits that he had to
give up his house in Aldgate and barter his pension for an
advance of cash. Yet his prudential abstention from politics may have lightened his fall, for he never seems to
have lost his position, somewhat nominal, I imagine, lat-
terly, in the royal household, and his little pensions
from the exchequer and the duchy of Lancaster enabled him
to live somehow.
 Very different was the fate of a brother man of letters,
Thomas Usk, in status a clerk, but engaged mainly in the
public service, being in turn secretary to John Northampton, the turbulent mayor of London (whom he betrayed),
king's sergeant-at-arms, and under-sheriff of Middlesex.
He was, therefore, if not quite a civil servant, engaged
in official work. He was a literary man, too, being, as
Dr Henry Bradley has proved, the author of that 'Testament
of Love', which in precritical days was ascribed to Chaucer. Usk, whose repeated treachery to his masters had
lost him all his friends, was one of the culprits whom the
Merciless Parliament of 1388 condemned to a cruel end.
The chronicler expatiates on the piety shown by this
victim of the angry estates. As he was dragged to his
doom, he recited the penitential psalms, the *Te Deum*, and
other incentives to devotion at the hour of death, among

them, curiously enough, being the Athanasian Creed. He
was strung up on the gallows and cut down immediately,
when still conscious. His subsequent beheading was so
mishandled by a clumsy executioner that it was only after
thirty strokes of the sword that his sufferings were
brought to an end. The fate of this poet turned politi-
cian may well have convinced his friend Chaucer of the
wisdom of holding aloof from politics and ostentatiously
proclaiming his indifference to all but the daily official
task and the literary pursuits of his leisure hours.
There is no civil servant, clerical or lay, depicted in
the great gallery of portraits drawn in the General Prologue to the 'Canterbury Tales'.

We must now turn to a later stage of Chaucer's official
career. His worst trials were soon over, but for some
time it was thought prudent to keep him out of the way.
On July 5, 1387, he had letters of protection to go for a
year to Calais in the retinue of the captain of the
town.(3) However, he was back in England before the end
of the year, and, in 1389, the successful assertion by the
king of his right to choose his own ministers was soon
followed by Chaucer's restoration to place. He was not
put back in his old offices, but his appointment in 1389
as clerk of the king's works made him the successor of
William of Wykeham in the post which led his predecessor
to greatness both in church and state. Chaucer soon took
advantage of the not unusual permission to appoint a
deputy, but in 1391 he lost his controllership and was
again in financial difficulties. Henceforth, he ceased
to be a civil servant, for subsequent office, such as the
deputy keepership of a forest in Somerset, he owed technically, not to the crown, but to the young earl of March.
His other means of support were pensions, which were small
under Richard II and became adequate only when the accession of Henry of Lancaster was at once followed by marks
of royal favour that enabled the poet to end his life in
comfort in a home, under the shadow of the palace, and
within the precincts of the great abbey wherein he was
buried. Whether Chaucer's troubles in his public career
were accentuated, as some of his biographers suggest, by
his unbusinesslike ways which made further promotion difficult, it is hard to say. But chequered as was his official record, it had this importance that it gave him the
leisure to write what the world will not willingly let
die. But we know his public career only in outline and
from official documents. The rule of reticence as to his
personal affairs and his political attitude, already laid
down by him in 1384, was never broken. Yet his position
at court had this advantage for his stock that it gave to

Thomas Chaucer, whom I cannot but regard as his son, a
rich wife and a great estate in Oxfordshire, an almost
permanent position as 'knight' of that shire in parliament, and ultimately the speakership of the Commons at
the period of their greatest activity under the early
Lancastrians. The marriage of Thomas' daughter Alice to
William de la Pole, earl and afterwards duke of Suffolk,
raised the granddaughter of the poor poet to the highest
circle of the nobility, and Alice's son's marriage to
Edward IV's sister might have made her grandson heir to
the throne, but for the Tudor revolution. Altogether,
this is not a bad record for an official whose father was
a tradesman in the city of London. And yet people still
talk of the Middle Ages as the time of the domination of
an hereditary caste. Even the lay official could find
opportunities for his kin, hardly surpassed by the direct
avenue to power and position afforded by the church.

In the literary circle of which Chaucer was the chief
star, many lesser lights revolved. Some at least among
them had administrative affinities of a kind. Among them
some have been inclined to place Ralph Strode, common sergeant of the City of London, though he, even more than
Thomas Usk, was an officer of the city rather than of the
state. But this depends on identifying the scholastic
Oxford writer, Wycliffe's opponent, Chaucer's 'philosophic
Strode', with this successful lawyer, and fathering him in
addition with the authorship of anonymous poems of rare
poetic quality. Sir Israel Gollancz has not hesitated to
maintain for some thirty years that there was only one
Ralph Strode who did all these things. My sympathies go
with him, but my intelligence does not allow me to have
implicit faith in the identification. All one can say is
that if the one Ralph Strode did all these things he was
a very remarkable man. But I find it hard to believe that
a clerk of established position would leave the university,
start a new career as a common lawyer, abandon his clergy
for a wife and a family, and find time to write poetry in
his leisure. Something more positive than conjuncture is
necessary to carry conviction. More relevant to us is
that literary dining-club called the 'Court of Good Company,' which included Thomas Hoccleve among its members
and was entertained at dinner on May Day, 1410, by Henry
Somner, chancellor of the exchequer, still a civil servant
at that period, and not the political minister that he has
become in these later days. Chaucer was already dead, but
we may feel sure that he would not in his lifetime have
been lacking at such a feast.

Notes

1 'Essays in Mediaeval History presented to Thomas
   Frederick Tout' (Manchester University Press, 1925).
2 My reason for having, rather unfairly, traversed Mr
   Manly's argument, since it appears in a book of public
   lectures which he modestly says is not for specialists,
   is that it is a theory about which he seems fairly con-
   fident. He expounds it so clearly that I do not think
   I can have mistaken his arguments, in spite of the
   popular form in which they are cast. This question of
   Chaucer's education is one where the literary and
   administrative historians meet on common ground, and
   it is one on which, therefore, stress must inevitably
   be laid in this address. I read with delight Mr
   Manly's invigorating book, which I regard as an excellent illustration of the way our knowledge of Chaucer
   has been amplified and humanised by the researches of
   a host of workers into the records of the state. Among
   these Professor Manly and his colleague, Professor
   Rickert, occupy places of distinction.
3 This is a new fact due to a discovery of Professor E.
   Rickert, first revealed in her paper in the 'Times
   Literary Supplement' (September 27, 1928). Though I
   was of course unaware of it when this address was
   delivered, it rounds off the statement as to Chaucer's
   disgrace so well that I have ventured to incorporate
   it in my narrative.

46. WILLIAM EMPSON, THE AMBIGUITY OF CHAUCER

1930

William Empson (born 1906), educated at Magdalene College,
Cambridge, was Professor of English Literature in the University of Sheffield, 1953-71. His 'Seven Types of Ambiguity' (arising out of undergraduate essays) offers one of
the most brilliantly original and perceptive pieces of
incidental criticism of Chaucer ever written. Beginning
with a close inspection of the poetic text, Empson re-
discovers the riches of ambiguity, commonplace, hyperbole, pun, existing in Chaucer's apparently plain and
simple style, all of which calls for interpretation, not

visualisation. This piece marks the beginning of the end
of the domination of Neoclassical ideas in criticism.
Reprinted from 'Seven Types of Ambiguity', Chatto & Windus,
(1930) pp. 74-87, by permission of the publishers; and of
New Directions Publishing Corporation, New York.

(p. 74) One is tempted to think of these effects [of ambi-
guity] as belonging to the later stages of Renaissance
refinement, as something oversophisticated in the manner
of Caroline shape-poems; and due to a peculiar clotting of
the imagination. It is worth while then to produce
examples from 'Troilus and Criseyde', as one of the most
leisurely, simplest as to imagery, and earliest poems in
English literature. In the first love scene between the
two, Criseyde says petulantly she doesn't know what she's
expected to say; what does he mean, now, in plain words?

    What that I mene, O swete herte dere?
    Quod Troilus. O goodly fresshe free.
    That with the stremes of your eyen clere
    You wolde frendly sometimes on me see;
    And then agreen that I may be he....(iii. 128),

and so on for three verses, an enthusiastic and very
moving statement of the chivalric evasion of the point at
issue. *Stremes* has the straightforward meaning of
'beams of light' ('Compleynte unto Pite', line 94). The
N.E.D. does not give this meaning, but shows *stremes* as
already a hyperbolical commonplace use of blood and
tears, or 'beams of sweet influence,' like those of the
Pleiades; but after *fresh* and *free,* there is some implication of a stream (Naiades) that he can drink of and wash
in, cleansing and refreshing, so that one glance of her
eyes recovers him as by crossing a stream you break the
spells of black magic, or the scent by which the hounds of
your enemies are tracking you down; and so that the ready
tears of her sympathy are implied faintly, as in the
background.
    At the climax of the great scene in the second book,
when Pandarus has got his ward alone to talk to her about
her money affairs, mysteriously congratulated her on her
good luck, and gradually led her through the merits of
Troilus to an appeal to her pity for his unhappiness,
Cressida seems suddenly to guess his meaning and makes a
great display of outraged virtue. One must not suppose,
of course, because Chaucer shows us her machinery - 'I
shal fele what he meneth, I-wis' - 'It nedeth me ful

sleyly for to pleye' - that we are not to believe in the
reality of the virtue, or that it is not the modest and
proper machinery.

> What? Is this al the joye and al the feste?
> Is this your reed, is this my blisful cas?
> Is this the verray mede of your biheste?
> Is al this peynted proces seyd, alas,
> Right for this fyn?   (ii. 421.)

The last three lines, I submit, are extremely Shake-
spearean; they have all the concentrated imagery, the
bright central metaphor steeped and thickened in irrelevant incidental metaphors, of his mature style. I thought
at first the meanings might have been quite simple in
Chaucer's English, and have acquired a patina of subtlety
in the course of time; it would have been fun to maintain
that Shakespeare learnt his style from a misunderstanding
of Chaucer; but the N.E.D. leaves no doubt that (whether
Shakespeare was influenced by it or not) time has faded
rather than enriched the original ambiguity.

Reed, of course, is advice; he had told her her *cas* was
blisful, to have caught the eye of the prince; *mede* meant
at that time wages, a bribe, merit, a meadow and a drink
made with honey; *biheste* meant a vow, a promise, and a
command; *proces* meant a series of actions, the course of
a narrative, proceedings in an action at law, and a procession; and *fyn* meant generally 'end,' with accepted
derivatives like the object of an action, death, and a
contract; by itself it would not suggest a money penalty
before 1500, but it might suggest 'money offered in the
hope of exemption.' Thus the materials are ample enough,
but this is not to say they were all used.

I shall pause to illustrate the force of *beheste* and
the harangue of Pandarus that has gone before:-

> Now understand, that I yow nought requere
> To binde ye to him thorough no beheste,
> But only that yew make him bettre chere,
> Than ye had don er this, and more feste,
> So that his life be saved, at the leste.

Either 'I do not ask it, as a *command* from your guardian,
that you should bind yourself to him (permanently or
sinfully),' or 'I do not ask you to bind yourself to him
with anything so definite as a *vow*.'

> Think eke, how elde wasteth every houre
> In eche of yow a party of beautee;

And therefore, er that age thee devoure,
Go love, for olde, ther wol no wight of thee.
Lat this proverbe a lore unto yow be;
'To late y-war, quod Beautee, whan it paste';
And elde daunteth daunger at the laste.

It is not at first plain why there is so much power of
song in the poetical commonplace of the first four lines;
why its plainest statement seems to imply a lyric; so that
the English reader feels the pre-Raphaelites in it, and
Chaucer felt in it his Italians ('Filostrato', ii. 54).
A statement of the limitations of human life is a sort of
recipe for producing humility, concentration, and sincerity in the reader; it soothes, for instance, jealousy,
makes the labours of the practical world less pressing
because less likely to make any real difference (games
have the same mode of approach); sets the mind free,
therefore, to be operated on by the beauty of the verse
without distraction; and makes you willing to adopt,
perhaps to some slight extent permanently, the point of
view of the poet or of the character described, because,
having viewed your limits, marked your boat's position
with regard to distant objects on the shore, you are able
without losing your bearings to be turned round or moved
to another part of the bay.
    Further, to think of human life in terms of its lowest
factors, considered as in themselves dignified, has a
curious effect in dignifying the individual concerned;
makes him a type, and so something larger and more significant than before; makes his dignity feel safer, since
he is sure he has at least these qualifications for it;
makes him feel accepted and approved of by his herd, in
that he is being humble and understanding their situation
(poor creatures); makes it seem likely, since he understands their situation, because he feels it in himself,
that they will return to him also this reserved and detached sympathy; makes him, indeed, feel grander than the
rest of his herd, for a new series of reasons; because by
thinking of them he has got outside them; because by forming a concept of them he has made them seem limited; because he has thereby come to seem less subject to the
melancholy truths he is recognising; because to recognise
melancholy truths is itself, if you can be protected somehow, an invigorating activity; and (so that we complete
the circle back to humility) because to think about these
common factors has a certain solidity and safety in that
it is itself, after all, one of the relevant common factors of the human mind.
    However, it is the mode of action of the last two lines

which is my immediate business.

   Y-war may mean prudent or experienced; *too late*, 'Then
first when too late,' or 'going on until too late.'
'First prudent when too late' - I have found that one
should be careful to avoid risks, perhaps such as that of
never getting a lover, but, more strongly, such as are
involved in unlawful satisfactions. 'First conscious
when too late' - I have found too late that one should be
determined to obtain satisfaction. 'Having been prudent
until too late' - I have found that one can wait too long
for the safest moment for one's pleasures. 'Having been
conscious till too late' - I have found that one can seek
one's pleasure once too often. Pandarus, of course, only
meant the second and third; Chaucer (it is shown not as
irony but as a grand overtone of melancholy) meant all
four. (This, by the way, is the fourth type of ambiguity,
but I am taking the whole passage together.)

   And elde daunteth daunger at the last.

Daunt means subdue or frighten; *daunger* at this time had
a wealth of meaning that it has since lost, such as disdain, imperiousness, liability, miserliness, and power.
'Old age will break your pride, will make you afraid of
the independence you are now prizing; the coming of old
age is stronger than the greatness of kings, stronger
than all the brutal powers that you are now afraid of,
stronger even than the stubborn passion of misers that
defeat it for so long; you must act now because when you
are old you will be afraid to take risks, and you may take
heart because, however badly you are caught, it will be
all the same after another century; even in your own lifetime, by the time you are an old woman you will have lived
down scandal.' Or taking *elde* as an old woman, not as the
age that defeats her, the phrase interacts with the passing of beauty, whether after a life of sin or of seclu-
sion (there appear to have been no alternatives) in the
preceding line, and the old hag is finally so ugly that
all the powers in *daunger* shrink away from the gloom of
her grandeur, are either lost to her or subdued to her,
and the amorous risks and adventures will be at last
afraid to come near.
   The line is a straightforward ambiguity of the second
type, and I hope the reader will not object that I have
been making up a poem of my own. Mr. Eliot somewhere says
that this is always done by bad critics who have failed to
be poets; this is a valuable weapon but a dangerously
superficial remark, because it obscures the main crux
about poetry, that being an essentially suggestive act it

can only take effect if the impulses (and to some extent
the experiences) are already there to be called forth;
that the process of getting to understand a poet is precisely that of constructing his poems in one's own mind.
Of course, it is wrong to construct the wrong poem, and I
have no doubt Mr. Eliot was right in his particular accu-
sations.

> Is this the verray mede of youre beheste?
> Is this your reed, is this my blisful cas?

replies Cressida, to these ambiguities of Pandarus; 'Is
this the wage that is offered to me in return for obeying
your commands? Is this my inducement to be a good ward,
that I must continually have the trouble, and pain, to
think you so wicked, of repelling solicitations? Is this
what your advice is worth? Is this what your promise to
look after me is worth?' The honest meaning (wage)
carries contempt; the dishonest meaning (bribe) an accusation. 'Is this why the prince has been so friendly with
you? Is this what you stand to make out of being my guardian?' And if *mede* carries any echo of meaning (it is
impossible at this distance of time to say) from the natural freedom of the open meadow, or the simple delight-
fulness of that form of beer, we have, 'Is this the
meadow, or the beer, you had promised me, or proposed for
yourself? Is this my blissful case you have described?'
It is the two meanings of *beheste* which give her so powerful a weapon against Pandarus, in his double position of
guardian and go-between.

> Is all this peynted process seyd, alas,
> Right for this fyn?

These two lines have a lesser but a more beautiful complexity; Pandarus' great harangue is seen, by using the
puns on *fyn* and *process*, as a brightly-coloured procession
(*peynted* would suggest frescoes in churches) moving on,
leading her on, to dusty death and the everlasting bon-
fire; and behind this simple framework, that gives the
movement, the immediate point, of the phrase, *process*
hints at a parallel with legal proceedings, ending where
none of the parties wanted, when at last the lawyers, like
Pandarus, stop talking and demand to be paid; and rising
behind that again, heard in the indignation of the phrase,
is a threat that she may expose him, and *peyn*-ted and *fyn*
suggest legal pains and penalties.
    'To whom do they suggest these things?' the reader may
ask; and there is no obvious reply. It depends how

carefully the passage is supposed to be read; in a long
narrative poem the stress on particular phrases must be
slight, most of the lines do not expect more attention
than you would give to phrases of a novel when reading it
aloud; you would not look for the same concentration of
imagery as in a lyric. On the other hand, a long poem
accumulates imagery; I am dealing with a particularly
dramatic point where the meaning needs to be concentrated;
and Chaucer had abandoned his original for a moment to
write on his own.

It is a more crucial question how far *peynted*, in a
proper setting, can suggest 'pains'; how far we ought to
leave the comparatively safe ground of ambiguity to examine latent puns. The rule in general, I believe, is that
a mere similarity of sound will not take effect unless it
is consciously noticed, and will then give an impression
of oddity. For it is the essential discipline of language
that our elaborate reactions to a word are called out only
by the word itself, or what is guessed to be the word
itself; they are trained to be very completely inhibited
by anything near the word but not quite right. It is only
when a word has been passed in, accepted as sensible, that
it is allowed to echo about in the mind. On the other
hand, this very inhibition (the *effort* of distinction, in
cases where it would have been natural to have taken the
other word) may call forth effects of its own; that, for
instance, is why puns are funny; may make one, perhaps,
more ready, or for all I know rhythmically more and less
ready, to react to the word when it comes. Thus I have
often wondered whether Swinburne's 'Dolores' gets any of
its energy from the way the word Spain, suggested by the
title and by various things in the course of the poem,
although one is forced to wonder what the next rhyme is
going to be, never appears among the dozen that are paired
off with 'Our Lady of Pain'. But so little is known about
these matters that it is rather unwise to talk about them;
one goes off into Pure Sound and entirely private associations; for instance, I want to back up my 'pains' from
peynted by calling in 'weighted' and 'fainted,' and the
suggestion of labour in *all that painted*. The study of
subdued bad puns may be very important, but at the moment
it is less hopeful than the study of more rational ambiguities, because you can rely on most word associations
being called out (if one's mind does not in *some* way run
through the various meanings of a word, how can it arrive
at the right one?), whereas the puns, in a sense, ought not
to be there at all.

A good illustration of this point, not that most people
will require to be convinced of it, is given by the words

'rows' and 'rose'; 'rows' suggests regimentation, order,
a card index system, and the sciences; 'rose' suggests a
sort of grandeur in the state of culture, something with
all the definiteness and independence of Nature that has
been produced within the systems of mankind (giving a
sort of proof of our stability), some of the overtones of
richness, delicacy, and power of varying such as are
carried by 'wine'; various sexual associations from its
appearance and the 'Romaunt of the Roos'; and notions of
race, dignity, and fine clothes as if from the Wars of the
Roses. These two words never get in each other's way; it
is hard to believe they are pronounced the same. Homo-
nyms with less powerful systems of association, like the
verb 'rows' and the 'roes' of fishes, lend themselves
easily to puns and seem in some degree attracted towards
the two more powerful systems; but to insist that the
first two are the same sound, to pass suddenly from one to
the other, destroys both of them, and leaves a sort of
bewilderment in the mind.

On the other hand, there was a poem about strawberries
in 'Punch' a year or two ago, which I caught myself liking
because of a subdued pun; here what was suggested was a
powerful word, what was meant was a mere grammatical convenience:-

Queenlily June with a rose in her hair
Moves to her prime with a langorous air.
What in her kingdom's most comely? By far
Strawberries, strawberries, strawberries are.

I was puzzled to know why the first line seemed beautiful
till I found I was reading *Queenlily* as 'Queen Lily,'
which in a child's poetry-book style is rather charming;
'the lily with a rose in her hair,' used of a ripening
virgin and hence of early summer, in which the absolute
banality of roses and liles is employed as it were heral-
dically, as a symbol intended not to be visualised but at
once interpreted, is a fine Gongorism, and the alternative
adverb (a swan against panelling) sets the whole thing in
motion by its insistence on the verb. It is curious how
if you think of the word only as an adverb, all this playful dignity, indeed the whole rhythm of the line, ebbs
away into complacence and monotony.

It is a little unfair, perhaps, to use Chaucer for my
purpose; I have used him because he may give the impression these effects are somehow part of the character of
the language, since they were so much in evidence so
soon, and in a writer apparently so derivative from the
French and Italian literatures, which don't seem ambiguous

in the same way. I admit it is much easier to muddle
one's readers when using the unfamiliar stresses of fourteenth-century speech, and when dealing with unfamiliar
uses of words. This, for instance, I thought at first
was an ambiguity, when Troilus' sickness, caused by love
of Criseyde, and used to arrange a meeting with her, is
announced to the assembled company: -

> Compleyned eke Eleyne of his sycknesse
> So feithfully, that pitee was to here,
> And every wight gan waxen for accesse
> A leech anon, and seyde, 'in this manere
> Men curen folk; this charm I wol yow lere.'
> But there sat oon, al list hir nought to teche.
> That thoughte, beste coude I yet been his leche.
>
> (ii. 1576.)

Access in the fourteenth century meant some kind of fever-
ish attack, and I believe is not used in any other sense
by Chaucer; but it was used by Wyclif to mean the act of
coming near, or the right of coming near, and acquired
later the meaning of accession to an office of dignity.
So that it might mean that everybody said they knew how
to cure fevers so as to seem dignified at the party, so as
to put themselves forward, and perhaps so as to be allowed
to visit the prince on his sick-bed. The break of the
line which separates *accesse* from *leech* and connects it
with *gan* helps this overtone of ironical meaning, which is
just what the social comedy of the passage requires; and
if you wish to stress the influence of Chaucer as a stylist, it is these later meanings, and not the medical meaning, which were most prominent by the sixteenth century;
this, for instance, is just the suggestive way Shakespeare
would use a Latinised word. But to Chaucer at any rate, I
believe, the joke was strong enough to stand by itself,
and too pointed to call up overtones; I have put it in to
show a case where a plausible ambiguity may be unprofit-
able, and the sort of reasons that may make one refuse to
accept it.

Rather a pretty example turns up when Cressida is reflecting it would be unwise to fall in love (ii. 752). I
am, she says,

> Right yong, and stand unteyed in lusty lese
> Withouten jalousye or swich debaat.

Lese, among the absurd variety of its meaning, includes
lies, a snare for rabbits, a quantity of thread, a net, a
noose, a whip-lash, and the thong holding hunting dogs;

one would take with these *lusty* in the sense of amorous.
Or *lese* may mean a contract giving lands or tenements
for life, a term of years, or at will (hence guaranteed
permanence and safety), open pasture-land (as in leas),
picking fruit, the act of coursing (she is her own mistress), or a set of three (the symbol of companionship as
opposed to passion): one would take with these *lusty* in
the sense of hearty and delightful, its more usual meaning
at the time. Thus, while the intended meaning is not in
doubt, to be *in lusty lese* may be part of the condition of
being *unteyed* or of being *teyed*. I have put down most of
the meanings for fun; the only ones I feel sure of are:
'I am not entangled in the net of desire,' and 'I am dis-
entangled like a colt in a meadow'; these are quite enough
for the ambiguity of syntax.

You may say that these meanings should be permuted to
convey doubt: 'I am sprawling without foothold in the net
of desire,' and 'I have *not* been turned out to grass in
the wide meadow of freedom.' But in paraphrasing these
meanings I have had to look for an idiom that will hide
the main fact of the situation, that she is *unteyed*.

Or you might say that *stand* attracts *in*, so that *lese*
must be taken only with *unteyed*. But *withouten* suggests
a parallel with *unteyed*, which would make *lese* go with
teyed.

It would have been consistent enough with Criseyde's
character to have been expressing doubt, but about this
line, whatever its meaning, there is a sort of complacency and decision which convince me it is only of the
second type.

At the same time, I admit that this is a monstrously
clotted piece of language; not at all, for instance, a
thing it would be wise to imitate, and it would be unfair
to leave Chaucer without reminding the reader of something
more beautiful. It is during the scene, then, leading to
the actual seduction of Criseyde, when she has no doubt
what she wants but is determined to behave like a lady,
when Troilus is swooning about the place, always in despair, and Pandarus sees no immediate prospect of pushing
them into bed together, that this sheer song of ironical
happiness pours forth from the lips of their creator.

But now pray God to quenchen al this sorwe.
So hope I that he shall, for he best may.
For I have seen of a full misty morwe
Folwe ful ofte a merie somer's day,
And after winter folweth grene May.
Men sen alday, and reden eke in stories,
That after sharpe shoures ben victories.

It is the open and easy grandeur, moving with the whole
earth, of the middle lines, that made me quote them; my
immediate point is *shoures*. It meant charge, or onslaught
of battle, or pang, such as Troilus' fainting-fits, or the
pains of childbirth; if you take it as showers of rain
(I. iv. 251), the two metaphors, from man and the sky,
melt into each other; there is another connection with
warriors, in that the word is used for showers of arrows;
there is another connection with lovers in that it is used
for showers of tears.

I hope I have made out a fair case for a poetical use
of ambiguity, in one form or another, as already in full
swing in the English of Chaucer; so that it has some claim
to be considered native to the language. I really do not
know what importance it has in other European languages;
the practice of looking for it rapidly leads to hallucina-
tions, as you can train yourself always to hear a clock
ticking; and my impression is that while it is frequent in
French and Italian, the subsidiary meanings are nearly
always bad grammar, so that the inhabitants of those countries would have too much conscience to attend to them.
At any rate it is not true, obviously enough, that Chaucer's ambiguities are copied from Boccaccio; I found it
very exciting to go through my list in a parallel text and
see how, even where great sections of the stuff were being
translated directly, there would be a small patch of invention at the point I had marked down.

47.   JOHN LIVINGSTONE LOWES, A POWERFULLY ASSOCIATIVE
MEMORY

1930

J.L. Lowes (1867-1945) the famous US scholar and critic,
learnt and taught first mathematics and theology before
graduate work on Chaucer at Harvard University, where he
was eventually, in 1918, appointed to a chair from which
he retired in 1939. He excelled in tracing Chaucer's
relation to his French and Italian sources, rather as he
traced Coleridge's sources in his famous book 'The Road
to Xanadu' (1927). In the first Sir Israel Gollancz
Memorial Lecture Lowes surveys the raw material of Chaucer's art and the forms available. His special contribution lies in his scholarly recognition of the richness

and variety of Chaucer's resources, and his recognition of
the associative power of Chaucer to combine them in poetry.
Reprinted by permission of the British Academy from 'The
Proceedings of the British Academy', XVI (1930), pp. 297-
8, 302-3. 306-19, 322-6.

THE ART OF GEOFFREY CHAUCER

(p. 297) One of the glories of English poetry has been the
interpenetration in it of personal experience - call it
for brevity life, if you will - and of books. Through the
one, poetry acquires its stamp of individuality; through
the other it is dipped in the quickening stream of tradition which has flowed through the work of all the poets
from Homer and pre-Homeric days until now. The continuity
of poetry, through its participation in that deep and perpetually broadening current, is a fact perhaps more important than the newness of the channels through which from
time to time it flows. The greatest poetry is, indeed,
steeped in the poet's own experience and coloured by the
life of his times. But it also participates in a succession almost apostolic, in which there is an authentic if
incorporeal laying on of hands:

> Go, litel book...
>   ...no making thou n'envye,
> But subgit be to alle poesye;
> And kis the steppes, wher-as thou seest pace
> Virgile, Ovyde, Omer, Lucan, and Stace.

That is from the close of a masterpiece which is at once
sheer Chaucer and an embodiment of the tradition of the
elders from Homer through the Middle Ages to a contemporary fellow poet, Boccaccio; and I suspect that no one
in the long and splendid line of English poets more strikingly exemplifies than Geoffrey Chaucer the characteristic interplay, in great verse, of life and books. For he
was, on the one hand, a widely experienced, busy, and
versatile man of affairs, and he was also one of the most
omnivorous readers in that company of glorious literary
cormorants who have enriched English letters. Had he been
either without the other - had there been lacking either
the immediate and manifold contacts with life, or the zest
of a *helluo librorum* - he would doubtless still have been
a poet. But in that case not one of the poems by which he
is known could even remotely have been what it is. Let
me, then, rehearse as necessary background, even at the

risk of seeming for the moment to abandon poetry, a few of
the familiar facts....

(p. 302) But this wide range of his experience carries
with it another consequence. We need constantly to remind
ourselves of the degree to which in Chaucer's day communication had to be by word of mouth. And so the people whom
he knew were also channels through which came to him news
of his world - news not only of that 'little world' which
to Shakespeare's John of Gaunt was England ; not only,
either, of that 'queasy world' (in Margaret Paston's vivid
phrase) across the Channel; but also of that now looming,
menacing, always mysterious world beyond, which was the
Orient. And few men have ever been more strategically
placed for its reception. That news of England or Wales
or even Ireland should so reach him is too obvious to
dwell on, fascinating as is the use he makes of it. How,
for example, did he get to know of that 'Colle tregetour'
- Colin the magician - whom he saw in his dream in the
House of Fame?

> Ther saugh I Colle tregetour
> Upon a table of sicamour
> Pleye an uncouthe thing to telle;
> I saugh him carien a wind-melle
> Under a walsh-note shelle.

But Colle was actually no piquant figure in a dream. He
was, as we now know, thanks to Professor Royster, a contemporary Englishman, and he later exhibited his tricks,
'par voie de nigromancie', at Orleans, precisely as the
Clerk of Orleans in the Franklin's Tale produced his
illusions, 'Swiche as thise subtile tregetoures playe'.
And Chaucer's apposite choice of Orleans as the school of
his own magician is not without interest. How, too (to
draw on the House of Fame again), did he get to know of
Bret Glascurion and of Celtic wicker houses? Did that
Welsh vintner of London tell him - Lewis Johan, who was at
least a friend of Chaucer once removed; or did Sir Lewis
Clifford or Sir John Clanvowe, both close friends of his,
and both of whom held offices in Wales? Who can say!
Chaucer's London was his own vast House of Rumour, only on
a smaller scale.

But men, among them scores whom Chaucer knew, were constantly going out of England and coming back to it - going
out for reasons of war, or trade, or chivalry, or religion, and coming back along the trade routes and the
pilgrim roads and from their military exploits, with
stories, and tidings, and even manuscripts, as well as
with stuffs, or spices, or cockle-shells, or battered

arms. And such knights as the stately figure of the Prologue were among the great intermediaries between Chaucer's England and the rest of the world. Europe was being
menaced from three directions at once....

(p. 306) How this or that particular tale or bit of
information came to Chaucer, it is far from my present purpose to inquire. He was at the centre of a rich and varied
and shifting world, and in ways without number, of which
these are bare suggestions, his personal and official experience lent material to his art. And there were also
books.

The range of Chaucer's reading is as extraordinary as
the scope of his activities. He read in three languages
besides English - French, Latin, and Italian. French he
probably both knew and spoke from his childhood. Latin
with little doubt he learned at school. It has hitherto
been assumed that he picked up Italian in Italy, during his
first visit in 1372-3. It is possible, though not yet
proven, that he may have known it earlier. But in either
case, the bulk of his known reading, until the great
Italians swam into his ken, was French, with a good deal of
Latin besides. And French he never abandoned, and Latin
he read copiously to the end. The French and Italian works
which he knew may best for our purpose be considered later.
His wide and diversified reading of Latin, however, is both
typical of his varied interests and important for its contributions, and I shall rapidly summarize it here.

Of the classics, he knew in the original Ovid, especially the 'Metamorphoses' (his 'owne book', as he called
it), and the 'Heroides'. Virgil he knew, but apparently
only the 'Aeneid'; the 'Thebaid' of Statius; Claudian;
and either in Latin or French or both, the 'Pharsalia'.
Cicero's 'Somnium Scipionis' he read in a copy of the commentary of Macrobius which he or somebody else had thumbed
to pieces - 'myn olde book to-torn', as he refers to it.
Horace he quotes half a dozen times, but I doubt whether
he knew either Horace or Juvenal at first hand. Dante, or
John of Salisbury, or the *florilegia* may well have been
intermediaries. But for Virgil, Statius, and Lucan, and
also for Ovid, he had two strings to his bow. For the
Middle Ages seized upon the Latin epics and made them over
into their own likeness as romances. And so there was,
for the 'Aeneid', the 'Roman d'Eneas', in which both Dido
and (especially) Lavinia sigh, wake, and 'walwe', like
Chaucer's own Dido in the 'Legend', in the throes of
heroic love. For the 'Thebaid', too, there was the 'Roman
de Thèbes', and for the 'Pharsalia' the 'Roman de Julius
Cesar'. And the Homeric story of the Trojan War passed by
devious ways into the 'Roman de Troie' of Benoit de Ste-

Maure, and thence to Guido delle Colonne. The 'Metamorphoses' were transmogrified into the interminable and portentous triple allegory of the 'Ovide moralisé', on which
Machaut had freely drawn for his classical lore. They are
all, as I can testify, diverting documents, after their
fantastic fashion, even yet, and Chaucer, who probably in
his salad days read French more readily than Latin, and
who also would be apt to read what his fellow pages and
squires at Court were reading, certainly knew and freely
used the 'Roman de Troie', and drew, on occasion, upon the
'Ovide moralisé'. He also read - I feel sure myself on
grounds which have no place here - the 'Roman d'Eneas'
and the 'Roman de Julius Cesar'. And there is evidence
that he knew the mythographers, and was not unfamiliar with
the mass of misinformation accumulated in the medieval
commentaries on the classics. It was, in fact, more than
once Servius or Lactantius or Junius Philargerius who
either directly or indirectly first made for him his mistakes. For few things about Chaucer are more important to
remember than the fact that even the classical authors whom
he read in the original were deeply coloured in his mind
through the various medieval metamorphoses which they had
undergone.

His reading in the medieval Latin authors was far too
extensive for enumeration here. But nothing in his deal-
ings with them is more characteristic than his trick of
suffusing with his own inalienable humour his borrowings
from the dullest and most arid documents. He knew well
both the 'Anticlaudianus' and the 'De Planctu Naturae' of
Alanus de Insulis, and especially remembered, as he would,
the concrete bits, and enriched them, as he also would,
with an added liveliness. He read Martianus Capella on
the Nuptials of Philology and Mercury, and Nigel Wireker's
diverting Mirror of Fools, with the adventures of Dan
Burnel the ass; and a scrap of the Eclogue of Theodulus
once leaped back to his memory, endowed with an exquisite
humour which he did not find in his original. He knew,
as a student of his art, who did not 'pipe but as the
linnets sing', the 'Nova Poetria' of Geoffrey of Vinsauf,
whom he calls his 'dere mayster soverayn', and he made
irresistible mock-heroic use, in the Nun's Priest's Tale,
of one of his master's *exempla*. He at least dipped into
the vast encyclopaedic reaches of Vincent of Beauvais, and
he read with obvious gusto and astounding results St.
Jerome's tractate against Jovinian on the subject of virginity. He was thoroughly familiar (to shift the key)
with the Vulgate, and with the service and especially the
great hymns of the Church, which inspired - in each case
interwoven with lines from the crowning vision of the

'Paradiso' - at least two of his loftiest passages.
Whether he saw as he read the rich potentialities of his
documents, or whether his stores came pouring back to
memory as he composed, or whether both processes went on
together, we can never know. But if any one ever read
(in the current phrase) 'creatively', it was he.

And to all this evidence of abounding vitality and
energy must be added the almost incredible list of his
translations. The refrain of the 'Balade' which Eustache
Deschamps addressed to Chaucer and sent by the hand of Sir
Lewis Clifford, is the line: 'Grant translateur, noble
Geffroy Chaucier.' It was as a translator only, it would
seem, that his fame had reached Deschamps. And the
'Balade' itself makes it clear that Deschamps had in mind
that translation of the 'Roman de la Rose' which, in the
Prologue to the 'Legend', gave such offence to the God of
Love. And the God of Love's anger makes it further clear
that Jean de Meun's huge continuation was included. As
if this great task were not enough, he translated Jean de
Meun's French version of Albertano of Brescia's 'Liber
Consolationis', and also (for his tastes were richly
catholic) the fierce misanthropy of Pope Innocent's 'De
Contemptu Mundi', at which gloomy treatise Deschamps too
had tried his hand. And there were besides the now lost
translations of a work of Origen on Mary Magdalene, and
of Machaut's 'Dit dou Lyon'. But above all the rest
stands Boethius 'On the Consolation of Philosophy'. He
translated it, as Alfred the Great and Jean de Meun had
done before him, and with the aid of Jean de Meun's
French version, and he drew upon it, as in another fashion
he levied tribute on the 'Roman de la Rose', until he
ceased to write.

His reading in the science of his day is in some respects, I am inclined to think, the most remarkable of all.
His singularly broad yet minute knowledge of medieval
medicine, in which he anticipated Burton, I have elsewhere
had occasion to discuss. But far more than his acquaintance with 'the loveres maladye of Hereos' is in point.
Fourteenth-century medicine, like its twentieth-century
descendant, was half psychology, and in its emphasis on
dreams as a means of diagnosis anticipated Freud. And
Madame Pertelote's diagnosis, by means of his dream, of
Chauntecleer's malady, as well as her inimitable discourse on dreams as symptoms, is scientifically accurate.
So is her *materia medica*. The herbs which she prescribes
- 'Pekke hem up right as they growe, and ete hem in' - are
the medically proper herbs. And the quintessential touch
is her inclusion in Chauntecleer's dietary of 'wormes' for
'a day or two'. For worms - you may read a learned and

matter-of-fact chapter on *Vermes terrenae* in the 'Medica Materia' of Dioscorides - were among the recognized correctives. It is easy enough to slip into one's narrative as evidence of erudition an excerpt from some learned document. But such casual exactness, imbued with delicious humour to boot, is not something which one gets up over night. In alchemy - witness the Canon's Yeoman's Tale - Chaucer was no less deeply grounded than in medicine. He had read enough in the alchemical treatises of Arnoldus de Villanova, for example, his 'Arnold of the Newe Toun', to refer to one of Arnold's treatises a highly picturesque and abstruse dictum which he quotes, when he had actually read it in another. As for physics, one of the very best pieces of exposition, as exposition, which I know in English is the erudite Eagle's discourse in the House of Fame on the transmission of sound, and that again is founded on accepted authority. So is Chaucer's astrology, and in astronomy proper he could point with just pride to that Treatise on the Astrolabe which he wrote, with its charming Preface, for his 'litel son Lowis', using freely a Latin translation of the Arabian astronomer Messahala. These are the barest shreds and patches only. The scope and thoroughness of Chaucer's scientific reading would still be remarkable, had he read nothing else.

There, then, are the raw materials of his art - men and their doings, and books - God's plenty of each, in all conscience. And since he began with books (with which, to be sure, he never ended) it is much to the point to consider how he read. Did he have the books on our list, for example, in his own possession, and therefore ready at hand for pleasure or need? Without question a large, perhaps a very large proportion of them were his own. He declared, fairly late in his life - or rather, the God of Love asserted for him - that he had in his chest 'sixty bokes, olde and newe', and there is no reason to doubt the statement. But that number may easily have represented three or four times sixty 'books', in the sense in which we use the word. For book, as Chaucer employs the term, must be thought of in the light of medieval manuscripts, and a single manuscript was often a small library in itself. The 'boke' which Chaucer was reading when he fell asleep over the tale of Ceyx and Alcyone was an omnium gatherum of verse, and lives of queens and kings, and 'many othere thinges smale'. The 'book' (and again the word is the same) which the Wife of Bath's fifth husband revelled in contained, she declared, Valerius 'ad Rufinum', Theophrastus, Jerome against Jovinian, Tertullian, the mysterious Crisippus, Trotula, the

Epistles of Eloise, the Parables of Solomon, and the 'Ars
Amatoria' - 'And alle thise were bounden in o volume'.
And one need only recall, among extant examples, the
Auchinleck MS., with its more than forty separate pieces,
or, for that matter, Harley 7333 among the manuscripts of
the Canterbury Tales. Chaucer's library was a rich one
for his day, and like his own clerk of Oxford who had 'at
his beddes heed' his 'Twenty bokes, clad in blak or
reed', and like that clerk of another kidney, 'hende
Nicholas', who likewise kept in his lodgings 'his Alma-
geste, and bokes grete and smale... On shelves couched at
his beddes heed', one may be fairly sure that Chaucer's
sixty books were not far from his hand.
   But is there any way of knowing, aside from these more
or less material considerations, how he actually read?
There are two subjects, and two only, on which Chaucer
vouchsafes us personal information about himself - his
love of books, and his imperviousness, real or assumed,
to love. On those two topics he is, in William Wordsworth's phrase but with a difference, 'right voluble'.
And two passages are especially in point. In one, that
preternaturally intelligent bird, the Eagle of the House
of Fame, gently chides him for his habits. He knows
nothing now, says the Eagle, of what is going on about
him; even 'of thy verray neyghebores That dwellen almost
at thy dores, Thou herest neither that ne this'. And then
follows, under cover of the Eagle's irresponsible loqua-
city, the most precious autobiographical touch that Chaucer left:

> For whan thy labour doon al is,
> And hast y-maad thy rekeninges,
> In stede of reste and newe thinges,
> Thou gost hoom to thy hous anoon;
> And, also domb as any stoon,
> Thou sittest at another boke,
> Til fully daswed is thy loke,
> And livest thus as an hermyte,
> Although thyn abstinence is lyte.

That picture - the account books of the customs exchanged
after hours for vastly different books (the Eagle's
'another' is pregnant), and Chaucer reading on, oblivious
of all else, until his eyes dazzle in his head - that picture tells more than pages, not merely of the intimate
relation in which his books stood to his business, but
also of the absorbed intentness with which he read. And
there is another passage which illuminates yet another
quality of his reading. 'Not yore agon', he writes in the

Parlement of Foules,

>..hit happed me for to beholde
>Upon a boke, was write with lettres olde;
>And ther-upon, *a certeyn thing to lerne,*
>The longe day *ful faste I radde and yerne.*

I do not know which is the more characteristic of Chaucer - the fact that he was reading with the definite purpose of learning a certain thing, or the fact that he was
reading fast and eagerly. The two belong together. You
cannot divide his invincible zest from his incorrigibly
inquiring spirit - that 'besy gost' of his, as he called
it once, 'that thrusteth alwey newe'. And because he
brought both to his books, his reading became a live and
plastic thing for his art to seize on.
He was gifted, finally, with another quality of mind
which is peculiarly bound up with his art. He possessed,
in a word, like Virgil and Milton and Coleridge, a powerfully associative memory, which played, as he read, over
the multitude of impressions from previous reading, with
which his mind was stored. And the zest with which he
read gave freshness to his recollections, and one can
sometimes almost see the hovering associations precipi-
tate themselves as he reads. A single phrase in Boccaccio (and I am speaking by the book) calls up the lines of
a famous passage in Dante in which the same phrase occurs,
and the result is a *tertium quid* of his own, enriched
from the spoils of both. He finds in Boccaccio's 'Filostrato', as he works it over into his own Troilus, the
lovely Virgilian simile of the lily cut by the plough and
withering. But Dante, in a canto of the 'Inferno', the
opening lines of which Chaucer elsewhere quotes, has a
simile of falling, withering leaves. And again, through
a common element, Boccaccio's lines recall the lines of
Dante, and the falling leaves replace the fading lily in
Chaucer's simile. And Boccaccio and Dante in turn had
each in like fashion recalled his simile from Virgil.
It would be easy to rehearse such instances by the score
- instances, too, in which with his reminiscences of
books are interwoven his recollections of experience.
For that continuity of poetry of which I spoke consists
in the perpetual enrichment, through just such incremen-
tal transformations, of the present through the past.
And one of the happiest gifts of the gods to English
poetry, at the strategic moment of its history, was that
prehensile, amalgamating memory of Chaucer's which had
for its playground the prodigious array of promiscuous
writings which a moment ago I ruthlessly catalogued.

What now of his art in its larger relations? For
everything that I have so far said has been said with that
definitely in view. It is perilous, in the first place,
to divide Chaucer's poetic biography mechanically into
periods. There was nothing cataclysmic about his development. He was not a new creature, as Professor Kittredge
once observed, when he came back to London from his first
visit to Italy, nor does the poet of the Canterbury Tales
startle us by a 'leap of buds into ripe flowers'. Rather
- if I too may yield to an association - 'Morn into noon
did pass, noon into eve'. Transitions there were, of
course, but they were gradual. French poetry yielded
first place to Italian, and both to an asorption in human
life, in which books and men were fused as in a crucible.
But even after his momentous discovery of Boccaccio and
Dante, the influence of French poetry went on, though its
character changed - changed (to put it briefly) from the
mood of Guillaume de Lorris and Machaut to the mood of
Jean de Meun and Deschamps and the *fabliaux*. And *pari
passu*, as his powers developed, there came a significant
shift of values, and his reading of books played a lesser
and his reading of life a larger role in his art. But
throughout his career, that art kept curiously even pace
with his active life. It was dominantly French while he
was in personal attendance on a court where French was
still the more familiar language. His so-called Italian
period, which was never Italian in the sense in which the
earlier period had been French, coincided roughly with
those activities - his missions and the customs - which
brought him into various relations with Italy, Italians,
and Italian letters. And when his broadening affairs
afforded wider opportunities for observation, his art,
keeping all that it had won from France and Italy, became
at once English and universal.

Everybody knows that Chaucer began as a follower of the
contemporary French school of poetry, and that the most
powerful influence upon that school was the thirteenth-
century 'Roman de la Rose'. But the 'Roman de la Rose'
was influential in two entirely different ways. Guillaume
de Lorris, who began it, was a dreamer of dreams and a
poet of exquisite grace and charm. Jean de Meun, who continued it and multiplied its length by five, was a caustic
and disillusioned satirist, trenchant, arrogant, and
absolute master of a mordant pen. If Pope had taken it
into his head to complete the 'Faerie Queene', or if
Swift had been seized by the fancy of carrying on the
'Vicar of Wakefield' in the mood of Gulliver's fierce misanthropy, we might have had an adequate parallel. And
the fourteenth-century French Poets, as a consequence of

this strange duplex authorship, fall roughly into two
schools - the sons of Guillaume de Lorris and the sons of
Jean de Meun. But common to them all, and giving the
framework to half their verse, was the allegorical love
vision.

The contemporary Frenchmen whose influence on Chaucer
was farthest reaching were three: Guillaume de Machaut,
an elder contemporary; Jean Froissart, his coeval; and
Eustache Deschamps, who was younger. Machaut, who like
Chaucer was courtier and man of affairs as well as poet,
and who with his master, John of Bohemia, had 'reysed',
like the Knight, against the 'mescreans' in Prussia and
the Tartars in the snows of Lithuania, was the most influential French poet of his day. And he was so chiefly by
virtue of a highly sophisticated, artificial, exquisitely
elaborated technique. Froissart, whom Chaucer probably
knew at Court as the protégé of Queen Philippa, was an
incomparably less finished craftsman than Machaut, to
whose school he belongs. When he tells a story, like that
in the 'Dit dou Florin', of his reading aloud to Gaston
Phebus, Count of Foix, night after night for weeks, his
interminable 'Méliador', the tale becomes, through the art
of the chronicler, vivid with firelight and candles and
flagons; and when he writes of his boyhood and young manhood - of the games that he played, and of the maiden whom
he one day found reading the 'Cléomadès' - his verse is
suffused with personal charm. But when he falls into the
vein of the school, he can be both long-winded and very
dull. And finally Deschamps, who calls Machaut his
master, but who was really of the tribe of Jean de Meun,
was an inordinately prolific versifier, with the skill of
a virtuoso, but without music, grace, or charm; could be
as minutely circumstantial as Mistress Quickly over her
silver-gilt goblet; and was possessed by a passion like
that of Pepys for autobiographical memoranda. Of the
three, Machaut was Chaucer's earliest master; from Froissart he effectively borrowed more than once; and Deschamps twice furnished him with subject matter to which,
on the two occasions, each time with a technique already
mastered, he gave consummate form. There were others, of
course, but these three were the chief influences during
the period when Chaucer was saturated with the later
French poetry of courtly love, even while maintaining an
amiable impermeability all his own to its inherent absurdities. And I am far from sure that it was not to these
very absurdities that Chaucer's genius owed the turn which
from the first it took.

For he found in his French models, and especially in
Machaut, the framework of the vision, as that had come

down, with growing elaboration on the way, from Guillaume
de Lorris. And he used the machinery of the vision in the
Book of the Duchess, the House of Fame, the Parliament of
Fowls, and in the first version of the Prologue to the
Legend of Good Women. It was the most popular and, in
Machaut's expert hands, the most sophisticated device of
his day, and Chaucer was then writing for a sophisticated
audience. But the visions were allegorical love visions,
and as such they were thick sown with artifices at which
Chaucer balked. And the more thoroughly one is steeped in
Chaucer, so that one sees in a measure with his eyes, the
more readily one understands the impossibility of his
acquiescence in the then current artificialities of the
genre. The framework of the vision, to be sure, offered
freedom in both choice and disposition of subject matter.
But it was precisely in the character of the French subject matter, to judge from the cold shoulder which Chaucer
turned to it, that one source of his disrelish lay. For
it was obviously as barren of interest to Geoffrey Chaucer
as interminable subtilizings about love - especially when
nothing comes of them - have been and are to any normally
constituted Anglo-Saxon. Moreover, the visions are
thickly peopled with personified abstractions. Esperance, Attemprance, Mesure, Douce Pensée, Plaisance,
Desirs, Franchise, Pité, Loyauté, Espoirs, Raison, Suf-
fisance, Patience, Paour - those are the denizens of less
than half of Machaut's 'Remede de Fortune'. Like Criseyde listening under trying circumstances to the 'wom-
manisshe thinges' of her feminine callers, Chaucer must
have 'felte almost [his] herte dye For wo, and wery of
that companye'. Nor was it subject matter alone which he
found alien. The phraseology, too, was remote alike from
his tastes and his aptitudes. There is nothing I know
which rivals in its tireless facility of recurrence the
later vacabulary of courtly love. If one read long
enough, one is obsessed by the uncanny feeling that the
phraseology walks alone, without need of the poet's
intervention, and carries the poet with it of its own
momentum. Specific meaning disappears. Machaut's
Peronne, in that amazing Goethe-and-Bettina correspondence, the 'Voir-Dit', is 'en douceur douce com coulom-
belle, En loyauté loyal com turturelle'. But the same
columbine phrases slip from his pen, when, in 'Prise
d'Alexandrie', he describes the Emperor Charles I of Lux-
embourg. He too, like Peronne, is 'humbles et piteus
Plus que turtre ne colombele'. In that ineffably affected
jargon discriminations vanish. 'Thought and affliction,
passion, hell itself, [are turned] to favour and to prettiness.' And that was not Chaucer's way.

What he found, then, in the French vision poems, was a
frame - a frame which possessed admirable potentialities,
but which for him, to all intents and purposes, was empty.
And Chaucer, who in his way was not unlike Nature herself,
abhorred a vacuum. He proceeded, accordingly, to fill the
frame, and incidentally to set one of the great traditions
of English poetry. And into the vision framework, instead
of consecrated phrases, wire-drawn subtleties, *ragiona-
mente d'amore,* and the more fantastic elements of the
courtly code, he poured the stores of that reading and
observation on which we have dwelt so long. 'For out of
olde feldes' - and this was his discovery, as 'the longe
day ful faste [he] radde and yerne' -

> For out of olde feldes, as man seith,
> Cometh al this newe corn fro yeer to yere;
> And out of olde bokes, in good feith,
> Cometh al this newe science that men lere.

And into the old bottles Chaucer poured with lavish hand
a new and heady wine.

What happened may best be seen by a glance at his first
three vision poems. His earliest essay, the Book of the
Duchess, was made before he went to Italy, when his reading was almost wholly French, and when Machaut in particular was at his finger tips. It is a vision poem, with all
the paraphernalia of the *genre,* and it is also an elegy -
an elegy on the death of the Duchess Blanche, the first
wife of his patron, John of Gaunt. But into the conventional frame he fits, with tact and feeling, and with conspicuous skill in adapting them to his ends, materials
drawn from what was then his reading - to wit, in this
instance, from no less than eight of Machaut's poems and
one (at least) of Froissart's. Save for scattered reminiscences of the Bible, the 'Roman de la Rose', Boethius,
and Benoit, there is little else. His instinct from the
beginning was to enrich, and those were the stores which
he then possessed. But his borrowings are interwoven with
such art that for more than five hundred years nobody suspected that the poem was not all of a piece. And even
when his appropriations are most unmistakable, they are
still miraculously Chaucer and not Machaut. The little
whelp that came creeping up, as if it knew him, to the
Dreamer, and 'Hild doun his heed and joyned his eres, And
leyde al smothe doun his heres' - that bewitching English
puppy is Chaucer's metamorphosis of a fantastic lion,
which Carpaccio would have revelled in, native to the
bizarre landscape of the 'Dit dou Lyon' of Machaut. And
into his version of Machaut's catalogue of those remote

regions to which the courtly lovers were dispatched to
win their spurs, Chaucer has slipped that precious bit of
hearsay about the Dry Sea and the Carrenar. The Book of
the Duchess is not a masterpiece, but it is significant
far beyond its intrinsic merit. For in it for the first
time, with the still limited resources at his command,
Chaucer loaded every rift with ore. And now the ore grew
steadily richer.

For Chaucer went to Italy, and learned to read Boccaccio and Dante, and all the while that knowledge of books
and men on which we have dwelt was broadening and deepening. The French influence waned as that of Italy waxed,
but the shift of emphasis was gradual, and the vision
poems still went on. And into the three that followed
the Book of the Duchess poured those steadily growing
stores....

(p. 322) From Machaut and his French contemporaries
Chaucer had taken over a form which for him was relatively
empty of content. In Boccaccio and Dante he found for
the first time among his moderns architectonic powers
which in the case of Dante were supreme, and which
Boccaccio in narrative exercised with a master's skill.
Moreover, in Boccaccio, and superlatively in Dante, the
greatness of the form was inseparable from the richness
of the content, and that content was now no longer interminable lucubrations in a vacuum, but men and women, and
their actions and their fates. And in the 'Filostrato'
he found a story richer in possibilities than any on
which he had yet exercised his powers. Into none had so
many strands been woven by earlier hands, from its far-
off inception in the 'Iliad', down through a provocative
catalogue of names in Dares, to three of which Benoit,
through one of those inscrutable promptings of genius
which set in motion incalculable trains of consequence,
had attached a story of faithless love. And then Boccaccio, through his own 'Filocolo', poured into it the passion of his long eventful intrigue with Maria d'Aquino.
And as the inevitable consequence, his Criseida and
Troilo and Pandaro *live,* as his Palamon and Arcita and
Emilia never do. In the 'Filostrato' Chaucer at last
had flesh and blood to deal with.

What the 'Filostrato' did, accordingly, was to awaken
as nothing else yet had done, his own creative powers.
For the Troilus is a magnificently independent reworking
of Boccaccio's narrative, bearing to its original, indeed,
a relation not unlike that in which 'King Lear', for
example, stands to the earlier play. For Chaucer had
thought deeply through Boccaccio's story before he set
pen to parchment for his own. Boccaccio's Criseida is a

fair and fickle woman, conventional alike in her beauty
and her faithlessness; Chaucer's Criseyde, in her baffling
and complex femininity remains unrivalled, save in Shakespeare and one or two of the great novelists. And by a
change as simple as it is consummate in its art, Chaucer
opened the way for another transformation - the metamorphosis of a conventional young man-about-town into a
masterpiece of characterization which he equalled only,
if I may hazard my own opinion, in the Wife of Bath. For
Boccaccio's Pandaro was Criseida's cousin; Chaucer's Pandarus is her uncle. And through that simple-seeming shift,
not only is the irony of the situation deepened and the
tragedy enhanced, but Pandarus also becomes what a younger
man could never have been - the vehicle of Chaucer's own
humour and urbanity and worldy wisdom, and of his inimitable raciness of speech. Somewhere, among his courtly
friends in England or in Italy or both, he had come, one
feels, to know the type to which he gave immortal individuality. It is in the Troilus, too, that one also feels,
again for the first time, that detachment which is also
the distinctive note of the greater Canterbury Tales -
that wise and urbane detachment with which Chaucer came in
the end to view the human comedy. And often when Pandare
speaks, one is curiously aware of something in the background - like Meredith's Comic Spirit with its 'slim
feasting smile' - which is playing the game with Pandare
no less urbanely and ironically than he with Troilus and
Criseyde. And those are but hints of what Chaucer's
reading of life lent to his reading of Boccaccio.

Moreover, no sooner had he set out to write than his
mind began to race beyond the text he was translating.
In scores of stanzas, even in the first book, he will
follow Boccaccio for three or four or five lines of his
stanza, then go his own gate for the rest of it, as if his
thought in its eagerness overleaped Boccaccio's. And
often, before he returns to his text, he has carried on
alone for three, four, or a score of stanzas. And when,
in the great second and third books, he comes to the
heart of the drama as he conceives it, he leaves Boccaccio
almost wholly aside, and the great bulk of those two
crucial books is Chaucer's own. And nowhere else, save in
the plan of the Canterbury Tales, does he exercise such
sovereign constructive powers. Life and his reading of
the great Italians had made him master of his art.

And that mastery of an art which has for its end the
portrayal of life is peculiarly manifest in his dialogue....

And in nothing that he ever wrote did his possession at
once of the scholar's and the artist's gifts stand him in

better stead than in his weaving into one the complex
strands which underlay his story. And as he wrote,
phrases and ideas, Boccaccio's or his own, kept calling up
to his memory associated fragments of his reading, and the
'Divine Comedy', and the 'Convito', and the 'Teseide', and
a sonnet of Petrarch, and Ovid, Virgil, Statius and Boethius, and the 'Roman de la Rose' and the 'Roman d'Eneas'
and even Machaut himself (to name no more) contribute to
the sense which we have in the Troilus of a richness like
God's plenty, which pervades the poem.

When Chaucer ended the Troilus, he was in possession of
a mastered art. To the question which I asked in the
beginning - What aside from genius made the poet of the
greater Canterbury Tales? - I have attempted, within my
limits of time and understanding, to give an answer. The
supreme art of that crowning achievement had been learned
through the independent exercise of his own powers upon
given materials - upon form and content of conventional
types or specific poems, which the accident of courtly
connexions or business in Italy had offered. And through
the poet's gift of seeing the latent possibilities in
everything he touched, and through the scholar's passion
for facts, and through his own invincible eagerness of
spirit which spared no pains, his masters and his models
slipped steadily into the background, and on the threshold of the Canterbury Tales the theme towards which his
face was turned was *life* - that life above all which
through years of intimate contact with it he had learned
to know; not French life nor Italian life, but English.
And instead of any longer filling empty forms or reconstructing full ones, he drew straight from life a framework of his own - the one form in all the world to give
free play to his disciplined and ripened powers, and room
for all that wealth of reading and experience with which
this tale began. And as if with one lingering look
behind, he begins his masterpiece - I wish I knew whether
he so meant it - with an exquisite *ave atque vale*:

> Whan that Aprille with his shoures sote
> The droghte of Marche hath perced to the rote,
> And bathed every veyne in swich licour,
> Of which vertu engendred is the flour;
> Whan Zephirus eek with his swete breeth
> Inspired hath in every holt and heeth
> The tendre croppes...

and on through the lovely lines still redolent of their
April freshness after five hundred years. That is the
stock introduction - *sed quantum mutatus ab illo* - to a

hundred love-vision poems! But instead of ushering in
Plaisance and Esperance and Douce Pensée and their crew
of fellow abstractions, it opens the door of the Tabard
Inn to Harry Bailly and the Wife of Bath and the Miller
and the Pardoner and their goodly fellowship. There could
be no better symbol than those opening lines of the continuity, through steadily maturing powers, of Chaucer's
art. And it is that continuity of evolution, up to the
full flowering of his genius in the Canterbury Tales, that
I have essayed to describe.

48. CLIVE STAPLES LEWIS, WHAT CHAUCER REALLY DID TO
'IL FILOSTRATO'

1932

C.S. Lewis (1898-1963), literary historian, novelist, and
popular theologian, was educated at University College,
Oxford, and became Professor of Medieval and Renaissance
English in the University of Cambridge, 1954-63. Of many
learned, witty, and imaginatively generous books, his
'Allegory of Love' (1936), in which he developed the
theory of 'courtly love', earlier set out by W.G. Dodd
and adumbrated even earlier, has been perhaps the most
influential. In the present essay, the forerunner of
'The Allegory of Love', Lewis presents 'courtly love' as
an example of essentially medieval interest, and in re-
creating the medieval interest in poetry, different from
that of the twentieth century, he also emphasises the
historical, rhetorical, sententious aspects of Chaucer's
poetry. Reprinted from 'Essays and Studies 1932' (1932),
pp. 56-75, by permission of the English Association.

WHAT CHAUCER REALLY DID TO 'IL FILOSTRATO'

A great deal of attention has deservedly been given to
the relation between the 'Book of Troilus' and its original, 'Il Filostrato', and Rossetti's collation placed a
knowledge of the subject within the reach even of undergraduate inquirers. It is, of course, entirely right and
proper that the greater part of this attention has been

devoted to such points as specially illustrate the individual genius of Chaucer as a dramatist and a psychologist.
But such studies, without any disgrace to themselves,
often leave singularly undefined the historical position
and affinities of a book; and if pursued intemperately
they may leave us with a preposterous picture of the
author as that abstraction, a *pure* individual, bound to no
time nor place, or even obeying in the fourteenth century
the aesthetics of the twentieth. It is possible that a
good deal of misunderstanding still exists, even among
instructed people, as to the real significance of the
liberties that Chaucer took with his source. M. Legouis,
in his study of Chaucer to which we all owe so much,
remarks that Chaucer's additions 'implied a wider and more
varied conception' than those of Boccaccio; and again
'Chaucer's aim was not like Boccaccio's to paint sentimentality alone, but to reflect life'. I do not wish
to contradict either statement, but I am convinced that
both are capable of conveying a false impression. What
follows may be regarded as a cautionary gloss on M. Legouis's text. I shall endeavour to show that the process
which 'Il Filostrato' underwent at Chaucer's hands was
first and foremost a process of *medievalization*. One
aspect of this process has received some attention from
scholars,(1) but its importance appears to me to be still
insufficiently stressed. In what follows I shall, therefore, restate this aspect in my own terms while endea-
vouring to replace it in its context.

   Chaucer had never heard of a renaissance; and I think
it would be difficult to translate either into the
English or the Latin of his day our distinction between
sentimental or conventional art on the one hand, and art
which paints 'Life' - whatever this means - on the other.
When first a manuscript beginning with the words *Alcun
di giove sogliono il favore* came into his hands, he was,
no doubt, aware of a difference between its contents and
those of certain English and French manuscripts which he
had read before. That some of the differences did not
please him is apparent from his treatment. We may be
sure, however, that he noticed and approved the new use
of stanzas, instead of octosyllabic couplets, for narrative. He certainly thought the story a good story; he
may even have thought it a story better told than any
that he had yet read. But there was also, for Chaucer, a
special reason why he should choose this story for his
own retelling; and that reason largely determined the
alterations that he made.

   He was not yet the Chaucer of the 'Canterbury Tales':
he was the *grant translateur* of the 'Roman de la Rose',

the author of the 'Book of the Duchesse', and probably of
'many a song and many a lecherous lay' ['C.T.', I, 1086].
In other words he was the great living interpreter in
English of *l'amour courtois*. Even in 1390, when Gower
produced the first version of his 'Confessio Amantis',
such faithful interpretation of the love tradition was
still regarded as the typical and essential function of
Chaucer: he is Venus' 'disciple' and 'poete', with whose
'ditees and songes glade...the lond fulfild is overal'.
And Gower still has hopes that Chaucer's existing treat-
ments of *Frauendienst* are only the preludes to some great
'testament' which will 'sette an ende of alle his werk'
['Conf. Am.', viii, 2941-58]. These expectations were,
of course, disappointed; and it is possibly to that disappointment, rather than to a hypothetical quarrel (for
which only the most ridiculous grounds have been assigned),
that we should attribute Gower's removal of this passage
from the second text of the 'Confessio Amantis'. It had
become apparent that Chaucer was following a different
line of development, and the reference made to him by
Venus had ceased to be appropriate.

It was, then, as a poet of courtly love that Chaucer
approached 'Il Filostrato'. There is no sign as yet that
he wished to desert the courtly tradition; on the contrary, there is ample evidence that he still regarded himself as its exponent. But the narrative bent of his
genius was already urging him, not to desert this tradition, but to pass from its doctrinal treatment (as in the
'Romance of the Rose') to its narrative treatment. Having
preached it, and sung it, he would now exemplify it: he
would show the code put into action in the course of a
story - without prejudice (as we shall see) to a good deal
of doctrine and pointing of the amorous moral by the way.
The thing represents a curious return upon itself of
literary history. If Chaucer had lived earlier he would,
we may be sure, have found just the model that he desired
in Chrestien de Troyes. But by Chaucer's time certain
elements, which Chrestien had held together in unity, had
come apart and taken an independent life. Chrestien had
combined, magnificently, the interest of the story, and
the interest of erotic doctrine and psychology. His successors had been unable or unwilling to achieve this union.
Perhaps, indeed, the two things had to separate in order
that each might grow to maturity; and in many of Chrestien's psychological passages one sees the embryonic
allegory struggling to be born.(2) Whatever the reason
may be, such a separation took place. The story sets up
on its own in the prose romances - the 'French book' of
Malory: the doctrine and psychology set up on their own in

the 'Romance of the Rose'. In this situation if a poet
arose who accepted the doctrines and also had a narrative
genius, then *a priori* such a poet might be expected to
combine again the two elements - now fully grown - which,
in their rudimentary form, had lain together in Chrestien.
But this is exactly the sort of poet that Chaucer was; and
this (as we shall see) is what Chaucer did. The 'Book of
Troilus' shows, in fact, the very peculiar literary phenomenon of Chaucer groping back, unknowingly, through the
very slightly medieval work of Boccaccio, to the genuinely
medieval formula of Chrestien. We may be thankful that
Chaucer did not live in the high noon of Chrestien's celebrity; for, if he had, we should probably have lost much
of the originality of Troilus. He would have had less
motive for altering Chrestien than for altering Boccaccio,
and probably would have altered him less.

Approaching 'Il Filostrato' from this angle, Chaucer,
we may be sure, while feeling the charm of its narrative
power, would have found himself, at many passages, uttering the Middle English equivalent of 'This will never do!'
In such places he did not hesitate, as he might have said,
to *amenden* and to *reducen* what was *amis* in his author.
The majority of his modifications are corrections of
errors which Boccaccio had committed against the code of
courtly love; and modifications of this kind have not been
entirely neglected by criticism. It has not, however,
been sufficiently observed that these are only part and
parcel of a general process of medievalization. They are,
indeed, the most instructive part of that process, and
even in the present discussion must claim the chief place;
but in order to restore them to their proper setting it
will be convenient to make a division of the different
capacities in which Chaucer approached his original.
These will, of course, be found to overlap in the concrete;
but that is no reason for not plucking them ideally apart
in the interests of clarity.

I.   Chaucer approached his work as an 'Historial' poet
contributing to the story of Troy. I do not mean that he
necessarily believed his tale to be wholly or partly a
record of fact, but his attitude towards it in this respect is different from Boccaccio's. Boccaccio, we may
surmise, wrote for an audience who were beginning to look
at poetry in our own way. For them 'Il Filostrato' was
mainly, though not entirely, 'a new poem by Boccaccio'.
Chaucer wrote for an audience who still looked at poetry
in the medieval fashion - a fashion for which the real
literary units were 'matters', 'stories', and the like,
rather than individual authors. For them the 'Book of
Troilus' was partly, though of course only partly, 'a new

bit of the matter of Rome'. Hence Chaucer expects them to
be interested not only in the personal drama between his
little group of characters but in that whole world of
story which makes this drama's context: like children
looking at a landscape picture and wanting to know what
happens to the road after it disappears into the frame.
For the same reason they will want to know his authorities. Passages in which Chaucer has departed from his
original to meet this demand will easily occur to the
memory. Thus, in i. 141 et seq., he excuses himself for
not telling us more about the military history of the
Trojan war, and adds what is almost a footnote to tell his
audience where they can find that missing part of the
story - 'in Omer, or in Dares, or in Dyte'. Boccaccio had
merely sketched in, in the preceding stanza, a general
picture of war sufficient to provide the background for
his own story - much as a dramatist might put 'Alarums
within' in a stage direction: he has in view an audience
fully conscious that all this is mere necessary 'setting'
or hypothesis. Thus again, in iv. 120 et seq., Chaucer
inserts into the speech of *Calkas* an account of the
quarrel between *Phebus* and *Neptunus* and *Lameadoun*. This
is not dramatically necessary. All that was needed for
Calkas's argument has already been given in lines 111 and
112 (cf. 'Filostrato', IV, xi). The Greek leaders did
not need to be told about Laomedon; but Chaucer is not
thinking of the Greek leaders; he is thinking of his
audience who will gladly learn, or be reminded, of that
part of the cycle. At lines 204 et seq. he inserts a
note on the later history of *Antenor* for the same reason.
In the fifth book he inserts unnecessarily lines 1464-
1510 from the story of Thebes. The spirit in which this
is done is aptly expressed in his own words:

>   And so descendeth down from gestes olde
>   To Diomede. (v. 1511, 1512)

The whole 'matter of Rome' is still a unity, with a
structure and life of its own. That part of it which the
poem in hand is treating, which is, so to speak, in focus,
must be seen fading gradually away into its 'historial'
surroundings. The method is the antithesis of that which
produces the 'framed' story of a modern writer: it is a
method which romance largely took over from the epic.
    II. Chaucer approached his work as a pupil of the
rhetoricians and a firm believer in the good, old, and
now neglected maxim of Dante: *omnis qui versificatur suos
versus exornare debet in quantum potest*. This side of
Chaucer's poetry has been illustrated by Mr. Manly (3) so

well that most readers will not now be in danger of neg-
lecting it. A detailed application of this new study to
the 'Book of Troilus' would here detain us too long, but
a cursory glance shows that Chaucer found his original
too short and proceeded in many places to 'amplify' it.
He began by abandoning the device - that of invoking his
lady instead of the Muses - whereby Boccaccio had given a
lyrical instead of a rhetorical turn to the invocation,
and substituted an address to *Thesiphone* ('Filostrato',
I. i-v, cf. 'Troilus', i. 1-14). He added at the beginning of his second book an invocation of *Cleo* and an
apology of the usual medieval type, for the defects of
his work (ii. 15-21). Almost immediately afterwards he
inserted a *descriptio* of the month of May (an innovation
which concerned him as poet of courtly love no less than
as rhetorician) which is extremely beautiful and appropriate, but which follows, none the less, conventional
lines. The season is fixed by astronomical references,
and *Proigne* and *Tereus* appear just where we should expect
them (ii. 50-6, 64-70). In the third book the scene of
the morning parting between the two lovers affords a
complicated example of Chaucer's medievalization. In his
original (III. xlii) Chaucer read

> Ma poich' e galli presso al giorno udiro
> Cantar per l'aurora che surgea.

He proceeded to amplify this, first by the device of *Cir-*
cuitio or *Circumlocutio; galli*, with the aid of Alanus de
Insulis, became 'the cok, comune astrologer'. Not content with this, he then repeated the sense of that whole
phrase by the device *Expolitio*, of which the formula is
Mutiplice forma Dissimuletur idem: varius sis et tamen
idem (4) and the theme 'Dawn came' is varied with *Lucifer*
and *Fortuna Minor*, till it fills a whole stanza (iii.
1415-21). In the next stanza of Boccaccio he found a
short speech by *Griseida*, expressing her sorrow at the
parting which dawn necessitated: but this was not enough
for him. As poet of love he wanted his *alba*; as rhetorician he wanted his *apostropha*. He therefore inserted six-
teen lines of address to Night (1427-42), during which he
secured the additional advantage, from the medieval point
of view, of 'som doctryne' (1429-32). In lines 1452-70
he inserted antiphonally Troilus's *alba,* for which the only
basis in Boccaccio was the line *Il giorno che venia male-*
dicendo (III. xliv). The passage is an object lesson for
those who tend to identify the traditional with the dull.
Its matter goes back to the ancient sources of medieval
love poetry, notably to Ovid, 'Amores', i. 13, and it has

been handled often before, and better handled, by the
Provençals. Yet it is responsible for one of the most
vivid and beautiful expressions that Chaucer ever used.

> Accursed be thy coming into Troye
> For every bore hath oon of thy bright eyen.

A detailed study of the 'Book of Troilus' would reveal
this 'rhetoricization', if I may coin an ugly word, as
the common quality of many of Chaucer's additions. As
examples of *Apostropha* alone I may mention, before leaving this part of the subject, iii. 301 et seq. (*O tonge*),
617 et seq. (*But o Fortune*), 715 et seq. (*O Venus*), and
813 et seq. where Chaucer is following Boethius.

III.   Chaucer approached his work as a poet of *doctryne*
and sentence. This is a side of his literary character
which twentieth-century fashions encourage us to overlook,
but, of course, no honest historian can deny it. His contemporaries and immediate successors did not. His own
creatures, the pilgrims, regarded *mirthe* and *doctryne*,
['Canterbury Tales', B 2125] or, as it is elsewhere
expressed, *sentence* and *solas*, [ibid., A 798] as the two
alternative, and equally welcome, excellences of a story.
In the same spirit Hoccleve praises Chaucer as the *mirour
of fructuous entendement* and the universal *fadir in
science* ['Regement', 1963 et seq.] - a passage, by the
by, to be recommended to those who are astonished that
the fifteenth century should imitate those elements of
Chaucer's genius which it enjoyed instead of those which
we enjoy. In respect of *doctryne*, then, Chaucer found
his original deficient, and *amended* it. The example
which will leap to every one's mind is the Boethian discussion on free will (iv. 946-1078). To Boccaccio, I
suspect, this would have seemed as much an excrescence
as it does to the modern reader; to the unjaded appetites
of Chaucer's audience mere thickness in a wad of manuscript was a merit. If the author was so 'courteous
beyond covenant' as to give you an extra bit of *doctryne*
(or of story), who would be so churlish as to refuse it
on the pedantic ground of irrelevance? But this passage
is only one of many in which Chaucer departs from his
original for the sake of giving his readers interesting
general knowledge or philosophical doctrine. In iii.
1387 et seq., finding Boccaccio's attack upon *gli avari* a
little bare and unsupported, he throws out, as a species
of buttress, the *exempla* of *Myda* and *Crassus*.(5) In the
same book he has to deal with the second assignation of
Troilus and Cressida. Boccaccio gave him three stanzas
of dialogue ('Filostrato', III. lxvi-lxviii), but Chaucer

rejected them and preferred - in curious anticipation of
Falstaff's thesis about pitch - to assure his readers, on
the authority of *thise clerkes wyse* (iii. 1691) that *felicitee* is felicitous, though *Troilus* and *Criseyde* enjoyed
something better than *felicitee*. In the same stanza he
also intends, I think, an allusion to the *sententia* that
occurs elsewhere in the Franklin's Tale ['C.T.' F 7621].
In iv. 197-203, immediately before his *historial* insertion about Antenor, he introduces a *sentence* from Juvenal,
partly for its own sake, partly in order that the story
of Antenor may thus acquire an exemplary, as well as a
historial value. In iv. 323-8 he inserts a passage on
the great *locus communis* of Fortune and her wheel.

In the light of this sententious bias, Chaucer's
treatment of Pandarus should be reconsidered, and it is
here that a somewhat subtle exercise of the historical
imagination becomes necessary. On the one hand, he would
be a dull reader, and the victim rather than the pupil of
history, who would take all the doctrinal passages in
Chaucer seriously: that the speeches of Chauntecleer and
Pertelote and of the Wyf of Bath not only *are* funny by
reason of their sententiousness and learning, but are
intended to be funny, and funny by that reason, is indisputable. On the other hand, to assume that sententiousness became funny for Chaucer's readers as easily as it
becomes funny for us, is to misunderstand the fourteenth
century: such an assumption will lead us to the preposterous view that 'Melibee' (or even the Parson's Tale)
is a comic work - a view not much mended by Mr. Mackail's
suggestion that there are some jokes *too* funny to excite
laughter and that 'Melibee' is one of these. A clear
recognition that our own age is quite abnormally sensitive to the funny side of sententiousness, to possible
hypocrisy, and to dulness, is absolutely necessary for
any one who wishes to understand the past. We must face
the fact that Chaucer's audience could listen with gravity
and interest to edifying matter which would set a modern
audience sleeping or sniggering. The application of this
to Pandarus is a delicate business. Every reader must
interpret Pandarus for himself, and I can only put forward my own interpretation very tentatively. I believe
that Pandarus is meant to be a comic character, but not,
by many degrees, so broadly comic as he appears to some
modern readers. There is, for me, no doubt that Chaucer
intended us to smile when he made Troilus exclaim

What knowe I of the queene Niobe?
Lat be thyne olde ensaumples, I thee preye. (I. 759)

But I question if he intended just that sort of smile
which we actually give him. For me the fun lies in the
fact that poor Troilus says that I have been wishing to
say for some time. For Chaucer's hearers the point was a
little different. The suddenness of the gap thus revealed
between Troilus's state of mind and Pandarus's words cast
a faintly ludicrous air on what had gone before: it made
the theorizing and the *exempla* a little funny in retrospect. But it is quite probable that they had not been
funny till then: the discourse on contraries (i. 631-44),
the *exemplum* of Paris and Oenone, leading up to the
theme 'Physician heal thyself' (652-72), the doctrine of
the Mean applied to secrecy in love (687-93), the *sentences* from Solomon (695) and elsewhere (708), are all of
them the sort of thing that can be found in admittedly
serious passages, [cf. 'C.T.', I 140-55] and it may well
be that Chaucer 'had it both ways'. His readers were to
be, first of all, edified by the doctrine for its own
sake, and then (slightly) amused by the contrast between
this edification and Troilus's obstinate attitude of the
plain man. If this view be accepted it will have the consequence that Chaucer intended an effect of more subtility
than that which we ordinarily receive. We get the broadly
comic effect - a loquacious and unscrupulous old uncle
talks solemn platitude at interminable length. For Chaucer, a *textuel* man talked excellent doctrine which we
enjoy and by which we are edified: but at the same time
we see that this 'has its funny side'. Ours is the crude
joke of laughing at admitted rubbish: Chaucer's the much
more lasting joke of laughing at 'the funny side' of that
which, even while we laugh, we admire. To the present
writer this reading of Pandarus does not appear doubtful;
but it depends to some extent, on a mere 'impression'
about the quality of the Middle Ages, an impression hard
to correct, if it is an error, and hard to teach, if it is
a truth. For this reason I do not insist on my interpretation. If, however, it is accepted, many of the speeches
of Pandarus which are commonly regarded as having a purely
dramatic significance will have to be classed among the
examples of Chaucer's doctrinal or sententious inser-
tions.(6)

    IV. Finally, Chaucer approached his work as the poet
of courtly love. He not only modified his story so as to
make it a more accurate representation in action of the
orthodox erotic code, but he also went out of his way to
emphasize its didactic element. Andreas Capellanus had
given instructions to lovers; Guillaume de Lorris had
given instructions veiled and decorated by allegory;
Chaucer carries the process a stage further and gives

instruction by example in the course of a concrete story.
But he does not forget the instructional side of his work.
In the following paragraphs I shall sometimes quote parallels to Chaucer's innovations from the earlier love literature, but it must not be thought that I suppose my quotations to represent Chaucer's immediate source.

1. Boccaccio in his induction, after invoking his mistress instead of the Muses, inserts (I. vi) a short request for lovers in general that they will pray for him.
The prayer itself is disposed of in a single line

Per me vi prego ch'amore preghiate.

This is little more than a conceit, abandoned as soon
as it is used: a modern poet could almost do the like.
Chaucer devotes four stanzas (i. 22-49) to this prayer.
If we make an abstract of both passages, Boccaccio will
run 'Pray for me to Love', while Chaucer will run 'Remember, all lovers, your old unhappiness, and pray, for the
unsuccessful, that they may come to solace; for me, that
I may be enabled to tell this story; for those in despair,
that they may die; for the fortunate, that they may per-
severe, and please their ladies in such manner as may
advance the glory of Love'. The important point here is
not so much that Chaucer expands his original, as that he
renders it more liturgical: his prayer, with its careful
discriminations in intercession for the various recognized stages of the amorous life, and its final reference
ad Amoris majorem gloriam, is a collect. Chaucer is
emphasizing that parody, or imitation, or rivalry - I
know not which to call it - of the Christian religion
which was inherent in traditional *Frauendienst*. The
thing can be traced back to Ovid's purely ironical worship of Venus and Amor in the 'De Arte Amatoria'. The
idea of a love religion is taken up and worked out,
though still with equal flippancy, in terms of medieval
Christianity, by the twelfth-century poet of the 'Concilium Romaricimontis',(7) where Love is given Cardinals
(female), the power of visitation, and the power of
cursing. Andreas Capellanus carried the process a stage
further and gave Love the power of distributing reward
and punishment after death. But while his hell of cruel
beauties (*Siccitas*), his purgatory of beauties promiscu-
ously kind (*Humiditas*), and his heaven of true lovers
(*Amoenitas*)(8) can hardly be other than playful, Andreas
deals with the love religion much more seriously than the
author of the 'Concilium'. The lover's qualification is
morum probitas: he must be truthful and modest, a good
Catholic, clean in his speech, hospitable, and ready to

return good for evil. There is nothing in *saeculo bonum* which is not derived from love:(9) it may even be said in virtue of its severe standard of constancy, to be 'a kind of chastity' - *reddit hominem castitatis quasi virtute decoratum*.(10)

In all this we are far removed from the tittering nuns and *clerici* of the 'Concilium'. In Chrestien, the scene in which Lancelot kneels and adores the bed of Guinevere (as if before a *corseynt*)(11) is, I think, certainly intended to be read seriously: what mental reservations the poet himself had on the whole business is another question. In Dante the love religion has become wholly and unequivocally serious by fusing with the real religion: the distance between the *Amor deus omnium quotquot sunt amantium* of the 'Concilium', and the *segnore di pauroso aspetto* of the 'Vita Nuova',(12) is the measure of the tradition's real flexibility and universality. It is this quasi-religious element in the content, and this liturgical element in the diction, which Chaucer found lacking in his original at the very opening of the book, and which he supplied. The line

That Love hem bringe in hevene to solas

is particularly instructive.

2. In the Temple scene (Chaucer, i. 155-315, 'Filostrato', I. xix-xxxii) Chaucer found a stanza which it was very necessary to *reducen*. It was Boccaccio's twenty-third, in which Troilus, after indulging in his 'cooling card for lovers', mentions that he has himself been singed with that fire, and even hints that he has had his successes; but the pleasures were not worth the pains. The whole passage is a typical example of that Latin spirit which in all ages (except perhaps our own) has made Englishmen a little uncomfortable; the hero must be a lady-killer from the very beginning, or the audience will think him a milksop and a booby. To have abashed, however temporarily, these strutting Latinisms, is not least among the virtues of medieval *Frauendienst:* and for Chaucer as its poet, this stanza was emphatically one of those that 'would never do'. He drops it quietly out of its place, and thus brings the course of his story nearer to that of the 'Romance of the Rose'. The parallelism is so far intact. Troilus, an unattached young member of the courtly world, wandering idly about the Temple, is smitten with Love. In the same way the Dreamer having been admitted by Ydelnesse into the garden goes 'Pleying along ful merily'(13) until he looks in the fatal well. If he had already met Love outside the garden the whole allegory

would have to be reconstructed.

3. A few lines lower Chaucer found in his original the words

> il quale amor trafisse
> Più ch'alcun altro, pria del tempio uscisse. (I. xxv)

Amor trafisse in Boccaccio is hardly more than a literary variant for 'he fell in love': the allegory has shrunk into a metaphor and even that metaphor is almost unconscious and fossilized. Over such a passage one can imagine Chaucer exclaiming, *tantamne rem tam negligenter?* He at once goes back through the metaphor to the allegory that begot it, and gives us his own thirtieth stanza (I. 204-10) on the god of Love in anger bending his bow. The image is very ancient and goes back at least as far as Apollonius Rhodius.(14) Ovid was probably the intermediary who conveyed it to the Middle Ages. Chrestien uses it, with particular emphasis on Love as the avenger of contempt.(15) But Chaucer need not have gone further to find it than to the 'Romance of the Rose':(16) with which, here again, he brings his story into line.

4. But even this was not enough. Boccaccio's *Amor trafisse* had occurred in a stanza where the author apostrophizes the *Cecità delle mondane menti,* and reflects on the familiar contrast between human expectations and the actual course of events. But this general contrast seemed weak to the poet of courtly love: what he wanted was the explicit erotic *moral,* based on the special contrast between the hubris of the young scoffer and the complete surrender which the offended deity soon afterwards extracted from him. This conception, again, owes much to Ovid; but between Ovid and the Middle Ages comes the later practice of the ancient Epithalamium during the decline of antiquity and the Dark Ages: to which, as I hope to show elsewhere, the system of courtly love as a whole is heavily indebted. Thus in the fifth century Sidonius Apollinarus in an Epithalamium, makes the bridegroom just such another as Troilus: a proud scoffer humbled by Love. Amor brings to Venus the triumphant news

> Nova gaudia porto
> Felicis praedae, genetrix. Calet ille *superbus*
> Ruricius.(17)

Venus replies

> gaudemus nate, *rebellem*
> *Quod vincis.*

In a much stranger poem, by the Bishop Ennodius, it is not
the hubris of a single youth, but of the world, that has
stung the deities of love into retributive action. Cupid
and Venus are introduced deploring the present state of
Europe

> Frigida consumens multorum possidet artus
> Virginitas.(18)

and Venus meets the situation by a threat that she'll
'larn 'em':

> Discant populi tunc crescere divam
> Cum neglecta iacet.(19)

They conclude by attacking one Maximus and thus bringing
about the marriage which the poem was written to celebrate. Venantius Fortunatus, in his Epithalamium for
Brunchild reproduces, together with Ennodius's spring
morning, Ennodius's boastful Cupid, and makes the god,
after an exhibition of his archery, announce to his
mother, *mihi vincitur alter Achilles*.(20) In Chrestien
the rôle of tamed rebel is transferred to the woman. In
'Cligès' Soredamors confesses that Love has humbled her
pride by force, and doubts whether such extorted service
will find favour.(21) In strict obedience to this tradition Chaucer inserts his lines 214-31, emphasizing the
dangers of hubris against Love and the certainty of its
ultimate failure; and we may be thankful that he did,
since it gives us the lively and touching simile of
proude Bayard. Then, mindful of his instructional purpose, he adds four stanzas more (239-66), in which he
directly exhorts his readers to avoid the error of Troilus, and that for two reasons: firstly, because Love
cannot be resisted (this is the policeman's argument - we
may as well 'come quiet'); and secondly because Love is
a thing 'so vertuous in kinde'. The second argument, of
course, follows traditional lines, and recalls Andreas's
theory of Love as the source of all secular virtue.

5. In lines 330-50 Chaucer again returns to Troilus's
scoffing - a scoffing this time assumed as a disguise. I
do not wish to press the possibility that Chaucer in this
passage is attempting, in virtue of his instructional purpose, to stress the lover's virtue of secrecy more than he
found it stressed in his original; for Boccaccio, probably
for different reasons, does not leave that side of the
subject untouched. But it is interesting to note a difference in the content between this scoffing and that of
Boccaccio ('Filostrato', I. xxi, xxii). Boccaccio's is

based on contempt for women, fickle as wind, and heartless. Chaucer's is based on the hardships of love's *lay*
or religion: hardships arising from the uncertainty of
the most orthodox *observances*, which may lead to various
kinds of harm and may be taken amiss by the lady. Boccaccio dethrones the deity: Chaucer complains of the sever-
ity of the cult. It is the difference between an atheist
and a man who humorously insists that he 'is not of
religioun'.

6. In the first dialogue between Troilus and Pandarus
the difference between Chaucer and his original can best
be shown by an asbtract. Boccaccio (II. vi-xxviii) would
run roughly as follows:

T. Well, if you must know, I am in love. But don't
    ask me with whom (vi-viii).
P. Why did you not tell me long ago? I could have
    helped you (ix).
T. What use would *you* be? Your own suit never
    succeeded (ix).
P. A man can often guide others better than himself
    (x).
T. I can't tell you, because it is a relation of
    yours (xv).
P. A fig for relations! Who is it? (xvi).
T. (after a pause) Griseida.
P. Splendid! Love has fixed your heart in a good
    place. She is an admirable person. The only
    trouble is that she is rather *pie* (*onesta*): but
    I'll soon see to that (xxiii). Every woman is
    amorous at heart: they are only anxious to save
    their reputations (xxvii). I'll do all I can for
    you (xxviii).

Chaucer (I. 603-1008) would be more like this:

T. Well, if you must know, I am in love. But don't
    ask me with whom (603-16).
P. Why did you not tell me long ago? I could have
    helped you (617-20).
T. What use would *you* be? Your own suit never
    succeeded (621-3).
P. A man can often guide others better than himself,
    as we see from the analogy of the whetstone.
    Remember the doctrine of contraries, and what
    Oenone said. As regards secrecy, remember that
    all virtue is a mean between two extremes (624-
    700).
T. Do leave me alone (760).

P. If you die, how will she interpret it? Many lovers
    have served for twenty years without a single kiss.
    But should they despair? No, they should think it
    a guerdon even to serve (761-819).

T. (much moved by this argument, 820-6) What shall I
    do? Fortune is my foe (827-40).

P. Her wheel is always turning. Tell me who your
    mistress is. If it were my sister, you should have
    her (841-61).

T. (after a pause) - My sweet foe is Criseyde (870-5).

P. Splendid: Love has fixed your heart in a good place.
    This ought to gladden you, firstly, because to love
    such a lady is nothing but good: secondly, because
    if she has all these virtues, she must have Pity
    too. You are very fortunate that Love has treated
    you so well, considering your previous scorn of
    him. You must repent at once (874-935).

T. (kneeling) Mea Culpa! (936-8).

P. Good. All will now come right. Govern yourself
    properly: you know that a divided heart can have no
    grace. I have reasons for being hopeful. No man
    or woman was ever born who was not apt for love,
    either natural or celestial: and celestial love is
    not fitted to Criseyde's years. I will do all I
    can for you. Love converted you of his goodness.
    Now that you are converted, you will be as conspi-
    cuous among his saints as you formerly were among
    the sinners against him (939-1008).

In this passage it is safe to say that every single
alteration by Chaucer is an alteration in the direction
of medievaliasm. The Whetstone, Oenone, Fortune, and the
like we have already discussed: the significance of the
remaining innovations may now be briefly indicated. In
Boccaccio the reason for Troilus's hesitation in giving
the name is Criseida's relationship to Pandaro: and like
a flash comes back Pandaro's startling answer. In Chaucer
his hesitation is due to the courtly lover's certainty that
'she nil to noon suich wrecche as I be wonne' (778) and
that 'full harde it wer to helpen in this cas' (836).
Pandaro's original

    Se quella ch'ami fosse mia sorella
    A mio potere avrai tuo piacer d'ella (xvi)

is reproduced in the English, but by removing the words
that provoked it in the Italian (E tua parenta, xv) Chaucer makes it merely a general protestation of boundless
friendship in love, instead of a cynical defiance of

scruples already raised (Chaucer, 861). Boccaccio had delighted to bring the purities of family life and the profligacy of his young man about town into collision, and to show the triumph of the latter. Chaucer keeps all the time within the charmed circle of *Frauendienst* and allows no conflict but that of the lover's hopes and fears. Again, Boccaccio's Pandaro has no argument to use against Troilo's silence, but the argument 'I may help you'. Chaucer's Pandarus, on finding that this argument fails, proceeds to expound the code. The fear of dishonour in the lady's eyes, the duty of humble but not despairing service in the face of all discouragement, and the acceptance of this service as its own reward, form the substance of six stanzas in the English text (lines 768-819): at least, if we accept four lines very characteristically devoted to 'Ticius' and what 'bokes telle' of him. Even more remarkable is the difference between the behaviour of the two Pandars after the lady's name has been disclosed. Boccaccio's, cynical as ever, encourages Troilo by the reflection that female virtue is not really a serious obstacle: Chaucer's makes the virtue of the lady itself the ground for hope - arguing scholastically that the *genus* of virtue implies that *species* thereof which is *Pitee* (897-900). In what follows, Pandarus, while continuing to advise, becomes an adviser of a slightly different sort. He instructs Troilus not so much on his relationship to the Lady as on his relationship to Love. He endeavours to awaken in Troilus a devout sense of his previous sins against that deity (904-30) and is not satisfied without confession (931-8), briefly enumerates the commandments (953-9), and warns his penitent of the dangers of a divided heart.

In establishing such a case as mine, the author who transfers relentlessly to his article all the passages listed in his private notes can expect nothing but weariness from the reader. If I am criticized, I am prepared to produce for my contention many more evidential passages of the same kind. I am prepared to show how many of the beauties introduced by Chaucer, such as the song of Antigone or the riding past of Troilus, are introduced to explain and mitigate and delay the surrender of the heroine, who showed in Boccaccio a facility condemned by the courtly code.(22) I am prepared to show how Chaucer never forgets his erotically didactic purpose; and how, anticipating criticism as a teacher of love, he guards himself by reminding us that

> For to winne love in sondry ages
> In sondry londes, sondry ben usages. (ii. 27) (23)

But the reader whose stomach is limited would be tired, and he who is interested may safely be left to follow the clue for himself. Only one point, and that a point of principle, remains to be treated in full. Do I, or do I not, lie open to the criticism of Professor Abercrombie's 'Liberty of Interpreting'?(24)

The Professor *quem honoris causa nomino* urges us not to turn from the known effect which an ancient poem has upon us to speculation about the effect which the poet intended it to have. The application of this criticism which may be directed against me would run as follows: 'If Chaucer's "Troilus" actually produces on us an effect of greater realism and nature and freedom than its original, why should we assume that this effect was accidentally produced in the attempt to conform to an outworn convention?' If the charge is grounded, it is, to my mind, a very grave one. My reply is that such a charge begs the very question which I have most at heart in this paper, and but for which I should regard my analysis as the aimless burrowings of a thesis-monger. I would retort upon my imagined critic with another question. This poem is more lively and of deeper human appeal than its original. I grant it. This poem conforms more closely than its original to the system of courtly love. I claim to prove it. What then is the natural conclusion to draw? Surely, that courtly love itself, in spite of all its shabby origins and pedantic rules, is at bottom more agreeable to those elements in human, or at least in European, nature, which last longest, than the cynical Latin gallantries of Boccaccio? The world of Chrestien, of Guillaume de Lorris, and of Chaucer, is nearer to the world universal, is less of a closed system, than the world of Ovid, of Congreve, of Anatole France.

This is doctrine little palatable to the age in which we live: and it carries with it another doctrine that may seem no less paradoxical - namely, that certain medieval things are more universal, in that sense more classical, can claim more confidently a *securus judicat,* than certain things of the Renaissance. To make Herod your villain is more human than to make Tamburlaine your hero. The politics of Machiavelli are provincial and temporary beside the doctrine of the *jus gentium*. The love-lore of Andreas, though a narrow stream, is a stream tending to the universal sea. Its waters move. For real stagnancy and isolation we must turn to the decorative lakes dug out far inland at such a mighty cost by Mr. George Moore; to the more popular corporation swimming-baths of Dr. Marie Stopes; or to the teeming marshlands of the late D.H. Lawrence, whose depth the wisest knows not and on whose bank the hart gives up his life rather than plunge in:

paer maeg nihta gehwaem nithwundor seon
Fyr on flode!

Notes

1   Dodd, 'Courtly Love in Chaucer and Gower', 1913.
2   'Lancelot', 369-81, 2844-61; 'Yvain', 6001 et seq.,
    2639 et seq.; 'Cligès', 5855 et seq.
3   'Chaucer and the Rhetoricians', Warton Lecture XVII,
    1926.
4   Geoffroi de Vinsauf, 'Poetr. Nov.', 220-5.
5   This might equally well have been treated above in our
    rhetorical section. The instructed reader will recog-
    nize that a final distinction between *doctrinal* and
    rhetorical aspects, is not possible in the Middle
    Ages.
6   From another point of view Pandarus can be regarded as
    the *Vekke* of the 'R.R.' (cf. Thessala in 'Cligès')
    taken out of allegory into drama and changed in sex,
    so as to 'double' the rôles of *Vekke* and *Frend*.
7   'Zeitschrift für Deutsches Alterthum', vii, pp. 160
    et seq.
8   Andreas Capellanus, 'De Arte Honeste Amandi', ed.
    Troejel, i. 6 D2 (pp. 91-108).
9   Ibid., i. 6 A (p. 28).
10 Ibid., i. 4 (p. 10).
11 'Lancelot', 4670, 4734 et seq.
12 'Vit. Nuov.' iii.
13 'R.R.' 1329 (English Version).
14 'Argonaut', iii. 275 et seq.
15 'Cligès', 460; cf. 770.
16 'R.R.' 1330 et seq.; 1715 et seq.
17 Sid. Apoll. 'Carm.' xi. 61.
18 Ennodius, 'Carm.' I, iv. 57.
19 Ibid. 84.
20 Venant. Fort. VI, i.
21 'Cligès', 682, 241.
22 A particularly instructive comparison could be drawn
    between the Chaucerian Cresseide's determination to
    yield, yet to seem to yield by force and deception,
    and Bialacoil's behaviour. 'R.R.' 12607-88; speci-
    ally 12682, 3.
23 Cf. ii. 1023 et seq.
24 'Proceedings of Brit. Acad.', vol. xvi, Shakespeare
    Lecture, 1930.

49.   GILBERT KEITH CHESTERTON, NEVER A LESS TYPICAL POET

1933

G.K. Chesterton (1874-1936), educated at St Paul's
School, London and at the Slade School of Art, was a man
of letters, novelist, poet, and journalist. His entertaining evocation of a cheerful, Christian, patient Chaucer, both spiritual and practical, is an agreeably old-
fashioned exercise in literary appreciation, which estab-
lishes with penetration some differences between Chaucer
and modern literary culture. Reprinted from 'All I
Survey' (1933), pp. 174-8, by permission of Miss D.
Collins.

On Mr. Geoffrey Chaucer

The challenge of Chaucer is that he is our one medieval
poet, for most moderns; and he flatly contradicts all
that they mean by medieval. Aged and crabbed historians
tell them that medievalism was only filth, fear, gloom,
self-torture and torture of others. Even medievalist
aesthetes tell them it was chiefly mystery, solemnity and
care for the supernatural to the exclusion of the natural.
Now Chaucer is obviously *less* like this than the poets
after the Renaissance and the Reformation. He is obviously more sane even than Shakespeare; more liberal than
Milton; more tolerant than Pope; more humorous than
Wordsworth; more social and at ease with men than Byron or
even Shelley. Nay, some have doubted whether he is not
still more humane that the very latest humanists; whether
his geniality does not exceed the rosy optimism of Aldous
Huxley or the ever-bubbling high spirits of T.S. Eliot.
     Chaucer was, above all, an artist; and he was one of
that fairly large and very happy band of artists who are
not troubled with the artistic temperament. Perhaps there
was never a less typical poet, as a poet was understood in
the Byronic tradition of dark passions and tempestuous
raiment. But, indeed, that Byronic generalization was
largely founded upon Byron, or rather, on a blunder about
Byron. It would be much truer to say that practically
every type of human being has been also a poet, and that
Byron was a Regency Buck plus poetry. Similarly, Goethe
was a German professor plus poetry, and Browning was a

rather commercial-looking bourgeois plus poetry, and
Heine was a cynical Jew plus poetry, and Scott was a
rather acquisitive gentleman farmer plus poetry, and
Villon was a pickpocket plus poetry, and Wordsworth was a
noodle plus poetry, and Walt Whitman was an American
loafer plus poetry - for, in the art of loafing, Weary
Willie could never have stood up against Unweary Walt. I
have not yet heard of an American dentist or a shop-walker
in a large draper's who is a poet, and I have no doubt
that both of these deficiencies will soon be supplied.
Anyhow, the general rule is that almost any trade or type
of man can be an artist - yes, even an aesthete.
    But once or twice there appears in history the artist
who is the extreme antithesis of the aesthete. An artist
of this kind was Geoffrey Chaucer. He was a man who
always made himself useful, and not only ornamental.
People trusted him, not only in the moral, but in the more
purely practical sense. He was not the sort of poet who
would forget to post a letter, or post an unstamped ode to
the cuckoo instead, had the penny postage existed in his
day. He was not only given many responsible posts, but
responsible posts of many kinds. At one time he was sent
to negotiate the delicate finances of ransom and peace
with a great prince. At another time he was sent to
oversee the builders and workmen in the construction of a
great public building. It has been conjectured that he
had some technical knowledge of architecture, and I think
the descriptions of various pagan temples and royal pala-
ces in his poems support the conjecture. It is certain
that he knew a good deal about the official precedence
and etiquette of the Chamberlain's Office; he was a witness upon a point of heraldry in an important trial.
Though his relations to the Court, during and after the
débâcle of Richard II, are covered with some obscurity, it
is certain that, for the greater part of his life at
least, he performed job after job, of the most quaintly
different kinds, to the increasing satisfaction of his
employers. He was emphatically, as the vulgar phrase
goes, a man of the world.
    But through all these tasks the lyric element flowed
out of him quite naturally, as a man will whistle or sing
while he is potting a shrub or adding up a column of figures. He never seemed to have felt any particular strain
or dislocation between the world in which he was a man of
the world and that other world of which he was one of the
immortals. He had that sort of temper in which there is
no antithesis of Sense and Sensibility. He does not seem
to have quarrelled with many people, even in that very
quarrelsome transition time; and he does not seem to have

quarrelled with himself. Being a Christian, he was ready
to accuse himself when he was seriously considering the
question; but that is something quite different from the
sort of constant unconscious friction between different
parts of the mind which has marred the happiness of so
many artists and poets.

I do not mean merely that the poetry of Chaucer, like
the poetry of Dante, was in the higher sense a harmony.
I mean that it was in the ordinary human sense a melody.
It remained not only unspoilt, but unmixed; uncomplicated
by the complexities of living, whether they were actually
there or no. It is unfortunate that the word 'mood' is
almost always used of a sombre or secretive mood; and that
we do not convey the idea that a man was in merry mood
when we say merely that he was moody. For there was truly
a special thing that may be called the Chaucerian mood,
and it was essentially merry. There are any number of
passages of pathos, and one or two passages of tragedy,
but they never make us feel that the mood has really
altered, and it seems as if the man speaking is always
smiling as he speaks. In other words, the thing which is
supremely Chaucerian is the Chaucerian atmosphere, an
atmosphere which penetrates through all particular persons and problems; a sort of diffused light which lies on
everything, whether tragic or comic, and prevents the
tragedy from being hopeless or the comedy from being
cruel. No art critic, however artistic, has ever succeeded in describing an atmosphere. The only way to
approach it is to compare it with another atmosphere.
And this Chaucerian mood is very like the mood in which
(before it became merely vulgarized by cant or commer-
cialism) some of the greatest of modern English writers
have praised Christmas.

Chaucer was wide enough to be narrow; that is, he
could bring a broad experience of life to the enjoyment
of local or even accidental things. Now, it is the chief
defect of the literature of to-day that it always talks
as if local things could only be limiting, not to say
strangling; and that anything like an accident could only
be a jar. A Christmas dinner, as described by a modern
minor poet, would almost certainly be a study in acute
agony: the unendurable dullness of Uncle George; the
cacophonous voice of Aunt Adelaide. But Chaucer, who sat
down at the table with the Miller and the Pardoner, could
have sat down to a Christmas dinner with the heaviest
uncle or the shrillest aunt. He might have been amused
at them, but he would never have been angered by them,
and certainly he would never have insulted them in irritable little poems. And the reason was partly spiritual

and partly practical; spiritual because he had, whatever
his faults, a scheme of spiritual values in their right
order, and knew that Christmas was more important than
Uncle George's anecdotes; and practical because he had
seen the great world of human beings, and knew that wherever a man wanders among men, in Flanders or France or
Italy, he will find that the world largely consists of
Uncle Georges. This imaginative patience is the thing
that men want most in the modern Christmas, and if they
wish to learn it I recommend them to read Chaucer.

50. THOMAS STEARNS ELIOT, IS CHAUCER LESS SERIOUS THAN WORDSWORTH?

1933

T.S. Eliot (1888-1965), poet and critic, was educated at
the Universities of Harvard and Paris, and at Merton
College, Oxford. His significance as a twentieth-century
literary figure is such that any remarks he made must be
of interest: it is clear that he accepts Chaucer as an
important poet, and equally clear that Eliot, so intensely
literalistic and Neoclassical a critic, and no doubt the
last major figure in that line, has not a scrap of sympathy with or interest in Chaucer. His view of Dryden's
Chaucer may be contrasted with Housman's (No. 51). This
comment is reprinted from 'The Use of Poetry and the Use
of Criticism' (1933), pp. 24, 40, 116-17, by permission
of Faber & Faber Ltd, and Harvard University Press.

(p. 24) In England the critical force due to the new contrast between Latin and vernacular met, in the sixteenth
century, with just the right degree of resistance. That
is to say, for the age which is represented for us by
Spenser and Shakespeare, the new forces stimulated the
native genius and did not overwhelm it. The purpose of
my second lecture will be to give to the criticism of
this period the due which it does not seem to me to have
received. In the next age, the great work of Dryden in
criticism is, I think, that at the right moment he became
conscious of the necessity of affirming the native element

in literature. Dryden is more consciously English, in his plays, than were his predecessors; his essays on the drama and on the art of translation are conscious studies of the nature of the English theatre and the English language; and even his adaptation of Chaucer is an assertion of the native tradition - rather than, what it has sometimes been taken to be, an amusing and pathetic failure to appreciate the beauty of the Chaucerian language and metric. Where the Elizabethan critics, for the most part, were aware of something to be borrowed or adapted from abroad, Dryden was aware of something to be preserved at home....

(p. 40) The essay of Sidney in which occur the passages ridiculing the contemporary stage, so frequently quoted, may have been composed as early as 1580; at any rate, was composed before the great plays of the age were written. We can hardly suppose that the writer who in passing showed not only a lively appreciation of 'Chevy Chase', but also of Chaucer, singling for mention what is Chaucer's greatest poem - 'Troilus' - would have been imperceptive of the excellence of Shakespeare....

(p. 116) This is not the place for discussing the deplorable moral and religious effects of confusing poetry and morals in the attempt to find a substitute for religious faith. What concerns me here, is the disturbance of our literary values in consequence of it. One observes this in Arnold's criticism. It is easy to see that Dryden underrated Chaucer; not so easy to see that to rate Chaucer as highly as Dryden did (in a period in which critics were not lavish of superlatives) was a triumph of objectivity for its time, as was Dryden's consistent differentiation between Shakespeare and Beaumont and Fletcher. It is easy to see that Johnson underrated Donne and overrated Cowley; it is even possible to come to understand why. But neither Johnson nor Dryden had any axe to grind; and in their errors they are more consistent than Arnold. Take, for instance, Arnold's opinion of Chaucer, a poet who, although very different from Arnold, was not altogether deficient in high seriousness. First he contrasts Chaucer with Dante: we admit the inferiority, and are almost convinced that Chaucer is not serious enough. But is Chaucer, in the end, less serious than Wordsworth, with whom Arnold does not compare him? And when Arnold puts Chaucer below François Villon, although he is in a way right, and although it was high time that somebody in England spoke up for Villon, one does not feel that the theory of 'high seriousness' is in operation. That is one of the troubles of the critic who feels called upon to set the poets in rank: if he is honest with his own sensibility he must now and again violate his own rules of rating.

There are also dangers arising from being too sure that
one knows what 'genuine poetry' is.

51.   ALFRED EDWARD HOUSMAN, SENSITIVE FIDELITY TO NATURE

1933

A.E. Housman (1859-1936), was educated at St John's
College, Oxford. Classical scholar, poet and textual
critic, he was Professor of Latin in the University of
Cambridge, 1911-36. Like Eliot (No. 50) Housman approaches Chaucer through Dryden, and by implication praises
Chaucer's 'sensitive fidelity to nature' and his capacity
to express human feeling, revealing a genuine response to
the 'realistic' side of Chaucer's genius, and a not incomparable wit. The comment is reprinted from 'The Name
and Nature of Poetry' Cambridge University Press (1933),
pp. 22-5, by permission of the Society of Authors as
literary representative for the Estate of the late A.E.
Housman.

(p. 22) [Eighteenth-century style] was in truth at once
pompous and poverty-stricken. It had a very limited,
because supposedly choice, vocabulary, and was consequently unequal to the multitude and refinement of its
duties. It could not describe natural objects with sensitive fidelity to nature; it could not express human
feelings with a variety and delicacy answering to their
own. A thick, stiff, unaccommodating medium was interposed between the writer and his work. And this deaden-
ing of language had a consequence betyond its own sphere:
its effect worked inward, and deadened perception. That
which could no longer be described was no longer noticed.
    The features and formation of the style can be studied
under a cruel light in Dryden's translations from Chaucer.
The Knight's Tale of Palamon and Arcite is not one of
Chaucer's most characteristic and successful poems: he is
not perfectly at home, as in the Prologue and the tale of
Chauntecleer and Pertelote, and his movement is a trifle
languid. Dryden's translation shows Dryden in the maturity of his power and accomplishment, and much of it can

be honestly and soberly admired. Nor was he insensible
to all the peculiar excellence of Chaucer: he had the wit
to keep unchanged such lines as 'Up rose the sun and up
rose Emily' or 'The slayer of himself yet saw I there';
he understood that neither he nor anyone else could
better them. But much too often in a like case he would
try to improve, because he thought that he could. He
believed, as he says himself, that he was 'turning some
of the Canterbury Tales into our language, as it is now
refined'; 'the words' he says again 'are given up as a
post not to be defended in our poet, because he wanted
the modern art of fortifying'; 'in some places' he tells
us 'I have added somewhat of my own where I thought my
author was deficient, and had not given his thoughts
their true lustre, for want of words in the beginning of
our language'.

Let us look at the consequences. Chaucer's vivid and
memorable line

The smiler with the knife under the cloke

becomes these three:

Next stood Hypocrisy, with holy leer,
Soft smiling and demurely looking down,
But hid the dagger underneath the gown.

Again:

Alas, quod he, that day that I was bore.

So Chaucer, for want of words in the beginning of our
language. Dryden comes to his assistance and gives his
thoughts their true lustre thus:

Cursed be the day when first I did appear;
Let it be blotted from the calendar,
Lest it pollute the month and poison all the year.

Or yet again:

The queen anon for very womanhead
Gan for to weep, and so did Emily
And all the ladies in the company.

If Homer or Dante had the same thing to say, would he
wish to say it otherwise? But to Dryden Chaucer wanted
the modern art of fortifying, which he thus applies:

He said; dumb sorrow seized the standers-by.
The queen, above the rest, by nature good
(The pattern formed of perfect womanhood)
For tender pity wept: when she began
Through the bright quire the infectious virtue ran.
All dropped their tears, even the contended maid.

Had there not fallen upon England the curse out of
Isaiah, 'make the heart of this people fat, and make their
ears heavy, and shut their eyes'?

52. ROSEMOND TUVE, CHAUCER AND THE SEASONS

1933

Rosemond Tuve (1903-64), educated at the Universities of
Minnesota and Johns Hopkins, and at Somerville College,
Oxford, was a member of the faculty of Connecticut
College, 1934-63, and Professor of English in the University of Pennsylvania, 1963-4. Her first book 'Seasons
and Months', Paris 1933, examines the multiple strands
that constitute seasonal descriptions in earlier English
poetry. The multiplicity of Chaucer's resources and the
subtle balance of 'nature' and 'convention' are demonstrated with detailed verbal analysis, while the book
also pioneers that close comparison of literature with
the visual arts which has become fruitful in later criticism. Reprinted by permission of Dr Richard L. Tuve from
'Seasons and Months', Paris, 1933, reprinted D.S. Brewer
Ltd, Cambridge (1974), pp. 181-7.

Section IV. We have now to see how there came into
English seasons poetry that courtly and sophisticated
element which seems so alien to the temper of the earlier
references in lyrics and romances, but which is so invariably present in Lydgate and in the Scotch school, scattering spring formulas and worn-out metaphors even through
Elizabethan pastoral descriptions. The principal channel
in Chaucer's own case was surely the 'Romaunt of the
Rose', important and early in his literary development.
The translation in the long May passage is very close
(vv. 49ff.); we find here a different phraseology from

that which he inherited from earlier English uses of the
motif. There are conceits he is not to forget, and a kind
of diction which will persist in his spring descriptions
until his later period. Busk and hay will be 'shrouded';
the ground will have a 'queynt robe and fayr' ('cointe
robe faire'), many-hewed, of flowers and grass; nightingale, chelandre and papingay will sing blithely. The
'erthe wexeth proud' ('s'orgueille') forgetting its 'pore
estat' in winter; 'love affrayeth alle thing' ('toute rien
d'amer s'esfroie'). This is the spring into which all the
courtly-love and dream-garden poets have waked, from the
early lyrics to Froissart. The 'Book of the Duchesse'
shows the same predominating influence, as one would
expect. In the charm of Chaucer's description, the birds
'upon the tyles, al a-boute' seem particular with him;
this 'moste solempne servyse' is universal and customary,
however, and has been in progress many seasons. The walls
need not have been painted with the 'Romaunce of the Rose',
for it shows plainly in the reference to the dwelling
of Flora and Zephirus, or in the proud earth outdoing
heaven in gaiety, forgetting 'the povertee That winter...
had mad hit suffre[n]', now green through 'sweetnesse of
dewe' (291ff., 398ff.).

A slightly different tradition, and one of even more
ancient heritage, predominates in the 'Parlement of
Foules' passage on spring - the earthly paradise motif
(which had, of course, also attached itself to the Garden
of Love). 'Grene and lusty May shal ever endure' in this
garden, with its many kinds of trees, its river, its
heavenly harmony of birds, stringed instruments of
'ravisshing swetnesse', its small beasts playing, its
spices and 'attempre' air, its freedom from disease and
age, and its train of allegorical figures around the well
of Cupid - with the lovers of all times 'peynted over al'
(130ff.). As in Froissart or Machaut, these details have
become a characteristic part of the convention. The
appearance of Aleyn's 'noble goddesse Nature' re-empha-
sizes the fact that it was Chaucer's habit to put together
if he pleased settings of very different provenance; but
both are stage-sets and neither carries its original force
of purpose. In the Prologue to the 'Legend of Good
Women', one would of course expect a court of love, since
the God of Love himself is to appear, in one version gar-
landed with 'rose-leves Steked al with lilie floures
newe' (A 160) like the April or May of late 'Horae', in
the other 'corouned with a sonne' (B 230). The songs to
St Valentine, the Zephirus and Flora, the forgotten 'pore
estat' of winter (B 125, A 113), all belong to the convention as we have seen it in French courtly romances;

the 'swerd of cold', for example, probably comes either
directly from the 'Roman de la Rose', or from Machaut(1).
The 'smale foules', in Prologue B, go on to a long and
artificial court scene, with swearing of troth on the
blossoms, and reconciliations through the 'ruled curtesye'
that is the chief statute of the love court proper (left
out in Prologue A); but their songs in despite of the
'fouler' are in a manner that is not second-hand, however
conventional the situation. The 'observaunces' to be done
to May in the 'Knight's Tale' are like those of the
courtly figures of 'Guillaume de Dole'; they are very
different from those of the junketings that Chaucer may
have seen on Mayday. 'May wol have no slogardye a-night'
(184) has a background of Provençal complaint (strained
through many filters) rather than of early hawthorn gathering and love-making in the country; the 'joly wo' and
'lusty sorwe' that kept Pandarus awake on a 'Mayes morwe'
was that of Petrarch for Laura not of Jack for Jill
('Tr.' II, st. 157).

But this is only one color in the complex tissue that
makes up Chaucer's contribution to English seasons poetry.
The 'Prologue' to the 'Tales', fully as characteristic, is
written in another idiom; and the months with their qualities of cold or hot, moist or dry, the humor in the bud-
ding trees, the sun running its course, now half through
the sign of Aries, remind one that Chaucer was interested
enough in the sciences of his day to write not only a
'Knight's Tale' grounded on aspects and conjunctions but
a treatise on the astrolabe. In 'Troilus and Criseyde'
also 'Phebus doth his brighte bemes sprede Right in the
whyte Bole', and 'ful of bawme is fletinge every mede'
(II, 8;...). The 'Squire's Tale' passage is even more
closely related to diagrams and tables such as those
that illustrate calendar treatises:

> Phebus the sonne ful joly was and cleer;
> For he was neigh his exaltacioun
> In Martes face, and in his mansioun
> In Aries, the colerik hote signe...(40ff.)

Similarly, the 'gardin ful of leves and of floures'
'Which May had peynted with his softe shoures' (in the
'Franklin's Tale')(2) contrasts with the longer description of the 'colde frosty seson of Decembre' (179, cf.
516ff.). Into this, Chaucer has put suggestions from
December and January feast scenes in the 'Horae' or other
calendar series, and their declining sun taking his course
through Capricorn; and while he doubtless observed for
himself the 'bittre frostes,.... sleet and reyn' of actual

English winters, destroying 'the grene in every yerd', it
is equally questionless that he had seen the bare trees
and brown earth of the winter landscapes in the 'Horae'.
We have seen how often, in the manuscripts, 'Janus sit by
the fyr, with double berd, And drinketh of his bugle-horn
the wyn', while 'Biforn him stant braun of the tusked
swyn'. Also, when Chaucer and other poets, in the line
immediately before or after the description of a month,
note the position of the sun in the zodiac, they are not
merely obedient to a literary convention. They also
follow an artistic tradition. Some of the descriptions
are earlier in date than the more elaborate pictures(3)
which we still possess, in which Phebus does actually
drive through the degrees on the circle of the zodiac and
alight full pale in Capricorn. But e.g. in MS. Douce 62,
a 'Book of Hours' of the late xiv. c., use of Paris, the
rectangular 'labor' of the month contains, besides the
zodiac sign, a redfaced sun varying in size, with 'stremes'
which increase and decrease; long, strongly-marked rays in
May or July give place to shorter slighter ones in November and December. The gradual strengthening of the 'yonge
sonne' as he runs his course is marked in B. Mus. MS.
Arundel 157 by inscriptions under the zodiac signs (under
the ram, for example, '...ore commence li soleil a montrer
sa force'; MS. before 1220, English). Bodley 614 (Engl.,
last quarter xii.), whose series of occupations (folios
3-16) has not been completely filled in (but includes a
January 'with double berd' eating 'by the fyr'), pictures
Sol on f. 17 as a gold-crowned nude in a chariot, with
four leaping horses and a staff with a gold pennon; on
f. 23 he is a figure with two gold torches, surrounded by
personified planets. It is true that none of the pictures
like these which were seen by Chaucer and Lydgate and
Hoccleve and Spenser suggested *new* ideas to them; it was
the frequent seeing of them that made them conventions -
which only to us seem recondite. We realize the relative
parts played by observation of 'nature' and by convention
more clearly if we recognize that in such a familiar description as that here considered, observation is much
likelier to embellish than to originate, to add striking
details than to see independently.

One other Chaucerian figure seems thrice as familiar
after seeing a great number of 'Horae' manuscripts, - the
Squire, a 'lovyere, and... lusty bacheler' ('C.T., Prol.',
80), 'with lokkes crulle, as they were leyd in presse',
'embrouded... al ful of fresshe floures, whyte and rede',
'of twenty yeer of age', 'singinge... or floytinge, al the
day', in 'short... goune, with sleves longe and wyde',
well knowing how to 'sitte on hors, and faire ryde', with

him a 'yeman'. The month of May in Queen Mary's
'Psalter' (MS. Royal 2 B vii, early xiv.), with curly
yellow hair, in a wide-sleeved, decorated short gown,
rides a horse, hawking; his two attendants also have
hawks. The May of a St. Omer 'Book of Hours' (B. Mus.
Addit. 36684, after 1318) is also a youth with curly
yellow hair, in short gown and wide sleeves, on a horse,
with hawk and rose. In the May of Lansdowne 383 (mid-
xii., Shaftesbury Abbey), the horse is gaily caparisoned,
the saddle red, the wide-sleeved gold and blue embroidered gown slit to the thigh, the hair wavy. In B. Nat.
MS. f. lat. 1076 (English, xiii.) May has a chaplet of
red flowers; in B. Nat. f. lat. 745 (xiv., f. clxxix) his
gown is plaited and has puffed sleeves; in both B. Nat.
f. lat. 1077 (xiii.) and Bodleian Canon. Lit. 126 (xiv.,
Neth. ?) he has a musical instrument.(4) Perhaps Chaucer's squire was 'as fresh' as a very particular 'month
of May' ('C.T., Prol.', 92).

Those who echoed the seasons-descriptions of Chaucer
and of the French poets whose works he helped to make
popular in England, mingled the traditions as casually if
not as skillfully as he had. *Pastourelles* in English
perhaps show only this last influence; they are late and
formalized. They are often 'upon a morning in May', but
only occasionally have seasons-passages of any fresh
ness.(5)

Notes

1 'R. de la R.' has (5942-4, in a passage translated
   from Alanus' 'Anticlaudianus', v. notes, II. 345):
   'E quant Bise resoufle, il fauche Les floretes e la
   verdure A l'espee de sa freidure'. Cf. Machaut's
   'Jugement dou Roy de Navarre' (*v.* appendix 64; also
   noted by Fansler, 'Ch. and the R. de la R.', 99).
   The same metaphor occurs again in the 'Squire's Tale'
   (48).
2 *V.* Lowes' discussion of Chaucer's relation here to the
   'Teseide'; cf. also his comparison of Chaucer's December description with Boccaccio's October reference,
   ('The Franklin's Tale', the 'Tes.', and the 'Filocolo',
   'Mod. Phil.' XV, 689ff., esp. 698-9 [1917-18]....
3 In later 'Horae' - of the Jean Pucelle school, for
   example, and more especially in the Duc de Berry MSS.
   V. the 'Très riches heures du Duc de Berry', Musée
   Condé, Chantilly; 'Petites heures', B. Nat. MS. f.
   lat. 18014, fin. by 1402; 'Grandes heures', B. Nat. f.
   lat. 919, dated 1409; *v.* Delisle, 'Les livres d'heures

du Duc de Berry; Herbert', 250 f.; Leroquais, II,
175ff.
4   *V.* also, among many others, Royal I D x (xiii.), Harl.
2332 (early xv., standing), Lansdowne 431, B. Mus.
Addit. 38116 (after 1280; on dappled horse, with hawk
and short gown, gloved and curly-haired), Addit.
33992 (xiv., red gown above knees).
5   Perhaps 'in ane symmer sessoun, quhen men wynnis thair
hay' is mildly interesting when one remembers the
labors of June, July, and August (ed. Laing, 'Early
Pop. Poetry', I, 113; first half xv., according to
Sandison, 130; *v.* there also no. A 37, *c.* 1303, A 22,
c. 1400).

Index

The index has been divided into two parts. The first index contains material on Chaucer: biographical details, literary qualities and themes and his works. The second index contains general topics, people, books and periodicals.

1. GEOFFREY CHAUCER

2. GENERAL INDEX

THE CRITICAL HERITAGE SERIES

GENERAL EDITOR: B. C. SOUTHAM

Volumes published and forthcoming

Smalley

McWilliams

Lockwood

GE(

artridge